~~£1.50~~

50p

C28

Juvenile Justice Management

JUVENILE JUSTICE MANAGEMENT

Edited by

GARY B. ADAMS, D.P.A.
Assistant Professor of Criminology
California State University at Long Beach

ROBERT M. CARTER, D. CRIM.
Associate Professor, School of Public Administration
Director of the Delinquency Control Institute
Director of the Center for the Administration of Justice
University of Southern California

JOHN D. GERLETTI, ED. D.
Professor, School of Public Administration
University of Southern California

DAN G. PURSUIT, M.S.S.A.
Associate Director of the Delinquency Control Institute
School of Public Administration
University of Southern California

PERCY G. ROGERS, D.P.A.
Major, United States Air Force
Washington D.C.

CHARLES C THOMAS · PUBLISHER
Springfield · Illinois · U.S.A.

Published and Distributed Throughout the World by
CHARLES C THOMAS • PUBLISHER
Bannerstone House
301-327 East Lawrence Avenue, Springfield, Illinois, U.S.A.

ISBN 0-398-02773-0
Library of Congress Catalog Card Number: 72-93200

Printed in the United States of America
PP-22

CONTRIBUTORS

HARVEY M. ADELMAN, Ph.D.
Associate Professor of Business
Pepperdine University

LEE P. BROWN, D.Crim.
Director, Administration of Justice Program
Howard University

JACK COCKS, M.S.
Chief, Eastern Division
Los Angeles County Probation Department

LaMAR EMPEY, Ph.D.
Professor of Sociology
University of Southern California

JOSEPH FINK, Ph.D.
Senior Research Associate
School of Public Administration
University of Southern California

NEELY GARDNER, B.S.
Professor of Public Administration
University of Southern California

ALBERTO GUERREIRO-RAMOS, Ph.D.
Professor of Public Administration
University of Southern California

JOHN P. KENNEY, Ph.D.
Professor of Criminology
California State University at Long Beach

MALCOLM W. KLEIN Ph.D.
Chairman, Sociology and Anthropology Department
Professor of Sociology
Senior Research Associate, Social Science Research Institute
University of Southern California

LYLE KNOWLES, Ph.D.
Associate Professor of Public Administration
Pepperdine University

MARTIN LEVINE, LL.B.
Professor of Law
University of Southern California

CATHERINE LOVELL, Ph.D.
Associate Professor of Public Administration
California State University Pomona

STEVEN G. LUBECK, Ph.D.
Research Associate
Gerontology Center
University of Southern California

DAVID MARS, Ph.D.
Professor of Public Administration
University of Southern California

ALEX McEACHERN, M.A.
Associate Professor of Public Administration
University of Southern California

BURT NANUS, D.B.A.
Director, Center for Futures Research
University of Southern California

E. K. NELSON, J.D. and D.P.A.
Dean, School of Public Administration
Professor of Public Administration
University of Southern California

LLOYD OHLIN, Ph.D.
Professor of Sociology
Harvard University

RAYMOND OLSEN, M.P.A.
Program Officer, Delinquency Control Institute
University of Southern California

EMERY E. OLSON, J.D.
Emeritus Dean, School of Public Administration
University of Southern California

CARL SHAFER, D.S.W.
Associate Professor of Social Work
University of Southern California

WILLIAM B. STORM, Ph.D.
Professor of Public Administration
University of Southern California

WILLIAM J. WILLIAMS, D.P.A.
Associate Professor of Public Administration
University of Southern California

THEODORE B. WILSON, M.P.A.
Program Officer, Delinquency Control Institute
University of Southern California

CLASS MEMBERS

President—Bruce D. Kennedy, Detroit, Michigan Police Department

Vice President—Thomas C. Kendra, Culver City, California Police Department

Secretary—G. Helena Ashby, Los Angeles County, California Sheriff's Department

Sergeant At Arms—Frank Locantore, Jr., Camden, New Jersey Police Department

Gerald E. Barrentine, Inglewood, California Police Department

DePriest Bernard, Los Angeles County, California Probation Department

J. Walter Bryan, North Carolina Department of Juvenile Corrections

Robert Cleary, San Jose, California Police Department

Terrence K. Colley, Cincinnati, Ohio Police Department

David Patrick Geary, Ventura, California Police Department

Edward Glasgow, Costa Mesa, California Police Department

Lawrence L. Haines, Concord, California Police Department

Frances L. Hollis, Los Angeles County, California Department of Community Services

Ruth E. Kranovich, California Youth Authority

Fred N. Neuhaus, Los Angeles, California Police Department

Raymond L. Silagy, Torrance, California Police Department

David W. Sirinek, St. Louis, Missouri Juvenile Court

Otis M. Tipton, Oxnard, California Police Department

William L. Woodmansee, Hampton, Virginia Police Department

PREFACE

THIS TEXT IS THE PRODUCT OF grants made by the Youth Development and Delinquency Prevention Administration, Department of Health, Education and Welfare, to the Delinquency Control Institute, Center for the Administration of Justice, School of Public Administration of the University of Southern California. The Institute, Center, and School are components of the Von Kleinsmid Center for International and Public Affairs. The period covered by the grants was from May 1970 to June 1971, with grants # 75-P-45034/9-01 and 02.

The major purpose of this Training Project in Juvenile Delinquency was to develop meaningful educational materials for leaders in the juvenile justice system such as commanding officers of police juvenile units and middle managers in probation, institutional care, and parole. There has, heretofore, been a minimum of materials focusing on the important roles of these significant middle managers.

The text was designed for use by training officials in police and sheriff's departments, probation departments and state juvenile correctional agencies as well as in educational institutions providing courses for criminal justice personnel. Such uses should help to generate the quality of coordination needed to make the administration of juvenile justice more effective.

The content was developed from numerous surveys and inquires involving juvenile justice midlle managers, top criminal justice executives and professional associations in the field to ascertain the major problems and issues which should be dealt with in the experimental curriculum.

The first Juvenile Justice Middle Management Course was conducted by the Delinquency Control Institue in the twelve week period from March 29 to June 16, 1971. Nineteen students comprised the class, fifteen from police and sheriff's departments, three from corrections and one from the field of community organization. These experienced middle managers participated actively in helping to determine the most appropriate course content.

Faculty members from the University of Southern California and California State University at Long Beach represented a broad interdisciplinary group of scholars and local practitioners deeply committed to effecting change in the juvenile justice system.

The Staff consisted of the following: John D. Gerletti, Ed. D., project director, 5/1/70 to 10/31/70; Robert M. Carter, D. Crim., project director, 11/1/70 to 6/30/71; Dan G. Pursuit, M.S.S.A., project coordinator; Gary B. Adams, M.P.A., Robert M. Brown, M.P.A. and Percy G. Rogers, M.P.A. research assistants.

As with most editors, our manuscripts had to be deciphered and typed by very patient secretaries. We are deeply indebted to three girls who performed this task, Fredricka DeVega, Sharon Ellison and Patricia Smith. We are also indebted to many authors who have granted us permission to reprint selections of their work in this volume.

Finally, we all owe a great deal to the students who endured the training session, brought us together, and provided the stimulus for our work.

Gary B. Adams
Robert M. Carter
John D. Gerletti
Dan G. Pursuit
Percy G. Rogers

INTRODUCTION

ALTHOUGH THERE IS CONSIDERABLE discussion and writing by academicians, administrators, and researchers about the *system* of criminal and/or juvenile justice, the United States does not have a single system of justice. Each level of government, indeed each jurisdiction, has its own unique system. These many systems—all established to enforce the standards of conduct believed necessary for the protection of individuals and the preservation of the community—are a collectivity of some forty thousand law enforcement agencies, probation and parole departments, correctional institutions and related community-based organizations. It is clear that our *system* of criminal and juvenile justice sacrifices much in the way of efficiency and effectiveness in order to preserve local autonomy and to protect the individual.

The many systems of justice in existence in the United States as we enter the 1970's are not the same as those which emerged following the American Revolution. Although American justice systems have traditionally tried to insure justice for all citizens, the systems have not developed or evolved uniformly or consistently or, for that matter, always in the same direction. Parts of our systems, such as trial by jury and the principle of bail are relatively old and date back to our European heritage in general and the English Common Law in particular, while probation and parole began in the nineteenth century and the juvenile court is a twentieth century innovation. Some of the innovations and changes in our systems have been generated by judicial decisions and legislative decrees; others have evolved more by chance than by design.

Coupled with the numerous criminal and juvenile justice systems in the United States and their uneven development is the separation of functions within the systems. There are similar components in all systems ranging from police at input, through prosecution and courts, to correction at outgo. Although these major components and subcomponents are interwoven and interdependent one with the other, they typically function independently and autonomously. This separateness of functions, which on one hand prevents the possibility of a *police state,* on the other leads to some extraordinarily complex problems. Not the least of these is that the systems of justice are not really systems—integrated, coordinated, and effective entities—but rather are fragmented non-systems and collections of agencies tied together by the processing of an increasing number of adult and juvenile offenders. These non-systems are marked by an unequal quality of justice, inadequate fiscal, manpower and training resources, shortages in equipment and facilities, lack of relevant research and evaluation to provide some measure of effectiveness and, until recently, a general indifference and apathy on the part of the public which the systems were designed to serve.

As if the *non-system* problems were not sufficient cause for concern, we are confronted with large increases in reported crime. Nationwide, the Federal Bureau of Investigation reports a population increase of 13 percent, a crime rate increase of 120 percent, and an increase in the number of index offenses reported of 148 percent between 1960 and 1969.

The data on juvenile and youthful offenders are equally distressing. The FBI reports a nationwide increase of ninety percent in the number of persons under the age of eighteen arrested between 1960 and 1969 for the seven index offenses. In 1969, persons under the age of fifteen accounted for almost ten percent of the total arrests reported; persons under eighteen accounted for one-fourth of the total arrests.

It is clearly appropriate to inquire about the future of criminal and juvenile justice in the United States. The crime and delinquency explosion since World War II in general and in the 1960's in particular makes imperative and unequivocally demonstrates the need for extensive planning of justice operations: projections of the current crime and delinquency situation may serve as a foundation and catalyst for such planning. To the extent that reported crime and delinquency continue to increase in the future as they have in the recent past and our systems of justice continue to function without substantial change, a very probable answer to our inquiry is that the criminal and juvenile justice systems will collapse from sheer input and uncoordinated processing of offenders.

If crime and delinquency continue unabated into the future as they have grown in the recent past and the components of a multiplicity of justice systems continue to operate autonomously and in an uncoordinated fashion, a disaster of major proportions may lie ahead. We are confronted with difficulties which are increasing not only in number but in magnitude and seriousness. Systematic interventions into the operations of the justice systems, if achieved, could ameliorate some difficulties, but the level of detail of available statistics and data is so meager that specific changes and their potential outcomes are at best uncertain or are at such a level of abstraction that the consequences of change may be estimated only grossly. And again, changes in policies, procedures and practices in one agency of a justice system are likely to have unanticipated consequences for the operations of other agencies in the same or related systems.

The uncertain future of justice may be illuminated by development of a blueprint which *terminates criminal and juvenile justice provincialism and requires systematic and cooperative planning by all agencies concerned with crime and the criminal and delinquency and the delinquent.* The end of provincialism and beginning of integrated planning includes the establishment of comprehensive, across-the-board information systems to provide sophisticated levels of data describing the nature and dimensions of current justice activities and to allow evaluation of the effectiveness of these activities. It also includes the demise of purely law enforcement, judicial, and correctional-oriented thinking and the emergence of system-wide orientations and perspectives which consider the total implication of the responses to criminal and delinquent behavior. Reasoned legislative action to include possible redefinitions of criminal and delinquent behavior and the creation of systems parallel to and cooperating with the justice systems, broadly based community support, and an inclusive attack on the conditions which generate crime and delinquency are requirements which may more readily be achieved when sponsored by justice systems which themselves have clear directions and goals for the future.

American society is currently experiencing violent upheaval and change. Our social-political institutions—including the justice systems

—must respond appropriately to new demands and pressures or be cast aside. The decision to be made at this point in time is not whether the systems should or should not be changed, but rather the nature of the changes which must ensue. The justice systems, broadly conceived, can respond and react to external pressures or they can themselves be the vehicle for initiating relevant and significant change.

For the first time in our history the Federal government has significantly responded to the enormous problems confronting agencies of the criminal justice system. The Omnibus Crime Control and Safe Streets Act of 1968 not only provides resources for experimentation and change, but more importantly requires that comprehensive justice planning be conducted at local, regional, state and national levels. Although much of the justice planning conducted to date has been based upon inadequate information on how these systems function, the scientific and technological capability exists to overcome this planning deficiency.

The projections provided in this report suggest the extent of the crime and delinquency problem confronting us in the immediate future; these projections, and others like them, may be used to direct the planning efforts which are necessary to avoid the potential collapse of criminal and juvenile justice.

Considering both the criminal and juvenile systems overall, a single observation may be made on the basis of these projections: the inevitable changes which are suggested by the convoluted growth of these systems will occur before 1985, a year in which a number of output statistics throughout the systems exceed the specific inputs from which they are derived. This is not intended as an Orwellian prediction, but simply as a conclusion drawn from the nature of the *real* systems and their present growth rates.

At press time the National Advisory Commission on Criminal Justice Standards and Goals, U.S. Department of Justice, released a series of valuable reports which should provide implementation challenges to lay leaders and professional justice personnel at all levels of government.

CONTENTS

SECTION FOUR

Youth Development and Delinquency Prevention

SECTION FIVE

Training

SECTION SIX

Community Relations

SECTION SEVEN

Diversion

SECTION EIGHT

Corrections

SECTION NINE

Research and Evaluation Methods

SECTION TEN

Legal Aspects

Juvenile Justice Management

SECTION ONE

WHAT IS JUVENILE DELINQUENCY?

CHAPTER 1

NATURE AND EXTENT OF JUVENILE DELINQUENCY

JUVENILE DELINQUENCY IS one of the nation's major unsolved problems. It is more than a headline issue, more than a matter of public safety. Nor is delinquency a single problem which calls for a single answer.

Delinquency is a tangle of profoundly interwoven problems that are inseparable from the social system in which we live. It is a chronic problem that will not yield easily to efforts of prevention and control. Neither can it be resolved by crash programs leaving underlying social causes unchanged.

Delinquency is not a new or uniquely American problem. The particular forms and varieties of youthful antisocial behavior may change with the times, but delinquency remains an intrinsic part of industrial society. Today's expanding youth population, and the increasing complexities of modern life, call for innovative long-range programs—as well as immediate action—for dealing with youth problems.

There are different ways of looking at delinquency and its manifestations. One possible approach is to suggest that societies which place a high premium on freedom, initiative, and success should hardly expect to contain all of its members in a conventional mold. According to this approach, delinquency is one form of breaking out of the mold. Another related approach is to suggest that democratic

*From Annual Report 1970, Youth Development and Delinquency Prevention Administration, U.S. Department of Health, Education, and Welfare.

societies always have to tolerate a fairly high percentage of non-conformity among youth. However, in any approach to delinquency, while nonconformity and unconventional behavior are factors to be recognized, the protection of society comes first. Ways must be found to deal with deviant behavior which leads to the destruction of property; criminal acts; or violence.

Destructive behavior needs to be channelled into constructive activity in order to reverse the effects of this social blight in our future generations.

Planning for the prevention of delinquency must be based on the realistic appraisal of the problem. Resources for coping with the problem must be adequate; and feasible programs need to be undertaken. However it is approached, the problem of juvenile delinquency needs to be recognized as a fundamental challenge to our ability to make the American dream mean something in a nuclear society.

The Size of the Delinquency Problem

With the single exception of 1961 the upward trend in juvenile delinquency rates has continued.

The FBI's Uniform Crime Reports andD/HEW's Juvenile Court Statistical Reports show not only spiralling rates of delinquency but increasing involvement of youth in serious crimes.

During the past decade (1960 thru 1969) the volume of police arrests of persons under eighteen years of age for all offenses except traffic violations increased at a pace almost four times the precentage rate of increase in the national population. While the number of young people in the age group 10 to 17 increased 27 percent during this period, the arrest rate of persons under the age of 18 doubled. When only the Crime Index offenses are considered in computing this long-term trend, the rate of increase registers a startling 90 percent, for the decade.[1]

Similarly, during the same period of time, juvenile arrests for violent crimes increased 148 percent, while arrests for property offenses increased 85 percent. While the total youth population aged 10 to 17 constituted approximately 16 percent of the total population of the United States in 1969, persons under 18 years of age were involved in 32 percent of the Crime Index offenses which were solved.

TABLE 1-1

1969 Arrest Rates for Persons Under Age 18
for Crime Index Offenses*

Offense Charged	Percentage of Persons Under Age 18 Arrested in 1969	Increase 1960 1969 (percent)
Murder	9.4	151
Aggravated Assault	16.4	123
Forcible Rape	20.1	86
Robbery	33.4	13
Burglary	53.7	72
Larceny-Theft	53.1	100
Auto-Theft	58.0	63

*Uniform Crime Reports—1969

A similar trend is indicated by Juvenile Court Statistics—1969, the latest year for which complete statistics are available. Nationally, the volume of juvenile court cases increased 9.9 percent over the previous year. Boys' cases registered at 10.1 percent increase, girls' cases a 19.0 percent increase. Delinquency, however, continues to be primarily a male problem—with four times as many males as females being referred to the juvenile courts in 1969.[2]

Who Are The Delinquents?

Although the problem of juvenile delinquency remains concentrated primarily in the urban areas of the country, the statistics indicate a problem of considerable magnitude in the rural and suburban areas as well. According to the 1969 Uniform Crime Report:

> Nationally, persons under 15 years of age made up 10 percent of the total police arrests; under 18, 26 percent; under 21, 39 percent, and under 25, 51 percent. In the suburban areas, the involvement of the young age groups in police arrests is again markedly higher than the national figures with the under 15 age group represented in 13 percent; under 18, 35 percent; under 21, 50 percent; and under 25, 63 percent. In the rural areas, the distributions were lower for the younger age groups, with the under 15 group being involved in 5 percent of the cases; under 18 in 21 percent; under 21 in 38 percent; and those under 25, 53 percent. When only the serious crimes are considered 22 percent

of all arrests in 1969 were for persons under the age of 15 and almost one-half were under 18 years of age (p. 33).

Likewise, the 1969 Juvenile Court Statistics show that juvenile court cases increased in all areas of the country. Nationally, juvenile court cases increased 9.9 precent in that year; urban courts experienced a 9.8 percent increase, while the increase in semi-urban courts was 9.2 percent and rural courts registered an 8.8 percent increase. The number of juvenile court cases handled by predominantly urban areas, however, was almost three times higher than in the rural areas. Sixty-six percent of all the cases were handled by the urban courts, 28 percent by semi-urban courts, and 6 percent by rural courts.

Drug offenses, too, are becoming increasingly prevalent among young people, as evidenced by the statistics contained in the 1969 Uniform Crime Report. In 1964, 23 percent of the persons arrested for Narcotic Drug Law violations were under 21 years of age; by 1969, the percentage had jumped to 55 percent. When marijuana offenses alone are considered, 27 percent of the persons arrested were under 18 years of age, and 63 percent were under 21.

Statistics, however, tell only part of the story. As the President's Commission on Law Enforcement and Administration of Justice pointed out in *The Challenge of Crime in a Free Society,* "These reports (The Uniform Crime Reports and the Juvenile Court Statistics) can tell us nothing about the vast numbers of unsolved crimes or about the many cases in which delinquents are dealt with informally instead of being arrested or referred to court."[3]

Indeed, various self-report studies indicate that approximately 90 percent of all youth commit acts for which they might be brought to the attention of juvenile courts if apprehended.

Alarming as these juvenile delinquency statistics may be, however, it is necessary to view them in perspective.

In part, these increases are the result of better statistical reporting and better record keeping systems adopted by police departments and other official agencies. In part, they may stem from increased formal actions on the part of law enforcement agencies. In part, too, they are the product of a phenomenal increase in the youth population in recent years—a rate of increase which is significantly higher than for the adult population. And, in part, they are the consequence of an increasing urbanization which has exacerbated conditions in which delinquency rates have traditionally been high.

Moreover, despite the increasing involvement of juveniles in Crime Index Offenses, the majority of youth continue to be apprehended for *minor* crimes, and a significant number are arrested for actions which, if committed by an adult, would not be considered criminal.

In 1969, boys under eighteen years of age were most often arrested for larceny and burglary. Large numbers, however, were also apprehended for disorderly conduct, curfew and loitering violations, and running away. Similarly, while a large number of girls under eighteen were arrested for larceny, a significant proportion of both boy and girls were arrested for other violations of State and local laws which are not broken down in the Uniform Crime Reports, but rather are classified as "all other offenses, except traffic." This category encompasses such offenses as truancy, ungovernable behavior, and similar activities, as well as other offenses which pertain to both adults and juveniles.

Finally, the fact that a large percentage of juvenile crimes are committed in groups—the estimates range from 60 to 90 percent—may also result in *inflated* statistics which are out of proportion to the number of crimes actually committed.

Delinquency and the Inner City

Despite the rise in suburban delinquency, more often than not the world around the delinquent is the inner-city slum.

By 1980, seventy-five percent of the population the United States will live in metropolitan areas. As has already been indicated, crime and delinquency rates are considerably higher in the more deprived centers of these metropolitan areas where slum conditions prevail.

In inner-city areas where income is low, unemployment high, housing poor, health resources inaccessible, and recreation facilities inadequate, the crime and delinquency rates are staggering.

In other words, where crime and delinquency rates are highest, one is certain to find all the other evidences of social disintegration.

As the Crime Commission report made clear: ". . . Negroes who live in disproportionate numbers in slum neighborhoods account for a disproportionate number of arrests. Numerous studies indicate that what matters is where in the city one is growing up, not religion or nationality or race" . . . It found that, "for all groups, delinquency rates were highest in the center and lowest on the outskirts of the city." The Commission report then noted:

> . . . but for Negroes, movement out of the inner-city and absorption into America's middle class have been much slower and more difficult than for any other ethnic or racial group.[4]

One of the gravest challenges facing the nation today, then, is to be found in the interlocking problems of poverty, discrimination, and the cities.

Few things cause more concern, or are more frightening and real than violent crime in our cities. The twenty-six cities with populations of 500,000 or more contribute about half the total reported major violent crimes, yet comprise only about one-fifth of the total reporting population. That violent crimes in the city are committed primarily by young persons between the ages of eighteen and twenty-four, followed by youth in the fifteen to seventeen group, is a gloomy portent for the future.

Such crime is overwhelmingly committed by males, usually with poor education, and little or no employment skills. Violent crime rates for Negroes appear to be considerably higher than for whites.

The urgent need to reduce violent crime among urban non-white youth is obvious, requiring a total effort toward changing their demoralizing conditions and life patterns, the unequal opportunity and discrimination they confront, and the over-crowding and decay of the urban ghettos in which most of them live.

Middle Class Delinquency—Suburbia

The Crime Commission report observed: "It is likely that the official picture exaggerates the role played by social and economic conditions since slum offenders are more likely than suburban offenders to be arrested and sent to juvenile court. In fact, recent self-report studies reveal suburban and middle class delinquency to be more significant a problem than was ever assumed."[5]

Many suburban communities find themselves faced with a rapid population growth. This rapid growth has made it difficult for suburbs to increase the level of services needed by their residents—including resources to meet pressing problems such as delinquency.

A study of delinquency in an education conscious and middle class suburb revealed that two-thirds of the delinquents were from the least affluent families.[6] Thus, special problems arise for poor youth in middle class communities. Failure in education in a community which emphasizes education for the college bound puts special pressure on both parents and children.

Since current trends are toward movement from the city to the suburbs, the pattern of delinquency in middle class suburban communities is likely to become more pronounced. There is a grave need not only for more information about the quantity and quality of delinquency in suburban areas but also for the provision of services to meet the special needs of suburban delinquents and their families.

Changing Patterns of Youthful Behavior

This century has seen a period of unprecedented rapid social, industrial, ideological and political change.

During the post-war era, the pace of change has increased still further, transforming the world in a way that no one twenty-five years ago could have anticipated. These years have brought to the more advanced nations of the world an affluence never before dreamed of. They have seen the liberation—often accompanied by violence—of the majority of the world's population from colonial rule. They have seen a time of such extraordinary scientific and technological innovation that physical, human, and social environments have been profoundly transformed.

During the 1960's, Americans lived in mounting historical crisis. The symptoms were everywhere: poverty and urban deterioration in the world's richest nation, racism in a society committed to equality, civil disturbances in the streets of urban slums, campus unrest, and the growing disaffection and alienation among those from the best educated generation in history.

This rapid pace of change has produced new forms and expressions of youth revolt and protest—ranging from rejection of society and withdrawal from the community, to attempts to overthrow the *system* through violent confrontations. The shifts in youthful behavior have been so frequent and sudden that adults often have been unable to perceive, much less understand, what is happening.

Institutional Response to Youth

Youth protest and rebellion, whether it takes the form of student violence or disengagement and alienation from society, is often the response of youth to institutional systems that exclude them or that they perceive to be degrading.

Youth deeply resent the definitions, categories and restrictions that have been assigned to them. If, on the other hand, they are accepted as legitimate partners, as they were in the past when their labor was required by a less efficient society, they are more likely to participate in, and give support to, the key systems of the community.

Young people are not content to have things done for them; they want a share in shaping their destinies. They are seeking one of the most important of all human needs: to be taken seriously, to have their voices heard.

Whether adult society and youth can bridge the gap depends in large part upon the capacity of our institutions to develop procedures that will enable those who seek change to be part of the process of change. Special efforts must be made to find ways of including those who have suffered the most from exclusion and who have traditionally been labeled as deviant. Youth who have little or no hope or confidence in themselves, or their situation, must be convinced that they are of value and worth, not only to themselves, but to their community and its institutions.

An effort to involve youth in the community and its institutions is part and parcel of a total effort as institutional change.

Institutional change is defined for the purposes of this report as the effort to improve institutional practices, procedures and policies in such a way so as to improve their responsiveness to youth and delinquent needs, to improve their effectiveness in combating juvenile delinquency, and to improve their abilities to provide meaningful and constructive youth roles in the carrying out of their activities.

In the modern world, the family has become a focal point where a great many institutional influences meet but the way in which families function depends on the way they are influenced by various community institutions.

Today, the family and local community can no longer exercise any strong control over the activities and content of education, industry, recreation, health services, or law enforcement. It is just the other way around. This is especially true of poor families, since their functioning is almost completely dependent upon public institutions. When they need help, they have neither the resources or know how to make independent choices among both public and private alternatives.

Many of the agencies serving the poor are unable to serve them well. Restrictive regulations, inadequate budgets, personnel shortages, and fragmentation among the public services also serve as barriers to adequate assistance. Families who are exclusively dependent upon public services that cannot provide adequate solutions to their problems are especially subject to the feelings of hopelessness and surrender that are often instrumental in promoting marital conflict and inability to assume meaningful parental roles.

The Official Response to Delinquency—Labeling and Stigma

When official agencies respond to certain behaviors by placing a youth in the delinquent category, they attach a label that seriously affects his future opportunities and conduct.

Once a youth is stamped delinquent, the police, the court, the school, and other official agencies respond to him on the basis of that label in a manner different from the way they respond to those without it. The label also become known to the public which then views the youth with suspicion.

Further, the young person may begin to perceive himself as different or *bad* and act accordingly. Having a record makes it more difficult for a youngster to walk conventional paths and have equal access to the opportunities of society. Faced with this dilemma, the young person may be propelled to act out further the delinquent role he has been assigned.

Without the evidence to show that official actions by police and courts are successful in preventing further delinquency, the exercise of caution in determining when young people are to be labeled assumes overwhelming significance.

There is reason to believe, on the other hand, that the very act of official intervention has an impact directly contrary to that which it is designed to create. While the court may see its intervention as helpful and rehabilitative, prospective employers, for example, tend to view less benignly the fact that the youth *has a record.*

The schools may view with suspicion the youngster who has been pronounced delinquent. Further, it is important to draw the distinction between engaging in one delinquent act and the repetitive commission of delinquent acts.

Many young people may engage in one or two delinquent acts as a relatively normal part of their adolescence. Occasional and minor delinquency need not presage a delinquent career. To funnel such youth into the formal juvenile justice and correctional system may have the unfortunate and unnecessary consequence of contributing to the development of a career in delinquency.

Correctional Agencies

The field of youth corrections faces two serious problems. First, funds and facilities are inadequate to the demands placed on correctional institutions by the community. Second, the validity of the techniques of present day corrections has been seriously challenged.

Even with its swing away from large institutions to smaller correctional facilities, the correctional process still segregates and labels those in its custody. It still stands as the last resort—the end of the line for those unfortunate enought to enter its jurisdiction.

The Crime Commission report stated that: ". . . for the large bulk of offenders, particularly the youthful, the first or minor offender, institutional commitments can cause more problems than they solve. Institutions tend to isolate offenders from society, both physically and psychologically, cutting them off from schools, jobs, families and other supportive influences and increasing the probability that the label of criminal will be indelibly impressed upon them."[7]

In many communities, however, youth are referred to the correctional system because no treatment alternatives exist. This is true most frequently in the poorer residential areas where the lack of social walfare resources and other alternatives often require the police to send children to court; and the courts, in turn, often have no alternative but to send these children to correctional institutions.

"The Statistics on Public Institutions for Delinquent Children—1969", the latest year for which complete statistics are available—indicates that approximately 52,000 children and youth were living in residental correctional institutions in that year, a four percent decrease over the previous year. Of these youth, the preponderant majority—43,000—were in training schools; an additional 1,500 were in forestry camps and ranches; and 3,200 were in reception and diagnostic centers.

Such institutional care is expensive. The 1969 figures show that approximately $258.2 million was spent on public institutions serving delinquents in that year, at a per capita cost of $5,031.

Even more important is the fact that the traditional forms of institutionalization are relatively ineffectual in rehabilitating most delinquent youth. The recidivism rate for youth released from public and private residential institutions ranges from an estimated fifty percent to eighty percent. The 1968 Uniform Crime Report stated:

> The younger the age group, the higher the repeating rate, has been documented many times, as it is here . . . of the offenders under 20 released in 1963, 74 percent were rearrested by 1969, 72 percent of those 20 to 24, and 69 percent of the offenders 25 to 29 years. When viewed by race, the Negro rearrested rate, 71 percent, was higher than the white offender rate of 61 percent. All other races, made up primarily of Indian Americans, had a rearrest rate of 82 percent between 1963 and 1969. Of the 1,419 female offenders released in 1963, 47 percent had been rearrested for new offenses by 1969.[8]

Correctional services for youth should be an integral part of the network of services for all youth in the community.

Correctional treatment should be closely related to the other systems that exist to reintegrate its charges into the main currents of society. Youth in training schools or in a community-based facility should have available to them the same breadth of services offered to their peers on the outside.

Support must be given to the search for alternative methods of providing services to achieve this integration of correctional systems into broader services offered in the community. States and local communities must be given the opportunities and incentives to innovate and experiment with these methods; and to develop correctional programs that are incorporated into the community so that the isolation, alienation and disassociation that often follow from traditional correctional experiences do not disconnect young offenders from society.

Finally, much of the help that probationers and parolees need can come from community institutions—help from schools in acquiring the education necessary for employment, and help from employment services and vocational training facilities in finding jobs. If probation and parole officers are to mobilize community resources to deal more effectively with offenders, they must develop new work styles that reach out to community resources and relate them to the needs of their caseloads.

New approaches to rehabilitation may make possible the assignment of probation and parole officers to specific target communities to act as advocates and mobilizers of resources for problem youth living in these communities. The role of the community corrections worker might be analagous to that of the Ombudsman, a spokesman for the target population in the larger community. New approaches might also make it possible for courts and correctional agencies to recruit and train both professional and nonprofessional workers to carry out these and other new roles in the community.

FOOTNOTES

[1]UNIFORM CRIME REPORTS, Federal Bureau of Investigation, U.S. Department of Justice (Washington, GPO, 1969).

[2]JUVENILE COURT STATISTICS, National Center for Social Statistics, Social and Rehabilitative Service, U.S. Department of Health, Education, and Welfare (Washington, D.C., 1969).

[3]President's Commission on Law Enforcement and Administration of Justice, *The Challenge of Crime in a Free Society,* (Washington, GPO, 1967).

[4]*Ibid.,* p. 57.

[5]*Ibid.*

[6]Stanton Wheeler, Leonard Cottrill, and Ann Romasco, *Juvenile Delinquency: Its Prevention and Control* in *Task Force Report on Juvenile Delinquency and Youth Crime* to the President's Commission on Law Enforcement and Administration of Justice (Washington, GPO, 1967), p. 44.

[7]President's Commission, *The Challenge of Crime.*

[8]UNIFORM CRIME REPORTS 1968, p. 39.

SECTION TWO

ORGANIZATION AND MANAGEMENT

CHAPTER 2

MODERN ORGANIZATION AND MANAGEMENT

HARVEY M. ADELMAN
JOSEPH FINK

Introduction

MANAGEMENT WITHIN AN organization is generally accepted as that part of the structure where the administrative, executive, decision-making responsibility lies. Todays' organizations, using as a model any large structured hierarchy, develop decision-making as a behavior that is public and planned—an identifiable *process*. Management seeks to apply both the recent systems theories and the older concepts of the behavioral sciences. The term *modern* as used with management organizational behavior today usually means the closer involvement of systems and behavioral sciences.

The movement toward management systems is more than a conceptual undertaking. The use of computerized quantitative methods enables planners to view management as a specific system (or a subsystem) with its own behaviors and processes rather than an attachment to existing structures. This document will attempt to present some of the system behaviors and the psycho-social processes within the management functions.

In the discussions which relate to the location of decision-making it should be clear that all the decisions are not made by a few top-echelon executives, but that there is a delegation of such responsibilty to managers on other levels. A prime consideration of management—

one which underlines almost all of its behavior—is that it administers this function and as much as making decisions it manages the decision-making activities.

Management and Organizational Size

An important area of organization study which seems to get less consideration than it should, is in the limitations imposed by management on organization size.

Since expenditures of time and energy are finite, there are limits on the numbers of subordinates or units that can be effectively managed. Koontz and O'Donnell call this the Span of Management.[1]

As the numbers of personnel increase there are often resulting increases in the numbers of levels in an organization. A limitation crops up because of the additional communications that become necessary, and to this is added the concerns with cost and efficiency.

The problem to be resolved is the optimum organizational size that can be appropriately managed for a given output. Three areas need to be dealt with to maximize efficiency:

A. Socio-political Factors. The social aspects of organization are being treated with some newer emphasis. Exactly how the span of management or its size influences the productive behavior of organization members is not understood, but these are issues in group psychology and need to be recognized.

B. Communication. Lengthening organization chains often change communication content, decisions made without *going up* leave higher levels of management unaware of what may be happening, and when a manager's capacities get saturated there are impediments to the flow of information.

C. Management Personnel. When the span of management is reduced an increase is required in the number of supervisors. Such added expense can only be justified by an increase in productivity of the organization supervised. Costs of added management personnel have the greatest impact on smaller organizations.

As a general proposition, the restrictions resulting from socio-political factors are hard to pin down and the costs of additional management tend to be absorbed as an organization gets larger. The primary reasons for inefficiency that are left stem from problems of communication and the frequency and complexity of the interactions between a manager and his subordinates.

However, there are a number of factors in regard to personnel that can have an important influence on these problems without (in a given situation) suffering from a loss of efficiency. These are:

1. Subordinate Training
2. Planning
3. Delegation of Authority
4. Lateral Communication
5. Objective Standards
6. Management Staffing
7. Direct Access

All of the factors above, which might act in an efficient manner, are subject to *diminishing returns*. The question is whether or not an organization can expand without incurring increased inefficiencies up to the limits of its operation. It is usually sufficient to demonstrate that management is not the limiting factor in organizational size.

D. Organization Variables. Two examples will be considered which fit most academic organizational and administrative management theories. The variables grow out of the concept of structuring an organization into *departments* and delegating functional authority so that a process can be carried out.

The variables, as discussed by a number of authors are that of *self-containment and specialization.* It should be readily apparent that departmentalization which provides the highest coordination and is self-contained, may suffer when compared to the economy obtainable through specialization. However, as an organization gets larger, there are greater efficiencies to be gained from self-containment since coordination costs begin to increase.

E. The Role of the Individual. Associated with the above is the way in which organization members have tended to be regarded. The employee may be viewed as a static unit whose function is the performance of assigned tasks. He may also be considered as an invariant rather than a reactor to the dynamics of the situations.

Some of the behavioral aspects of organizations are lost when the functioning individual is not considered as a variable and when relationships of people and equipment to performance are considered as *fixed.*

Leadership

Research on organizational performance has concentrated for many years on the qualities of the manager as a supervisor, on the relationship between the leader and the subordinates, and on the rules (or lack of them) which seem related to optimum results. The quality of leadership comes out as being among the attributes with greatest importance. There is some contention that it is the basic behavior pattern of the leader that produces results, with little regard to the criteria of productivity, employee satisfaction and/or absenteeism.

The principal leadership quality involved is the focus on the personal aspects of the subordinates and on the effort to build goal-oriented work groups. *Employee-centered* supervisors as contrasted to *job-centered* leaders have been the subject of much study.[2]

Leaders whose concept of management follows the job-centered concept have units with relatively poor production records, while the best performance records seem to appear with *interest in people* operations.

The Organization of Decision Making

Some authorities propose that *authority* may not be the basic principle of organization and management and that command systems should be subordinated to information and decision systems. An overview of most of the ingredients of such systems seems to suggest a typology based on the characteristics of the process of making decisions. The steps in this organizational process are embraced in the following seven items:

1. Goals must be specified.
2. The attainment of these objectives must be studied.
3. Alternate solutions should be surveyed.
4. Selection of a solution should follow after evaluation.
5. Acceptance and authorizations are required.
6. The activity gets implemented.
7. The outcomes must be evaluated.

The decision-making process falls within more than one set of activities—however, the unifying characteristic is its problem solving nature. This will remain true even though the decision area may vary from a production process to development of a chemical or engineering product to psycho-social problems.[3]

A. PERT SCHEDULING. A document on modern management would be remiss without a few words on Program Evaluation and Review Technique (PERT), one of the *modern* system buzz words. Today's organizational emphasis on time scheduling requires each decision maker to be current with methods for planning, monitoring and controlling a complex problem environment. PERT, originally designed to coordinate Polaris missle contractors, is a principle vehicle for such monitoring. PERT's outstanding feature is the use of time estimates in a schedule for the duration of activities that have not been undertaken before and have no existing time standards. In general it can be described as follows:

1. A complete project survey is made and tasks identified.
2. These tasks are arranged in a network of named *activities* and *events*.
   a. The actions required to go from one event to another are named (activity).
   b. The accomplishments at a specific point in time are named (events).
3. *a* and *b* above are put into a network diagram in sequence.
   a. Arrows connecting two or more events represent activities.
   b. Directionality indicates the order of undertaking.
4. The sequence is rigidly adhered to with following events not completed until all of its preceding events are finished.
5. Each network activity has a time estimate. (Sometimes several estimates [high-low] are made.)
6. A critical path is formed by linking those events that take the longest time in a sequence. Other expected activity times can sometimes be delayed by shifting emphasis from them to the critical path.

The entire concept of PERT which is an advanced development of planning and control techniques is especially useful for performance evaluation in terms of time (i.e. men and money) for management decision-making.[4]

Automation, Management and Organization

Since the time that man became a tool-user and began to develop organized behaviors he has been using *machines* to supplement his own physical (and now mental) efforts. Managers, bosses in a pre-industrial revolution sense, always seem to be oriented toward both increased productivity and the replacement of workers by machines. The problems of relationships between management and labor caused by technological shifts in employment and social policies, and impacted on by automation, can be anticipated to continue as one of the underlying dynamics of our society.

Another class of automation impact is that of cybernation* in the information science revolution which enables management to acquire greater control over the decision-making processes in policy planning and administration. Cybernation is the use of machines to perform or assist in all the processes in information management.

The most positive effect of automation is an increase in productivity. The human labor organization no longer is as essential to produce good and services. Industrial robots (machines) have been welcomed by labor in many areas of production where physically demanding tasks make the expenditure of human effort less appropriate to the sense of technological advancement. The requirement for a management organization in the newer automated textile mill, for example, has completely disappeared. The dislocation of people and skills, as a result of mechanization, requires the private sector to make a continuing reappraisal of its role, (on the other side of the argument, automation and mechanization lead to increased productivity which makes it feasible for a greater private involvement in the overall social problems of technological change).

Management has to consider some new roles in regard to the automating of information handling and its subsequent effects on decision-making. More effective problem solving because of automated information systems leaves room for many things that management may not have regarded as a necessity before. Lang range planning may become a more highly considered organization behavior. New entrants in management will undergo a different education than present

---

*A term credited to Donald Michael, CRUSK, University of Michigan.

managers—and education to equip them for the new technologies. The type of decision that middle management has customarily dealt with will undergo an upgrading as the minutiae of information becomes less burdensome.

The decision process itself, which is the cornerstone of management, is undergoing some subtle changes. A great deal of concentration is being given to the design and implementation of the information management system behind the decision process because the effectiveness of the organization will depend on it.

A. The Management Information System. One of the most important new assists to come into the inventory of managers decision-making tools is Automated Data Processing (ADP).

Information storage and retrieval (IR) via the electronic computer is only recently starting to make inroads into the problem of the executive decision making process.

Of course, storage and retrieval and the indexing and filing required is *made to order* for ADP capabilities at a low level. System implementation for management systems, however, even with complete understanding, is much more difficult than the description of library IR procedures. This kind of storage and retrieval is quite simple. A set of key words is used to identify documents. These are put into an index which also locates the material. After these are stored in a computer memory one can search and locate by key word. Abstracts (if abstracts are entered) can be an output. However, a tremendous programming effort has to be considered for the development of indexing systems.

Routine data processing in a management system is usually occupied with furnishing statistical reports about internal operations. To go several steps beyond this requires a recognition that it is not the *hardware* but the information management system which can contribute to problem resolution. There are few automatic functions in management. The documented material is neither compact nor homogeneous and will often be as wide-ranging and diffuse as the character of the decision-making.

B. Program Planning Budgeting Systems (PPBS): Modern organizations have become increasingly interested in setting objectives to guide their behavior with respect to goods and services. Most of these objectives imply criteria which provide for measurements of how effective the organization is functioning. In most cases, however, the organization cannot totally reach all objectives because of the scarcity of monetary and personnel resources at their disposal. Consequently, they are forced to make trade-offs, or suboptimize their behavior toward the complete range of desired goals. In making the trade-off decisions each organization usually keeps in mind both the benefits of their programs as well as the costs of implementing them over the required period. Thus, these decisions are circumscribed by the budgets which essentially picture the allocations that management has made to the various goals.

Most organizational budgets, however, may be described as the traditional sort, i.e., yearly allocations assigned to personnel and items. This budget has been referred to as *line item* budgets. As such they are not designed as aids to decision making but rather as support to auditors and comptrollers. This budget does not support policy decisions and may be used only elliptically as a management device. Further, the one year purview does not seem to support long range planning and seemingly ignores both the administration of large scale programs and the optimization of the use of scarce resources. In short, the traditional budget would seem to ignore its potential use as a device for improving planning and operational effectiveness.

A relatively recent budget innovation has been PPBS. This approach views budgeting as a framework for making management decisions.[5] One of its basic objectives is to evaluate systematically the relative merit of separate programs by comparison of the relative costs and benefits and consequences of alternative decisions over an extended time period, e.g., five years or longer. The system relates to quantifiable objectives or what the organization wishes to achieve. Expenditures are designed accordingly. Data is then collected on how well the program is meeting its objectives. The process of implementation and reevaluation is continuously iterated until the objectives are either reached or considered untenable.

The major contribution of PPBS is its stress on programs instead of organizational entities such as departments, bureaus, and offices. Programs such as delinquency prevention have components in many departments and not just within criminal justice agencies. The analysis necessary to prepare the PPBS documents must uncover these and assign the resources to the more general program with its specific objectives. The result has been less duplication of effort, more realistic assignment of responsibility, and greater articulation of performance. With information about progress more readily available and with desirable outcomes stated, management can now make decisions in the presence of reasonable estimates of outcome. The budget can thus serve the dual function of providing for cost control while at the same time allowing for long range planning and meaningful management decisions. Consequently, the end result of PPBS is a framework for making decisions based upon predicated impact of various allocation alternatives.

Evaluation As A Management Function

Perhaps the most important part of the management of an organization is the evaluation of the work done or the services of items provided. In the presence of specifically stated objectives it is necessary to determine how effectively the organization is performing and, if not, what needs to be changed to pursue the goals. In organizations whose output is a specified product, evaluation is relatively simple. In those dealing with social phenomena or services, evaluation becomes much more difficult. It is the latter case that confronts much of society today and since evaluation is difficult it is typically omitted from consideration. The result has been poor understanding of problems and only feeble attempts at solution.

Two points about evaluation should be clearly understood: 1. the concept of evaluation is rapidly changing, becoming in particular much more pervasive and less quantitative; and, 2. the methodologies available are extremely poor and urgently need reformulation. Traditional concepts of evaluation have denoted two complementary operations. The first is a comparison of some results, output, or product, with a set of standards—in an absolute sense. A test score is an example. The second involves a comparison between two or more methods of producing identical results, output, or product, in a relative sense. The operations have usually implied the collection of initial status data for comparison with later data of the same sort.

Generally, the traditional rules of experimental design and field control are rigorously invoked.

In dealing with organizations that have broad programs, evaluation should be viewed in a broad manner. In this view the results of evaluation are related to decision-making. Thus, the first step toward evaluation becomes an identification of the class of decisions at issue, such as whether to continue a program, choose among competing programs, and so forth. Then sub-decisions are identified concerned with feasibility, quality, effectiveness, and efficiency or other attributes of the major decision. The process of collecting and interpreting data relevant to those attributes is seen as the substance of evaluation.

In most public agencies services are provided in relation to a problem to be solved. The effectiveness of any program is the degree to which the problem in question has been impacted. Thus, a program of evaluation should be directed toward a determination of the conformance between community need (problem) and actual performance of the organization(s) in question. In a *system* philosophy the following steps in the evaluation process are identified:

1. Identification of need (problem)
2. Statement of objectives concerning how the organization wishes to impact the problem
3. Development of remedial programs
4. Implementation of the program
5. Measurement of the effect of the program (evaluation)

Psycho-Social Bases for Management Behaviors

It has long been apparent that those who are interested in management and organizations are basically concerned with the psychological (and sociological) bases of human behavior. Entire graduate curricula, leading to advanced degrees, are now built about such requirements. The practical applications take place in a widespread environment, in both the public and private sectors. Some of the areas given prominent consideration are motivation, sensitivity training, conflict, behavior theory, attitudes, etc. One of these concepts, conflict, is presented as a brief example.

A. Conflict. Conflict is used in many ways by organizational theorists. Katz and Kahn view conflict as a behavior that results from the relationship of rules and regulations to human needs, while Dahrendorf[6] associates conflict with dominance roles—an authority concept. Thus, conflict is seen as both a behavioral consequence of feelings and as an antecedent to other behavior. Coser[7] has pointed out both functional and dysfunctional aspects of conflict as interpreted from selected subgroups. It would thus appear that little agreement exists as to what *conflict* denotes and what kind of behavior it entails. Does conflict reside within a person, between organizational entities, or external to both? How can a manager in viewing behavior understand that conflict is somehow associated with what he is observing?

The concept of conflict is interwoven with motivation in regard to the property of stimulating behavior. Like motivation, conflict involves both *approach* behavior (goal directed) and *avoidance* behavior (escape). The responses that one observes is a result of the interaction of approach and avoidance tendencies. Some basic understanding of these two behaviors is necessary to a meaningful conceptualization of the term conflict.

Approach—as one nears a desirable goal the motivation to continue gets stronger.

Avoidance—as one nears the object to be avoided the tendency toward escape grows correspondingly higher. When these two tendencies occur toward the same goal objects the resulting behavior may be said to be some function of *conflict.* The following are some examples:

1. *Approach - Approach*—this type of conflict occurs when two equally desirable alternatives are available. Usually there is some hesitation in decision making but once an alternative is chosen the conflict is resolved.

2. *Approach - Avoidance*—this type of conflict is the most insidious. Essentially, the closer you approach the goal the more you wish to avoid it. The more you avoid the greater the tendency to approach once more. For example, if you desire a date with a beauty queen but you are afraid of a rebuff, an approach/avoidance conflict can be said to exist.

3. *Avoidance - Avoidance*—this type of conflict is a function of equally undesirable decision alternatives. For example, failing school

and engaging in study behavior may present two unwanted choices. Consequently, the individual may go to the movies, or, in the parlance of the psychologist, leave the field.

It would thus appear that the concept of conflict can be applied to a knowledge of antecedent conditions on the one hand and resultant behavior on the other. The term is useful when it is related to behavior it purports to explain, and can markedly improve administrative understanding of organizational behavior.

Conclusions

A discussion of *Modern Organization and Management* leads to a conclusion that the *administration of decision-making* in a very wide variety of behaviors and forms is the essence of organizational functions. There are many areas that need extensive consideration which have been briefly alluded to in this coverage. Among the important ones are the Systems Concepts, the Psychological Bases of Organizations, Personnel Management and the Executive Function of a multi-level bureaucracy.

Above all, implicit in all analyses of organizational functions is the emerging role of the person, whether subordinate, middle manager or top executive, as an *individual* whose personal goals and behaviors must be considered as the paramount function to be kept in the proper perspective.

FOOTNOTES

[1]H. Koontz, and C. O'Donnell, *Principles of Management,* McGraw-Hill, New York, 1964.

[2]D. Katz, and R. L. Kahn, *The Social Psychology of Organizations,* New York, John Wiley & Sons, Inc., 1966.

[3]J. G. March and H. Simon, *Organizations,* Wiley, New York, 1958.

[4]P. P. Schoderbek, *Management-Systems,* Wiley & Sons, New York, 1968.

[5]Henry S. Rowen, *PPBS What and Why, Civil Service Journal,* Jan-March, 1966.

[6]R. Dahrendorf, *Toward a Theory of Social Conflict, Journal of Conflict Resolution,* 1958, pp. 170-183.

[7]L. Coser, *The Functions of Social Conflict,* New York, Free Press, 1956.

CHAPTER 3

PLANNING, PROGRAMMING, BUDGETING SYSTEM FOR LOCAL GOVERNMENT (PPBS)

HARVEY M. ADELMAN
JOSEPH FINK

MOST LEVELS OF GOVERNMENT, whether national or local in scope, are concerned with what may be termed *substantive* areas. Some of these may be health, education, welfare, criminal justice, or countless others. The major societal concerns are usually embedded in statements about desirable goals such as, *improve the quality of life, pursuit of excellence in education,* or *decrease the rate of juvenile recidivism.* These statements are generally referred to as objectives and, in a theoretical sense, should key organizational behavior accordingly. Thus, the attainment of the stated objectives should encompass the basic structure of the agencies involved with the goals in question. However, most local government organizations are somewhat constrained in pursuing objectives by the scarcity of resources at their disposal. They are thus forced into making decisions concerning various priorities, the allocation of remaining resources, and the impact or trade-offs resulting.

However, current decision-making, even minor decisions, may have impact or consequences for many years to come. Thus, each decision alternative must take into account a minimum of two considerations:

1. The benefits of the program considered for implementation.

2. The costs of the various programs.

In addition, the impacts of both implementing and not implementing any given alternative must also be treated in a similar manner. It would thus appear that decisions regarding courses of action necessarily involve the budget process. This is true even though most government agencies do not appear to predicate their decisions upon these important considerations.

At any level of government, according to Rowen,[1] the budgeting process can and should provide a guide for public policy decisions and a tool for effective management. Since decisions, as previously stated, have long-range implications, it follows that the budgeting process should also support long-range planning. But this is not the case with current practices. Public budgeting on the local level seems to be based upon yearly consequences and seems to relate more to the cost accountant and the comptroller rather than management. The following descriptions seem to characterize the traditional budget:

1. The budget is organized at the highest executive level and typically excludes the substance considerations of lower level agencies.
2. Each specific class of expenditure is articulated with special emphasis on personnel, supplies, travel, and so forth.
3. The time period for budget use is usually one fiscal or calendar year.
4. The traditional budget is input oriented. That is, amounts of money are allocated to categories of expenditure.

Thus, the major focus of the traditional budget appears to surround those factors that must be brought together to achieve some level or organizational performance. That level is defined, in a somewhat circular fashion, in terms of what the resources can accomplish for the budget period. The major divisions of these budgets seem to be the department level where large public organizations are concerned.

With the changing nature of bureaucracy, this form of budget process and use has become somewhat archaic and unsatisfactory in general. Some of the reasons follow:

1. The names and missions of departments and subordinate elements often reflect purposes of years before and are no longer representative of current functions and practices.

2. Monies allocated to line items such as personnel reflect little of actual performance for the involved functions.
3. The one year character of the budget destroys continuity from year to year and reflects little about significant money decisions.
4. Decisions based upon this budget typically ignore the interrelationships between various parts of the organization.

In sum, the traditional line item budget does not really reveal whether we are spending the right amount of money for the right thing. It is for these reasons that the Planning Program Budgeting System (PPBS) was introduced.

The development of PPBS essentially involved an orderly progression through a number of relatively distinct phases. The *first* phase encompassed those attempts to control expenditures through the application of accounting techniques.[2,3] Accountability of dollars for public expenditures was a dominant concern in the early twenties and that tradition has carried over even into the more advanced concepts of control and management. The *second* major development was based partially on management needs for efficiency control.[4] This phase can be termed a performance phase and it was concerned with work measurement, cost control and other basic techniques of the time and motion period of the late twenties and early thirties. The *third* phase was oriented to planning and the setting of objectives.[5] In effect this philosophy resulted in budgets being oriented toward the *effectiveness* problem rather than the *efficiency* problem of phases one and two. The stress on objectives to key budgets began in the early 1900's, but only became important when the techniques of system analysis, operations research and others were available to aid in implementation. PPBS contains remnants of all three phases denoted above.

By way of defining the PPBS, it should be stated from the outset that planning and programming are part of the same process. Planning is the selection of courses of action through a rather systematic consideration of alternatives. Programming is concerned with the specific determination of methods of implementing selected alternatives. Part of the programming task is the selection of dollar amounts for the alternatives. The budget format is differentiated from the traditional format by its orientation to output. That is, the activities of the various departments are aggregated in terms of specific programs or subprograms at various performance levels. These programs and subprograms are in turn related to a minimum of five years of projected expenditures or for a shorter period if the objectives considered are realizable in that time frame.

The major purpose of the PPBS is for providing more effective information and analysis to support management decisions in resources, needs, and allocation among competing claims. This system is predicated upon three fundamental assumptions:

1. The existence in each articulate agency of an analytical capability which carries out continuing in-depth analyses of the objectives and various forms of programs designed to meet these objectives. This input/output/feedback process is consistent with system theory and the ongoing process is keyed to behaviorally stated objectives and criteria.
2. The existence of a multi-year planning process which uses an information system to provide data for decisions. This system is data bound whether that data is available in computerized or manual form. Decisions are viewed as a relatively trivial consequence of necessary and sufficient data.
3. The existence of a traditional budgeting process to transform the program budget into financial terms. Thus, planning for expenditures involves broad program decisions but the money is spent by cost accounting oriented categories.

PPBS is built upon three types of documents:

1. *Program Memoranda*—major programs within the context of objectives, alternatives, and relative contribution of the alternatives to the achievement of these objectives.

2. *Program and Financial Plans*—a periodically updated summary of agency programs in terms of outputs and costs.

3. *Special Studies*—analytic groundwork for decisions reported in program memoranda.

The program and financial plans (PFP) of each agency is a quantitative statement, largely in tabular form, of the programs of the agency, organized according to the main purposes of the agency. Data should be shown for the current year and as far into the future as it is useful to project. This plan expresses objectives and planned accomplishments, wherever possible in quantitative terms (output) and financial terms (input). For a juvenile rehabilitation agency, for example, a description of additional capacity would include recreational facilities, number of youths to be given job training, number of youths to be medically rehabilitated, and so forth. Where quantitative data is difficult to obtain, *softer* data may be used but should be as specific as possible. *Expert* ratings are one example of such a quantitative criterion.

Program Memoranda should also be as concrete as possible. They can be described as analytic, quantitative documents that describe needs, define objectives in precise terms, analyze cost and effectiveness, and state explicit priorities. Assumptions and criteria for choices should be articulated and uncertainties identified. In many cases, social theory may be employed to elucidate certain relationships.

For example, the relationship between education and job levels, those between education and delinquency, expenditures for retraining, and the specific effects on an agency may be clearly drawn. Adequate analysis of this kind is obviously difficult and time-consuming. Therefore, it may take several years to derive adequate memoranda statements. Nevertheless, the desired end products may be reached by a temperate process of successive approximation characterized by gradually improving the documentation with newly acquired data availability.

In considering the application of the PPBS to problems of juveniles we will utilize Churchman's model.[6] The concerned agency must first obtain a statement of objectives even though the initial attempts may result in provisional statements. A decrease in recidivism of juvenile offenders might very well be one of the objectives of a Juvenile Justice Agency, for example. With this preliminary definition accomplished, management must turn to the kinds of activities which will affect—either positively or negatively—juvenile behavior. In the language of the PPBS these activities will be called programs. The first approximation of programs may be obtained from social theory and may be represented as follows:

1. *Prevention* of juvenile delinquency.
2. *Rehabilitation* after delinquent acts.
3. *Control* of delinquency through medical, social, legal, or other activities.

4. *Research* on the problem of delinquency.
5. *Administration* for support to recidivism activities.

These five general programs have been broadly stated. The next task confronting management is therefore to define these programs by a set of subprograms for each. For example, education, new legislation, and new programs of taxation could very well become subprograms under the prevention programs. Initial attempts for the remaining four programs can be equally obvious. The major purpose of further definition is to arrive at activities that are in some manner quantifiable. Thus, the management of an agency wishes to arrive at educational activities in dollars, rehabilitation activities, in terms of in-patient time (days), and so forth. In all of these subprograms, there are several choices for quantifying the amount of activity, but management should choose the ones with the heaviest overall contribution to the major objective of decrease in recidivism.

The new task of management is to determine how much of each subprogram exists in the current system. Care must be exercised that the determination should be directed toward *all* concerned agencies and not just those internal to the Juvenile Justice Agency. Therefore, the program planner assigned to budget development must begin to look to other departments and agencies to assess the amount of activity. It should now be apparent what program budgeting entails. Obviously, no budgeting has yet been considered. Only a description of total current activity has been accomplished. In this regard, it is sometimes helpful to develop a matrix such as illustrated in Table 3-1.

TABLE 3-1 *A Performance Matrix*

PROGRAM	*AGENCY*			
A. Prevention	Law Enforcement	Parole	Probation	Education
1. Sub-Programs				
a. Education	x	x	x	x
b. Legislation	x		x	
c. Taxation		x		x
B. Rehabilitation				
1. Sub-Programs				
a. Training	x	x	x	x
b. Therapy		x	x	x
c. Education	x		x	x

The major purpose of this matrix is to determine how much of each subprogram is divided among the agencies under budgetary concern. Consequently, each program listed under the program axis is described and the amounts of those programs in each agency listed under the agency axis is noted. In Table 3-1, each *X* represents the existence of the specified activity in the agency. Obviously, only two programs were considered as well as only representative agencies. The list on each axis should ordinarily be exhaustive. The next task is to replace the *X's* by some measure of activity from the view of the budgeter.

Obviously, the first step as denoted by the matrix should be stated in terms amenable to data collection. The next step, then, is to construct another matrix, a requirements matrix, which indicates the number of individuals to be handled, or, more specifically, the total hours demanded by each individual for each subprogram. For example, under the education subprogram, a certain demand exists for service. This demand should be assessed in terms of the amount of activity required to meet the stated objectives. Where possible, the assessment should yield dollar estimates of all activities as well as estimates of contribution to objectives. The completed matrices should relate in terms of the requirements in one and the amounts of effort in the other.

In the actual practice of program planning and budgeting, the requirements matrix is compared with the performance matrix to arrive at judgments concerning costs and benefits of each activity. The cost of each activity includes all expenditure items stated in dollar amounts. The benefit is a quantification of the results of the expenditure also stated in dollars. Included in the benefit side of the ratio are seeming intangibles such as *community effect*. The result is a benefit-to-cost ratio which should be maximized for the chosen activities, i.e., the activity alternatives chosen should be those with the highest ratio. Cost benefit judgments may necessarily involve considerable activity in economic analysis of the contribution of each activity. What results then is a third matrix in which each activity's benefits can be compared to its costs.

The advantages of PPBS over the traditional budget has been stated. However, in the absolute sense, many managers feel uncomfortable about the implied judgments which characterize PPBS. It should be remembered that program budgeting is but one techinque among many. Serious knowledge gaps exist and will be pointedly obvious during the budget cycle. Nevertheless, it is reasonable to use the *expert* manager to supply the judgmental efforts where gaps in information exist. Perhaps then the understanding and identification of those gaps is a principle output of PPBS. Special studies may then be performed to complete the data required for sound judgments based upon a multi-year set of programs and budgets.

FOOTNOTES

[1]Henry S. Rowen, *PPBS: What and Why, Civil Service Journal,* January-March 1966.

[2]Committee for Economic Development. Budgeting for National Objectives, New York, CED, January 1966.

[3]W. Hanna, *The Workmen's Compensation Laws of California,* Matthew Bender and Company, 1967.

[4]A. Schick, *The Road to PPB: The Stages of Budget Reform, Public Administration Review,* Vol. XXVI, December, 1966.

[5]F. Mosher, *Program Budgeting: Theory and Practice,* New York: Public Administration Series, 1954.

[6]C. West Churchman, *The Systems Approach,* New York: Delta, 1968.

REFERENCES

Churchman, C. West, *The Systems Approach,* New York: Delta, 1968.

Committee for Economic Development Budgeting for National Objectives, New York: CED, January, 1966.

Hanna, W., *The Workmen's Compensation Laws of California,* California: Bender, 1967.

Hovey, H., *The Planning-Programming-Budgeting Approach to Government Decision Making,* New York: Praeger, 1968.

Mosher, F., *Program Budgeting: Theory and Practice,* New York: Public Administration Series, 1954.

Rowen, Henry S., *PPBS: What and Why, Civil Service Journal,* January-March, 1966.

Shick, A., *The Road to PPB: The Stages of Budget Reform, Public Administration Review,* Vol. XXVI, December 1966.

CHAPTER 4

EFFECTIVE COMMUNICATION

HARVEY M. ADELMAN
JOSEPH FINK

Introduction

EFFECTIVE COMMUNICATION is treated in this paper through brief presentations of its more basic concepts. The primary need is to examine the way persons and groups communicate, the characteristics and restrictions of communication networks, and the control of what is transmitted.

The more universal behavior of individuals in a human society is the sending and receiving of information and it is useful to investigate the psycho-social nature of these transactions.

The following material deals briefly with what some authors may feel are the fundamental issues.

What Is Communication?

Society can be defined as the world of people, and communication is a social affair. A variety of different systems of communication have developed to enable man to live as a social being. The most important system is speech and language. This is more than the inborn reflexes of blushing, or grinning, and more complicated than signs like smiling or crying.

In reviewing the varieties of communication, speech and writing are the principal vehicles, although habits of gesture, hand and face movements, may be even more common.

Tokens for communication in economic systems may be coins, bonds, letters of credit. In the technological world, communication depends on the transmission media. For practical purposes, it is only through communication that business proceeds, education is possible, and law and order are maintained.

The various aspects of communication as studied in different disciplines do not form a unified study and sometimes it becomes difficult to find an acceptable spot from which to review the wealth of material.

Some Concepts. A few of the concepts we deal with need to be understood in their ordinary usage before what we think of as *communication* can also become an element, which, in a circular fashion, communicates to us. Some brief dictionary definitions can serve as a starting point:[1]

Communication—Act of imparting (especially news); information given.
Message—Oral or written communication.
Signal—Preconcerted or intelligible sign conveying information.
Knowledge—Person's range of information.
Sign—Written mark conventionally used for word and phrase; symbol; thing suggested as representation of something; motion or gesture used instead of words to convey information.
Language—A vocabulary and way of using it.
Code—Set of rules on any subject; systematic collection of statutes.

Other communication systems and concepts need to be recognized without any necessity of trying to incorporate them. Among different systems of communication are those that belong to specialists; ornithologists think of the homing of pigeons and physiologists consider the integrative aspects of the nervous system.

Also, apart from natural languages, we have many systems of signs and rules, usually of an inflexible kind. A deck of playing cards is a set of signs and the rules of the game ensure communications and predictable behavior among the players. Every motorist applying for a driver's license gets a book of rules of the road and adherence to these rules is supposed to produce predictable behavior. The patterned flow of communication is often decided by a structured functional relationship between individual (e.g., "Private Jones has the Sergeant's permission to speak to the Captain").

Dictionary definitions of words, as used above, are in connection with *human* communication. Whatever system we deal with, what comes to mind is an interaction of sending and receiving information; letters, newspapers, radio, etc. are examples of how the linkage is created.

Restrictions On Communication

Communication must take into account how a social system functions and the specific needs of its subsystems. Organized communication expects some inhibition among its members.

The following example is of such restriction. Suppose we have a group of sixty people, unorganized, and moving about at random in a conference room. The number of potential two-way communications is N (N-1)/2 or 1770. If the workshop is organized into twelve groups of five persons each, so each person is interdependent with four other people, the number of communication channels is reduced to 120. If each person in a work group is serially dependent, then the number of channels is 4 in each group, or a total of 48. The point is being made that a movement from an unorganized condition to an organized state requires some restrictions to influence random communication into channels appropriate for the accomplishment of organizational purposes.

There are a number of examples that can be used to illustrate the concept of restriction. One with which we all have some acquaintance, is the *national political system.* Its loose organization reflects a requirement of full communication. Every fourth year the major parties nominate two presidential candidates. This is in effect a restriction and channeling of the communication process. Once candidates are selected, factional groups unite and communication to the candidate is restricted. The rank and file does not communicate up the line or get much information down the line except the projected images of the candidate and the party. If all groups and factions had their own parties and representatives in Congress, there would be more communication between the people and their elected leaders, but there would be tremendous problems of system stability.

Communication Network Characteristics

The major characteristics of communication networks are: 1—size, 2—kind, 3—open or closed character, 4—efficiency, and 5—fit between network and function.[2]

1. *Size.* Communication networks may cover an entire system, or only a subsystem. Some nets exist only in top echelons. There is often a discrepancy between the size of a network as seen at the top and its actual size. Executives usually overestimate the number of persons they can reach in their communications.

2. *Kind.* A large communication net may reach an entire system through repetition. In one net the information may go from the top down and be reissued at each level to the one below it. In another net different patterns appear where the messages undergo some translation at each level. The size of the nets is the same but there is a provision for modification of messages. The first pattern is simple and uniform; everyone is exposed to identical information, but a simple system may be advantageous only for simple problems. Complex material repeated uniformly across several subsystems may not be uniform in its meaning and may require modification.

3. *Open or Closed.* A communication circuit has a dominant direction, but it may also involve a circularity. Reaction to a transmission can furnish feedback to the sender. Closure can be a fixed response of acceptance or a report of inadequacy. In the latter, the open case, the cycle is completed and if a fault is fed back the circuit is reactivated. The closed net is one in which the cycle is not open to change once it has been initiated.

4. *Efficiency.* A different aspect of communication nets is their efficiency. This can be measured by the number of links in a network. Earlier we mentioned that restriction in the communication process was part of the essential nature of social organizations. Experiments generally support an hypothesis that the smaller the number of communication links in a group, the greater the efficiency of a group in task performance.[3] Differing number of links can be seen in the following three typical patterns (After Leavitt)[4]

5. *Fit.* A network may be too large and involve irrelevant people or too small, omitting key positions. A common unproductive arrange-

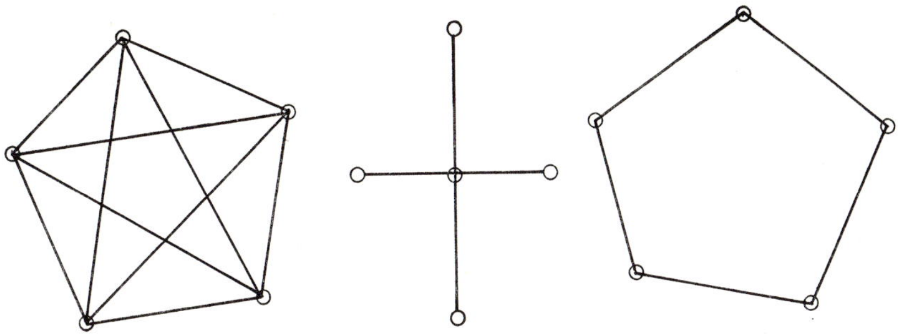

Figure 4-1

ment is a net of disproportionate size with respect to the message. Executives may issue directives to an entire organization when a transmission is only necessary to their immediate subordinates.

Communication Flow

There are three directions in which information can flow in a communication network.[5]

From Top to Bottom. Communications from top to bottom are generally of five types:

1. Information about the organization.
2. Instruction about specific tasks.
3. Explanations about tasks.
4. Performance evaluations to subordinate.
5. Indoctrination information.

Lateral. Communication across peer levels in an organization is often necessary for a system to operate effectively. Unrestricted interactions of a lateral nature can detract from efficiency—but where tasks are of a team variety it may be only through such transmissions that coordination can be effected.

If task coordination is not the problem then unrestricted lateral communication may create confusion and organizational dysfunction. Such communications are usually in a closed network ignoring other levels in an organization.

From Bottom to Top. There are many forms of communication that go up but the most frequent are the grievance and organization behavior categories. Upward communication is basically in conflict with an hierarchical structure. The subordinate role is not conducive to transmitting information to the executive level nor are executives in the habit of listening. Since up the line communication is often used for control purposes there are many self and peer imposed restraints on a free information flow.

Despite efforts to provide upward channels, such expression is not notable in structured organizations. The net is usually small and goes no further than the next level supervisor. Any higher transmission is often in a modified form. Although many executives might contend that their communication networks extend to all subordinate levels, it is usually a theoretical system and in practical operation there are few top echelon open doors.

Psycho-Social Units Of Communication

The following matrix illuminates most of the possibilities for communication between persons and groups. Each unit can transmit and receive information, and the flow is not only in both directions, but can also represent feedback and closure.

The entire range of communication units can be subsumed into this matrix. All of the communication networks considered here, except one, have the quality of being publicly observable in their behaviors. This matrix is one convenient way to describe such networks and can provide a more appropriate alternative for personal/organizational communication undertakings.[6]

Ego. The exception to public observation is the privacy inherent in a person communicating with himself. We make generalized statements about internal communication processes because people are basically alike with behaviors that are caused, motivated and goal directed.

People are also different. Although born with similar physical needs, they acquire a large number of differing social behaviors. We also perceive *facts* differently. One of the most important determinants is relevance to one's needs. Changing perceptions in ourselves and others may be the most important function of the internal communications network.

PERSON-TO-PERSON. The focus of these communications shifts from

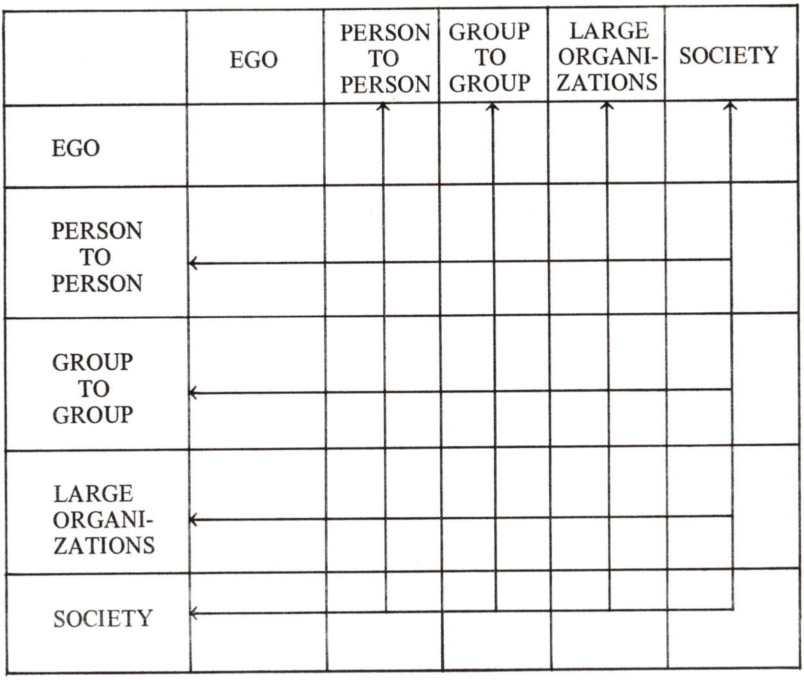

Figure 4-2

one person to the relationships between two or more people and the network that influences and changes the behavior of others. Much energy is devoted to communicating with others—for a purpose. All of the attributes of communication networks may be involved here since people begin, modify, and end relationships by communicating with one another. The mechanism of change and influence is communication.

GROUP-TO-GROUP. From the organization viewpoint communication is usually not to individuals one at a time. Communication is through staff meetings, committees and planning groups. A single person is often not in a position to get all the facts and act on decisions. The problem-solving group has become a new managerial communication tool with a structure for communication and a network for operation.

LARGE ORGANIZATIONS. An organization is a system of tasks, structures, and people. All the behaviors that it must deal with are qualitatively the same as the ego, person-to-person and group-to-group interactions. The units of communication remain much the same and the psycho-social processes for information are not exclusive to any structure.

Most of the interactions we have, as individuals, are acts of communication. This is also true of the behavior of organizations. Communication becomes the very essence of organization and all the forms of social interaction such as the exertion of leadership, influence, or cooperation, can be subsumed under it.

SOCIETY. Communication is not only a process between a sender and a receiver, but also an activity in relation to the social system in which it occurs. Our principal interest in societal interactions is the knowledge that they are usually actions or reactions to a system of controls.

Social control is the capacity of society to manipulate the environments of other persons or groups so as to achieve a planned goal. This normally involves changes in the information received to change in some way the perceptions or values so that there is a response in a desired manner.

The Content Of Communication

So far the material has been a variety of attributes of communication such as structure, direction, composition, restriction, etc. It is the substance, the content of communication, that is behind all the vehicular activity for processing it. What kind of information should be transmitted? What to do with information that is not relevant? After feedback, channel, network and direction problems have been solved, what should the communication be?

It is possible to treat the substance of communication by specific topics. However, the specifics of content do not identify general rules to follow (or avoid).

NOISE AND REDUNDANCY. Identifiable communication contents are the noise and redundancy components of information. To information theorists, sounds that do not communicate any content, and interfere with what one is listening to, are considered *noise*. One has to question whether noise is relevant to the solution of a problem. If not, what should be done about it? In addition to being noisy, group communications tend to be redundant. The same information is discussed over and over. The same point gets made in several ways at different times in the course of a discussion.

Noise and redundancy look like signs of inefficiency in the communication process. We expect to find groups that solve problems like intelligent individuals following a set of reasonable decision rules. The group should learn from its communications, so that it can deal with new problems better than it did with the old ones.

These behaviors do not always happen. So much group activity seems devoted to noise and redundancy that orderly problem-solving processes become obscure. It is understandable that group leaders would like to see noise and redundancy cut to a minimum as quickly as possible, so people can get on with solving the problem at hand.

Maximizing Content. The most common procedure is simply to set up rules. The rules may be formal parliamentary ones or they may be informal. The manager (or group leader) says, "We will stick to the topic in this meeeting. We will not permit people to talk too long." His purpose is to eliminate noise, and his weapon is his authority to enforce organizational rules.

Noise-making behavior by people in groups, like all other behavior, is goal-directed. When several people join to coordinate a task through group communication there may be one central problem common to everyone, but there are also individual problems that each member brings in with him. The noise in a group may therefore be made up, to a large extent, of efforts of individuals to satisfy their personal needs.

It is not practical to exclude all individual noise from group discussion by force or by parliamentary procedure. If these approaches eliminate noise, they eliminate it at the cost of much relevant information.

The other choice is to let the channels carry whatever people want to say. Identify the different classes of information, so that everyone knows what is being discussed. When people have had the opportunity to relieve the *noise* need, they will stop and begin to communicate on the group task.

Groups that operate with fairly free communication follow a somewhat different pattern from more controlled groups. They may start more slowly, usually with noticeable disturbance and not much progress. But they can accelerate fast once they reach the appropriate topic. Controlled groups, in contrast, show steadier progress that apears more orderly from the observer's viewpoint.

Man-Machine Communication

The recent important additions to information handling are the automated forms of communication interchange. These have, in the past two decades, come to occupy a central place in the art. Man-machine relationships are one development of the science of cybernetics, and the carrying of information via electronic data processing equipment is an aspect of man's continual progress toward control of his environment.

We can conceive of the individual's environmental system in terms of a man-machine relationship with the machine as a projection of the personality, normally subject to human control, and capable of converting a given input into a more utilitarian output.

All of the attributes of communication as a concept apply to the qualities of man-machine systems, especially in the automated computer areas. Although no attempt is being made here to develop the theme attendant on the *information explosion* and the problems that it poses for society, it may be useful to point out the communication impact. In 1960 about 1,200,000 articles appeared in 60,000 books and 100,000 research reports. In the United States alone, scientific and technical publications have doubled in size about every twenty years since 1800. Communicators treat some of the problems of handling this expansion of communicable material as *Information Input Overload,* an interesting and complicated sub-topic in communication.

Conclusion

Communication is considered as one of the higher-order forms of behavior between human beings and is, in many senses, their principal activity. The use of effective communication as an instrument of social control is often the goal of the purposive activity of individuals and groups.

The organization of communication into its appropriate dimensions —such as structure, direction, restriction, etc. is a requirement if more than a random state is desired.

The important consideration of the psycho-social nature of communication is its use as an intervening variable, contributing to equilibrium or creating dysfunctional tension, according to the goals and perceptions of the participants.

We often assume that many of our problems are the result of inadequate and faulty communications. The assumption is common where there is a doctrine of universal education, freedom of speech, and a belief that truth will out if everyone has ready access to all the relevant information.

But problems may not be resolved solely as a result of uninhibited communications flow. Exchanging information is not only a way to eliminate problems, it can also reveal them. While communication is often employed for change, it often only changes images (e.g. the very public display on television of the employment of minority group members). Full information flow can be measured in its data transformation sense but there needs to be a qualitative appraisal of its relevancy. While the general principles of communication (as a psycho-social process) often define the limits within which people and societies operate, the application needs to be correct, i.e. relevant, in the transactions between individuals and groups.

REFERENCES

The material in this chapter is based on many sources. The publications in this field are voluminous. Several of the volumes mentioned account for almost 2,000 bibliographic references—and a query about published materials using the term *communication* in their titles would lead to tens of thousands of items.

[1]C. Cherry, *On Human Communication,* New York: Wiley, 1957.

[2]H. J. Leavitt, *Managerial Psychology (Rev.),* Chicago: University of Chicago Press, 1964.

[3]R. Dubin, *Stability of Human Organizations,* In M. Haire (ed.) Modern Organizations Theory, New York: Wiley, 1959, pp. 215-253.

[4]H. J. Leavitt, *Some Effects of Certain Communication Patterns on Group Performance,* J. Abt. Soc. Psych, 1951, pp. 48, 53-60.

[5]H. J. Leavitt, *Managerial Psychology (Rev.),* Chicago: University of Chicago Press, 1964.

[6]D. Katz and R. L. Kahn, *The Social Psychology of Organizations,* New York: Wiley, 1966.

CHAPTER 5

POLICE ADMINISTRATIVE ORGANIZATION

JOHN P. KENNEY

POLICING IS A PHENOMENON of man's passage from the state of nature to the civil state which brought about substitution of justice for instinct in his conduct, and by the giving of his actions the modesty they formerly lacked.[1] Society became a necessity for the preservation of the peace with the subsequent formation of governments and their institutions essential for the maintenance of ordered liberty and the provision of services.[2] Basically the function of policing is concerned with acts against the safety of persons or property. In the simple societies the acts are labelled wrongs against a member or members based upon custom and tradition of what constitutes wrongs. Modern complex societies have codified these acts into laws and regulations and have called them crimes or offenses against the state. Such acts must be antisocial in nature.

Much of the world's population is still policed in much the same manner as society has policed itself since the beginning of societies. It is a folk system for policing which relies on control methods established by the family, the community or the tribal leaders or councils. The prevailing customs prescribe the system. The basic feature of such systems is that people police themselves. Even in more complex societies many features of the *folk* system are found in that control is collectively exercised through the folkways, mores and traditions of particular groups.

Maintenance of ordered liberty clearly has emerged as the overriding role of police in modern society. Traditionally, the police view and society's view of the police role has emphasized criminal law enforcement. However, law enforcement really covers only a relatively small portion of the police activities which contribute to the maintenance of order. Activities may be described as either coercive or non-coercive. Coercive activities include criminal, traffic, regulatory and juvenile law enforcement: keeping the peace and intelligence gathering. Non-coercive activities include social service, crime prevention, participation in the development of an environment of security and stability, and the provision of services. In addition, the police have a major responsibility to protect personal liberties and civil rights. A clarification and understanding of the police role in society gives direction for the administration of the police function and provides the basis for development of the essential programs for the police operations.

Administration of the police function is a result of a government empowering its police agency or agencies to exercise authority in dealing with the challenge of crime and criminal behavior to internal order. Basic responsibility for performance of the police function rests, in the United States, with the state government. However, a myriad of relationships are found between the federal governmental police agencies, and state and local agencies.

Basic responsibility for performance of the police function rests with the state governments. State laws for the most part, regulate crime and criminal behavior and the authority for creation of sheriff's offices and local police forces emanates from state constitutions and statutes. The federal government has been generally precluded from performance of the primary police functions except in jurisdictions under its direct control such as territories and in the District of Columbia. Federal policing agencies have limited policing responsibilities.

A complex matrix of relationships exists between the federal, state and local agencies which is as uneven as the distribution of the agencies. States have established state police and highway patrols and other agencies with limited law enforcement responsibilities which have concurrent jurisdiction for the enforcement of laws in local jurisdictions. In addition states have created bureaus of identification, statewide communications and information systems and state laboratories to assist local agencies. States have also established standards for recruitment and training. Enforcement of federal laws is a responsibility of state and local police agencies as well as of federal agencies. The federal government provides a central repository of criminal information and provides a considerable amount of training for local police personnel. More recently, the federal government has given direct support to state and local police agencies for research and development of new police techniques and improvement in training programs.

Police administration in its broadest sense embraces all of the activities of the federal government and state and local governments related to performance of the police function. By established usage, however, police administration has come to signify primarily the organization, personnel, practices and procedures essential to effective performance of the law enforcement and other traditional police functions by those agencies to which the responsibilty has been entrusted.[3] Generally, reference to the subject of police administration is limited to those agencies responsible for criminal law enforcement and does not include other administration by criminal justice agencies which perform law enforcement functions but with purposes which are otherwise.

Police administration also signifies relationships and interaction between city councils and commissions, county boards of supervisors and commissioners, city and county managers and administrative officers, mayors, boards of police commissioners, governors and other agencies or individuals which have executive responsibilities for administering police agencies. Police departments and other law enforcement agencies do not operate as singular agencies within their governmental units. They are dependent upon a number of other agencies for support and direction.

Basic policies or guidelines for administration of the police function are provided by the *Federal Constitution, State Constitutions, City Charters,* state laws and local ordinances. Administrative policies of local legislative bodies and chief administrators provide direction for administration. Departmental policies provide internal guidelines under which departments perform the police functions. Modification of policies and guidelines is continuous. Court decisions continually impose change on policies, practices and procedures. Public pressures influence change both in laws and ordinances and in administrative and operational policies and practices.

The *police administrator's role* is complex. The major thrust of his efforts is dealing with people and their behaviors in the organizational setting in which he works. He must also cope with the institutional environment which imposes sanctions upon him and formally defines the contexts within which he works. And he lives in a third world of processes which are his major tasks of management which bridge the gap between the behavioral and institutional worlds. To perform his role he must play the game according to the *rules* set by the social milieu with its values and attitudes.[4]

The police administrator is constantly in face to face relationships with people. He is either interacting with personnel of the department, with other department heads or administrators, legislators or legislative bodies, community leaders, or large or small community groups. He must also interact with ethnic, religious and racial groups, each posing different problems. The interplay is dynamic and success or failure depends on how he sees himself, how he sees others and how they see him.

In the context of the behavioral world the police administrator is concerned with power relationships, struggles for position or favor, perceptions of people about their roles, personal intrigue and a whole host of interactions between himself and other people and between other people as such relationships affect the operation of the department. At one time it may be a confrontation between the chief of police and a ghetto riot leader, moments later it may be a meeting with the mayor followed by a meeting with top staff aides. The behavioral relationships between a sergeant and his men, a detective and an armed robber, a juvenile officer and a lost child or the chief's aid and an irate citizen are all part of the police administrator's world of behavior.[5]

The institutional world of the police administrator differs significantly in many ways from his behavioral world, and also influences it greatly. For the most part it has already been established. Seldom does the police administrator share in its building. It includes the legal framework—constitutions, charters and statutes—within which the department must operate, the city or county governmental organization or state or federal agency within which context the administrator must work. These and many other institutional factors impose sanctions and restrictions on the administrator. For example, the Bill of Rights by its very nature circumscribes the behavior of all police personnel. Federal and state supreme court decisions continuously impose changes upon police operations. Defined relationships between the police department, other city departments, the city manager and the city council are other examples.

The world of processes are the tasks of management. The major processes of management include: communicating, coordinating, motivating, and controlling. They provide general categories for guiding and analyzing behavior or personnel and an understanding of the operation of the department.

The police administrator is provided a number of tools and techniques to aid him in the management of the affairs of the department. He has support personnel, he has information, and he has control over personnel. Organization becomes a key tool for establishing inter-relationships, programming activities and directing operations. Relating the real world of operation to the procedural concepts of management provides the important means by which the chief integrates his department.

Police administration then is the meshing of these diverse worlds together, organizing if you will, to accomplish the objectives and purposes of the department. It is the relating together of those elements of laws, of city government, of the community, of police officers, of detectives, of secretaries, and a multitude of activities, situations and incidents in order to provide police service.

Organization: Orthodox Approaches

Police agencies have traditionally viewed themselves as *semi-military* organizations. The implications are that there shall be an hierarchical, job-task related structure with an emphasis on well defined superior-subordinate relationships. A dedication to the *principles* of organization predominates. Acceptance of human relations concepts as modifying forces has come slowly. Emphasis has been on formal organization which is the official organization as viewed by top management of the department. The informal or prevailing social organization which describes personnel relationships has received little attention and is more often than not completely ignored.

However, a larger problem in discussing police organization is arriving at an understanding of what is meant by organization. A simple definition is that formal organization is a network of relationships between things, people, jobs, groups and processes arranged to accomplish a common objective. However, organization is really more. It includes the behavioral patterns of people toward each other. Such patterns influence and modify structure and objectives and, in fact, are an integral part of organization. Because police agencies vary so much in size, definitions and prescriptions with respect to organization become somewhat meaningless, thus emphasis will be on several approaches to organizing.

Influence of Formal Organization Theory[6]

The police have had a dedication to the *principles* of organization and have adhered closely to the concepts of formal organization theory developed in the first half of the twentieth century. Initially, the police looked to the military for organizational guidelines. Classifying themselves as a *semi-military* organization, this came naturally. Military ranks were adopted to go with the uniform.

As management and organization theory began to appear in the public administration literature in the 1920's and 1930's, the police were exposed to it and the few writers in the police field adopted concepts for police organizations. With the appearance of the first edition of *Municipal Police Administration* published by the International City Managers' Association initially in 1938, formal organization theory was universally accepted as the guide. Publication of O. W. Wilson's *Police Administration* in 1950 further amplified on its soundness. The two publications with their succeeding editions have been the principal influencing factors in police organization.[7]

Formal organization theory emanates from the *machine model* which is descriptive of the nineteenth century approach to organization. Basically, organization in that period was authoritarian, emphasizing command, control, direction, and communication through channels. Workers were viewed as automatons with organization based on jobs and tasks and the position of the basic unit. Workers were expected to adjust to the job, behavior was to be ignored and leaders' orders were not to be questioned. Communication was downward, except for reporting of accomplishments. There was no room for acceptance of man as a very complex organism.

Succeeding models developed a broader rationale for concepts of the *machine model* and provided additional rationale for the features of formal organization. Max Weber introduced the term *bureaucracy* and recognized power as an important feature of organization. His ideal type bureaucracy placed emphasis on form and introduced the concepts of hierarchy, specialization of tasks, a specified sphere of competence, established norms of conduct and provided for a record of action.

The Mooney and Reiley Model introduced the idea of *principles* to explain organization concepts. Their *principles* were as follows:

1. *The Coordination Principle* emphasized unity of command and pursuit of a common purpose. The need for authority and leadership is embodied in the concept; but coordination is realized as much by the unifying focus of doctrine, spirit and morale.

2. *The Scalar Principle* has reference to hierarchy with the subprocesses of leadership, delegation and functional definitions. It refers to the vertical division of authority and definite arrangement of duties to organization units.

3. *The Functional Principle* is the concept of specialization. Police organizations specialize in patrol, traffic, investigation, juvenile, records, etc.

4. *Staff and Line.* Staff represents advice and ideas and in the police organization, generally refers to administration, personnel and training and planning and research. Line represents authority and in police organizations refers to units which perform the basic police work such as patrol, traffic and investigation.

The influence of the Mooney and Reiley *principles* on police organizations is quite pronounced.

The Public Administration Model developed from the great wave of governmental reorganization in the 1920's and 1930's. Emphasis was on giving the executive more authority, control and direction over the multitude of diverse autonomous or semi-autonomous agencies which had proliferated in the federal and state governments and in some cities. The main features of the model were as follows:

1. *Executive leadership of administration.* The objective is to make the executive the administrative leader as well as political chief. In council-manager cities the manager is the chief administrative officer.
2. *Unity of command.* Emphasis here is that someone should have sole ultimate responsibility for coordinating agencies or organizational units.
3. *Hierarchical confirmation.* The channels of administrative authority in the hierarchical structure are to be adhered to.
4. *Span of control.* The number of organizational units or persons reporting to a manager or supervisor should be small enough so that the person can give each adequate attention.
5. *Coordination through the budget* gives the chief administrative officer control over agencies or departments.
6. *Boards are for advice* but not for administration.
7. *Staff serves as an instrumentality for coordination and control.* This means that the central budget, accounting and personnel units may maintain rather detailed supervision over line activities.
8. *Departmentation by general purpose.* All of the activities devoted to the same purpose should be grouped together in the same department, i.e., agriculture, public works and policing.
9. *Separation of politics and administration.* Inference of this concept was that politicians tended toward corruption whereas administrators ran clean operations. Special emphasis has been given over the past half century of *keeping politics* out of the police. However, the concept has been criticized as not being realistic since administrators by the nature of their interaction with people are involved in the political process and political leaders of necessity influence the administrative process.

The emphasis in these formal organization models is on hierarchy. Structure is the key based on jobs, positions, processes and procedures. People and their influence on organization have been largely ignored. The models have had a major impact on reorganization studies of police departments and the police literature continues to emphasize formal organizations. The President's Commission on Law Enforcement and the Administration of Justice emphasized the concepts of formal organization, suggesting that there is an essential need to examine internal police organizations in order to determine whether:[8]

—The force's work is apportioned among the various individuals and units according to a logical plan.
—Lines of authority and responsibility are made as definite and direct as possible.
—The number of subordinates who can be effectively supervised by one officer is not exceeded.
—There is *unity of command* throughout the organization.
—Responsibility, once placed, is accompanied by commensurate authority, and that once delegated the user is held to account for the use he makes of it.
—The efforts of the organizational units and of their component members are coordinated so that all will be directed harmoniously toward the accomplishment of the police purpose. The components thus coordinated will enable the organization to function as a well-integrated unit.

To the previously discussed structures must be added the formalized concepts of job-task, rank, skill and pay. They are an integral part of formal organization and complete the emphasis on form as contrasted with recognition of the influence of the behavior of people on organization.

Police Organization Models

Police agencies have adopted the formal organization models in several ways leading to what may be referred to as five approaches to police organization. The wide variation in sizes of police agencies and the different approaches to administration has made this inevitable. The model designators are arbitrary but are descriptive of the police approaches.

The Traditional Model. Until the 1950's and 60's the more common approach to structuring police departments was to create a specialized unit for each functional operation. Both large and small departments adopted the structure. Special units were established for patrol, traffic, vice, detectives, juvenile, records, communications, property and whatever other function which appeared to be sufficiently large to warrant separation. Work was very much segmented and management and supervising personnel proliferated.

Field operations is highly specialized under the model. The patrol unit has responsibility for field patrol and preliminary case investigations. All follow-up investigations are a responsibility of the detective and juvenile units. The vice unit has overall responsibility for vice case investigations. Traffic enforcement and accident investigation is generally an exclusive responsibility of the traffic unit.

Staff activities are similarly specialized, with separate units for the support activities of records, property, communications, and custody. Staff units for budgeting, personnel, training, and planning are separate even though the units for each may consist of a single person.

Since most departments adopting the traditional model have not had a professional view toward police work, a state of confusion with respect to coordinated efforts to achieve a common objective prevails. Control of operations is limited and overall management is at best mediocre. Fortunately, the days of *overspecialization* resulting from the traditional model are passing and adoption of the Vollmer or the modified model to be described next is increasing.

THE MODIFIED POLICE MODEL. The modified model is similar to the Vollmer Model in that the structure is basically the same. The three divisional arrangement of investigation, field and services is followed with an office of chief of police containing the staff activities of budgeting, planning, personnel and training.

The model basically calls for a relatively high degree of specialization. The patrol unit is responsible for general patrol activities and preliminary case investigation. Follow-up case investigations are a responsibility of the detective and juvenile units. Vice is commonly an exclusive responsibility of the vice unit. Traffic enforcement and accident investigation are responsibilities of the traffic unit. The record unit does not share in the control of case investigations and the other service activities perform their responsibilities as in the Vollmer Model.

The modified model is the more common in the medium-sized departments consisting of between forty and two hundred to three hundred personnel. Obviously, a number of variations from the description provided is found but the basic structural scheme prevails. Specialization is emphasized and overall management generally can be described as mediocre with the specialized units guilty of *empire building* and noncooperation with other units. The task of coordination at best is difficult.

THE VOLLMER MODEL. August Vollmer as Chief of Police in Berkeley, California from 1905 to 1932 developed a unique approach in organizing the department. He established the uniformed field officer as a *criminologist* responsible for the performance of all police functions on the beat. Ideally, each field officer was required (1) to be thoroughly familiar with all criminal and delinquency problems on his beat; (2) to be thoroughly familiar with resources on the beat and other resources available to deal with criminal and delinquency problems which did not require law enforcement action inserting individuals into the criminal justice system; (3) to be capable of resolving criminal and delinquency behavioral problems with the help of available local resources without referral to agencies in the criminal justice system except when absolutely necessary; and (4) to be responsible for performing all of the essential field functions.

The patrol division is the principal and only line unit responsible for performance of all line functions. The detective, traffic, and juvenile units are considered staff in a sense that their primary responsibilities are to aid and assist the patrol division in the performance of the basic police functions. Only in the investigation and processing of specified cases predetermined by policy decisions would any of the units other than patrol have full responsibility for case investigations and case processing.

Control over the investigation process is shared by the patrol division, detective, traffic, juvenile and record units. A follow-up report review clerk reviews all reports for completeness and thoroughness of investigations. If errors are found or additional investigation is required the clerk so notifies the field officer and the notification in effect constitutes an order. Other units by their involvement in the aiding and assisting of the investigation process and case review exercise control.

Cases remain a responsibility of the uniformed field officer until closed or action is suspended. Officers in other units aid and assist the field officer when expertise may be required or established policies and procedures require their involvement in the investigation or disposition process.

Structurally, the Vollmer Model is quite traditional. The field division consists of the patrol and traffic units. The traffic unit, however, does not have operational traffic enforcement and accident investigation responsibilities. It is primarily an analytical unit and has responsibility for safety education and a bicycle licensing and safety program. The investigation division consists of the detectives and juvenile units, which as previously indicated provide support for the field officers and in the traditional sense must be viewed as staff units. The third component is the services division into which has been integrated the records, property, communications, and custodial support functions and are staff in the traditional sense. The traditional staff functions of personnel, training, budgeting and planning have been incorporated into an office of the Chief of Police.

The Model implies staffing of the department by *professionals*. The term *criminologist* suggests a person broadly educated in the social sciences and qualified to deal with a multitude of behavioral problems.

It was Vollmer's thesis that police work required professionally trained personnel and to this end he recruited many college and university educated personnel and dedicated his professional life to the improvement of the police service in many areas.

THE SMALL DEPARTMENT MODEL. The majority of the police agencies in the United States are small with personnel of from one to forty. There can really be no description of the structure of the very small department but departments with personnel of from fifteen to forty follow a general structural pattern.

The small department model provides for a generalist approach to police operations with a minimal specialization. Staff-line concepts do not apply. The department is divided into three shifts which from a very practical standpoint are self contained. All situations requiring police attention must be handled by the personnel on duty. Any follow-up investigation or case processing may involve a singular specialist designated as the department's investigator or the chief of police wears a multiple of *hats* and in addition to his administrative responsibilities serves as the departmental investigator.

There can be no such thing as staff or specialized units. All of the support activities such as records, communications, property and custody must be performed by a single individual on duty on each shift. One individual may be designated as responsible for records or property. Budgeting, personnel, training, and planning are a responsibility of the chief of police.

The essence of the small department model is that all personnel must work as a team prepared to perform all of the essential police functions as situations demand. The implications are that a small department needs highly qualified personnel since all of the tasks performed in a larger department must be performed by the small department even though infrequently. The responsibilities of the chief of police are broad in that he must fulfill an operational responsibility as well as provide the expected staff needs of the department.

The Larger Department Model. The twenty-five or so departments in the United States are unique in cities with over 500,000 population. They are big organizations. They can benefit from the large body of organization theory which has been developed in the past fifteen or twenty years. They meet the specifications of an organization in that they are large, bureaucratic, do not permit face to face relationships, their organization is complex, they attempt to meet a *conscious rationality;* the organization has a purpose and it has a universality. Organization can be defined for the large police department as ". . . the pattern of ways in which a large number of people, of a size too great to have intimate face-to-face contact and engaged in a complexity of tasks relate themselves to each other in the conscious, systematic establishment and accomplishment of mutually agreed purposes."[9]

However, the large departments have not been too different from departments which follow the modified model. The difference is that the larger departments are decentralized into precinct or district stations and that there exists a higher degree of specialization. A multiplicity of specialized units prevails at headquarters and precinct or district unit relationships show a complex set of relationships.

Basically, the large department has centralized the support and administrative staff functions. The traffic control and accident investigation functions are a centralized responsibility. Administrative direction and control over follow-up investigations remains with the headquarters units even though there is a decentralization of units responsible for such activities. There is a high degree of centralization of the vice, narcotics, and intelligence functions. Almost all of the administrative staff functions of personnel, budgeting, training and planning are centralized.

The structure reflects an emphasis on functional specialization. Each major functional activity is represented by a divisional or bureau unit each on par with the other. Major divisions are patrol, administration, personnel and training, custody, detectives, traffic and services. The trend has been for the chief of police or superintendent, whatever the title may be, to operate with a minimal staff depending upon the functional units to provide the traditional staff support.

The structure of the large departments decentralizes the patrol operation with the precinct or station under the patrol bureau. The detective, juvenile, and vice operation also may be decentralized but the pattern varies. The usual pattern is for there to be a detective, juvenile, and vice unit in each precinct or station responsible to the headquarters unit. Variations of this pattern exist with some vice precinct or station units being under control of the division commander.

Detective operations of a specialized nature are almost always centralized. Major crimes, narcotics, intelligence and city wide vice investigations are a responsibility of headquarters units.

All of the support and administrative staff activities are centralized. Precinct or station division is operationally oriented and almost completely dependent upon centralized units for support. Administrative staff support is universally a function of headquarters.

Thus, the large department model can find its counterpart in big business, industry and other governmental agencies with respect to organization. The theoretical concepts of organization as reflected in the literature apply to the large department. However, the large police organizations in the United States have developed somewhat like *Topsy* and still retain many of the features of the traditional and modified models previously described. The primary difference is in bigness. Conscious attempts to adopt and adapt developing theories of organization by the police agencies have been slow.

Some change is taking place. A few of the larger departments are consolidating investigation functions at the precinct or station level, removing centralized control over investigations. Juvenile investigations are being integrated into the detective function upon the premise that most offenses when reported do not signify a juvenile or an adult as an offender. Traffic enforcement and accident investigation responsibilities are being assigned more to the uniformed patrol unit.

Organization: The Changing Nature

The traditional classical approaches to organization have been subjected to considerable review and modifications over the past four decades. The advent of the human relations approach in the 1930's recognized the organization as a social entity in which the socio-psychological behavioral patterns of man influenced relationships on the job. The structuralist approach which began in the 1950's is an attempt at synthesis of the classical formal approaches and the human relations informal approaches. It reflects a recognition that there can be compatibility between organizational and personal needs, a melding together of formal and informal organizations.

The ingredients for change in police organizations are increasing. Improvements in personnel standards and training are injecting new and higher quality personnel into the organization. Societal demands for changes in police operations and relationships between the police and the public suggests a greater emphasis on human relations. Research in crime prevention, field operations and the investigation process suggests a break with the traditional classical approaches. The emerging impact of technology, especially the application of automatic data processing is bringing about a considerable realignment in structural relationships.

The Human Relations Approach

Recognition that man is a social as well as a physical being in organizations is the key feature of the human relations approach. It introduced the ideas and the concepts that man was motivated by other than economic rewards, that group behavior influenced organizational relationships and that specialization does not necessarily become the most efficient form of division of labor. The human relations approach was based upon the assumption that the most satisfying organization is the most efficient.[10] In it workers are happy and the organization is one big *happy family*. The informal nature of organization is considered as important as the formal.

Informal organization refers to the social relations that develop among people in the organization which are above and beyond those formally prescribed or which have evolved as a consequence of the interaction between workers and the pressure of interpersonal relationships which follow from formal or prescribed relationships. Informal organization introduces the complex factors of human behavior which work on the formal organization, and which reflect the nature of interpersonal relationships with a recognition of outside pressures including personal preferences, interaction patterns, individual capacities, power struggles and communication. It brings into perspective relationships between the specialist and operational personnel, recognizes that there are decision and power centers other than those formally prescribed and that channels of internal communication are often quite different than outlined formally. The socio-psychological behavioral features of man are thus recognized as important elements of organizations influencing the relationships between individuals, groups and formally established units. Such relationships are in addition to and supplemental to organizational patterns designed by management which in essence is formal organization.[11]

The literature on informal organization has in general provided a means for analyzing organizations. Informal organization is viewed separately from formal organization with the *ideal* being that the two meld perfectly together. The fact that the *ideal* seldom exists has not deterred the separatist approach to analysis. The formal organization is generally deemed to be the principal determinant of relationships, and although informal factors may predominate, formal organization is usually allotted credence.

That the police view of organization gives credence to formal organization is generally accepted. However, police organizations have felt the influence of the human relations approach and where there exists a formal police organization there also exists an informal organization. The nature of police organizations is highly susceptible to external and internal pressures because they primarily revolve around people interacting in face to face relationships both within and outside of the organization.

The informal group is a key feature of the human relations approach. In police organizations informal groups evolve primarily along functional lines. Uniformed patrol officers have their after shift *beer* parties, the detectives meet regularly at their favorite restaurant for lunch or the *monthly* dinner, motorcycle officers have their own *support* group and so on.

Basically, informal organization reflects how relationships really are. More often than not the relationships are at variance with the blueprint or formal organization specified by management.

The Structuralist Approach

The structuralist school raised systematically the question of the relationships between formal and informal organizations and provided an approach for the synthesis of the two. Basically, the structuralists suggested that the human relations approach did not provide a full view of the organization. They see organization as a large, complex social unit in which many social groups interact, and that a synthesis and integration of these group interactions in an holistic manner reflecting both management and the workers expectations is the desirable approach to organization. Realistically then, organization to the structuralists is singular, accommodating the features of both the traditional formal organization, and the human relations informal organization.[12]

Robert T. Golembiewski, the more recent of the structuralists, introduced the colleague model of staff-line relationships which does not prescribe a particular pattern of behavior but implies a continuous bargaining situation with respect to the decision making process resulting in a fluidity of organizational relationships. The model in effect discards the classical models and molds the concepts of the human relations approach into a new theory of formal organization. The design of the colleague structure calls for organizing around subunits focusing on program activities traditionally referred to as line with integration of essential sustaining (staff) activities into each sub-unit.[13]

Essentially the colleague model is based on a team approach to organization. Relationships are circular rather than hierarchical. The top level of organization reflects an assemblage of top management personnel each with particular expertise in a functional or program area working together to provide direction to the organization. The lower levels of an organization are discrete sub-assemblies for the performance of specific programs. Essential expertise is included in each lower level team.

The team or teams at the top level are responsible for resolving substantive issues, that is, the development of policies and comprehensive plans for implementation by the lower level teams. Left for the lower level teams is the responsibility for resolving technical issues which include development of sub-policies and procedures for program implementation. Delegation is the key.

The colleague model requires a new way of thinking about organization. Emphasis is of necessity on programs rather than upon functions. Structure evolves from a recognition and clarification of program activities. For example, investigation of offenses is perceived as a singular program instead of in terms of preliminary and follow-up investigations with attendant assignments to the patrol division and detective divisions. Community relations is viewed as a total departmental effort rather than a functional activity of a specific unit.

Essential sustaining or staff activities become an integral part of each team both at the top level and the lower levels. For example, personnel management is not a function of a single unit; rather the essentials of personnel management are dispersed throughout the organization such as a program of career development which is implemented by all teams. The sustaining activities are integrated with the program activities.

The colleague model presupposes a professional quality of employees at all levels. Teams reflect the necessary expertise required to perform all essential activities. For example, an operational team for performance of police activities in the field may consist of a number of generalist patrolmen to perform routine activities, investigation experts for the more involved types of case investigations and records and communication specialists. Each team would in essence be self contained for performance of all essential police activities and collectively would share responsibility for performance. Supervision and direction for achievement of specific case investigations would revolve to the individual who possessed the necessary expertise to accomplish the job.

The colleague model substantially changes relationships. First, horizontal integration of program and sustaining activities is reduced to a minimum if not alleviated. Second, the tendency toward vertical fragmentation of functional units is reduced, that is, the personnel identify across the organization rather than *within* and *upward* in the functional unit, i.e., motorcycle traffic officers forming an *elite* corps with loyalties primarily within the unit rather than to achievement of the overall departmental goals. Third, horizontal integration of activities is encouraged, i.e., the investigation program requirements are met by a team approach rather than separated into functional unit responsibilities as has been traditional. Fourth, the colleague concept encourages sustaining (staff) personnel to work more closely with program (line) personnel, especially at the upper management level leading to smoother operations. Fifth, overall tensions created by the separatist nature of the functional units formed in the classical models are reduced.[14]

Team Policing Organization Model

Team policing is based on a phenomenon of accepting the premise that all personnel have a contribution to make to the policy and operational decision making process. It presupposes that all personnel have a contribution to make to the operation of the department, are capable and motivated to make that contribution and that there will be acceptance, if worthy, of the contribution. It is a continuing process whereby involvement of all personnel takes place, a continuous input of ideas, suggestions and constructive criticism is fostered, and new ideas and concepts are ingested into the system. Management personnel assume responsibility for broad policy making, planning of operational activities, for dealing with substantive issues regarding personnel, operations, budget and unusual situations and community relations. Operational personnel become concerned with routine day to day operations and implementation of broad policy guidelines laid down by the management team.

Team policing suggests that all personnel will be removed from a nice neat box which prescribes specific and limited jobs, tasks and duties. All personnel will be perceived as having a major contribution to make to the success of the organization and capabilities will be examined. It is recognized that each person in the organization has talent, develops an expertise, has a basic know-how and a quality of leadership and an ability to contribute to the total operation of the department. Capitalizing on the talents of all persons in the organization is the key to success. It is essential that the potential and actual talents be ascertained.

Can a police department match these lofty concepts? A break from tradition is required. The structures of the traditional and orthodox concepts of organization are being challenged. The giving up of command authority—not responsibility—in the traditional sense changes organizational relationships. Participative and collegial decision making replaces orders by administrative fiat. Operational activities involve the maximizing of the expertise of the individual members of the organization; the development of a system whereby the most capable, not necessarily the highest ranked, officer is called upon to decide and handle specific situations.

Superior-subordinate relationships dealing with concepts of command and supervision are questioned. The emphasis is placed upon work to be done rather than the bureaucratic relationships of *who is responsible to whom*. Dealing with specific situations replaces emphasis on command relationships. Elaborating on this issue, program goals become the principal focus of operation. Personnel work as a team is dealing with problems and situations rather than being concerned with the chain of command.

Team policing is not necessarily a new concept in organization; rather, it incorporates many features of current approaches to police organization and integrates a broad range of ideas from recently developed organization and management theory. Team building has long been essential for police operations but for the most part has taken place outside of the existing formal structure except in the smaller departments where a team approach has been required from a practical standpoint. Writings in organizational theory recount that team building innovations in structure work.

The *team policing model* incorporates the characteristic role features of Golembiewski's colleague model[15] which provide that in some situations line units or personnel may be dominant over staff; however, the most suitable characteristic role for the model is acceptance of the concept of *consensus about alternation of roles.* Traditionally the police emphasis on team activities has accentuated the dominance of the line units or personnel. Only occasionally does one find the line in a subservient position to staff. Basically, reference here is to a recognition that units and personnel other than those directly charged with program (line) operations may often be in a better position to make appropriate decisions than the line unit or personnel.

The Vollmer model varied the team approach by identifying the field uniformed unit and personnel as the line, making the traffic and investigation units and personnel, staff, along with the other traditional staff activities such as personnel, training and planning. However, the interrelationships of the line and staff personnel under the Vollmer model implied a *concensus about alternating roles* between the investigators, traffic, and services personnel and the uniformed officer.

The emergence of the office of chief of police, incorporating the administrative staff activities into the chief's office, suggests movement towards the *Alter Ego Model* in which the staff unit personnel assist the chief in his exercise of command, a middle ground between the orthodox organizational models and the colleague model. Staff personnel become much more intimately involved in the decision process often dominating line activities.

Movement toward the team policing model suggests changes in perception about line and staff and the introduction of new terminology which is more descriptive of line and staff concepts. The traditional view of staff as advisory and aiding and assisting without *authority,* and line as having sole responsibility for operations, is too delimiting. Rather, an abandonment of the traditional line-staff relationships in favor of a distinction between *program* and *sustaining* units acting within a network of power is in order. Briefly, programs develop from establishment of goals and refer to the functions and policies related to what is to be done, whereas, sustaining activities are concerned more with the development of methods, skills and techniques. A team approach to the meeting of agency goals and objectives is suggested, in which *programs* and *sustaining* activities are reflected in a grid or *network of authority.*

Police programs have traditionally been perceived along functional lines. That is, the patrol unit performs the patrol function, the traffic unit the traffic function, the investigation unit the investigation function and so on. Sustaining activities are reflected in separate functional units. The fact that in actual operation the sustaining and program functions are intertwined is often overlooked. The means overshadow the goals. The tendency is toward overspecialization. However, an analysis of informal relationships which pertain in many departments, suggests that team efforts do prevail but are not officially recognized.

The Vollmer organizational model does in fact recognize a team approach to police organization. In a sense the programs are identified in terms of field unit responsibilities; to wit: that primarily all operational police work is a responsibility of the field unit. Thus, the patrol, traffic, investigation and services program are the field unit's responsibility. Sustaining (staff) activities are designed to support the field operations. This includes the follow-up investigation function for both juveniles and adults as well as traffic support activities. All units perform their jobs for a definite purpose.

However, conceptualization of programs in discrete terms has been weak in most police departments. As indicated, the emphasis has been on vertical program sub-divisions rather than horizontal integration. More specifically, for example, an investigative program has been viewed in terms of the preliminary investigation considered a patrol unit program function, and follow-up investigation an investigation unit program function. Although the Vollmer model does not differentiate on such terms, the program issue is clouded.

What appears to be needed is a statement of the police agency role followed by a *clarification of goals and objectives.* If the police role is perceived as maintenance of ordered liberty which requires performance of coercive and non-coercive activities and the protection of personal liberties and civil rights, a basis is provided for the establishment of goals and objectives. Coercive activities include criminal, traffic, regulatory and juvenile law enforcement, keeping the peace and intelligence gathering. Non-coercive activities inclule social service, crime prevention, participation in the development of an environment of order and stability, and the provision of services.

With the establishment of goals and objectives departmental programs follow logically. For example, an investigation program is essential for achievement of law enforcement goals and objectives; a community relations program becomes essential for achievement of crime prevention and participation in the development of an environment of order and stability. A program may be perceived differently by different departments but programs can be operationally defined, an important process in changing structure.

Clarification of sustaining activities and their relationship to programs is necessary. Orthodox organizational models reflect sustaining activities in terms of functional units. Thus, the personnel and training functions are perceived as a responsibility of a singular unit. Record management is perceived as a function of the records unit. Integration of the sustaining activities with program operations and goals suggests a broader perception. For example, a career development activity, a personnel function, is not a singular function of the personnel unit. All units of necessity must be involved. This is also true of training. Likewise, records management may be integrated into program operations to provide a more meaningful support for program activities, a most feasible operation with the advent of automatic data processing.

Thus, in developing a team policing organizational model, it is in order to perceive program and sustaining activities as integrated and intertwined. However, this does not just happen. Continuous planning is the key to success including a continuous monitoring of all activities for control and coordination purposes. Planning does not just take place as a function of a planning unit. *To be successful all segments of the organization should be involved.* True, basic guidelines must be developed by sustaining personnel and *staff* work is necessary for data processing and preparation of reports, directives and procedures. Basically, long range planning is a function of top management and day to day operational planning a responsibility of operational personnel. However, the most successful planning both of a long range and operational nature takes place when all concerned personnel are involved or at least are aware of what is taking place. Long range plans of necessity must be resolved into operational plans, and often these plans require or lead to the development of long range plans.

Although there may be no one best way to structure for the team policing model, a circular arrangement for the top management team and the operational teams is suggested. The circular nature of the structure suggests that the continuous exchange of views and bargaining relationships will prevail between the members of each team, with all members intimately involved in the decision making process. The top management team will be primarily concerned with the policy decisions and the operational teams with the operations decisions.

First, a look at the top management team. Normally, the team will consist of the chief of police and the top command personnel of a department. The command personnel will not have the traditional command responsibility but will bring to the team the *expertise* of their functional specialty which will be utilized in planning, directing, coordinating and controlling an integrated operation. In essence the team will be constituted as a *board of directors* with a collective responsibility for overall management of the affairs of the department.

The chief of police is the *chairman* of the top management team. He may be perceived as the hub of the circle surrounded by other team members. His function is to provide leadership for the team as well as the department as a whole. The *buck* stops with him but more importantly he is responsible for creating a management environment in which the top management team members may tackle and resolve major departmental issues. It is up to him to provide a proper balance in the resolution of issues to assure that no one program is overemphasized and that the operation of the department proceeds in a reasonably smooth fashion.

The other members of the top management team will be responsible for designated program areas for which their background of experience and education reasonably provide them with an expertise. Using the orthodox organization's command officers as examples, the commander of the investigation division would bring to the team expertise in investigation and juvenile programs; the commander of the operations division, expertise in patrol and traffic programs; the commander of the services division, expertise in records and property management, communications and custody; and the head of the management services division, expertise in personnel, training, planning and budget. Each, in a sense, would become the *director* of their individual program area. One *director,* more than likely the expert in operations in a medium sized department, would become *director of operations* with responsibility for coordinating and directing the work of the operations teams. Departmental size would dictate the number of personnel in the team and program areas of responsibility for each team member. Necessary support personnel would be provided to perform *staff* work.

How would the team function? Each member of the team would be responsible for inputting into the planning and policy decision making process program requirements for his area of *expertise.* Each input would be *evaluated by the team as a whole vis-a-vis all other inputs.* The ultimate team decision with respect to each input would assure that implementation provides for a balanced operation. It is presupposed that there is a continuous flow of information on all operations and activities to the top management team.

Although the *director of operations* would have primary responsibility for coordinating and directing operational teams, all other directors would engage in a continuous process of monitoring the operation of their program areas. This would be done by review of information and by inspections. In essence, the top management *circle* would revolve for the purposes of a continuous evaluation and integration of all programs to assure a proper balance in operations.

The question arises, would not the dominant *director* usurp leadership of the team leading to an imbalance in program emphasis? This could happen. However, the role of the chief of police is to minimize such a tendency, and since there is collective responsibility for the whole operation, the other *directors* would probably join together to assure a reasonable balance in program development and direction.

The operations teams are responsible for program implementation. The number of operations teams, their personnel complement, and responsibilities would vary depending upon departmental size, planning and agency requirements. For the most part, teams with overall program responsibilities are suggested, however, specialists teams may be required on a continuing basis or to meet specific needs depending on agency size and problems.

The basic operational team will consist of a manager and personnel with the necessary expertise to implement program requirements as designated by the top management team. The manager will be responsible for organizing the team and planning its operation with involvement of all team members. It should be emphasized that the manager and his team members are delegated full responsibility and authority for operations.

The responsibility of the basic operational team under one concept would consist of the performance of substantially all programs and sustaining activities essential for fulfilling the police role in the community and achieving departmental goals and objectives. In effect each team will be self-contained with respect to performing all operational functions. The field operational personnel will consist of generalist patrolmen capable of performing the basic traditional field tasks including traffic enforcement and accident investigation. Personnel, traditionally performing investigation duties including juvenile, will become an integral part of the field team. Thus the field personnel will have the capability to handle all routine operations and major investigations. Preplanning calls for development of a case assignment system whereby the expertise of the most capable officer on duty will be assigned to handle each case. Routine cases will be handled by the generalist officer. The officer in charge of each case will in effect supervise the investigation of that case.

One may ask what about supervision? The team approach suggests that basic supervision will be accomplished through a system of *peer control*. However, the model suggests that a *lead officer* approach could be used to supplant the traditional first line supervisor, which calls for a clearly defined superior-subordinate relationship. A clear delineation of the superior-subordinate relationships does not appear necessary when all personnel become a collegial body equally responsible for the success or failure of operations. Furthermore, careful preplanning of relationships in which all personnel participate in the decision making process can reduce confusion and tension situations. In addition, a system can be preplanned for meeting emergency situations requiring precise leadership and supervision.

Sustaining personnel performing records, communications, property, crime laboratory and custodial functions will be an integral part of the operations team responsible for supporting the field operations. They too will function under the general direction and in cooperation with the team manager. Again, reliance is on the most capable or qualified person to give direction on the performance work related to his field of endeavor.

As indicated, the number of basic operational teams will depend on departmental program workload, then divide the department into two teams, each responsible for a twelve hour period, seven days a week, throughout the year. Development of personnel and scheduling of assignments would be a responsibility of each team. Preplanning should take care of overlapping responsibilities.

Another approach might be to follow the traditional three shift pattern with appropriate distribution of personnel to meet shift loads. This appears to be somewhat cumbersome since there would be unequal teams, but, it may be the best approach under certain circumstances.

Inevitably there will be certain activities which may be incompatible for the basic operation team structure. Narcotics, vice and intelligence activities are probably better performed by use of specialist teams. The same could be true of warrant service, forged document investigations, and other types of activities which do not lend themselves to operational team activities.

In the larger department with substations or precincts, a number of structural relationships may be feasible. One approach could be for headquarters to consist of the top management team, and to provide specialist support through a number of specialist teams. The substations or precincts could use the approach of having a *minor* top management team and then constitute several basic operational teams to provide 24 hours coverage of designated *areas,* workload to be relatively equal. Sustaining activities could be performed for all basic operational teams by a station team. Careful preplanning for designation of responsibilities and inter-team relationships would be required.

What about sustaining activities as recruit and in-service training, budget preparation, and purchasing? Again, specialist teams under the general direction of one of the top management directors may be the answer. Each department will have to decide. However, it must be remembered that insofar as is feasible the sustaining functions should be performed as an integral part of each operational team's activities.

The team policing organization model is a drastic breach with tradition. However, it does provide an *ideal* to be strived for which can reduce the rigidity and the tension building features of current approaches to organization. It provides a means for involving the *new breed* of police officer who brings to the department talents and potential capabilities superior to his predecessor. It makes possible a continuous input of ideas and observations about the community, the operations and agency relationships which have been severely restricted and which are becoming extremely vital for meeting the dynamic and changing demands of society on the police. Admittedly, many problems are posed in changing over to adoption of the model. Serious questioning of many current practices must take place and a number of *myths* challenged. However, the end result may be a more viable, meaningful and dynamic organization.

FOOTNOTES

1Samuel H. Jameson, *Man and Society* (Totowa, New Jersey: Littlefield, Adams and Company).

2See Jean Jacques Rousseau, *The Social Contract.*

3Fritz M. Marx (ed.), *Elements of Public Administration* (2nd ed., Englewood Cliffs, New Jersey: Prentice Hall, 1963), p. 7.

4Robert T. Golembiewski, Frank Gibson, and Geoffrey Cornog (eds.), *Public Administration: Readings in Institutions Processes and Behavior* (Chicago: Rand McNally and Company, 1966), p. 13.

5John M. Pfiffner and Frank Sherwood, *Administration Organization* (Englewood Cliffs, New Jersey: Prentice Hall, 1960), Chapter II.

[6]*Ibid.,* Chapter IV.

[7]O. W. Wilson, *Police Administration* (2nd ed.; New York: McGraw Hill Book Company, 1963), and *Municipal Police Administration* (4th ed.; Chicago: International City Managers' Association, 1969).

[8]The President's Commission on Law Enforcement and Administration of Justice, *Task Force Report: The Police* (Washington: Government Printing Office, 1967).

[9]Pfiffner and Sherwood, *loc. cit.*

[10]Amitai Etzioni, *Modern Organizations* (Englewood Cliffs, New Jersey: Prentice Hall, Inc., 1964), Chapter 6.

[11]Robert T. Golembiewski, *Organizing Men and Power: Patterns of Behavior and Line-Staff Behavior* (Chicago: Rand McNally and Company, 1967); Chapter 7.

[12]*Ibid.,* p. 232

[13]*Ibid.,* Chapters 3, 4, 7,. See also F. J. Roethlichberger and W. J. Dixon, *Management and the Worker* (Cambridge: Harvard University Press, 1939).

[14]Golembiewski, *loc. cit.*

[15]*Ibid.*

CHAPTER 6

DEVELOPING CORRECTIONAL ADMINISTRATORS

E. K. NELSON AND CATHERINE H. LOVELL

THIS SECTION REPRESENTS selected materials from a special study of correctional administrators made by Elmer K. Nelson, Jr. and Catherine H. Lovell of the University of Southern California for the Joint Commission on Correctional Manpower and Training. The report, "Developing Correctional Administrators" was published in 1969.*

The Joint Commission on Correctional Manpower and Training, incorporated in the District of Columbia, consisted of 95 national, international, and regional organizations and public agencies which joined together to address one of the most serious social problems of our day: How to recruit and retain enough trained men and women to increase correctional effectiveness and thus reduce the incidence of crime and delinquency in the United States.

Recognizing the importance of this problem, the Congress in 1965 passed the Correctional Rehabilitation Study Act, which authorized grants through the Social and Rehabilitation Service, Department of Health, Education, and Welfare, for a broad study of correctional manpower and training. The Joint Commission had been funded under this Act and through grants and contributions from private foundations, organizations, and individuals. The aim of this study

*Now being distributed by the American Correctional Association.

was to clarify the roles correctional administrators play, the problems they encounter, and the theoretical and practical skills they need for successful performance of their demanding duties.

The report should be viewed in the context of two broad movements. The first is the movement of the correctional field away from its isolating, institution-based system of custodial confinement and toward a goal of reintegrating the offender into the fabric of community life.

The second is a profound shift in ways of thinking about the role of the administrator in American society. This shift is away from the traditional view of the administrator as one who mechanically performs specialized functions in officially prescribed ways within closed organizational systems. The movement is toward a conception of the administrator as a creative and highly skilled professional who works within organizations which are *open* in the sense that they interact dynamically with myriad forces around them. The convergence of these two movements may well bring about a renaissance of management in correctional programs within the next decade.

The total number of correctional administrators whose questionnaires were analyzed was 393. One-half were administrators in institutions (32 percent adult, 18 percent juvenile), 42 percent in probation and parole settings, and nearly 8 percent in state headquarters. Of the sample, 34 percent were top administrators and 66 percent were middle-level managers (assistant heads or administrators of operating units).

Organizations were nominated to the sample by representatives of the National Council on Crime and Delinquency.

Corrections and the Development of a Science of Management

As corrections has evolved and changed, producing new styles of management and proliferating new environments for administrators, so also have there been pervasive changes in theories of formal organization and in concepts related to administrative leadership and behavior. The evolution of correctional management has moved along pathways which run generally parallel to this larger movement. In fact, there is reason to believe that the generic management sciences have something to learn from correctional administration, which has had to address change within encapsulated systems where the dynamics of power and compliance are highly concentrated and executive mistakes are heavily penalized. But the reverse, of course, also is true, and our perspective on correctional management should include an effort to place it in the context of the larger theoretical movement.

Conceptions of formal organizations and of the roles of their managers have changed radically in the past half-century. Taylor's *scientific management* movement portrayed the administrator as a highly skilled technician who insured the smooth operation of such organizational processes as planning, organizing, staffing, directing, coordinating, reporting, and budgeting.[1] Seen from this vantage point, the ideal executive is a *rational* individual who manipulates the levers of a human machine, correcting deficiencies by rearranging the span of control, the line of command, or the interrelationships of the structural components. Taylor's emphasis was on the anatomy of the system as symbolized by the organization chart. The pyramidal form, with its built-in caste system of status graduations, was sacrosanct.[2] The basic human tendency not to conform to official specification was ignored, a fact which contributed greatly to the early demise of the scientific management movement.

The so-called *human relations* movement which followed proclaimed somewhat pompously (as it now seems) that the needs and predilections of the human participants within formal organizations exert a powerful influence, and management would do well to recognize and accommodate them.[3] Especially, it was argued, the workers' need to find rewarding *social* satisfaction in their relationships with each other operates as a strong determinant of morale, and therefore of production. Research findings soon reinforced this position.[4]

An undoubted contribution of this school of thought was an elaboration of the idea of *informal organization,* which takes account of the myriad ways in which the actual dynamics of status and influence differ dramatically from the static juxtaposition of lines and boxes on an organization chart. The boss's secretary, it was pointed out, may exercise great influence, though she has little formal status, because she can control the access of people and information to her superior.

In recent years, more sophisticated theories and research methodologies have been brought to bear upon the informal side of organization life. Just as penal institutions came to be conceived of as social systems, generic theories of organization began to define all of the systems within which men join together to accomplish work goals as *complex* and *open*.[5] It was asserted that such organizations strain toward equilibrium and survival, and that change, far from being easily initiated and controlled, usually results from the cumulative effects of those internal and external forces which produce disequilibrium.

This way of thinking about organizations directed attention to many variables which had not been considered by the earlier, more formalistic theories. The modern systems conception of organization opened a number of new areas for study, such as the communications network, the processes by which conflict is generated and resolved, the nature of the elites within the organization, the expectations people have of each other, and the sanctions they use in efforts to influence each other.[6]

Concern for the psychological and social ingredients of organization life gave rise to ideas which differed sharply from the mechanistic and authoritarian doctrines of the scientific management era. Increasing emphasis was placed on the responsibility of management to create conditions under which participants could use their capacities fully and creatively.[7] Attention was given to the dilemma of satisfying the legitimate requirements of the individual and the organization concurrently.[8] In contrast to the former preoccupation with hierarchy and the downward flow of authority, modern theorists argue that organizations should be seen as composites of problem-solving groups in which the leaders are primarily concerned with generating wide participation among the members and decisional power is shared genuinely with them.[9]

Management Theories Basic To This Study

Some recent information concerning management techniques seem especially applicable to developments in the field of corrections and therefore help to provide a context of the research reported upon here. Schein has pointed out that the work styles of managers reflect the assumptions which they make about people.[10] He sets forth four views or assumptions about the nature of man which seem to have been operative in correctional management.

The first view sees man as *rational* and *economic* in nature, primarily motivated by materialistic rewards, requiring from management a firm structure of incentives and controls in order to carry out predetermined tasks.

The second view sees man as *social*, primarily motivated by his need for meaningful relationships with others, requiring from management a concern for his feelings and a structuring of work to bring about satisfying human interactions and group experiences.

The third view sees man as potentially *self-actualizing*. After satisfying lower-level needs, such as survival, self-esteem, and autonomy,[11] man responds to internal forces in seeking a sense of achievement and meaning in his work. The function of management, under this view, is to facilitate the efforts of organization members to use their energies in creative and productive ways.

The fourth view sees man as *complex* and, while capable of self-actualization, highly varied in his responses to different situations. This view challenges management to develop diagnostic skills and wide flexibility in meeting the needs, and thereby maximizing the contribution, of different organization members under constantly changing circumstances.

Some aspects of all of these views can be found in correctional administration, both historic and contemporary. The staffs of large, routinized institutions have generally been treated by management as rational-economic. Smaller institutions (especially those for juvenile offenders) and community-based correctional programs have moved toward the view that employees are motivated by social as well as economic satisfaction. Some of the most interesting experimental programs (for example, institutional efforts to develop *therapeutic communities*, and demonstrations of intensive treatment on probation or parole) have given the staff many opportunities for self-actualization. Some managers, as will be shown in the research reported here, do view their staff as complex and seek to use varied skills and methods in working with them, along the lines suggested by Schein.

We must remember, of course, that correctional administrators have managerial relationships not only with staff but with offenders. Indeed it is the balancing and harmonizing of these two sets of relationships that creates some of the most difficult problems, perhaps because administrators (consciously or unconsciously) adopt one view of man when dealing with staff and another when dealing with offenders. Consider, for example, the dynamics which might occur in an institution where the management treats staff as motivated by social and economic needs, while viewing inmates as capable of responding only to coercion.

The historic and contemporary picture of correctional management's view of offenders seems even more varied than its views of staff. Many offenders have been, and still are, viewed as responding only to force or threat of force. Both the time-honored penal work programs, which provide opportunities for small earnings on a sliding scale, and the practice of reducing the time of incarceration *(giving good time)* for conforming behavior stem from a rational-economic view of inmates.

One of the most significant developments in correctional rehabilitation, the use of small group process to bring about changes of attitude and behavior, seems to rest on the concept that offenders are social men. Other innovations, such as furloughs for work or study, have overtones of both the self-actualization and the complex views of man.

The position implicit in our research is that correctional management will be most effective if it is generally consistent in its view of *all* participants (whether staff or offenders) and if it seeks to develop approaches to them based on the assumption that, while complex, they are capable of self-actualization.

Another formulation from management theory which seems useful in assessing trends in correctional administration is the typology of organization and management styles suggested by Likert.[12] Distinguishing basically between authoritative and participative organizations, Likert posits four approaches to management, each with specified consequences for the motivation of participants, their job satisfaction, communication, decision-making, production, and other variables. The four types, which Likert views as stages of development, from ineffective and pathological to effective and healthy management are: (1) exploitive-authoritative; (2) benevolent-authoritative; (3) participative-consultative; and (4) participative-group.

It appears that aspects of all four approaches are to be found in contemporary correctional organizations. The general trend, however, has been away from type 1, which is illustrated by the traditional prison with its dependence on coercive uses of authority, and into types 3 and 4 through a mixture of benevolently applied authority and limited democratization of the management process. The use of inmate advisory-councils, the delegation of case management authority to probation and parole officers, and the involvement of junior staff in long-range planning are examples of the participative-consultative practices adopted in many correctional agencies, particularly those based in or closely tied to the community. The general pattern in corrections, however, seems closer to Likert's benevolent-authoritative type than to any of the other three.

Some progressive correctional programs operate along lines very similar to Likert's fourth type, participative-group. Examples of such an approach can be found in the New Jersey Highfields experiment,[13] the Pinehills project in Utah,[14] and the California Community Treatment Project.[15] While differing from each other in many ways, these and similar experimental ventures distribute influence and decisional power widely among the staff and the offenders involved and make extensive use of group process in guiding operation.

The research reported here is based on the assumption that correctional administrators should seek to develop participation at all levels within their organizations. It should be recognized, however, that much empirical research is needed (both in correctional administration and in generic management processes) to refine understanding of how participative techniques may be employed successfully and how they may be adapted to the realities of particular programs. As has already been noted, precipitous efforts to democratize correctional organizations not only tend to be dangerous but are usually destined to fail. The introduction of participative methods into programs which are oriented toward the goals of revenge and restraint requires great sensitivity to the forces at work in the organization and in its environment.

A final theoretical formulation of relevance to the development of correctional administration is Etzioni's typology of organizations (and, implicity, of management styles) based upon the kinds of power used by administrators and the kinds of compliance or *involvement* exhibited by the *lower participants.*[16] Etzioni suggests that there are three major ways in which power may be used: (1) *coercively,* through force or the threat of force; (2) *remuneratively,* through manipulation of economic and related rewards; (3) *normatively* through the use of symbols (e.g., the goal of reintegrating offenders into the community) to which the lower participants become committed.

Each type of power, according to Etzioni, elicits a distinctive and *congruent* response from those involved. The use of coercive power (as illustrated every day in the authoritarian prison) elicits an alienative response characterized by distrust and psychological distance between the managers and those who are managed. The use of remunerative power (as illustrated by administrative process in a factory producing goods on a piecework basis) elicits a calculative response in which the commitment of the employees is related to their desire to secure designated materialistic benefits. The use of normative power (as illustrated in a university faculty which is committed to such symbolic norms as *academic excellence)* elicits a moral response from participants who conform to organizational requirements because they have a personal commitment to them, rather than because of force or economic incentive.

Applying Etzioni's theory to corrections, again we see a mixed picture. Some prisons, indeed some entire correctional systems, clearly appear to be close to the coercive-alienative mode.[17] Other correctional organizations seek to *purchase* conformity, at least temporarily, by the manipulation of materialistic sanctions. Still other programs, however, seem to be pushing toward the normative-moral pattern by management methods which are designed to gain the commitment of all who are involved to the people-changing goals of the system.

Obviously, there is a great deal of similarity and overlapping among the formulations of Schein, Likert, and Etzioni. All three are reviewed here not only because they are largely consistent but mainly because, taken together, they provide a context for thinking about the general directions of change needed in corrections today. The lines of conceptualization, and the limited research available to support them, suggest that correctional managers should seek to create conditions leading to participative, normative organizations in which all participants are perceived as complex and capable of self-actualizing behavior.[18]

Conceptualization And Design Of The Research

The research reported upon here was of necessity exploratory in nature, since there has been little systematic inquiry into correctional operations[19] or into the management process of that field. Thus, we could not develop precisely defined theoretical premises or specific hypotheses to test through our data. Nevertheless, a number of assumptions underlie the study and should be made clear to those interested in results.

Assumptions Underlying the Research

The first set of assumptions concerns the future of the correctional field and its nature as a working environment for administrators. The second set has to do with the nature of the managerial role and involves the postulation that administrators work in, and must deal with, a complex force field. The final set of assumptions has to do with the behavior of managers and involves the postulation that they must be effective strategists in order to attain their goals.

The Future of Correctional Management. We stress the vital importance of fundamental change in the correctional field and identify the potential role of correctional administrators as change agents. Thus we have assumed that prospective correctional administrators should acquire the skills associated with change rather than merely those required for maintenance of the system. We have further assumed that change is not a task which corrections can undertake and then be done with, but rather a constant and ongoing process characterized by corectional agencies' attempts to adjust to a never-ending array of new and complex problems. The caseload of offenders reflects all of the movements and the turbulence of our social order—urbanization, the tensions of race relations, the upward striving of the poor, the state of the economy, the mvriad habits, cults, and vices which preoccupy the people in bewildering, kaleidoscopic succession.

In attempting to understand the knowledge and skills required of correctional managers, we wished to look to the future as well as at the present. Thus we focused our research on the administrative functions which presumably will be increasingly important as the system changes. We draw our assumptions about the nature of the correctional system of the future primarily from the *directions for the future* recommended by the President's Commission on Law Enforcement and Administration of Justice.[20]

Assumption 1. The correctional system of the future will attempt to reintegrate offenders into the community. The functions of individual restraint and treatment will be adapted to that purpose. Although the correctional system will still be expected to serve as a deterrent to criminal activity, its function as an instrument of revenge will gradually fade, once the public exerts less pressure for use of correctional services as a means of retribution.

Implications for management. In a recent study on the establishment of a resocializing community within a corectional institution, Studt, Messinger, and Wilson conclude that current organization and management practices are not suited to the reintegration model.

> The traditional bureaucratic form of management currently adopted by correctional agencies is severely limited as a means for facilitating the process of social and personal change established by the resocializing community. The bureaucratic organization necessarily focuses on the orderly performance of established routines that often become ends in themselves. . .
>
> The relationships between the resocializing community and its organizational environment are critical for the emergence and maintenance of a resocializing culture within the community. When there are ultimate decision-makers outside the resocializing community, the system pressures on them, their goals and orientations, and the processes for communication between them and the smaller unit are critical for what happens within the community itself. Any successful resocializing community must give high priority to designing its relationships with the higher authorities who determine its fate.[21]

If traditional organizational form and management style are relatively ineffectual for the reintegration model, how can we replace them? Although we must speculate, the major elements seem apparent.

The managers of reintegrating programs need to cooperate with the varied centers of influence which control the resources needed by individual offenders. These centers of influence can exist within the correctional system or within the general community. In the research of Studt and her colleagues, the influence centers were located within the larger institutional system in which their experimental program was embedded. In the case of community-based correctional efforts, the relevant influence centers are dispersed throughout the community: in schools, neighborhood centers, employment services, and recreational facilities. The managers must understand the makeup, the operating *etiquette,* and the constituencies of these varied institutions; and above all, they must understand how to establish enduring and truly reciprocal relationships with them.

The correctional field must develop more collaborative, less hierarchical administrative regimes in order to implement its reintegration programs. The hierarchical format was developed to achieve the goal of production and orderly task performance. When individual change is the prime purpose of the organization, this format is inappropriate for people cannot be *ordered* to change strongly patterned attitudes and behavior. Nor is change apt to come about through the ritual performance of a series of tasks.

The managerial requirements of operating collaborative programs seem extremely severe. Power must be shared rather than hoarded. Communication must be open rather than restricted. Role and status often become blurred rather than explicit, an outcome which appears threatening to those who have strong investments in hierarchical or functional position. Thus the managers of reintegration programs will need the skills of co-optation, communication, and collaboration. And they will need to have a tolerance for ambiguity, conflict, and ferment; for the process of change is not smooth and orderly. Even more demanding will be the administrators' need to encourage collaborative regimes while still maintaining their credibility as agents of public protection, something which cannot be achieved without holding to *reasonable* requirements of order and control. The management of the process of reintegrating offenders might well be called *the administration of dilemma.*[22]

Assumption 2. The correctional system of the future will differentiate between kinds of offenders and between kinds of intervention more precisely than the present system does.[23] The diagnosis of individual offenders will be supplemented by increasingly refined typologies of their problems and corresponding forms of intervention. Some offenders will require rigorous control and supervision; others, little or none. Some will benefit from group therapy; others will require individual counseling. Some will be helped mainly through assistance in finding work and in establishing themselves in legitimate circles.

IMPLICATIONS FOR MANAGEMENT. At present, the programming of offenders is highly routinized. In spite of a preoccupation with individualized treatment, alternative ways of handling offenders are quite limited in most correctional systems. Assignments to supervisory caseloads are typically made on the basis of geographic location rather than individual need. The use of intervention typologies is limited to a small number of experimental programs. The correctional manager of the future will need to understand the theories underlying typological systems, theories relevant both to problems that require intervention and to kinds of intervention indicated. It might be argued that the correctional administrator does not need such specialized knowledge so long as his staff has it. But managers cannot create the conditions for differential handling of offenders without a grasp of the rationales for doing so. Armed with such knowledge, the administrator may be able to modify in creative ways such traditionally static factors as length of intervention, closeness of control, and type of assistance.

Assumption 3. The correctional system of the future will emphasize fairness and objectivity in the handling of offenders. This concern will be implemented through procedures designed to protect individual rights, particularly in connection with decisions affecting liberty. While there will be some increase in judicial involvement in the correctional process (e.g., the right to be represented by counsel at parole revocation proceedings and increased juristic review of decision-making that affects degrees of freedom from custody), most of the added emphasis on fairness will come in the form of administrative action. Written records will be required to support key decisions. There will be an increase in administrative reviews of such decisions. The offender involved will have more access to relevant information and the right to challenge evidence which is antagonistic to his position. In order to avoid an unmanageable burden of legalistic interference, corrections will itself take responsibility for protecting the individual from bureaucratic arbitrariness and insensitivity. Selznick has suggested that, far from being only a grudging acquiescence to legal due process requirements, increased concern for fairness on the part of correctional officials would add strength to efforts to resocialize offenders.

> A concern for fairness and civic validation should permeate the entire administration of criminal law, including the daily life of the prisoner. That treatment will be most effective which does the most for the inmate's sense of self-worth and responsibility. Nothing contributes more to these feelings than a social environment whose constitutive principle is justice.[24]

Implications for Management. Some present-day correctional administrators are uneasy about the encroachment of legalistic constraints upon their actions. They assume that the system is essentially fair and benevolent in its orientation to the offender. They tend to resist adversarial proceedings, sometimes on logically dubious grounds, as, for example, when they claim that allowing the inmate to have an attorney at his parole hearing *would be the same as trying his case all over again.*

Future administrators will need to be better informed and more secure about the substantive procedural ingredients of due process. Thus, they will need to be familiar with relevant areas of law and procedure. They will have to be aware of the growing practice of supplementing administrative procedures with judicial process in other managerial arenas, as in the work of the regulatory agencies of government. They will need to incorporate into administrative practice varied procedures to secure, test, and disseminate information for decision-making and to provide for dispassionate review of such decisions once they are made.

Assumption 4. The correctional system of the future will have a configuration of numerous, quite autonomous subsystems operating to maximize cooperation and interchange. Given the realities of a federal system and of the centrifugal pressures described earlier, we ought not to expect a monolithic correctional apparatus for the United States in the future. But remedies must and will be found for the present problems of fragmentation. They will take the form, we predict, of a large repertoire of reciprocal arrangements between the parts of the total system. These new arrangements will be used flexibly and with much less reverence for the sanctity of organizational and governmental boundaries than is evident today.

Offenders with special requirements will be sent to specialized facilities capable of meeting their needs, regardless of the jurisdictional niceties involved. Offenders whose primary requirement is to reestablish themselves in their home communities will be routed there and supervised by local authorities. The federal and state governments will facilitate the efforts of local governments to develop strong community-based programs and will backstop them with resources they cannot provide; for example, a fully staffed center for screening and diagnosis of offenders or an institution for mentally ill offenders.

Implications for Management. The administrators of a cooperative correctional system would need to understand the national network of services of which their particular program would be an integral part. They would need to be aware of the laws, policies, and procedures through which cross-jurisdictional cooperation could be implemented. They would need to participate in those public and private organizations which address the problems of coordinating correctional efforts across the country and carry out planning and information-gathering activities. In sum, they would need to be outwardly directed, rather than concerned only with local activities. They would need to work with the totality of corrections-related activities rather than with the happenings of their own organizational enclave.

Assumption 5. The correctional system of the future will follow a strategy of search[25] *to determine which new techniques and pro-*

grams to undertake, and which existing services to dispense with. The outcomes of this strategy will be:

1. Evaluative data on the effectiveness of ongoing operations,
2. Experimental trials of promising innovations,
3. Well-developed feedback on the results of both ongoing and experimental activities, and
4. A management style which places a high value on being responsive to the results of evaluative and other research and which scrupulously prevents interference by vested program interests with the progress of research and consideration of change indicated by that research.

IMPLICATIONS FOR MANAGEMENT. Today, research has gained a foothold in correctional operations, but it remains a strange and somewhat frightening specter to most administrators in the system. Research, they tend to believe, is worthwhile to support, but its methods, its vocabulary, and many of its advocates cause them a great deal of apprehension. Furthermore, correctional administrators are worried about the consequences of its widespread use. When administrators support extensive research, they admit the uncertainty of existing knowledge about the management and rehabilitation of offenders. Such an administration raises questions about the necessity of operations on which large amounts of money have been spent over the years, and therefore about the wisdom and credibility of those who urged such expenditures.

Nevertheless, administrators of the future will have to adjust themselves to the tentativeness of available knowledge. They will need to understand basic research methodology and its capacities and limitations. The administrator will not need to be a researcher, but he will need a firm hold on certain concepts such as representativeness in sampling, tests of significance in data analysis, and the functions of questions and hypotheses in determining the targets for research activity.

In addition to the grasp of basic research methods, future administrators will need a broad understanding of knowledge and theory in the social and behavioral sciences. They will need special comprehension of scientific knowledge about deviant behavior and its treatment. The correctional administrator who is aware of past efforts to understand and control criminality can avoid impulsive commitment to the succession of seemingly new *solutions* which achieve a transitory visibility and then pass from sight. Hopefully, he will be equally able to recognize genuine innovations when they do appear.

The Force Field of Correctional Management. We have made a second set of assumptions about the role and environment of the correctional administrator: *each administrator occupies a focal point within a complex field of forces.* Thus we have tried to view the functions the administrator performs, the problems he encounters, and his needs for education and development through an analysis of the forces around him and the dynamics of his interaction with them.

The concept of the force field is well supported both by prior conceptualization and by a growing trend in organization theory to view the systems within which men work as open configurations of highly interdependent parts.[26] Organizations, understood in this way, strain to maintain an equilibrium but are constantly bombarded by forces from within and without, which (unless they compensate for and neutralize each other) produce disequilibrium.

In such a model of organizations a major determinant of managerial effectiveness is the administrator's capacity to deal effectively with the constantly shifting forces around him. Lewin has conceived of organizational change as a process of *unfreezing* existing patterns, *moving* to incorporate an innovation, and *freezing* the new element into the repertory of the organization.[27] Given such a view of change, we would ask: What are the administrative functions and capabilities required to unfreeze, move, and refreeze bureaucratically patterned events in the field of corrections? Various formulations such as this, generally stemming from the construct of a force field, influenced the lines of inquiry in the research reported here.

One aspect of force field analysis was especially potent in shaping the research. It was our belief that conflict manifestation and conflict management are key variables in the process of organizational change. This view, anticipated in early writings on administration by Follett[28] and Barnard,[29] has subsequently been reaffirmed and refined through research on administrative roles. William G. Scott, for example, typifies conflict management as "a process which reconciles and maintains structured interrelationships among the many forces that make up the organization."[30]

Our stress on conflict manifestation, management, and resolution is also well grounded in the correctional field itself. There is reason to believe that the field of corrections presents an environment for management in which powerful forces often are held delicately in balance and particular kinds of managerial adroitness are required even for survival, to say nothing of change. The strong gravitation of the corrections field toward the traditional goals of revenge and restraint makes really significant change extremely difficult to induce. Times of crisis and turbulence in and around a correctional organization may at times provide the only viable opportunities for significant change.

Seen at closer range, the everyday manifestations of conflict may typically help to place correctional administrators in *binds* and impasses which immobilize them for all but the most system-conserving activities. The contradictory goals set for the corrections field by the divergent forces in its environment may create powerful pressures which act to cancel each other out, creating an equilibrium which is sometimes tense, sometimes relatively inert, but unchanging with respect to its content, goals, and methods. Such a milieu may encourage highly expediental forms of administrative behavior in which the manager sees himself as a mediator rather than a user of conflict. By *cooling out* stressful situations and avoiding confrontations in which goal questions become sharply focused, the odds for survival of the organization (and the administrator) are improved, but opportunities for important change may be lost.

Martin has suggested that, in order to implement the reintegration ideology of correctional intervention, the field would need to move from *order theory to conflict theory* as a basis for determining activities and priorities.[31] The implications of this formulation for correctional managers are sizeable. Under the conflict theory, administrators would play roles as advocates (perhaps even instigators) of the kinds of change in institutional subsystems which would make reintegration of offenders truly feasible. They might seek out public confrontations on controversial issues, rather than avoiding them. They might reach deeply into their organizational environments to develop constituencies favorable to their goals and thus bring leverage to bear upon historically unresponsive power centers.

In order to understand the forces which surround correctional administrators we drew from the increasingly large literature on role analysis, literature which has contributed both depth and rigor to organizational research in recent years.[32] Most research on work roles, like that reported here, views the role occupant as the central figure in a *set,* which Katz and Kahn liken to "a vast fish net, in which each knot represents an office and each string a functional relationship between offices."[33]

Use of this conceptual tool avoids the temptation to account for variance in the behavior of organization members on the basis of personality factors alone. Rather, role analysis focuses on the expectations held for the focal person by the significant others around him. It helps to determine these expectations through the study of the positive and negative sanctions which each actor (individually or in concert) can apply in bargaining transactions with other actors, and it balances these sanctions against the actors' perceptions of the legitimacy of the expectations (Do they have a *right* to expect that of me?).

Prior research in role analysis has helped to delineate the kinds of conflict with which the occupant of any organizational role must contend. Conflicts may be engendered by discrepancies in the expectations of a single member in the relevant force field. They may arise when expectations in one part of the field are incompatible with those in another or when different roles assumed by a given individual are incompatible. Conflicts are also generated when role requirements are at odds with the *needs, values, or capacities* of the role incumbent.[34]

Our research sought to identify the disparate sources of expectation in the force field and to discover the nature of the expectations and the kinds of sanctions used to enforce them. We were especially interested in the responses of the administrators to various forms of conflict and in the feelings of inadequacy generated by such experiences.

The force field, for purposes of the research, was depicted in terms of the significant relationships which the administrators had with others in work situations. It is possible to conceive of the field of forces of correctional administrators in a somewhat more abstract way, and indeed Conrad has done so recently, as indicated in the following paradigm.[35]

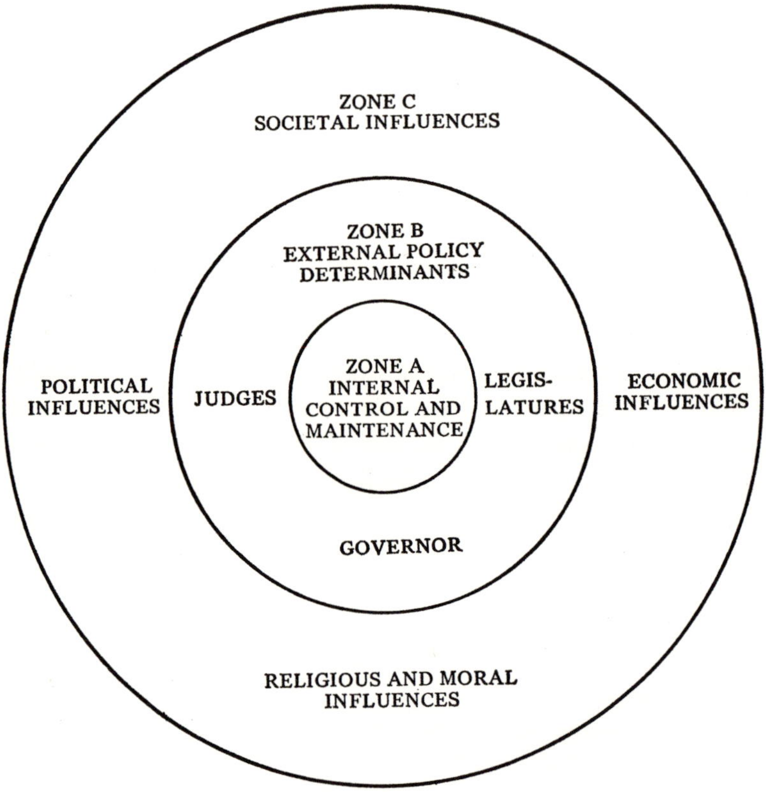

Figure 6-1 The field of forces of correctional administration

Our effort to chart the force field of each administrator we contacted began with an exploration of the working relationships which he identified as most important to him in seeking to attain his goals. Usually superiors, subordinates, and administrative peers were named as very significant. Beyond these, the relevant relationships varied considerably according to the role and status of the individual. Some perceived relationships with legislators as extremely significant; others were equally concerned with relationship with offenders. Still others perceived relationships with mass media, public and private agencies related to corrections, and *service* agencies, such as personnel and finance departments, as significant.

Having gained a sense of the topography of these relationships, we sought to understand their content. What problems arose in each of them? What kinds of influence were attempted from both ends of given relationships, and with what consequences? What types of skill, *knowhow,* and information were needed by the administrator in order to achieve successful transactions? What kinds of education or developmental experience, in his view, might be expected to increase administrative effectiveness?

While embedded in a broad theoretical context, the research had a strongly pragmatic orientation. Many critical incidents and short case studies were collected in the interview phase of the project in an effort to gain a *close-in* view of specific interactions between administrators and those others upon whom they had to depend in order to achieve their goals. We sought particularly to examine the kinds of relationships and interactions which would be of special importance in introducing change in the field of corrections and in performing successfully in the correctional system of the future. For example, we were less interested in the story of how an impressively efficient penal security system was developed than in an account of innovative efforts to blur the line between confinement and freedom in the community.

THE STRATEGIC DIMENSION OF CORRECTIONAL MANAGEMENT. Our view of the administrator as situated in a complex force field led to a final set of underlying assumptions. We assumed that an administrator's effectiveness, particularly in efforts to change the system, will depend greatly upon his skill in using tactics and strategies which give him some measure of control over the forces around him. We studied strategic behavior through an analysis of the problem-solving activities of the administrators we interviewed. As Phelan has said, the organization can be viewed as a "complex information-processing system," and when so considered can be evaluated "in terms of its effectiveness and efficiency in problem-solving."[36]

We defined the term *problem* broadly. For purposes of the research, we assumed that a problem could arise in any part of the force field or could be self-initiated by the administrator; that the problem could involve either maintenance or change of the organization; and that the attempted solution could involve the use of either programmed or unprogrammed procedures.[37] All of these possibilities, in fact, became foci for data collection.

We attempted to study the process of problem-solving through critical incidents and short case studies, seeking to make determinations about such factors as:

1. Whether the administrator sought to define the nature of the problem before acting upon it.
2. The extent to which he scanned alternative solutions before selecting one.
3. The extent to which he sought validation of either his diagnosis of the problem or his chosen solution, and the extent to which he sought *feedback* on the results of the action taken.
4. His perception, looking backward on the episode, of what he might do differently should a similar problem arise again.

While our effort was to describe the process of problem-solving in a step-by-step fashion, we were, nevertheless, guided by some assumptions about the nature of administrative decision-making. We assumed that the constraints imposed by limited time and information make problem-solving only partly rational and that most solutions tend to be satisfactory rather than optimal.[38] We further assumed that the process of searching for and selecting among alternatives is pragmatic or intuitive, involving the rules of thumb learned in previous situations.[39] Finally, we assumed, that the introduction of research and sophisticated information systems into correctional organizations will increase opportunities for finding more nearly optimal solutions to management problems.[40]

Perhaps the major factor in structuring our study of the problem-solving behavior of correctional administrators was our strong interest in the capacity of the administrators to exert influence on the forces around them. This, in turn, was related to our desire to understand the ways in which they were able to function as agents of change. We wished to determine what strategies they employed in different parts of the force field and with different problem situations. For this purpose, we thought of the force field as a competitive environment, where *bargaining* takes place in the pursuit of organizational goals and where the advantage goes to the administrator who is armed with *political* and strategic skills. [41] Our orientation, in this respect, was not unlike the recent tendency to view the force field of organizations as a marketplace, where resources essential to organizational functioning must be secured from *suppliers* and the product must be made attractive to *consumers*. Indeed, one highly placed administrator in our sample had conceptualized his operations in these very terms.

Before designing data-collection procedures which would reveal how correctional administrators exercise influence, we reviewed voluminous literature on influence and leadership in formal organizations. Two formulations on the subject seemed especially suited to our need.

The first was the classification of influence styles by Harold J. Leavitt,[42] who suggests that there are three basic ways in which organization members attempt to influence each other. The first method is the use of formal *authority* vested in the individual seeking to exercise influence as a result of his organizational role. Leavitt suggests that this method is limited because the repeated use of restrictive one-way authority tends to alienate those on the receiving end. Second, individuals may seek to exercise through the use of *manipulation*. The individual who uses this approach keeps his goals hidden while building relationships or otherwise laying a basis for getting what he wants. Unfortunately for its users, this method tends to lose its effectiveness when those on the receiving end perceive that they have been manipulated. The third influence style in Leavitt's view is *collaboration*. The definition of this method seems more nebulous, but it does involve the establishment through open communication of genuinely reciprocal problem-solving efforts.

We have very little empirical data on how widely any of the three methods are used or what their consequences may be. Our findings, for example, indicate that manipulation is much used (though seldom admitted) and that its negative effects vary widely according to the type and duration of the relationship involved.

The other formulation of managerial influence which assisted us was the concept of a *psychological contract* advanced by Schein.[43] He asserts that complex sets of expectations develop between management and those whose assistance management requires to attain its goals. The expectations which make up such a contract may be extremely subtle and usually are implicit rather than explicit. While these expectations are honored, the realtionship remains viable. When they are violated, the continuation or the productivity of the relationship is cast in doubt. Thus it seemed to us that the strategies and influence patterns exhibited by a given administrator in transactions with any part of his force field should be examined in terms of the psychological contract extant between him and the others involved. For instance, a prison warden might use direct authority most effectively in dealing with the captain of his custodial force but meet with disastrous consequences in attempting to do so with a newspaper reporter who was looking into problems in the institution.

An analysis of existing psychological contracts would be useful, we believed, not only in providing insights into existing influence styles but also in thinking about ways to induce needed change. For instance, how might the warden develop a different psychological contract with the captain or, for that matter, with the representative of the press?

Because we were interested in the tactical and strategic behavior of correctional administrators, we had to develop a definition of *strategic* and to designate at least generally the kinds of administrative behavior which would be considered nonstrategic. One concern, in this regard, was the danger of equating *strategic* with *expediential.* On the one hand, an administrator might be extraordinarily adept at maneuvering his way through his force field toward short-run goals but totally unable to construct or work toward long-range objectives. On the other hand, an administrator might be quite successful in setting long-range objectives and still be hopelessly ineffective in working with the *here and now* exigencies of administration.

Etzioni has offered a formulation which helps to deal conceptually with this problem. He points out limitations in two currently popular interpretations of the management function: the rationalistic and the incrementalist. His criticism of rationalistic models seems particularly relevant to correctional administration. The assumption that alternative courses of action can be precisely weighed and compared by rational methods ignores the fluidity and ambiguity of the values which necessarily underlie all criteria for such evaluations in corrections.

In his discussion of incrementalism, which he characterizes as an accumulation of small steps, Etzioni identifies still another major problem in current correctional management.

> . . . incrementalism would tend to neglect basic societal innovations, as it focuses on the short run and seeks no more than limited variations from past policies. While an accumulation of small steps could lead to a significant change, there is nothing in this approach to guide the accumulation; the steps may be circular—leading back to where they started, or dispersed—leading in many directions at once but leading nowhere. Boulding comments that, according to this approach, "we do stagger through history like a drunk putting one disjointed incremental foot after another.[44]

Etzioni suggests a strategy of mixed-scanning, by which he means that management should attend both to immediate problem-solving and to high-order policy choices. Because of its concern for change, evaluative information, and avoidance of dogmatic value assumptions, mixed-scanning provides a useful method of thinking about the behavior of the correctional administrators whom we have studied. While the exploratory nature of our project made it undesirable to adopt any single conception of *ideal* administrative behavior, it was helpful to ask what the data indicate about the manager's capacity to deal both with immediate problems and with long-range changes.

In an effort to achieve some comparability in the data collected on the administrators' problem-solving behavior, we developed a typology consisting of the following nine strategies:

1. *Compromise:* adjustment and concession among the parties involved.
2. *Involvement-Commitment:* gaining the participation and cooperation of the parties involved and thus securing their commitment to the solution
3. *Direct Authority:* using the rewards and penalities attaching to a formal position and rank in the organization.
4. *Dilemma Management:* using the increased attention generated by

a problem or crisis as a means of bringing about a desirable solution.

5. *Expertise:* introducing new information or calling upon persons with specialized knowledge or skills.
6. *Integration:* a new approach which recognizes the competing interests involved and seeks to avoid diminishing any legitimate ones.
7. *Manipulation:* not fully revealing all the purposes sought, while skillfully influencing others to achieve the desired goal.
8. *Invoking Standards and Norms:* calling upon widely accepted standards and beliefs to bring about the desired result.
9. *Delay:* Delaying action until a more opportune time or until a natural solution emerges.

The administrators interviewed were asked to indicate the degree to which they used each strategy in each of the relationships which made up their force fields. In a later portion of the interview, when we asked administrators to describe critical incidents in their own experience, we used the same typology of strategies to analyze each problem-solving episode.

We did not view the strategies as mutually exclusive, but rather we assumed (and this later turned out to be the case) that they would be used in varying combinations under different circumstances and with different relationships. We also assumed that an administrator might shift from one pattern of strategies to another (or simply vary the degrees to which he used those initially selected) during the course of a problem-solving episode. Not only did this turn out to be true, but it also appeared that many administrators made substantial shifts over time in their dominant mode of strategic behavior, e.g., from heavy reliance on authority to increased reliance on involvement and commitment.

Locals or Cosmopolitians?

It seems clear from the data that correctional administrators are for the most part *locals* in organization life. The majority face inward toward the organization, responding to the norms and loyalties which it imposes as a system; they are very little in touch with the fast-moving *outside* world. Correctional administrators seem little involved with the efforts of the social and behavioral sciences to understand and explain defiant behavior and to develop concepts to guide intervention in that complex set of problems. They are also isolated from organized efforts to advance and refine general understanding of administration, especially public administration.

The findings tell us that, if the new requirements and goals of the field are to be understood and pursued, correctional administrators must be helped to become more "cosmopolitan" in their understanding of management precepts, of relevant social science theory and methodology, and of the distribution of power and resources in American society. Ways must be found to supply the time, opportunity, and motivation to bring the administrators into contact with the world of literature and ideas which relate to their work. In turn, those who write and teach in the management and social sciences fields must demonstrate the relevance of what they have to say to the exacting problems which the administrators experience. Correctional administrators need new affiliations, perhaps organizations different from any of those which now exist, through which to reconcile the dilemmas of theory versus practice and to explore avenues leading to change which now are blocked by widely respected dogma. Any program for change in correctional administration must certainly address these problems.

How The Administrator Uses His Time

In order to understand the correctional administrator at work we viewed him from still another perspective. What does the administrator do? How does he spend his time? What are his conflicts about its use? How would he like to organize his days differently? Answers to such questions reveal a great deal about both the manager and the system within which he works. In order to look at this area in detail we gathered information on the weekly schedule of a selected group of 42 administrators.

The perception of time as a scarce resource is apparent among administrators everywhere. Books on administration are filled with suggestions for better use of time. The most common complaint of administrators is lack of time to do all that should be done. The way time is spent indicates something about the value system of the administrator in his organizational role. Since time, as perceived in our culture, is ultimately scarce, its expenditure requires the establishment of priorities so that more valued goals can be pursued at the expense of less valued ones. Relative use of time can be one indicator of the importance assigned (consciously or unconsciously) to various activities. As Heirich has suggested, time use in and of itself may not be suffiicient to establish the existence of causal relations between other variables, but it can add strong evidence for or against a relationship already postulated.[45] Changes in proportionate allocation of time use over a given period can also indicate a changing attitude on the part of the administrator toward the relative importance of various activities.

Studies have shown that the value of time as a resource varies according to level in the organization, since roles differ in expectation and possibilities for the use of time. The higher the level, the more possibilities exist for choices in the use of time, and therefore the more time pressure is felt. Yet the higher-level executive is perceived by the general public as having more control over the use of his time than do those at lower levels.

Sherwood has pointed out the heavy demands on executive time exerted by the very nature of the role, with pressures coming from both inside and outside the organization.[46] In modern management the leadership role tends to be one of *linkage*—tying the various parts of the organization together—and one of *problem-solving*—of facilitating and arbitrating. Both these functions take a tremendous amount of time. Accessibility has obvious time implications, and information demands are such as to make serious intrusions on time. Time is especially valued or seems especially scarce when synchronization factors—coordinating needs—are considered. In today's organizational world the most stringent organizational controls are imposed through time mechanisms: deadlines, meeting schedules, appointments. It has been suggested that "in modern industrial society, time becomes not only a mode of control but the central commodity; resources, both natural and human are measured in temporal units which become the criterion of scarcity."[47] Time has become so central in importance and so effective as a control mechanism that some administrative writers have even suggested that political bargaining between individuals and departments often takes place in terms of time priorities.

In this study, a detailed time analysis form covering a seven-day period was collected from each of the fourty-two selected administrators in institutional, probation and parole, and headquarters settings. Each executive was asked to record his time (in most cases the actual recording was done by his secretary), indicating the type of activity, who initiated it, with whom he talked or conferred, and the substance or objective of the activity. He was asked to indicate the type of activity by using the following code:

1. Individual reflection and planning
2. Discussion with one other individual
3. Group discussion
4. Telephone discussion
5. Paper work
6. Observation of programs (inspection, etc.)
7. Away from organization
8. Other

At the conclusion of the week he was asked to tell us whether or not he felt that he had substantial control over how his time was distributed among the activities and, if not, what factors tended to limit his control. He was also asked to say what he felt to be the most significant activities and the least significant. Additionally he was asked to describe work-related time usage outside of work hours (professional and community organizations), and finally, he was asked to comment on any changes he would like to make in the ways he allocated his time.

In addition to a straightforward tabulation of how time was actually used and with whom, the data were analyzed along three other dimensions. *The first* was the degree to which time was used in routine-programmed activity or, alternatively, in innovative-creative activity. *The second* was the relationship of time spent within the organization to the amount of time spent in dealing with external environment.

Finally, we look at which conflicts about time imperatives seem to be uppermost in the correctional administrators' minds.

The General Pattern. The records collected seemed to give a rather good picture of how these forty-two administrators spent their time. Most of the administrators worked more than a 40-hour week directly on the job. Outside job-related activities consumed another large period of time each month, at least six hours and in some cases over fifty hours. Administrators in the juvenile institutions and in the field settings and headquarters operations spent slightly more time on the job and on outside job-related activities than did the adult institutional executives. If time is one of the primary factors by which organizational or job commitment may be measured, as suggested by Gouldner,[48] the correctional administrator is highly committed. Of course, differences in structure and functions of organizations result in differences in executive use of time. The apparent adherence of the adult institutional executive to a stricter time schedule than that of the field or headquarters administrator seemed to be relatetd to the stricter time allocation in the adult institutional setting, where custodial and security requirements and long-honored traditions dictate rigorous scheduling.

All of the executives spent more of their time than we had expected in their offices. They spent very little time out of the office in reading, thinking, or in research activities. Perhaps public service executives, because of high visibility, public expectations, and civil service regulations, feel more constrained than do private business executives in deciding how to allocate their time. They seem to accept more restrictions on their freedom in using time as being in the nature of their publicly financed jobs.

The level which the administrator occupied in the organization did apparently have an effect on his use of time. The higher the job level, the longer the administrators were apt to work.

The greatest amount of time was spent in one-to-one conversations, primarily with subordinates; the next largest block of time was spent in meetings and conferences. These conferences took, on the average, 1½ days of each week. Time spent with offenders ranged from 20 percent on the part of a warden to 80 percent on the part of the head of a functional unit. Headquarters administrators, of course, spent little time with offenders.

Finding time to spend alone seemed to represent a problem for nearly all of the executives. In the great majority of cases, well under 25 percent of their work time was spent alone.

With the exception of the headquarters executives, less than 10 percent of the executives' time was spent with people from outside of the organization. Most external contact seemed to occur on the executive's *own* time. The higher the level, the more external contact took place.[49] Assuming reintegration of the offender into the community as the primary goal in the corrections of the future, a drastic change seems indicated in the amount of time spent by the administrators in dealing with community forces external to his organization. It appears that in the future much of an executive's time will be spent establishing communication and developing cooperative efforts with the people and organizations who control the resources needed by individual offenders in order to become reintegrated into community life. As the research points out, only the highest levels, and primarily those who work at the state level, now spend a significant proportion of their time with *outsiders* such as legislators, courts, community groups, and the press.

Most of the administrators indicated that they initiated over half of their time-consuming activities. The head administrators, as might be anticipated, indicated slightly more initiation than did the assistant heads. Most initiation took the form of scheduling staff meetings and conferring with individual staff members. Juvenile institutional administrators seemed to be more flexible and more self-initiating, and to participate in more external activities than did adult institutional managers.

Only half of the respondents said that they felt that they had control over their time. Most of the adult institutional heads did feel they had control, while most of the juvenile institution heads said they did not. Most field administrators and nearly half the headquarters executives believed that they did not have control.

SOME IMPLICATIONS OF TIME USE. Turning now to some of the possible implications of the findings, we will examine them along the three dimensions suggested at the beginning of this section.

The first dimension, determining the proportion of time devoted to routine programmed activity in relation to the proportion used for innovative creative activity, proved to be a difficult distinction to make. It is difficult, for example, to say whether time spent with a subordinate in solving a personnel problem was routine or innovative.

One would need to know the exact details of each case. But it is possible to get some impressions from the time records, which, while less than absolutely accurate, do seem to confirm the findings of a number of other time-use studies.

Modern writers in management talk a good deal about the distinction between programmed and unprogrammed decisions and activities. Herbert Simon writes that decisions are unprogrammed to the extent that they are novel, unstructured, and consequential; that is, decisions for which there is no cut-and-dried method for handling the problem because it has not arisen before, because its precise nature and structure are elusive or complex, or because it is so important that it deserves a special treatment.[50]

The same kind of dichotomy is applicable to the way time is spent. Simon goes on to say that an executive usually starts with a clean slate in a new organization and gradually accumulates a host of routine *maintenance* activities. He must take steps periodically to free his time from these *growing barnacles of programmed activity.* There is, therefore, a need for conscious effort on the part of executives to allocate time to innovation and to the development of an atmosphere of creativity.

As previously mentioned, it has been argued that there is a Gresham's law by which programmed activity drives out unprogrammed. March reports on a laboratory experiment in which participants were given three different types of jobs to do.[51] The first in order of importance was the development of changes in procedure that seemed indicated; the second, reassignment of personnel to maintain approximately equal work load; and the third, routine communication. The executives were instructed to spend equal time on each of the tasks, and the rate of work was varied systematically. The investigators found two things:

1. No matter what the rate of work and despite the instruction to spend only one-third time on routine communication, the percentage of time was heavily skewed toward routine.
2. As the rate of work was increased, the percentage of time spent on routine increased until, at peak load, unprogrammed activity was virtually eliminated.

Other evidence could be provided that points in the same direction. In our study several of the administrators spent as little as 10 percent of their time on what appeared to be unprogrammed or innovative activity. The most time spent by any administrator in such activity was 30 percent. This ratio, coupled with the findings that most of the executives spent less than 25 percent of their time in individual reflection and planning, seems to indicate rather clearly that most time is spent on a combination of disruptive, externally programmed activities (problem-solving, information-furnishing) and in largely self-programmed but rather routine coordinative activities. The least amount of time goes to innovative, developmental activities.

Along the second dimension, the relationship of time spent within the organization to the amount of time spent with the external environment, some interesting interpretations might also be made. Viewing our executive against the widely held assumption that the correctional field will move away from its isolating institution-based system of custodial confinement and toward the goal of reintegrating offenders into the fabric of community life, the amount of time the administrator spends with the *external world* becomes significant. In the conceptualization of this study we have assumed that corrections must secure an improved mandate from the public in order to carry out the new programs that are more community-oriented. We have assumed that corrections must work out effective partnerships with many community resource systems so that their services may be mobilized to assist in the rehabilitation and reintegration of offenders.

The time study reveals in one sense what might logically be expected: the institutional executives spent the least time on external contacts. The juvenile institution executives spent slightly more time in the external environment that did the adult institution executives. The field administrators spent slightly more external time, but still a surprisingly small amount, in most cases under 15 percent. The headquarters executives spent the most time with individuals and groups outside their own organization, primarily with legislators and governmental officials. They also spent time as speakers and resource persons at meetings of outside organizations.

Modern management literature is pressing for executives themselves to generate a developmental or change-oriented attitude. If the organization is to adapt to environmental imperatives for change and is constantly to re-think and re-address its goals, the organizational leader must spend a good deal of time searching the environment and working out new approaches. If the direction of change in the corrections field is indeed toward more emphasis on rehabilitation and reintegration of offenders, the need for executives to carry out probing, planning, and mobilizing functions within the wider community is obvious.

On the third dimension, the conflicts about time imperatives which were uppermost in the correctional administrators' minds, the summary of their managers' comments is helpful. The administrators repeatedly said that their most significant time expenditure was on planning and program review, although almost to a man they deplored the *lack of time* for planning, for study of trends in corrections and management theory, and for time alone to think. One rather typical remark from the head administrator of a large probation agency was: "I need to be able to reserve more time for individual reflection and planning. I find that I require stimulation by meeting with others, both within and outside this agency, to discuss ideas and test our ideas which can then be considered for incorporation into programs. I have difficulty reserving time for myself to prepare adequately for such meetings. My role as director of probation requires that I be available during the office hours to certain key groups and officials as well as being visible out of the office in either branches of this agency or with outside organizations. My schedule is thus built around this prerequisite. The time required for individual thinking is best found outside the office."

Another executive in a headquarters setting felt he did not control his own time. He felt his most significant work was on program-planning and personnel matters, yet he said, "The reason I can't control my time is that routine matters have developed into emergencies simply because of staff shortages, i.e., not enough staff is available so that planning and implementation of routine administrative matters can take place in an orderly way."

The assistant head of a large prison felt that she could not control her time, "because the span of administrative control is too wide, with diverse or different program units and with lack of sufficient undergirding by middle management." Her main conflict was over "time wasted in meetings in which staff give blow-by-blow descriptions of events."

A boys' school program head felt his time was out of his control because "approximately twenty hours per week are scheduled meetings requiring me to be present." He preferred to spend some of that time planning, reviewing program, and counseling with the boys. Functional heads, such as physicians and educators, to a man, deplored the amount of time spent in administrative duties (meetings and paper work) rather than on their *real jobs*.

To summarize, the main conflicts seemed to arise around whether or not the executive can actually control his own time and his inability to allocate his time for things he considers significant and those he considers insignificant. His pulls seem to be similar to those expressed by other executive groups as revealed in other recent studies.[52]

The administrators' time conflicts might be listed thus:

Unprogrammed Pulls	*Programmed Pulls*
Probing environment	Custodial and security requirements
Developing new alternatives	Conflict management
Planning	Facilitation activities
Improving climate	Communication activities
Improving self	Bureaucratic responsibility
	Day-to-day problem-solving

Expressed through conflict in time use

Time alone	vs	Meetings and interpersonal contacts
Doing own project	vs	Helping work of others
Seeking out problems	vs	Waiting for problems
Thinking innovatively	vs	Doing routines
Personal problemsolving	vs	Insuring system responses

The Correctional Administrator As Strategist

The nine strategies used in the interviewing provided a satisfactory framework for the examination of problem-solving behavior. Virtually all of the actions reported by the interviewees could be classified within this typology, as recapitulated below:

1. Compromise: Adjustment and concession among the parties involved.
2. Involvement-Commitment: Gaining the participation and cooperation of the parties involved and thus securing their commitment to the the solution.
3. Direct Authority: Using the rewards and penalties attached to a formal position and rank in the organization.
4. Dilemma Management: Using the increased attention generated by a problem or crisis as a means of bringing about a desirable solution.
5. Expertise: Introducing new information or calling upon persons with specialized knowledge or skills.
6. Integration: Using a new approach which recognizes the competing interests involved and seeks to avoid diminishing any legitimate ones.
7. Manipulation: Not fully revealing all the purposes sought while skillfully influencing others to achieve the desired goal.
8. Invoking Standards and Norms: Calling upon widely accepted standards and beliefs to bring about the desired result.
9. Delay: Delaying action until a more opportune time or until a natural solution emerges.

The rather cryptic definitions given above, however, usually were not sufficient to communicate the operational meanings which we had established for each strategy. Typically there was considerable discussion between the interviewer and the interviewee to clarify these definitions.

As previously indicated, some of the data collected on the strategic behavior of the administrators was appropriate for quantitative analysis. For instance, each interviewee had been asked to indicate on a five-point scale the degree to which he employed each of the nine strategies within each relationship which he had defined as significant in his work activities. Although the interview sample was too small to permit statistical comparisons of many subgroups, we were still curious to learn whether there were patterns in the strategic behavior of the interviewees. Did top administrators differ from those working at the second echelon? Were the administrators working in institutional settings significantly different from those employed in community-based programs (probation and parole)? Were those administering programs for juvenile offenders different from adult correctional administrators? We also wished to determine whether certain strategies were employed predominantly in certain relationships. For instance, was manipulation used more frequently in dealing with relatively remote parts of the force field, such as legislators, than in more intimate relationships, such as those with subordinates and superiors?

The overall patterns of strategic behavior are discernible in Figures 6-2 through 6-5. Figure 6-2 indicates the number of times given strategies were employed at the highest level of relative frequency by the administrators in the various settings in dealing with particular relationships. Figure 6-3 indicates the number of times given strategies were employed at the middle range of relative frequency in the various settings. Figure 6-4 indicates the number of times given strategies were employed at the lowest level of relative frequency in

COMPROMISE	INVOLVEMENT	DIRECT AUTHORITY	DILEMMA	EXPERTISE	INTEGRATION	MANIPULATION	STANDARDS AND NORMS	DELAY	PROBLEM SOLVING STRATEGY / SETTING
–	8	–	–	–	2	–	3	–	INST ADULT
–	9	–	3	–	–	–	–	–	INST JUVENILE
–	9	–	1	2	–	–	1	–	PROB-PAROLE
–	9	–	2	–	–	–	2	–	HEADQUARTERS

BASED ON TABLES 5.1 – 5.4

Figure 6-2 Frequencies of highest rankings of strategies, compared by setting

SETTING / PROBLEM SOLVING STRATEGY	COMPROMISE	INVOLVEMENT	DIRECT AUTHORITY	DILEMMA	EXPERTISE	INTEGRATION	MANIPULATION	STANDARDS AND NORMS	DELAY
INST ADULT	4	–	–	5	1	2	1	–	–
INST JUVENILE	–	–	1	1	2	5	–	3	–
PROB-PAROLE	5	–	–	–	–	5	–	3	–
HEADQUARTERS	2	–	–	–	–	5	–	2	–

BASED ON TABLES 5.1 – 5.4

SETTING / PROBLEM SOLVING STRATEGY	COMPROMISE	INVOLVEMENT	DIRECT AUTHORITY	DILEMMA	EXPERTISE	INTEGRATION	MANIPULATION	STANDARDS AND NORMS	DELAY
INST ADULT	–	–	8	–	–	–	4	–	1
INST JUVENILE	–	–	–	–	–	–	6	–	6
PROB-PAROLE	–	–	11	–	–	–	–	–	2
HEADQUARTERS	–	–	10	–	–	–	–	–	2

BASED ON TABLES 5.1 – 5.4

Figure 6-3 Frequencies of middle rankings of strategies, compared by setting

Figure 6-4 Frequencies of lowest rankings of strategies, compared by setting

the various settings. Figure 6-5 presents the same information but divides the sample of administrators by management level rather than by setting.

Despite the limitations imposed by the smallness of the sample, some interesting findings emerged from these analyses. Viewing the sample as a whole, without distinguishing between top and second-level administrators, the interviewees relied upon two strategies—involvement-commitment and invoking standards and norms—more

COMPRIMISE	INVOLVEMENT	DIRECT AUTHORITY	DILEMMA	EXPERTISE	INTEGRATION	MANIPULATION	STANDARDS AND NORMS	DELAY	PROBLEM SOLVING STRATEGY
–	11	–	1	–	–	–	1	–	TOP
1	10	–	2	–	–	–	–	–	MIDDLE

HIGHEST RANKING

COMPRIMISE	INVOLVEMENT	DIRECT AUTHORITY	DILEMMA	EXPERTISE	INTEGRATION	MANIPULATION	STANDARDS AND NORMS	DELAY	PROBLEM SOLVING STRATEGY
5	–	–	2	2	3	–	1	–	TOP
–	–	–	1	3	3	–	6	–	MIDDLE

MIDDLE RANKING

COMPRIMISE	INVOLVEMENT	DIRECT AUTHORITY	DILEMMA	EXPERTISE	INTEGRATION	MANIPULATION	STANDARDS AND NORMS	DELAY	PROBLEM SOLVING STRATEGY
–	–	10	–	–	–	1	–	2	TOP
–	–	8	–	–	–	4	–	1	MIDDLE

LOWEST RANKING

BASED ON TABLES 5.5 AND 5.6

Figure 6-5 Frequencies of rankings of strategies, compared by level

than the others. They relied least upon direct authority, delay, and manipulation.

One of the most striking findings was the general similarity in the strategic behavior employed by both top and second-level administrators. Nevertheless, interesting differences did appear in the data. Top managers in their relationships with parole board members used involvement-commitment, integration, and invoking standards and norms more than did the second-level managers in the same relationships. Top managers used dilemma management more in their relationships with peers than did second-level managers in the same relationship. Top managers used integration more with both subordinates and superiors than did the managers working at the second echelon.

It is interesting to note that in most cases the top managers appeared to make greater use of methods which are preferred in current management literature such as involvement-commitment and integration. We can conceive of a number of possible explanations. Perhaps these individuals find their way to headship positions partly through a greater reliance on such strategies. It is also possible that the role of top administrator poses problems and provides opportunities for learning which elicit the preferred methods of problem-solving. The critical incident data support the second explanation most strongly. Many of the top administrators reported discovering that the methods they had depended upon in more junior assignments simply did not suffice when they rose to the top position in their organization.

Our analysis of variations in the use of different administrative strategies also produced interesting results. Viewing the sample as a whole, delay and compromise where by far the most variably used strategies among different settings. The importation of new expertise was the strategy most consistently employed by both top and second-level administrators, with no statistically significant differences among the various organizational settings.

There was great variation among the different settings in the selection of strategies for dealing with offenders. Administrators at work in correctional institutions for adult offenders used significantly more direct authority than did those working in institutions for juvenile offenders or in community-based correctional programs. Community-based administrators used the least amount of direct authority; they also reported less use of manipulation with offenders than did either the administrators of juvenile institutions or those working in adult institutions. Administrators working in institutions for juvenile offenders reported more use of the strategy of integration in dealing with offenders than did either community-based administrators or those employed in institutions for adult offenders. It should be noted, however, that none of these administrators perceived himself as having a significant operating relationship with parole boards, and therefore their force field consisted of twelve rather than thirteen significant relationships.

Such disparities in the posture of differently situated officials toward offenders both reflect and accentuate the discontinuities and goal contradictions which characterize corrections today. Finally, the administrators differed markedly in their choice of strategic behaviors as directed toward people with whom they had a close and continuing relationship in contrast to those who were physically and socially more remote. The correctional administrator apparently uses a more standardized and programmed set of strategies in dealing with relatively distant relationships than with those which are more intimate and more sustained over time; e.g., subordinates and peers. One question for those concerned with executive development might be: How can public administrators be helped to develop a larger repertoire of strategies and become more versatile in using them with such groups as legislators, the press, and special interests in the community?

We will close this section of the report with two impressionistic points. First, on inspecting the data, we suspected that certain of the strategies may have been overly endorsed because they reflected ideas which are currently in vogue in the management literature of today. We do not imply that such concepts are wrong, or even that they are inaccurate. We are concerned, however, that such techniques as involvement-commitment might have been mentioned because of a positive halo rather than because they actually were used to the extent reported in the activities described.

Similarly, some of the strategies seemed to reflect currently non-prestigious styles of problem-solving. This seemed particularly true of manipulation, the use of direct authority and, to some extent, delay. The critical incidents, as will soon become apparent, contained a large number of problem-solving episodes which utilized these methods. And yet, perhaps understandably, the interviewees were reluctant to identify themselves with premises which supported their behavior. Thus, we may not have been supplied with correct information about the uses of strategies. By relying on incorrect information we may have interpreted the data inaccurately. There does not seem to be any satisfactory solution to this issue of inaccurate reporting, given the type of data which we have collected and must rely upon.

Putting aside such concerns, however, we wonder whether one function of development for correctional administrators might not be to *put on the table* for candid examination whole categories of administrative behavior around which administrators have developed feelings of anxiety or self-depreciation. If some correctional administrators feel inadequate because they rely on problem-solving strategies which their inner values tell them are unworthy, perhaps one task of executive development may be to increase their skills in understanding and using other methods more congruent with their drives for self-actualization.

We shall now turn to a discussion of each of the nine problem-solving strategies employed in the interviewing. The major data base for this discussion is the tape-recorded series of problem-solving episodes reported by the interviewees. A protocol was developed for each interviewee by monitoring the tapes and reviewing the questionnaire materials collected from that individual. The monitoring was systematized through the use of a coding sheet which provided a description of the strategies used, changes in their use during the course of events from the beginning to the end of the episode, and the effect of the experience on such dependent variables as communication, influence, and trust of participants in each other. The comments of the interviewees concerning their retrospective evaluation of the incident were also recorded. Of particular importance were their views of the implications of the experience for the training of administrators and their reactions to the question: "What would you do differently if you could relive the incident?"

The Method of Compromise

Adjustment and concession as an approach to problem-solving appeared much more heavily in the incidents than in the generalized self-perceptions of the interviewees. The administrators disliked the label of compromise but made frequent use of the method, an outcome which seemed connected with their view of correctional management as having to satisfy multiple and often contradictory goals. Believing that it was impossible to maximize any single goal at the absolute expense of others, the administrators inevitably found themselves operating as arbiters of conflicting forces.

The foci of conflict reported in the incidents were numerous and varied, but one predominated: the traditional struggle between treatment and control in the management of offenders, as described in Chapter 1. This was not a particular problem for the administrators of agencies in which the rehabilitation of offenders was addressed only in token ways, but it was a continuing and often a volatile problem in the programs which had made major commitments to both goals. The following are examples of types of problems in which compromise solutions frequently occurred.

1. A plan is developed to send institutionalized boys out to a nearby community for work and recreation. Some members of the community, including the press, react with alarm and opposition. Some of the older members of the custodial force of the institution also oppose the plan and seek in covert ways to subvert it.

2. The newly appointed administrator of treatment services in an institution launches a group therapy program, believing it can go far toward changing negative attitudes and behavior among the offenders who participate and that it can help to bridge a very wide gap between staff and offenders. In the first few weeks of the new program much opposition and criticism develops. Schedules are dislocated as the new program competes for the time of the offenders with established programs. The movement of offenders within the institution is changed and complicated, to the dismay of the custodial personnel.

3. A parole administrator determines that his staff are spending far too much time in their offices writing reports and fulfilling bureaucratic requirements. Offenders are dealt with in routinized ways which are not varied according to their individual needs. In fact, very little counseling and help is actually being provided to parolees. In his effort to restructure the work of the parole officers, the administrators encounters a great deal of adverse reaction from those who have a vested interest in the ongoing system. The issue becomes polarized around the assertion that the new plan is *social work oriented,* while the old system was commendable in that it took a realistic and firm approach to offenders. Some members of the parole board identify with this position and bring pressure to bear upon the administrator involved.

A study of the approaches taken toward solving problems such as those reconstructed above revealed that the administrators involved used compromise frequently in very different ways. For some it seemed to be the dominant approach to problem-solving. Not only did they meet crises by trying to placate and satisfy the minimal requirements of those involved, but they allocated rewards and penalties in such a fashion that no interest prevailed but no interest ever really lost out entirely. This type of administrative behavior often seemed to be used together with direct authority and manipulation. It appeared to be most effective at system maintenance and quite ineffective in producing significant changes.

Another pattern involving the use of compromise was conspicuously different. Here concession and negotiation appeared as a *fallback* strategy to be used when preferred approaches became ineffectual. Typically, the administrator would move aggressively toward change goals and draw back only when mounting resistance instructed him that he had lost momentum. Then, however, he would scan the resistance, send out *feelers* to ascertain what the most imperative needs of opposing forces were, and enter into compromise in a manner calculated to consolidate his gains. The resulting pattern was a combination of integration and compromise.

In this second pattern, compromise seemed to be accompanied by a variety of other strategies. Though the data are unclear on this point, it would seem that integration was the major preferred strategy in such cases and that all of the other strategies (perhaps unhappily including manipulation) were brought to bear on the problem according to the administrator's perception of which method would serve his purposes most effectively and expeditiously.

There were some administrators in the interview sample who both rejected compromise as a label for their strategy and described their behavior in a manner which indicated that they actually avoided adjustment and concession in the real-life arena. Like the *moralist* administrators in the study of school superintendents by Gross, Mason, and McEachern,[53] these interviewees seemed to believe that they knew what was best for all involved and inferred, therefore, that compromise was both ethically and psychologically unacceptable. Not surprisingly, these individuals tended to nominate the use of direct authority as their most preferred strategy for problem-solving. We cannot help but believe that such inflexibility most often hinders effective administrative action.

The Method of Involvement-Commitment

As has been stated, the interviewees selected the strategy of involvement-commitment in describing their own behavior more frequently than any other problem-solving method when confronted with a forced choice. With very few exceptions, they seemed to be aware of the concept of *participative management* which is so much in vogue in the literature today and regarded it as a prestigious style of administration.

In contrast to the findings regarding compromise, however, the critical incidents revealed much less use of involvement-commitment data than did the statistical data based on generalized self-perceptions of the interviewees. Examination of the incidents made it clear that we must distinguish between many different kinds of involvement in the problem-solving process. It was possible to place the incidents in which the involvement-commitment strategy was reported into four rough categories differentiated with regard to the depth and authenticity of the involvement process.

The first level of involvement, the most superficial, consisted of bringing people together to inform them of decisions already made. This category could be sub-divided into two groups. In the first, it was made clear that the only involvement expected was to hear the decisions which had been made unilaterally by the administrator and then take part in the process of dissemination and implementation. In the second (and this appeared quite frequently in the incidents), there was ritual involvement of others in discussing the desirability of decisions which in fact had already been made. In these cases, it would appear that a very small amount of involvement-commitment was combined with a large amount of manipulation. When this approach was observed in staff meetings we attended, however, it appeared that the manipulation aspect usually was ineffectual, since those involved were well aware that the decision-making was unilateral.

A second level at which the involvement-commitment strategy was used consisted of the involvement of others, usually subordinates, in devising and carrying out a plan for the implementation of decisions which were made unilaterally. An interesting feature of this strategy was that some of the time the administrators who reported it seemed convinced that the process had been fully democratic, even though what they described clearly was a limited use of the principle of participation.

A third level in the use of the involvement-commitment strategy consisted of those cases in which the administrator did in fact involve others in the making of decisions about change. Some of the interviewees, in fact, tended to look upon their managerial careers as evolutionary in the sense that they started at what we have defined here as level 1 and progressed to level 3. In such cases, there tended to be expressions of satisfaction with the greater utilization of others in the problem-solving process. A typical comment would be:

> In the beginning I thought I had to do it all myself and went around acting like the great leader. It was a great relief when I found out that I could get others to help in making the decisions, and I think the place runs a lot better this way because everybody has a stake in what we decide to do.

The fourth level of involvement of others was similar to the category just described but had the additional feature of the involvement of others in the diagnosis of problems and change needs. This did not appear very clearly in specific incidents, but in the case of some of the interviewees was an essential aspect of their administrative styles. One top administrator described his approach to problem-solving cogently:

> I try to make everyone feel that they have as much at stake in what goes on in this agency as I do and that they have as much responsibility for finding out how to get the job done better. We are working in a very primitive field in corrections and have a lot to learn. No one should feel that he has all the answers, especially the top man.

As observed in staff meetings, this administrator did in fact not only allow participation by his immediate subordinates but required it. And, though it is proper that we should avoid evaluative statements as to effectiveness since our data do not permit them, it did seem clear to the two interviewers involved that there was a high level of commitment to organizational goals in this management team.

It also seemed useful to classify the incidents in which the strategy of involvement-commitment was employed on the basis of who was involved. The great preponderance of those who were brought into the problem-solving process by the reporting administrator were subordinates. In fact, the *mind set* of most interviewees with respect to the involvement of others was that this method was appropriate only for subordinates. In particular, second-level managers usually avoided involving their peers and tended to approach their superiors very cautiously about unsolved problems. The most obvious gap in the incident data on involvement-commitment was in the area of including offenders in problem-solving. Here we had few incidents indeed! Nevertheless there were incidents reporting the use of involvement-commitment with all relationships, indicating perhaps that it is an extremely valuable and versatile strategy which could be used much more widely than it is today.

A few administrators whose work brought them into close contact with offenders described revealing examples of involving them in problem-solving at all of the four levels defined above. These examples made it clear that the gulf between staff and offenders is so wide and so imbedded in the social structure of the two groups that involvement-commitment is extremely difficult to implement. The typical inmate advisory council seemed to operate at levels 1 and 2 as described above. But there were examples of staff-offender interaction in living units in which decisions vital to the life of the institution were made collaboratively. Clearly, in such cases, the interviewees were reporting the evolution of new roles for both staff and offenders. The vested interests of staff in retaining the roles of superior and treater (interests of which apparently they are not fully conscious) raise provocative questions for those concerned with professional training and development.

The limited number of incidents in which the involvement-commitment strategy was employed in dealing with superiors was interesting. Administrators working in headquarters settings sometimes sought to involve the governor or other political executive above them in the activities of the correctional system. Similar approaches were attempted with legislators who served on key committees and whose understanding and support were required for the funding of new programs. The incidents reported in this area were not always successful, and indeed it would appear that correctional administrators often feel frustrated by their inability to make effective calls on the time and attention of their superiors, at least until a crisis occurs.

One top administrator in a headquarters setting described a lengthy process through which a work furlough plan for inmates to return to community life was enacted into law. Much learning and development were involved for the administrator, since this represented his first major attempt at change and brought him into contact with the governor and the legislature for the first time in his role as director. His approach to the task of obtaining new and, for his state, unprecedented legislation depended heavily upon the involvement-commitment strategy. He contacted citizen groups concerned with community welfare and, while he presented the work furlough idea to them as an already conceived goal, he solicited their support in getting it enacted into law. He contacted numerous legislators with explanations of the proposed legislation and its probable benefits in reducing costs of the correctional process while increasing opportunities for rehabilitation of offenders. Some legislators who were already friendly to the proposal were asked to contact others who were not. Similarly, the governor was persuaded of the desirability of the idea at an early stage, and he was asked to make personal contact with a limited number of legislators whose support was regarded as critical. The director spent a great deal of time working on these contacts himself and, when the time came for legislative hearings, devoted almost all of his time in advocacy for the bill and neutralizing hard centers of resistance.

The director in this incident spoke of his own development along two major dimensions. First, he admitted that in the beginning he was ill at ease and somewhat anxious about contacts with the governor and the legislators. He gained confidence and self-assurance by *becoming immersed in the battle.* In addition to this psychological dimension, a cognitive factor was involved. In the beginning, the world of partisan politics and the legislative process were unfamiliar to the director. He simply did not understand very much about the ways in which influence is exercised in order to achieve desired changes in public policy. He felt not only that he was *desensitized* emotionally by the rough-and-tumble involved in playing the advocate role, but that he learned a great deal by doing so. This last point seems important because most of the administrators in the study appeared to enter the political arena only reluctantly and tended to feel vulnerable while in it.

In general, the involvement-commitment strategy was used much more in the internal force field than in the external one. Administrators who were comfortable and felt that they had experienced success in working collaboratively with external interests such as legislators, the press, and special community groups appeared to have a much higher capability for bringing change about than did those who either avoided such relationships or used less preferred strategies in them.

Several administrators reported spending large proportions of their time in efforts to mobilize a wider base of support for correctional programs. Examples of such efforts were: the development of trade advisory councils through which both management and labor unions were brought into contact with the training of inmates and their placement on jobs in the community; the development of an extensive program for the use of lay volunteers in the probation supervision process; and the co-optation of employers and employment service argencies in a substantial effort to open up job opportunities for released offenders.

One interesting aspect of the use of involvement-commitment by the administrators in our sample was that they often viewed staff members in their organizations as potential links to points in the surrounding force field where support or assistance was required. The director of food services in one institution became extremely effective at placing offenders in jobs in the food service industry because he had entree with the *gatekeepers* to those jobs. His superior was quite prepared to have him spend a large part of his time in the community rather than performing the tasks listed in his job description, because the superior saw the major goal of the institution being better served in that manner.

The involvement-commitment strategy seemed most satisfying and appeared to be practiced most authentically when it was accompanied by the strategy of manipulation. Paradoxically, some of the administrators who made good use of the involvement-commitment approach also used direct authority at times. One such administrator spoke of the relationship between the two strategies in an insightful manner when he said:

> It has seemed to me that the idea of participation sometimes gets to be an excuse for avoiding your responsibility as the administrator. At times one can't get the involvement he would like because time and circumstances make it impossible. And even when there has been a lot of involvement and people have contributed a great deal to the working out of a plan, a decision still has to be made.

The substantial gap between how administrators would like to behave with respect to involvement of others and the way in which they actually behave reveals major opportunities for executive development. Dependence on less preferred methods of problem-solving needs to be understand in terms of felt inadequacy to practice the art of involving others and gaining their commitment to goals of change. An upgrading of both personal skills and knowledge of the groups and individuals whose cooperation is needed seem necessary.

The Method of Direct Authority

The majority of interviewees seemed highly ambivalent about the exercise of influence through the use of rewards and penalties attached to their administrative positions. A minority of those interviewed voiced no such concern and seemed comfortable with the idea that authority and responsibility should be commensurate and that the administrator who shrinks from exercising the former thus abdicates the latter. Such conceptions may seem simplistic or plainly inaccurate in the light of modern management theory, yet the incidents which we collected indicated that such theory, at its present stage of development, does not give sufficient attention to distinctions between positive and negative uses of authority.

Some interesting incidents on the use of authority were reported by administrators who worked in the more traditional and custodial programs. These incidents help us realize that authority is a major variable in correctional administration. The maintenance of control over captive offenders in such settings (where participative management is wholly alien to the normative structuring of social interaction) appears to involve quite delicate judgements, a deft hand, and a measure of good luck. In incidents involving the reestablishment of formal authority over mutinous inmates, the frequency with which certain vignettes appeared made them seem almost apocryphal.

Typically, inmates involved in a work stoppage, a sit-down strike, or a refusal to eat the prison food were approached on the basis of *divide and conquer.* The more amenable inmates were first brought under control and were well rewarded for their conformity (e.g., by a steak dinner), while those who continued on strike went hungry. Through such a process the hard core of the dissidents was separated out and eventually brought under control. Those who reported such stories seemed much more preoccupied with the tactical aspects of maintaining or regaining control than in understanding the dynamics through which it was threatened or lost. Nevertheless, the feeling came through that administrators who were seasoned by such difficult experiences developed a shrewd, if unevenly tempered, insight into the human fabric of their organizations.

Incidents involving the direct use of authority as the only or the primary method of solving problems occurred almost entirely in settings where revenge and restraint were the major goals of organizational activity. When reform and reintegration were legitimatized as goals, direct authority did not seem sufficient even to maintain the system, much less to change it in ways congruent with those goals. In fact, it appeared that some of the most powerful tensions and conflicts reported in the incidents were generated by the continuation of authoritarian regimes in programs wherein both staff and inmates had come to believe that participative methods of management would be introduced. This point can be illustrated through combining elements from a series of connected incidents collected in our research.

The resulting fabricated case study involved the appointment of a new warden in an old and highly repressive prison. The new appointee was described as an extremely dynamic, articulate, and charismatic individual. Coming to his post with a mandate to reform the system and develop rehabilitative programs, he received a great deal of attention from the press. He spoke out against capital and corporal punishment, both of which had been administered for many years in his institution. He called for community volunteers to help with educational and recreational activities for inmates. He embarked upon a program of staff training through which university faculty members came to the institution to instruct the custodial force in a variety of subjects generally associated with the reform model of correctional practice. Needless to say, the inmates were keen observers of both the publicity and the actual changes which took place. The power elite of the inmate population consisted of a group of individuals on the *max unit,* almost all of whom had long been committed to criminal careers.

Within only a few months it became clear that the new warden's efforts to supply leadership toward a changed system were not well understood or imitated by subordinate administrators and certainly not by the most influential inmate leaders. The method of direct and coercive authority which had been practiced for decades in the institution continued to be the dominant approach to securing compliance from those within the system. Rewards and penalties were meted out in well-elaborated ways. The small number of *treatment staff* whom the warden had brought with him to his new assignment were accorded superficial respect but were actually viewed with considerable amusement and condescension by the informal coalition of staff and inmates which maintained control over the belief system of the institution.

As the disparity between the original statements about change and the actual results became more evident, considerable tension and dissatisfaction began to develop among both staff and inmates. They were no longer sure that familiar principles would govern their efforts to *make out* in the system, but it seemed to most of them that the new approach was not making much headway either. One of the old-time guards said: "It's like trying to conquer China; the invaders get enveloped in the old system and disappear."

The new warden was reported to have shifted his own administrative style as these developments occurred. He still remained an extremely active and *charismatic* figure, involving himself deeply in many aspects of the program. Nevertheless, his own problem-solving behavior began to shift more and more toward the direct use of authority, often in punitive ways which reflected the long-standing norms of the institution. While still holding to his original goals in public pronouncements, he was sometimes heard to say that he had tried to move too fast and that some of the old approaches *make pretty good sense*. He told the professional associates from outside the prison, "You just don't change these people right away by bringing social work into the place."

Never very skillful in the participative involvement of subordinates in problem-solving, nevertheless the warden had established numerous committees and endorsed the use of group process; e.g., including *every inmate on any unit who wants to get involved* as a way of changing from the old regime to a modern, treatment-oriented program. Now, however, he sometimes showed impatience with the slowness of committee work and at times impulsively issued terse, unilateral orders much in the tradition of the previous warden.

The behavior of the new warden shifted somewhat in still other ways which were highly visible to the inmates and the line custodial staff and were laden with strong symbolic meaning for them. While continuing to oppose corporal punishment as a governmental policy, he made increasing use of it as a punishment for violation of institutional rules. He adopted the policy of personally attending sessions where the paddle was applied, saying that he did so as a way of protecting inmates against excessive brutality. He explained the difference between his public position and his operating policy on the rationale that tradition-bound systems must be changed incrementally rather than precipitously.

The end result of this sequence of events was an explosive and highly destructive riot in which costly property damage occurred and a number of personal injuries were sustained. The leaders of the riot were the hard core of inmates who previously had shared power with the old-line custodians and felt their influence slipping in the new regime. The followers, however, were the mass of inmates who (although confused and largely unable to articulate the reasons for their hostility) plainly felt that they had been promised benefits which were not forthcoming.

Most of the incidents involving the use of authority were not so dramatic as the one recounted above but perhaps have more relevance for everyday practice in modern correctional programs. A number of patterns of authority use appeared in the incidents, varying to a great extent in the way in which authority was combined with other strategies to obtain desired results.

A majority of administrators at the second echelon considered the use of authority as an essentially undesirable approach to problem-solving and believed that involvement-participation was the preferred method. One interviewee asserted, "Once you have to resort to authority, you have lost the game. The trick of administration is to bring people together to decide what needs to be done and then give them their heads in doing it." This attitude seemed particularly prevalent among administrators with professional training, especially those whose backgrounds were in social work. We wonder, however, whether such a complete avoidance of the use of formal sanctions might not constitute an abdication of certain kinds of administrative responsibility. In fact, incidents collected from management teams composed of members holding such a view and others favoring the use of authority suggested that, when an administrator denies sanctioning as a part of his role, that function is assumed by others. One division head described the situation of an administrative peer by saying: "John thinks he is operating completely democratically, but what is really happening is that his assistant cracks the whip and gets things done. And he is the fellow everyone knows really runs the division."

Another pattern appeared to be the combination of authority with manipulation, the latter often flying under false colors as involvement-commitment. One top administrator, in incidents reported both by himself and by others in his management team, demonstrated a clear and apparently long-standing tendency to shift back and forth between arbitrary order-giving (backed up by equally arbitrary rewarding and penalizing) and an affection of commitment to democratic management. In the *democratic* phase, the administrator would call numerous meetings in which he spoke at length and quite repetitiously about the virtues of staff participation, then finished by instructing his division heads on what to do. It was said that his sense of timing was so finely developed that *to his regret* there was never any time left for questions and certainly none for critical reactions to his edicts.

A much preferred pattern of authority use, on the basis of precepts set forth in Chapters 1 and 2 (that management should establish participative conditions and view men as self-actualizing), was one in which that approach to problem-solving was combined with the method of integration. The use of outside expertise and the invoking of standards and norms also appeared as a part of this pattern in some incidents. Frequently involvement-commitment (without the unauthentic overtone introduced by manipulation) constituted an intervening phase during which the goal of integrating diverse interests was pursued and the direct use of authority was avoided.

An example of this more complicated method of problem-solving behavior occurred in a large institution which had moved by fits and starts over the years from a totally repressive regime to one in which, while the excesses of sadism and mortification of inmates were relinquished, only the smallest beginnings had been made in working toward the goals of reform and integration. At this juncture a new superintendent was appointed who had demonstrated unusual competence in a previous assignment as an institutional administrator and who, while quite pragmatic and eclectic in his approach to management, was generally committed to the idea of no substitute for personal occupancy of the *lonely* executive role. We were persuaded that at least some of the learning involved therein could be achieved through imaginative simulation of real events.

The Method of Introducing Expertise

The importation of specialized knowledge or skill, whether in the form of human resources or some inanimate carrier such as literary or visual materials, was frequently nominated as an approach to problem-solving and was given a relatively high priority in the forced-choice rankings made by all interviewees. Moreover, it was spread rather uniformly across a wide range of relationships.

Expertise was employed in a wide variety of ways in the incidents. Correctional administrators often find themselves in at least nominal control of services which affect every aspect of human life. Institutional managers, in particular, must provide and maintain quality control over the feeding, housing, recreation, training, employment, and protection of the inmates under their charge. Beyond these functions, many administrators also seek to provide psychological and spiritual retraining. And all of this must be done in the potentially incongruous context of custodial containment and control.

Even the administrators of probation and parole programs must have concern for this same broad spectrum of services. While not working in encapsulated environments such as correctional institutions, the community-based administrators have the added problem of mobilizing a variety of resources over which they have no direct authority. Thus the securing of needed employment, training, and medical assistance requires that their staff (the supervising probation and parole officers) be knowledgeable about these resources, skillful in determining which are needed, and most of all, able to secure them. To say that a great deal of specialized expertise is required in the performance of these functions is something of an understatement.

Many of the institutional administrators who reported incidents expressed frustration in their efforts to attract needed expertise from typically indifferent outsiders. This was particularly the case with respect to consultation related to rehabilitative programs. In part, this reflected an uncertainty about the relative effectiveness of different rehabilitative techniques. There was a tendency for many administrators to have on their desks some of the recent works concerning crime or delinquency, and to refer to them in conversation, but we found few examples of well organized and implemented programs to bring such materials to the attention of staff or to help them consider the implications of current research and theory for local operations. Some of the incidents concerned the development of staff training programs and libraries, but in general it did not seem that such activities made a vital difference in the direction or velocity of change in the general programming of the agency. Most staff libraries which we saw were dusty and out of date.

The introduction of needed expertise seemed to be more relevant to actual needs when it arose out of a particular, vexing problem. In one incident a panel of experts on dietetics and nutrition redesigned the food service program of an institution after it had come under severe criticism from inmates and their families. In another incident an interdenominational committee of clergymen was called in to help deal with a charge that time and physical space in an institution were inequitably allocated as between Protestant and Roman Catholic interests. Thus, expertise injected with the purpose of solving a specific problem seemed more potent than expertise introduced for the general good of the organization.

In incidents reported by community-based administrators, the successful co-captain of needed expertise seemed at times to depend upon the administrator's ability to identify intersections of interest between his own agency and others in the force field. One parole administrator described a situation in which his staff needed psychiatric consultation in order to deal more effectively with emotionally disabled clients. Budget constraints made it impossible to meet this need through the employment of qualified psychiatrists. In scanning alternative solutions, the administrator discovered that the psychiatric training program of his state university needed real-life opportunities for psychiatric interns to apply their generic skills to the problem of crime and delinquency. The discovery of these intersecting needs provided a basis for a series of workshops and seminars in which parole officers interacted with young psychiatrists to the considerable satisfaction of all parties involved.

We obtained additional insights through an examination of incidents which were designated as *ineffective* by the interviewee. Two factors contributed to unsuccessful outcomes: the lack of relevance of the available expertise to the problem which needed solution, and the low quality of the *expert* input. Demonstrations of the irrelevance of *experts* occurred during incidents where otherwise competent and well-intentioned outsiders simply could not develop solutions that were really pertinent to specific problems. For example, a parole administrator described a large-scale effort of his department to enlist the efforts of service clubs in obtaining employment for offenders. A number of such organizations were contacted and persuaded to give carefully prepared talks. Parolees were called in to describe the problems encountered by offenders in obtaining jobs. All of this resulted in a sizable effort on the part of service club members to open up job opportunities for probationers.

The difficulty, however, was that the membership of the service clubs did not really constitute an appropriate power base for significantly changing the employment system for ex-offenders. In retrospect, the reporting administrator somewhat ruefully recognzied that "most of those who set out to help us were small businessmen who had a highly limited number of jobs available within their own organization." This experience, he said, helped him to recognize that *the real brekthrough* would have to come through obtaining advice and subsequently active assistance (a combination of expertise and involvement-commitment) from such authentic *gatekeepers* as the officials of large industrial unions, the heads of organizations employing hundreds or even thousands of workers, the personnel directors of these same organizations and, finally, the public employment agencies which provide a large and highly bureaucratized network of contact points between potential employers and those in need of employment.

The factor of quality, as illuminated by the *unsuccessful* incidents, seemed to reflect the fact that our society is replete with *experts* of all kinds, not a few of whom turn out to be duds or frauds, however invincible their *paper* qualifications seem to be. If the tone of this comment seems unduly sour, it is because our interviewees had a number of convincing stories to tell about entreprenurial outsiders who assured the solution of complex problems concerning which they had only meager understanding. Some interviewees may have been resentful partly because the correctional field tends to shift its allegiance in decidedly fickle fashion from one *omnipotent* source of expertise to another—education, psychiatry, sociology, management consultation, and, most recently, computerized information-processing.

In any case, many of the incidents involving the use of outside expertise were rather sad tales of flirtation with outsiders who, as it turned out, possessed no magic solution to long-standing problems. So numerous and diverse are the purported experts around the correctional field that a plausible goal of executive development might be to increase the sophistication and awareness of administrators concerning their relative strengths and limitations.

A final observation is in order concerning the introduction of expertise as an approach to problem-solving. Some of the incidents made it clear that in dealing with outside experts the administrator must be sensitive to the reactions of such inside power centers as the legislature, service and control agencies, and others who might be negative to the influence of the *expert* or the *consultant*. Indeed, it appeared that rather delicate judgment may be required to distinguish between the times when *expert* evidence carries the day and the times when it alienates those whose cooperation is most needed. The importance of this variable is reflected in the fact that perennial consultants to correctional agencies, such as representatives of the National Council on Crime and Delinquency, have learned to defer to the overriding importance of local needs and traditions and have become skillful in adapting their conceptions of *the best way* to indigenous circumstances.

Some of the incidents which were judged as less than successful by those who reported them involved events in which legisators, control agency officials, representatives of the local press, or others concluded that "our situation is special and we really don't care how they do it in some other place." The lack of sure and proven knowledge concerning what works and does not work in correctional practice suggests that this may not be an unreasonable position much of the time.

The problem for executive development lies in developing an ability to identify forms of outside assistance which are both relevant and of good quality. Even when these criteria are met, however, the problem remains of using the influence of outside experts in such a fashion as to persuade rather than alienate *inside* decision-makers. Viewing this function as a task for executive development, the administrator might be seen as playing the role of mediator between local and outside forces. The great limitation apparent in our sample of administrators with respect to the performance of this task was their parochialism and lack of contact with authoritative opinion, research data, and experience in other jurisdictions. There seemed to be a clear contrast between those administrators who were knowledgeable and in touch with developments relevant to their work, and those who were essentially insular in outlook. The former seemed to generate in their staffs a spirit of inquiry and an appetite for finding connections between their correctional enclave and the outside world. In such settings, small talk at coffee breaks included, for example, references to a professor's comments at an evening lecture, a book on management read over the weekend, a newspaper story about efforts to change programming for mentally ill patients from an institutional to a community-based approach. In the settings in which management did not provide models for such *reaching out* behavior, discussion over coffee tended to revolve more around local gossip and intrigue, preoccupation with such concerns seemingly substituting for the harder questions of program policy that were left unaddressed.

The Method of Integration

Within our conceptual scheme the integration of disparate interests and goals was a highly preferred approach to administrative problem-solving. Our use of the term integration in the classification of incidents is based upon Mary Parker Follett's work in distinguishing integration (contrasted with domination and compromise) as an administrative strategy.[55]

Administrators who were skillful in integrating legitimate but seemingly irreconcilable interests usually did so by probing the context within which the problem was moving rather than through a rigid application of predetermined values and priorities. This is not to say that such administrators had no concern for values and goals; the opposite seemed to be true. But the administrators with integrative capability seemed to bring their value positions to the problem situation as general referents rather than as polarizing influences. In the case of nonintegrative interviewees, predetermined positions were rigidly applied, with the result that solutions could only be achieved either through an authoritative edict (domination, in Follett's terms) or a scaling down of legitimate aspirations on the part of the parties involved, i.e., compromise.

The incidents classified under the heading of integration included a variety of types of conflict. The great majority, however, fall under the following headings: (1) conflicts about the management of offender between treatment and control orientations; (2)) conflicts between those who favored the conservation and maintenance of the organization within its force field and those who perceived a need to change its direction and mode of operation; and (3) conflict between concern for production and task performance versus concern for the morale, welfare, and development of the human participants in the situation. Conflicts of the last type presented particularly difficult problems of definition. The social worker attached to an institutional living unit tended to think of production as a change in inmate attitudes and behaviors. The custodial officer attached to the same unit thought of production as cleanliness, order, and discipline on the unit and argued that the creation of these conditions amounted to exactly what the social worker was seeking. Conflicts in this case centered not so much around long-term images of desired change as around the intervening processes which were thought likely to produce those results.

TREATMENT VS. CONTROL. The incidents which revolved around conflicts between the goals of helping and controlling offenders provided more examples of compromise than of integration. Many of the organizations studied seemed to have institutionalized these functions in a way that insured their separateness. Periodic skirmishes occurred along divisional boundaries when one side or the other considered its interests to be in jeopardy, but the paucity of collaborative problem-solving between administrators in peer rank was notable.

However, the relatively rare instances of integrative problem-solving in which the functions of control and treatment were merged rather than compromised were extremely interesting. One institutional administrator, for example, described a series of events in which disciplinary infractions by inmates escalated sharply and feelings between the custodial staff and the inmates became exacerbated. Many representatives of the treatment-training component sympathized with the inmates and at times subverted the custodians in the efforts to enforce rules.

In discussion with the staff involved and with members of the inmate advisory council, the warden found opinions so polarized and feelings so strained that there seemed little basis for fact-finding and negotiation. The inmates asserted angrily that the officers were "always on our back," while the officers maintained that "the place has been getting completely out of hand and we have to make it clear who is in charge here."

Members of the treatment division seemed torn by the conflict between hierarchical loyalties to the institutional rule system and the dicta of their profession which moved them to oppose, as one of them put it, "authoritarian handling which aggravates the inmate's tendency to be hostile and reinforces his tendency to be immature and dependent."

Almost everyone involved seemed to be talking in terms of slogans and abstract principles, all of which sounded high-minded and virtuous. The warden was angered by the extent to which all parties seemed bent on frustrating each other rather than working out a solution to the problem. He confessed that he also felt somewhat afraid because he could feel tension building and believed that there might be a series of explosive incidents before long in which people would be seriously injured.

One morning the warden received a request for an interview from an *old con* who, although not on the inmate advisory council and certainly not much involved in rehabilitative programs, had prestige in the inmate society because of his accomplishments in crime and because he was a *loner* who always said what he meant. This inmate told the warden that he and *other old timers like myself* were interested in doing *quiet time.* He said that the continuing animosity between the young *orangutangs* and the *stupid screws* was making life very difficult, and he thought that something should be done about it. Asked for advice on what steps might be taken, he offered to serve on a small committee of inmates and staff who would study the situation and bring in recommendations to the warden.

After a night's thought, the warden decided to move along the lines suggested by the inmate. He appointed to the study committee the inmate who had made the suggestion, the head of the inmate advisory council, and two middle-management staffers (one from custody and one from treatment) who tended to be moderate and reasonable in their approach to other people. The warden announced this move publicly at an evening movie attended by most of the inmates, and subsequently he gave considerable personal attention to the work of the committee.

This process did not suddenly solve the problem, but it set in motion a series of events which eventually led to a much more satisfactory disciplinary program. One of the major features of the new program was strong participation of the inmates in defining, modifying, and implementing the rule system of the institution. Eventually inmates actually sat on disciplinary boards and, at a living-unit level, made the major decisions about penalties to be imposed for rule infractions by their fellows, subject only to general review by designated staff members. There seemed, in this situation, good reason to believe that the goal of maintaining reasonable order and control had indeed been integrated with the goal of helping the offenders involved to learn about self-control, not only at an individual level but in terms of the institutionalization of this function within a miniature society.

Incidents involving the integration of control and treatment within community-based correctional programs were somewhat more obscure. Elliot Studt has referred to parole officers as *Janus figures* because they face both ways on the status passage which the offender is expected to traverse from the position of prison inmate to that of responsible citizen. The strain experienced by the officers in their efforts to police the conduct of the offender, thus protecting the public while still assisting him in making a successful adjustment to community life, appeared to be exceedingly severe in several incidents reported to us.

The ways in which these officers managed at times to integrate the function of control with that of treatment were human rather than bureaucratic. The rules and conditions of probation and parole stood as a kind of formal structure for both officers and offenders, but the real-life struggles through which the offenders attempted to come to terms with the expectations of their families, employers, friends, and acquaintances obviously presented continuing dilemmas for all involved.

One probation officer told of approaching his job in an unconventional way which allowed him to monitor and set limits on the behavior of his juvenile charges while still providing them essential emotional support and much-needed opportunities for ventilating pent-up feelings. He explained that he was then working in an area where most of the juvenile probationers came from middle- or upper-class families. He said that the parents, and particularly the fathers, tended to be neglectful of their sons and out of touch with them. Therefore he made himself available to boys in this situation, only some of whom were probationers. Being a relaxed person and genuinely interested in young people, he spent long hours talking with them at drive-in restaurants, recreation spots, and around school. He felt that not only was he able to fill some of the gaps left open by indifferent parents but that he found opportunities to help the youngsters evaluate the feelings of anger and deprivation generated in previous inadequate relationships.

The probation officer's close contacts with the boys at times made him privy to their interest in law-violating activities. He was *tested* by them numerous times with reference to his own commitment to societal rules and quickly learned that he could be a useful model for the boys only if his own attitudes were clear and unambiguous around the need to support authority.

He cited this experience as an exception to the usual process of probation supervision, pointing out that the high caseloads and the bureaucratic requirements for reporting that were established by administrative decree tend to make officers act as surveillance agents (with occasional office interviews, defined as *therapy*) rather than true integrators of help and control.

System Maintenance vs. Change. Turning now to the integration of system maintenance with change, as revealed in the incidents, we may note first that the capacity to blend the two seemed to be present more often at top administrative levels than at the second level. Perhaps this is more a matter of role than aptitude, since it seems reasonable to believe that top administrators are better positioned to comprehend needs for both conservation and innovation than are subordinates whose responsibility is limited to particular sectors of the organization.

Two major types of integration appeared in the incidents. The first involved instances in which an administrator managed to blend maintenance and change concerns through the direct exercise of his own influence. The second consisted of efforts to institutionalize the integration of these two concerns within appropriate organizational structure.

With respect to the exercise of personal influence, there were a number of incidents in which administrators reported a conscious avoidance of *oversell* in presenting proposed new programs to the legislature, fiscal control agencies, or other groups whose support was required for approval. Obviously, such restraint was difficult, since administrators are conditioned to fight hard for a share of the public revenue in a highly competitive environment. Nevertheless, certain administrators told us that in the long run it was better to justify proposed new programming on the basis that "we don't know for sure how effective it will be, but the best evidence we can obtain suggests that it will substantially improve our operations." It was admitted that often it is possible to coax or force a particular program through with grandiose promises, but the integration-minded administrators suggested that eventually they might pay a heavy price for such action. Legislative and other relevant reviewing authorities might become cynical about the administrator's *puffing* statements and discount them in the future. They asserted that the administrator who oversells for short-term gains loses his credibility in the very parts of his force field where he needs it most.

It seemed clear that maintaining the reputation and integrity of the agency while still being an effective advocate for needed changes is an extremely difficult function. The neophyte administrator, particularly, faces many seductions when he is cast in the role of correctional expert and asked to defend his proposals for a better system. It is much more satisfying to claim unequivocally that a proposed innovation will work than to place qualifications upon its possible success. The administrators who sought to integrate the functions of system maintenance and system change seemed at times to define themselves as teachers, in the broadest meaning of the term. They saw as essential the need to provide key legislators, budget reviewers, members of the press, and others with opportunities to gain a more sophisticated understanding of the crime problem and of the tentative character of present knowledge about correctional techniques. They were well armed with facts about the inadequacy and costliness of the present system and argued that we must take risks in moving toward a better system but that these risks should be calculated ones and that we should continually evaluate the success of new and experimental ventures.

Some administrators who approached change in this fashion spoke of developing satisfying partnerships with those in the external force field who had previously been regarded as critics. Long-term change, in fact, seemed to depend upon establishing a coalition of interests in which the administrator was no longer a lone voice for needed reforms but had developed commitment on the part of numerous others capable of exercising influence at key decision points.

With regard to activities taking place within their own organizations, the administrators who sought to combine system maintenance with change appeared to exercise considerable personal influence in the sense of providing models for a *strategy of search*. During contacts with staff who represented particular program interests, these administrators communicated the idea that it is not necessary to maintain a facade about effectiveness and that it is highly desirable to seek better ways of doing the job.

One administrator told at length of his contacts with a group of subordinates who were overzealous in their advocacy of a vocational training program for offenders. They bombarded visitors to the institution with glowing statements about the training and with *success stories* about ex-inmates who had obtained highly paid jobs. While still maintaining a generally supportive attitude toward the program, the administrator began to ask for *hard data* on the number of trainees who obtained employment in their specialty, the length of time they had such jobs, and other information related to success. Gradually the staff involved began to ask such questions themselves and reportedly experienced a sense of relief in discovering that their program did not have to be a total success so long as it was being reviewed objectively. They then became more capable of devising ways of improving training and job placement. The same administrator also indicated that he made it a practice to move staff about to different jobs in order to keep them from developing too much vested interest in a particular program.

The incidents which involved an effort to institutionalize the integration of system maintenance and change were typically not reported as highly effective. Rather, they seemed to represent somewhat primitive efforts to build change dynamics into organizations in which the idea of change was basically alien and threatening.

A long incident (really a case study) about the development of an action research program within a large correctional system provided many insights about the difficulties involved in such efforts. Defensiveness and suspicion between researchers and those in action roles appeared very clearly. An early tendency for the researchers to proceed unilaterally rather than in collaboration with program operators in defining research questions led to serious consequences in the form of lack of cooperation from those in action roles when data collection was carried on. The most successful integration of action and inquiry seemed to occur when the researchers became deeply involved in the real-life problems of program staff and the latter became involved in research activities. Such collaborative activities developed mutual trust and support as well as greater awareness by all involved of the problems and dilemmas of inquiry and evaluation. Nevertheless, it appeared to us that research as a way of institutionalizing change in corrections has made only a small beginning and the problem of integrating concerns for system maintenance with the hard questioning of systems operations which is implicit in research activities has not been satisfactorily resolved in any operating agency.

Another institutionalized approach to the integration of system maintenance and change in corrections was the establishment of special organizational units for planning and development. Some of the interviewees in our sample reported assigning specially qualified staff to the task of looking ahead, assessing the adequacy of available resources in terms of the projected workload, and thinking generally about the future without being overly constrained by present realities. It appeared to us that some of these efforts were not making much headway, that the staff involved in planning and development were relatively remote, not only from ongoing operations but also from the information required to make realistic projections into the future.

Nevertheless, there were incidents in which important changes apparently came about through such arrangements. In one case, the head of planning and development in a department of corrections was brought to that role from many years of varied experience in both institutional and community-based correctional programs. Long an outspoken and intelligent critic of agency programs, he was asked to evaluate the entire system, talk to anyone he wished to, and make recommendations to the director for new legislation and for policy changes. His rapport with operating personnel and his intimate knowledge of the system prepared him to make recommendations which, although far-reaching in nature, were congruent with the basic commitments and goals of the organization. By contrast, some planning and development efforts seemed ineffectual because they were carried on by persons who made their recommendations on the basis of extremely superficial understanding of the existing system.

A general and quite basic limitation of studies and surveys as instruments for introducing needed change appeared to be that ideas about change were largely formulated within the framework of current ideology. It seemed difficult for those identified with the reform movement in corrections to take a fresh and objective look at ongoing operations. Perhaps a consortium of insiders and outsiders might make a more effective planning and development team than most of those which have operated thus far on the correctional scene.

Production vs. Human Welfare. The integration of concern for production and concern for human welfare and morale was revealed in a number of incidents, although as previously stated, there was a good deal of *muddiness* in the data with regard to the meaning of the terms. Perhaps the best way to approach a discussion of this dimension would be to note that much of the incident data reflected no effort to integrate these two concerns. Some business managers, for example, seemed totally oriented to the maintenance of good fiscal records and the balancing of the budget. But one *elder statesman* in this group offered a number of ingenious examples of ways in which he was able to advance the treatment and training program for the offenders in his agency by his handling of the fiscal system. He said, "The job really started to be fun when I decided that these young fellows involved in treatment (meaning both the staff and the offenders) were not my enemies and that there were lots of ways that I could help them." He seemed to derive his major job satisfaction from being able to supply fiscal support for needed innovations rather than, in typical fiscal management behavior, playing a role of denying and restricting. It did appear, it must be added, that he made personal and perhaps quite arbitrary judgments about which treatment programs were worthy and which were not.

If the major *production* of a correctional organization really is the changing of offender attitudes and behaviors, then it is apparent that lesser production goals, which are really only means to that end, need to be subordinated. Problems occur when these lesser goals are made dominant. Thus, great tension and animosity developed in one institution when the farm manager became so preoccupied with crop production that he neglected opportunities for inmates assigned to this activity to learn skills which might have helped them to secure employment after release. The ability of administrators both in institutions and in the community to establish the goal of reintegration of offenders as a major orientating point for all staff seemed critical. With the reintegration goal as the major reference point for all participants, there was a basis for determining which priorities were more justified than others. Without it, diverse interests tended to compete with each other in ways which were frequently destructive, and the climate and morale of the organization was adversely affected. In this sense the integration of production with human welfare seemed to depend very greatly upon the administrator's ability to use the strategy of invoking standards and norms in such a manner as to generate consensus about and commitment to the goals of the agency.

The Method of Manipulation

While many of the interviewees were reluctant to identify themselves with use of manipulation, as operationally defined in our research, the incidents which they reported frequently revealed intricate manipulation strategies. Some of the interviewees were refreshingly blunt in saying, in effect, that in a competitive, pluralistic system there is sometimes great advantage in *concealing part of your hand.* Still others spoke of this practice in more bland terms; e.g., "It is wise to cultivate goodwill from people whose help you will need later."

It is difficult to assess this strategy, or the possibilities for refining it through developmental experience, because it is so negatively stereotyped in our society. The interviews indicated that manipulation is most appropriate and effective when used in relationships in which the parties deal at arm's length and the caveat of potential exploitation is well understood on both sides. Yet the quantitative data based on forced-choice rankings of strategies show the use of manipulation slightly more frequently with relationships in the internal force field than in the external one.

Paradoxically, even those administrators who were predominantly oriented toward a preferred set of strategies, such as involvement-commitment, integration, and use of expertise, seemed to make use of manipulation when the problem context was highly competitive or antagonistic. In these situations, problem-solving was so structured that in order for the administrator to win, someone else would have to lose. Just as a good chess player does not tell his opponent the moves he expects to make ahead of time, the administrator who reported manipulation strategies seemed to regard concealment as a major advantage. An example may help to clarify this point.

One day an administrator received a call from a newspaper reporter who told him that the head of a newly formed private association which purported to help offenders reestablish themselves in the community had been sharply critical of the correctional organization headed by the administrator. The group had charged that the policies of his organization were antagonistic to the purposes of the private program and demanded a public explanation. The administrator, while irritated and somewhat threatened by the communication, affected an unruffled manner and said that he would like an opportunity to study the charges and meet with those who had made them in order to see what might be done. Having already formulated a negative opinion of the private group, however, he instead proceeded to make a number of telephone calls to officials in other jurisdictions where groups affiliated with the same private organization were operating. In this way he obtained anecdotal information from credible sources which cast doubt upon the integrity and responsibility of the group. He then called in the reporter who had contacted him and in an *off the record* interview made available to him the new sources of information, saying that he did not want to be quoted since he had no firsthand knowledge of the allegations. With the reporter following these new and more attractive lures, the administrator engaged in delaying tactics with the private association, whose originally clamorous demands for attention subsided after a few days.

It may be helpful to consider our data on manipulation in the light of management literature associated with the concept of social exchange.[56] If we assume, as does the concept of social exchange, that those operating in the administrative arena interact with each other in terms of complex desires to achieve gains and avoid losses, it becomes clear that certain of these interactions will be competitive or even antagonistic in nature. Our incidents tended to bear this out. The administrator dealt more openly with legislators with whom there was a prospect of mutual gain (e.g., securing approval of a new institution to be located in the district of a friendly assemblyman) than with those who had no particular reason to be supportive of correctional program expansion. While openness and candor might be advocated as general principles by an administrator, he was much more apt to practice them with a newspaper reporter who was friendly than with one who was *looking for trouble*. We heard many references to such tactics; e.g., "protecting our flanks against that young assistant in the governor's office who wants to build his empire," or "Tom Jones (a subordinate working in one of the institutions) is a troublemaker and would discredit his superiors if we put him into a position where he could do so."

In final appraisal of our incident data on manipulation, two contradictory themes predominated. First, it seemed clear that there were numerous occasions when all of the administrators believed it necessary to be guarded rather than open and to use influence indirectly rather than directly. At the same time, several ineffective incidents (some of them reported about other administrators rather than the interviewees themselves) indicated that it is disastrous for an administrator to become known as deceptive and as one who works behind the scenes to undercut others. We heard a great many approving descriptions of other managers who were admired because "you can trust him," or "even if he disagrees with you, you always know where he stands," or "he always operates out in the open."

While our data do not provide a basis for reconciling the basic inconsistency of such attitudes toward manipulation and the practice of it, they do suggest some plausible explanations. First, certain relationships seem to require a higher level of openness than do others. An administrator who amiably supplied critics of his program with ammunition to use in a legislative hearing was perceived by his associates as *naive* rather than as possessed of great integrity. Secondly, openness seemed to depend greatly upon individual personality and style. Some administrators naturally operated in an open and spontaneous way which apparently was contagious and allowed them to deal directly and above board in a wide range of relationships. Others were much more cautious and reserved, becoming relatively open only as a result of long-term contact with other individuals. A style which generated universal disapproval among our interviewees, however, was that in which a facade of openness masked calculative and manipulative strategems for dealing with others.

The Method of Invoking Standards and Norms

We found that the administrators studied, particularly those with innovative capacity, made wide and varied use of the strategy of invoking standards and norms. *Authoritative* standards such as those promulgated by the American Correctional Association, the National Council on Crime and Delinquency, and the U. S. Children's Bureau frequently constituted the primary basis for requesting a better staffing ratio, a new institution, or some other desideratum. The administrators who were orientated toward change tended to speak about their operations in comparative terms; e.g., "we have better job placement services than the Employment Service" or "our school program has been accredited in the top category for this country."

It was obvious, however, that most of the standards and norms which are pertinent to the rehabilitation or reintegration of offenders rest on rather flimsy evidence, and most of the administrators seemed well aware of this limitation. One interviewee said:

> I stand up in front of the Ways and Means Committee and tell them that we simply have to hire enough additional officers to get the caseload size down to that recommended by NCCD, but I know damn well that if they ask me for proof that this would reduce recidivism, I wouldn't have much to say.

The administrators who were most attracted to the idea of building a research capability into their organizations seemed to be most skeptical of the sanctity of existing standards.

We identified a small number of interviewees for whom the invoking of standards and norms seemed to be the primary strategy used in problem-solving. For every problem, with these individuals, there seemed to be an appropriate axiom of principle to produce the answer. Frequently in these cases the invoking of norms was at a highly abstract level and at times seemed to have a pontifical tone. Without exception, all of the incidents which we obtained from administrators who appeared to depend primarily upon the invoking of standards and norms had to do with organizational maintenance rather than change. The following incident is illustrative.

One interviewee described a situation in which boys committed to a forestry camp became recalcitrant and difficult to manage. Responsibility for their supervision and programming was divided between paid staff and volunteers from a nearby community. It was reported that the problems started when volunteer supervisors allowed the boys to get out of hand during the evening recreational period. Work efficiency in reforestation projects then dropped sharply. Liquor (possibly stolen from nearby vacation cottages) appeared in the camp and there was furtive drinking in the barracks. Boys began to run away. Word that all was not well found its way back to the headquarters and also came to the attention of a number of private citizens who, as a result, became critical of the correctional system.

The administrator's description of his resolution of these difficulties was paternalistic in tone. He indicated that his subordinates had chosen volunteer workers who were "goodhearted, but didn't understand how to handle these boys." In subsequent meetings with both professional staff and volunteers, the administrator reported *educating* them along lines which seemed clear-cut to him. There is a *right way* to handle rebellious boys, he explained, indicating that a combination of firmness and paternally allocated benevolence was the correct formula. He also detailed a number of specific standards for the conduct of work and recreation programs, standards which "have to be observed if you are going to avoid problems."

The troubling aspect of this and related incidents was that those administrators who depended so heavily upon preformulated axioms frequently were regarded by their associates as *rigid* and lacking in capacity to introduce truly significant innovations. We gained the impression that some correctional organizations make a token display of rehabilitative programs but in major substance retain the practices and the climate of authoritarian regimes. One key to such conditions may be the presence of administrators who, in seeing themselves as the source of all legitimate prescription and authority, keep hierarchically subordinate staff and offenders in dependent and relatively uncreative roles.

A seemingly preferable use of standards and norms in problem-solving appeared in instances of administrative behavior which emphasized search for more effective methods rather than treating existing dogma as immutable. Administrators conforming to this pattern made much use of standards and norms to solve particular problems (in some cases tending to be somewhat manipulative when seeking to influence naive interest groups) but tended to regard them as tentative *rules of thumb* which can be improved upon as knowledge about correctional intervention techniques advances. In this pattern the invoking of standards and norms tended to be combined with integration, involvement-commitment, the use of expertise and, at times, manipulation.

The Method of Delay

The use of delay was reported persistently, though with a relatively low frequency, by administrators in discussing many relationships. An amusingly constant response to the interviewer's suggestion that deciding not to decide was a possibility, came in such statements as "yes, I've learned that's so, and I don't charge in like I used to in the beginning."

It appeared that some respondents actually were reporting an avoidance of problems rather than a well-conceived strategy of solving them through delay. On the other hand, a few administrators had given a great deal of thought to the timing of efforts to bring about change and reported quite elaborate strategies in which delay was combined with such other methods as dilemma management and involvement-commitment. These administrators placed a great deal of importance upon preparatory work which enabled them to move strongly and decisively when the time for action finally arrived. Activities carried on in the preparatory period included gathering facts and arguments to support a change when the time came to advocate it openly, helping staff to be ready to implement a major new program by a prior period of development and training, and *softening up the public* as, for example, in preparation for a work furlough law, through a series of educational programs about the causes of crime and the potentiality of many offenders for successful reintegration in the community.

It seemed to us that the use of delay was especially characteristic of administrators who had been seasoned in bureaucratic battles and, while still preserving a zeal for reform and change, had learned to bide their time and develop needed support. Some of the ineffective incidents reported by such administrators from their earlier careers were intended to document the idea that ill-considered efforts to introduce change which result in failure are more harmful than no effort at all.

One crusty elder in correctional management suggested that there has been a tendency for administrators in the field to move impulsively on the belief that *the guys with the white hats always win.* He spoke at some length about the disadvantages which correctional executives face in competing with a multitude of other more attractive programs for public funds. He argued for long-term planning and urged that administrators desiring to develop and change their programs should be objective in calculating the chances of success before taking overt action.

In our incidents, successful use of the strategy of delay seemed to depend more than anything else on a shrewd ability to appraise the movement of forces which might be mobilized for or against a given project and on a fine sense of timing in moving from preparation into action. It appeared that the skillful use of delay in the interest of change objectives was closely related to the strategy of compromise employed for the same purpose. Trygve Lie is reported to have observed that "you have to make compromises that in the long run will serve the principles for which you stand." Change-minded administrators seemed to be stoic about delay on the same premise. We will close this section with an episode of administrative behavior which illustrates this point.

An administrator who had responsibility for both institutional and community-based correctional programs was visited one day by a prominent businessman who said that he "wanted to do something serious about getting offenders back on the right track." He explained that he had read publicity released by the President's Crime Commission concerning the woeful condition of the nation's institutions and the lack of personnel for effective rehabilitative work in the community. Explaining his concern for human predicaments by saying that he was an alcoholic who had *learned to handle the problem,* he indicated that he would like to organize a select committee of business leaders who would work to open up job opportunities for ex-offenders and promote better understanding of their problems *in the respectable part of town.*

The administrator was delighted with this opportunity. The two men proceeded to lay out a plan of action which involved launching the new program at a press conference with the governor and a series of supportive news stories based on cases of men who had made a successful transition from the role of prison inmate to that of responsible citizen.

In moving to implement the plan in the following days, however, the administrator encountered two rather discouraging reactions. First, his enthusiastic explanation of the plan to the governor elicited only a lukewarm response. The governor made it clear that, while he himself was not campaigning for reelection, nevertheless he was involved with the campaigns of lesser officials within his party. He pointed out that the issue of law and order was *touchy,* with *a lot of real idiots* doing most of the talking about the need to get tough with criminals. He said to the administrator, "You know that I've always been on the right side of these questions, but just be sure you don't put me in a spot which will be embarrassing to my friends in the party."

The second negative reaction came from a reporter on the staff of the major newspaper in the area where the committee of businessmen was to be formed. He had always been more or less friendly to the administrator, and they had worked together effectively in the past. This time, however, he listened to the *pitch* of the administrator in a rather perfunctory manner and indicated that his paper already had plans for a major series about crime. Somewhat in the same vein as the governor's comments, he said that he would be glad to stop by and talk further if the administrator wished him to but added that "this may not be the best time to do what you want." Only two days later the first of the series to which the reporter had referred appeared in the press, and the administrator discovered to his discomfort that it was to consist of interviews with a number of prominent law enforcement officials who were highly critical of recent Supreme Court decisions concerning the investigation and adjudication of crimes, and generally were negative to correctional programs.

The administrator then asked the businessman who had suggested the new program to come in for further discussion. They quickly agreed that it would be a bad time to launch a major effort of the kind proposed and addressed themselves to the problem of laying a solid groundwork for later implementation of the plan. The businessman agreed to talk informally with a number of his friends and solicit their support. The administrator indicated that he would assign some staff members to work out more effective liaison with employment agencies and to identify a number of inmates who might be suited for the kind of help which later would be furnished.

At the time of the interview, the select committee had still to be appointed and the program was being held in abeyance. But the administrator already was *reading the signs up ahead* and had concluded that the time was nearing when the governor would see considerable payoff in identifying himself with an alliance of businessmen interested in helping ex-offenders. The administrator also had little doubt that the press would be willing to give good coverage to the new program. He roughly paraphrased the old adage by saying, "There are times when you have to back away in order to fight again another day."

The Change-Capable Administrator

The major purpose of this section is to summarize the attributes of administrators who appear capable of bringing about needed changes in corrections. Before doing so, however, we shall present information on attitudes of the administrators studied which are relevant to change capability.

Attitudes Affecting Change

To secure such information, we sought to ascertain what the administrators feel to be the goals toward which corrections should move and the degree to which they themselves are committed to change.

Goals for Corrections. As we have previously pointed out, the correctional field has been plagued by the contradictory pressures imposed by the goals of revenge, restraint and reform. More recently, the goal of reintegrating the offender into the community has emerged as a primary referent. This goal requires the correctional worker not only to attend to the offender but also to make the resources of community institutions, such as schools, recreation facilities, and employment services, more readily available to offenders and to those who are potential recruits to criminal careers.

It is within the vortex of these often conflicting goals that the administrator must carry on his work. Administrators, more than any other group, are involved in the setting of goals and the determination of the means by which the goals will be reached. The administrator works along the boundary lines which separate his organization from related services. He must serve as a mediator of the conflicting values which are constantly asserted through the process of policy formulation and implementation. These realities provided the context for our queries to the administrators concerning goals.

We asked the administrators to indicate the present goals of their organizations and to tell us which goals they thought should be given greater emphasis. They were asked to indicate the degree to which restraint, treatment, and integration are *now* emphasized and *should* be emphasized, and to rank them in order of present emphasis. Restraint was defined as the application of custodial control, containment, or surveillance over offenders. Treatment was defined as the effort to change offenders into law-abiding persons by correcting individual defects or supplying needed skills and personal resources. Integration was defined as the effort to influence the policies and practices of community institutions (e.g., employment, schools, recreation) to make their resources more available to offenders.

Some interesting differences among organizational settings and between top and second-level management appear in the rankings of the present emphasis attached to the three goals.

In general the administrators thought that restraint should be emphasized slightly less than it is, although the middle-level administrators in both juvenile institutions and headquarters thought that it should be emphasized slightly more than it is.

The majority of the administrators in both settings believed that treatment is now emphasized strongly. The second-level administrators believed that it is emphasized slightly less than did their superiors in all settings. Juvenile administrators emphasized treatment the most, adult institutions the next, headquarters still less, and probation and parole the least of all the settings.

Across the board the administrators would like to see treatment emphasized much more than it now is, with over 60 percent wanting it to be emphasized *very* strongly.

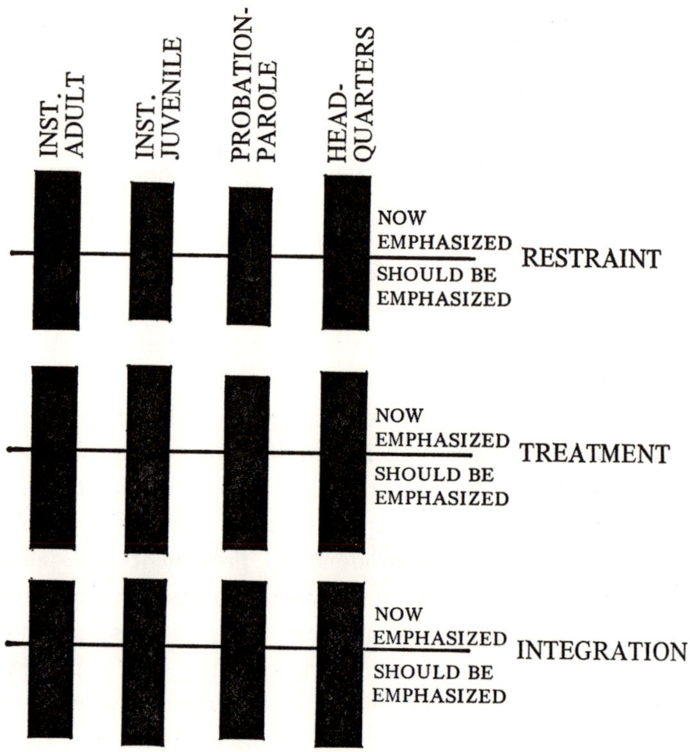

BASED ON TABLE 6.1

Figure 6-6 Goal Emphasis

There was more disparity in the degree to which integration is now emphasized and the degree to which it should be emphasized than on the same dimension with respect to either restraint or treatment.

A majority of the respondents in all the settings indicated that integration is at least fairly strongly emphasized now. The second-level administrators in all settings except probation and parole perceived integration as stressed less than did their superiors. Over 90 percent of the administrators in every setting believed that integration should be emphasized strongly or very strongly, and all indicated that it should be stressed much more than it is.

One of the interesting findings about goal emphasis is the small

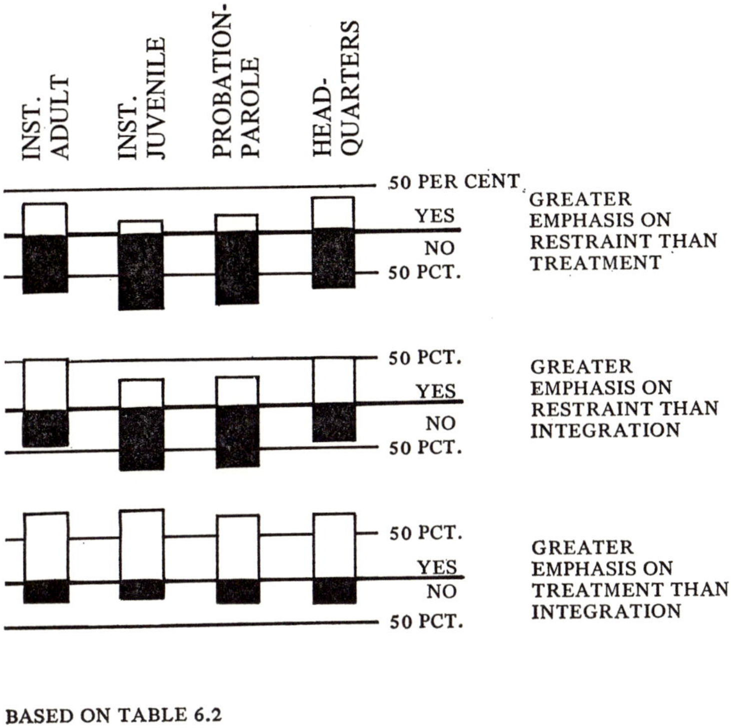

Figure 6-7 Goal emphasis

but significant difference between the perceptions of the second-level and the top administrators. The second-level managers appeared to feel slightly more strain between what exists and what should be, and they generally rated their organizations' orientation toward the goals of treatment and integration lower than did their superiors.

An additional way of estimating how much consensus or disagreement exists about goals is to obtain a measure of the amount of agreement among the administrators within a given setting. Cross-perception data were collected from forty-eight administrators in eight settings, a state headquarters unit, a large parole agency, a large probation department, a large juvenile male institution, a small juvenile male institution, a small juvenile female institution, a large adult male institution, and a large adult female institution. Each administrator was asked to rate each other administrator with whom he worked on the extent to which the goals of restraint, treatment, and integration appeared to be emphasized in their work. The scale used was: not at all, very little, moderately, strongly, or very strongly. The data were analyzed by a consensus method developed by Gross, Mason, and McEachern in their well-known study of school boards and school superintendents.[57] We were able to learn to what extent the top administrators differed in goal emphasis from the rest of the management team; the extent to which the management team members differed among themselves as to goals; and the goals around which the most consensus and disagreement exists.

In three of the eight settings the top administrators perceived the goal emphasis hierarchy slightly differently than did the management team as a whole. In the other five settings the top administrator and the rest of the team agreed on their rankings, all indicating that treatment received the most emphasis, integration the second most, and restraint the least. In all eight settings restraint was emphasized least by both top managers and the teams as a whole.

In the three settings in which top managers' evaluations disagreed with the rest of the management team, the disagreement was about whether treatment or integration was most emphasized. In two of the settings the leader believed that integration was emphasized more than did the rest of his administrative team. In one, the top man saw treatment given much more emphasis than was perceived by his associates.

Although restraint received the least emphasis in all settings, in only three was it stressed less than moderately. In the rest of the settings it was stressed at least moderately or strongly.

In most of the settings the top administrator saw the management team as having much greater goal agreement than the team members saw among themselves. In only three of the eight groups did the second level as a group see themselves as more in agreement about goals than did their leader. The most consensus existed around the goal of treatment and the least around the goal of integration. Obviously, some disagreement existed around all the goals in all of the settings studied.

In summary, the administrators at all levels seemed to recognize clearly that they must deal with multiple goals, somehow balancing out or neutralizing the contradictions which plural goals impose, rather than maximizing one goal over all of the others. They appeared to understand that the mandate to rehabilitate offenders cannot be retained and enlarged if the control function permanently loses credibility with the public, particularly with such critical power centers as the legislature and the press. Rather delicate problems present themselves in this respect, since many administrators see what the public does not know: that the really potent controls lie within the offenders themselves, individually and through well-elaborated social structures.

The ability to handle strains imposed by dissonant goals must be ranked very high in any hierarchy of skills posited for correctional administrators. Consequently it is a most important problem for those concerned with executive development. The interview data discussed in the previous chapter suggest that some administrators handle such strains purely on the basis of expediency, *cooling out* conflict situations and avoiding confrontations in which goal questions become sharply focused. The limitation of this approach is made clear by looking at the data on goals just reported. Most administrators are not content with the present *mix* and wish to move more strongly toward the goals of treatment and integration. This cannot be accomplished simply by keeping the force field in a state of equilibrium.

It was interesting to note that the administrators not only embraced and wished to accelerate movement toward the goal of integration but indicated that they were already significantly involved in addressing that goal. In emphasizing the importance of integration, they were in agreement with the reports of the President's Commission on Law Enforcement and the Administration of Justice. In believing that they are substantially seeking that goal today, however, they were in disagreement with the Commission reports.

Correctional administrators need to know more about the methods of mobilizing community resources, about how to increase their managerial effectiveness in the force field external to their own organizations. There is much to be learned, obviously, beyond the often prosaic courses in community organization offered as part of university curricula today. Perhaps corrections can take lessons from the experiences of antipoverty programs at the community level.

Perhaps it can make use of innovations in delivery of needed services to offenders which shortcut defeating bureaucratic process (e.g., a technique pioneered by the Vocational Rehabilitation Service in directly purchasing needed services from whatever source is available).

Changes in goals and functions will have far-reaching implications for the policies of correctional organizations and for the way in which administrators perceive their roles. New administrative problems will be generated as corrections moves into such new functions as serving as mediator between the offender and community resource systems, acting as the advocate of offender needs or even as a strong adversary to those who block entrance to legitimate assistance or impose negative labels and self-fulfilling prophecies of failure upon offenders. New skills are needed, and new ways of teaching and learning them must be found.

CONSERVATION VS. CHANGE. The general disparity between desired and actual goals as perceived by the administrators studied suggests that a majority have developed a strong commitment to change. Such indeed was the case according to our data.

In response to the question, "What degree of responsibility do you have for conserving the organization?", 30 percent of the administrators indicated at least a strong emphasis on conservation and another 30 percent a fairly strong emphasis, while the remaining 40 percent felt only a weak obligation to conserve the system. The second-level administrators indicated more emphasis on conservation functions than did top management.

Probation and parole administrators emphasized conservation slightly more than did those working in any other setting, this pattern appearing in the case of both top and second-level managers. The adult institution administrators placed the second heaviest emphasis on system maintenance, and headquarters managers by far the least.

To gauge the strength of emphasis on change, the related question was asked: "What degree of responsibility do you have for changing the organization into something new?" Nearly half of the administrators said that their commitment to change was strong or very strong. In all settings the second-level executives felt less responsibility for change then did those at the top level, with the most disparity occurring in the adult institutions. In comparing the different settings

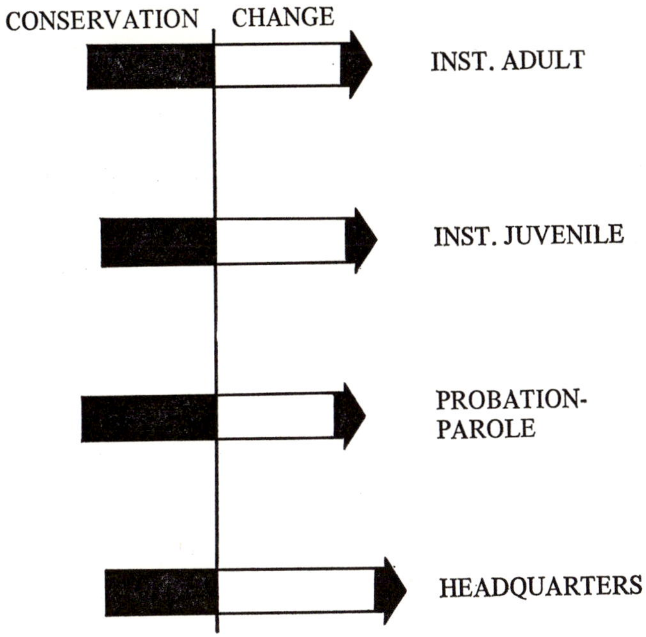

BASED ON TABLE 6.3

Figure 6-8 Change emphasis

we found that the headquarters group emphasized responsibility for change the most, with juvenile institutions next and the administrators of probation and parole and adult institutions slightly lower in their commitment to change.

The administrators were also asked to indicate on a forced-choice basis whether they placed greater emphasis on conservation or change at the present time. The results are depicted in Figure 6-9. Again, change was the favored response by an impressive margin. Nearly 70 percent of the respondents said they placed a greater emphasis on change than on conservation. Headquarters administrators stressed change the most and probation and parole administrators the least. Top administrators reported a change emphasis more often than did those working at the second level in all settings.

These data should be examined with considerable caution. Prob-

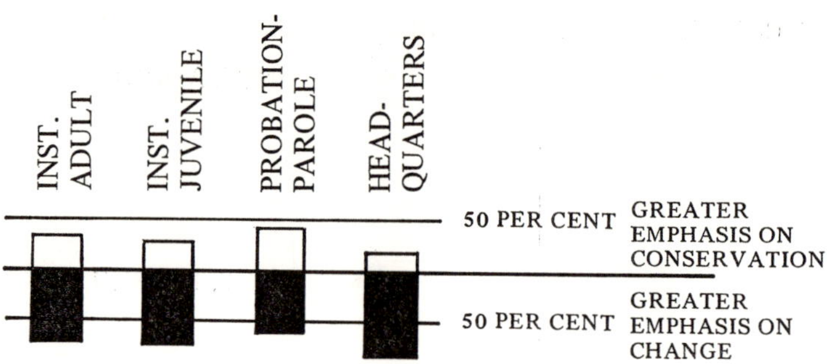

Figure 6-9

ably the idea of change wears a positive halo for most of the respondents (especially when they communicate with researchers who express an interest in change), while the conserving function may seem rather too stodgy to be identified with. From the depth interviewing, however, our impressions are that most of the administrators do have great concern for change and like to think of themselves as change agents. Probably there is a considerable gap between aspiration and accomplishment in this respect; we found evidence in the critical incidents of much frustration generated by a myriad of obstacles.

While the data indicate considerable attention to change, it is obvious that the administrators are far from unconcerned with the maintenance of their systems. In examining the appendix, it is important to note that a good deal of emphasis is placed on conservation by a sizable minority of the administrators. We noted earlier that the analysis of how the administrators used their time revealed that the bulk of it actually was allocated to sustaining and protecting their organizations.

Some interviewees wanted to avoid dichotomous thinking about conservation and change, feeling effective system maintenance lays the basis for needed changes, while in the long run change may be essential to organizational survival. This theme is developed more fully in the following section.

Profile Of The Change-Capable Administrator

The purpose of this section is to identify the attributes which characterize correctional administrators who are effective in bringing about changes within their organizations. These findings have been derived mainly from an analysis of the varied descriptive data on administrators who appear to be especially effective as agents of change. It must be admitted that the criteria of effectiveness which we employed are not only subjective but somewhat circular. Certain administrators were classified as change-capable when their administrative styles and protocols of strategic behavior reflected both concern for change and skill in bringing it about. To some extent, we also considered the reputation of some of these administrators within the correctional community for effectiveness in introducing needed change. Granting the limitations imposed by these criteria, we feel reasonably confident of our ability to offer a tentative prototype of the change-capable administrator. The profile presented below is divided into two major parts: (1) factors affecting the readiness of the administrator to bring about change; (2) factors associated with the implementation of change.

THE READINESS PROFILE. Careful scrutiny of the interview data made it clear that effectiveness in the induction of change consists of more than actionist skills. Equally critical are the orientation of the administrator toward events which open up possibilities for change and his characteristic way of working with the people and forces around him. The most important of these *readiness* variables are discussed below.

THE CONCEPTUALIZING MIND. An important but somewhat hazy attribute of the change-capable administrator seemed to lie in his having a durable conception of his organization, its mission, and its long-range goals. This attribute appeared in the data as a kind of intellectual frame of reference which enabled the administrator to look at what was going on in the force field around him, to *make sense* of it, and thus to formulate premises for action in meeting particular problems. Such an administrator might say to himself, for example, "Morale is getting bad in the juvenile hall because . . ." The *because,* in such a case would have to do with a well-established and consistently applied set of beliefs about human behavior and the forces which affect it, about the *mission* of a juvenile hall, and about the function of leadership.

This capacity to understand, to integrate disparate pieces of information, and to envision the consequences of projected courses of action may be the most fundamental of all cognitive prerequisites to change capability. The administrators in our sample who lacked at least a modicum of this capacity appeared in numerous critical incidents to be at the mercy of events which they seemed incapable of interpreting, much less influencing.

THE POWER OF KNOWLEDGE. The previous paragraphs stressed the importance of the administrator's having an intellectual frame of reference within which to process information and form judgment about cause-and-effect relationships. The interview data also documented another cognitive attribute—that of being thoroughly informed about and up to date on the myriad activities which join together to make up the dynamic life of the organization. It would appear that a commitment to desirable goals may accomplish little unless the administrator also has the facts not only about current operations but about trends which help to forecast the future.

Again and again in the interview incidents, advantage seemed to go to the administrator who did his homework consistently and conscientiously. It was not so much that he needed to be better informed than all others in the situation (for this, of course, is impossible) but that he needed to be able to probe, test, and validate the positions taken by others on the basis of his own reach and grasp of the situation. Obviously a sizable amount of interest and curiosity was required to keep the administrators informed about their operations and about the environmental events which helped to determine opportunities for and constraints on change. Relevant were such diverse kinds of information as crime rates, governmental budgets, population movements, political campaigns, research on correctional innovations, and union negotiations with public organizations. It was our impression that many administrators who might otherwise have been effective changers became impotent in that role because they had insufficient knowledge to deal competently with the problems confronting them.

SCANNING ALTERNATIVES AND DEVELOPING PLANS. Many of the descriptions of problem-solving activity which we collected associated the successful accomplishment of change with the timely development of workable plans. The change-capable administrator characteristically would report that "I could not have taken advantage of that opportunity if I had not already developed a plan of action and a set of justifications." The picture that emerged was one in which such administrators constantly scanned the needs of their organizations for change and developed plans for meeting needs which were well buttressed by relevant supporting data. Typically, these plans were tentative and, more often than not, they were never formally proposed. Sometimes they served as trial balloons through which efforts to secure essential support were given a rigorous provisional testing before any public commitment to the program was made.

MAINTAINING CREDIBILITY AND GOOD WILL. An important aspect of readiness to induce change for the correctional administrator seemed to be his ability to develop and sustain personal credibility throughout the force field around him. The incidents and case studies collected in our interviewing indicated that this capacity had a number of dimensions.

First, it seemed that the credibility of the administrator depended partly upon his reputation for openness. The converse of this was the apparent proclivity of many administrators to be secretive, *hiding* their operations from view as evidenced by reluctance to share information with such outsiders as members of the press, interested legislators, and special interest groups from the community.

Some change-capable administrators, on the other hand, almost made a fetish out of communicating the idea that *we have nothing to hide*. Typically this approach took the form of saying that the administrator's organization was afflicted with numerous problems and limitations. This, then, became a basis for arguing that something needed to be done in order to remedy these difficulties. which might include additional staff, a new facility, or whatever might be on his agenda.

A second and quite different dimension of credibility might be described as *protecting the flanks* of the organization while awaiting opportunities to move toward change goals. In part, this function was served simply by good housekeeping. It was important to keep the process of financial administration in good order, to observe accepted norms in recruiting and selecting personnel, and generally to keep open the channels of communication with service and control agencies. In a different and more strategic sense, the function of protecting flanks also involved not being outmaneuvered in establishing and maintaining good relationships with those who influence decisions vital to the survival of the organization. Particularly in the competition for operating budgets, it seemed imperative for the administrators to be aware of the actions of potentially competitive agencies, to stay in touch with the political echelon and the key legislators involved, and to keep the needs of their organization before the public intermittently through favorable stories in the press.

A final aspect of credibility which appeared frequently in the interview data had to do with the personal image of the administrator. This variable is difficult to define because it took many forms. To some extent, it seemed to be the quality of charisma, but it also included more mundane elements such as the ability to project a reputation for not letting things get out of hand and for not *going overboard on far-fetched ideas.* Later, in the implementation of change, the ability to make otherwise *far-fetched ideas* palatable as respectable innovations seemed equally important. Charisma seemed especially important for the maintenance of the administrator's credibility in the eyes of his staff. Their sense of hope and their belief that change was possible appeared to turn significantly upon whether they perceived the administrator as able to accomplish notable gains in the face of difficult odds. In this respect the stance of *happy warrior* sometimes seemed more important than a record of pragmatic achievement in winning battles.

THE DEVELOPMENTAL APPROACH. Still another attribute of administrators associated with the capacity to bring about change was concern for the growth and development of organization members. This was much in contrast to non-change-oriented administrators, who seemed preoccupied with their own status and power. The developmental approach manifested itself in involving subordinates in a variety of tasks which allowed them to try their wings, to play unfamiliar roles, and to make unorthodox contributions to the solution of problems. A tolerance for human error often appeared to underlie this ability.

Behind this approach to subordinate staff (and sometimes offenders as well) seemed to be a flexible view of the things people might do to advance the common cause. The business manager was not assumed to have insights and capabilities which those near the top of the ladder did not have. And some administrators clearly wished to make offenders participants in the people-changing work of the organization rather than mere recipients of staff effort directed toward that goal.

We could not help but feel, as the interview data related to this point were reviewed, that this characteristic was greatly determined by the personality of the administrator. Those who were genuinely warm in their relationships with other people, and consequently interested in their development, gravitated naturally toward this approach. The administrators who were relatively isolated and self-centered in their interactions with others did not make much headway along this line despite giving lip service to the idea. In any event, when opportunities for change presented themselves, a clear advantage seemed to go to the administrator who was able quickly to mobilize human energy toward implementation of the new idea. And this could not be done unless a groundwork for it had been laid. There were numerous incidents in which administrators who apparently had not been developmental or participative in their approach to staff and offenders inaugurated an innovation, only to have it falter and eventually disappear. Change of the kind defined as significant in this study, it would seem, cannot be preemptorily *ordered in.*

THE QUALITY OF IMPATIENCE. A final characteristic associated with readiness for the induction of change, as reflected in the study findings, was a persistently nagging dissatisfaction with the status quo and a corresponding impatience to find a better way. It is difficult, perhaps impossible, to determine the extent to which impatience is a constitutional or an acquired trait. That it is central to the induction of change, however, seemed little in doubt. The descriptions of problems, the portrayal of strategies, the remembrance of incidents which seemed critical to given administrators—almost inevitably seemed to lead to such a dichotomy. Many of the administrators interviewed were essentially content with the system as it was. Their efforts were bent mainly toward protection and conservation. The others, those who were *impatient,* seemed chronically discontent. In this, they demonstrated a prime qualification to act as the leaders of change. Nevertheless, it was the combination of impatience with at least a minimal supply of the skills associated with conservation of the organization which seemed to create optimal qualifications to serve as leaders of change.

THE IMPLEMENTATION PROFILE. The line between qualities associated with readiness to bring about change and those required for the actual implementation of change cannot be sharply drawn. Typically, the readiness factors continued to stand the change-capable administrator in good stead during the frequently more stressful events leading to change. Nevertheless, certain variables seemed much more closely associated with action than preparedness.

CAPITALIZING ON OPPORTUNITY. A common characteristic of the change-capable administrator seemed to be their capacity to take advantage of opportunities for innovation created by forces within the organization or in its environment. Frequently this was the mechanism through which the scanning process described in the previous section was translated into action. Administrators who were less oriented to change tended to make adjustments aimed as maintaining equilibrium. The change-capable administrators, by contrast, more often acted decisively to turn temporary disequilibrium into action of a kind previously identified as desirable.

For example, the retirement of a long-entrenched institution superintendent was seen by one departmental director as an opportunity to *make changes from top to bottom in that program.* As had been anticipated in interviewing concerning the dilemma management strategy, the change-capable administrators frequently turned adversity to advantage. Mutinous behavior among prison inmates was used to persuade the legislature that additional funds for staff were required. An attack on the organization from unfriendly sources was used to command space in the mass media for affirmative declarations of program goals. It is not suggested that change was never self-initiated by the administrators. But even when it was, the change-capable group seemed much more concerned with timing and assessment of potential support and resistance than were the less change-oriented administrators.

Risk-Taking. A related characteristic was the tendency for the change-capable administrators to take risks and, in a real sense, to gamble in order to bring about change. It must be added that some of the incidents collected in the research described risk-taking which ended in disastrous losses. The most successful form of risk-taking, by contrast, seemed to be one in which there was a calculation of danger and an effort to protect against the most unacceptable consequences. Such calculations also seemed to attach considerable importance to the amount of payoff perceived by the administrator. Risks were ventured in high-gain situations which would have been considered unacceptable under low—or zero-gain circumstances.

Even in the light of such qualifications, however, the change-capable administrators as a group clearly seemed willing to take chances which their less change-oriented counterparts were not prepared to take. This appeared in many ways: the appointment of an inexperienced but gifted subordinate to a key post; the reduction of severe custodial restraints in the face of predictions of calamity from old-line staff; the frank communication to the public of problems and failures; a candid and assertive confrontation with an unfriendly legislator in a public hearing; the placement in community treatment of youngsters previously defined as *too dangerous to be released*. All of these are examples of risk-taking which appeared in the critical incidents.

Catalyzing. The change-capable group of administrators seemed often to act as catalysts once the process of change was under way. Frequently different parts of the organization, or forces in its environment, were opposed or indifferent to the proposed change. This problem was dealt with much of the time by getting people together to talk it out, identifying payoff for those who previously had seen no reason to participate in the change effort, or making clear that the administrator himself was thoroughly and authentically committed to change.

Somewhat different catalytic skills seemed to be required when the administrator sought to co-opt those outside his own organization. In dealing with the press, the legislature, and special interest groups within the community, where administrators had few sanctions to employ, persuasion was much more used. And knowledge of the force field and credibility with those in key power positions were extremely important. Several administrators spoke of arranging to be introduced by some mutual friend to someone whose help was required in the solution of a problem. Others called attention to the importance of *knowing where the bodies are buried* in different power systems. It was clear that influence was exerted in a variety of ways by the more ingenious of the interviewees. One head of a large correctional organization, for example, kept careful records of the familial and friendship connections of all of his staff members with legislators and others who were influential in state government, and he put this information to good use in myriad legislative encounters.

BUFFERING. The process of change seemed to be accompanied by tension and anxiety on the part of those who were entangled in it. The upsetting of familiar ways of doing things, the dislocation of organization members from their accustomed roles, the general fear of unknown consequences—these factors created considerable human travail when the process of change was inexorably under way.

While the change-capable administrators seemed to believe that innovation could not be achieved without a certain amount of tension, they often took action to keep it within bounds. They were aware that fear can become endemic in an organization and that it can reach levels at which those affected become either destructive or immobilized in their dealings with each other.

Buffering often was achieved by approaching the change goal in an incremental fashion and making clear to those involved that their personal problems would be worked out as events moved along. At times, buffering consisted of the administrator himself absorbing the pressures of unknown consequences while maintaining an optimistic front with his staff. At other times, buffering took the form of systematically provided opportunities for ventilation of the tensions generated by change. Some administrators described their behavior during stressful episodes in a way which made them appear clinical and therapeutic in their relationships with the others involved. It seemed equally clear that these same administrators could have benefited from opportunities to express their own concerns, and that the loneliness of their roles often constituted a heavy burden for them.

INTEGRATING. Several of the most impressive incidents of change involved a high level of integrative ability on the part of the administrator. The ability to satisfy contradictory needs through some previously unseen solution was an important element of successful change, albeit not a common one in our data.

Of course all administrators face the problem of facilitating disparate needs and strivings within the force field which they occupy. The management grid which was given to the administrators in our sample tapped the contradictory pulls of concern for people and concern for production. In addition to this generic conflict, however, correctional administrators seemed to be faced with a much larger than ordinary number of dilemmas and contradictions of purpose. This, no doubt, is part and parcel of the problem of multiple goals toward which the field is oriented. The effort to reconcile punishment with treatment of offenders appeared in numerous incidents. The difficulty of blending control with treatment was a related problem. To some extent, dilemmas of this kind were more a problem of satisfying highly differing expectations from the force field than of actually devising appropriate programs of intervention.

The majority of solutions to the conflicts which appeared in the interviews were characterized more by compromise than integration. Faced with pressures to both help and punish inmates, institutional staff typically tried to provide a little of each. But many incidents did portray an administrator struggling seriously with the task of integration, of finding optimal solutions to all legitimate needs without diminishing any of them.

One attribute of the administrator who worked toward integration seemed to be flexibility. Such administrators were not locked into programmed solutions to all problems. They looked about them, seeking stimulation and guidance from a variety of sources, and sometimes produced quite unconventional answers to long-standing problems. This quality of open-mindedness and of desire to find creative solutions may also be near the apex of administrative talents related to change-capability. We did note that administrators who felt a desire to seek integrative solutions worked very hard and were deeply concerned at all times about outcomes. In the total universe of activity samples, it seemed much easier for the administrator to compromise than to integrate.

INSTITUTIONALIZING. The implementation profile of the change-capable administrator may be completed, so far as our findings are concerned, by noting capactiy for bringing the innovation into the main stream of organizational activity, a function which we have described as *institutionalizing*. Many of the interviewees spoke with an air of frustration about the fact that encouraging changes sometimes were brought about, only to disappear within a relatively short time. An examination of their interview responses tended to reveal that little had been done to diffuse the new approach throughout the organization or to provide the manpower, funding, and management attention required to make sure that it remained ongoing after the aura of newness had evaporated.

A variety of institutionalizing devices appeared in the data. Some administrators inaugurated training programs to bring a new program or technique to the attention of staff members who had not been involved in initial experimentation with it, and to work through the problems encountered in adapting it to the requirements of different situations. Some administrators pointed out the importance of bringing those concerned with budgeting for future operations into the discussion of program innovations *early in the game*. Thus, questions of forward financing on a larger scale were addressed well ahead of the presentation of a new program to the legislature, and the staff (both within and outside the organization) who had responsibility for review of budgets were allowed to participate in the excitement of starting a new program. Perhaps most fundamental of all, so far as the institutionalization of innovations was concerned, was the tendency of change-capable administrators themselves to *carry the word* about new ideas throughout the organization and into its environment. The personal support and enthusiasm of the administrator for the innovation seemed to be a highly significant factor in eliciting the support of others who previously had been content to remain uncommitted spectators.

Achieving Change Capability

The research on which this report is based has been aimed at clarifying the role which the correctional administrator plays and understanding more fully the environment in which he works. During the study we looked closely at a group of top administrators and their associates working in adult and juvenile institutions, probation and parole programs, and headquarters units in various parts of the United States. We attempted to set forth for the reader a portrait of correctional administrators in the United States—their educational backgrounds, professional careers, reading and joining habits, how they think about their jobs, the problems they face, how they spend their time, what styles of leadership they use, and the kinds of strategic behavior in which they engage as they seek to solve day-to-day problems in their organizations. We have also presented the attitudes of the administrators toward the need for change and their beliefs about the goals toward which change efforts should be directed. Finally we have attempted to appraise the capacity of the administrators to serve as leaders of change and to identify the special capabilities they will require to perform this vital leadership function as the corrections field seeks to meet the burgeoning demands of our complex society.

The present chapter, after briefly reviewing the generic functions which administrators must perform, suggest some steps which seem indicated if correctional administrators are to muster a greater capability for achieving organizational change. The suggestions are directed both to the development of correctional managers and to the modification of the organizational environments in which they work. These prescriptions regarding the locus of responsibility for change provide a basis for some of the specific recommendations contained in the major report of the Joint Commission on Correctional Manpower and Training, entitled *A Time to Act.*

The Role of the Administrator

The basic conceptualization underlying this research viewed the administrator as the occupant of a focal role within a complex field of forces. Efforts to understand the functions any administrator performs, the problems he encounters, and his needs for education and development must include an analysis of the forces around him and the dynamics of his interaction with them.

The organization in which the correctional administrator works is an increasingly open system, a structure of roles, resources, and technology in constant interaction with its environment. The goals of the organization are developed and changed as a part of this dynamic process.

Every organization has multiple functions: carrying on the work, insuring maintenance of the structure, obtaining environmental support, adapting to environmental change, and coordinating and controlling the activities of its members.[58] Each of these functions tends to become differentiated into appropriate organizational subsystems. The major type of work that gets done by the organization develops as a productive subsystem. The activities which insure the survival of the organization—e.g., the recruitment and socialization of new members—become a maintenance subsystem. The monitoring of changing forces which may and should affect the organization is performed by an adaptive subsystem through research and planning activities. Cutting across all of the subsystems is the managerial process which coordinates all of their activities, both in relation to one another and to the external world.

We have suggested throughout this report that individual administrators in similar authority positions differ in the amount and kind of influence which they are able to exert and in their readiness and capability to serve as innovators. In considering how a greater capacity for leadership might be developed, however, it seems helpful to distinguish between two types of managerial roles.

Pfiffner and Presthus have suggested that the distinction which is found in business between "corporate-level" and "operating-level" management functions might well be embraced in the administration of public organizations.[59] They describe the corporate-level functions as planning, policy formulation, conduct of public relations, securing an adequate and continuing supply of resources, and evaluating operations in relation to present and changing goals—in essence, the externally faced activities. Operating-level functions include the supervision of day-to-day activities, the implementation of the overall goals and the goals of the various subsystems—in essence, the internally faced activities.

Katz and Kahn also make a similar distinction between "policy-making" and "routine" administration.[60] Policy-making is the formulation of substantive goals and objectives and the development of procedures and devices for achieving goals and evaluating performance. Routine administration is the application of existing policies to ongoing operations and the making of residual ad hoc decisions.

Obviously many administrators perform both policy-making and operating administrative functions. The exact position in the organizational hierarchy does not necessarily determine the specific way in which the role is performed. The personality of the individual administrator combines with the situational context to create actual role performance.

The change-readiness and change-implementation profiles postulated in the previous chapter, which form a highly tentative prototype of the change-capable administrator, seem to us to describe attributes particularly applicable to the policy-making administrator. But it is through the interaction and cooperation of the two levels, through the mesh of their quite distinctive functions, that the mission of the organization is determined and carried out. Before suggesting ways of developing dynamism for needed change in correctional organizations and managers, it may be helpful to review the functions which management must perform. Specifically, top and second-level administrators have a joint responsibility to:

1. Establish and maintain organization structure;
2. Make some of the broader and more important decisions regarding the content of the organization's work;
3. Formulate organizational objectives and values which guide decisions at lower levels in the organization;
4. Coordinate functions of members of the organization so that the products of specialized roles will coalesce and contribute to the accomplishment of the overall organizational purposes;
5. Negotiate with outside agencies to insure an adequate supply of resources;
6. Monitor and adapt to changes in the environment which require a modification of methods or goals;
7. Influence the outside environment so as to help it become more amenable to the organization's goals and methods.

These generic administrative functions can be understood fully only when viewed in relation to the characteristics of particular organizations and the forces in their environments which influence and constrain them. Correctional organizations differ from setting to setting, but in their efforts to develop and change they face certain common and stubborn problems.

The correctional organization is an integral part of the criminal justice system and is therefore subject to the diverse goals and activities of that larger system. Additionally, correctional agencies are (or profess to be) people-changing entities and suffer problems peculiar to all organizations with this purpose, particularly the problems of operationalizing goals and measuring effectiveness. Correctional goals tend to be both contradictory and intangible and therefore difficult to translate into programs and methods which structure day-to-day work. New goals constantly are being added and old ones modified or relinquished. Valid and reliable techniques for measuring effectiveness are difficult to devise and often must be conducted in environments which are unfriendly to research and evaluation.

With these ideas in mind concerning the functions which all managers are required to perform, together with the special problems faced by correctional administrators, we will turn to a consideration of ways of upgrading correctional management and strengthening its capacity to bring about needed changes in the handling of offenders.

This final section of the report identifies some of the actions which might be taken to move from the status quo in corrections into an era in which both correctional systems and the administrators who manage them will have a greater capability for bringing about the changes required to implement the reintegration model described previously. It is obvious that major changes indeed will be required if such a movement is to take place, changes not only in the structure and function of correctional agencies but in the way in which their needs are serviced by universities, personnel officials, and others concerned with manpower development. We shall discuss proposals for action at two levels: first, the development of individual administrators; second, the introduction of essential changes in the institutional arrangements for carrying on correctional programs. We conceive of the administrators as both the instigator and the target of such changes. While at least potentially a key figure in launching and guiding change, it is equally true that his capacity to perform such functions depends upon varied kinds of organizational *backup* and facilitation.

Executive Development

A review of the literature on executive development and an evaluation of existing concepts and techniques in this area suggest that certain approaches to the education and upgrading of administrators are especially relevant to the development of the attributes specified in the profile of the change-capable administrator set forth in Chapter 6. These approaches are given special emphasis in the discussion which follows.

Attempts to develop executive abilities must be based upon sound conceptions of how people learn and develop. Learning seeks a relatively permanent change in behavior that occurs as a result of practice or experiences.[81] Learning and training may be conceptualized in terms of system methodology,[62] revolving around the establishment of goals for and by the learner, with feedback utilized so that the learner and instructor may adjust the learning process to ensure that the goals are being met. Although goals may be established externally, the learner must share the goals if effective learning is to take place. Lippitt and This have compiled a list of generally accepted conditions for learning, which includes the following, among others:

> The individual must be motivated to learn.
> Learning is an active process, not passive.
> Normally the learner must have guidance (feedback).
> Time must be provided to practice learning.
> The learner must secure satisfaction from the learning.
> The learner must get reinforcement of the correct behavior.
> Standards of performance should be set for the learner.
> There are different levels of learning, and these take different times and methods.[63]

Learning and attitude change are major paths toward behavior change; learning without attitude change does not result in managerial improvement.[64] Learning is best translated into action when the learner has the opportunity to practice what he has learned or the opportunity to use the skills, theories, concepts, and ideas he has developed in training sessions.[65] Thus, management development should attempt to change the individual's knowledge, attitudes, ability and job performance to meet selected goals.[66] Strong support from top management is essential in order to provide the kind of environment required for the conduct of executive development programs and the utilization of developed skills. Resistance to management development activities is commonly recognized, and numerous comments volunteered by our interviewers made it clear that correctional administrators have not always had positive experiences in the limited contacts they have had with such programs. The lack of development programs in corrections today is often attributable to previous negative experiences of staff, inability to translate knowledge into action, or a feeling of futility generated by the lack of upward mobility in the organization.[67] This constraint is certainly apparent in corrections. As previously made clear, the findings in this study show that correctional executives see lack of opportunity for career advancement as one of their most severe personnel problems. Blake and Mouton, who have a long and successful history as executive trainers, add further empirical evidence indicating that.

> Those who appear to want development the least seem to need it the most. Darwin's survival of the fittest theory is constant with these results. Organizations and individuals alike might well review their attitudes toward development in light of the Darwinian thought.[68]

A second essential requirement is the proper selection of participants for development programs. Accepting only those who volunteer is one means, although it must be noted that those who do not volunteer are self-selected out for reasons which necessarily remain obscure. Certain predictive factors have been identified which can help select those individuals who are most likely to benefit.[69] Unless personnel mobility patterns change in corrections so that lateral entry is much more fully utilized, recruiting for executive development programs should be directed toward a variety of organization members including those who have not yet indicated a desire for managerial responsibility.

Motivation to be selected and to perform well in development programs no doubt has a number of bases. There is evidence that people in training tend to perform more effectively in programs when "performance is believed to be a means to the attainment of some externally mediated reward such as higher pay, promotion, or approval by their associates than when it is believed to be unrelated to these rewards."[70] The link between training and rewards which are meaningful to those participating must be made clear. The success of leadership training depends upon the degree to which the trainee perceives tangible personal, social, or economic payoff, and the degree to which such payoff actually occurs to reinforce the learned behavior during and after training.[71] When the environment does not support the newly learned behavior, evidence indicates that there may be decreased job performance and increased stress between the returned trainee and the members of his organization with whom he must interact.[72]

Lundberg has developed a matrix of executive skills which includes nine areas for management development attention.[73] Our own profile of the change-capable administrator leads us to modify the Lundberg dimensions somewhat, while staying within his basic framework of technological, human relations, and conceptual attributes, as indicated in the listing below.

Dimensions of Administrative Capability

Technological	*Human Relations*	*Conceptual*
1. Facilitative skills	1. Leadership style	1. "Explanation and theory"
2. Correctional program knowledge	2. Interpersonal skills	2. Mixed scanning
3. Management process knowledge	3. Group process skills	3. Strategic *know-how*

The implications of our data with regard to executive development needs along the nine dimensions listed above emerge fairly clearly later in the chapter. Some additional comments are offered below to concretize prescriptions needed for action.

Technological Capability

Correctional executives must recognize that they are indeed the managers of extremely complex organizational activities. Additional study in social work, education, criminology, or other specialized fields may not be the most effective way to develop their skills as managers. In a survey conducted by Louis Harris and Associates for the Joint Commission on Correctional Manpower and Training, top and middle managers placed management-supervisory techniques and the dynamics of human behavior at the top of their list of subjects needed for in-service training programs, and public administration first on the list of needed categories of formal education.[74] Obviously course work in these areas in nearly all universities is to be encouraged as one of the basic methods of continuing development.

O'Leary, in a discussion of training of parole officers, noted one technique for development of managerial competence:

> Participants work extensively in various small group combinations on practical parole problems. The focus is on principles rather than "how to" answers, thus enabling participants to generate broad concepts which can be applied to the unique situations each confronts in his own jurisdiction. A combination of relevant content and the laboratory method of examining group decision-making has been enthusiastically received by participants. Further, formal evaluations conducted at the end . . . indicate progress in meeting the defined goals of the program. . . .
>
> The methods employed in this training effort seem to indicate considerable promise in effecting substantial simulation toward critical analysis of existing programs and for promoting a willingness to experiment in the adaptation of new concepts. Of particular importance has been the unfolding of realistic methods of encouraging a dialogue between the world of research and theory and that of practice.[75]

These types of training sessions can be sponsored at a relatively low cost to the local jurisdiction. Accommodations and facilities can be obtained, usually, for the total cost of per diem, leaving payments to trainers as the only additional cost.

Another technique which has been useful is the seminar in which individual administrators present their own programmatic and administrative ideas, discuss them, and get feedback from the group.[76]

Although the use of regular work hours gives training the high status it merits, the use of a lunch or evening meeting, perhaps half on the organization's time and half on the individual's time, may be feasible alternative. Countless variations on such arrangements can be devised if sufficient priority is given to training activities.

In short, all possible techniques must be employed to help the executives to open themselves to educational opportunities in both program and management fields. Recent college graduates in the system may be asked to present papers on specific issues, both to inform older staff of new trends and to provide developmental experiences for those who perform the teaching role. When a training need is clearly recognized, appropriate methods of meeting it can be discovered.

Human Relations Capability

Understanding and skill in human relations is pivotal for the good executive. Cleary suggests that:

> . . . emphasis should be on the understanding of motivations. The individual who understands his own motivations and increasingly tries to assess the drives, physical forces, and values that motivate others, possesses a skill for examining human behavior, his own and that exhibited by others. Thus, he is aided in selecting appropriate behavior for himself and anticipating its effects upon others.[77]

Two generic techniques (and innumerable variations of them) are increasingly being used to upgrade managerial effectiveness in dealing with vital human resources: role-playing and sensitivity training. Mounting evidence indicates that changes do occur in the behavior of participants in sensitivity training groups and that such changes can be transferred (although often with great difficulty) into work situations.[78] Frequently there is resistence to participation in sensitivity training sessions. Such reluctance may be found among those who have little or distorted knowledge about the processes involved, but in any case selective use of the technique seems indicated at the present time.

Sensitivity training has at least three basic goals: (1) to develop greater and more accurate knowledge of one's self: (2) to understand one's self in relation to others and others in relation to self: and (3) to gain more knowledge of groups and group processes. Argyris sees the major objective of sensitivity training as the development of effective, reality-centered leaders.[79] Studies provide a variety of data indicating that changes as a result of sensitivity training may include the following: increased sensitivity to others; more democratic attitudes; improved skills in communication and leadership methods, group maintenance and task direction skills; increased openness: receptivity to and tolerance of individual differences: interpersonal relations skills; improved understanding and awareness of interactive processes in groups; increased awareness of one's own impact on others: listening tolerance and flexibility; and better understanding of one's own values and the values of others.[80] Much more research is needed to validate these trends.

It is often suggested that the learning from sensitivity group sessions can be better transferred to work sessions if those who work together are trained together.[81] Intensive sessions might be scheduled on weekends to make this possible. Members of the external correctional force field might be included; for example, legislators, judges, parole board members, and community leaders. The inclusion of offenders in such groups might add greatly to their power to influence attitudes and behavior.

Many innovations have been introduced in sensitivity group techniques in recent years. One such innovation is video-taping of administrators at work, with later replay and group discussion. An example of the application of such a technique in management is the experience at TRW Corporation in California where staff behavioral scientists attend certain problem-solving work sessions, with full opportunity to intervene and raise the human relations issues which occur in the course of group discussion.

Role-playing is being used increasingly to develop greater interpersonal skills among managers. It can be used for several purposes, including teaching specific skills, such as interviewing and negotiation or as a tool for human relations instruction. The playing of a role before others helps develop self-reliance as well as the insight provided by constructive feedback.[82] A related technique, spontaneous role-playing, in which there is confrontation with unexpected problems and challenges, coupled with opportunities for critique and review, seems particularly helpful to managers at senior levels.[83]

Role-playing can be utilized at relatively little cost to the organization. Short role-play situations can be presented at any time of the day—even during lunch. For example, *dry runs* for legislative hearings in which correctional staff play all of the key roles (i.e., advocate, opponent, decider) could help not only to sharpen strategic skills but also to sensitize participants to the imperatives felt by others in a position to influence the final outcome.

It may be of special value to executives to play the unfamiliar roles of prisoners, parolees, community resource leaders, or budget officers, to enable them to gain empathy for those in their immediate force field. Cleary considers this technique the most powerful developmental tool for improved human relations skills.[84]

An additional aspect of human relations skill is the ability to generate truly reciprocal communication and the development of multi-channel communication networks. The technique discussed above is helpful in developing communication skills, but there is an additional need to provide continual feedback and evaluation concerning the fidelity of both written and verbal communications. A recent survey of top business executives found that they saw no aspect of managerial performance more important to effectiveness and ultimate success than skill in communications.[85]

The quality of empathy is at the heart of human relations. It is an important attribute in all management activities, but especially so in the field of corrections because of the vast diversities in cultural background and life style which tend to differentiate the offenders from the staff of corrections organizations. Empathetic administrators are able to put themselves in the position of others, to perceive their needs, and to understand the social system in which they live. The empathetic administrator is able to recognize the critical importance of meaningful participation in the system by those who are hierarchically subordinated, especially offenders.

The racial problems which have erupted in American society[86] are reinforced, indeed often multiplied, in corections because of the high proportion of minority group persons in the offender population. Open disscussions of ethnic relations should be a common occurrence in corrections. Not only must executives be helped to examine their own attitudes and behavior, but they must be made more aware of institutional discrimination and the techniques necessary to change prejudicial attitudes of workers in daily contact with offenders. Many of the human relations techniques discussed above can help change prejudiced attitudes. For example, one study of sensitivity training demonstrated a significant increase in positive attitudes on the part of white management toward Negroes and toward the problem of segregation.[87]

Training to develop empathy requires imagination and the use of innovative techniques. In addition to the suggestions above, the ideas of the Peace Corps in creating transcultural learning environments[88] may suggest some new approaches to corrections. Why not, for example, train prison executives in the prisoner's home environment, in ghettos, or in juvenile detention homes? Why not arrange for correctional administrators (and perhaps legislators, judges, law enforcement officers, and community leaders as well) to play the role of offender for a few days, unknown to the criminal justice officials who deal with them? Such techniques might well be painful and unpleasant for the participants, but the limited experimentation which has taken place along these lines indicates that dramatic gains can be made in sensitivity to the position of alientated persons.

One of the underlying assumptions of this research has been that much of the time of the administrator is spent in the role of a problem-solver. The successful administrator must have the capacity to recognize problems, and, as often as possible, to anticipate them. No problem has a perfect solution. Each *solution* only sets up a temporary equilibrium from which new problems emerge. Every act, including problem solution, must be expected to generate unsought consequences that may give either satisfaction or dissatisfaction.[89]

Effective problem-solving brings into play all the skills discussed thus far. Pfiffner has characterized this function of the administrator as requiring three qualities: the search for truth, the study and understanding of values; and a grasp of the political process.[90]

Some techniques are particularly helpful for training problem-solvers. The case study and incident methods, for example, may be used to study real situations in correctional organizations. Few materials of this kind have been developed for use in corrections, but it should not be difficult to do so. Some of the incidents from the present research might be adapted as a start in that direction.

Simulation games that use computers for analysis and feedback have proven to be useful devices in business training, but only recently have public management games begun to be developed. These games provide useful training in problem-solving as well as in organizational planning. They train the players for high-speed thinking and decision-making, teach them to recognize and understand cause-and-effect relationships, encourage executive teamwork, and permit analysis of the behavior of others.[91] Correctional systems might consider the development and use of management games and the adaptation of some general management games to correctional problems.

The *syndicate system* is a device which has a larger value than in problem-solving development alone. In this technique groups of executives research, analyze, and discuss problems of significance in their jobs. The groups are usually divided into interdisciplinary committees to address specific tasks. After completing its work, each committee reports to the general committee and attempts to integrate its report with that of the other syndicate groups.

The advantages of this technique seem to include broadening of knowledge and experience, development of understanding between those from various disciplines, refinement of the team approach to management, and practice in the assimilation of ideas and their presentation in concise form at a target date.[92] The technique seems appropriate for corrections in that it thrives on participation by representatives from different organizations within a system and encourages focus on critical intersystem issues. A team, for example, composed of officials from probation, parole, prisons, professional societies, the university, the legislature, and perhaps the office of the governor or budget analyst, faced with a challenge to develop *a solution to crime in the streets* within certain specific limitations (e.g., money, manpower, and time), should have a challenging and developmental experience.

Such a syndicate might prove to be far superior as a learning experience to the familiar conferences held to discuss *recent developments* or to hear conventional papers presented by outside *experts.* Syndicate sessions, running from one week to several months and utilizing library, academic, and specialist resources, might lead to some highly innovative solutions to longstanding problems.

Creativity is an especially prized managerial quality, although difficult to define and harder yet to bring about. Managers should not only develop their own creative abilities but also learn to foster an organizational climate which encourages creative thinking and problem-solving on the part of all involved.[93] Rigid bureaucratic systems and rules work against creativity and drive away those who need an open environment in order to make their best contribution to the organization.

One experimental technique, *synectics,* seeks the release of creative abilities both for developing ideas and solving problems. To date, it has been used chiefly in industrial and scientific situations, but its elements could be applied to public organizations. The synectics group is a task-oriented sensitivity group. The participants, however, are interested in the group process only a a means of encouraging creativity:

> They have a definite goal: the attainment and testing of creative breakthrough. The group's session is task oriented. . . . An objective is to create a successful group that can function independently over a period of time and produce useful concepts and models that serve the ends of the sponsoring organization.[94]

Several devices are employed in the synectics group e.g., role-playing, brainstorming, problem-focusing, and the use of moot proceedings—but the key ingredient to creativity is an organizational atmosphere in which original contributions are both encouraged and rewarded.

Conceptual Capability

To conceptualize is to step back, to think about the stream of organizational events and problems, and to place them (however tenatively) in an explanatory framework of theory and ideology. Top managers, especially, must have conceptual ability. They must be able periodically to rise above habit and dogma. Ward and Honey suggest that, in education for conceptual skills,

> The objective . . . is that of making the executive into a man of broader perspectives with a greater capacity to see the issues he must deal with in an enlightened, multi-dimensional manner.
> There is a widespread assumption that exposing the executive to the literature and ideas associated with liberal education and perhaps to an additional especially designed course or seminar will accomplish this goal. The executive thus "liberalized" will be able to play a leadership role in the public service in a far more effective way than he would otherwise. . . . The evidence . . . seems to support this thesis.[95]

The development of conceptual skills may come about in a variety of ways. It is most likely to occur in an atmosphere in which task performance is subordinated to thoughtful reflection upon the issues and choices which underlie decisions. The use of sabbatical leaves, for example, is one way in which the executive can confront new learning experiences and engage in personal reflection and expansion of his total self.

Chowdry points out that executives at critical stages of their career "feel the need of an intermediary period, a psycho-social moratorium through which they could deal with the stress, conflicts, and problems of identity."[96] Goldwin seconds this idea and suggests giving executives an opportunity to develop their ideas through reading and discussion with others and to study under a guided program carefully designed to meet needs—needs of which they may not even be aware.[97] Stair suggests that extended leave should be granted to some civil servants as a time of leisure for thinking and for reassessment of the self, before returning to new positions of greatly expanded responsibility.[98] Randall goes further to suggest time off for direction of civic campaigns, participation in community affairs, and the like.[99]

In summary, we have described some selected techniques of development directed toward the individual leader. This presentation is intended to be suggestive only. It rests on the assumption, however, that a great deal can in fact be done to upgrade correctional administrators and, further, that the administrators themselves can play a vital role in initiating, encouraging, and implementing the needed programs.

Changing the System

Research has shown that training effects fade and deteriorate if the results of the training are not compatible with the goals of the organization as a whole. Bennis points out that there is a tendency to diagnose problems as functions of faulty individuals rather than as symptoms of malfunctioning social systems.[100] It should be clear from reading the development proposals in the previous section that the possibility of carrying out many of them is dependent on changes within the correctional system and other systems in its environment. We need to remember that each administrator works within an organizational context which he has only limited ability to influence. The goals of his organization are set by a combination of public attitudes, history and traditions, laws, funding capabilities, geographical settings, personnel capacities, requirements of related organizations which deal with the same offenders, and so on. Many of the rules, regulations, and procedures which control a large part of the manager's everyday operational life have become habits in the organization. They have often been formulated by groups beyond the organization—by legislatures, other political bodies, civil service commissions, personnel boards, and budget and control agencies.

As this research has discovered, most correctional administrators reflect the bureaucratic orientation of their organization. Typically, they entered the correctional field in a lower level and progressed slowly up the hierarchical ladder. They are understandably responsive to the web of rules, regulations, and procedures which makes up a large part of organization life. Many patterns of administrative behavior are explainable less in terms of personality traits than of conditions in the social context in which they are embedded.

In most of the correctional settings the incentives for innovative, creative, highly energetic behavior appear to be minimal. Ways must be found to build such incentives into the system and to develop the kinds of standards and values that will support the change-capable administrator.

Personnel Administration

Changes in the personnel systems (civil service for the most part) are at the heart of many needed program changes. Those elements of personnel systems which limit effective executive development require fundamental change. Corson and Paul's suggestions for improvement of the federal service in general are transferable in large part to corrections.[101] Their suggestions would lead to: (1) aggressive recruitment, based on research and good manpower planning, together with the encouragement of lateral entry from the outside; (2) levels of compensation comparable to those in the private sector; (3) an emphasized policy of career-long development; (4) higher standards of promotion or continued service, including program competency, knowledge of the internal and external environment with which executives must cope, management process competency, and the ability to apply knowledge. They suggest procedures for selecting out through rigorous evaluation the 10 to 20 percent of top executives who are no longer developing, and placing them in positions suited to their level of competence.

Obviously, there will never be persons with potential for executive roles if recruitment is not actively pursued. We cited earlier the Harris study on the negative public view of corrections and the difficulties presented by these attitudes for recruiters. Those responsible for future manpower face difficult odds. Internal changes such as improved salaries, more rapid upward mobility, and certain intangibles such as an aura of experimentation, challenge, and progress, would help to attract potentially outstanding people. Many recruitment techniques proved successful by business firms, could be adapted, including energetic activity on college campuses with a special emphasis on seeking executive potential at the entry level.

Lateral entry, especially at upper levels, is the exception rather than the rule in corrections today. Our research found that the administrator sees lack of advancement opportunities as one of the key problems in his organization, yet the organizations fill top positions mostly from within. Lateral entry—which serves to bring in new blood, with new perspectives, different experience, and added skills—is generally considered one of the most beneficial personnel devices for upgrading the pool of executive talent. In corrections it appears that lateral entry should be combined with imaginative job-rotation programs. Even within the constraints of public organizations, innovative rotational programs can be established if appropriate effort is made. In corrections, job rotation might start among the various parts of the correctional system. The ultimate goal, however, should be to encourage and facilitate exchange among the administrative levels of police departments, welfare agencies, prisons, social work agencies, probation offices, and eventually all components of the corrections system and related fields. Rotational or exchange systems should be designed on a principle of reciprocity, so that those who participate can do so without losing status or economic benefits.

Data in this study have indicated that a critical problem in corrections is the narrow experience of most executives. Job rotation is one of the best ways to counteract this problem, since it broadens the knowledge of the individual and renews his interest and motivation. Some public organizations now depend on job rotation to protect their staff room stagnation. The military and the foreign service rotate their officers. The Peace Corps systematically moves its executives around and limits the tenure of any one of them to five years. The U.S. Information Agency encourages management interns to continue selective rotation as they advance up the career ladder.

A major qualification concerning the use of job rotation should be noted. As persons rotate through job assignments there are forces which work against the individual continuing in the rotation pattern. Good men are scarce and tend to be siphoned off to attractive jobs inside or outside the system, or held to a particularly interesting position. Therefore, the use of *planned experience* might be a preferred alternative to rotation at times. Here the individual tapped for executive development is given experiences in a number of positions as he works his way up the ladder.[102] This might include sitting on high-level committees, planning a major conference, acting in various positions while their incumbents are on vacation or while the job is temporarily vacant, or undertaking major assignments outside the organization, such as legislative liaison work.

A group of civil service systems related to correctional organizations at the city, county, state and federal levels might combine their resources to facilitate both rotation and planned experience. The Committee for Economic Development suggests personnel exchange between all levels of government.[103] A bill by Senator Edmund Muskie, that is now before Congress would encourage improvements in governmental personnel systems by providing financial and technical assistance for personnel systems with the stipulation that there be interchange between federal, state, and local governments. Corrections should ready itself to take advantage of this type of legislation.

Management intern programs are good devices to bring bright young persons into corrections. Extended programs should be developed to permit the young recruit to rotate through work assignments in a number of the offices of the agency and to get exposure to other organizations in the system, while perhaps at the same time doing assigned reading to develop knowledge in depth of the overall agency program. Corrections can also consider *farming out* developing personnel to outside organization.[104] Young executives can receive excellent experience by spending a year with a legislative committee, in university administration, or with a management consulting firm, although the previously mentioned risks should be noted.

For those executives who prefer to journey out on their own, correctional organizations should guarantee, as most civil service systems do, that seniority and other rights are maintained through leaves of absence. Not only the informal leave of absence but the *sabbatical leave* on full or part salary can be authorized. The individual on such a leave could pursue his academic interests, join VISTA, engage in an intensive group development experience, meditate, travel—in short, meet his needs for growth and renewal in a wide variety of ways. One year out of corrections on sabbatical leave might be worth many times the cost to the organization through increased productivity. The question might be asked whether twenty years in corrections is indeed twenty years of experience or is in fact four or five years of experience multiplied four or five times.

Civil service regulations should be modified where necessary to permit time off from work to attend classes and even to permit tuition reimbursement. Pay could be increased incrementally for completed university courses.

Finally, correctional personnel systems might consider working toward the establishment of a corrections Senior Civil Service, similar to California's career executive assignments, in which top career officials, who themselves carry rank and salary as individuals, perform those tasks throughout the system which require top managerial talent.[105] This approach might be implemented in a variety of ways.

The least difficult plan to install would cover just one jurisdiction, requiring modification of only one set of personnel procedures. However, the greater the transferability of executive staff between agencies and jurisdiction, the richer the opportunities for growth and development of administrators.

Financing Change

It is obvious that many of the reforms suggested would require additional funding. Increased appropriations must be sought and different ways of allocating present funds must be devised.

Salaries high enough to attract talented personnel from the entry level to top managerial positions are essential. Money must be found to support recruitment and developmental programs, in-service training, leaves of absence, paid time off for school, tuition reimbursements and academic scholarships. In some cases financial trade-offs can take place within existing budgets, for example, using for management development activities unexpended personnel funds which may accumulate due to job vacancies. In some cases, funds accumulated through unused per diem might be used to offset costs of staff training. Several jurisdictions might pool their resources to develop more effective programs. Combined programs, perhaps with some financing from community organizations or local business groups, could be used to subsidize small jurisdictions unable to support their own programs.

Fundamental to these proposals and to many other potential alternatives is the idea that budgeting requirements and organizational rules and regulations must be flexible enough to permit transfer of money among categories. Rules and regulations must be designed to encourage leaders in the organization to use available funds to increase the capabilities of personnel. Besides making the rules flexible enough to encourage rather than to prohibit experimentation, some positive forms of financial assistance can be devised. Matching funds, provided by state systems or outside organizations, to help finance developmental activities might be an effective form of assistance. Moreover, provision of sufficient money for evaluative research is essential not only to good management but to the development of good managers. Research forces people to think, to speculate about alternatives, to experiment with new ways of doing things.

Ways must be found to pay for the outside resources required for good training programs: qualified instructors, imaginative curriculum materials, special equipment (e.g., the videotape), and contacts with people and environments which bring a new and different perspective to bear upon old problems. Some programs, as has been pointed out, can be undertaken for little cost but they face the initial obstacle of inertia, the problem of making a beginning. Consultants need to be made available to correctional organizations to help them decide what they want to do and how to accomplish it. The Correctional Training Resource Center sponsored by the American Correctional Association, the National Council on Crime and Delinquency, the Federal Bureau of Prisons, and the Joint Commission on Correctional Manpower and Training constitute significant resources for such purposes, but the need remains great.

Allocation of money is a reliable indicator of the worth attached by policy-makers to a given activity. If management capability, and in particular change capability, is considered a crucial variable in the future of corrections, money will be allocated to do the things necessary to attract and develop qualified administrators. If little value is placed on this goal, or if it is not explicitly recognized as a goal, money will be allocated elsewhere—perhaps in building bigger and more secure prisons.

Coordination of Change

Much more cooperation must be developed within the presently fragmented correctional system and between it and organizations in the wider community. Many of the development activities suggested above could be undertaken jointly, thus making it possible for the executives to get acquainted with each other's ideas and experiences. The cooperation called for will not be easy to achieve. The thousands of political jurisdictions responsible for correctional services vary greatly both in quality of operations and capability of implementing change. There are many human and organizational barriers to co-operative endeavor.

A similar need exists for development of relationships with organizations outside of the core correctional system. Correction needs to import ideas from agencies with experience analogous to its own, and secure assistance of widely varied kinds throughout the force field explored in this research. In reintegrating the offender, corrections and the community must work together. A challenge for executive development is to provide an open system perspective to the correctional manager. As John Gardner has said, the upgrading of executive ability requires the individual to develop a dialogue with his environment.[106] One of the best ways to provide this enlarged outlook is to have people from community organizations participate with corrections in varied training, research, and program activities.

Conclusion

In this section we have suggested some of the ways to develop more change-capability in correctional administrators. We have suggested that many programs and activities can be directed to the individual administrator to enlarge his outlook and experience, to stretch his mind, and to supply or sharpen needed skills. We have also suggested that programs to change the individual administrator must be accompanied by organization changes in order to promote and sustain new kinds of managerial behavior.

Other documents published by the Joint Commission make recommendations concerning the locus of responsibility for bringing about change. In one sense, however, it is the individual manager himself who must recognize the essentiality of continuing development and of struggle against the specter of personal obsolescence. Ultimately the goal is to build a self-renewing corrections system in which positive and negative feedback continually adjusts the system's path, keeping it pointed toward existing goals and helping it to establish new ones. A self-renewing system will require self-renewing managers. This is the quality of change capability which we have sought to understand and describe in the research reported here.

FOOTNOTES

1Frederick W. Taylor, *The Principles of Scientific Management* (New York: Harper, 1911).

2L. H. Gulick and L. F. Urwick, *Papers in the Science of Administration* (New York: Institute of Public Administration, 1937).

[3]For a more recent series of papers illustrating and testifying to this point of view, see Robert Dubin, *Human Relations in Administration* (Englewood Cliffs, N.J.: Prentice-Hall, 1951).

[4]Fritz J. Roethliesberger and William J. Dickson, *Management and the Worker* (Cambridge University Press, 1939).

[5]Daniel Katz and Robert L. Kahn, *The Social Psychology of Organizations* (New York: Wiley, 1966).

[6]James G. March and Herbert A. Simon, *Organizations* (New York: Wiley, 1958).

[7]Douglas McGregor, *The Human Side of Enterprise* (New York: McGraw-Hill, 1960).

[8]Chris Argyris, *Integrating the Individual and the Organization* (New York: Wiley, 1964).

[9]Rensis Likert, *New Patterns of Management* (New York: McGraw-Hill, 1961).

[10]Edgar H. Schein, *Organizational Psychology* (Englewood Cliffs, N.J.: Prentice-Hall, 1965).

[11]Abraham H. Maslow, *Motivation and Personality* (New York: Harper and Row, 1954).

[12]Likert, *op cit.*, pp. 223-224.

[13]Lloyd W. McCorkle, Albert Elias, and F. Lovell Bixby, *The Highfields Story: An Experimental Treatment Project for Youthful Offenders* (New York: Holt, 1958).

[14]Empey, *op cit.*, pp. 37-40.

[15]The development of the Community Treatment Project is reported in a series of "Community Treatment Reports" issued by the Division of Research, California Youth Authority, Sacramento, California, 1962-1968.

[16]Amitai Etzioni, *A Comparative Analysis of Complex Organizations* (New York: Free Press, 1961), p. 12.

[17]It should be noted, however, that coercive power in the traditional prison in reality is shared by the staff with an elite of prisoners. See Sykes, *op. cit.*, chs. 3,4. For a useful analysis of the dynamic of power in a youth institution, see Allen F. Breed, "Inmate Subculture," *California Youth Authority Quarterly*, XVI, (1963), pp. 3-16.

[18]While the participative and *normative-moral* models of organization seem most desirable for future correctional organizations, knowledge remains too limited to permit hard, doctrinaire conclusions. For example, some impressive results are now appearing in correctional agencies which use behavior-modification techniques involving various sanctions to reward desired behavior and to penalize that defined as unacceptable. For a description of such a program at the National Training School for Boys in Washington, D.C., see *Task Force Report: Corrections*, p. 53.

[19]See Don M. Gottsfredson, *Current Information Bases for Evaluating Correctional Programs* in *Research in Correctional Rehabilitation* (Washington: Joint Commissions on Correctional Manpower and Training, 1967), pp. 28-33.

[20]President's Commission on Law Enforcement and Administration of Justice, *Task Force Report: Corrections* (Washington: U.S. Government Printing Office, 1967), pp. 6-16.

[21]Elliott Studt, Sheldon L. Messinger, and Thomas P. Wilson, *C-Unit: Search for Community in Prison* (New York: Russell Sage Foundation, 1968), p. 278.

[22]For a discussion of the dilemma posed by conflicting goals in prisons, see John Galtung, *The Social Functions of a Prison,* Social Problems, V (958), pp. 127-140.

[23]See *Inquiries Concerning Kinds of Treatment for Kinds of Offenders,* Monograph No. 2, Board of Corrections (Sacramento: California Department of Corrections, 1961). It should be noted that the Community Treatment Project referred to is predicated on a refined typology of offenders and intervention strategies. See also J. Douglas Grant and Marguerite O. Grant, *A Group Dynamics Approach to the Treatment of Nonconformists in the Navy, Annals of the American Academy of Political and Social Science,* CCCXXII (1959), pp. 126-135.

[24]Philip Selznick, In Studt, Messinger, and Wilson, *op. cit.,* foreword, p. viii.

[25]See LeMar T. Empey, *Alternatives to Incarceration,* Office of Juvenile Delinquency Studies in Delinquency (Washington: U.S. Government Printing Office, 1967), pp. 79-82.

[26]See Daniel Katz and Robert L. Kahn, *The Social Psychology of Organizations* (New York: Wiley, 1966), p. 13.

[27]Kurt Lewin, *Quasi-stationary Social Equilibrium and the Problem of Permanent Change* in *The Planning of Change,* Warren G. Bennis, Ed. (New York: Holt, Rinehart and Winston, 1964), p. 237.

[28]Mary Parker Follett, *Constructive Conflict* in *Dynamic Administration: The Collected Papers of Mary Parker Follett,* Henry C. Metcalf and L. Urwick, eds. (New York: Harper and Row, 1940), pp. 30-49.

[29]Chester I. Barnard, *The Functions of the Executive* (Cambridge: Harvard University Press, 1938).

[30]William G. Scott, *Organization Theory, A Behavioral Analysis for Management* (Homewood, Ill.: Richard D. Irwin, 1967), p. 235. See also Daniel Katz, *Approaches to Managing Conflict* in *Conflict Management in Organizations,* Elise Boulding, ed. (Ann Arbor, Mich.: Brown and Brumfield, 1961), p. 12.

[31]John M. Martin and Joseph P. Fitzpatrick, *Delinquent Behavior: A Redefinition of the Problem* (New York: Random House, 1965), pp. 183-186.

[32]For a definitive work in this area, see Neal Gross, Ward S. Mason, and Alexander W. McEachern, *Explorations in Role Analysis: Studies in the School Superintendency Role* (New York: Wiley, 1958).

[33]Katz and Kahn, *op. cit.,* p. 174.

[34]*Ibid.,* pp. 184.

[35]John P. Conrad, "Research and the Knowledge Base of Correction," *Crime and Delinquency,* XII (1967), 448. Figure reproduced by permission of the author and publisher.

[36]Joseph G. Phelan, "Problem-Solving: Management's Prime Responsibility," *Personnel Administration,* XXIX (1966), pp. 49-52.

[37]For an analysis of the difference between *programmed* and *non-programmed* decision-making techniques, see Herbert A. Simon, *The New Science of Management Decision* (New York: Harper, 1960), p. 8.

[38]For a discussion of Simon's principle of bounded rationality, see Donald W. Taylor, "Decision-Making and Problem-Solving," in *Handbook of Organizations,* James G. March, ed. (Chicago: Rand McNally, 1965), pp. 60-62 (cited hereafter by title).

[39]See Harold J. Leavitt, *Management Psychology* (Chicago: University of Chicago Press, 1967), p. 74. See also Charles L. Lindbloom, "The Science of Muddling Through," *Public Administration Review,* XIX, (1959), p. 79.

[40]In a research project funded by the National Institute of Mental Health and under the auspices of the Institute for the Study of Crime and Delinquency, Sacramento, California, Dr. Harland Hill currently is conducting an analysis of information needs and computer applications in the California state correctional services. For an imaginative application of computer technology to organizational problem-solving (called *Leviathan* by its originators), see Beatrice K. Rome and Sydney C. Rome, "Leviathan: An Experimental Study of Large Organizations with the Aid of Computers" in *Studies on Behavior in Organizations,* Raymond V. Bowers, ed. (Athens, Ga.: University of Georgia Press, 1966), p. 257.

[41]See "Studies in Interpersonal Bargaining," *Journal of Conflict Resolution,* VI (1962), 52-76. For an analysis of varying degrees of rationality in competitive problem-solving situations, see Anatol Rapoport, *Fights, Games and Debates* (Ann Arbor, Mich.: University of Michigan Press, 1961). For an elaboration of the argument that the administrator need not be *fettered* by the forces around him but has the option of viewing many of them as *variables over which he has some control,* see Robert Tannenbaum and Warren H. Smith, "How to Choose a Leadership Pattern," *Harvard Business Review,* XXXVI (1958), pp. 95-101.

[42]Leavitt, *op. cit.,* pp. 165-205.

[43]Edgar H. Schein, *Organizational Psychology* (Englewood Cliffs, N.J.: Prentice-Hall, 1965), p. 11. For a helpful analysis of the difference between *influence by persuasion* and *influence by ecological control* (both pertinent to the research reported here), see Dorwin Cartwright, "Influence, Leadership, Control" in *Handbook of Organizations,* pp. 18-20.

[44]Amitai Etzioni, "Mixed-Scanning: A 'Third' Approach to Decision-Making," *Public Administration Review,* XXVII (1967), 387. Quotations from Kenneth E. Boulding is from "A Strategy of Decision," *American Sociological Review,* XXIX (1964), 931. For a discussion of circularity and faddism in correctional program development, see E. K. Nelson, "Strategies for Action in Meeting Correctional Manpower and Program Needs," *Crime and Delinquency,* XII (1966), 224: "Current program offerings in the field of correction are pretty much of a smorgasbord of *good things* to help *bad people.* Implicit in these programs are highly general and frequently contradictory ideas about the problems which are the targets of change."

[45]Max Heirich, "The Use of Time in the Study of Change," American Sociological Review, XXIX (June, 1964), 386-397. (18) See Herbert Simon, *The New Science of Management Decision* (New York: Harper and Row, 1960).

[46]Frank P. Sherwood, "The Clock and the Specialized R and D Society" (Unpublished paper prepared for the University of Southern California, 1967).

[47]John G. Grinnell, "Time and the Concept of Development" (paper prepared for presentation to the Comparative Administrative Group of the American Society of Public Administrators, April 1966), pp. 1-66.

[48]Helen P. Gouldner, "Dimensions of Organizational Commitment," *Administrative Science Quarterly,* V (1960), pp. 467-490.

[49]Katz and Kahn, *op. cit.,* (Ch. 7, especially p. 192) discuss the top executive at the boundary position in the organization.

[50]Simon, *op. cit.,* pp. 5-6.

[51]J. G. March, "Business Decision-Making" in Harold J. Leavitt and Louis R. Pondy, eds., *Readings in Managerial Psychology* (Chicago: University of Chicago Press, 1964), pp. 447-456.

[52]See Sherwood, *op. cit.* We are indebted to Professor Sherwood for this paradigmatic method of summarizing the findings.

[53]Neal Gross, Ward S. Mason, Alexander W. McEachern, *Explorations in Role Analysis: Studies of the School Superintendency Role* (New York: Wiley, 1958), pp. 281-318.

[54]We are indebted to Richard A. McGee for the articulation of this idea and for numerous pointed examples of its application in various relationships and problem areas.

[55]See *Dynamic Administration: The Collected Papers of Mary Parker Follett,* Henry C. Metcalf and L. Urwick, eds. (New York: Harper, 1940), pp. 30-49.

[56]For a further discussion of this concept, see Peter M. Blau, "Social Exchange" (under "Interaction") in *International Encyclopedia of Social Sciences,* 1968, VII, 452-457; James A. Davis and Kenneth Boulding, "Two Critiques of Homans' Social Behavior: Its Elementary Forms," *American Journal of Sociology,* LXVII (1961), 454-461; Frank Sherwood, "'Social Exchange in the Institution-Building Process" (paper prepared for the Comparative Administration Group, American Society for Public Administration, June 1967).

[57]Neal Gross, Ward S. Mason, and Alexander W. McEachern, *Explorations in Role Analysis: Studies in the School Superintendency Role* (New York: Wiley, 1958), pp. 167-175.

[58]See Daniel Katz and Robert L. Kahn, *The Social Psychology of Organizations* (New York: Wiley, 1966); particularly ch. 4.

[59]John M. Pfiffner and Robert Presthus, *Public Administration,* 5th ed., (New York: Ronald Press, 1967), p. 191.

[60]Katz and Kahn, *op. cit.,* ch. 10.

[61]Bernard M. Bass and James A. Vaughn, *Training in Industry: The Management of Learning* (Belmont, Calif.: Wadsworth, 1966), p. 8.

[62]Gabriel O. Ofiesh, *Programmed Instruction, A Guide for Management* (New York: American Management Association, 1965).

[63]L. E. This and G. L. Lippitt, "Learning Theories and Training," *Training and Development Journal,* XX (1966), pp. 10-17.

[64]Robert J. House, "Management Development Is a Game," *Harvard Business Review,* XLI (1963), p. 139.

[65]British Institute of Management, *Management Training Techniques* (London: The Institute, 1962), p. 49 (cited subsequently by title).

[66]House, *op. cit.,* p. 139.

[67]W. F. Bennett, *Manager Selection, Education and Training* (New York: McGraw-Hill, 1959), p. 23.

[68]Robert Blake and Jane Mouton, "The Rich Grow Richer," *Training and Development Journal,* XX (1966), p. 2.

[69]John B. Miner, *Studies in Management Education* (New York: Springer, 1965), p. 189.

[70]V. H. Vroom, *Motivation in Management* (New York: American Foundation for Management Research, 1965), p. 47.

[71]Robert J. House, "Leadership Training: Some Dysfunctional Consequences," *Administrative Sciences Quarterly,* XII (1968), p. 571.

[72]*Ibid,* p. 567.

[73]C. C. Lundberg, "Management Development Refocussed," *Personnel Administration,* XXIX (1966), pp. 39-44.

[74]*Corrections 1968: A Climate for Change* (Washington: Joint Commission on Correctional Manpower and Training, 1968), pp. 29, 31.

[75]Vincent O'Leary, "A National Training Program for Parole Officials," *State Government,* XXVII (1964), pp. 116-117.

[76]R. E. Miles and L. W. Porter, "Leadership Training: Back to the Classroom?" *Personnel,* XLIII (1966), pp. 27-35.

[77]F. D. Cleary, *Blueprint for Better Learning* (Metuchen, N.J.: Scarecrow Press, 1968), p. 160.

[78]Peter B. Smith, "The Effects of T-Group Training" in Galvin Whitaker, ed., *T-Group Training: Group Dynamics in Management Education* (Oxford: Basil Blackwell, 1965).

[79]Chris Argyris, "T-Groups and Organizational Effectiveness," *Harvard Business Review,* XLII (1964), pp. 60-74.

[80]See, for example, Douglas Bunker, "Individual Applications of Laboratory Training," *Journal of Applied Behavioral Science,* I (1965), pp. 131-148; Edgar H. Schien and Warren Bennis, *Personal and Organizational Change through Group Methods* (New York: Wiley, 1965), pp. 17-19; and Peter B. Smith, *op. cit.*

[81]R. B. Morton, "Organizational Training Laboratory," *Advanced Management Journal,* XXX (1965), pp. 58-67.

[82]Joel Kibbee, *Management Games: A New Technique for Executive Development* (New York: Rheinhold, 1962), p. 40.

[83]*Management Training Techniques.*

[84]Cleary, *op. cit.,* p. 167.

[85]John Felden, "What Do You Mean, I Can't Write?" *Harvard Business Review* XLII (1964), pp. 144-156.

[86]See *Report of the National Advisory Commission on Civil Disorders* (New York: Bantam Books, 1968).

[87]C. M. Hampden-Turner, "An Existential Learning Theory and the Integration of T-Group Research," *Journal of the Applied Behavioral Sciences,* II (1966), p. 380.

[88]Donald R. Shea, "The Preparation of Peace Corps Volunteers for Overseas Service," *Annals of the American Society of Political & Social Science,* CCCLXV (1966).

[89]For further discussion of this concept, see Chester I. Barnard, *Functions of the Executive* (Cambridge: Harvard University Press, 1962), p. 20 and passim; and Robert Merton, *Social Theory and Social Structure* (Glencoe, Ill.: Free Press), pp. 19-83.

[90]John M. Pfiffner, *"The Role of the Administrative Generalist"* (unpublished paper, University of Southern California, 1967).

[91]Smode, Dunlap and Associates, '"Recent Developments in Training Problems and Training Methodology" in Robert Glaser, ed., *Training Research and Education* (Pittsburgh: University of Pittsburgh Press, 1962).

[92]P. A. Tobin, *The Syndicate System in Management Training* (Lahore: Pakistan Administrative Staff College, 1964), p. 58.

[93]David Mars, "Creativity, Leadership and City Managers," *Public Management,* XVII (1964), pp. 102-108.

[94]John Mann, *Changing Human Behavior* (New York: Scribner, 1965), p. 133.

[95]Stewart Ward and John C. Honey, *University Sponsored Executive* Development Programs (Washington: U. S. Office of Education, 1966), p. 21.

[96]K. Chowdry, "Management Development Programs: Moratorium for Executives," *Human Organization,* XXIII (1964), p. 254.

[97]Robert A. Goldwin, *Toward the Liberally Educated Executive* (New York: New American Library, 1960) quoting Wilfred D. Gillen.

[98]Joseph Stair, *Handbook of Training in the Public Service* (New York: United Nations, 1966), pp. 103-104.

[99]Clarence B. Randall, *The Executive in Transition* (New York: McGraw-Hill, 1967), p. 119.

[100]Warren G. Bennis and Philip E. Slater, *The Temporary Society* (New York: Harper and Row, 1968), p. 116.

[101]John J. Corson and Paul R. Shale, *Men Near the Top: Filling Key Posts in the Federal Service* (Baltimore: Johns Hopkins Press, 1966) pp. 158-159.

[102]Interview with Professor Neely Gardner, School of Public Administration, University of Southern California.

[103]Committee for Economic Development, *Better Management of the Public's Business* (New York: The Committee, 1964), p. 31.

[104]See Bennett, *op. cit.,* p. 100.

[105]Commission on Organization of the Executive Branch of the Government, *Personnel and Civil Service* (Washington: U.S. Government Printing Office, 1965).

[106]John Gardner, *Self Renewal* (New York: Harper & Row, 1964), p. 11.

CHAPTER 7

CREATIVITY AND THE MIDDLE MANAGER

DAVID MARS

THIS PAPER WILL MAKE the following points: (a) the need for creativity in modern society, (b) the need for creativity in modern organizations, (c) the responsibility for organizational leaders to take steps to provide an organizational climate conducive to creativity, and (d) the particular responsibility of middle managers to help in the maintenance of such a climate. The first three points will serve to introduce the last point, upon which particular stress will be placed. The first three points have generally been dealt with rather substantially in various writings, and need only be reviewed here; what the middle manager can do about creativity has not been dealt with in the literature, and will be the special focus of this paper.

Nothing will be said in particular about middle managers in the juvenile justice system, nor about organizations specifically within the juvenile justice system. We make an assumption that such organizations generally resemble other organizations in our society and that what may be said in favor of creativity within those other organizations applies equally forcefully to the juvenile justice organizations. Similarly, what is said in general about the role of middle managers in developing and maintaining creativity should be taken to apply with equal force and logic to juvenile justice middle managers. Indeed, one creativity test which the juvenile justice middle manager might well set for himself is the creative adaptation of some of the ideas in this paper to his own organization.

Need for Creative Society

Why be concerned about creativity in modern society? Basically, the need stems from the ever-increasing number and complexity of problems which have come to characterize modern life, and from the great increase in the rate of change.

Whence came these problems? A number of factors might be cited, among which might be included the following: growth in population and qualitative changes in the make-up of the population; great advances in technology, particularly in the fields of automation, communication, transportation, and public health (these advances have all been positive goods, but have also brought hazardous, and potentially destructive, side effects); increased mobility of the population; changes in morality and value systems held by large segments of the population; increased pressures and demands from hitherto-neglected groups and segments of society; increased numbers of governmental entities involved in public programs. The list is by no means exhaustive; probably each reader could add to this list at length, from his own personal experience. (Another possible creativity test!)

When change is rapid and problems abundant, society must be creatively adaptive, or fall further and further behind.

Almost two decades ago, Carl Rogers, founder of an important modern school of psychotherapy, called attention to the necessity for creativity in modern society. He approached the problem by stressing the dangers of conformity, for which he saw much evidence in the United States. In words which seem as relevant today as when they were written, Rogers poses a *so what* question about conformity and then answers the question himself very cogently:

> Why be concerned over this? If, as a people, we enjoy conformity rather than creativity, shall we not be permitted this chohice? In my estimation such a choice would be entirely reasonable were it not for one great shadow which hangs over all of us. In a time when knowledge, constructive and destructive, is advancing by the most incredible leaps and bounds into a fantastic atomic age, genuinely creative adaptation seems to represent the only possibility that man can keep abreast of the kaleidoscopic changes in his world. With scientific discovery and invention proceeding, we are told, at the rate of geometric progression, a generally passive and

> culture-bound people cannot cope with the multiplying issues and problems. Unless individuals, groups, and nations can imagine, construct, and creatively revise new ways of relating to these complex changes, the lights will go out. Unless man can make new and original adaptations to his environment as rapidly as his science can change the environment, our culture will perish. Not only individual maladjustment and group tensions, but international annihilation will be the price we pay for a lack of creativity.[1]

More terse, but no less salient, is the statement by the noted British scientist Fred Hoyle, "The nation that neglects creative thought today will assuredly have its nose ground into the dust of tomorrow."

Need for Creative Organizations

The United States has been referred to as an organizational society. Much of our national effort is expressed through organizations of all types and sizes. If there is a need for a society to be creative in modern times, there is equally clearly a need for its organization to be creative.

This is not to say that in our society individuals are not important nor that individual creativity should not be encouraged and rewarded. We know that many signficant innovations, social as well as technological, have come from individuals working alone.

What we intend to say is that since so much of modern society's work is carried forward through organizations, it behooves us all (but particularly our organizational leaders, as stressed below) to try to make these organizations as creative and adaptive as possible.

It is important to consider together creativity both in society and in organizations because in important ways they interact. Robert Presthus goes so far as to define organizations as "miniature societies in which the dominant values of society are inculcated and sought in a more structured, spatially restricted context" and as "miniature social systems that meet many of the most basic needs of their members and expect in return loyalty and conformity." Pointing to organizations as important reinforcers of the various pressures put upon individuals by their social structure, he states further: "Contemporary organizations have a pervasive influence upon individual and group behavior, expressed through a web of rewards, sanctions, and other inducements that range from patent coercion to the most subtle of group appeals to conformity."[2]

Another reason for considering the need for creativity in organizations as well as in society as a whole is because no organization, no matter how large, represents all of society. It represents only a small part, and is dependent on the larger society, including society's resources and markets, for its support. Hence, it must be effective both in sensing change in its social environment and in adapting to change. A non-creative organization is neither sensitive nor adaptive. And, if the signs are right that the future holds even more drastic change, then clearly we need to stress organizational creativity.

What about those signs? Almost every writer who gazes into the future sees it as being even more dynamic and changeful than the present and the immediate past. Warren Bennis, forecasting the next twenty-five to fifty years, envisages continuation of rapid technological change, with the environment characterized by interdependence and turbulence, more mobility, more other-directedness, more ambiguity and conflict over goals and effectiveness criteria, and major changes in organizational structures.[3]

So too Daniel Bell, Chairman of the Commission on the Year 2000 (American Academy of Arts and Sciences), concludes that society in the year 2000 will be "more fragile, more susceptible to hostilities and to polarization among many different lines." After looking at various predictions and extrapolations, Bell concludes, "The only prediction about the future that one can make with certainty is that public authorities will face more problems that they have at any previous time in history." But rather than despairing, Bell is hopeful that we will be able to deal with these problems, because the power to do so "is latent in the flexibility of the American political system, its adaptability to change, and its ability to create new social forms to meet the challenges. . . ."[4]

The implication is very clear: organizations which are creative and adaptive can view the future with the confidence that they will be able to cope with it; organizations which are not creative and adaptive will probably not see the changes coming in the first place, and when these changes arrive, will be overwhelmed by the stresses which they will create.

Responsibility of Organizational Leaders

Having established the need for creativity both at the societal and organizational level, we now deal with where to focus the responsibility for maintaining such creativity. We begin this section with a series of assumptions. Though labeled here as assumptions, they do have substantial support in the literature on psychology and organizational behavior. They are as follows:

(1) Creativity is spread unevenly throughout all human organizations; some persons are more creative than others; probably everyone has some attributes of creativity.

(2) Creativity can, to a certain extent, be isolated, identified, tested, and measured.

(3) Creativity can be increased in various ways, including specialized training and educational experiences.

(4) Creativity can, within certain limits, be encouraged or discouraged, rewarded or punished, turned on or turned off.

(5) Members of organizations in large measure take the cues for their behavior within the organization from its leader and administrators.

We stress the last two assumptions. Taken together with earlier statements in this paper on the need for creativity today, they make the case that *the modern leader or administrator is responsible for providing the kind of leadership and administration which will maximize the creative behavior of members of his organization.* This is a responsibility which cannot be delegated; no matter how supportive and encouraging an employee's peers may be, he must be convinced clearly that the leadership of his organization values creativity before he can be expected to behave creatively.

How can the modern organizational leader provide a climate within which creativity can flourish? Elsewhere I have written in detail on this point.[5] For our present purposes, that discussion can be summarized, as follows:

1. The administrator must try to improve his own creativity, through specialized readings in the field, practice exercises, seminars, and other kinds of training experiences.
2. The administrator needs to de-emphasize the bureaucratic orienta-

tion of his organization, because this stands in the way of innovation and creativity.

3. The administrator needs to attempt to restructure the reward system in his organization, for the typical rewards of status, power, and money encourage jockeying for position, pleasing of superiors, conformity, *not making waves,* precisely the types of activities which discourage innovativeness and creative behavior.

4. The administrator will to a much greater extent have to incorporate into his organization delegation and decentralization, not simply of tasks, but rather of influence and power.

5. The administrator, difficult though it might be, will have to take a long hard look at the departmental structure of his organization, and attempt to make it less rigid.

6. The administrator will have to think of some changes in the administrative practices of his organization, changes based in general on a lessening of control and the introduction of the four d's: democracy, delegation, decentralization, and dispersal.

In other words, both by word and by deed, the organizational leader must demonstrate to his entire organization (and to the world) that he encourages, supports, and rewards creative, innovative, and adaptive behavior.

Such a posture is not without risk. Generally, organizations and the individuals which constitute them tend to be characterized by inertia and by resistance to change. It is much easier to do nothing or to mobilize in favor of retention of the status quo than it is to create a climate for change. Thomas Jefferson recognized this in the Declaration of Independence, when he wrote "all experience hath shown, that mankind are more disposed to suffer, while evils are sufferable, than to right themselves by abolishing the forms to which they are accustomed."

But the risk must be taken. And it is the particular responsibility of organizations' leaders to light the way in this effort.

The Middle Manager and Creativity

This section will deal with two matters: the general and particular responsibility of the middle manager with respect to creativity, and some more practical suggestions on how to go about the accomplishment of a creative organizational climate.

The general matter is easily disposed. We simply assume here that the middle manager is a part of the structure of organizational leadership. Hence, everything said earlier about the responsibility for such leadership to take the steps required for the creation and maintenance of creativity within their organizations also applies to the middle manager.

The particular responsibility of the middle manager stems from his peculiar position within the organization: the traditional man in the middle. This position carries with it a triple responsibility, which appears in sharp outline when dealing with such a sensitive matter as creativity: toward his superiors, toward his fellow middle managers, and toward those members of the organization whom he supervises.

In the first place, the middle manager must believe in creativity with the same strength and intensity as his superiors (assuming that they do!) He must also act in a way which clearly demonstrates that belief. For example, in transmitting communications dealing with creativity, he must make it clear that he supports the spirit and the letter of these communications. He must be careful to avoid any statements or behavior which will be read by others as modifying the intent of these communications. As stated earlier, the top leadership of an organization has a non-delegable responsibility to maintain a creative climate. But an important ingredient in the maintenance of such a climate is the support given to it by the organization's middle managers. Even if they consciously support it, they can—if not careful—unwittingly behave in such a way that it is eroded.

With respect to his peers, the middle manager has two tasks: trying to persuade them to behave in the way just described for himself, and trying to generate creative ideas within the middle management group. A brief comment about each of these thoughts is in order here. First, lacking any organizational authority over his fellow managers, he must rely upon persuasion to win their support of creativity within the organization. In doing this, he will be able to give free rein to his own creativity. Given the general tendency in favor of the status quo, the middle manager will have to be creative in presenting his ideas on creativity within his particular organization, even in the context of top leaderships having taken a position in favor of creativity.

Second, consonant with the earlier statement about the distribuiton of creativity within human organizations, we cannot assume that organizations' top leadership have a monopoly on creativity. Creative ideas can be developed at all levels in the organization, including the middle management level. The creative middle manager not only produces creative ideas himself; he also helps his peers and colleagues produce such ideas. Some hints on how to help with such production are given below.

One caution must be introduced here. The middle manager must avoid a perception by his peers that in encouraging them to generate creative ideas he is trying to win particular recognition or reward for himself, or that he is somehow *superior* to them. In order to do this, he will have to develop his interpersonal skills, including such matters as the effective use of group sessions, meetings, and conferences.

With respect to the middle manager's responsibility vis-a-vis persons over whom he has supervisorial authority, again two points must be made: help in the generation of creative ideas, and open and sympathetic transmission of such ideas to top leadership. Once again, a brief comment is in order. First, the creative middle manager will assist subordinates in the production of creative ideas, much in the same way as he works with his own peers. The nature of the interaction will of course be different, since in meetings with subordinates, he will have to guard particularly against his superior organizational status getting in the way of the creative flow.

Second, once creative ideas are generated, whether by his own efforts, the efforts of a subordinate, or the result of subordinates' group interaction without his involvement, the middle manager must play an active and sympathetic role in seeing that the ideas are transmitted to top leadership. Simple transmission without his clearly stating his support might jeopardize a fair reading of the idea by top leadership and thereby reduce the chances of its adoption. Even more dangerous is the failure to transmit creative ideas at all or their transmission with so much negative comment that the ideas are doomel. Such behavior has a negative impact on the flow of creative ideas from the bottom up in an organization in two significant ways: the particular ideas involved are lost, and in addition—and much more important— the production of future ideas is severely inhibited, because the producers of the ideas will feel that their efforts are not appreciated or valued.

Finally, we consider some practical suggestions for the middle manager interested in increasing creativity in himself and in his organization. Some of these have already been summarized in the action "Responsibility of Organizational Leaders." They may be recapitulated here simply by saying that the middle manager who is interested in creativity can take a number of positive steps.

First, he should consult the burgeoning literature on creativity. There is now a journal specifically devoted to this subject. The quarterly, *The Journal of Creative Behavior,* is published by the Creative Education Foundation, State University College at Buffalo.[6] The Journal is an important reference, not only because of the articles, notes, and reviews which it publishes, but also because it in turn points the way to additional sources of help. For example, the Summer 1970 issue of the Journal (in an article entitled "Films on Creativity—Do they Exist?") includes an annotated list of ninety films on creativity, with the names and addresses of their producers.

The section "News and Notes" calls the reader's attention to happenings of note related to creativity, and the book review section deals with the latest research and literature in the field. In addition, the Journal has periodically published bibliographies on the subject of creativity.

The Creative Education Foundation is a rich source of material on creativity. In its own words, the Foundation "has served as the focal point for the dissemination of pertinent information in the field of creativity." The Foundation distributes many different types of material on request, and a letter of inquiry directed to it would bring a rich reward to the writer.

In addition to publishing *The Journal of Creative Behavior* and reproducing other interesting material in the field, the Creative Education Foundation operates an annual creative problem-solving institute. Now in its seventeenth year, the institute runs for a week in Buffalo. It offers a rich variety of experiences for those attending, but a great deal of the material generated is also available to a wider audience. Besides the annual institute, the Foundation also operates a number of workshops, seminars, and institutes throughout the year, all held at Buffalo.

In addition, the University of Utah has during the past fifteen years sponsored a series of conferences on creativity, and the papers presented at these conferences include much interesting and valuable material on the subject. Also important in the literature on creativity are the Studies of Creative Thinking sponsored by the University of Minnesota.

Articles and books on creativity are being produced in increasing quantities; the interested middle manager should familiarize himself with the standard books, authors, and periodical literature.[7]

Second, a growing number of courses in creativity and creative problem-solving is now available, both on a credit and non-credit basis, at colleges, universities, research organizations, and industrial organizations. Many of these courses offer very practical suggestions for the middle manager interested in improving his personal creativity and increasing the creativity in his organization. Information on these courses may be secured in a variety of ways.[8]

One interesting thing to be borne in mind in connection with these two suggestions is both their actual and symbolic value. The middle manager who works at the literature or takes courses in creativity heightens his personal creativity. But he also symbolically communicates to his organization (and to the world at large) the great value he places on creativity and his personal investment therein. Here as in many other areas of human endeavor, a person's behavior may speak even more loudly than his words.

Third, and last, the middle manager may find great profit in the technique known as *brainstorming*. Many persons have achieved great success in generating creative ideas within their organizations by the use of this technique. The middle manager interested in this approach to creativity should familiarize himself with *Applied Imagination,* written by Alex Osborn, noted writer on creativity and generally acknowledged as the father of brainstorming.[9]

To summarize: creativity is important to our society and in our organizations; organizational leaders have a responsibility to encourage and maintain creativity within their organizations; middle managers share in this responsibility; middle managers can take significant steps to help discharge this responsibility. Lest this sound too solemn, we close on the following note: delving into creativity and its applications in organizational settings can be personally rewarding, exciting, and fun.

FOOTNOTES

[1]Carl Rogers, "Toward a Theory of Creativity," *ETC: A Review of General Semantics,* Vol. XI, No. 4 (Summer 1954), p. 250.

[2]Robert V. Presthus, *The Organizational Society: An Analysis and a Theory,* (New York: Random House, 1965), pp. 7, 3, 95.

[3]Warren Bennis, "The Decline of Bureaucracy and Organizations of the Future," in *Changing Organizations: Essays on the Development and Evolution of Human Organization* (New York: McGraw-Hill, 1966), pp. 3-14. See also: Warren Bennis and Philip Slater, *The Temporary Society* (New York: Harper and Row, 1968); Alvin Toffler, *Future Shock* (New York: Random House, 1970).

[4]Daniel Bell, "The Year 2000: The Trajectory of an Idea," in Stephen Graubard, ed., *Toward the Year 2000: Work in Progress, Daedalus,* Summer 1967, pp. 645-646.

[5]David Mars, "Creativity and Administration," *Public Administration Review,* Volume XXVII, Number 3 (September 1967), pp. 252-256.

[6]Address: 1300 Elmwood Avenue, Buffalo, New York 14222.

[7]The reader interested in pursuing the subject of creativity in greater detail might well consult a comprehensive bibliography on the subject. The most comprehensive, listing 4,170 items, is Taher A. Razik, *A Bibliography of Creativity Studies and Related Areas* (Buffalo: State University of New York at Buffalo, 1965.)

Readers interested particularly in the question of how to maintain an organizational climate conducive to creativity might consult: David Mars, *Organizational Climate for Creativity,* Occasional Paper Number Four (Buffalo: The Creative Education Foundation, 1969). The paper lists 56 annotated sources dealing with the subject, and in an appendix lists 25 bibliographies on creativity, for those who want to pursue the subject further.

[8]One way is directly to contact colleges and universities in the area. Another is to direct an inquiry to the Creative Education Foundation. In addition, the Winter 1968 issue of *The Journal of Creative Behavior* included *a survey of problem-solving courses* (pp. 33-51). The report on which this article was based is available from SRI Publications, 333 Ravenswood Avenue, Menlo Park, California 94025.

[9]Alex F. Osborn, *Applied Imagination: Principles and Procedures of Creative Problem-Solving* (New York: Charles Scribner's Sons, 1953). This book has gone through a large number of revisions and reprintings. In 1959, Sidney J. Parnes published *Instructor's Manual for Semester Courses in Creative Problem-Solving,* designed to accompany *Applied Imagination.* This book has now been revised, expanded, and republished as *Creative Behavior Guidebook* (New York: Scribner's, 1967). In its expanded version, the guidebook is no longer merely an instructor's manual, but can be used as a self-teaching device.

CHAPTER 8

NORMATIVE POSSIBILITIES FOR TOMORROW'S PUBLIC ADMINISTRATION*

WILLIAM B. STORM

During the past few years a number of books have appeared which deal with today's youth and what is happening—or likely to happen—to them. Roszak's *Making of a Counterculture* and Reich's *Greening of America* are well-known examples of this literature. We are all aware that the youth of this period are manifesting in a broad range of ways a marked alienation from the main stream of contemporary American culture and these and other writers have supplied us a frame of reference for comprehending this phenomenon. Futurists vary in their interpretations of what is happening but few doubt that a distinct change in *values* is represented among the youth, while some cite a change in *consciousness* which they predict will have profound effects in the near future. Certainly Reich's Consciousness III represents such a change, as does Hampden-Turner's *Radical Man.*

In this paper I have a very specific purpose: to raise the possibility that these developments, already well under way, will result in a schism between government, as represented by public employment in this case, and the youth of this coming era, and to suggest possible ways of avoiding this catastrophe. This breach appears certain to

---

*Paper presented at the National Conference of The American Society for Public Administration, Denver, Colorado, April 18-21, 1971.

occur if the values and practices which attend our public programs are not substantially altered, and if current trends continue among our youth. Already we may fairly wonder whether there is a place in today's typical public agency for the Parenthetical Man (Guerreiro-Ramos), Consciousness III (Reich), Radical Man (Hampden-Turner), the Proactive Man (Bonner), or any of a number of other models of new men who may frequent our future. I believe this should be a matter of concern to students and practitioners in public administration.

While the counterculture contains a range of types and qualifications, we must acknowledge that these various authors are talking about a certain kind of man, part real and part possibility, who is developing throughout Western society, a man possessing qualities different from those typical of his predecessors. This man may yet be small in numbers but as a type he is very promising—and he is most common among members of the counterculture. This person seeks independence, the freedom to find himself, to be creative, to take risks, to experiment. He strives to find the existential meaning in his experiences; he is much concerned with those elemental societal values which deal with the self, with the individual's maximum growth and development. Perhaps as much as anything, he is concerned with authenticity, with putting proper labels on the phenomena around himself. He is inclined to reject much of what we call human experience. Thus employment in typical, structured, bureaucratic settings, where neither organizational purposes or processes appear socially significant, often proves anathema to him.

We are developing a situation in which employers are less willing to employ this new man—and in which he, in turn, is less willing to work. If this situation continues to develop we will rapidly reach a condition in which the members of the counterculture are almost completely excluded from the working world. This could be acceptable, perhaps, if the numbers involved were small and if there was real indication that this movement would simply go away; but such is not the case. Indeed, there is much evidence which suggests that these few are the forerunners of many, that before long the counterculture may represent our culture, at least in substantial portion. This has tended to be the history of Bohemian movements in the past; their deviant ways become increasingly the norm.

With attention both to the obvious qualities of present members of this movement and to the probability that their numbers will increase, I propose, in this paper, that the public service pay attention to what is happening in this situation and begin some adaptive adjustments which will make these persons more likely to seek participation in the public endeavors of their time. The very nature of many of our social problems and the responding public programs implies that these may be the very kind of persons most appropriate to staff the agencies! It seems inconceivable that we would allow our stereotypes and procedures to cause us to exclude them from participation.

In order to emphasize the notion of *possibility* in this situation, I propose to develop the arguments of one author who believes that we are moving swiftly along a route which will take us to a world largely populated by persons who are unwilling to work in the conventional sense of that term. My author is Gunther S. Stent, professor of genetics at Berkeley, whose book, *The Coming of the Golden Age: A View of the End of Progress* (New York, 1969), seems especially useful to my purpose here. I choose Stent's work rather than other excellent alternatives because he addresses matters related to what is happening to the younger generation but takes them up in a unique manner, one which stimulates the imagination and extends our awareness of possibilities. When considered as *possibility,* his work offers a useful take-off point for my normative notions about possibilities for public administration.

In brief, Stent argues that the achievement of a high level of affluence as well as almost unlimited technological capability is creating a condition which is antithetical to the will to power and economic security which has motivated Faustian man for the past two centuries. In effect, the extraordinary exertions of this man have created the conditions for his demise. The basic reasons appears to relate to freedom: man has achieved a fair degree of social and economic freedom with his technology, which has caused him to reject the Faustian stance.

Further, Stent establishes an effective case in support of his notion that scientific progress (in the sense of adding to the theory on which we base control of our physical world) is almost exhausted. Meanwhile, scientific and technological progress which has already been achieved has contributed immeasurably to man's freedom. Stent also looks hard at the world of art (painting, drama, poetry, literature, etc.) and demonstrates an evolutionary pattern which literally precludes additional important statements (artistic breakthroughs) in those fields. He argues that each of these areas has evolved through various stages of discipline to a condition of randomness where events become *happenings,* subject to the individual interpretations and meanings of observers. Here again the central variable is freedom; both artist and spectator manifest almost total freedom as they present and interpret their forms of artistic expression.

A further argument Stent offers relates to the acceleration of progress, measured in terms of energy use. He points out that our current rate of use is 100,000 times what it was in the year 1000 BC and one-thousand times what it was early in the eighteenth century—but we have only to project another ninety years to multiply our current use by one-thousand, while a projection of about two-hundred years multiplies our rate by at least one million times! This argument is intended to demonstrate two things: that the very kinetics of the acceleration of progress will tend to place a brake—and possibly a maximum—on this process; and the speed of accleration of progress has caused an increasing rate of alienation among persons unable to achieve sufficient spiritual and cultural assimilation to *keep up.*

As man makes progress, according to this argument, he achieves new levels of freedom, which, in turn, reduce his need and desire for more progress. This is manifested where technological achievement reduces the burden of the individual and his responsibility for performance of certain kinds of work, where sexual freedom removes restraint and frustration, where intellectual freedom relieves man of the disciplines which orthodoxy imposed upon his predecessors, and so on. In sum, a manifestation of Maslow's need hierarchy is involved here: as man achieves certain levels of freedom and capability, his commitment to certain kinds of activity diminishes.

Granting this, we still must recognize that there is a double edge to our argument here. While the high *level* of progress diminishes man's need for progress, the high *rate* of progress diminishes his ability to assimilate and participate. Stent argues that Bohemianism first manifested itself in the nineteenth century simply because it took that long for the rate of progress to reach a level where personal accommodation became difficult. As the rate accelerated, the proportion of disengaged persons has increased. The Beatniks and Hippies are subsequent manifestations of this phenomenon. When one looks at the acceleration-of-progress curve, one has to ask himself where on that curve most of the rest of us will disengage. In effect, this condition appears to imply that the rate of progress is limited by the alienation process, though probably a much higher proportion of the population will have to have *checked out* before the rate is diminished in a substantial way.

Our point here of course, is not to prove anything but only to raise a possibility. What Stent is arguing in overall summary is that these various processes—the apparent end of scientific and artistic breakthroughs, the kinetics of progress, the phenomenon of Bohemianism, the ending of the Faustian will to power, etc.—add up to the real possibility that we are confronting a time not far from now when a large portion of the population will simply disengage from work as we have known it. They simply won't be interested in it or will reject it because of what it is supposed to achieve. We appear to be confronting a true Age of Leisure, with all the possibilities such a condition implies.

This possibility is enhanced by the argument of Norman Brown* who suggests that the day of Apollonian man is about over and we should begin to replace him with Dionysion model. Somewhat overly simplified, Apollonian man is the man who negates his instincts, postpones his rewards and hews to rational civilized forms of life. His is a world of sublimation. The Dionysian man represents life *complete and immediate.* This man does not sublimate or negate; he affirms life and enjoys his rewards as they come. Indeed, he seeks them and relishes them. The Dionysian ego cannot be synthesized with the Apollonian; they are too different. We can manifest one but not both. Thus Brown's argument, seen inconjunction with Stent's and many others, again reinforces the notion that we may be on the brink of profound changes in the kind of person *available* for public

*Norman O. Brown, *Life Against Death; The Psychoanalytical Meaning of History* (New York, 1959).

emploment and their *willingness* to participate in our public endeavors.

C.E.M. Joad has written that "work is the only occupation yet invented which mankind has been able to endure in any but the smallest possible doses." The clear implication is that man will have difficulty with his newfound leisure. Certainly the nature of the leisure world these writers envisage is cause for sober reflection. We in public administration must, I believe, ask ourselves what this new phenomenon means for our own activities and for our public institutions. We have, after all, been aware of the probable shortening of the work week—and many people have considered the implications of increased leisure time in tomorrow's society. But here, in this argument, we are faced with a possibility which is very threatening to much of what we hold central to our scheme of things. Very few of us have really anticipated that this new leisure world might be made up of a few workers plus a lot of non-working drone-types who are living in apathetic indifference (or open hostility) to the existing system—or in a psychedelic netherland of drugs and other escapes. For Stent's world has a large category of persons who are simply consumers making either no contribution to progress or a very nominal one. His Golden Age is a sort of Polynesian paradise transferred to apartments supported by technology and the efforts of a few.

There is evidence which suggests that we are further along the *Road to Polynisia* than we think. Indeed, many would argue that much of the malaise of our time stems from our failure to recognize our real location on that road.

I do not wish, however, to convey the impression that I am predicting this Golden Age. I have reviewed it because it is a well-developed construct which suggests possibilities dramatically different from those we might readily expect and because there are signs that some of what is predicted is taking place. The argument is very suggestive of some possible developments in public administration which perhaps we should begin to think about.

By this I mean only that we who are concerned with our public affairs might benefit from beginning to consider things we might do which would help the public service (and through it the country at large) to accommodate *proactively* to the kinds of conditions which many writers are beginning to describe. This does not mean we have to throw in the towel and give up. On the contrary, I believe the implication is neither more nor less than that we must consider very carefully our premises and processes in the light of the possibility that we may have increasing difficulty recruiting the kind of commitment and qualification we need to continue to operate our public programs. I believe we are coming into a critical interface between our traditional ways of thinking and doing and a broad new set of possible ways which will be needed both to *induce participation* and *solve problems* tomorrow.

In the remarks which follow I will assume that I am talking about the possibility of developing and maintaining a positive public service in the face of the kinds of trends I have mentioned. At the same time, I cannot refrain from noting that I believe the alternatives I mention in this paper would be appropriate innovations in public administration in this country without regard to the specific trends I have described. It simply happens that I am inclined to be influenced by the prolifery of arguments like that of Stent, Reick and others. I am convinced that a polarity is developing among and within young people—whether to dedicate oneself to the job and to progress or to dedicate oneself to need-fulfilling behavior which appears possible only outside the system. I see this as an either/or thing for many of them, and I posit the notion that there is yet time to integrate and synthesize the goal of *both* rather than one *or* the other. In other words, rather than work *or* play or within the system *versus* outside the system, I suggest that current developments imply that we develop a self-directed work/play employment model which is *both* inside and outside the established organizational system in its operational sense. I suggest we consider how we may combine the self-directed worlds of work and leisure in order to avoid a catastrophic dichotomy. And I suggest the public service is the proper, even natural environment within which to experiment with this possibility. In the remainder of this paper, I will attempt to develop this and suggest some ways to bring it about.

To begin, we might pause a moment to note that the contemporary environment of much of public administration is *inert, dull, fatuous or torpid,* as Henry Kariel recently wrote of his field, political science.

Our field is ridden with bureaucratic process, political anachronisms, programs assiduously devoted to carrying out bad policies, people long since committed to cynicism or despair at the prospect of progress, people given to indifference, ignominious behavior, bitterness, hostility, carelessness, and so on. Certainly there are high points as well as low at every level of government, but too often good people and good programs get buried, politics overrules appropriate action, private interests obliterate new possibilities, and the processes of pluralism grind out inadequate, incremental adjustments which barely satisfice and rarely solve problems.

The point of this excursion is to emphasize that we may expect to have difficulty recruiting into this environment people representing the new consciousness, the proactive or self-actualizing posture, or the pleasure-seeking Polynesians, including the Beats and Hippies. As we address the question of what we might do, I think it will be useful for us to assume we have an important issue and that the range of possible cures must be almost unlimited. I believe, too, that we must assume that we should not give up but that we should proceed to develop some normative possibilities for increasing the employment appeal of public programs for the particular kind of man who may be both the most common type before long—and valuable in helping our programs.

To supply an illustration of the separation which appears to be taking place, I cite an associated press article which appeared in the *Los Angeles Times* a few days ago. The article was concerned with the kind of management trainee which General Motors Corporation looks for; it was entitled *Corporate Trainee: Simple Virtues First.* In the article, one Dennis Allen is described as typifying what this corporation is seeking for its new management cadre. Allen is a true-believer type. He was a C student in college, but he paid his own way through all four years. He is a dedicated, hardworking young man who relishes his job, arriving at 6:30 AM and leaving after five in the evening. Frequently he returns to work to complete tasks after supper. He is described as a *clean-cut conservative* in both dress and politics. Only one of his trainee group have smoked marijuana (he didn't like it); only one (a black) had ever participated in any college or other demonstration; literally all had voted republican (all generally agree with Spiro Agnew and the President). Most of the trainees support the Vietnam war. All (except one black) believe they have an excellent chance to become president of GM. None of the group feels any alarm over pollution, believing that private enterprise will solve such problems. The group is almost totally from small towns and the middle classes. They are the *good guy* type, drinking beer and following sports with their fellows. The placement officer from the corporation described young Allen as the perfect prototype for their management purposes.

Dennis Allen sounds like a decent, well-meaning fellow, certainly. The issue I am raising here is simply that already one giant corporation has cut one large and growing category of young persons out of its range of employable persons. It is not that the members of the counterculture would make great executives or that they are all bright, creative, self-actualizing people who should be encouraged. On the other hand, many would indeed make first-rate executive and many would make other kinds of contributions. I have mentioned that the same forces which are creating the counterculture are forming or contributing to many contemporary problems. The members of this group are logical participants in the battles we must fight. While the General Motors Corporation does not have to solve social problems and can afford the luxury of narrow choice, the public service does have to confront the problems of the day; it cannot afford such luxury.

The Question of Values and Premises

Perhaps I might best begin my normative possibilities with a consideration of a few alternative values or premises for our field. We cannot probe these in detail in this limited space, but we should look at some possible variations in our familiar themes. In the first place, many of our current values tend to deny the individual and emphasize the so-called *product* of our endeavors. They place a high value on work and the postponement of rewards. They subjugate man to system. In this sense, they reinforce the Faustian or Apollonian model of man. The typical values in our field simply do not address the whole individual. Were they to do so, taking into account individuals both inside and outside our public programs, we would need to fall back upon more fundamental considerations—those concerned specifically with the self. Thus such values as the development of self-awareness, empathy, personal congruence, responsibility, etc.—values purely associated with personal development—might be termed *meta-values,* which such traditional values as freedom, production, order, etc., while significant, might be seen to be of a different order of magnitude; they are not fundamentally related to individual growth but are a form of *social myth,* fabricated to meet other needs than the maximum development of the person. Some of them might, in fact, be antithetical to individual growth. It appears reasonable to consider whether we have not now progressed to the degree that we can move from emphasis on the more general societal values to more individually-oriented concerns. Were we to do so to the degree that meta-values of the sort mentioned above were indeed realized in our society, the kinds of remedial programs which are the focus of much of public administration would be less necessary. The very achievement of these fundamental human values would diminish the field. One might argue that normal program pursuit in any of our traditional line agencies would have this same kind of effect—but this has not been the case as a rule. Perhaps we might try this other way for a change, focusing more specifically on the development of the individual. We would have to experiment, of course, since we do not know all we would need to know to maximize the possibilities for individual development and contribute to man's becoming. We know only that bureaucratic organizational styles have not done this, so we have a beginning.

Another area of values where we might spend some time relates to where our field, public administration, may differ from administration in the private sector. We have allowed ourselves to accept many of the values and premises of the entrepreneurial world without scrutinizing them with sufficient care. Thus in public as in private programs we encounter many situations where social costs are not borne by the program but are passed along to other public agencies or the public at large. If we feel—as many seem to feel—that the time may have arrived when the private enterprise should be required to anticipate and absorb more of its social costs, we might agree that it is past time for the public program to give more attention to this.

In this vein, Kenneth Boulding has drawn a sharp distinction between what he terms the *cowboy economy* and the *spaceman economy.* The former is our contemporary consumption-oriented economy with its assumption of unlimited resources, affluence, and the rights of unrestricted entrepreneurialism. The latter sees the earth as a place of limited resources whose development and use are dependent on a variety of distinctly *finite* conditions. The cowboy economy depends upon technology, changing, and resource use; the spaceman economy implies equilibrium, balance with nature (a man-nature symbiosis), and the husbandry approach. While we can readily comprehend the business culture's sponsorship of the cowboy model, one wonders whether public administration in general should not be based on the spaceman frame of reference. If the public programs of this country do not choose this path, who will? Certainly this alternative appears relevant to our current problems, does it not? We may fear this issue as a choice between continued progress *versus* the end of progress, but I do not believe the matter should be cast in that light. I see this as a question of a nation's approach to resource use: whether we see the objective as controlling and exploiting nature or as understanding and working with nature. Boulding would term it a contest between the myth of affluence and the reality of scarcity!

We have selected only two general areas to illustrate the possibility of value changes which might enhance the appeal of public employment for persons with a less Faustian outlook on the world of work. There are many additional values which would need to be adjusted in much the same manner as those mentioned here, were we to attempt this task, but these point the way.

The Rejection of Bureaucracy

Enough has been written on the problems of bureaucracy to reduce my responsibility for treatment of this subject here. On the other hand, some of the alternatives which are common in the literature today do not necessarily solve our problem of combining the work/play dichotomy, so we might address that aspect.

In the first place, one major theme we should consider is that sponsored by Warren Bennis: the notion of the *changing organization.* While this formulation has implicit in it the rejection of traditional bureaucracy, it does not necessarily follow that the model offers sanctuary for those seekers of relevance and enjoyment in their work. Indeed, the *changing organization* seems dangerously reactive, a means merely of accommodating to the exigencies of an unstable environment. It appears a natural feature of Boulding's cowboy economy. One cannot sense that life would be especially interesting, fun, or even challenging in such a setting. On the contrary, one suspects that it offers the very environment least likely to appeal to those elements of the society most likely to *cut out* in the future. One sees the possibility that meta-values might receive greater attention in this changing situation, but that is not implicit in the concept.

Are there alternatives? Possibly. For one thing my graduate students have convinced me that we should offer choice rather than change as the central denominator of a new public administration organization model. They argue that while change is an external and institutional process, choice is internal and individual. The temporary society tends towards a value-free posture, thereby precluding choice by individuals. This could represent going in the opposite direction to that which long-term goals and meta-values would adjudge most central to our interests. One could even argue, I believe, that a period of frenetic accommodation would inevitably accompany the sharp rise in the rate of progress (change) described in my introduction and that this would continue until it became impossible to keep up and more manageable alternatives were selected. Thus the notion of the changing organization may represent nothing more than a last gasp of Faustian man and his highly structured organizations—trying desperately to keep going a model which has evolved into obsolescence.

Perhaps what we must begin to consider (I hope I am doing so here) are some of the dimensions of what is being termed the *post-change* society. In such an environment the reactive processes of changing must surely have been supplanted by the proactive process of choice. Perhaps we might assume that the processes of *planned* change, emphasizing choice, might have replaced morphogenic changing where choice is hardly possible. In any case, in the process of moving into the post-change condition, with its emphasis on man *and* nature, equilibrium and proactive confrontation with problems, we may find it imperative to refine our skills at *planned* organizational change rather than *automatic* change.

When one considers alternatives to bureaucracy, he finds himself aware that many of the suggestions in the literature are not necessarily truly new modes or forms. One exception to this may well be the so-called sociotechnical system with its autonomous work groups. This approach has received relatively little attention in the literature as yet but is the subject of considerable interest and experimentation in such places as Norway and Yugoslavia (and even in a new branch of Procter and Gamble about to open in California.)

The socio-technical system appears to offer a number of exciting possibilities. Certainly its underlying premises are different from those which characterized traditional bureaucratic organizations. The socio-technical model does not appear merely an adjunct to the established system, a means of coopting people in a new way. Rather, such systems appear to offer an environment wherein meta-values are paramount, where there is room for experimentation and risk-taking, where policy is planned rather than expediential, and where choice at all levels is paramount. Further, this model is more skillfully contrived to account the symbiosos between man and his systems, between the social and technical. The system is designed to maximize man. Some have wondered whether this organizational form can be made to work in a political context. We cannot say as yet but we should observe carefully what happens abroad and be prepared to experiment here. In Norway, they are already claiming a variety of social spin-offs resulting from the impact of the autonomous work groups on their members. The Norweigians claim they find themselves more likely to take positive attitudes toward people in general, to see them as good and to trust them, as a result of working in a more autonomous, people-oriented group. They believe they are more able to behave as individuals and to treat others as individuals. If developments such as these are real, they are clearly on the track we have set for ourselves here—to fit the work and play environments together around the individual person. It would appear that keeping track of what happens in these various developments is of potential value for students and practitioners in this country.

This brings me to a final point I want to mention in this section of my paper. Harold Leavitt attended a meeting of organization theorists in Europe last year and subsequently wrote that the most interesting thing they agreed upon was that we should begin to introduce a far greater degree of *playfulness* into our organizations, both public and private. This seems a remarkable conclusion but it is one I embrace with pleasure. It is remarkable because it represents a very substantial change of direction from established theory. It represents commitment to the idea that the organization environment includes the possibility of real pleasure for organization members. It puts faith in the individual. It rejects the primacy of systems and techniques, the grey, somber goals and formalisms of so many modern organizations. I embrace his suggestion because it offers the combination I am seeking in this paper. Playfulness implies the qualities of creativity and innovation as well as humor and informality. Hal's suggestion should appeal to the Dionysian spirit!

I was delighted to find Henry Kariel using this same term as he wrote about *creating political reality.** Admittedly, he is talking about a different subject, but much of what he said has relevance for my purposes here. He is talking about the importance of political man being a *value-creating being.* He argues that such a model would direct attention to current non-decisions and induce us to transform present organizational structures and attitudes . . . in order to create new meanings and to construct new realities. . ." He urges "frankly provocative, intrusive strategies" and says that were we "to value this imagination . . . we would move lightly and playfully through new territory, receptive to its promise, proceeding . . . in ever-widening circles." He even urges us to consider politics as play and to put quotation marks around our "most precious obsessions," such as "the democratic process," "private property," and even "reality." He might certainly be talking about public administration instead of political science (indeed, in part of his article he *is*); his paper might just as well have been presented at this panel, with but minor editing. The point is that we all seem to take what we do so seriously that we forget that the real point is problem-solving, a process which is

*Henry S. Kariel, "Creating Political Reality," *American Political Science Review,* Vol. 64 (1970), pp. 1088-1098.

stultified by rules and formalism and pomposity. It is the very thing which will drive out the new man we will soon want to induce into our programs.

Treating the Individual

Another major theme I want to develop relates to the manner in which we perceive and treat the individual in our public organizations. Such organizations are characteristically highly structured and riven with formalisms. Inevitably, they tend to reject participation and creative input. They are formed in terms of distrust of individual motivation and capability—indeed, of the individual as apart from the group or system. The person in the system is bent to the technique and goal.

We might begin more seriously to question our organizational relationships, the structures of power established both within our public organizations and between them and the political and clientele relationships. We might consider new ways for building up individuals and then rely on their capability and dedication to perform on their own. This applies both inside and outside our organizational structures. Here I am talking about the emphasis on meta-values rather than skill and technique training. If, as Norman Brown argues, Apollonian man is to be replaced by Dionysian man, we must learn to understand this latter form. Perhaps as important a starting point as any is recognition that the Apollonian represents the rational negation of instinct while the Dionysian sponsors the fulfillment of instinctual pleasures (this mirrors the conflict between the Faustian and Polynesian approaches to work and living). Our question is whether accommodation of Dionysian man in our organizations in a positive fashion is possible. No conclusive answer is available as yet but one senses that with certain changes in our values and processes it can be done. I believe the matters I have raised here are pertinent to this accommodation.

One possible way of helping to further this cause may be for we in public administration to accept the notion that for much of what we do in our public agencies, *process may be our most important product.* We have become used to sublimating the individual to the organization and its goals, yet many programs are not in fact involved with activities where goals are achievable in the sense we have in mind for production organizations. Even where goals *are* being achieved one wonders whether the exchange of individual sublimation (reducing the employee's *self)* for goal purposes is necessary or, in the long run, rewarding to the organization or society.

My argument here is that were we to attempt in all of our public programs to work with the people in the system in ways which seem functional to them and their peers (in growth and development terms) we would absorb much of the social cost now sloughed off and we should be able to contribute considerably to society. The organization models thereby developed might offer incentives to organizations throughout society, with beneficial returns.

To illustrate what I am getting at here, let me mention a situation I witnessed in a particular public organization with which I was associated a couple years ago. This organization employs a thousand or more persons for a certain routine task. Initially they had used white males for this task but in rapid succession they cycled through black males, white females, and finally, to black females, all because each successive group could be employed at a lower price. When I explored this situation to determine what if anything was being done to improve the general capability (as employees, citizens, mothers, human beings, etc.) of these black women, people in the agency thought I was either putting them on or on the edge of madness! I continued to wonder, however, why this large and seemingly responsible public agency should function just as a private business enterprise would function in this same regard. Why should they risk contributing to a problem which is already the focus of attention of a substantial number of major public programs? Why should not this organization be expected to work with these employees in such ways as to assist them with some of the problems they suffer, to strengthen their capability in such ways as possible in that context?

Again, obviously, the question of values and premises is uppermost here. The process model would assume that man is always becoming, that he is a learning, growing person rather than a finished product to be used and abused by such organizations as he joins. It would assume that the proactive stance is preferable to reactive behaviors and that organizational efforts to teach, facilitate and reenforce proactive behavior is socially useful—and valuable to the organization, if you will. The process emphasis would sponsor individual choice in a context of freedom, partly because that offers a stronger appeal for persons critical of the Faustian organization model and its imperatives, and partly because that helps develop better citizens in a free society. Maybe you do it simply because, as Bob Biller says, "Organizations come and go, but men persist!" In any case, the organization offers a great place to apply McLuhan's dicta that "the medium is the message."

In Summary

In these remarks I have considered changes in values and premises underlying public administration, the rejection of the bureaucratic organizational form, and some new approaches toward the development of the individual. My purpose has been to suggest some possible adjustments which might render public employment more meaningful and attractive for the organization man who may well be developing as the prototype of the (near) future.

I reiterate that my argument is not so completely tied to the possible rise to majority of this new man that it will be meaningless if he fails to show up. I stand on most of these arguments as relevant for improved public administration regradless. It simply happens that change is more likely when duress is involved so I have considered some possible sources of duress.

Needless to say, there are many additional matters I should spend time on—in either or both of these contexts. I am much concerned with the public policy process, with the problems of racial and sexual discrimination in public programs, with the rise of public service unions to positions of power, and with many additional matters which appear to reduce man and which would need to be altered in order both to induce participation in public administration and improve its quality. I would like also to be able to include in this paper consideration of the concept of possibility both as a teaching device and as a frame of reference for scholars and practitioners. I believe this concept offers an interesting and useful means to challenge our stereotypes and enlarge our qualities of perception

—both useful in the activity I am sponsoring here. But time is running out and I will refrain from further speculation.

Let me conclude by noting that the test of our ability to attract participants and survive as viable organizations may be at stake in the near future. In these remarks I hope I have offered some possible means to meet this problem. One of Kariel's observations seems appropriate for my conclusion. He remarks on the annoying fact that all kinds of unaccredited persons outside political science seem to have shown powers of observation and surmise in various matters relating to that field which were better than those of professionals in the field. I think that this may also be true for public administration and I believe the implication is that we should try to get as broad a range of people as possible into our act to capture the benefits of their variety.

SECTION THREE

PLANNING AND COORDINATION

The absence of adequate planning and effective coordination has long been a major weakness in the juvenile justice system. This section presents materials directed at the improvement of the planning and coordinative functions of all agencies in the system.

CHAPTER 9

JUVENILE DELINQUENCY PLANNING*

Foreword

THIS PUBLICATION IS intended to serve as a basic statement of the necessary elements for the comprehensive juvenile delinquency planning process. Apart from its contribution to effective delinquency prevention and control, such planning is a required element for participation in the Federal assistance programs under the Juvenile Delinquency Prevention and Control Act of 1968 and the Omnibus Crime Control and Safe Streets Act of 1968. Under the former, States must submit comprehensive delinquency plans in order to assume responsibility and distribute funds for implementation of prevention and rehabilitation programs. Under the latter, States must develop comprehensive law enforcement improvement plans, of which juvenile delinquency planning is a required and major component. In both cases, local units of governments and public agencies must be conversant with planning techniques to develop programs acceptable for Federal support, whether directly or through State planning agencies designated under the two acts. Indeed, most States have established common agencies to carry forward the planning

*A joint publication of the: U.S. Department of Health, Education, and Welfare, Social and Rehabilitation Service, Youth Development and Delinquency Prevention Administration and the U.S. Department of Justice, Law Enforcement Assistance Administration.

process under the Juvenile Delinquency and Omnibus Crime Control Acts, thereby minimizing fragmentation and duplication of effort.

The publication should be of special value to those who are newly involved in the planning process, particularly members of groups, agencies, and organizations who will be called upon to participate. To those who have been involved in delinquency planning throughout their careers, most of what follows will be familiar, but should serve as a useful summary of what constitutes good planning.

This work is not intended to serve as a how-to-do-it recipe book for developing a comprehensive plan. Actual and specific planning of a comprehensive anti-delinquency program is the proper province of planners who are familiar with their communities, its needs and objectives. But this publication should provide a guide to the basic and necessary steps to follow if good and effective planning is to be accomplished.

The Youth Development and Delinquency Prevention Administration (of the U.S. Department of Health, Education, and Welfare) and the Law Enforcement Assistance Administration (of the U. S. Department of Justice) are pleased to publish this booklet jointly as part of their ongoing efforts to supply important and useful information to those working in the areas of delinquency planning, prevention, and rehabilitation. Readers may refer also to other planning aids issued by the sponsoring agencies, such as the YDDPA's guidelines and regulations concerning the format and content of State plans, and LEAA's "Correctional Planning and Resource Guide" (February 1969) and training manual on "Long Range Planning for the Criminal Justice System" (September 1970).

ROBERT J. GEMIGNANI,
Commissioner
Youth Development and Delinquency Prevention Administration
U. S. Department of Health, Education, and Welfare

RICHARD W. VELDE **CLARENCE M. COSTER**
Associate Administrators
Law Enforcement Assistance Administration
U. S. Department of Justice

* * * * * * * * * *

Introduction

Juvenile delinquency is one of the Nation's major problems. The 90th Congress of the United States, in enacting the Juvenile Delinquency Prevention and Control Act of 1968, states:

> The Congress finds that delinquency among youths constitutes a national problem which can be met by assisting and coordinating the efforts of public and private agencies engaged in combating the problem, and by increasing the number and extent of the services available for preventing and combating juvenile delinquency. It is, therefore, the purpose of this act to help State and local communities strengthen their juvenile justice and juvenile aid systems, including courts, correctional systems, police agencies, and law enforcement and other agencies which deal with juveniles, and to assist communities in providing diagnosis, treatment, rehabilitative, and preventive services to youths who are delinquent or in danger of becoming delinquent, to encourage the development of community-based rehabilitation and prevention programs to provide assistance in the training of personnel employed or preparing for employment in occupations involving the provision of such services, to provide support for comprehensive planning, development of improved techniques, and information services in the field of juvenile delinquency, and to provide technical assistance in such field.[1]

Under the Omnibus Crime Control and Safe Streets Act of 1968, States are enjoined to develop comprehensive plans and programs of law enforcement and criminal justice improvement, including efforts relating to prevention, control, or reduction of juvenile delinquency.

Nature of Juvenile Delinquency

The incidence of juvenile delinquency appears to have shown a dramatic rise over the years. Today, as in the past, juvenile delinquency rates are rising in all areas, with the highest in the cities, followed by the suburbs and rural areas.

The following single statistic, perhaps, illustrates the problem of juvenile delinquency today. *During a recent eight year period, the increase in arrests of youngsters under eighteen was almost double the increase in adult arrest.*

Authorities in the field predict: The rapid expansion of metropolitan areas almost certainly will continue to contribute to the growing rate of delinquency; one out of every six boys will end up in court for other than a traffic offense sometime before his eighteenth birthday; the maturation of suburbia coupled with a sense of alienation of middle-class youth will also contribute to the growing rate of delinquency.

Other official statistics reveal: Boys are most often sent to juvenile court for committing larceny, burglary, and motor vehicle theft; a significant number are referred for truancy and ungovernable behavior; girls are most often sent to juvenile court for running away, ungovernability, larceny, and sex offenses.

The cost of juvenile delinquency is *expensive,* both in terms of human resources and money. In terms of human resources, the cost is *incalculable.* In monetary terms, it is estimated that the cost of a single juvenile career of crime costs the governmental system $11,000. In the aggregate, juvenile crime costs this Nation an estimated $4 billion annaully, and this does not include the inestimable cost to the victims of delinquent acts of violence against their person or property.

These facts substantiate the Congressional finding that juvenile delinquency is a national problem that transcends local, regional, and State lines. The continued drain of public funds and loss of valuable human resources due to delinquency justified a Federal commitment to assist the States.

To assist the States in addressing these problems of juvenile delinquency, the Congress enacted the Juvenile Delinquency Prevention and Control Act of 1968 and the Omnibus Crime Control and Safe Streets Act of 1968, with considerable emphasis on *comprehensive planning.*

The Role of the Planner

Planners in the field of juvenile delinquency have been given the very difficult task of instituting comprehensive planning for programs dealing with multiproblem people and involving multiagencies at the local and State levels.

The function of the planner is to:

Gather background material on the subject of delinquency prevention, control, and treatment from a variety of sources including other local, State, national and international governmental and private agencies and organizations;

Analyze such material in relation to the community for which he has planning responsibility;

Evaluate existing programs in the community;

Identify needs of the community which are not being met by existing programs;

Develop programs to meet the needs of the community;

Serve as a channel of communication to those interested in or affected by the communities' programs;

Involve the affected organizations or individuals in the development of a comprehensive plan;

Provide leadership in the development of a comprehensive plan for delinquency prevention and rehabilitation.

The Objective of Comprehensive Planning

The objective of comprehensive planning is to *facilitate* the process by which a State, region, or local community establishes an effective system, public and private, to *prevent, control and reduce* delinquency, and to *rehabilitate or treat* juvenile delinquents or youth in danger of becoming delinquent. (Figure 9-1 illustrates these elements which should be considered in the planning process.)

Planning is necessary both to achieve these objectives and to serve as an effective motivating force to improve delinquency programs.

Planning in juvenile delinquency should provide for *balance* in the

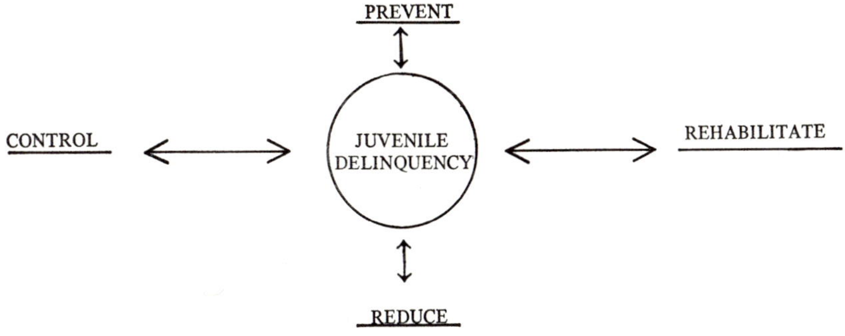

Figure 9-1 The objective of comprehensive planning is to facilitate the process by which a State established an effective system, public and private, to;

achievement of the program objectives of prevention and rehabilitation.

Planning should include a system for the development of *alternatives* to inclusion in existing juvenile justice systems and to divert youth from correctional systems.

Planning in juvenile delinquency should be comprehensive both in terms of program and coverage. That is, with regard to program comprehensiveness, the plan should consider *all* services, programs, and activities which contribute to the control, prevention, and reduction of delinquency. Geographic comprehensiveness requires that the plan cover all of the area within the community engaged in the planning process.

Planning should be ideal in that it looks to the full satisfaction of the established goals and objectives. However, while final plans should recognize constraints, they should also direct attention to the elimination or modification of such constraints as they impede the achievement of the plan's objective. The final formulated plan should reasonably approximate what can be accomplished with the available resources (personnel and money) and the legislative or statutory basis of the program within a given period.

Thus, planning should be *realistic* in relation to the resources. The plan should show what steps and intermediate activities are necessary to achieve the desired results from the resources.

Planning should also be *complete,* showing all the resources and program activities required to achieve the planned results, although they may involve a variety of agencies, public and private.

Planning should be *concrete*. It should state definitely that certain resources are to be scheduled for certain periods. It must indicate specifically what *results* are expected from these resources and when.

Unfortunately, few guidelines or standards have been conceptualized in the area of delinquency planning which would provide criteria by which comprehensive planners could assess their planning. The Juvenile Delinquency Prevention and Control Act of 1968 and the Omnibus Crime Control and Safe Streets Act of 1968 facilitate the development of the comprehensive planning process through the introduction of Federal financial support in this important activity.

The Written Plan

In the field of delinquency prevention and rehabilitation a written plan is essential to success since:

The written plan is a result or record of decisions and assignments made;
Decisions on goals and objectives are stated;
Written plans provide an orderly history which is readily available. Future plans are better made when it is possible to go back over what has and has not worked in the past. Referring to past plans insures that more care and thought will be put into current plans and wiser decisions can be made concerning the priorities of service to be rendered;
Written plans promote increased probability of success since there is more certainty that plans will in fact be made if they exist in writing;
Written plans promote an increase in leadership ability. The skills of those involved in planning will be sharpened and leadership growth in administration and in elementary human relations will be accelerated;
Written plans provide a vehicle for communicating what is done, and why, to all parties concerned in the implementation of the plan.

In delinquency planning, the written plan should provide *in narrative form* an answer to these questions:

1. What is to be done?
2. Who is to do what?
3. How is it to be done?
4. When is it to be done?

The careful formulation of the answers to these four questions should provide a comprehensive plan related to the needs of the community.

What Is To Be Done?

The rational planning process begins with an evaluation of the nature and scope of the problem of delinquency in the community engaged in the planning process. Specifically the plan must take cognizance of:

Youth population, present and projected;[2]
Youth unemployment;[3]
Youth arrest, rate of increase in delinquency, and number of institutionalized youth;[4]

Youth school dropout and truancy rates;[5]
Family status and income.[6]

In some states the above information may not be available uniformly for the entire State. However, skilled planning technicians have the capacity for observation and analysis. This will permit them to utilize the available data or to project such data to the total community which is engaged in the planning process. The absence of basic information, however, indicates that the development of an information system should be given high priority.

In addition to the above quantitative data, the following should be available for planning:

A description of the nature and scope as well as the adequacy of prevention projects and programs in the community for youth in danger of becoming delinquent, including existing educational, vocational, training, preventive health, social, and youth service programs, and other programs for youth;
A description of the nature and scope of current rehabilitation projects and programs in the community for delinquent youth, including programs in institutions relating to the custody, care, treatment, and supervision of delinquent youth.

In the light of the above information, an evaluation should be made as to the *adequacy* of existing prevention and rehabilitation services and facilities, the *gaps* in services and facilities, and the *projected needs* for services for delinquent youth or youth in danger of becoming delinquent.

Based on this analysis, a general statement of priorities for the distribution of funds among projects and programs through the State or locality with respect to location and type can be made in order to give emphasis to the areas of increased need. In securing such material, efforts should be made to determine whether there already exists statewide studies of such programs. If not, there are a number of national agencies which perform such services.[7]

An integral part of the planning process is *the defining of what the plan is to achieve.*

A well-conceived comprehensive plan will contain a definition of the goals and objectives of the community in youth development and juvenile delinquency prevention. It will be complementary to or supportive of existing programs or activities in the community.

The goals and objectives of delinquency planning should be stated whenever possible in *quantifiable* terms. A clear statement of the goals and objectives of the plan enables more clear communication of goals and objectives to staff, other public agencies, and the community. It also facilitates the measurement of success in achieving the stated goals.

Who Is To Do What?

There are at least two dimensions to this question. The first is who should be represented and participate in the planning process and the second is what resources are available to carry out the plan.

I. *Who should be represented on and participate in the planning process?* Experience to date suggests that it is desirable for all those who are *affected* by a comprehensive plan for youth development and delinquency prevention to be involved in the planning process.

Goals and objectives formulated in this way have a much better likelihood of success *when all who are affected are heard,* especially in the early stages of discussion. In this way a more binding commitment to the implementation of plans can be achieved.

Since planners are dealing with a complex social issue, prevention and control of delinquency, broad community participation, including ideas from a variety of sources, facilitate formulation of an effective plan. When alternative points of view are raised, the more rigorous is the analytical process necessary to adequately incorporate them into program goals and objectives. With a variety of points of view expressed early in the planning progress, it is possible to take them into account in considering alternative solutions of problems.

The ideal answer to the question of who should participate in the planning for juvenile delinquency prevention and rehabilitation thus becomes: courts; law enforcement agencies; public and private agencies familiar with the field of juvenile delinquency and associated fields; welfare agencies; education depatments; health departments; mental health departments; recreation departments; job training departments; job placement departments; corrections departments; and youth.

Youth themselves are too often neglected as a community resource. Therefore, when identifying the nature and scope of activity of existing public and private agencies and organizations involved in juvenile delinquency planning, and in making assignments, the possibilities for better utilization of the young people should not be overlooked since: They are most closely linked to the problems that are of their generation; they are more and more willing to express their points of view; they are a vast source of largely untapped manpower and ideas.

In addition, outside consultants, specialists in fiscal matters, public information, research, statistical analysis, and other related program personnel might be invited to serve on the planning board or as *ad hoc* consultants.

The service of a full-time, paid staff is essential for effective planning. Such staff should include a director or chairman, other staff technicians and secretarial help. The director must be able to provide skilled leadership, and to keep the process moving in spite of divergent points of view and a variety of vested program interests. In addition, housekeeping duties must be carried out, such as the appointment of committees, the assignment of duties, the completing of reports, setting meetings, and developing agendas.

The following list identifies the many community entities that collectively comprise the *who* in comprehensive planning (and the plan *must* take into careful account how each affects the juvenile): home; courts; employers; welfare; recreation centers; corrections; religion; school; youth organizations; law enforcement; community youth centers; health facilities.

II. *Who in the community is a resource to assist in carrying out the plan?* Seeking an answer to this question in the planning process results in an *assessment of the resources* in the community which are available to deal with the problem. This requires an identification of the nature and scope of existing public and private agencies, organizations, and programs concerned with delinquency prevention and treatment.

In the planning process, it is common to catalog existing organizations dealing with or concerned about the area of delinquency prevention and treatment.

As illustrated through the above listing, the juvenile may be viewed as the central individual in a theoretical construct of a system in juvenile delinquency. The various components of the system (called sub-systems) are integral parts of the system. A comprehensive plan should take into account how each segment of the system affects the juvenile and which resources are to be applied.

In considering resources needed to achieve plan goals and objectives, it is common to find deficiencies or gaps in resources. It therefore appears desirable to organize as part of the plan a process by which additional resources are identified and developed to meet the needs of the community.

In developing a comprehensive plan the answer to *who is to do what?* will identify personnel and organizational resources which should be engaged in formulation and execution of the plan.

How Is It To Be Done?

Consideration of the question of how the plan is to be put into effect throughout the planning process is highly desirable. Experience suggests that planning done with a view toward eventual implementation has more *likelihood* of implementation than a plan which lacks such consideration.

In the planning process, as the goals and objectives of the plan are agreed upon and resources are identified by which the community hopes to achieve the stated goals and objectives of the plan, it is necessary to consider how utilization of resources will achieve the goal. In other words, merely stating goals and listing resources is not enough. The plan should describe what it is that a given resource is expected to *achieve*.

In developing this portion of the plan, it is essential that the individuals and organizations which constitute the resources in the plan *participate* in consideration of how they or their programs will be an integral part of the plan.

Success of implementation is facilitated by effectively considering and answering the *how is it to be done?* question throughout the planning process.

How the plan is to be implemented should also identify *who* is responsible for marshaling the identified resources and providing leadership in the effort. The interaction and interdependence of the various groups and elements of the plan must be stated as precisely as possible. The sources and interrelationships of funds must be similarly stated. For example, the responsibility of detailed planning for beginning and operating a youth center may be assumed by a voluntary group. The funding may be the responsibility of the State. The *how to* must show the interaction of these two activities, including timing and the mechanics of justification, approvals, and follow-up.

The implementation plan should also consider how the program will be *evaluated*. This will include a method for gathering statistical data on the program that will enable later analysis of *how well* the program is achieving its stated objectives. This is important for continued justification for the program and to make indicated changes and improvements for future activities, plan for resource allocations, and conduct community relations and publicity.

When Is It To Be Done?

Having determined the goals and objectives of the plan, identified who and what resources are to perform specific functions, and described how the plan is to be implemented, it is then necessary to determine *priorities* among the various programs or activities which constitute the plan.

Frequently it is impossible to do all a community would like to do at once. The establishment of *realistic priorities* is an integral part of a comprehensive plan and permits the community to allocate resources consistent with its judgment on what should be done first. Ideally all programs and activities should be implemented within the period of the plan. When this is the case, the setting of priorities will facilitate an evolutionary fulfillment of the plan.

Integral to this phase of the plan is to provide schedules in as much detail as possible. Milestone dates should be set and, if possible, specific accomplishments tied to the milestones should be identified. For example if a youth center is to be established, the plan should identify when detailed planning will be completed, when funding will be provided, when the center facilities will be ready, when the center will be in operation, when maximum number of youths to be served will be achieved, and when the first evaluation of the center can be made.

The establishment of milestones in the planning process provides a mechanism for forcing rational thinking through of the problem and insuring that plans will be realistic. Milestone dates also provide motivation for all involved to become achievement oriented against specific measurable points of time and to take indicated corrective action when necessary to achieve the milestones. Milestone planning also lends motivation and direction to establishing when data should be collected and analyzed to determine how well the program is achieving its goals and what changes in directions and resources might be necessary.

In the process of planning the plans themselves, the establishment of schedules is desirable, if not mandatory. In this case, *backward schedule planning* is useful. Such planning might begin with an assumption of when the submission of a final plan is required, based on Federal requirements, State legislative hearings, State budget calls, or other considerations. The resulting date would dictate all other possible prior activities as shown in the schedule contained in Figure 2. This sample schedule shows each preceding activity and event in descending order and that the activities leading to a final plan might begin as early as four months prior to the completion and submission of a comprehensive State plan. Of course, the length of time allowed for each of the activities depends on the judgment of the planning group, the complexity of the plans, the normal operating mode of the State and its agencies, and any other factors bearing on the reality and validity of the planning process. The fundamental logic contained in the simplified schedule system can also be applied to the implementation of the plans themselves, although they may more often be in the form of *forward planning*. Naturally statewide comprehensive plans may not have details as specific as those used in the example for specific projects, but the milestone concept should be used for whatever level of specificity is appropriate.

Plans and schedules should also, where possible, contemplate the long-range goals of the program. If it seems that to achieve goals, more than a year will be required, then the original plan should take this into account. Specifics for the first year should be as detailed as possible with more general objectives, milestones, costs, etc., stated for later years. The plans prepared in the subsequent years can then be more detailed and accurate as experience is gained.

The process of updating a comprehensive plan is facilitated when the original plan contained all the essential elements described above. If the plan being updated is deficient in one or more factors, the deficiency, of course, should be corrected.

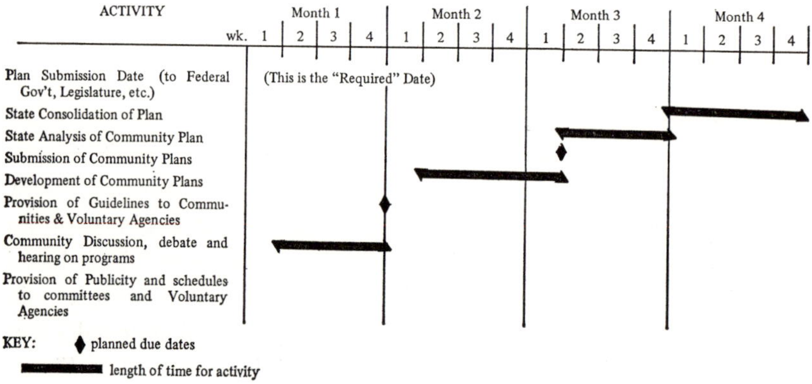

Figure 9-2 Sample planning activity schedule

Summary

Comprehensive planning is a necessity for:

Establishing realistic goals and objectives;
Measuring accomplishments;
Meeting goals and objectives on schedule;
Justifying programs to the *resource providers;*
Matching goals and resources and applying required resources;
Refining and improving continued and subsequent programs;
Communicating to all concerned;
Motivating all concerned to achievement of stated goals.

Figure 3 represents a summary of the sequence of the *kinds of consideration* which must be taken into account in the planning process. The final *form* of a plan is not as important as the *content* of the plan which should demonstrate as well as possible the logic utilized by the planners; their assumptions; their expectations for the program; the definitiveness of their plans; and the realism of their plans in terms of resources required and available, and achievable schedules. Planners should always keep in mind the key questions of:

> Is this plan credible and understandable to resource providers?
> On this basis will they provide the resources?
> Will the community understand, accept, and act on the comprehensive plan and its constituent local level plans?

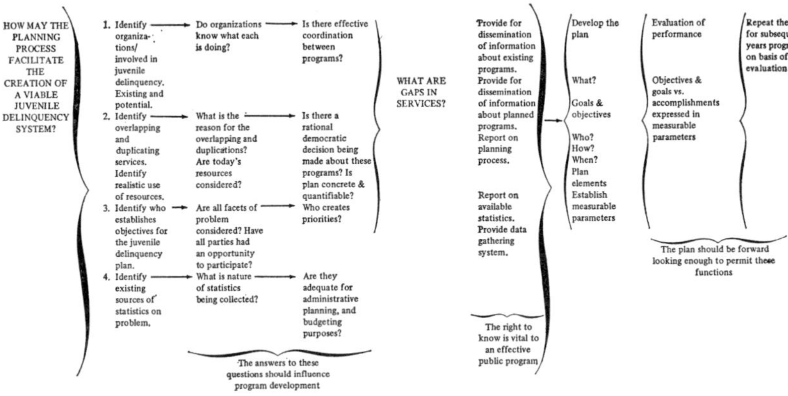

Figure 9-3 The planners task

FOOTNOTES

[1]Sec. 2, Public Law 90-445, 90th Congress, H.R. 12120, July 31, 1968.

[2]Information concerning this item may be secured by writing to the Bureau of Census, Population Division, Washington, D.C. 20233.

[3]Information concerning youth unemployment may be secured by writing to the Department of Labor, Bureau of Labor Statistics, Washington, D.C., 20212.

[4]On youth arrests, information can be secured by writing to Uniform Crime Reports, Federal Bureau of Investigation, 9th and Pennsylvania Ave. N.W., Washington, D.C. 20525. Information on the rate of increase in juvenile delinquency and the number of children institutionalized in the State may be secured by writing to Program Statistics and Data Systems, U.S. Department of Health, Education, and Welfare, Washington, D.C. 20201.

[5]State figures on truancy rates may be secured by writing to Reference Estimates and Projections Branch, National Center for Educational Statistics, U.S. Office of Education, Washington, D.C. 20202; information on dropout rates is more difficult

to secure. Some information may be available from State and local boards of education.

[6]Information concerning family status and income may be secured by writing to the Bureau of Census, Population Division, Washington, D.C. 20233.

[7]For information write to Youth Development and Delinquency Prevention Administration, U.S. Department of Health, Education, and Welfare, Washington, D.C. 20201.

CHAPTER 10

THE ROLE OF POLICE AND CORRECTIONAL PERSONNEL IN COMMUNITY PLANNING

CARL M. SHAFER

ONE OF THE MOST STRONGLY supported new developments in the fields of law enforcement and corrections has come to be known as community relations. The activities described by this term are aimed at achieving and maintaining a continuous exchange of views between professional law enforcement personnel and all segments of society. This development is in keeping with a shift in orientation of all systems of remedial social control to an increasingly broad view of their functions as being related to all segments of the community.[1] This approach places the police department at the focal point of community organization efforts to deal with problems of crime, delinquency, and anti-social behavior, and involves professional police and correctional personnel in a community planning process.[2]

Simply stated, the goal of community planning is community problem-solving. The organizational activity which develops and implements policies dealing with a wide variety of social ills also is termed community organization. In the past, the major responsibility for this activity has been assigned to community planning and coordinating councils at local levels. Governmental organizations carry major planning responsibilities on state, regional, and national levels.

Applied to juvenile delinquency, it is well established that planning is necessary to achieve prevention, control, and reduction of delinquency, and to rehabilitate juvenile delinquents or young people in danger of becoming delinquent. Without the participation of police and correctional personnel in this planning process, an important dimension of such planning would be missing.

The mandate for participation in planning, broadly conceived, has led police departments generally to select special officers to carry out public speaking assignments and to organize committees of citizens that function as discussion groups in which ideas mgiht be exchanged. Perhaps it is due to the selection process by which citizens find themselves on such committees, or it may be due to difficulty in communication, but such efforts have not proven effective in involving the community in planning.

In some instances, community relations units have aimed at developing positive relationships with *grass roots* elements of the community in order to reduce tensions between certain groups in the community and the police department.

While both these approaches are beginning efforts toward planning with the community and are useful as ways to make a start, they cannot be viewed as effective beyond establishing a first step toward planning with the community. The method of community planning requires much broader community participation in planning that deals with problems that contribute to individual and family breakdown as well as with problems resulting from individual anti-social or asocial behavior.

Two Strategies in Community Planning

Most social problems sooner or later manifest themselves in the behavior of individuals. Because of this phenomenon, it has been widely accepted (and many still hold this to be true) that the problem resided within the individual. Programs of rehabilitation or treatment, and corrective punishment have therefore received heavy emphasis. A supporting philosophy to this approach has been our belief in individual effort and free choice as the major determinants of a man's success or failure.

It is not surprising that our major community planning efforts have been characterized by the *social problem management* approach.

This strategy plans community resources available for solving social problems around some definable risk population. The chronically unemployed, the mentally retarded, the juvenile delinquent, the alcoholic—all are examples of the wide variety of risk populations at whom social, health, and correctional services might be aimed.

A second strategy begins with the assumption that a breakdown in certain vital functions of the social system contributes to the production of social problems. It can be referred to as the *community development* model since its approach is to examine the requisite social necessities that insure wholesome community life for everyone and develop programs and services to provide them.

It is obvious that both these strategies are useful in any attack on social problems. Their inherent weaknesses are that they cannot be effective without having enormous material and personnel resources available to them, and they require techniques for analysis and intervention that are not yet adequately developed. Both, however, show promise of increasing our ability to cope with social problems as the process of social planning gains in participation from important segments of the community such as police and correctional personnel. Only then will the data necessary to develop more effective techniques become available.

Obstacles to Community Planning

In spite of the clear advantages that community planning seems to have over the random, disjointed incrementalism[3] that has characterized community service development in the past, a number of obstacles remain in the path of rational approaches to community problem-solving. Several of these will be noted and briefly discussed as background for presenting the essential elements of the community planning process.

1. Obsolete services. In every field, and the field of criminal justice is no exception, there are obsolescent services and procedures that perpetuate and aggravate the very problems they were designed to alleviate. Having existed for a long time, they have succeeded in developing a community power base that protects their organizations against attempts form the outside to change them. Their purpose seems to be organization maintenance rather than goal achievement.

2. PRESSURE TO FIND CONTROL MEASURES. The urgency that accompanies problems associated with anti-social behavior makes a community impatient with plans from law enforcement and correctional agencies for time to find basic solutions to problems of crime and delinquency. We therefore find ready support for short-term control measures that produce immediate, if temporary, results. Unfortunately, most measures of control require coercion in increasing amounts that ultimately results in undesirable consequences while the underlying social problem goes unattended.

3. SERVICE FRAGMENTATION. Our failure to see the connections between problems that appear to be different but may be associated with some common social variables has led us to develop an allegiance to and preference for single problem structures in law enforcement, correctional and social welfare agencies. Such fragmentation of services has made coordination impossible and has fragmented the client in a way that forces him to fit his problem to the service rather than the other way around. Similarly, fragmentation of authority among services has reduced their capacity to be responsive to changing needs, changing techniques and efforts to plan for comprehensive attacks on social problems. As an example, although it is well established that delinquent behavior in a young person has important causal relationships with his family life, many services to delinquent youth provide no direct service to his family. Or in instances in which it is clear that a child should not be returned to his own home, he is nevertheless returned there with no service provided to correct the conditions in the home deemed inimical to his well-being.

4. REDUCTION OF CITIZEN INVOLVEMENT. As our communities have become more crowded, life in them has become more impersonal. The idea of the community itself seems to be disappearing. It is thus more difficult to involve citizens representing a wide spectrum of people from the community in the planning process. This has resulted in planning *for* rather than *with* people with the consequence that programs growing out of such partisan planning are rejected and fail. The erosion of citizen interest is only one manifestation of the sense of powerlessness and separation from the sources of power that most people feel today. In such a situation it is not surprising that alienation from society, and strong feelings of frustration and anger

are widespread. These are not the circumstances that enhance trust in the planning process.

The Process of Community Problem-Solving

Effective community organization requires that strategies in problem-solving must be broadened from social problem management to include a community development approach.[4] That is, to plan effectively for problems like juvenile delinquency, the scope of the planner's consideration must go beyond ways to simply control the range and consequences of the delinquent's behavior. He must examine the degree to which the problem may be associated with some system dysfunction. The inability of the community to provide certain basic necessities—physical and social—often is considered as a contributing factor to serious maladaptive behavior of individuals and groups.

Carrying this idea further, the problem of delinquency may be viewed as being caused in four different ways, each of which may be a true but insufficient explanation.[5]

1. Delinquency sometimes is seen as a consequence of insufficient concern for youth, and inadequate functioning of youth-serving agencies. This perception of the cause of delinquency directs the planner to identify where the failures exist and hopefully to enlist the aid of interested citizens to plan for provision of improved recreational, cultural, and spiritual programs in the community. This approach places the planner in the role commonly identified as an *enabler* because of the primacy placed upon enabling groups to become effective in planning for community needs.

2. The failure of social organizations such as courts, schools, public housing projects, the outmoded approaches of some organizations serving young people, and political factors are considered primary causes of delinquency by some individuals and groups. The idea of a power deficit is central to this position. It is thought that delinquency is a response to powerlessness at the hands of social institutions. The planner's role can be described as an *advocate* from this point of view. He becomes identified with goals of social change through channels that legitimately challenge established institutional practices.

Demonstration projects that highlight new and improved ways of serving the community may be included among the advocate's efforts.

3. When delinquency is thought to be a symptom of basic societal defects, it is seen as primarily a defensive or compensating strategy against unfair circumstances and failure of the power structure to remove oppressive elements in society. This position contains a sense of deep social pathology and calls upon the planner to be an *organizer* who mobilizes grass roots' militant action against the identified sources of social defect. Various civil rights movements characterize this approach.

4. Finally, delinquency may be viewed as being related to family or local community influences that create anti-social attitudes and values, and promote delinquent behavior. An individual exposed to such influences is thus not permitted by his environment to develop appropriate social responses. Included in this view is the idea that some individuals may make delinquent choices because of some personal character defect that has developed out of faulty family experiences or a genetic deficiency. Following from this position, the planner assumes the role of *developer*. His goal is to involve the community in an understanding of its problem, and to work with indigenous community interests to achieve a solution to the problems that concern them, and on their own terms. The key to this approach is in persuading local people to assume responsibility in the planning process.

To take the position that any one of these explanations of delinquency contains the root cause of all delinquent behavior is to oversimplify an extremely complex social problem. However, all of them taken together provide a broad base from which planning can take place. This would direct the planner to consider each of the four planning roles—enabler, advocate, organizer, and developer—as appropriate at various times and places.

To control anti-social behavior, however, management strategies are necessary to protect society and at the same time provide opportunities for the delinquent to become rehabilitated and to grow into a normal, productive adult. But for prevention, broad development strategies are more appropriate. The strategy of community development aims toward development of policies and programs that would reduce the number of youth who become delinquent. This requires active collaboration of police and corrections personnel with other professions. It also requires intervention into institutions having crucial roles in the lives of youth. Schools, the courts, and the church are examples of social institutions which are necessary participants to such planning.

Required Tactical Activities

Unfortunately, one of the most common methods for decision-making in the field of public policy is reliance upon intuition. Little or no effort is made either to structure the problem or to determine cause and effect relationships. The intuitive approach allows a solution to evolve out of a subconscious process based upon acquaintance with the problem. When using this method, the decision-maker relies mainly on *practice-wisdom* and *living with the problem* as principal sources of data. Such decisions are inherently subjective and contain reflections of personal or group bias that may contribute more to the problem than to the solution. This process is in no sense analytic. Reliance on expert opinion or committee studies are alternative approaches that may reduce bias to the extent that they engage in a reasonable and impartial examination of the facts.

In contrast to these alternatives, the analytic approach is accessible to critical examination and can be replicated by others. It, too, is subjective to the extent that human judgement must augment the findings of any public policy study. But scientific analysis can reduce judgemental error in a way that simple intuition cannot.

The process of *systems analysis,* then, becomes the basic tactical activity in any strategy of community problem-solving. It consists of five elements of analysis that are present in every analysis of choice.[6]

1. *The Objectives.* In selecting a course of action, systems analysis requires first a determination of what objectives the decision-makers are or should be attempting to attain through the options that are open to them. The determination of objectives then forms the basis on which later considerations dealing with costs and benefits can be evaluated.

2. *The Alternatives.* The range of means by which the objectives can be attained are the alternatives. They need not perform the same

functions or be substitutes for one another. For example, to reduce juvenile delinquency, early engagement of youth in occupational careers, early identification and treatment of family breakdown, and increased recreational resources are all possible alternatives.

3. *The Costs.* When thinking of costs, analysis must include not only money costs of a particular alternative but also the cost of additional resources that will no longer be available for other uses. Thus we must consider what opportunities are being precluded in some future time period by each alternative we might select, for this too is a cost.

4. *The Model.* To the extent possible, the analyst develops a model that abstracts the features of the situation relevant to the problem under study. Its role is to estimate the consequences of a choice—the costs and the power of each alternative to achieve the objective. Models may be constructed as gaming exercises, pencil and paper constructs, or pilot demonstrations.

5. *Criteria.* To order or rank the alternatives under consideration, rules or standards for ranking must be established. These become the criteria which provide the means of measuring cost and performance of the alternatives under consideration.

The process of analysis advances by successive approximation through five stages that overlap but also are distinct. (1) In the *conceptual phase,* objectives are clarified, issues are defined, and the limits of the problem are set. (2) In the *research phase,* a search is made for information, relationships, and promising alternative programs of action. (3) The *analytic phase* involves evaluation of alternatives, examination of models, prediction of consequences of various actions, and comparison of alternatives. (4) In the *judgement phase,* interpretations are made and a course of action is selected. (5) Finally, in the *verification phase,* the program is evaluated, tested for effectiveness and either carried on or modified. The following figure illustrates the process of analysis as a process of successive approximation and advancement to further planning.

Application of Analytic Process to Juvenile Delinquency

It is seldom that the activities are so neatly separated as the illustration would suggest. Once an effective process of planning is in operation, many of the phases of the process occur simultaneously.

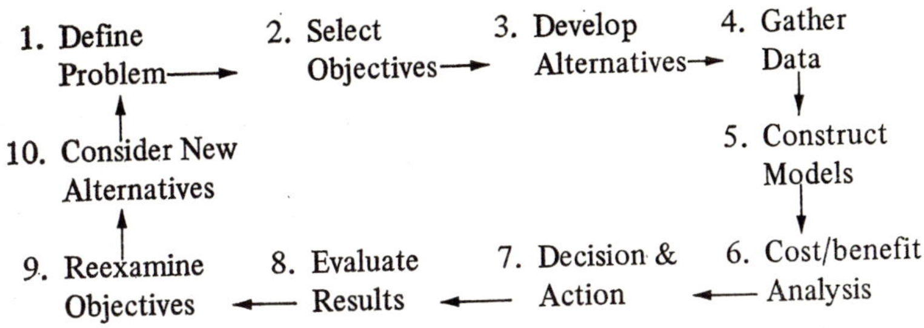

Figure 10-1 The process of successive approximation

It is typical, for example, that the search for data permeates the whole analysis process. Applied to the problem of juvenile delinquency, the planning task might be outlined as follows:

1. Define and limit the problem. Are we contributing to the development of a wide range assault on basic causes of delinquency or is the decision limited to improving and extending a promising existing program?
2. Classify the objectives or goals to be achieved. Are we striving to control, manage, and deter delinquency and limit its social consequences, or are we aiming for a more comprehensive preventive program?
3. Forecast the social and political environment in which the proposed system is to operate. Are we to consider scenarios in which there is a degeneration of community stability and an accompanying increase of crises, a reduction of community tensions, or a stable and relatively unchanged set of social circumstances?
4. Establish ways to measure the degree of goal attainment based upon some standard level of law violation by youth.
5. Identify and describe the alternative programs that hold promise of achieving the established goals, and develop appropriate criteria for choosing from among these programs.
6. Select the most promising approaches. Shall they be compared on the basis of a fixed budget or shall goal achievement effectiveness be the primary consideration?
7. Explore the money costs of the program and of anticipated related changes and development costs. Estimate non-monetary costs such as the use of resources that will no longer be available for other desirable purposes. Are there important resource and technological

restraints? Are there undesirable consequences that may interfere with other programs?

8. Identify the risks and indicate the time span for development. Are we seeking to develop techniques that are departures from current practice and knowledge, or are we aiming to improve current capabilities?

9. Thoroughly explore major uncertainties, and test the proposal for its sensitivity to the problem.

10. Consider all factors against what we think we have some knowledge about in terms of outcomes and program effectiveness.

11. Decide what can be recommended on the basis of the analysis.

12. Make explicit and document the analysis including the rationale and assumptions on which the work was based. Clearly describe the important features of the proposal, its expected capabilities, the costs and resources needed in order that the analysis can be seen to form a clear imperative for the recommended choice.

The Contribution of Law Enforcement Personnel to Community Planning

The analysis of a social problem described in the previous section can be seen as giving guidance to the planning group to the extent that consequences of various options open to the planners have been evaluated. The analysis should form the basis for cooperative planning among the interested segments of the community.

However, even after the study of the problem has been completed, there are still unanswered questions to be considered. Objectives must be agreed upon before means can be selected. The choice is thus between goals and objectives, though ostensibly it is between alternative programs. But decisions about objectives remain judgements, a process requiring participation by a broad range of interests; it is non-analytic. It is, rather a reconciliation of views, opinions, and interests.

For a number of reasons the ideas and purposes of police and corrections personnel are important to community planning. Quite apart from the public relations values of participation in citizen and professional planning groups, the police have important information to impart. Such participation enables police to interpret this role, encourage community support, and it gives them an opportunity to lend constructive influence to public policy formulation.[8] This casts police and corrections professionals in the role of participant experts in planning with a constituency made up of lay and professional community members.

The community planning process is not simply a matter of national consideration of social problems. Beyond the task of problem analysis is the process of reconciliation of goals, values, and priorities. To accomplish this effectively by satisfying the variety of community interests that generally are represented in such deliberations, participation of the representatives of the various constituencies must be present at all stages of the planning process. This requirement in community planning is a complication at the same time that it is an opportunity. Because of their action orientation, police may view the protracted discussions that attend the community planning process to be a needless expenditure of scarce manpower time. On the other hand, participation by police in planning can be of decisive significance in influencing policies that effect the community effort to reduce crime and delinquency. It also contributes to the education of all who participate in the process. Since police are as one with the community they serve, to benefit one is to enhance the other.

FOOTNOTES

[1]Egon Bittner, *The Functions of the Police in Modern Society,* Chevy Chase, (Nev.: NIMH Center for Studies of Crime and Delinquency, 1970), p. 114.

[2]John P. Kenney and Dan G. Pursuit, *Police Work With Juveniles and The Administration of Juvenile Justice* (Springfield: Thomas, Fourth Edition, 1970), p. 398.

[3]For a discussion of this concept, see David Braybrooke and Charles E. Lindblom, *A Strategy of Decision* (New York: The Free Press of Glencoe, 1963), Chapter 5.

[4]John B. Turner, "Relation of Health and Welfare Planning to Social Change and Social Development," *Social Work and Social Planning* (New York: NASW, 1964), p. 12.

[5]Irving, A. Spergel, *Community Problem Solving: The Delinquency Example* (Chicago: University of Chicago Press, 1969), p. 62 ff.

[6]E. S. Quade, and W. I. Boucher, eds., *Systems Analysis and Policy Planning: Applications in Defense* (New York: American Elsevier Publishing Company, Inc., 1968), p. 12.

[7]Adapted from E. S. Quade, *Ibid.*

[8]Kenney and Pursuit, *op. cit.*, pp. 405-407.

CHAPTER 11

GUIDELINES FOR DEVELOPING MORE EFFECTIVE COORDINATION IN THE JUVENILE JUSTICE SYSTEM

DAN G. PURSUIT

COMMANDING OFFICERS OF police juvenile units and middle managers in probation, institutional care and parole, must assume more dynamic roles in order to maximize coordination and understanding within the juvenile justice system.

Following are some suggested guidelines which could help to generate more effective relationships.

Departmental Training

Each agency might develop appropriate recruit and in-service training programs which emphasize improved understanding and appreciation of the purposes and functions of all system components.

Speakers from the various agencies could be invited to present their organizations' roles and clarify any misunderstandings. Distribution of departmental printed materials can also be most helpful.

Speakers need to explain how their departments inputs and procedures affect the work load of the other system components.

Police departments can also provide opportunities for court or correctional personnel to ride in squad cars to enhance understanding of daily police operations.

As the result of such training programs, staff members should begin to see themselves not only as police or correctional specialists but also as total system coordinators.

Joint Training

Experimental joint training programs for new employees might be established to include police, court and correctional personnel. Local colleges or universities could be involved in developing core curriculum materials which would be pertinent for all system employees. All such new employees would thus benefit from an early exposure to system concepts and would gain much from classroom interactions.

College and University Programs

Educational institutions can play an important role by expanding their offerings to include more courses and seminars on the criminal justice system as a whole. Whenever possible, efforts should be made to enroll students representing all of the components.

System concepts still need to be emphasized even in such specialized courses as Police Administration, etc.

Many undergraduate and graduate courses provide an opportunity for instructors to present speakers from the various agencies. In addition, field trips to the key departments can also be arranged to provide first hand knowledge of operations.

Organizational Structure

System effectiveness can be enhanced by new organizational structures which give greater emphasis to the coordinative function.

In this regard the International Association of Chiefs of Police reported an innovative trend in its 1971 publication, *The Police Role and Juvenile Delinquency* authored by Richard W. Kobetz. It described the trend to develop a bureau of crime prevention to emphasize crime prevention and community service activities and to serve as a communication source between the department and the public. Such a bureau consolidates similar functions into one unit: community relations and human relations, juvenile, public information and miscellaneous preventive activities such as police—school and crime prevention programs.

In carrying out these functions such a bureau could easily include efforts to maximize system coordination. Similar organizational restructuring could be implemented in correctional agencies.

Professional Relationships

More cooperative relationships can also be developed through some of the following activities.

— County, regional and state criminal justice councils provide a medium to plan innovative programs and help resolve selected conflicts within the system. (See Appendix for federal sources of funds to support new programs.)

— A panel of representative juvenile justice speakers might be organized for presentations before interested civic groups, service clubs, etc. so citizens can understand the need for system coordination.

— Work exchange experiences could be provided for selected personnel so that a police officer might spend a week or so in a correctional agency and vice versa.

— Monthly or quarterly luncheon meetings might be held for representatives of all components to focus on system improvement. These meetings could also be opened to educators, social workers, recreation leaders, etc.

— Professional associations might encourage associate or honorary memberships for personnel from other professions or disciplines. Thus an association of police juvenile officers might have some members from the courts and from corrections.

— Professional conferences could include speakers or panels representing all system components.

— Professional associations might provide a special award for leaders who develop innovative programs which increase system effectiveness.

— Joint planning between system leaders needs to be done to develop incentives which would motivate police executives to encourage greater use of diversion policies. County or state subsidies to local police departments for innovative prevention and diversion programs might be considered.

— System representatives should also participate actively as members of community organization entities such as coordinating councils, welfare planning councils, councils of social agencies, etc.

It is through these broad planning organizations that leaders in the juvenile justice system can develop more effective relationships with leaders in interfacing systems such as health, welfare, recreation, employment, etc.

SECTION FOUR

YOUTH DEVELOPMENT AND DELINQUENCY PREVENTION

The Youth Development and Delinquency Prevention Administration of the U.S. Department of Health, Education, and Welfare is making concerted efforts to develop more effective strategies to prevent delinquency.

This section is devoted to three current statements on this challenging task, beginning with the Administrations own national strategy and followed by presentations prepared with YDDPA support by eminent sociologists: LeMar T. Empey and Lloyd Ohlin.

CHAPTER 12

NATIONAL STRATEGY FOR YOUTH DEVELOPMENT AND DELINQUENCY PREVENTION

Youth Development and Delinquency Prevention Administration

PROGRAMS FOR THE EFFECTIVE prevention and control of juvenile delinquency and youth crime continue to elude decision-makers at the national, state, and local levels. Despite rapidly expanding efforts during recent years, illegal behavior by young people has grown more extensive since the post World War II period. During the past decade, especially, the problem has been further confounded by the emergence of new patterns of group dissidence on the part of many young people who were formerly free of highly visible forms of illegal activity. Moreover, among some youths today, both relatively rich and poor alike, dissidence in far too many instances has been replaced by collective withdrawal and sometimes calculated violence. Thus, today as yesterday, the vast bulk of young violators continues to be involved in petty theft, truancy, and in some instances, vandalism. But there have now been added to these familiar forms of delinquency such violations as massive drug abuse and planned violence against established institutions.

Clearly, a fresh look at the problem is warranted. This needs to be based on a reassessment of present public policies for dealing with youthful deviance and on the development of new linkages between an understanding of what causes such activities and what can and should be done about them in policy terms at the Federal, State, and local levels. Unfortunately, much of what is known is not presently being used to direct intervention strategies. Much of what needs to be learned is not even being addressed in a systematic and comprehensive manner.

The development of a national strategy with respect to these problems should begin by addressing the question of why and under what conditions young people lead essentially lawabiding lives, not the question of why so many of them violate the law. The most widely accepted answer appears to be that most of the nation's youth avoid participating in patterned delinquent activities because they have been provided with ready access to socially acceptable, responsible, and personally gratifying social roles in the areas of family life, education, recreation, religion, and eventually work.

Second, access to such roles seems simultaneously to furnish their incumbents a degree of legitimate social protection from the consequences of their occasional illegal behavior. Thus, they avoid the entrapment of being *labeled* as out-of-step and troublemakers by the schools, the police, the courts, and subsequently being placed on probation or committed to the care of various correctional agencies or institutions. The avoidance of such labels and commitments by diversion from the juvenile justice system reduces the likelihood of mutual rejection and alienation between young people and the representatives of the adult world. In this way, for most of the youth group the often escalating and reciprocal processes of individual and group estrangement are not activated and accentuated.

These propositions furnish a basic perspective on the problem of delinquency by linking it firmly to specific types of failure on the part of specific social institutions as they seek to relate to young people, and, in turn, to the negative reactions of young people to such institutions when they find them wanting. It follows from this that the development of a viable national strategy for the prevention and reduction of delinquency rests on the identification, assessment, and alteration of those features of institutional functioning that impede and obstruct a favorable course of youth development for all youths, particularly those whose social situation makes them most prone to the development of delinquent careers and to participation in collective forms of withdrawal and deviancy.

This institutional focus does not overlook the importance of direct work with individuals and families. Attention must be given to services directed at the prevention of individual delinquency as well as to the rehabilitation of youths already involved with law enforcement or correctional agencies. The institutional focus emphasized in this strategy identifies those features of the social environment whose interaction with human personality produces malignant behavioral effects, and calls attention to the need to deal with such conditions on three levels of intervention: community, family, and individual. In brief, a youth development approach to delinquency prevention takes an institutional focus as its point of origin, considers the compounding effects of institutional failure, and traces the effects of such failure through to their outcomes in human personality and behavior.

Further, a strategy of delinquency prevention that focuses on institutional misalignments in no way denies the importance of effective law enforcement. This is essential for the protection of the community. There exists a necessary and useful division of labor between such agencies of formal control as the police, the judiciary, and corrections, on the one hand, and the institutions responsible for delinquency prevention and youth development on the other. At the same time it must be recognized that the manner in which control functions are performed may frequently confound the problem of prevention. Overly aggressive police action often mobilizes defensive opposition to law enforcement; hurried and perfunctory judicial proceedings frequently fail to communicate a sense of fairness and justice to the young; and corrections commonly intensify delinquent attitudes by radically isolating offenders from law-abiding peers. Methods of control require careful and continuous review with respect to their capacity to reverse law violating patterns of behavior.

Just as various sources of weakness in the social fabric may operate as causes of delinquency, the contexts in which delinquent behavior occurs are similarly varied. Four such contexts, or social settings, may be identified: the inner-city slum areas; the suburbs; the rural community; and the college and high school campus. In each of these social settings, the elements that obstruct youth development and operate to weaken the young person's tie to the social order, as well as the types of events and situations that precipitate episodes of delinquent or destructive activity, combine in many different ways. Each of these contexts has unique features; no single type of program of intervention is likely to be able to deal effectively with all. Neither the patterns of delinquency nor their significance for the career of the person or the safety of the community are identical in each of these social settings. Within each of these social settings, moreover, it is possible to specify the types of institutional activities that have the most direct and immediate impact on the emerging commitment of many youths to violate the legal norms of society. These activities may be thought of as occurring in and around distictive *arenas of action,* wherein adolescents forge their identities with respect to their support or rejection of lawful activities.

In inner-city slum areas, for example, a primary arena of action is the school, notably the secondary school, where the educational processes of ranking and rating frequently tend to segregate nonachievers into depreciated status groups. A wealth of available evidence clearly indicates that such status groups have persistently served as centers for the development of oppositional and often explicitly delinquent subcultures.

A second arena in the slum, integrally related to the first, but much less formal in its social structure and organization, is the local community or neighborhood. Here, for a variety of reasons, group and cultural support is given to youthful alienation, withdrawal, and delinquency. Here linkages are forged between younger youths who are in the market for a delinquent solution and older, more established and sophisticated career deviants. Here the more conventional socializing agencies of family and church, for example, frequently fail to perform adequately their functions and the culture of the street takes hold.

A third arena of critical activity in slum communities is represented by encounters between the young and the law enforcement, judicial, and correctional agencies. The central problems here turn on questions of the deterrent effect of invoking the official machiney of the juvenile justice system in response to particular types of offenses, as opposed to more informal procedures for dealing with infractions through the involvement of more informal and less stigmatizing mechanisms. Related questions pertain to the purposes, program content, and efficiency of official control agencies, specifically the police, courts, and corrections.

For the three other social settings—the suburbs, the rural community, and the college and high school campus—the developmental problems of youth which may eventuate in delinquency would seem to require specification of crucial arenas of action peculiar to each setting. Most likely each of the social settings, with its particular crucial arenas, represents a distinctive problem which, in turn, requires a different local approach and strategy. Yet, it seems likely that the three underlying principles described earlier—access to acceptable social roles, escape from the entrapment of labeling, and avoidance of the reciprocal processes of rejection, alienation, and estrangement—are applicable in central ways in all four social settings. However, the current state of knowledge, as well as the *state of the art,* do not permit altogether confident prescription. What is clearly called for is a carefully differentiated approach keyed to what may become recognized with experience as basic differences in the four social settings identified.

Such a differentiated approach requires not only a capactiy to distinguish between the significant features of different social settings, but also the capacity to distinguish between more conventional or traditional forms of delinquency and more recent cultural, political, and social developments which have added novel features to those that have characterized youth and delinquency problems for some time. Of these, two may be tentatively identified: growing ideological hostility among youths to what is globally referred to as the *establishment;* and the politicalization of some forms of serious illegal activity in response to the prejudice endemic in American society.

These developments are not merely novel in themselves. They also pose new problems of control and prevention. They tend to generate massive collective infraction of law, manifested in widespread violations of the drug abuse laws, campus riots, violent street gang, activity now justified by reference to racial injustice, and prison rebellions similarly justified. In effect, delinquency promises to become increasingly politicalized. It may be anticipated as a consequence that interaction between control agencies and some youth groups will move increasingly to the collective level, generating unprecedented problems of prevention as well. With increasing frequency the juvenile justice system is likely to be confronted with individuals and groups whose dissident, deviant, and illegal acts received collective ideological support. This trend is currently in an incipient, but highly visible, stage. Should it continue to grow, the problem of delinquency is likely to be transformed in part from the conventional and familiar one of the control of the individual to a massive problem at the political level.

These developments suggest that the range of elements affecting youth development and delinquency prevention has been decisively widened during the past decade. Elements that have been added appear to be related to possible changes in the cultural values of American society to which many youth groups are most sensitively attuned. Such change may be responsible for the appearance of new social types and social roles whose function, in part, has been to innovate and legitimate novel modes of dissident and deviant behavior. Transformations of this kind are too recent in origin to permit accurate analysis of their full meaning and nature. As a basis for evolving a satisfactory national strategy for dealing with this problem, there is need for a continuing assessment of the youth scene, conducted in a sustained and systematic manner.

In the meantime, one possible approach to this problem is suggested by the fact that there is currently in the structures of Federal, State and local governments no agency which can claim a wide constituency among youth. This situation contrasts starkly with agency-constituency relationships involving business and commerce, labor, agriculture, and even such special interest groups as war veterans. Shifts in relationships among social classes, ethnic groups, interest groups, and age groups, all consequent to ongoing social change in American society, have produced in the past innovations in the structure and functions of government agencies. At the present juncture one possibility may be to provide youth groups with an established channel of access to government and other bureaucratic decision making. Such a move may serve to reduce the hostility and suspicion that some of the most problem-solving segments of the youth groups now direct toward government, colleges, and industry, and serve to restore the credibility of these institutions in the eyes of youth.

The foregoing analysis of the youth development and delinquency prevention problem has identified as its central feature certain weaknesses and inadequacies of institutions crucial in the socialization of the young, and the reactions of the youth to these failures. The implied theory of institutional misalignment suggests as the appropriate strategy of intervention efforts to alter constructively those features of agencies and institutions having predictably negative consequences. The strategy focuses explicitly on those aspects of institutional design, program, and procedure that have been seen to generate alienation in the youth population.

The content of programs at the local level capable of implementing this strategy can be indicated at the moment in only the most general terms. Needed, therefore, as the initial phase in the orderly development of a national policy is a preliminary period for the demonstration and testing of the approach proposed here. Since the problem of youth development and delinquency prevention exhibits different features in various social locations, combining the elements obstructing favorable youth development in different ways, the intervention strategy should itself be similarly differentiated.

Required as a first step in the identification of a minimum set of representative social and/or geographic niches in the structure of society whose unique features may be ascertained and addressed. As has been indicated, these have been identified as the inner city, the rural community, the suburbs, and the college and high school campus. No single program format is likely to be responsive to the distinctive problems indigenous to each of these settings.

The most expedient way of moving rapidly toward the specification of useful program content is to establish a set of program planning and monitoring task forces to demonstrate and test effective procedures in each of the social settings specified. One task force or group for each of the four social settings identified would be charged with mounting programs in that setting under the most viable of local auspices. A fifth overall task force with more general responsibilities for advancing the new national strategy and for evaluating program outcome would also seem appropriate.

CHAPTER 13

DELINQUENCY PREVENTION STRATEGIES

LAMAR T. EMPEY AND STEVEN G. LUBECK

IN SETTING THE STAGE for this paper, I should like to present a body of sociological theory on delinquency which, in addition to its interest to the scientific community, has enjoyed rather wide acceptance among non-scientists as well. Then, before attempting to assess the relevance of the theory for preventive purposes, I should like to review it in light of emerging evidence, especially in terms of the detailed test of the theory involving such disparate groups as serious delinquents and non-delinquents in largely rural Utah, and similar groups in urban Los Angeles. This review will provide a useful preface to a discussion of prevention strategies.

The Theory

Without going into all the subtleties of the theoretical argument, its main points might be summarized as follows:[1]

1. Official delinquency is primarily a lower-class phenomenon (Shaw and McKay, 1942; Dirksen, 1948; Wattenberg and Balistrieri, 1950; Burgess, 1952; Cohen, 1955; Eaton and Polk, 1961). As the President's Crime Commission (1967) put it, "Delinquents tend to come from backgrounds of social and economic deprivation. Their families tend to have lower than average incomes and social status . . . It is inescapable that juvenile delinquency is directly related to conditions bred by poverty."

2. Lower-class children do not possess the familial and other institutional resources by which to acquire the requisite cognitive and social skills to cope with grade school environment, or to succeed in other ways defined as important by American society (Deutsch, 1967; Dennis, 1960; Goldfarb, 1953; Hunt, 1961). These disabilities are especially acute among those who eventually become delinquent (Shulman, 1949; Monahan, 1957; Toby, 1957; Reiss and Rhodes, 1961; Short and Strodtbeck, 1965).

3. The failure of these juveniles to achieve in school and community is productive of strain—a lowered sense of self-worth, alienation, and a loss of status (Merton, 1957; Cohen, 1955). As Cloward and Ohlin (1960) put it,

> The disparity between what lower-class youth are led to want and what is actually available to them is the source of a major problem of adjustment. . . . Faced with limitations or legitimate avenues of access to [conventional] goals, and unable to revise their aspirations downward, they experience intense frustration; the exploration of nonconformist alternatives may be the result.

4. Failing to find satisfaction in conventional pursuits, a significant number of these juveniles find refuge in deviant peer groups (Tannenbaum, 1938; Thrasher, 1927; Shaw and McKay, 1942; Cohen, 1955; Cloward and Ohlin, 1960). Membership in such groups serves as an alternative means for achieving the status, recognition, and sense of belonging which others achieve through conventional means.

5. Not all, but a significant proportion of the delinquent acts that are committed, derive their meaning from these groups. They provide the rationalizations, the techniques, and the socio-psychological support necessary to withstand the moral and legal encroachments of legitimate society (Cohen, 1955; Cloward and Ohlin, 1960). In summary, this theoretical argument might be diagrammed as follows:

Test of Theory

The sample. The theory was tested on a purposive sample of 482 serious delinquents (249 in Utah and 233 in Los Angeles), and 185

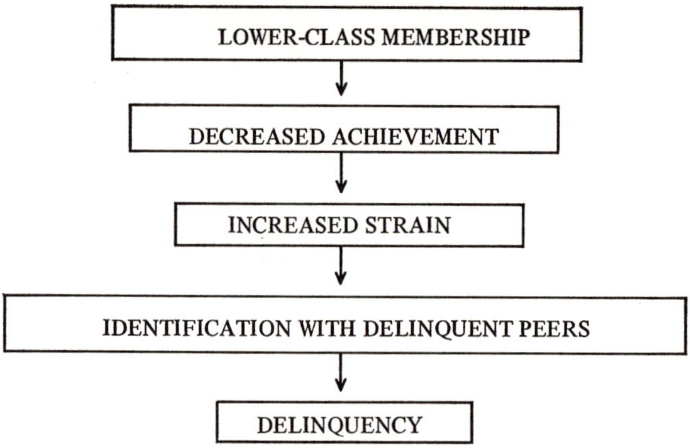

Figure 13-1

nondelinquents (100 in Utah and 85 in Los Angeles). While the overall sample was well distributed over the class structure—more than 1/2 from lower levels, about 1/3 from lower middle and middle levels, and less than 1/5 from upper levels—it may have been deficient in terms of minority representation. In Utah, there were virtually no minorities included, since few reside there; in Los Angeles, only about 1/4 were of minority status, mostly black.

The Findings. Perhaps the most significant finding was the fact that, in neither location, was social class of much explanatory value. It did not help to explain any of the major concepts of the theory: lack of achievement, a high degree of strain, identification with peers, or official delinquency itself. These factors were related as much to membership in other class levels as to lower class membership.

This result tends to support the findings of recent studies using self-reported, and thus non-official delinquency. These studies seriously question the existence of a universal, causal relationship between social class and law-violating behavior (Nye, Short, et al., 1958; Clark and Wenninger, 1962; Dentler and Monroe, 1961; Porterfield, 1946; Reiss and Rhodes, 1961; Empey, 1967; Empey and Erickson, 1966; Gold, 1966). They suggest that middle as well as lower class adolescents are involved in a large amount of illegal behavior. What is significant, further, is the fact that our finding, using official criteria, came up with much the same result.

It is of further interest to note that our findings are also similar to those of Polk (1965) in his study of official delinquency in Lane County, Oregon. As in this case, Polk found that delinquency was more highly related to poor adjustment in school than it was to social class. He concluded that social class, by itself, is simply too global a concept to be of much use as an explanatory variable. Theories and intervention models are needed which take better account of the interlocking configurations of economic, ethnic, familial, and educational variables as they operate within, as well as between, different class levels.

Beyond social class, there was some general confirmation for the theory in our findings: decreased achievement was associated with increased strain; increased strain was related to identification with peers; and identification with peers was related to official delinquency. However, the analysis also pinpointed certain subtleties that were not taken into account in the theory, subtleties which would require attention before the utility of the theory could be maximized.

First, we found that some of our measures of achievement, such as school awards, extra-curricular activities, and number of jobs held were relatively poor predictors either of other variables in the theory or of delinquency itself. Meanwhile, one measure—school grades—was highly predictive.

Second, we found that family separation and relationships with parents—variables which are not ordinarily included in sociological formulations—were highly predictive, especially of delinquency. Therefore, if one combined these family measures with school performance, as indicated by the hard criterion of grades, he would have a measure that was far more efficient in predicting both strain and delinquency than the singular measure of achievement.

Some other research findings were supportive of this notion. Short and Strodtbeck (1965), for example, found that gang boys, when compared with non-gang boys of a similar or different class level, were characterized by a long list of disabilities which led to, or were caused by, their lack of effective and rewarding ties with major societal institutions: limited social and technical skills, a low capacity for self-assertion, lower intelligence scores, and even a tendency to hold their own friends to low esteem.

In a similar way, Matza (1964) points out that juveniles, and especially delinquents, exist within a narrow life space centering around the family, school, and peers. Consequently, an especially difficult situation is created for any individual who is cut off from two of these three major sources of support. "Stripped of moral guidance . . . ," says Matza (1964), "he momentarily exists in a stark and frightening isolation." He oftens turns to his peers for moral guidance, but because of the problems they share with him, they cannot adequately fill the gap. The situation is such as to further exacerbate his mood of fatalism and strain, and to increase the likelihood of further deviance.

Third, our findings were such as to question the sequential development of delinquency as implied by the original formulation; that is, from lack of achievement or institutional ties, to strain, to identification with peers, to delinquency. If anything, the findings compounded that chain, suggesting a series of *feedback loops* which added great complexity to the delinquency developing sequence. These feedback loops seem to be most apparent at two places.

The first involved the relationship between lack of institutional ties and strain. The absence of satisfying relationships with parents and school produces strain, strain in turn feeds back and further worsens already tenuous, institutional ties. The result is a circular, and everworsening problem, which explains, we believe, the reason that both poor institutional ties and strain have an extremely high and direct relationship to delinquency, rather than always being mediated by the intervening variables of peer identification.

The second feedback loop is related to the one just described, but occurred further along the chain. The original, theoretical model suggested that peer identification was an intervening variable between strain and delinquency; that is, it could not be assumed that poor institutional ties and strain would lead directly to delinquency. The moral support of peers and the learning of techniques and rationalizations were a necessary, intermediate step. Our findings, however, suggest a modification of this notion.

While they did not discredit the importance of peers, they seemed to suggest that identification with peers may result from, as well as precede, being officially defined as delinquent. This idea was expressed by Tannenbaum a long time ago. At the outset, he argued, boys who are unintegrated into the institutional paths of society engage in mischievous and annoying behavior, breaking windows, truancy, defying authority. As the community imposed increasing sanctions upon them, especially when it officially defines them as delinquent, they are forced ever further into delinquent group associations as a refuge. Thus, a self-fulfilling prophecy—a second feedback loop—is set up which tends to evoke and make worse the very behavior which was complained about in the first place. That is why, as Tannenbaum suggested, the process of labeling a person deviant and then making him self-conscious of that label, may make the problem worse, not better. This is what Tannenbaum called the *dramatization of evil.*

If he is correct, then we would want to introduce the concept of *stigma* to the theory. If that were done then the second feedback loop might go from an initial and weak identification with peers to delinquency, to stigma, and then back again to strain. Like the first loop, it might imply an ever-worsening series of problems. The fact that we have a significant number of official recidivists, testifies to the necessity to be concerned with this feedback loop.

By way of summary, the reformulated theory might be diagrammed as follows:

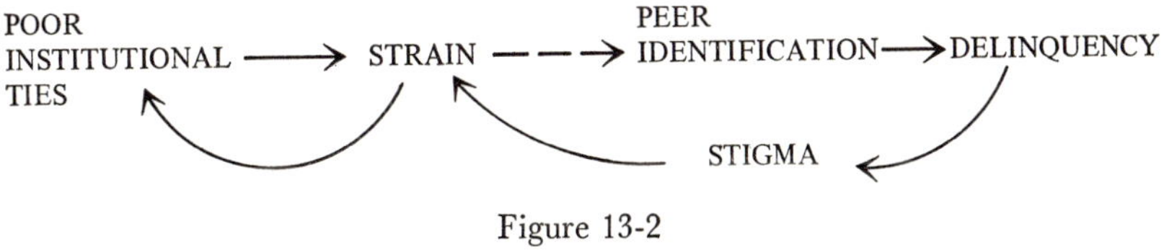

Figure 13-2

As can be seen, poor institutional ties with family and school produce strain; these factors comprise the first feedback loop. When children react to this strain, the first thing that is likely to occur is a worsening of the already tenuous ties. The loop is completed. This progressive deterioration leads, in turn, to an increasing association with other boys having similar problems. But while this association may be quite innocent in terms of the way the boys see it—they are in search, primarily, of companionship—it leads to increasing condemnation by people in authority. When that condemnation results in official sanctioning, suspension from school or, worse still, official adjudication as delinquent, then the problem, at least for many boys, is compounded; the second feedback loop is completed. Unless broken institutional fences can be mended, the stigma of official sanctioning only compounds the strain, strengthens ties to delinquent peers, and leads to a repetition of the whole pattern.

Priorities for Prevention

Since we are concerned primarily with prevention, how could such a formulation lead to the establishment of intervention priorities? The answer to that question would depend upon the age of the population one had in mind and whether one were interested in prevention or rehabilitation. For example, if one were dealing with pre-adolescents, especially young children, then the greatest attention should be focused upon preventing the first feedback loop by improving institutional ties. If ways could be found by which to enhance the beneficial effects of family and school, then one would have to worry less about the growth of strain and the negative effects of peer association and official processing. It might be possible to avoid the negative and spiraling effects described in the first feedback loop.

On the other hand, if one were concerned with an older, but as yet unadjudicated group of juveniles, one for whom institutional ties were already weakened and strain intensified, then the task would be more difficult. The further one goes down the chain, the more one has to be concerned with undoing, as well as preventing, difficulties. Methods would be required, not only by which to enhance institutional ties, but to reduce the negative effects of strain and the tendency to take refuge in deviant subgroups. Therefore, priorities in this case would concentrate:

a. upon improving institutional ties; and
b. upon reducing strain.

Finally, if one were concerned with preventing recidivism in a group of already convicted offenders, especially adolescents, he would have to be concerned with the whole chain. Program priorities and methods would again be made progressively more complicated and more costly and would:

a. re-establish and improve institutional ties;
b. reduce strain introduced by the lack of institutional ties and the stigmatizing effects of official labeling; and
c. alter and provide alternatives for the moral support, the rationalizations and the rewards which may have been obtained by delinquent peers and activities.

These different sets of priorities, and the differences in programming they imply, make it clear why no single strategy is universally applicable to all populations, even given the same theory. The things that must be done, the funds and staffing that would be required, would vary markedly. In moving to assess these matters, therefore, the next issue that must be addressed is how one goes about operationalizing a program, taking into account the fact that different priorities will be required depending upon the population involved.

The answer to this question involves several steps. In discussing them, I should like to relate them to the theory which has already been presented. However, it should be noted that they could be adapted to other theories as well. The important point is that a theoretical base is an essential prerequisite for following the steps.

STEP 1. Define the target population. With this particular theory, one would want to decide whether it is to be composed of a very young group, a middle range, or a convicted group.

STEP 2. Set up specific procedures by which to identify the juveniles to be included in the target population. This is not a difficult task, if handled systematically and with reference to theory. However, it is a task that is almost universally ignored. It can be accomplished in a two-stage process.

First, for the young and middle-range groups, teachers may be the best source of information regarding those whose behavior is disruptive, who are not performing up to capacity, and for whom parental relations seem to be poor. For the older, convicted group, official court and welfare records, as well as school nominations, could be used.

Second, initial nominations can be validated and problems identified with greater precision by conducting a small pilot study. For example, given the theory presented earlier, this study might include at least four things:

a. a comprehensive assessment of each nominee's intellectual achievements through the administration of standardized achievement tests;
b. a study of his sociometric standing among his peers—who his network of friends are, the degree to which he is accepted or rejected by others, and whether his friends are well or only marginally integrated into the school;
c. what his family resources are—whether from a broken or otherwise disrupted home; and
d. whether he has been officially recorded as a problem case.

Step 3. Using the information gained in Step 2, set objectives for the program. Obviously, it is impossible in this paper to know what those objectives might be; they would depend upon the population selected. However, certain things merit attention.

It is ludicrous, for example, to follow the common route of saying that the objective for a program is to prevent delinquency. While the objective is an obvious and necessary one, it is also so global as to be almost meaningless. Instead, objectives should be relevant, first, to one of the three target populations and, second, to the problems of specific individuals within each target group. If, as recommended, a pilot study is conducted, vital information will be available by which to devise intervention procedures and plot progress for individuals as well as for the total group. The point is that, if our prevention efforts are to become more efficient, the administrators, the practitioners, and the research people involved must have more specific and precisely defined objectives than they have enjoyed in the past.

Step 4. The fourth step is closely related. It involves the writing of a contract in which the various people to be involved in the program—the administrators, the funding sources, the practitioners, and the researchers—would be signatories to a common agreement. The goal would be to specify, in precise terms, the basic objectives of the program, the general methods to be used, the costs involved, and the obligations of each of the signatories to the overall operation.

While this may seem to be an excessively formal and difficult step, the disastrous consequences of previous efforts at innovation and collaboration would seem to argue in favor of trying it. All too often, the various actors involved have engaged in new programs only to see their efforts go awry because they shared different fantasies as to what, and how, something was to be accomplished. Because expectations varied widely, a violation of those expectations was inevitable.

The writing of a contract might serve as a check on those signatories—especially administrators, funding sources, and practitioners —who often share unrealistic aspirations as to what can be achieved in any new approach. Likewise, it would constrain those researchers who are disinclined to devote the time and effort necessary to study and feed back findings which have pragmatic as well as theoretical implications. Hopefully, a contract might set the stage for a more realistic and productive endeavor.

Step 5. The fifth step involves the derivation of an intervention strategy. This strategy should be logically related to theory and to a set of priorities as determined by one's target population; that is, if the target population is young children, then priorities will be different than if it is an older, adjudicated groups of offenders.

Such a strategy might be comprised of two kinds of building blocks; (a) a set of intervention principles, and (b) a set of operational guidelines. The principles would be comprised of an abstract set of statements, derived from the basic theory, and would indicate how the problems of the target population should be addressed. Operational guidelines would be concerned with translating principles into action. What is the nature of the organization that is needed to operationalize intervention principles? What kinds of staff are required, and what roles shall they be expected to play? What kinds of training will be required? How shall the new program be integrated into the organizational networks that already exist?

While it is impossible to sketch all of the principles and guidelines that might be derived from this or any other theory, since many different models are possible, the following are illustrative of principles and guidelines that might be developed for young children.

The reformulated theory sketched earlier suggested that the institutional linkage of those children most inclined to become delinquent is usually poor. Therefore, the first principle is self-evident: the institutional ties of problem-children should be strengthened. The second is closely related: the spiraling and destructive effects of strain —dropping out of school, worsening relations with parents, teachers, and successful peers—should be prevented. Yet, despite the obvious character of these principles, there is reason to question whether their implications are generally acceptable.

The increasing tendency for the public, indeed the schools and many other agencies, to look to the police, the courts and corrections for solutions is contradictory to them. Not only does this tendency tend to exclude the family, school, and community from responsibilty, but it overlooks the fact that the most effective social control occurs only when young people are linked to, and have a stake in, these institutions, not legal ones. The latter are totally peripheral to the life-space of the child. Thus, societal aspirations for the juvenile justice system far exceed its capacity to produce results. The search for answers will have to focus even more than it has in the past upon the home and school.

In terms of operational guidelines, therefore, the following might be considered for the young target population.

a. Since it is usually in the school where problems are first identified, the school should occupy a central position in the prevention program. Ameliorative efforts should be an *integral* part of the school, not an appendage to it.

b. Planning for any new program, and the conduct of the pilot study mentioned earlier, should involve the school from the very beginning.

c. Funding for a prevention program should provide a high level of support for the school so that it might address the difficulties of children in a more effective way.

d. The home situation of the child should be diagnosed and a combined program of intervention planned, involving joint cooperation between the home and the school. Any worker assigned to this linkage task should have as his objective the reduction of the levels of bureaucracy and social distance between the teacher and the parent. This might be accomplished most effectively by centering these linking activities around the home room of the child. Furthermore, it might be useful to develop a parent organization associated, not with the total school, but with the home room so that the teacher and any other professional personnel might have the assistance of an indigenous group of parents. They might serve as a better bridge to problem families than officially designated workers. If carefully selected, they might, at the very least, be an important resource.

e. Efforts should be made to improve the relations of the child who has problems with his more successful peers. This might be accomplished by asking successful children to act as a sponsor, a friend, and even a tutor for the difficult child. Conversely, as the subject improved, his role might be switched so that he might act as a sponsor or tutor. The idea would be to redefine his role by involving him in a network of relatively successful children.

f. Once basic problems have been identified for each child—scholastic, familial, and interpersonal—a specific set of objectives should be set for him, and steps toward these objectives assessed at definite intervals. This monitoring procedure would not only constitute an important source of information in implementing the program, but would partake of a hard measure of success, namely, the ability of the child to progress satisfactorily in his academic and extracurricular activities.

In summary, guidelines such as these would be designed to provide substance for the two major intervention principles. The objectives would be to do everything possible to keep children on the major institutional track in society, leading from childhood to adulthood. And the only way this could be accomplished would be to have efforts at intervention a part of, not tangential to, the major socializing institutions in society. Yet, it is also obvious that these guidelines oversimplify the steps at intervention that would be required.

Before any program could be implemented which made use of such guidelines, much greater detail would be necessary with respect to the parameters of the program, the staff that would be needed, the costs that would be required. Further, the guidelines that have been suggested would be much more complex were an older population being considered. The further along the theoretical change any population is, the greater would be the necessary elaborations. The parameters of this set of problems are such that they merit the same kinds of considerations that have been described for the younger group. However, rather than dealing with them here, let us consider the remaining step in setting up an experimental program, and return to them at the conclusion of the paper.

STEP 6. The sixth and final step would involve the definition of a research strategy. There are some compelling reasons why an innovation should include research. In the first place, we have failed so often to evaluate experimental programs, that it is difficult to indicate where we have been, to say nothing of having a sound, empirical base to suggest where we should go. As Wheeler and Cottrell (1966) point out, ". . . no responsible business concern would operate with as little information regarding its success or failure as do nearly all of our delinquency prevention and control programs. . . . We spend millions of dollars a year in preventative and correctional work, with little other than guesswork to tell us whether we are getting the desired effects."

In the second place, it is a foregone conclusion that whatever program is tried, it will not constitute a panacea. Consequently the more sensible way to proceed would be to gather data systematically so that while we may not have complete success, we could do more to indicate wherein we have succeeded or failed and with whom. In other words, the knowledge that might be gained from any program, whether successful or unsuccessful, might be more useful in the long-run than the program itself.

In order to improve the utility of programmatic research, there are several things that might be done. The first has to do with the conceptualization of the research. It can be improved if it is guided, as in an action program, by a sound, theoretical base. Just as a given theory serves as a framework from which intervention principles and guidelines are derived, so that theory can be use to guide research. In fact, the theory, the principles, and the guidelines can perform the invaluable function of helping to clarify the relation between action and research. While action would be concerned with implementing basic principles and guidelines, so research would be concerned with success and consequences of that implementation. The factors which give meaning to action would also give meaning to research. In terms of the steps for developing a program that have already been outlined, research could be used in the following ways:

a. It could be used to conduct the pilot study mentioned earlier. It could provide the invaluable function of clarifying the problems that the target population has, and in defining more precisely the kinds of intervention that would be required. Further, the data that were gathered could be used as a baseline by which to assess the progress of both individuals and the total program.

b. Research could be used to study program process. Heretofore, most efforts at intervention have remained mysterious, black boxes. It is impossible even for those who run such programs to know whether staff members are operating consistently with program guidelines; that is, to make sure they are doing the actual things that were prescribed for them on paper. There has been no means for *quality control;* research could perform that function.

   Second, process research is necessary as a means of documenting what was done so that others might benefit from it, either in terms of assessing the effectiveness of a program or attempting to replicate it.

c. Research could perform the invaluable function of measuring outcome. Did the program achieve its objectives? Were the institutional ties of children improved? Was strain reduced? Were delinquency rates for this population lower than might have been expected otherwise?

   The only way these questions can be answered with some certainty is to select experimental and control groups. After having defined and identified a target population, this population would be split into two groups on a random basis. The experimentals would receive the new programming, the controls standard programming.

   There are compelling reasons why such an experimental design should be used. In the first place, any intervention concerned with delinquency prevention runs the risk of defining its subjects as pre- or potential delinquents. There is danger of assigning a permanent label to subjects which could have serious and detrimental consequences. Thus, not only should such a program be defined as an educational program, or something of a similar nature, but its worth should be well-documented before it is ever applied on a mass basis.

   In this regard, previous evaluations of delinquency prevention programs indicate that they have been singularly *unsuccessful* in realizing their objectives (Miller, 1962; Berelman and Steinburn, 1968; Caplan, 1968; Klein, 1969). Therefore, this fact underscores not only the need for caution regarding implementation, but underscores the importance of approaching prevention on an experimental rather than a mass basis. The only ethical approach is one which contributes to the long-range search for solutions and minimizes possible detrimental effects. That is why, at this juncture, one of the major objectives of any program should be that of contributing to knowledge. That is why research is such an important part of any intervention model.

d. Finally, research could provide an important feedback function. It was suggested earlier, for example, that the progress of individuals in terms of academic achievement and improved ties with family and peers should be measured at regular intervals. Research could perform that function and provide the invaluable service of pinpointing specific problems and achievements, and of providing that information to operational staff.

In summary, research has an important role to play, both in improving program operation and evaluating overall outcome. However, research in the past has been an appendage, tolerated but not embraced. If it is to be made functional, therefore, it must be given stature equal to that of other program components. Its role as a monitor, while productive of discomfort, must be encouraged and protected.

Second, research must be financed adequately. Good research is expensive, especially the kind of research being suggested here. Therefore, in funding a program, research must be treated as more than an afterthought. It cannot make a contribution unless adequate staffing and resources are provided.

Recapitulation

This paper has attempted to demonstrate the ways in which theory and research findings might be used to develop prevention and rehabilitation programs. Perhaps of greatest importance were several steps which were suggested for operationalizing any program:

1. *Define the target population.* Decide whether it is to include young children, a middle range group, or older, convicted offenders.
2. *Conduct a pilot study* by which to identify and describe the particular children who fit the general characteristics of the target population.
3. *Define objectives* for the program. Include administrators, practitioners, and research people in the defining process.

4. *Write a contract* specifying the obligations and roles of each of these three sets of people.
5. *Derive an intervention strategy* based upon the general leads provided by the theory and the findings of the pilot study. Set forth specific principles and guidelines for intervention.
6. *Establish a research strategy* based upon the same principles and guidelines and concerned with studying the characteristics of the subject population, the program itself, and its outcome.

It was also promised that attention would be paid to some of the more global issues that confront anyone concerned with prevention. All too often, there is a tendency to ignore these issues by taking refuge in the process of applying yet another band aid to a large and festering wound.

Fundamental to the whole process of defining objectives for prevention is one basic question: Are these objectives concerned with preventing *law-violating behavior* or with preventing *official delinquency?* Official delinquency is defined by two essential elements: (1) it is behavior that violates legal norms; but (2) in order for it to become official, it must also evoke responses from one or more of the elements of the juvenile justice system. Delinquency, then, in official terms, does *not* occur until officials respond. This means that official delinquency and actual lawbreaking are two vastly different things.

A recent summary of the literature (Empey, 1967) indicates just how different they are:

1. The amount of juvenile lawbreaking in the U.S. is great and the degree of apprehension is low, likely less than 10 percent, perhaps even lower. Thus, there may be great differences between the body of offenders who are officially defined as delinquent and the larger number of juveniles who actually break the law.
2. When self-reported information on lawbreaking behavior is obtained from middle as well as lower class juveniles, the assumed relationship between being lower class and violating the law is reduced considerably. Middle may be as much involved in such behavior as lower class adolescents.
3. The fact that legal authorities are charged with responding to poor home and family conditions, neglect and truancy, as well as criminal behavior, may distort the epidemiological character of delinquency,

causing officials to focus upon that group at the expense of considering the larger problem of law-violating behavior.

4. A 1964 U. N. report (Kvaraceus, 1964) concluded that, "Even when statistics are judged with greatest reserve . . . their meaning is clear: delinquency is increasing everywhere." Furthermore, some of the "delinquency" is taking on political meaning (Polk, 1968). An increasing number of delinquent acts are associated with growing social protest over such issues as civil rights, educational and political policies. The increasing participation of black and Chicano students in such activities, for example, could be inclined positively as well as negatively. Their acts are far more goal-oriented now on social inequities than were many of the unthinking delinquencies of the past.

If these conditions are true, then there are grounds for trying to view the whole forest as well as a few trees. In addition to the steps that have already been suggested, we should not ignore the need for changes in our total response to juvenile behavior.

One difficulty has to do with the definition of delinquency. Given the broad mandate of the juvenile court, and the catch-all character of the statutes which define delinquency, there are virtually no non-delinquents. Juveniles have committed, and commit acts daily, which if detected could result in adjudication. Consequently, from the standpoint of social control, it is necessary to question the utility of legal norms about which there is such ambiguity.

Not only does that ambiguity erode respect for the legal system, as did the law against prohibition in the 1920's, but makes extremely difficult the roles of officials who are expected to enforce it.

The juvenile court, likewise, suffers from this state of ambiguity. In fact, the court, like its youthful clients, has not enjoyed much power or status. The furious conflict that has been occasioned by an ambiguous mandate, designed to make the court a legal pillar on one hand, and a social agency on the other, has not only pitted legalists against reformers, but has split both the legal and helping professions as well.

The crowning blow came with recent Supreme Court decisions which held that the juvenile court may have afforded the offending juvenile the worst of two possible worlds (George, 1968). He has enjoyed neither the constitutional protection of the adult, nor the solicitous and helpful care supposedly inherent in the special provisions of the court. In other words, the way in which the court has had to operate has not served to dignify its position either as a legal or as a helping agency.

Finally, as mentioned earlier, the increasing tendency for the public to look at the police, the courts, and corrections for effective solutions to its failure to socialize young people adequately has led to societal aspirations for the juvenile justice system that far exceed its capacity to produce results. The search for answers will have to look elsewhere.

Suggested Reforms

The suggested reforms, like the problems themselves, are not new:

1. The Second United Nations Congress on the Prevention of Crime and the Treatment of Offenders recommended in 1960 that juveniles should not be prosecuted and receive penal sanctions for behavior which, if exhibited by adults, would not be prosecuted. It recommended, instead, that the many problems of neglect, truancy, and obstreperous behavior should be dealt with by agencies other than the juvenile court; perhaps in terms of the kind mentioned above, or in recognition that some forms of protest have a positive as well as negative connotation.

2. Similarly, the recent Crime Commission (1967b) strongly suggested that the mandate of the juvenile court should be more narrowly defined. Judges and other legal authorities should not be placed in the primary position of having to decide what is moral and immoral conduct for young people, of imposing codes for youthful behavior, or in levying sanction against the youthful fads which wax and wane.

There is no better example of this problem than the one mentioned earlier. It was noted that, so long as we place such great emphasis on legal definition (even though no one can state with precision what the definition means), we run the risk in prevention programs of labeling children as potential lawbreakers long before a legal tag is actually applied to them. If statutes were changed, therefore, and if the role of the court were made narrowly circumscribed, then we could do a much better job of focusing upon the educational, familial, and other problems of children, and with much less likelihood of doing harm to them.

3. In this regard, a recent white paper, published by the Home Office of the United Kingdom, went even further (Morris, 1966). It recommended the total abolition of all juvenile courts for children under 16 in the belief that the problems they present can best be handled on a consensual basis between child, parents and the welfare authorities of the state; and that the hearings, the day in court, and the sentence are not necessary.

No one knows for certain what all the consequences of these recommendations would be. However, several things seem likely. First, the reduction of the range of offenses for which juveniles could be prosecuted, and the exercise of constitutional protections for them, would undoubtedly result in a decrease in the number of young people defined as delinquent. Official delinquency rates would be decreased because of changes in official rules and processing.

Second, a narrowing of the mandate of the juvenile court might also help both to clarify and to increase respect among the young for the role of law, and aid legal authorities in focusing upon those acts which are more clearly of a predatory and harmful character.

Third, many of the problems now handled by legal institutions would be shifted to others—familial, education, welfare, and political. From a theoretical standpoint, this makes sense because, in the last analysis, the prevention of harmful behavior depends more upon the effectiveness of socialization within, and the attachment of young people to, these institutions than to the imposition by legal authorities of constraints from without. Furthermore, such institutions are in a better position to redress some of the problems and inequities about which young people have a legitimate right to protest.

With respect to those who are concerned about the loss of social control over the young, it is important to note that it is theoretically inconceivable that society, or any organization for that matter, can operate without age-graded and other kinds of status differences. For example, we must rely upon the older generation and major societal institutions to socialize the young, to guide and help them become responsible adults. It goes without saying, therefore, that the young cannot expect to remove all status differences and to operate without adherence to social norms and various forms of authority.

On the other hand, the idea of resorting only to legal means for a solution to current problems is also ridiculous. The value conflicts which are generated by the competing belief systems of old and young may only continue to accelerate the amount of law-violating behavior if they are handled strictly as legal matters. Furthermore, it would be wise to remind ourselves that children *are* children, given to excess on occasion over matters about which they feel strongly. Therefore, what they need, in addition to punitive sanction, is guidance, plus active participation in the social institutions where they spend great portions of their lives.

Paradoxically, we see both young and old trying to escape this kind of mutual involvement and problem-solving. Weary adults attempt to deny the existence of change, or revert to old patterns and old routines. The police, they argue, have always maintained order in the past; hence, to maintain order now, we need only more police.

Youthful behavior is no less contradictory. For some, change becomes an end in itself; nothing about the old order is worth saving; any kind of new behavior, much of which may be destructive, is worth trying. For others, reversion to an idealized and bucolic past is the answer; small towns and pre-technological societies are venerated. In either case, for juvenile or adult, there are far too many for whom a neat, simple answer is the solution.

It seems clear, therefore, that prevention strategies which pay little attention to these kinds of problems may themselves be in search of a simple neat solution when, in fact, a reconsideration of the meaning of deviance and the dysfunctions of present means for dealing with it, is what is needed. The prevention of law-violating behavior may, in the last analysis, require a much greater alteration of existing institutional patterns than has been suggested in this paper.

REFERENCES

Berelman, William C., and Steinburn, Thomas W.
1968 *Delinquency Prevention Experiments: A Reappraisal.* Seattle: Seattle Atlantic Street Center.

Burgess, Ernest W.
1952 "The economic factor in juvenile delinquency." Journal of Criminal Law, Criminology and Police Science 43 (May-June): 29-42.

Caplan, Nathan
1968 "Treatment Intervention and reciprocal interaction effects." Journal of Social Issues, 24 (January): 63-88.

Clark, John P. and Eugene P. Wenninger
1962 "Socio-economic class and areas as correlates of illegal behavior among juveniles." American Sociological Review 26 (December): 826-834."

Cloward, Richard A. and Ohlin, Lloyd E.
1960 *Delinquency and Opportunity: A Theory of Delinquent Gangs.* Glencoe: Free Press.

Dennis, W.
1960 "Causes of retardation among institutional children." Journal of Genetic Psychology 19:47-59.

Dentler, Robert and Lawrence J. Monroe
1961 "Early adolescent theft." American Sociological Review 26 (October): 733-743.

Deutsch, Martin and Associates
1967 *The Disadvantaged Child.* New York: Basic Books.

Dirksen, Cletus
1948 *Economic Factors in Delinquency.* Milwaukee: Bruce.

Eaton, Joseph W. and Kenneth Polk
1961 *Measuring Delinquency: A Study of Probation Department Referrals.* Pittsburgh: University of Pittsburgh Press.

Empey, LaMar T.
1967 "Delinquency theory and recent research." Journal of Research in Crime and Delinquency 4 (January):28-42.

Empey, LaMar T. and Maynard L. Erickson
1966 "Hidden delinquency and social status." Social Forces 44 (June):546-554.

Empey, LaMar T. and Steven G. Lubeck
1970 *The Silverlake Experiment: Testing Delinquency Theory and Community Intervention.* Chicago: Aldine Press.

George, B. James
1968 *Gault and the Juvenile Court Revolution.* Ann Arbor: Institute of Continuing Legal Education.

Gold, Martin
1966 "Undetected delinquent behavior." Journal of Research in Crime and Delinquency 3 (January):27-46.

Goldfarb, W.
1953 "The effects of early institutional care on adolescent personality." Journal of Experimental Education 12:106-129.

Hunt, J. M.
1961 *Intelligence and Experience.* New York: Ronald Press.

Klein, Malcolm W.
1969 "Gang cohesiveness, delinquency, and a street work program." Journal of Research in Crime and Delinquency (In press).

Kvaraceus, William C.
1964 "World wide story." The Unesco Courier (May)

Matza, David
1964 *Delinquency and Drift*. New York: John Wiley and Sons.
Merton, Robert K.
1957 *Social Theory and Social Structure*. Glencoe: Free Press.
Miller, Walter B.
1962 "The impact of a 'total community' delinquency control project." Social Problems 10 (Fall):168-191.
Monahan, Thomas P.
1957 "Family status and the delinquent child: a reappraisal and some new findings." Social Forces 35 (March):257.
Morris, Norval
1966 "Impediments to penal reform." The University of Chicago Law Review 33 (Summer):628.
Nye, F. Ivan, James F. Short, Jr., and V. J. Olsen
1958 "Socio-economic status and delinquent behavior." American Journal of Sociology 63 (January):318-329.
Polk, Kenneth
1965. *Those Who Fail*. Eugene, Oregon: Lane County Youth Project (Unpublished manuscript).
Polk, Kenneth
1968 "International perspectives on crime and delinquency, or nothing succeeds like failure." Salem: Paper presented at the 1968 Annual Conference, Oregon Corrections Association.
Porterfield, Austin L.
1946 *Youth in Trouble*. Fort Worth: Leo Potishman Foundation.
President's Commission on Law Enforcement and Administration of Justice
1967a *The Challenge of Crime in a Free Society*. Washington, D.C.: U.S. Government Printing Office.
1967b Task Force Report: *Juvenile Delinquency and Youth Crime*. Washington, D.C.: U. S. Government Printing Office.
Reiss, Albert J. and Albert L. Rhodes
1961 "The distribution of juvenile delinquency in the social class structure." American Sociological Review 26 (October): 730-732.
Shaw, Clifford and Henry D. McKay
1942 *Juvenile Delinquency in Urban Areas*. Chicago: University of Chicago Press.
Short, James F., Jr. and Fred L. Strodtbeck
1965 *Group Process and Gang Delinquency*. Chicago: University of Chicago Press.
Shulman, Harry M.
1949 "The family and juvenile delinquency." Annals of the American Academy of Political and Social Science 26 (January):21-31.
Tannenbaum, Frank
1938 *Crime and the Community*. New York: Columbia University Press.

Thrasher, Frederic M.
1927 *The Gang.* Chicago: University of Chicago Press.
Toby, Jackson
1957 "The differential impact of family disorganization." American Sociological Review 22 (October): 505-152.
Wattenberg, William W. and J. J. Balistrieri
1950 "Gang membership and juvenile delinquency." American Sociological Review 18: 631-635.
Wheeler, Stanton and Leonard S. Cottrell, Jr.
1966 *Juvenile Delinquency: Its Prevention and Control.* New York: Russell Sage Foundation.

CHAPTER 14

A SITUATIONAL APPROACH TO DELINQUENCY PREVENTION

LLOYD E. OHLIN

EXPLANING DELINQUENT ACTS and devising measures to prevent them are complementary activities. Yet the relationship between them is neither obvious nor immediate. It is important to try to explain the source of delinquent conduct since in this process we gain insights into relevant personal and social conditions which may then become the targets of delinquency prevention programs. However, even after these targets have been identified, it is not at all clear how to achive the desired changes. At this point another set of theoretical issues arise.

The lack of a systematic body of theories concerned with social and behavioral change cannot of course be attributed solely to those concerned with delinquency prevention. However, the undeveloped state of such theories means that the planning of prevention programs must rely heavily on the insights, judgements, and experiences of practitioners such as clinicians, policemen, teachers, social workers, and administrators of programs of social reform. At this point I only want to note the great need to devote more time and resources to the task of building a well grounded set of theories of personal and social change to complement those theories concerned with the explanation of delinquent acts.

A Situational View of Delinquent Acts

For a number of years I have held the view that a situational schema for understanding delinquent acts and the frequency with which they occur is the most fruitful approach. We need some systematic way to relate the wide variety of factors and conditions which produce delinquent events. We also need some type of field theory approach to order the concepts and findings from studies on the personal, social, cultural and economic dimensions of the circumstances surrounding delinquent acts.

I have encountered in the recent literature in the field of criminology frequent references to a book entitled *Delinquency and Opportunity* which my colleague, Richard Cloward, and I wrote some ten years ago.[1] This book and the theories contained in it were, of course, not intended to explain individual acts of delinquency. Instead, it sought to account for the social distribution of delinquent norms embodied in different types of delinquent subcultures. It tried to build on the pioneer work of Albert Cohen who first raised to critical attention questions concerning the sources and persistence of delinquent subcultures.[2]

We theorized that the types of delinquent conduct preferred by different delinquent groups grew out of group responses to their problems with the social and cultural systems of their local communities. We tried to explain the origin of delinquent norms of behavior and their related justification and rationalizations. These stand most clearly revealed in the conduct of the ideal, role-models, the heros, of different types of delinquent groups. We were not trying to explain the occurrence or even the distribution of delinquent acts, but rather the origin and distribution of preferred forms of delinquent conduct.

The explanatory variables highlighted the relationship of potential delinquents to the social and cultural system of which they were a part.

The theory focused on the disparity between those expectations of the *good life* which are held out to persons residing in low income urban areas and their opportunities for achieving them. This gap can produce feelings of alienation and can lead to a withdrawal of a sense of legitimacy toward the institutions and practices of the established order. This tension and its alienative effects can establish the preconditions in which a group will develop a set of deviant rules of conduct and an image of a new hero to follow. What type of hero or role-model gains allegiance depends on the particular type of legitimate or illegitimate resources and opportunities which are still available to group members.

It proved difficult in developing this theory to remain sharply focused on the issue of the origin and persistence of different types of delinquent norms. In large part this was due to the lack of any data on the distribution of different types of delinquent norms of conduct throughout the population. Instead, it was necessary to rely on descriptions of juvenile gang activity backed up by such insights as might be gained from self-report studies and information about arrested delinquents. This made it appear at times as if we were trying to describe the distribution of delinquent acts or apprehended delinquents, when in fact we were using such data to infer the probable distribution of different types of delinquent norms. The accepted norms of conduct for particular situations and what a person actually does do not always match. One may accept as legitimate rules of conduct very seldom acted on in concrete situations and yet allegiance to these norms may lead one to lend encouragement to others who do act them out. Thus, the distribution of subcultural norms held to be legitimate may not be adequately indicated either by the distribution of frequency with which they are acted upon.

Similarly, from self-report studies of delinquent conduct, it is clear that the distribution of arrested delinquents does not necessarily correspond with the distribution of delinquent acts. There are many selective factors operating which lead these distributions to look quite different. Actually then there are three different types of distributions which are often confused with one another and sometimes used inappropriately as indicators for each other.

Cloward and I were forced to rely on existing research data since we aimed to produce a hypothetical statement marking the beginning of a research process rather than its termination. To carry out a proper test of that theory would have required the gathering of extensive survey data on urban youth combined with detailed organizational studies of opportunities in their communities. Futhermore, since the theory seeks to explain the development and persistence of a particular set of norms of conduct, it would require historical research as well. We still do not have adequate studies providing such data. We are still mixing up delinquent norms, acts, and persons, rather than treating them as separate social facts requiring special explanations as to their distribution and possible connections.

Thus it is inappropriate to regard the theoretical statements which Cloward and I presented in *Delinquency and Opportunity* as an attempt to explain either the occurrence or the distribution of delinquent acts.

The origin, location, and persistence of different types of delinquent subcultures constitute an important component of the situational field in which delinquent acts occur, but cannot be taken as the major determinant of these acts in individual cases. Undoubtedly these subcultures play a significant role in recidivism and the socialization process through which a delinquent career is developed. They may therefore assume considerable strategic importance as targets for delinquency prevention programs. However, their contribution to delinquency must be evaluated in relation to other influences and conditions that create the circumstances for delinquent conduct.

A schematic representation of key elements present in the situations in which delinquent events occur is shown in Figure 14-1. This diagram is not intended to define a flow of causal relationships. It identifies key components of the delinquent situation, variations of which may determine whether or not the event actually occurs. It is also a useful device for identifying significant areas of theoretical and research contributions to the understanding of delinquency which may aid the development of broadly based prevention programs.[3]

The Offenders

Most of the theoretical and research studies of delinquency have tried to differentiate the personality, situational and background characteristics in the life and experience of offenders from those of non-offenders.[4] Though much effort has been expended, the search has seemed remarkably unproductive. An especially severe handicap

Diagram of Situational Components of Delinquent Events

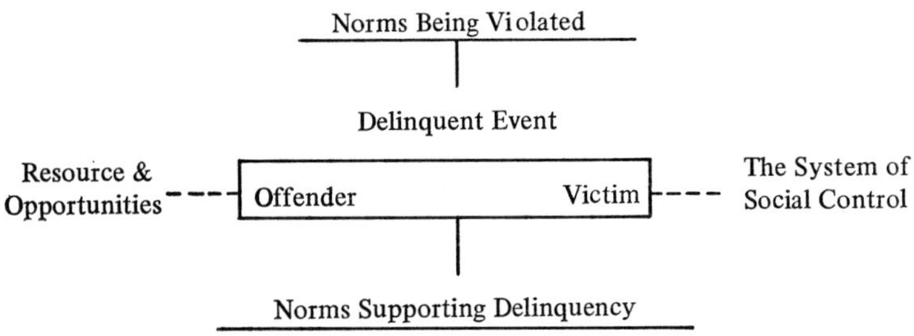

Figure 14-1

has been the inability to define and sample a realistic universe of those engaging in a particular form of delinquent conduct such as drug use, for example. The offender sample is ordinarily drawn from the aggregate of persons defined as juvenile drug users by the action of some official agency. However, the biases implicit in the available resources and discretion of these agencies mean that many drug users are undetected and unreported and therefore erroneously classified as non-deviants.

Some progress in dealing with this program has been made through the use of self-report studies in which surveys of different population groups have tried to elicit anonymous or confidential admissions to various types of delinquent acts. Though these studies suffer from a number of serious methodological problems, including the validity of the admissions, they have helped to give some insight into the types of biases operating in the selection of officially identified offenders. However, they have not on the whole produced systematic differences between offenders and non-offenders. Several delinquency self-report studies have suggested that while participation in minor acts of delinquency is very widespread, involvement in frequent and serious delinquent acts is concentrated among youth from families and neighborhoods with many other social problems as well. Less attention is now being devoted to explaining initial acts of delinquency and more to explaining the conditions which lead to the development of delinquent careers.

This concentration of research attention in the characteristics of offenders has been productive of many insights. It has not yielded, as one might have hoped, very clear differences between the biological, psychological, social, and developmental characteristics of offenders in contrast to non-offenders as a guide to prevention programs. However, it has yielded considerable insight into the way in which delinquency-prone youth are molded by their early developmental experiences and gradually socialized into adult criminal experiences and influences.

The Victims

Not all acts of delinquency have victims. A large number of recent studies have been exploring the *victimless* offenses, e.g., those in which a client wishes to purchase illicit goods or services. Ordinarily the seller of these services or goods is subjected to the heaviest penalties on discovery of the violation, as in cases of abortion, homosexuality, prostitution, pornography, and drug sales. However, there are obviously many other instances in which the person receiving the goods or services is also defined as an offender, as in the case of drug users, homosexuals and persons possessing pornographic material.

This current preoccupation with the area of consensual offenses has focused renewed interest on the relationship between the offender and the victim and the contribution which the victim himself makes to the precipitation and outcome of the delinquent event. Despite the clear definition of this problem by von Hentrick in 1939 with respect to more serious crimes, the part played by the victim in precipitating a serious offense has received relatively little systematic attention. In many acts of deviance the victim is a helpless and often innocent bystander, but in many others he plays a major role in the escalation of a chance encounter into a crime. There are still many unanswered questions concerning the circumstances under which this occurs such as the way in which the vicitm's role varies for different types of offenses, and whether there is a *victim proneness*. These and many other questions about victims essential to understanding the dynamics of delinquent events are still unexplored.

Surprisingly the agencies specifically charged with social control functions, such as public and private police forces, prosecutors and defenders, civil and criminal courts, and the correctional and treatment agencies, have received the least systematic study. The major exceptions are the adult and juvenile correctional services and the mental hospital system which have been subjected to a series of organizational studies over the last fifteen years. The most neglected agencies have been the police and the courts. However, several recent studies have been especially concerned with the way in which the agencies have exercised the discretion they possess to make dispositional decisions. They have also considered the types of organizational problems these agencies must solve in achieving the objectives of law enforcement and preservation of the public peace. Thus far only a bare beginning has been made in these organizational studies in comparision to the work accomplished in the area of industrial relations, for example.

However, a very productive line of recent investigation has explored the way in which agencies of social control may aggravate and foster many types of deviants by the measures they employ to control them. The idea that social actions taken to achieve control, deterrence, and respect for authority might in fact do as much to harden and perpetuate delinquent conduct by mobilizing a hostile public confrontation and a non-diffusable process of social stigma has a long history in sociological theory. However, empirical studies are beginning to explore the ramifications of this idea more fully, especially as it applies to the actions of the various agencies of criminal justice. Studies of the contribution of social control actions in schools and mental hospitals toward the creation of deviant self-identities have been concerned with the same problem.

Such studies need to be balanced by more intensive exploration of the deterrent effects actually achieved by these same control measures. Though our system of justice relies so heavily on the concept of deterrence for the justification of central features of its operation, virtually no systematic studies have been devoted to it. Use of survey techniques with the general population of adolescents and comparative analysis of the experience of cohorts of delinquents passing through the great variety of juvenile justice systems in the United States and other countries as well should permit a much more rigorous test of the idea of deterrence than has yet occurred.

Norms Being Violated

Interdisciplinary studies by lawyers, sociologists, and political scientists are just beginning to explore the origin, development, and institutionalization of official norms and sanctions. There is increasing interest in how different areas of personal and social activity become defined as so troublesome and problematic as to require control by formal sanctions. What is the process by which law is created to control new areas of social activity and what part is played by *moral enterpreneurs* in this process? This is a problem of increasing concern in our society as young people press for more immediate access to adult prerogatives and innovative new styles of public expression and consumption.

Public reaction to deviant conduct and the use of informal sanctions is also coming under closer scrutiny. What are the reactions of various segments of the general public to different forms of marginal conduct? And what forms of sanctions are they prepared to apply? How does one account for group differences in the definition of deviance and readiness of use sanctions? Though such questions are just beginning to form as subjects of serious study, answers to them will contribute significantly to a systematic theory of social deviance and control.

Norms Supporting Delinquency

Throughout the history of sociological studies of deviance, description, analysis, and theorizing about deviant norms have been a recurring theme. Recently renewed efforts have been made to explain the origin, content, and distribution of different types of deviant subcultures. The resulting theories have stimulated a number of studies aimed at defining the necessary conditions for the development and maintenance of these deviant norms.

As we have noted, this problem has special significance since such deviant subcultures are generally regarded as essential for the full development and maintenance of successful deviant careers. The subculture of the professional thief trains him in the attitudes and techniques needed to operate successfully. Thus from a practical standpoint understanding and control over the reinforcement provided by the deviant subculture may be the surest road to termination of prevention of the confirmed delinquent career.

Though a beginning has been made, identification of the various circumstances that join to create particular types of deviant cultures and the sequential process through which this occurs is still obscure and requires much more research as well as theoretical definition.

Most people take for granted that the opportunity to accomplish a legitimate job means having access to the tools, materials, and occasion to do the job. For the most part they would also assume this would be true if the intent was to steal a car, rob a bank, or run a loanshark racket. It would also be clear that the legitimate job would require training, a chance to get hired, promoted, and assigned responsibility to do the job. But to do something illegitimate is commonly regarded as available to anyone if he feels like it. What this view overlooks is that access to illegitimate opportunities for achieving one's desires may be as tightly controlled as legitimate ones. One needs to be chosen, trained, promoted, and assigned access and responsibility for illegitimate as well as legitimate opportunities.

This condition does not apply to all delinquent acts any more than it does to all conforming ones. However, it may apply more to those types of youthful offenders who are oriented at an early stage to the use of illegitimate means to achieve rewards of prestige, wealth, power, or fame. The descriptive studies carried out in urban slum communities demonstrate the pervasive hold of institutionalized forms of vice, corruption, and crime that constitutes an opportunity and a challenge to many slum youth to achieve by illegitimate means what cannot be won legitimately. Despite our awareness of the pervasive socializing effect of the everyday visibility of these institutions in the slum community, our theories of social control and deviance are badly handicapped because so little work has been done to map out the routes to success, the patterns of recruitment and induction, and the competitive criteria of achievement which make these institutions so pervasive, so strong, and so difficult to eradicate.

Nevertheless, even the poorest slum community is not solely an environment of pressures toward the utilization of illegitimate means to achieve personal or group goals. There are legitimate resources and opportunities and realistic visions of the achievement of success by such means. We still know too little about the distribution of such opportunities: who gets access to them and who does not; and what chances of reintegration arise after initial failures? Somehow our social system must incorporate the desires, needs, and capacities for growth in slum communities and suburban areas alike. To do so, much more must be known about the way in which established institutions distribute legitimate and illegitimate opportunities and what can be done to increase the capacity of young people to realize their true potential.

To discuss theory and research concerning the component elements of a situation of social action independently of one another obscures what may be learned by putting them together. It is now possible to think of recreating situational models within which different types of delinquency occur. Theoretically it may become possible to assign each component in this field an historically developed value such that at the time of the deviant event the interaction of these values may be seen as producing the event.

From another standpoint the occurrence of the delinquent act may be seen as a process in which the sequential order of involvement of different components is crucial in determining whether the act occurs or not, e.g., the patrol car stops and waits and the robbery set up falls apart.

Whether such new attempts at integration of different forms and levels of fact-finding and theorizing can yet be carried out successfully remains to be seen. The trend in theory development and research design seems to be moving in this direction, and it seems both a logical and a desirable one. To accomplish this will require a greater degree of investment in research in this field than at present. It will also require more interdisciplinary projects and a capacity to see a promising line of research through to the end. The field of deviance and control has suffered immensely from the intermittent, unsystematic character of its research enterprise. It is now at a stage where great progress can be achieved through more comprehensive, orderly development.

The schematic diagram employed in this presentation does not imply the desirability of an eclectic, multiple-factor approach to the causation of delinquent events. We have learned a great deal about different components of the delinquent situation and can begin to create a systematic view of this situation. Such an approach would certainly come closer to what individual offenders experience as reality. It should help us to assess more accurately the contribution of different factors to individual cases and the rates of different types of delinquencies. The components in the delinquent situation form a set of interacting influences such that the frequency and character of delinquent acts vary as changes occur in the various situational elements. We are probably not yet in a position to develop causation models in this degree of complexity. However, we should be moving in this direction. I am convinced that our prevention strategies would achieve great effectiveness if they were supported by explanatory models of the delinquency problem which took a systematic view. This would allow us to draw on many different types of empirical and theoretical contributions concerning the influence of different components in the situational context of the delinquent event.

Our primary need is the development of more realistic and more complete causation models for different types of juvenile offenses. There are important differences between consensual delinquent acts such as drug use, sexual, or liquor offenses, and predatory offenses such as robbery, burglary, larceny, and auto theft or solely juvenile offenses such as truancy, incorrigibility, stubborn child, runaway, and other labels for conflicts with adult authority. Development of situational models of causation for these different categories of juvenile offenses will make it possible to identify more precisely those targets of social action which the best available theory and research point to as the principal objects for prevention strategies.

Opportunity Systems

I would like to conclude these comments concerning explanation of delinquency by noting the key importance which I attribute to systems of opportunity and unrealized expectations as especially potent contributory factors in generating delinquency producing situations. The concept of opportunity itself is a very vague term that gains specifically only as it is related to particular ends which people may seek, such as economic rewards, prestige, fame, power, or affectional gratification. Opportunities for realizing such goals become institutionalized and controlled by organizations such as the family, school, employment office, and labor union.

A person comes to reflect the qualities of help, opportunity, and hope which are built into the institutions surrounding him. What can be the consequence for youth when schools do not train intelligence nor families feelings, when housing does not shelter nor sanitation clean, when police do not protect nor welfare support, when work offers no meaning and church no aspiration? In such circumstances, it is abundantly clear that the institutions of social life, which in modern society are the principal instruments for the achievement of human goals and for gaining satisfying and creative experiences, are not only defective and failing but are punitively unrewarding and alienative. Under such conditions the chance to exploit illegitimate opportunities for more immediate and tangible rewards may not seem a difficult choice to make.

There is a danger in exaggerating the deficiencies of the institutions found in urban slum communities. The fact is that some slum families are stable and creative environments for socializing children. Many young people are attracted to school. Many find exciting work prospects, adequate housing, police responsiveness, and understanding social services. However, we do not know enough about the criteria which control access to these effective types of institutional operations. Why do they exist for some and not others? What are the formal and informal criteria employed by the guardians of institutionalized services which repudiate some and admit others? These institutions tend to track people through interrelated systems of opportunities in ways which are insufficiently understood and infrequently challenged. Thus the concept of opportunity systems suggests the need to examine closely the types of reinforcement effects which institutions are capable of providing or turning off. Legitimate and illegitimate opportunity systems organized within the basic institutions of the community influence all of the basic components contained in a situational approach to delinquency prevention.

Strategies of Delinquency Prevention

Assuming the feasibility of a situational approach to delinquency events, a soundly based prevention strategy should be to produce a new system of influences and conditions more likely to control the frequency with which delinquent events occur. All communities have some type of existing system for both generating and controlling delinquency events. What prevention policies and strategies seek to do is to supplant the existing system with another that would produce more desirable effects.

General Assessment of Community Delinquency Problems

To prepare an appropriate prevention strategy, the initial task of the community planning group would be to secure information to answer a series of questions about the delinquency problem in the community and the responses now being made to it. It would be necessary to secure answers to such questions as the following:

1. What are the types of delinquency that occur most frequently or cause most harm? What types of delinquency concern the community most and what is the basis of this concern?
2. What is the community now doing about these offenses?
3. What do experienced persons say is the effect of the current measures now being used? What data exist to support this evaluation or other trends with regard to the delinquency problem?
4. Taking a situational view of these different delinquency problems, what are the aspects of the problem which are now being disregarded?
5. Considering the various components of a situational model of delinquency events which of these components seem to be most crucial for the different types of delinquency problems? Which appear to be most out of control? Which appear most accessible to strategic intervention?

Such an assessment of the general delinquency problem of the community will enable delinquency prevention planning to be guided by a sense of community priorities and an awareness of those problems likely to be most responsive to the resources available for achieving change. To illustrate how a situational approach to delinquency prevention might facilitate the development of a community plan for a delinquency problem, consider the problem of drug use by adolescents.

Prevention of Drug Use by Adolescents

In most communities throughout the country drug use by adolescents is spreading rapidly. New drug users are younger than before and more middle class children in suburban areas are experimenting with the use of drugs and often developing serious drug dependencies. Increasingly, adolescents seem to be turning from marijuana use to addictive opiate drugs, notably heroin. More drug related crimes of theft and robbery by adolescents are coming to the attention of the police. Several deaths from overdoses in the use of heroin have recently appeared. More adolescents are being hospitalized than ever before for psychotic episodes connected with drug use, such as suicide attempts, assaults, and other forms of mental and emotional trauma. More school dropouts and failures seem to be related to loss of motivation due to drug abuse.

The key fact in this situation appears to be a breakdown of formal and informal controls which have hitherto kept the problem of drug use in check. Up to now the police have been able to maintain heavy pressure on sellers of drugs and to intercept drug shipment transfers. Now, however, so many types of persons seem to be involved in the movement of drugs, that drugs have become more freely available and supplies have increased several-fold. Furthermore, there has been a rapid influx of the more addictive and dangerous drugs that have proved more difficult to trace. In addition to these enforcement problems there has been a noticeable weakening in the informal control system. Adolescents and many parents seem less fearful and uncertain about the possible effects of the drugs. Young people seem much more inclined to experiment with a variety of drugs and even to undertake experiments with heroin which was once widely viewed as far too threatening in its addictive consequences. This decline in the informal system of controlling beliefs about drug use has been accompanied by the growth of a set of subcultural norms favorable to drug use. Acceptance of such norms is spreading rapidly among young people, even reaching into the grammar school population.

Let us assume that the foregoing represents an accurate characterization of the problem confronting a community prevention planning group. Any intervention strategy must cope with these facts about the problem and especially those pertaining to the breakdown of formal and informal control.

1. Norms being violated. One of the first things to consider is the nature of the rules about drug use. Are these rules realistic? Do

they square with the experience of drug users? Are the penalities being used to respond to adult fears of what youth regard as a relatively harmless activity? To what extent are the drug prohibitions accepted as valid, realistic, and helpful by either adults or youth in the community? To what extent do they coincide with expert opinion in regard to this problem? To what extent is it politically feasible to affect a more closely matched and objective assessment by youth and adults of the need for different types of drug prohibitions?

2. Norms supporting violation. Where drug use is strongly opposed by adults and official agencies, drug subcultures develop to meet the needs of users for peer group support reinforcement. These subcultures also exist for the purpose of exchanging knowledge and lore about drug use and to provide safe channels for the distribution of drugs. Such drug subcultures can sometimes be infiltrated by control agents and disrupted temporarily. However, long range controls require the creation of conditions by which the supporting norms of this subculture and its system of beliefs about drug use can be effectively challenged. Encounter groups utilizing the experience and perceptions of ex-addicts represent one device for doing this, though they reach limited numbers of users, usually at very advanced stages of addicition. Counter education measures are necessary but unless they accurately reflect facts and experiences of users, they lose credibility and become ineffective. In addition many users find that drugs offer a symbolic opportunity to express defiance of authority. This may serve to give double reinforcement to the immediate gratification obtained from the drug use itself. Such complexities of the problem need to be exposed not only in contacts with users but in educational programs for adults.

3. Resources and opportunities. Careful consideration must be given to the existence of either legitimate or illegitimate resources and opportunities which give encouragement to the development of the drug culture. How are the illegal sources for obtaining the drugs organized to maintain distribution? What opportunities are available for learning about drug use and in what situations and circumstances do young people get inducted into drug patterns? What types of legitimate resources and opportunities might prove capable of competing with the rewards which youth are obtaining from the drug

subculture? What are the role models which members of the drug subculture are emulating? What are the attitudes, life-styles, career, and social adjustment patterns of these central figures? In what ways can their claims to legitimacy and allegiance from potential users be countered?

4. SYSTEM OF SOCIAL CONTROL. What type of assistance can be given the enforcement system? Are these possibilities for developing a more effective network for the exchange of information about drug use, the sources of drugs, and their distribution pattern among law enforcement agencies in the area? To what extent are the police enforcement efforts seen as helpful or threatening by young people throughout the community? Can the police establish procedures for identifying and referring users for treatment in ways which will be seen by parents and youth as a helpful service? Are the treatment opportunities for known users sufficient and effective?

5. VICTIMS. What are the characteristics of the users of drugs? Do they represent a special group in the community or in the school system? To what extent does it appear to be rooted in authority or personality problems of the victims themselves?

6. THE OFFENDER. What are the characteristics of those apprehended for selling drugs or otherwise known or believed to be selling drugs? What are the links in the distribution system of which the offender forms a part? To what extent does the character of the drug that is distributed and the levels of sophistication about use and distribution indicate the presence of organized criminal elements?

The problem of prevention of drug use provides a good illustration of the complex variety of questions that needs to be raised in developing prevention programs. The questions posed above are obviously illustrative rather than exhaustive since other possible program issues in each of the categories should be considered. Especially important is the need to be concerned about the inter-active effects of different prevention measures of one another. To what extent will the social control measures interfere with those taken to deal with the problems of both victims and offenders? To what extent can legitimate opportunities be developed so as to compete successfully with the illegitimate use of drugs? Will the increased education of adults and youth about drugs spread the risk of drugs use or decrease it?

The development of a successful prevention strategy and set of programs involves dealing with many parts of the problem at the same time and considering the way in which they reinforce or neutralize one another. Perhaps the most important prevention policy points to the need to build into the community a new set of positive reinforcements for non-drug use and easy reentry access to rehabilitation opportunities for those who become involved with drugs again.

The situational approach to delinquency causation and prevention is built on the concept of a system of components that constitutes a set of interrelated influences in the lives of potentially delinquent youth. The appropriate evaluation procedure would undertake a systems analysis approach to prevention activities. What this requires is a concerted effort to build objective indices of those key elements in the situation which affect delinquency and which are involved in the prevention strategy. These are the indicators that can be used to monitor changes in the situational components of delinquency and ultimately to test the effectiveness of the prevention strategies. As these indicators become more fully developed it should be possible to create simulated models of community conditions affecting delinquency. Such models could be used to learn much more about the interrelationships of these conditions and their related contribution to the occurrence of delinquent events. Eventually it may even prove possible to undertake computer simulations of the effects of introducing new resources and facilities at different points in the system of institutionalized opportunities and control measures.

A systems analysis approach closely tied to the operational phases of the program is likely to provide the most satisfying measure of effectiveness in the long run. In the short run it can yield effective feedback into police decisions. However, a complex delinquency prevention program such as that proposed here should not exclude the possible use of experimental and control group procedures. The experience of the California Treatment Project has shown that this approach can provide most useful insights concerning additional components needed in the treatment program. Also, as experience has accumulated, it has proved possible to handle a more complex research design and thus obtain more sensitive readings of the interactive effects experienced by various participants in the treatment program. In fact, the community treatment project provides a good example of the gradual expansion of the treatment system to include more of the pertinent influences facing the delinquent in the community. One virtue of such a program, now in its third phase, is that it represents the gradual accumulation of experience and knowledge concerning the effectiveness of certain varieties of treatment procedures.

It is clear that the payoffs are likely to be much more rewarding if treatment and prevention programs are permitted to grow over a number of years. We can no longer afford to launch short term projects that do not permit effective follow up studies and utilization of findings in further programs. Our procedures in the past have been wasteful of funds, trained personnel, and accumulated knowledge. I am hopeful that we are now entering a period when long range development of community prevention programs has become possible and that we can begin to institutionalize the process of programmed development and systematic evaluation and research.

In this paper I have not attempted to outline a particular theory of delinquency causation or a specific model of delinquency prevention planning and implementation. Instead I have proposed a long range strategy involving a systematic approach to future research on delinquency causation and planning for community based prevention programs. We do not yet possess all the knowledge we need about the various components of such an approach in explaining and preventing delinquency. Nevertheless it is time that we set this type of goal; that we assemble what we know about the various components in a situational approach to delinquency and begin to investigate the effects of such a program, not only on the causation of delinquent events, but on their control and prevention as well.

Ten years ago the Federal delinquency program urged the development of comprehensive planning processes in communities. At that time such a prospect was more a vision than a reality. We had neither the knowledge nor the trained personnel to undertake programs of such scope and complexity. In the intervening years we have learned much about what to do and what not to do in mobilizing communities to undertake prevention programs. I believe we can now be much more effective in the program designs we propose and the way we carry them out. With the new Federal funds now becoming available to communities throughout the country, I am hopeful that we will see a new readiness to collaborate on the part of all those concerned with delinquency problems, so that the system of pressures which produce and sustain delinquency can be effectively changed. It will require much imagination, experimentation, and a genuine commitment to work together.

FOOTNOTES

[1]Cloward, R. A. and Ohlin, L. E. *Delinquency and Opportunity: A Theory of Delinquent Gangs,* The Glencoe Free Press, 1960.

[2]Cohen, A. K. *Delinquent Boys: The Culture of the Delinquent Gang,* The Glencoe Free Press, 1955.

[3]The use of this schema to organize a brief review of research inquiries into problems of social deviance and control may be found in Neil J. Smelser and James A. Davis, ed., *Sociology:* A Report of the Sociology Panel of the Behavioral and Social Sciences Survey, Prentice Hall, Inc., Englewood Cliffs, N. J., 1969, pp. 72-78.

[4]In this review of the contributions to understanding different aspects of the delinquency situation, no attempt will be made to cite the sources of these contributions. To do so would amount to producing a set of citations for a comprehensive textbook on delinquency.

CHAPTER 15

THE ROLE OF THE JUVENILE COMMANDER IN DELINQUENCY PREVENTION

PERCY G. ROGERS

Because of his broad responsibilities, the chief of police or sheriff will usually want to delegate major responsibility for delinquency prevention planning to the commander of his juvenile division. It is through the juvenile commander that the department can be related effectively to all other components of the juvenile justice system and to the community at large.

The selection of the juvenile commander is a most important decision as he occupies a strategic position and has a complex role to play in the community. He should be as keenly interested in the prevention role as he is with his control role. He also needs to be committed to innovative changes in the total juvenile justice system.

The juvenile commander has two major delinquency prevention functions: (1) He needs to coordinate the police prevention activities with the existing or planned preventive functions of the total community, and (2) He should participate actively in the community organization process with lay and professional leaders to plan better prevention programs.

To do these well he must have a broad knowledge of his total department program as well as the community's education, health, welfare, recreation and employment resources. These resources will be in addition to his usual regular contacts with the justice system components such as the probation department, juvenile court and parole agency.

He should be an active member of such planning organizations as the Welfare Planning Council or Council of Social Agencies; Community Coordinating Council; and area Criminal Justice Council or one of its task forces. It is through these groups that he can best represent the interests of his department and plan programs to keep youth from committing unlawful acts.

He thus represents the juvenile justice system as it relates or interfaces with the health system, the education system, the welfare system, the employment system and the recreation system.

He can play an important role in planning a community Youth Services Bureau which was recommended by the President's Crime Commission in 1967. This Bureau would focus on the community's broad preventive function to provide multiple treatment services and other activities for youth with minor problems and thus divert them from the system. The Bureau would accept referrals from parents, schools, police and others so that many truants and incorrigibles could be helped without court intervention. The Youth Development and Delinquency Prevention Administration of the U.S. Department of Health Education and Welfare has published an excellent pamphlet on "Guides for Demonstration Projects for Youth Services Bureaus," which can help local communities in their planning.

The juvenile commander should also become adept at writing proposals for new prevention programs within his department. Funding is available for well planned projects through state criminal justice councils. He should seek the help of social science researchers to build in a sound evaluation process on the proposal.

The juvenile commander, with the aforementioned qualities and skills, can thus make a major contribution to improving his department's image while he helps to plan still more effective youth programs.

CHAPTER 16

CRIME PREVENTION: AN EVOLUTIONARY ANALYSIS

GARY B. ADAMS

CRIME PREVENTION IS no new phenomenon. Man has been concerned with crime prevention, in one form or another, from the very beginning of civilization. As the tribal customs and mores began to collapse, man instigated criminal law, which social groups have used to secure conformity in the conduct of their members. The criminal law to many was a deterrent against antisocial or deviant behavior in that a punishment was attached for violation.

Thorsten Sellen points out the fact that the criminal norms, i.e., the conduct norms embodied in the criminal law, change as the values of the dominate groups are modified.[1] The very fact that criminal law is changing and will continue to change simply means that all acts illegal today may not be so in the future. Crimes of yesterday may in fact be socially acceptable action of future generations.

What relevance does all this have for crime preventions? For the individual and the community in which he lives? Probably a great deal—maybe very little. A great deal in that it affects us all, whether we live in a large city or a small farm community. Very little in that no one seems to understand the causal factors or put together programs that have an impact on the problem. I will grant you that some of the proposed solutions have had, and will continue to enjoy, limited success but very few have been properly evaluated and thus we are left with the question, what relevance does all this have for crime prevention?

Programs designed to reduce delinquency have been many and varied in approach. One can almost say that the pre-Lombroso era was one characterized as a total community approach. Prior to the emergence of the Positive School of Criminology in nineteenth-century Italy, *Criminology* as a distinct scientific discipline did not exist. Crime was looked upon as one of the problems of the community, no different from the rest. Essentially what the great doctor did was create a specialty, one which viewed the criminal among us as *different,* a biologically distinct kind of human being—a subspecies of atavistic man. From that point in the history of man forward, wherever criminologists have gathered and organized themselves as separate from students of society in general, they have tended to study criminals as a type of group essentially different from other members in our society. The epistemological generates the ontological: special ways of knowing tend to create special kinds of things to be known.

Richard Korn, a noted Berkeley criminologist notes:[2]

> It seems logical to expect that a discipline which limits its study largely to persons especially nominated by society as responsible for crime and delinquency would be bound to discover such persons—and discover them precisely where society has placed them. Nor does it seem far-fetched to anticipate that the persons thus differentiated would rarely include those who are well-favored by society. By and large, criminologists have studied the trouble-makers who fail. With important exceptions they have limited themselves to the offenders of the socially or psychologically impotent.

Lombrosoism has never completely died. It is still with us today, in a somewhat changed form, but nevertheless still there. The criminologist in the early nineteen hundreds changed the model of operation from the positivist school of thought, in which the idea of sin and willful corruption was stressed, to the individualistic or analytical school. The emphasis was then shifted to unitary causes; physical disabilities, mental defects, etc. As one would suspect our efforts at the art of crime prevention followed the causal theories. Coming full circle we are now in the era of multiple causation, or by and large placing the blame for crime and delinquency back on the community.

Crime and delinquency prevention programs appear to fall into four rather broad time periods. The pre-1870's were almost exclusively devoted to identification of crime and the criminal as a community problem. 1870 to about 1925 seems to stress the elimination of the criminal mainly by identifying and preventing his birth. Detect and control attitudes prevail from 1925 up to the early forties, with August Vollner and the college trained cop holding the spotlight. The fourth and present period is characterized by efforts at behavior modification, again stressing the need for community involvement but with one major difference. The community is responsible for the problem, as before, but is also charged with its solution and hopefully its prevention. Let us now take a look at some of the programs and ideas as they have evolved in the past century.

"The true object of Municipal Law is to accomplish the ends of justice."[3] Mr. Reeves, writing in the *Annals* September 1892, points out that all men are created equal and that as soon as we begin to infringe on the rights of another, or seek to obstruct him in the enjoyment of his rights, that inequality begins.

"The true purpose of legislation," Mr. Reeves continues, "should be, the formulation of such laws as will prevent—as far as possible—such injudicious use of opportunities by each individual in providing for life, liberty, and in seeking substantial happiness, as will hinder others in their rights, and in this way tend to preserve equality."[4]

Mr. Reeves, while very concerned about preserving individual equality, then proceeds to ask, what is criminal? "One afflicted with moral obliquity of vision," is the reply. "One who, no matter what may be his apparent condition of bodily health, has such an anatomical and physiological arrangement of organs, as produces a perverted moral perception, or fails to produce any of sufficient strength to enable him to avoid offense."[5]

The solution to this problem, or at least one author's solution in 1892, was first to prohibit marriage by a known criminal, and others unfit for the relation; second, remove children from the custody of parents whose care will create, or whose environment leads to criminal mentality, or practices that prevent, pervert, or destroy moral perception.[6]

Edward Divine, *Survey*, January 1911, in writing about the new penology states, "the underlying idea of the new penology is social protection. The means to that end are three: prevention, reformation of the corrigible, and isolation of the incorrigible . . . the definite organization of preventive educational agencies, the socializing of our police, the very reform of government in order to bring it into closer accord with our ideals of justice—the unifying concept is social protection."[7] This will prove to be the forerunner of the community coordinating council movement in this country.

The use of community coordinating councils is not expressed in 1911 but nonetheless the seed appears to be planted. It is not until 1919 that the first coordinated community program, the Berkeley Coordinating Council, is formed to combat juvenile delinquency in the United States.

The Berkeley Council was set up to do research and conduct conferences and to explore the problems of children brought to its attention. The council was composed of three committees—the adjustment committee, the character-building committee, and the environment committee.

The council was typical of the community approach to crime prevention in that the problem was not tackled by one institution but rather handled as a community endeavor. Similar programs were set up across the United States and as of 1941 it was generally felt they were responsible for the decline of delinquency.

Preventive legislation was still being asked for in 1913 but not to prevent people from being born as criminals but rather to prevent families from breaking up. "If there is anything that reflects discredit upon America it is the fact that our homes are so easily broken up, marriage vows so readily dissolved and the children permitted to pursue their own course without supervision."[8] Adolph Eberhart, Governor of Minnesota, was asking for legislation which would tend to keep the home intact and bind the parents; thus having a direct bearing upon the reduction of crime as he felt the one great principle in crime prevention was maintenance of the home.

If the public does, in fact, want the prevention of crime, do they want the police charged with the responsibility? August Vollmer, 1926, was one of the first to answer in the affirmative and assert that police do have a crime prevention role. The Berkeley Chief stated, "Preventive phases of policing are beginning to be emphasized by policemen and this interesting function will engage the attention of more departments in the future." He went on to state, "A few departments have excellently trained officers who devote their entire time and attention to crime prevention." The visitation to schools by police officers was cited as one prevention program. Vollmer further stated ". . . if we are to prevent crime we've got to start with children."[9]

Nineteen thirty-one sees the prevention scene shift to the east coast as the New York Crime Prevention Bureau becomes a part of the Police Department. Headed by a woman, Henrietta Additon, the New York Bureau was one of the first crime prevention agencies to be created apart from law enforcement (created in 1930), and then placed under the Department for Coordination. The Bureau was charged with crime prevention from an environmental or social viewpoint.[10]

The early thirties witnessed the setting up of community coordinating councils across the nation based on the Berkeley Model. Los Angeles was one of those adopting such a plan. Instead of apprehending young delinquents as offenders, the officers should be trained to make referrals to proper social agencies for guidance according to Eliot Ness. The Chicago Police Department's Crime Prevention Bureau has stepped up patrol from 8 A.M. to midnight in high crime areas, but more important than the increased patrol was a program of increased education for juvenile officers. The Department in 1944 was giving its juvenile personnel and especially its policewomen a special twelve week course of instruction in dealing with juveniles, and referring them to social agencies.

Elizabeth Fajen, (chairman of a special committee of the lower west side District Health Committee, New York) writing in *Survey,* 1946, describes an unusual project to prevent youth's troubles.[12] The committee confronted two questions. First, can we identify at an early stage symptomatic difficulty that later may develop into serious behavior trouble. Secondly, in these cases, by mustering and coordinating the skills of the psychiatrist, psychologist, social worker, physician, vocation worker, and others, can we successfully diagnose the underlying difficulty in the child and his family, and offer a planned treatment service which will remove or modify that difficulty? The answer to both was an emphatic *yes.*[13]

The committee has a six step procedure which consists of first, the principal of the school selecting those students whose personality deviations indicate serious social or health problems. The case was then cleared with the social services exchange. Data about the student was gathered by either a committee member or a social worker and assembled and presented for clinical discussion. The fifth step is the formulation of a plan of action for the student and finally periodic reports were made to the committee on the child's progress. Basically the plan was an attempt to manipulate the environment of a child under stress, or stated in somewhat different terminology, to bring together all the resources of the community to aid the child. The program, according to the author, had enjoyed some success in that they had reached some children that otherwise would not have been aided by the community.[14]

The importance of getting aid to children and advice to parents at an early stage was the editorial opinion of *American City,* 1947.[15] The behavioral modification emphasis was pushed down to, or up at, as the case may be, the city fathers. Many cities were taking preventive action to head off the alarming delinquency trends. One such approach, the article continued, is revealed in *Children in the Community; The Saint Paul Experiment in Child Welfare.* The essence of the plan was that it established a *first aid station,* or referral center, to coordinate the community services for children and to provide individual assistance for boys and girls in trouble. The article concludes with the following statement, "There is no doubt that action must be taken on several fronts at once. The problem has now reached such proportions that no community can afford to ignore it."[16]

"One sociological theory, reminiscent of the Calvinist concept of original sin, maintains that a human being is born a criminal—in other words, entirely lacking in social adjustment." This was the opening statement of an October 1950 *Newsweek* account of Sheldon and Eleanor Glueck's new book entitled, *Unraveling Juvenile Delinquency.*[17] The book is the result of a ten year study by the Gluecks and others on their team to ascertain the causes of youthful criminality. It appears that up to this time most people were in agreement that something should be done about the youthful offender but no one had identified the problems except to state that they in fact did exist. The Gluecks found three factors prevalent among their 500 delinquents studied:

—The boys generally had poor family relations. Their fathers were needlessly harsh or completely lax in maintaining discipline, seldom firm but kindly. They received little parental love.

—They clashed with other people; were highly assertive, defiant, suspicious, destructive, and impulsive.

—They had turbulent personalities, were adventurous, extroverted, suggestible, stubborn, and emotionally unstable.

Two conclusions were made in the article. First, that detecting delinquency in its earliest stages is a job for specialists. It cannot be done, the Gluecks admit, by any simple, easily interpreted pencil and paper test. Secondly, the husband and wife team felt, that in delinquency society is faced not with predestination, but with destination. And probably destination can often be modified by intelligent early intervention.

The literature appears to be filled with intervention strategy during the late forties and early fifties. Among those writing was Dr. Edwin Powers (Annals, January 1949) in which he describes an experiment in the prevention of delinquency.[18] This particular ten year study called for 650 boys to be divided among ten counselors. (The essence of the relationship between the boy and his counselor was personal intimacy and friendship). Treatment consisted of the application of whatever skills each counselor was capable of supplying. Dr. Powers states, "In brief, it can be said that the treatment program, utilizing some of the best professional advice obtainable, comprised an unusually wide diversity of special services to boys and their families, from removing nits from boys' heads to preparing them for higher education."[19]

The conclusion of the study was somewhat vague in that, the counselors were unable to stop the rapid advance of young boys into delinquency with any greater success than the usual deterrent forces in the community. Some of the boys were evidently deflected from delinquent careers which, without the counselors help, might have resulted in continued or more serious violations. The researchers felt that although they were not completely successful in the first stage of delinquency prevention that in working with boys ages 8-11 later and more serious stages were to some degree curtailed.[20]

The Gluecks were in the forefront again in December, 1953. *U.S. News and World Report* carried an article entitled, "What Every Parent Should Know." Studies conducted at Harvard University by the husband and wife team concluded that delinquency started in homes that were characterized as follows:[21]

—6 out of every 10 juvenile delinquents have fathers who drink to excess
—3 out of 4 are permitted by parents to come and go as they please
—3 out of 5 are from homes where there is discord between parents
—7 out of 10 are from homes where there is no group or family recreation
—4 out of 5 have parents who take no interest in the children's friends
—4 out of 5 delinquent boys say their mothers were indifferent to them
—3 out of 5 delinquent boys say their fathers were indifferent to them
—Many have mothers who drink to excess
—Many come from broken homes
—Few get religious training of any kind

The solution was that only through the joint efforts of the home, the church and the general community can the youngster be insulated against the menace of crime. Stability in the home, the outreach of the church, youth organizations to keep the child busy outside the school—all of these have their place and help to bolster his sense of security.

Group action is working well in many places. There are suggestions for much more co-operative action: for a Youth National Institute on Juvenile Delinquency to explore the problem and develop a continuing program; for an organization of Delinquents Anonymous, patterned after Alcoholics Anonymous, to bring youngsters themselves into the work.

"What specialized role, if any, should the police play with reference to the problem of juvenile delinquency?"[22] This was the same question August Vollmer asked in 1926. Exactly twenty-nine years later the former police commissioner of New York, Francis Adams, was posing the same question. To answer the query the department launched an experimental project, extending over a period of three years, to gather data. Mr. Adams felt that no such data existed at that time and the experimental project would provide the means for effective evaluation of the questions at hand.

The United Nations International Conference on Prevention of Crime held in Geneva, 1956, gave priority to community organizations as a solution to the problem. The recommendations adopted include the following statement:

> The Congress recognized that the community provides the environment in which social institutions mold the child's behavior patterns of personality. The neighborhood in which young people live is perhaps the most fundamental phase of community influence. The factors which shape character derive very largely from these community influences as they operate through the family, the school, the church and other social institutions. Community action to prevent juvenile delinquency is to a great extent a matter of organizing a variety of community resources. . .[23]

Thus the International Conference went on record as favoring community action to prevent youth and adult crime.

The seed for what is later to become the Job Corps is planted in 1956 by the Citizens Union of New York for the Prevention and Cure of Delinquency. In an article appearing in *American City,* January 1956, in a listing of recommendations for preventing juvenile delinquency they mention the establishment of work camps for delinquent boys (similar to CCC Camps).[24] This in fact, was done in the early 60's with the formulation of the Job Corps but with a major modification of allowing all underprivileged youth, to take part of the advantage, to upgrade their education and at the same time learn a skill that would carry them through life.

The mid fifties to late fifties saw juvenile delinquency take a rapid increase and authors such as I. Richard Perlman (Then Chief of Juvenile Delinquency Statistics for the Children's Bureau) were calling for research into the problem.[25] More and better research was needed to test hypotheses concerning causal factors, to evaluate current programs of prevention and treatment, and to try out and evaluate new methods. Mr. Perlman points out the fact that the number of juvenile court cases reported to the Children's Bureau began to rise in 1948 and had more than doubled since 1950. "From all the evidence one is inclined to conclude that the problem of juvenile delinquency is tremendous and that it has been rising in recent years. But has the increase been real?" Mr. Perlman continues, "statements are often issued on the face of statistics that there has really been no real increase in delinquency." Rather, the statement implies, "the statistics merely reflect better reporting procedures, more public awareness, and increased law enforcement." The answer to the question is, yes there has been a rise in delinquency, and Mr. Perlman feels that it will continue in the years to come.[26]

The sixties see the closing of the circle. We have now traveled from delinquency and crime as a community problem thru the period of stressing the individual as being entirely responsible for all his criminal actions and now back to the community as the causal agent for our crime, both youth and adult.

Mr. James Symington, writing in *Survey,* February 1966, sees one of the major causal factors of youth crime as the high unemployment rate in the teenage group.[27] The largest group of today's unemployed is between sixteen and nineteen years old. Their unemployment rate is more than three times that for the labor force as a whole. One in three of these new young workers—an estimated twenty-six million of whom are entering the labor force during the 1960's—is a high school drop-out. "The relationship between unemployment and delinquency has not been precisely calibrated, but, like the predicted consequences of racial discrimination it rests on more than a hunch." Mr. Symington continues, "recognition of widespread delinquency and the probability of its increase brought about the establishment in 1961 of the President's committee to examine the delinquency problem."[28] The major result was the Juvenile Delinquency and Youth Offenses Control Act of September 1961.

Initially, under the 1961 Act sixteen major projects were developed in urban areas involving new techniques of job development, job training, education, and neighborhood organization.

"I come to you this evening to talk about crime . . . the goal of our nation is freedom and personal dignity for all our citizens . . . This year one out of every twenty juveniles will commit a criminal act. Juvenile crime is increasing 300 percent faster than the increase in the juvenile population." It was very apparent that John Mitchell, Attorney General of the United States, speaking before the Conference on Crime and Urban Crisis in San Francisco, 1969, was indeed concerned with the state of affairs.[29]

The Attorney General's solution was a simple yet very complex one, to involve the community as volunteers in the war against crime and especially youth crime. "We are approaching the limits of what government alone can do", the President has been quoted as saying in an earlier campaign speech. Mitchell continues, "In a recent poll conducted for the joint commission on Correctional Manpower, it was reported;[30]

> At least 10 percent of the public would be interested in serving as volunteer workers in juvenile programs, in helping to get jobs for ex-prisoners and in working on citizens' committees on organized crime—if asked.

Mr. Mitchell also proposed the establishment of a national United Anti-Crime Fund. This would serve the dual purposes of enlisting the aid of the private citizen and at the same time building a fund with which crime would be fought from a more effective approach.

The federal government has taken a more active interest in crime and delinquency prevention since 1960 when the Department of Health, Education, and Welfare submitted a Report to Congress on Juvenile Delinquency. Congress passed legislation in 1961 and 1964 to provide funds for research, demonstration, and training programs aimed at improving delinquency prevention and control programs.

As the outgrowth of the President's Crime Commission Report in 1967, Congress passed two major acts in 1968 which have generated progressive developments throughout the entire criminal justice system. These laws were (1) the Omnibus Crime Control and Safe Streets Act (Public Law 90-351) and (2) the Juvenile Delinquency Prevention and Control Act (Public Law 90-445).

An outgrowth of the Juvenile Delinquency Prevention and Control Act was the Youth Development and Delinquency Prevention Administration. The YDDPA has generated much interest in delinquency prevention in this country and is currenty funding many programs aimed at discovering more effective methods of keeping youth from committing unlawful acts.

As a result of the Omnibus Crime Control and Safe Streets Act, the Law Enforcement Assistance Administration was established and it is making funds available for crime prevention programs at the local levels of government.[31]

The decade of the 1970s should see much progress made in the challenging field of crime prevention.

FOOTNOTES

Note: This paper is an attempt to trace the phenomenon of crime prevention, mainly as it pertains to law enforcement. No in-depth analysis is intended.

[1]As cited by Barnes and Teeters.

[2]Richard Korn, *Juvenile Delinquency,* Crowell, 1968.

[3]C. H. Reeves, "Preventive Legislation in Relation to Crime", *Annals of the American Academy,* (September, 1892), p. 223.

[4]*Ibid.,* p. 224.

[5]*Ibid.,* p. 226.

[6]*Ibid.,* p. 227.

[7]Edward Divine, "The Correction and Prevention of Crime" *Survey,* (January 21, 1911).

[8]Adolph Eberhart, "Prevention of Crime" *Annals of the American Academy,* (March, 1913), p. 31.

[9]August Vollmer, "The Prevention and Detection of Crime as Viewed by a Police Officer" *Annals of the American Academy,* (May, 1926), p. 153.

[10]"Miss Deputy Commissioner Addition", *Survey,* (July 15, 1931), p. 379.

[11]Eliot Ness, "New Role of the Police" *Survey* (March, 1944), p. 77.

[12]Elizabeth Fajen, "Curing Delinquency at the Source" *Survey,* (October, 1946), p. 261-62.

[13]*Ibid.,* p. 261-62.

[14]*Ibid.,* p. 262.

[15]Children's Bureau of the Federal Security Agency, "The Saint Paul Experiment in Child Welfare" as cited in *The American City* (April, 1947), p. 118.

[16]*Ibid.,* p. 118.

[17]"Preventing Delinquency", *Newsweek,* (October 30, 1950), p. 56.

[18]Edwin Powers, "An Experiment in the Prevention of Delinquency" *The Annals of the American Academy,* (January, 1949), p. 81.

[19]*Ibid.,* p. 83-85.

[20]*Ibid.,* p. 83-85.

[21]"What Every Parent Should Know", *Newsweek,* (December 11, 1953), p. 37.

[22]Francis J. Adams, "New York Police Tackle Delinquency" *The American City,* (September, 1955), p. 5.

[23]As cited in "Recommendations for Preventing Delinquency", *The American City,* (February, 1956), p. 7.

[24]*Ibid.,* p. 7.

[25]Richard I. Perlman, "Delinquency Prevention: The Size of the Problem" *Annals of the American Academy,* (March, 1959), p. 1.

[26]*Ibid.,* p. 5-8.

[27]James Symington, "Youth, Crime, and the Great Society", *Survey,* (February, 1966), p. 41.

[28]*Ibid.,* p. 41-42.

[29]John Mitchell, "Crime Prevention" *Vital Speeches of the Day,* (March 1, 1969), p. 290-93.

[30]*Ibid.,* p. 290-93.

[31]John P. Kenney and Dan G. Pursuit, *Police Work With Juveniles and the Administration of Juvenile Justice.* Thomas: Springfield, 1970, p. 35.

SECTION FIVE

TRAINING

As program directors, justice middle managers have major personnel administrative responsibilities. They must determine program objectives and then relate these objectives to people. This means the development of job and position specifications and descriptions, the recruitment and selection of personnel to meet these specifications, the identification of skills, abilities, and training needs, and finally the employment of this total process. It is this process which overlaps into the greater personnel field that we will refer to as training; and therefore, this outline of training and educational material concerns itself with that part of the personnel function which focuses on the development of people through systematic training and education.

This section is included in outline form primarily because the subject matter would be a volume of its own, if expanded.

CHAPTER 17

TRAINING—MANAGEMENT'S TOOL FOR THE IMPLEMENTATION OF CHANGE

JOHN D. GERLETTI

Section I: Importance and Role of Training

THE TRAINING FUNCTION has been given as much lip service as any other single personnel function; but when it comes right down to hard facts of life, it is the most ignored of all management functions. In a very simple slow-moving world, the manager could be excused for ignoring the training function. However, operating in the dynamic world of management today, no manager can survive without completely understanding and being able to implement a continuous and effective People and Organization Development Program.

The world today is too complex, fast moving and ever changing to be able to afford the luxury of having each person learn the job as they grow up with it and without any guidance; thus, the emphasis on the importance of training in the life of today's manager. It is again to be emphasized that we are not trying to make fully qualified trainers of juvenile justice middle managers, but rather to acquaint them with the training process so that they can supervise and utilize this tool of management.

This training unit covers the following key points:

A. The growth and development of the training movement and its importance to management.
B. Limitations of training, or why training fails.
C. Training as a means to an end, not as an end in itself.
D. Training as a tool of management to implement change.
E. Training as a tool of management to improve employee satisfaction and employee morale.
F. Training as a tool for improved community relations.

Section II: Change—A Way of Life

Training by its very nature implies direction. It implies goals—not the goals of yesterday, or the day before, but the goals of today and tomorrow. It is therefore important that in this unit of effort we move away from the training function temporarily to take a long look at the world in which we live, work, play and some of the major changes that have taken place because these will dictate the need for new skills, abilities, and knowledge, and point up the increasing importance of training in today's world of management.

It is hoped that through the study within this section, we have an opportunity to trace the changing world of public administration and the role of government in our society plus the impact that technology has had upon the basic values of our lives. From this we can then develop a strategy for effective programs that are necessary to combat crime and delinquency in this ever changing world.

Outline:

A. The world today—the setting in which we work and live
   1. The growth and development of government in the United States—democracy at work
   2. The growth and development of the bureaucratic form of organization
   3. Democratic pluralism, or how decisions are made in a Democratic Society.
   4. The change agents at work—or the impact of technology after World War II.
   5. The world today and tomorrow and the implications for delinquency and crime prevention.

B. The development of organizational theory and its implications for training.
C. The impact of these changes on the problem of crime and delinquency, the need for community organization, state wide organization, national organization, and international organization to combat these problems.

Section III: Learning Theory and Change

Learning theory, by its very nature, is an extremely complex subject and probably more has been written in this area than in any other single area of training in the past four or five years. It is not important in this section that we master all of the learning theories that have been developed but rather that we understand the concepts which are most important to adult learning and especially to change and adjustment.

Outline:

A. Trial and error learning—the star experiment
B. Learning theory applied to the problems of youth
C. Learning theory applied to individual adult learning
D. Learning theory applied to organization development
E. Learning theory applied to community organization and coordination
F. Theories of motivation

Section IV: Kinds of Training

No systematic coverage of the area of training would be adequate unless we looked at what the literature refers to as the kinds of training that takes place in organizations. It is also important to clarify terminology from the education and training literature.

Outline:

A. Pre-Service education
B. Orientation training—breaking in the new employee, system, or organization model.
C. Induction or basic training
D. Job related or skill training—in service training
E. Technical and scientific training
F. Supervisory training and development
G. Executive development and leadership training

H. Attitude development or modification
I. Team training
J. Organizational development
K. In-service education programs
L. Inter-agency training

Section V: Training Methods and Their Application

When one thinks of training or education, one thinks of a classroom, an instructor, a blackboard, and a lecture. This of course is one approach to the educational process. However, it is only one of many methods and probably one of the most misused and abused. In the past few years, great progress in the education and training field has taken place in developing better methods, methods which are much more conducive to maximizing the learning process. In this section, we deal with the many varieties of methods which have been introduced into the education and training process, discussing their strong points, their weak points, and especially their points of application for maximum change and learning.

Outline:

A. Maximum learning and the choice of the training method
B. On the job versus off the job training
C. The lecture method
D. The conference method
E. The case studies method
F. Role Playing
G. Sensitivity Training—Human Relations Laboratory Training
H. Correspondence courses or home study courses
I. Supervised reading programs
J. Teaching machines, simulators, and programmed instructions
K. Management games
L. Syndicate or team training
M. Personal counseling or coaching
N. Job rotation
O. Internships—work study programs
P. Observational assignments
Q. Staff meetings
R. Apprenticeship training
S. The use of the diary
T. Formal education versus informal training
U. Instructional technology and its impact upon the entire learning process and training methods

Section VI: The Administration of Training Programs

All organizations have training programs, but in many cases they are not getting maximum return from their investment. This section deals with the key problems and issues in the establishment and the administration of a systematic training program.

Outline:

A. Who is responsible for training?
B. Why a training policy and the official essential elements of a training policy?
C. What is the ideal organizational structure for training?
D. Who should do the training?
E. Should training be centralized or decentralized?
F. Who should pay for the training?
G. Who should plan for training?

Section VII: The Availability of Training Resources

Training by its very nature is an expensive process. It demands a high degree of expertise which many organizations may or may not have. Therefore, a smart manager will look around and take advantage of every available resource. One of the great strengths of the American system of government is the provision of free public education, which is available to the young and old alike in the population centers of the nation. In addition to this, we have several other resources available to us.

In the following sections we discuss the location and utilization of these resources.

Outline:

A. Resources within an organization
B. Resources available from the educational institutions in the area, including the high schools, the junior high schools, the junior colleges, the four year institutions (private as well as public) and the public library
C. Resources available in other public institutions which have organized training programs
D. Resources available from suppliers of equipment and materials
E. The use of training consultants
F. Resources available from the professional societies

G. Resources available from the professional training organizations
H. Utilization of correspondence courses

Section VIII: Developing the Training Programs Based Upon Needs

The strategy of delinquency prevention and control calls for total community participation and involvement; therefore, we face the problem of developing competent juvenile justice leaders, teams of specialists, organizational effectiveness, and community-wide coordinated activities. This means that not one but several training efforts must be mounted and coordinated.

This section outlines an approach to meeting this complex problem.

Outline:

A. An analysis of the public and private organizations and citizen groups involved in delinquency prevention and control.
B. An organizational analysis of each of these groups determining their sphere of influence, their objectives and goals, etc.
C. The various approaches to determining the training needs of an organization.
   1. The management audit
   2. An analysis of the problems of managers
   3. Utilization of advisory committees
   4. Difficulty analysis of the field workers
   5. Difficulty analysis of the supervisors
   6. Difficulty analysis of the managers
   7. The use of examinations
   8. The use of counseling in employee evaluation
   9. The use of suggestion boxes, etc.
   10. Desk audits, job analysis, etc.

Section IX: The Development of Training Materials

One could settle for the fact that most of the training materials in this field are presented in texts in psychology, sociology, corrections, police administration, etc. However, this is not the case. When we speak of training materials, we are speaking of specific materials designed and developed to meet specific needs. Therefore, the major effort calls for the pulling together of all the available material that has been written and developed, isolating those areas which need additional development, and then through intensive training need surveys identifying the kinds of detailed problems which require better solutions. Finally, the best material from the literature and suggested solutions from experts as well as from juvenile justice personnel must be synthesized into an education and training package.

Outline:

A. The difficulty analysis and field survey approach of developing materials
B. The use of the group process in the planning and development of training materials
C. The utilization of training specialists and curriculum experts in the development of training materials
D. The development of training materials using the best of instructional technology
E. The printing and publication of training materials

Section X: The Development of Training Staffs

Who will be the trainers, where will they come from and how will they be developed is the concern of this section.

A. Selection and development of the training director for a large central training program
B. The decentralization of training and the development of training staff on the spot
C. The utilization of supervisors as trainers
D. The utilization of experts as trainers
E. The utilization of persons caught in the system, such as delinquents, etc. as trainers

Section XI: The Evaluation of Training

Evaluation is a must in any training program because it provides the feedback so necessary to measure effectiveness. This section concerns itself with the total process of evaluation, the various approaches to evaluation and the skills, knowledge, and abilities needed for evaluation.

Outline:

A. Evaluation as part of the learning process

B. Definition of goals, missions, and purposes so that programs can be measured and evaluated
C. A review of the statistics of evaluation
D. Methods of evaluation and the tools required

Section XII: The Legal Aspects and the Legislation Involved in Training

Industrial relations, community relations, and human relations are heavily tied up in national, state, and local legislation which impinges upon the training process. No program manager today can be effective unless he is aware of the implications of this legislation and especially how it bears upon the training process. Therefore, this section is devoted to a review and summary of the important legislation affecting training.

Outline:

A. A review of federal, state, county and city legislations
B. The development of training policies
C. The impact of Civil Service upon training
D. The development of needed legislation

REFERENCES

1. Applewhite, P. *Organization Behavior.* New York: Prentice-Hall, 1965.
2. Argyris, Chris. *Integrating the Individual and the Organization.* New York: Wiley, 1964.
3. Backman, R. O. *How to Train Supervisors.* New York: Harper, 1952.
4. Bennis, W. G., Benne, K. D., and Chin, R. *The Planning of Change.* New York: Holt, Rinehart and Winston, 1969.
5. Blalock, Hubert. *Towards a Theory of Minority-Group Relations.* New York: Wiley, 1967.
6. Boocock, S. S. and Schild, E. O. *Simulation Games in Learning.* Beverly Hills: Sage, 1968.
7. Breed, Allen F. *Guide for Conducting Youth Services.* California Youth Authority, 1969.
8. Browne, R. K. and Dr. Patterson. "The Evaluation of Training Programs," *Public Personnel Review.* July 1970, pp. 162-165.
9. Cassidy, R. "Manpower Planning: A coordinated Approach," *Personnel. September-October,* 1963, pp. 35-41.
10. Champagne, J. E. "Job Recruitment of the Unskilled," *Personnel Journal.* April 1969, pp. 259-268.
11. Craig, R., and Bittel, L. (eds.), *Training and Development Handbook.* New York: McGraw-Hill, 1967.

12. Crawford, C. C. *How to Make Training Surveys.* Crawford, 1954.
13. Dale, Edgar. *Audio Visual Methods in Teaching.* Dryden Press, 1969.
14. Dammond, Donald. "Three-Pronged Program Uncovers Talents on Minority Groups," *Employee Relations Bulletin.* Report No. 999, National Foreman's Institute, May 4, 1966.
15. De Phillips, F., Berliner, W., and Gribbin, J., Jr. *Management of Training Programs.* Homewood, Illinois: Irwin, 1960.
16. Doeinger, P. *Programs to Employ the Disadvantaged.* Englewood Cliffs, New Jersey: Prentice-Hall, 1969.
17. Dubin, R. *Leadership and Productivity.* San Francisco: Chandler, 1965.
18. Dworkis, M. P. "The Playback: A Technique of Management Training," *Personnel Administration.* November-December, 1962.
19. Eddy, W. B. "Beyond Behaviorism," Organization Development, *Public Personnel Review.* July 1970, pp. 169-175.
20. Emerson, Lynn A. *How to Prepare Training Manuals.* University of New York, 1952.
21. Gellerman, S. *Motivation and Productivity.* American Management Assoc., 1963.
22. Gerletti, John D., and Crawford, C. C. *Civil Defense Management.* University of Southern California, School of Public Administration, 1966.
23. Gerletti, John D. *Materials for the Study of the Problems of Juvenile Police Officers.* J. Gerletti, 1949.
24. Ginzberg, Eli, et. al. *The Middle-Class Negro in the White Man's World.* New York: Columbia University Press, 1967.
25. Golembiewski, R. "Organization Development in Public Agencies: Perspectives on Theory and Practice," *Public Administration Review.* July-August, 1969.
26. Golembiewski, R., and Cohen, M. *People in the Public Service.* Peacock, 1970.
27. Guerin, Q. W. "Focus on the Attitude of Change Process," *Personnel Journal.* February 1968, pp. 95-98.
28. Haskell, M. A. *The New Careers Concept: Potential for Public Employment of the Poor.* New York: Praeger, 1970.
29. Herzberg, F., Mausner, B., and Synderman, B. *The Motivation to Work.* New York: John Wiley, 1965.
30. Herzberg, F. "One More Time: How Do You Motivate Employees?" *Harvard Business Review.* January-February, 1968. pp. 53-62.
31. Hill, Wm. F. *Learning Through Discussion.* Sage Publications, 1969.
32. International City Manager's Association, *Municipal Personnel Administration.* 1960.
33. James, Howard. *Children in Trouble A National Scandal.* David McKay Co., 1970.
34. Jenson, Ollie A. "Cultural Bias in Selection," *Public Personnel Review.* Vol. 27, pp. 125-120, July-August, 1965.
35. Jones, R. "Developments in Government Manpower: A Federal Perspective," *Public Administration Review.* January 1967, pp. 134-141.
36. Katz, D., and Kahn, R. *The Social Psychology of Organizations.* New York: John Wiley, 1966.
37. Kirkpatrick, F., et.al. *Testing and Fair Employment.* New York: University Press, 1968.

38. Krislov, S. *The Negro in Federal Employment.* University of Minnesota Press, Minneapolis, 1967.
39. Likert, Rensis. *New Patterns of Management.* New York: McGraw-Hill, 1961.
40. Litwin, G., and Stringle, K. *Motivation and Organization Climate.* Cambridge, Harvard, 1967.
41. Lloyd, Betty J. "Womanpower Key to Manpower Shortage," *Personnel Journal.* April 1962.
42. Lockwood, Howard C. "Testing Minority Applications for Employment," *Personnel Journal,* 44:356-360, July-August, 1965.
43. Lynton, R., and Pareek, U. *Training for Development.* Homewood, Illinois: Dorsey Press, 1967.
44. Mager, Robert F. *Developing Attitude Towards Learning.* Fearon, 1964.
45. Mager, R., and Beach, K. M. *Developing Vocational Instruction.* Fearon, 1962.
46. Mager, Robert F. *Preparing Instruction Objectives.* Fearon, 1962.
47. Mailick, S., and Hoberman, S. "Executive Development and Organizational Development," *Public Personnel Review.* July, 1963, pp. 173-178.
48. Mangunn, G., and M. Glenn. *Employing the Disadvantaged in the Federal Civil Service.* (Policy Papers in Human Resources and Industrial Relations, No. 19) Ann Arbor, Michigan, Institute of Labor and Industrial Relations, Wayne State University and The National Manpower Policy Task Force, 1969.
49. Martin, A. "Morale and Productivity: A Review of the Literature," *Public Personnel Review.* January 1969.
50. Mathis, H. "The Disadvantaged and the Aptitude Barrier," *Personnel and Guidance Journal.* January 1969, pp. 467-472.
51. McFarland, D. *Personnel Management: Theory and Practice.* MacMillan Co., 1968.
52. McGehee, Wm., and Thayer, P. W. *Training in Business and Industry.* Wiley and Sons, 1961.
53. McGregor, D. M. *The Human Side of Enterprise.* New York: McGraw-Hill, 1960.
54. McPherron, D. "Jobs for the Disadvantaged—How?" *Public Personnel Review.* July 1966.
55. Megginson, L. *Personnel: A Behavioral Approach to Administration.* Irwin, 1967.
56. Meyer, H., and Kay, E., and French, J. "Split Roles in Performance Appraisal," *Harvard Business Review.* 1965, pp. 123-129.
57. Miles, M. B., *Learning to Work in Groups.* Teachers College Press, Columbia, 1967.
58. Miles, M. B. *Learning to Work in Groups.* Teachers College Press, Columbia, 1962.
59. Miles, M. B. *Learning to Work in Groups.* New York: Columbia, 1965.
60. Miller, N. R. "Sensitivity Training: A Case History," *Training Directors' Journal.* January 1963.
61. Mosher, F. *Democracy and the Public Service.* New York: Oxford, 1968.
62. Neff, W. S. *Work and Human Behavior,* New York: Atherton Press, 1968.
63. Nigro, Felix. *Public Personnel Administration.* Holt, 1959.
64. Paine, F. T., and Bassim, W. M. "Sensitivity Training: Theory and Practice," *Public Personnel Review.* 1965, pp. 78-82.

65. Parker, W. H. *Daily Training Bulletin of Los Angeles Police Department.* Thomas, 1961.
66. Pfiffner, John M. *The Function of Police in a Democratic Society.* School of Public Administration, University of Southern California, 1967.
67. Pfiffner, John M., and Fels, M. *The Supervision of Personnel—Human Relations in the Management of Men.* New York: Prentice-Hall, 1964.
68. Planty, E. G., and Funston, J. T. *Developing Managerial Ability.* Ronald Press, 1954.
69. Portune, Robert. *Changing Adolescent Attitudes Toward Police.* Cincinnati: W. H. Anderson Co., 1971.
70. Ricketts, E. F. "Performance Standards for City Employees," *Public Management.* August 1953, pp. 170-174.
71. Rowland, Virgil. *Managerial Performance Standards.* New York: American Management Association, 1960.
72. Rubin, Ted. *Law as an Agent of Delinquency Prevention.* California Youth Authority, 1970.
73. Scott, W. "Organization Government: The Prospects for a Truly Participative System," *Public Administration Review.* January-February, 1969.
74. Scully, William. *Monrovia Community Study.* California Youth Authority, 1969.
75. Seigel, G. "Management Development and the Instability of Skills: A Strategy," *Public Personnel Review.* January 1969.
76. Schein, E. H. *Organizational Psychology.* Englewood Cliffs, New Jersey: Prentice-Hall, 1965.
77. Seberhagen, L. W. "What Motivates Civil Service Employees," *Public Personnel Review.* January, 1970, pp. 48-50.
78. Sherwood, Frank. "The Role Concept in Administration," *Public Personnel Review.* January 1964, pp. 41-44.
79. Stahl, Glen O. *Public Personnel Administration.* Harper, 1963.
80. Tannenbaum, R., and Wechiser, T. R., and Massarik, F. *Leadership and Organization: A Behavioral Science Approach.* New York: McGraw-Hill, 1961.
81. Watson, N. G., and Sterling, J. W. *Police and Their Opinions.* I.A.C.P., 1969.
82. Wickert, F., and McFarland, D. (ed.) *Measuring Executive Effectiveness.* New York: Appleton-Century-Crofts, 1967.
83. Wiltich, W. A., and Schuller, C. F. *Audio Visual Materials.* New York: Harper and Row, 1967.
84. Yoder, Dale. *Personnel Principles and Policies.* Prentice-Hall, 1969.

SECTION SIX

COMMUNITY RELATIONS

CHAPTER 18

EVALUATION OF POLICE-COMMUNITY RELATIONS PROGRAMS*

LEE P. BROWN

THROUGHOUT THE NATION we have observed police departments striving to improve their relationship with the public. Even though many departments currently operate police-community relations programs, they are still searching for more efficient and effective methods of achieving this objective.

The purpose of this Chapter is to develop criteria for evaluating police-community relations programs. "This is probably the most difficult and the most neglected area in police-community relations."[1] Consequently, this represents the first attempt to identify specific criteria (e.g., measures of effectiveness) for evaluating the numerous community relations programs that have been developed by police agencies. Here, we will not be concerned with criteria for evaluating the overall relationship between the police and the public, rather we will focus on the development of criteria for evaluating the individual program components that make up a police-community relations program.

Presently, police departments are evaluating their community relations programs in the same manner they evaluate other police functions, vis-a-vis, the computation of statistics. The use of statistical data to analyze police activities was discussed by Neiderhoffer:

*Summarized from "Police Community Relations Project," LEAA-NI-075, prepared by Lee P. Brown, 1970.

> Every major police department spends a good portion of its time grinding out statistical reports: statistics of arrest, summonses, warnings, convictions, ambulance calls, fatalities. Each case is transformed into a number and reported whenever possible in a manner that enhances the glory of that department. The contemporary trend to seek a cure for every personal problem in *analysis* has invaded the police bureaucracy. But whereas a patient in psychonalysis supplies data by a system of consciousness, it is the never-ending stream of statistics that symbolizes police case histories. The analysis unit is the major arm of defense in the struggle of the department to justify itself. In any emergency the chief frequently turns for help to his specialized police bureau.[2]

Our research has shown that, in general, the police have not gone beyond this traditional reliance on statistical data for evaluating (and justifying) their community relations programs. Illustrative of this reliance on statistical data is the following excerpt.[3]

Community Relations Division

	NO. OF MEETINGS	NO. OF PEOPLE ATTENDING
Contact with Community Leaders		3,486
Civic and Citizen Association Meetings	21	4,054
Business Association Meetings	16	353
Civil Rights Meetings Attended	15	3,076
Church Meetings	15	1,441
Precinct Advisory Council Meetings	15	179
Participation in Community Workshops	16	14,972
P.T.A. Meetings	6	1,515
College Lectures	18	1,610
Schools Visited in Non-enforcement Program ..	7	2,191
Summer School Lectures	7	750
Demonstration Project of Student-Police Relations Program in Elementary Schools	36	2,716
Research Program in Senior High Schools	3	194
Tours of Headquarters, Elementary School Students		2,716
Tours of Ninth Precinct, Elementary School Students		1,492

Tours of Eleventh Precinct, Elementary School Students		1,224
Non-enforcement Contacts with Children other than in school	16	4,775
Radio and Television Appearances	6	
Programs honoring Citizens who aided the Police Department in the Apprehension of Criminals	1	

Community Relations Division

	NO. OF MEETINGS	NO. OF PEOPLE ATTENDING
In-Service Training of Police Officers by Members of this Unit	12	516
Block Club Meetings	3	940
Release Guidance Center (Parolees) Meetings	2	26
Tenant Council Meeting (N.C.H.A.)	8	5,068
Pre-Release Conference (Inmates D.C. Workhouse)	2	40
Others	4	755
Total Appearances	229	
Total Attendance		54,089

Several projects have focused on the overall evaluation of the police relationship with the community.[4] In addition, we were able to identify two police agencies that have evaluated the effectiveness of their police-community relations projects.[5] But to date, little has been written that attempts to identify specific criteria for police-community relations component analysis. In this Chapter we will discuss the criteria problem and attempt to identify meaningful means of evaluation that will stimulate additional efforts on the part of those concerned with the analytical side of police-community relations.[6] By no means, however, should the criteria provided here be considered either exhaustive or definitive. We must stress the point that considerably more effort must be addressed to the problem analyses of individual police-community relations components. Hopefully, this project will provide the starting point.

Evaluation should not be done for the mere sake of evaluation—it must have a purpose. Neither should evaluation be considered an end in itself—its purpose is to determine the value, effectiveness or quality of a program. The need is related to the decision-making process. Consequently, as we shall point out later, the objectives of the program itself provides the background for evaluation. The program performs certain functions and these functions are designed to accomplish certain objectives. Measuring the extent to which these objectives are being met is the essence of program evaluation.

In evaluating police-community relations programs, it should be understood from the beginning that a variety of research techniques are necessary. The complexity of police-community relations programming makes it virtually impossible to scientifically qualify the total research endeavor. Consequently, evaluation approaches utilized will be both quantitative and subjective.

Accepting the premise that portions of the evaluation process will be subjective, it follows that if an objective evaluation is to be made, the evaluation must be done by an agency or individuals external of the police-community relations program. In other words, in order to insure objectivity in the results it is necessary to have someone other than the police conduct the evaluation. Social scientists with expertise in the field of evaluatory research are readily available and willing to undertake such projects. College and university resources should be utilized primarily because of their interest and expertise in research, their availability, and their ready reservoir of knowledge. This position was voiced by Winston-Salem, one of the few cities that has concerned itself with program evaluation:

> All professional advice leads us to conclude that an outside evaluation team . . . is the best approach to gain an unbiased and professional appraisal.[7]

Under ideal conditions an evaluation component should be built into the police-community relations program from its inception. This would allow the establishment of a baseline from which to evaluate the effects of the program. In most cases, however, this is no longer possible since many departments have already initiated their programs without including in it an evaluation component. This should not preclude departments from undertaking program evaluation because the evaluation process should be a longitudinal undertaking. For those departments who do not have an evaluation component built into their program, the first evaluation will not only give insight into the effectiveness of their endeavors, but will also provide a baseline from which to evaluate the future operation of the program.

We have indicated that the evaluation of police-community relations programs necessitates a variety of techniques. Some of the data used in making an evaluation will be subjective in nature and others will be quantitative. The subjective data would come from systematic and direct observation; whereas the quantitative data would be collected by surveys and documentation.

Before developing our system for evaluating police-community relations programs, a few words should be said about evaluating the other four categories of programs we have previously categorized as not being police-community relations, although they are operated under the title.[8]

Public Relations

In order to establish criteria for evaluating a police department's public relations program, it is first necessary to define what we mean by the term. For purposes of this paper, public-relations, in its broadest sense, is a program designed to make the public aware of what the agency is doing, why it is doing it, and how it contributes to the welfare of the community as a whole. We do not intend to play down the importance of public relations for police agencies because they (the police) similar to business and industry have come to realize that it is not sufficient to just do a good job, the public must constantly be reminded of the good job it is doing. It is important, however, to keep in mind the fact that public relations will not solve any of the pressing community problems nor be acceptable to the subcultural groups who possess these problems.

Public relations, from the standpoint of private enterprise, is a method of selling a product. From the standpoint of the police, public relations is a method of selling the police image. Consequently, it is logical to assume that anything the police do from a public relations standpoint will be done to enhance their image. Stated negatively, the police will not develop a public relations program that will present a bad image to the public.

In that context, we do not deem it necessary to establish criteria for evaluating a police department's public relations program. Let it suffice to say that if the community relations is not good, the public relations will not be good. Public relations (a legitimate police function) does not attempt to involve itself in the problems of the community. It can be likened to a one-way street, or a broadcasting system. There is no real interaction, merely the police projecting its favorable image to the public. Such a program does not alleviate the tension between the police and the various enclaves who are at odds with the police.

Crime Prevention

It should be pointed out at the on-set that the police alone are not capable of preventing crime. Nevertheless, the police have a great responsibility in the area of crime prevention, a field which is relatively unexplored at this point. In the past and up until this date, the police have directed the vast majority of their efforts toward the after-the-fact policing. That is, matching a criminal act with an individual—with little effort directed toward before-the-act policing. This is true even though the police traditionally, in defining their goal, include the function of crime prevention.

Evaluation of the effectiveness of police-sponsored crime prevention programs is probably the easiest task to accomplish. Here, however, it is necessary that the department maintain adequate statistical data on the incidence of crime which their program is geared toward preventing. Evaluation, therefore, must be built into the program. For example, if a department develops a program aimed at reducing the shoplifting rate, the evaluation is simply a comparison of the rates before and the rates after the implementation of the program. The validity of the evaluation must be insured by controlling certain variables. An adequate period of time must be provided to show a relationship between the program and the results. The time element is also important in context of the monthly variations. For example, it would not be valid to compare the month of December prior to the initiation of the program with the month of October after the initiation of the program. The results would not be valid since during December, just prior to Christmas, the shoplifting rate generally increases greatly.

Essentially, evaluation of crime prevention programs is simply a matter of comparing the incidence rate of a particular crime before the initiation of a program with the rate after the program has operated for a period of time. The effectiveness of the program can be seen in a decrease in the crime for which the program is geared.

If the objective of a program is to reduce the crime rate in general (not focusing on one particular offense), ". . . then it would be appropriate to use crime rates as the major criterion (but not necessarily the only criterion) for evaluating activities aiming at these objectives."[9]

For example, if the program has as its objective: "To reduce the amount and effects of crime and in general to maintain an atmosphere of personal security from criminal behavior," the following criteria can be used:[10]

1. Annual number of offenses for each major class of crime (or reduction from the base in the number of crimes).
2. Crime rates, as for example, the number per 1,000 inhabitants per year, for each major class of crime.
3. Crime rate index that includes all offenses of a particular type (e.g., "crimes of violence," or "crimes against property"), perhaps weighted as to seriousness of each class of offense.
4. Number and percent of populace committing "criminal acts during the year. (This is a less common way to express the magnitude of the crime problem: it is criminal oriented rather than "crime oriented.")
5. Annual value of property lost (adjusted for price-level changes). This value might also be expressed as a percent of the total property value in the community.
6. An index of overall community "feeling of security" from crime, perhaps based on public opinion polls and/or opinion experts.
7. Percent of reported crimes cleared by arrest and "assignment of guilt" by a court.
8. Average time between occurrence of a crime and the apprehension of the criminal. (The major purpose of this criterion is to reflect the psychological reduction in anxiety due to the length of this time period.)

9. Number of apparently justified complaints of police excesses by private citizens
10. Number of persons subsequently found to be innocent who were punished and/or simply arrested.[11]

In examining the above, it should be noted that:

(a) Criteria 1 through 6 are criteria for evaluation of crime-prevention programs. Criteria 7 and 8 are aimed at evaluating crime control after crimes have occurred (i.e., when crime prevention has failed). Criteria 9 and 10 to some extent 6, aim at the avoidance of law enforcement practices that themselves have an adverse effect upon personal safety. Criterion 6, and to some extent 8, aim at indicating the presence of a fearful, insecure atmosphere in the locality.

(b) Some argue that the primary function of criminal apprehension and punishment is to prevent future crimes; and, therefore, that Criteria 7 and 8 would not be sufficiently "end oriented," but rather "means" oriented, and would not be included in the list.

(c) For many analyses it would probably be appropriate to distinguish crime activity by the type of criminal, including such characteristics as age, sex, family income, etc. (juvenile delinquency is an obvious subcategory).[12]

Youth Programs

Many police departments operating community relations programs are directing their major efforts toward the youth. We have previously identified programs geared for youth which start as early as St. Louis' pre-natal program and going as high as several college level programs.

This concern for the youth is understandable since the various national surveys conducted for the President's Crime Commission[13] indicated that the youth constitute one of the three critical areas of tension between the police and the community.[14] Also, some departments are concentrating their efforts on the youth because they feel their efforts directed toward the adult population are often fruitless. One community relations officer put it in these terms:

> We can give up on the adults. Their attitudes are already fixed and we aren't going to change them. The hope for the future rests with the youth. If we can reach them in the schools, we'll have a bright future ahead of us. We can reach the kids, but we can't reach the adults. Our greatest success has been with the kids.

The myriad of police-youth programs, excluding the police-school visitation programs (e.g., Officer Friendly) have two basic objectives: (1) to prevent juvenile delinquency, and (2) to instill in the youth positive attitudes toward the police. Closely related are the objectives of the police-school visitation programs:

> . . . to inform youth of their rights and responsibilities as citizens and to acquaint youth with problems of contemporary society and of measures taken to influence them in recognizing and adhering to a structure of law and order.[15]

The evaluation of police-youth programs, similar to the evaluation of any program must be based on the program objectives. If the objective of the program is to prevent juvenile delinquency, its effectiveness can be determined by the absence of illegal activity on the part of the participants in the program.

If the objective of the program is to instill in the youth positive attitudes toward the police, the effectiveness of the program can be determined by attitudinal measurements. The instrument used to measure attitudes should be administered at the inception of the program and again at a later date. From this, a comparison can be made to determine any attitudinal changes which occurred in the interim. The *before and after* testing should also be done with a control group. This would enable the evaluator to determine what effects the program had on the attitudes of those exposed to it, as contrasted with the control group which did not participate in the program.

Since several projects have been conducted on the effectiveness of police-youth programs, this project will limit its discussion of that topic. Reference is made to the Cincinnati Police-Juvenile Attitude Project[16] which includes a twenty question opinion sheet and the Chicago Board of Education's evaluation of their police-school pilot program.[17]

Police-Community Relations Training

Under the many programs operated under the title of police-community relations, we have previously identified several which we classified as police-community relations training programs. Before discussing the evaluation of police-community relations training programs, we will first discuss the objectives of such programs.

In developing a police-community relations training program, three conditions should be taken into consideration:

1. The diversity of men.
2. The diversity of need.
3. The diversity of the history of training in the department.

In considering the diversity of men, it should be remembered that all men are not the same. Therefore, individual differences should be taken into consideration before developing a police-community relations training program.

Along the same line, the needs of each department will differ; therefore, consideration should be given to the exact needs of the department for which the program is being developed.

Third, consideration should be given to the diversity of the department's history of overall training. If the department has a history of continuous training, then training in police-community relations will probably be more acceptable to the men. A community relations training program should not be a crash program—time is needed to prepare the course.

In developing the training program, certain questions should be considered. For example, does every man in the department have negative attitudes—are these attitudes to the same degree? Can these attitudes be changed? Our experience has shown that police-community relations training programs are more effective if the goal of the program is to create an awareness on the part of policemen of minority and community problems and the latent effect is generally an attitude change. The primary goal, however, should be to provide the mechanism whereby police officers become sensitive to the needs and feelings of the community:

> The overall needs of communities—better housing, more effective youth programs, et al, have a direct relationship to the problems with which law enforcement has to deal. Therefore, it is incumbent that peace officers acquire analytical tools, and educate themselves to the overall needs of the communities which they must police.[18]

The writer's personal observations lead him to believe that only a certain percentage of policemen (15 to 20 percent) have authoritative personalities. They, however, make such an impression that it seems as if everyone in the department has authoritative personalities. In addition, you will find the same number of men with just the opposite personality make-up. This leaves about 60 percent of the men in the middle. The challenge is to move the marginal men to the positive side and at the same time weaken the negative.

Unfortunately, we find that many cities are willing to spend large sums of money on riot control equipment, but not on police-community relations training. As a result, spotty training in community relations is a big problem for many police agencies. The typical response has been that when there is a crisis, then "We want a training program."

The ultimate goal of a community relations program should be to get *total* community relations in all aspects of police work. A comprehensive community relations training program should involve all people that train policemen. Community relations training should be an intricate part of *all* phases of the officers' training. This should include training in the area of arrest, search and seizure; use of firearms; citation writing; etc.

One of the biggest problems in community relations training is in the area of middle management (above sergeant and below deputy chief.) Therefore, it is necessary to understand that the same training program should not be given to all levels in the department. This is a lesson we have learned from large industry—the level of training must be geared to the level of the position the person holds within the organization. In developing the program, it is best to work with the command level officers first. Where a program is accepted at the top echelon, it is more readily accepted at the bottom of the organizational structure.

Training in police-community relations revolves around human problems—not just police problems. Such programs often deal with the attitudes of the men being trained. Consequently, the men tend to resist the attempt to change their attitudes (which is a normal reaction. This resistance can best be overcome by taking a survey of the attitudes that do exist, and then determining what needs to be accomplished. This would allow the trainer to determine the best solution to the problem. (Best solution equals quality times acceptance.) Through experience, we have found that the quality of the training program, in conjunction with the acceptance by the men, is the best solution to the problem. Everyone has an idea of what quality is, but what is important is acceptance. The level of acceptance relates to the quality of the solution—but no solution can be obtained without acceptance. It therefore, must be impressed upon the trainees that the program is designed to help them.

The question is often asked, "What is more important in a community relations training program, the content or the process?" We have found that the two cannot be separated. For example, the lecturer alone cannot accomplish the task, and many times he will find himself talking at the men; rather than with them. Discussion, problem solving and role playing are also important elements of a community relations training program.

The objective of a police-community relations training program should be to focus on the human relations factors which are so important to modern police work. It must be stressed throughout the program that good police-community relations is the responsibility of the total police department. It should be stressed that everything an officer does to eliminate misunderstanding and increase citizen confidence and support for the police will make his job that much easier.

Some of the objectives of a police-community relations training program should be:[19]

1. The development in police officers of an appreciation of the civil rights of the public.
2. The development in police officers the ability to meet without undue militance or aggressiveness police situations involving minority groups.
3. The development in police officers an adequate social perspective.
4. The development in police officers an awareness of individual and group differences.
5. The development of an understanding by police officers of how their words and actions may be perceived by the public.
6. The development in police officers a neutral, objective approach to integrated situations.
7. To develop in police officers a knowledge of the fact that their be-

havior will infuse similar inter-group behaviors and attitudes in other members of the police force.

8. The development in police officers a recognition and awareness of the role of associated community human relations agencies.
9. The development in police officers the skills required for anticipating and meeting the police-human relations aspects of (a) their work, (b) incidents rooted in factors of race, religion and national origin, (c) juvenile offenses, (d) civil rights complaints, and (e) community tensions.
10. The development in police officers an awareness of personal prejudice and bias prevalent on all sides of issues.
11. The development of an understanding by police officers of why certain groups purposely transgress the law and intentionally cause civil disobedience.
12. The development of an understanding by police officers the effects of firm, impartial law enforcement, as compared to lax, biased law enforcement.
13. The development in police officers the maintenance of a professional profile, regardless of the amount of stress or circumstances.

The ultimate goal of a community relations training program should be to teach the officer how to continue doing his job with the maximum effectiveness while building public confidence that fair and equal law enforcement is being maintained at all times.

Illustrative, but not representative, is the following topical outline of a police-community relations training program which was developed by the writer for a municipal police agency with a large Black community:

- I. Orientation to Class
  - A. Need for the course
- II. The Civil Rights Movement
  - A. An historical analysis
  - B. Present day demands
  - C. Causes
  - D. A Comparison of demands of civil rights movement in 1950's and 60's and the labor movement of the 1920's.
  - E. The Politics of Protest
    1. Black militancy
    2. White militancy
- III. Case Study of Four Active Organizations
  - A. NAACP
  - B. Urban League

C. Black Panthers
D. Nation of Islam

IV. Black History
A. To show contributions made by Blacks in the development of America

V. Police Officers Role in the Black Community
A. Ghetto conditions
1. Sociological
2. Psychological
B. Black attitudes toward the police
1. Nationally
2. Locally
C. Police attitudes toward Blacks
1. Nationally
2. Locally
D. Causes of police problems in the Black community
E. Race and crime

VI. Community Power and the Politics of Leadership
A. Approaches to the analysis of community power, changing patterns of political influence and resources, decision making within the context of local and national policies, myths and realities of political power.

VII. The Psychology of Human Development
A. Basic principles of developmental psychology
B. The psychology of perception and its relation to police performance
C. How attitudes are formed
D. How attitudes influence behavior
E. Basic principles of the psychology of adjustment
F. Knowing ourselves
G. Understanding others

VIII. The Mechanisms of Prejudice
A. To present a good working knowledge of the behavioral effects of prejudices which is essential for anyone whose job is the regulation of human behavior

IX. Professionalism and Ethics
A. The need for the inculcation of social awareness, expertise and ethical standards, concepts of police discretion and spot judgment

X. Practical Police Problems
A. Role playing

XI. Summary and Conclusion

Price and Lloyd have pointed out, "A major weakness of traditional, professional education programs is the failure to scientifically evaluate their impact on participants."[20] They concluded that a scientifically evaluated educational program would require three elements:[21]

1. A set of valid and reliable instruments which could be administered before and after the program and which would test changes in values, knowledge, skills and behavior.[22]
2. A control group of individuals who resemble in important respects the characteristics of the group being exposed to the program, but who would only be given the "before-after tests," should be maintained.
3. A follow-up study to determine long-term effects of the program would be desirable.

In essence, the evaluation of a police-community relations training program should cover perceptual, attitudinal and behavior measures before and after the program. In addition, the trainees should be allowed to evaluate the context and methods of instruction which are used. This *critique by participants* should be designed to point out the strengths and weaknesses of the program and provide recommendations for further improvements.[23]

Police-Community Relations

We have previously indicated that evaluation is the process of assessing the degree of achievements related to that which has been attempted.[24] The development of criteria for evaluating police-community relations programs, however, is greatly complicated by the many uncontrollable variables that influence the police relationship with the community. For example, what affect does other socio-economic conditions have on police-community relations (vis-a-vis, poor housing, unemployment, discrimination, lack of recreational facilities, poor schools, etc.)? That is to say, the nature of police-community relations, under our definition of the term, cannot be separated from the over-all problems of a given community. These other socio-economic variables may influence goal achievement (positively or negatively), thereby complicating any attempt to isolate a set of criteria that could emperically be used to determine the over-all effectiveness of a police-community relations program. For that reason, we have taken the position that evaluation should be geared toward assessing the effectiveness of individual police-community relations program components, and not the over-all relationship between the police and the community. The necessity of making this distinction can be seen in light of the need to make decisions—the need to change, modify or drop a particular program component. The evaluation of program objectives of the police-community relations programs (e.g., improving the police relationship with the community.)

Just as we have stated in our discussion of evaluating crime prevention programs, the criteria for determining the effectiveness of a police-community relations program must be directly related to the goals of the program. For example, what does the program seek to achieve? The goals should relate to the ends to be achieved and not to the means which are utilized to achieve the goals. The goal of police-community relations is to better the relationship between the police and the community, and not, for example, to establish a neighborhood advisory council. The establishment of a neighborhood advisory council may be one program component designed to assist in achieving this goal, but it is not an end in itself. A meaningful evaluation, therefore, would focus upon the effectiveness of the neighborhood advisory council as one component of the over-all police-community relations program.

The evaluation process is further complicated by the reluctance to experiment with new ideas:

> Thus, while evaluation is asked for, the assumption is made that it is really unnecessary because what is best or necessary is always known. What is *best* or *what is needed* is that which is selected to be done by those having sufficient power to see that their wishes are carried out.[25]

It is for that reason, as we have previously stated, the evaluation of police-community relations programs should be conducted by a person(s) or agency external of the police department. It is also essential to add at this point that the residents of the community must be involved in the evaluation process. Although the professionals may be more capable of defining the specific criteria to be used, the citizens are best able to point out the specific aspects of police and community relations which are of the most critical concern to them. The judgment of the residents must be reflected in both the program goals and also the criteria for assessing the achievements of these goals.

To merely say we must examine the end result of a police-community relations program is much too vague for effecting meaningful evaluation. It is therefore necessary to examine the criteria for evaluation in context of our definition of police-community relations. We have previously defined police-community relations as a meaningful program involving the police and the public—designed to identify the problems that create friction between the two groups—and then the working together to solve these problems.

It might be argued at this point that this definition is too broad and would complicate the evaluation process. In support of our definition, it should again be pointed out that the problems that create tension between the police and the public are many. Consequently, a meaningful police-community relations program should not be limited by virtue of definition. The problem is, "How can we use the resources at our disposal to alleviate the problems between the police and the community?"

In general, few police departments have built-in mechanisms for determining the effectiveness of their community relations programs.

Therefore, just as stated in our discussion of evaluating crime prevention programs, police-community relations programs should also have evaluation components built into them. We should ask, for example, "Are programs being established merely because other cities have tried them?" We pose this question because:

> There is within government neither a price mechanism which points the way to greater efficiency, nor competitive forces which induce government units to carry out each function at minimum cost.[26]

The absence of mechanisms for evaluation can also be seen in the following statement:

> In government, by contrast, there is no profit lure, and promotions or salary increases do not depend on profits. In most operations, an objective criterion of efficiency is not readily available, and even if it were, incentives to seek profitable innovations and efficient (least cost) methods are

> not strong. There is scope for *Parkinson's Law,* personal idiosyncrasy, and uneconomic preference of officials to take hold, because the costs of choosing ineffiicent policies do not impinge upon the choices.[27]

Stated differently, it becomes very easy to implement a police-community relations program by adopting program components that have been developed elsewhere and operating them with the assumption they will be applicable to any given city.

It is tempting at this point to follow the pattern set by industry and commerce who translate their objectives into dimensions of money and use the concept of *cost-benefit analysis* as an appropriate means of measuring the efficiency of police-community relations programs. Indeed, there are those who advocate this position, but far more reject it.

In lieu of cost-benefit analysis as a measurement of the efficiency of police-community relations programs, we offer the following measurement of performance:

A. Describe the problem which the program is designed to attack.
B. Establish quantifiable police-community relations goals and quantitative objectives of the various program components established to achieve the goals.
C. Determine the goal achievement by assessing the program results.

In consideration of the above, there are no perfect means of making such an evaluation and all criteria of measurements may be subject to some limitations. Even so, the criteria for determining the effectiveness of a police-community relations program must be directly related to the program goals. The goals of the program must be addressed to overcoming the problems that create friction between the police and the public. The criteria for evaluation must define and isolate the specific elements which are to be looked at, and then examined to determine the effectiveness of each program component.

In developing a police-community relations program, it is extremely important to know the attitudes of the community toward the police, yet that is not the specific purpose of this project. This is not to say, however, that an assessment of the community attitudes toward the police is not important:

It is not possible to plan effectively in the area of police-community relations unless we have a clear understanding and an accurate knowledge of the citizen's feeling toward the police.[28]

As further pointed out by Professor Mihanovich:

Too often, in the area of police-community relations, we program and sponsor activities primarily by ear, by touch, by "instinct" and by hearsay. We may know what a small injured minority thinks and feels and we may also know what the prominent citizen wants and believes. However, we do not know what the great masses between the two extremes of our population believe or think about the police. If we do not know what they think and they do not know the police, how can effective police-community relations be established?[29]

In order to survey the attitudes of the public toward the police, Professor Mihanovich has developed a thirty-five item questionnaire which we include in Appendix A. In addition to utilizing the questionnaire sampling technique, several other methods may be used to obtain an index of the public attitudes toward the police:

1. Number of complaints alleging police misconduct (number which are justified).
2. Number of minority group members joining police department.
3. Number and type of conflict between the police and the public (e.g., assaults against officers, rocks thrown at officers, etc.)
4. Frequency of citizens assisting the police (willingness to report crimes and/or suspicious circumstances, willingness to serve as witnesses, etc.)
5. Rumors directed toward the police (real or imagined).
6. Survey of police attitudes toward the public.

For a police-community relations program to be effective, it must involve the community. Obviously, some positive interchange between the police and the public is a prerequisite for any meaningful and positive program.

A paradigm for organizing a comparative perspective on the varieties of police-community relations programs can be illustrated by cross-classifying two of the notions included in our definition (1) the degree to which the community is involved with the police department, and (2) the degree to which police policy is influenced by citizen participation.

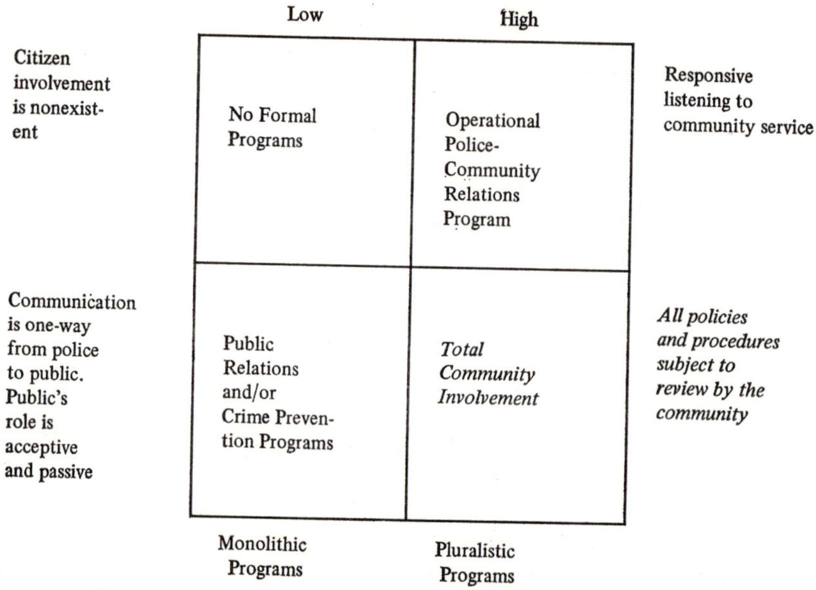

Figure 18-1 Degree to which citizens are involved with police

Of the types generated in the above classification, *No formal programs* refers to a police department that does not operate any programs designed to improve its relationship with the public. Such a classification, however, does not infer that the department is not efficient in its over-all police operations; rather, it only refers to departments that have not developed formal programs designed to involve the citizenry in the police operation. The classification of *Public Relations and/or Crime Prevention Programs* refers to police departments that have developed formal programs, but the involvement of citizens is passive and receptive. That is to say, the citizens do not play an active role—they are only the recipients of what ever information is given to them by the police. Such information is generally designed to project a favorable image of the police or information of a crime prevention nature (e.g., lock your car, pamphlets, etc.)

The classification of *Operational Police-Community Relations Programs,* refers to police departments that are responsive to the voice of the community. Most police departments that operate a formal police-community relations program fall into this category—to some degree. The degree of response, however, varies greatly.

The classification of *Total Community Involvement* refers to police departments where all police policies and procedures are subject to review by the community. Implementation of the concept of community control over the police would be necessary to reach this degree of community involvement.

The four types of police agencies depicted in the above paradigm may also be divided according to their beliefs about the distribution of police powers. A Monolithic Department (No Formal Programs and Public Relations and/or Crime Prevention Programs) have fixed notions about what information should be given to the public. Whereas, a Pluralistic Department (Operational Police-Community Relations Programs and Total Community Involvement) are responsive to both the ideal of decentralization of police power—to varying degrees—and the need to be sensitive to public opinion.

In conclusion, the evaluation of police-community relations programs must relate to the objectives of the program. The objectives of a program provide the background for evaluation. A program component performs certain functions and these functions are designed to accomplish the objectives. Measuring the extent to which these objectives are met is the essence of program evaluation.

We have consistently stated that evaluation must be an intimate part of the over-all police-community relations program. This is necessary in order to estimate its effectiveness (or lack of effectiveness). This will provide feedback which can be used to determine which program components are contributing to the accomplishment of the over-all goal. Inherent in this statement is the necessity for providing systematic input into the evaluation process. Such input must be twofold: (1) information relating to the day-by-day operation of the program, and (2) information relating to the progress made by the program components toward achieving its over-all goal.

Goal achievement, when viewed from a practical perspective, depends to a great degree, on the personnel assigned to work police-community relations and the methods by which they go about pursuing their task. Evaluation of police-community relations, in that context, might very well turn out to be an evaluation of police-community relations officers. The ultimate test of the effectiveness of the program, however, will be what effect it has on both the police department and the community.

APPENDIX A

PUBLIC ATTITUDES TOWARD THE POLICE

(Questionnaire)

Organization

Recruitment, Deployment, Stability, Leadership, Salary

The police should station their Negro men only in Negro neighborhoods.

By hiring non-city residents, the police department can build a more impartial police force.

Our policemen's futures are not too promising.

Police officers who wish to advance in rank have to play ball with city hall politics.

Our police are underpaid.

Adequacy, Efficiency and Techniques

Our police take advantage of their uniform and car.

Our policemen always seem to be picking on teenagers.

In few cases, the police are prompt when called by a resident for help.

The city is provided with inadequate police service.

Some of our police tactics, such as the use of unmarked cars, are dishonorable.

The police department has inadequate techniques in solving race problems.

Our police are overworked.

The decoy squad is one of the better ideas to come out of the police department.

The city police are well equipped to meet any situation.

Operation

Public Prestige and Image, Judgment, Ethnic and Race Relations

The city police, on the whole, do not have the respect of the people.

In most instances, the police do not protect the interests of the lower and uneducated classes of residents.

On many occasions the policemen are mean.

Our police seem to pay more attention to minor violations rather than major crimes.

Our police are not considerate in handling parking tickets in cases of very minor or unintentional violations.

________________________are proud of their police department.

Most residents of ________________________hate the police.

Our police tend to be bossy.

The city police go out of their way to show kindness to people who need it.

Most of the city residents seem to be afraid to contact their police.

In many cases policemen are arrogant.

Our police seem to be lazy.

In the performance of their duty, our police are discourteous.

In the majority of cases, the police of this city are cruel in the search and arrest of a suspect.

Our juveniles are given a helping hand by the city police whenever it is needed.

Dishonesty is one of the characteristics of many of our city police.

The police protect only those who have money.

The police do not care to understand the problems and feelings of the non-white.

Our police are courageous.

Our policemen have two methods of handling and investigating—one for dealing with white suspects, and one for dealing with Negro suspects.

FOOTNOTES

[1]Letter to the writer from Nelson A. Watson, I.A.C.P., October 13, 1969.

[2]Arthur Niederhoffer, *Behind the Shield: The Police in Urban Society* (New York: Anchor Books, 1967), p. 14.

[3]Washington, D.C. Metropolitan Police Department, *Annual Report: Community Relations Division,* Fiscal Year 1967, pp. 3-4.

[4]See for example, University of California at Berkeley, *The Police and the Community* (Washington, D.C.: U.S. Government Printing Office, 1966); Michigan State University, *A National Survey of Police and Community Relations* (Washington, D.C.: U.S. Government Printing Offce, 1967); Citizens' Committee to

Study Police-Community Relations, *Police and Public: A Report and A Program* (Chicago: City of Chicago, 1967).

[5]North City Congress, *North City Congress Police-Community Relations Program: Report of the Final Periodic Effectiveness Survey,* Philadelphia, Pa., March 31, 1969; Winston-Salem Police Department, *Community Services Unit: First Report and Preliminary Evaluation,* July, 1967.

[6]For an in-depth discussion of the criteria problem see: Charles J. Hitch and Roland N. McKean, *The Economics of Defense in the Nuclear Age* (Cambridge: Harvard University Press, 1960); E. S. Quade, ed., *Analysis For Military Decisions* (Chicago: Rand McNally and Co., 1966); Roland N. McKean, *Efficiency In Government Through Systems Analysis* (New York: John Wiley and Sons, 1958).

[7]A Proposal for the Second Year Funding of the Community Services Unit, Winston-Salem, North Carolina, p. 37.

[8]Information presented here is taken in part from: Lee P. Brown, "Evaluation of Police-Community Relations Programs," *Police,* Vol. XIV. No. 2, November-December, 1969, pp. 27-31.

[9]"Criteria for Evaluation in Planning State and Local Programs," A study submitted by the Subcommittee on Intergovernmental Relations to the Committee on Government Operations, United States Senate, July 21, 1967 (Washington, D.C.: U.S. Government Printing Office), p. 5.

[10]*Ibid,* p. 23.

[11]Note that it is not the purpose of this or any of these criteria to evaluate the efficiency of the police organization.

[12]*Supra,* Note 10, at p. 24.

[13]President's Commission on Law Enforcement and Administration of Justice, *Task Force Report: The Police* (Washington, D.C.: U.S. Government Printing Office, 1967).

[14]Minority groups and low income people constitute the other two areas.

[15]Chicago Police Department's Police-School pilot program on the secondary level.

[16]Robert Portune, *The Cincinnati Police-Journal Attitude Project: A Demonstration in Police-Teacher Curriculum Development,* A final report submitted to the Office of Law Enforcement Assistance, United States Department of Justice, Project #052, 1968.

[17]This evaluation was conducted by Barbara Johnson, Special Project Consultant for the Board of Education, City of Chicago.

[18]Marin County Human Rights Commission, "Police-Community Relations Training Proposal," Marin County, California, no date, p. 7.

[19]Nelson, A. Watson, *Police Community Relations,* (Washington, D.C.: International Association of Chiefs of Police), 1966.

[20]Kendall O. Price and Kent Lloyd, "Improving Police-Community Relations Through Leadership Training," a report prepared for the City of Covina, California, February, 1961, p. 29.

[21]*Ibid.*

[22]For examples of instruments used by Price and Lloyd, see *Ibid.*

[23]*Ibid.*

[24]This definition was used by: Leslie T. Wilkins, *Evaluation of Penal Measures* (New York: Random House, 1969, p. 114.

[25]*Ibid.*, p. 116.

[26]Charles J. Hitch and Roland N. McKean, *The Economics of Defense in the Nuclear Age* (Cambridge: Harvard University Press, 1960), p. 105.

[27]*Ibid.*

[28]Clement S. Mihanovich, "Management Measurements," *The Police Chief,* Vol. XXXIV, No. 5, May, 1967, p. 29.

[29]*Ibid.*

SECTION SEVEN

DIVERSION

CHAPTER 19

ISSUES IN POLICE DIVERSION OF JUVENILE OFFENDERS: A GUIDE FOR DISCUSSION

MALCOLM W. KLEIN

Introduction

SINCE THE ESTABLISHMENT of her State Almshouses and Reformatories, Massachusetts has assumed the guardianship of many thousands of indigent and unfortunate children, large numbers of whom have disappeared in the every-varying currents of human destiny, no accurate record of their locality, condition or life, having been preserved. Of their hopes and their struggles, their successes and their fate, no history exists. How many of them went forth to honor or to dishonor, to virtue or to vice, cannot now be known. 416*

This paper is designed more as a catalogue than as a manual. I am concerned not so much with techniques of diversion as with making explicit some of the problems raised by the philosophies and practices of diversion. My hope is that the paper can serve to spark and drive discussion so that those in a position to affect diversion procedures will do so on rational, well considered grounds. My experience over the past few years suggests that there is great need in this area for more considered and less doctrinaire approaches.

Before proceeding further, five critical terms require definition so

*All quotations at section headings are taken from Wiley B. Sanders (ed.), *Juvenile Offenders for a Thousand Years.* Chapel Hill, University of North Carolina Press, 1970.

that writer and reader can be in at least temporary accord on meanings. For the purpose of this paper:

1. We shall mean by *diversion* any process employed by components of the criminal justice system (police, prosecution, courts, corrections) to turn suspect and/or offenders away from the formal system or to a *lower* level in the system. This avoidance of greater involvement of the offender in the sequential components of the system can be and is practiced by each of the components, but this paper is concerned only with the diversion of juveniles by police agencies.[1]

2. We shall mean by *insertion* any process employed by components of the criminal justice system or by nonmembers of the system to introduce suspects and/or offenders into the system or into *higher* components of the system.

Complaints, arrests, bookings, petition filings, corectional placements and many other acts exemplify this simplistic notion of insertion. Since at every decision point in the criminal justice process there is a diminishing of the suspect/offender pool, it is obvious that the insertion rates at sequential decision points almost always decline, i.e., diversion constantly reduces the size and changes the quality of the offender population.[2]

3. We shall mean by *referral* any process by which a diverting agent initiates the connection of the diverted suspect or offender to another agent or agency, usually within the offender's community. Thus referral goes beyond the most common police diversion practice of *station adjustment, warning,* or *counsel and release,* in which the youngster is released without further significant action. A police officer who *refers* a youngster takes active steps to attach that youngster to someone else for preventive, rehabilitative, or reintegrative purposes.[3]

4. We shall mean by *absorption* the processes by which institutions in the community (family, educational, religious) or agencies (scouts, clinics, Big Brothers, etc.) take on offenders or suspects rather than reporting them or their acts to the police. To the best of my knowledge, the concept of *community adsorption* was first explicated by Carter who defined it as ". . . the attempt of parents, schools, neighborhoods, indeed, the communities, to address the problem of delinquent and deviant youth by minimizing referral to one of the

official State or County agencies designated to handle such youth; or, if there has been a referral to one of these agencies, the attempt to remove the offender from the official process by offering a solution, a technique, or a method of dealing with the offender outside of the usual agency channels."[4]

5. Finally, we shall mean by *normalization* the treatment of behavioral acts often though of as deviant or criminal as though they were not deviant or criminal and therefore not calling for sanctions or criminal processing. The reduction of criminal sanctions for marijuana possession is a move toward normalization, as is the treatment of alcoholism as a disease. The move to expunge consenting homosexuality, prostitution, and juvenile status offenses (acts which are not crimes if committed by adults) from the books represent pressures toward normalization. Fist fights among boys, petting among minors, and tearing down goalposts after a football victory are actionable behaviors ordinarily normalized by officials who recognize such behavior as *par for the course* in adolescence. The general spirit of normalization is captured in this statement, "Given the relatively minor, episodic, and perhaps situationally induced character of much delinquency, many who have engaged in minor forms of delinquency once or twice may grow out of this pattern of behavior as they move toward adulthood. For these . . . *a concerned policy of doing nothing* may be more helpful than active intervention, if the long-range goal is to reduce the probability of repetition of the acts."[5]

Obviously, the distinctions between these terms must remain a bit blurred. There is a certain arbitrariness in any set of nominal definitions. Sufficient clarity can be maintained if we remember that insertion is an act calling for further *formal* action; that the progression from diversion to referral to community absorption represents increasing levels of *non-formal* action; and that normalization represents a decision to deny the necessity for *any* action.

Given this foundation, there are two additional caveats to be mentioned before proceeding to the cataloging of issues in diversion. The first is that the current national intellectual trend toward diversion practices and policies is taking place in the absence of definitive proof that insertion is an *unsuccessful* policy. In almost every treatise on the criminal justice procedure, we read about the ineffectiveness of the deterrence and correctional apparatus of enforcement agencies, the judiciary, and especially correctional institutions and practices. Recidivism figures are cited to indicate a discouraging, even frightening, failure of the system to deal with delinquent and criminal populations. Indeed, the failure may be as advertised, but in all honesty we must admit that we cannot *know* this because we haven't tried genuine experiment *without* invoking punitive and restraining sanctions. To say that some percentage—50, 60, 80—of prison parolees eventually recidivate tells us little about what that percentage would be without imprisonment.

We live in a society—similar to most—in which genuine experimentation with immediate or early release of offenders is deemed unacceptable. Thus we turn to diversion practices for two reasons. First, we can compare their outcomes to those associated with normal insertion rates to determine comparative effectiveness among less serious offenders.[6]

Second, controlled field experiments are more feasible at those stages of the criminal justice process where diversion is currently legitimated. But let us remember as we proceed that the pressure toward diversion is more a function of our frustration with insertion than of any proof of its failure. We must turn to diversion in the spirit of testing its potential, not of accepting its preferability—not yet, at least.

The second caveat to keep in mind is that even as this is written and certainly as it is read, constant change is occuring in the legal foundations of the criminal justice system. Some of these changes can have momentous effects upon police diversion practices. Two examples will suffice:

From Florida comes a report of a new state law according to judges the discretion to release offenders convicted of felonies in their county. This is as close as we have ever come in modern times to being in a position to test the use of such discretion and its results on both the felon and the community.[7]

From the California Supreme Court comes a ruling (T.N.G. vs Superior Court, S.F. No. 22777) that prohibits criminal justice agencies, without express approval of the Juvenile Court, from releasing information to *any* other agencies about juveniles who have never been the subject of wardship proceedings. Thus, presumably, for that roughly 50 per cent of juveniles arrested by police but released without the filing of a petition, no referral or other police or community agencies can be made which would identify the youngster as a police contact. The more aggressive diversion practices now employed by some police departments are seemingly endangered by this ruling.*

The reader may easily think of other changes, recent or impending, that would effect the subject of this paper. The important point does not lie within any specific change—somehow we always manage to adjust—but rather in maintaining the flexibility of mind, of policy, and of practice that takes maximum advantage of such changes instead of being inhibited by their inevitability.

I. *The Appropriateness of Diversion as Police Work*

(It will not do to let them go unpunished; but it seems useless and endless, to inflict punishments which produce no reformation. . .)

Mayor C. D. Colden of New York City,
December 29, 1819. (330)

On the walls of a Sheriff's station in a western U. S. county hang signs saying *Think Referrals.* When told of this, reactions of police officials range from good-humored disbelief to enthusiastic approval. Whether diversion of juveniles is proper police work, to say nothing of how much and of what kind, is anything but a closed issue. If we can take departmental figures as an indication of policy and practice, then the lack of agreement on diversion becomes apparent in diversion rates. In 1969, a study of forty-eight police agencies in Los Angeles County revealed diversion rates ranging from a high of 82 per cent to a low of 2 per cent.[8] In this latter case, it was the policy of the department to insert *all* arrested juveniles into the system. Asked about the 2 per cent who seemed to escape insertion, the chief suggested that this might have been a clerical error.

That such variations in practice (and therefore presumably in

*In Los Angeles County as this report is being written, a cross-agency effort is being undertaken to obtain blanket approval from the juvenile court to release information for referral purposes to an extended list of approved absorption agencies.

philosophy) is widespread is shown in studies by Goldman (with insertion rates ranging from 8.6 to 71.2 per cent),[9] Bordua (nationwide data showing a range from less than 5 to more than 95 per cent diversion),[10] and McEachern and Bauzer (revealing not only departmental but officer-to-officer variations as well).[11] In view of such data, it would be foolhardy to maintain dogmatically, as I have heard many police officials do, that either diversion *or* insertion is *obviously* the appropriate police tactic. There is nothing obviously correct about either position nor, for that matter, about the more popular in-between position often stated as "well it depends on the circumstances of each individual case."

This much *is* clear however; a perusal of the available professional literature shows a preponderant preference for diverting youngsters at the point of police intake. Eldefonso cites a survey undertaken by the International Association of Chiefs of Police documenting the low level of active diversion practices. The kind of action diversion recommended by Eldefonso is illustrated in this excerpt:

> In preparing a child and his family for referral, the officer should do a constructive job of explaining the functions of the agency. He should describe the special skills of the workers employed in the agency and explain how they are able to help children and parents with specific problems. The officer should make it clear that problems can be solved only through the joint efforts of the agency and the child or his parents, and that the agency cannot undertake to help them without their active interest and participation.
>
> The officer should also provide specific information as to the name and address of the agency, the telephone number, and the person to contact. This information should be written on a card for the child and his parents. Once they have expressed their desire for help, the officer may telephone the agency to explain the case and, in certain instances, to make an appointment for them. A brief written summary of the case, as seen by the officer, may also be of value to the agency.[12]

In much the same vein, Kenney and Pursuit in their perennially popular text on juvenile procedures outline ten steps to be taken in the referral of diverted youngsters.[13] Like Eldefonso and many others, Kenney and Pursuit raise no question about the appropriateness of the diversion process. In his work, *Alternatives to Incarceration,*[14]

Empey cites the position of the Second United Nations Congress on the Prevention of Crime and Treatment of Offenders (1960) urging both the normalization of juvenile status offenses and the diversion of all such problems as truancy, neglect, and incorrigibility with referrals to schools and other non-criminal justice system agencies. The International Association of Chiefs of Police has also endorsed diversion practices in its Policy Guide No. 30 (see citation under Kobetz in bibliography).

Interestingly, it is the juvenile justice system itself, and especially the police, that in some sense may gain the most from successful diversion practices. This point is made nicely in a report prepared for the California Council on Criminal Justice:

> Concerning the responsibility of juvenile justice agencies, there is a growing conviction that any youngster who interacts with the juvenile justice apparatus is thereby stigmatized, and hence, any prevention program that is launched from a juvenile justice base may be self-defeating. Still, it is that same juvenile justice system that has, perhaps the greatest motivation to launch preventive efforts, for it stands to reap the ugly product of society's failure to prevent.[15]

Finally, there is an important point—almost a twist of the policeman's logic—made by Carter. Many police officers decry diversion practices—especially diversion without referral—as being antithetical to police goals and of no rehabilitative value. In fact, it is often suggested that to release youngsters without further action is tantamount to *rewarding* them or showing them that they *can* get away with their legal transgressions. Carter, viewing the situation in part from the offender's perspective, suggests a different outcome, one which puts the officers *one up* over the offender.

> It appears that the police have a *probation system* which is a specific expression of the policeman's discretionary power by which certain youth who come into contact with law enforcement agencies and are not formally proceeded against, are placed *on probation* to the police (to individual officers and the total agency). Violations of police *probation* by arrest for a new offense may result in entry of the offender into the official system for processing juveniles. While *police probation* is generally informal, records of contacts with youth who were handled informally and returned home may be recorded in *unofficial* pocket-size notebooks for

> further reference. The police *probation system* is quite simple, and the dialogue from officer to youthful offender runs along the lines of "I'm going to let you go this time, but if you get into more trouble, you will be processed as a delinquent." This violation of *police probation,* flagrant cases excluded, is seemingly one of the key factors in deciding which youth are returned home without formal action and those which are moved forward into the juvenile justice system.[16]

Lerman, in a variation on this theme, sees the police as often taking the role of *Dutch uncles.* He says "as a matter of historical fact, the hallmark of the American system is the intriguing combination of limitless scope of our delinquency statutes and enormous discretion granted in their enforcement and administration. Out statutes appear to reflect the image of the stern Puritan father, but our officials are permitted to behave like Dutch uncles—they are so inclined."[17]

The question remaining of course, is *how* to play this discretionary role. We can use the past as one guideline, useful at least in that it demonstrates directions which diversion might take. Lerman cites data from the U. S. Children's Bureau that at least a quarter of the cases reaching juvenile courts involve juvenile status offenses—offenses which are not criminal, not punishable if committed by adults. Further, these data reveal that from 40 to 50 per cent of the detentions awaiting dispositional hearings do not involve criminal acts and that 25 to 30 per cent of the commitments to juvenile correctional institutions do not involve criminal acts.[18] The implications for increasing diversion levels are obvious.

Other guidelines come from reviewing the factors which seem to account for diversion rates. As one example, one can cite Goldman's analysis. Describing diversion/insertion decisions as depending upon ". . . the attitudes of the policeman toward the offender, his family, the offense, the juvenile court, his own role as a policeman, and the community attitudes toward delinquency," Goldman specifies thirteen sets of influencing factors which certainly are not part of any legislative intents.

> A. *The policeman's attitudes toward the juvenile court.* This may be based on actual experience with the court or on ignorance of court policies. The policeman who feels the court unfair to the police or too

lenient with offenders may fail to report cases to the court since, in his opinion, nothing will be gained by such official referral.

B. *The impact of special individual experiences in the court, or with different racial groups, or with parents of offenders, or with specific offenses, on an individual policeman.* This may condition his future reporting of certain types of offenses or classes of offenders.

C. *Apprehension about criticism by the court.* Cases which the policeman might prefer, for various reasons, not to report for official action may be reported because of fear that the offense might subsequently come to the attention of the court and result in embarrassment to the police officer.

D. *Publicity given to certain offenses either in the neighborhood or elsewhere may cause the police to feel that these are too "hot" to handle unofficially and must be referred to the court.* In the discussion of police interviews it was indicated how this factor might operate to bring into court an offense of even a very insignificant nature.

E. *The necessity for maintaining respect for police authority in the community.* A juvenile who publicly causes damage to the dignity of the police, or who is defiant, refusing the *help* offered by the police, will be considered as needing court supervision, no matter how trivial the offense.

F. *Various practical problems of policing.* The fact that no witness fees are paid policemen in juvenile court was mentioned by a small number as affecting the policy of some police officers with respect to court referral of juveniles. The distance to the court and the detention home and the availability of police personnel for the trip were likewise indicated as occasionally affecting the decision of the policeman.

G. *Pressure by political groups or other special interest groups.* Such pressure may determine the line of action of a policeman will follow in a given case. He considers it necessary to accede to such pressures in order to retain his job.

H. *The policeman's attitude toward specific offenses.* The reporting or non-reporting of a juvenile offender may depend on the policeman's own childhood experiences or on attitudes toward specific offenses developed during his police career.

I. *The police officer's impression of the family situation, the degree of family interest in and control of the offender, and the reaction of the parents to the problem of the child's offense.* A child coming from a home where supervision is judged to be lacking, or where the parents—especially the mother—are alcoholic, or one whose parents assume an aggressive or *uncooperative* attitude toward the police officer, is considered in need of supervision by the juvenile court.

J. *The attitude and personality of the boy.* An offender who is well mannered, neat in appearance, and *listens* to the policeman will be considered a good risk for unofficial adjustment in the community. Defiance of the police will usually result in immediate court referral. Athletes and altar boys will rarely be referred to court for their offenses. The minor offenses of feeble-minded or atypical children will usually be overlooked by the police. Maliciousness in a child is considered by the police to indicate need for official court supervision.

K. *The Negro child offender is considered less tractable and needing more authoritarian supervision than a white child.* He is generally considered inherently more criminal than a white offender. Exceptions to this general attitude were found in the upper-class residential area and also among white policemen in the crowded Negro slum area of Pittsburgh. The statistical data, except for the small mill town, do not corroborate these discriminatory attitudes expressed by the police.

L. *The degree of criminal sophistication shown in the offense.* The use of burglar tools, criminal jargon, a gun, or strong-arm methods, or signs of planning or premeditation, are generally taken by the police to indicate a need for immediate court referral.

M. *Juvenile offenders apprehended in a group will generally be treated on an all-or-none basis.* The group must be released or reported as a whole. Some police may attempt to single out individuals in the gang for court referral. Such action, however, exposes the policeman to the censure of the court for failing to report the others involved in the offense.[19]

Goldman's list might be looked upon as a cafeteria of topics from which one could choose implications for changing diversion rates. Such a cafeteria makes it abundantly clear that one cannot retain any mythology about police response to juvenile offenses being a function only of the nature of those offenses.

If it is true that there has been much written on the advisability of diversion, and as we have seen there is much leeway for changing current diversion rates, we might next look at some of the specific pros and cons so that they may be weighed against each other. The task force on delinquency under the President's Crime Commission notes the following as the primary issues:

With respect to the pre-judicial function of the police, it can be argued that discretionary power increases their influence over the behavior of juveniles. Deployed about the city and county, the police have frequent contacts with juveniles and stand a better chance to identify the serious crime risks than do officials more removed; it follows that they may judge more wisely which juveniles to leave alone and which to divert to nonjudicial tracks. This line of reasoning suggests that police discretion should be enlarged in cities where existing policy requires automatic court referral for many crimes and other types of misbehavior.

Opponents of substantial discretionary police powers argue that informal dispositional duties divert police from primary law enforcement tasks. The authoritative mantle of the police, moreover, is said to make them appear to the public as figures of control, hence unlikely agents of help. Internal bureaucratic pressures may produce a predominantly punitive ethic. The subtle character of screening judgments calls for different personalities and preparation and for administrative checks of a sort than can be monitored more efficiently within the juvenile court.[20]

Other arguments in *favor* of police diversion include the clear fact that lack of diversion would quickly overload the courts, the belief among police generally that one offense still leaves room for reformation, and the opinion of many that insertion into the courts is insertion into an ineffective deterrence and rehabilitation system.[21] The possibility of stigmatizing youngsters through insertion is an additional major argument which will be treated throughout this paper.

Additional arguments *against* diversion include the observation that police departments are not well organized for the referral aspect of the diversion process, the view that diversion does not fit with the *normal* role assigned to enforcement personnel, and the growing absolutist or universalistic principle that all offenders should be treated alike, without attention to individual case differences.

A few additional points need to be considered. For instance, my own experience indicates the police chiefs are not, as a rule, very concerned with nor interested in juvenile matters. More often than not, they delegate most of the responsibility for juvenile matters to others so that rewards for increasing diversion or community referrals are seldom forthcoming.

Another consideration is that diversion with referral should also involve follow-up procedures and activity to increase referral resources, i.e., aggressive rather than passive diversion. But such activity requires time and effort that presumably could otherwise go into more direct detection, apprehension, and enforcement activities.[22]

Finally, this point: discussions this writer has had with juvenile officers and commanders have revealed a common tendency to equate diversion with treatment, or at least to confuse the two. Diversion does *not* mean treatment; those police officials who shy away from diversion practices because they object to the treatment role for police make an understandable error of logic. Diversion can be seen as a legitimate exercise in police discretion. Whether or not it results in treatment is a function of the absorption end of the spectrum, to be discussed later.

II. *Separatism Versus A Place in the System*

There has been a marked tendency among the various components of the criminal justice system to draw clear boundaries between the mandates and practices of each. More recently, the emphasis has been upon breaking through these boundaries to facilitate a full *system* of criminal justice administration. Among the police, the separatist approach has been strengthened by an increasing interest in police professionalization. The professionalized department has been described by James Q. Wilson: "A *professional* police department is one governed by values derived from general, impersonal rules which bind all members of the organization and whose relevance is independent of circumstances of time, place or personality."[23]

In comparing data from two cities, Wilson illustrates that the more professional department of the two ended up processing and arresting a far greater proportion of juveniles, although the crime rates were almost identical. Careful scrutiny of Wilson's data[24] suggests that the more professional department normalizes and diverts less, inserting more juveniles into the court system. I would suggest that this results in part from a narrow reading of appropriate police work in the more professional department. A broader perspective, stressing the police as a part of a larger processing mechanism which starts in the community, would lead to greater diversion rates. In particular, it is the police/community connections which require strengthening. Many components of the community—the potential absorption agencies and institutions—should be viewed as part and parcel of the juvenile justice system.[25] As an example of separatism, we can report that in thirty-one interviews with juvenile officers in the two largest police agencies in Southern California, fully one quarter of the officers could name *no* community resources and only two of the thirty-one used direct referral practices. Forty-five per cent said they made *no* referrals, direct or indirect.

We can contrast these figures with post-adjudication referrals reported by community agencies. In a survey of these agencies in Los Angeles County, 119 returns yielded an annual figure of five referrals from these two police agencies but 6,142 from probation, court, and correctional components of the system.

That the diversion rate can be increased substantially has been demonstrated recently by a special project in Los Angeles. The Sheriff's Department and the County Department of Community Services have launched a pilot project at a Sheriff's station in East Los Angeles. In 1969, this station had a below-average diversion rate of 38.6 percent, and made only an occasional juvenile referral to a church or to the Salvation army.

During the pilot project, a Sheriff's Lieutenant was placed in the station with the explicit mandate to see what might be done to increase the diversion rate. He investigated potential resources in the community and worked closely with the juvenile officers. Within the first forty days of the project, thirty-five were diverted to ten agencies, a remarkable change in organizational behavior. Only three of these failed to make the agency connection.[26]

We cannot afford to discount the importance of this project by the Sheriff's Department. A report of the State of California reveals that almost two-thirds of all prevention agencies in the state are private.[27] Thus successful diversion with referral *requires* making viable connections between the private and public components of the justice system, specifically between absorption agencies and police agencies.

Of the public agencies, the schools represent the greatest potential as absorbers of diverted youngsters and therefore a prime target for working to break down separatist attitudes. MacIver reports results of a police-school liaison project in Flint, Michigan. After introduction of the liaison, the area encompassed by the project reportedly yielded 1/8 as many offenses among school students as was the case in outside areas.[28]

This is not to say, of course, that increasing the connections between police and community raises no problems. Cicourel, for example, has illustrated very clearly that departmental procedures with juveniles can be and often are affected by local politics and by internal administrative wrangles occasioned by reaction to those politics.[29] The President's Crime Commission adds to this the point, that, "From an administrative perspective the enlargement of discretionary power entails dangers of . . . inconsistent law enforcement and the resultant evils of disrespect for and distrust of legal institutions."[30] But negative experience and *possible* dangers seem insufficient justification for withdrawal from the community. Such withdrawal usually leads to an increase in numbers of insertions into the system, as has recently happened in California,[31] and the effect of this system overload is desired by none. Here, the Crime Commission makes our point quite convincingly:

> Discretionary judgment also provides a necessary steam valve in the juvenile justice system. Just as the administration of criminal justice is strained by growing criminal populations, so too the increasing volume of juvenile offenders builds up pressure within police departments, juvenile courts, and all of the other institutions with responsibility to control delinquency. Neither police ranks nor the number of judges and auxiliary staff of juvenile courts has expanded at a rate commensurate with the increase in recorded delinquency. Informal determinations as to which cases demand official action are inevitable, and in the process many juveniles are diverted to non-judicial sources of control and service.[32]

The Commission's report also points out (pg. 16) that greater diversion can lead to distinct advantages for the police, the prosecution, and the courts because of the additional time and energy freed up for ". . . greater emphasis on official handling of the more serious and intractable offenders. Improvements in the several stages of the predispositional process would result in more selective and discriminating judgments as to those who should be subjected to formal and authoritative surveillance in the interest of community protection."

All of this points to some restructuring, modifying, or change in emphasis in the police role with juveniles in a number of departments. In particular, it calls for the police to conceive of community components as a part of *their* juvenile justice system, to conceive of the police not as the first or entry component of the system but as the second component, following the absorption components. Lohman's statement suggests much the same emphasis:

> The juvenile police officer's role as a professional is to be reconstructed so that he functions as a catalytic agent, through whom the resources, services, and institutions of the community can be activated in behalf of the needs of problem children. Hence, the target is no longer the act, nor its perpetrator, but *the condition of the child.* The answer is no longer a single type of agency solution but those aspects of the community's total resources which relate to a particular child's needs.
>
> In short, we should increase the capacity of the community to serve the needs of its problem children by increasing the capacity of the police to draw upon the totality of the community's resources.[33]

What we have suggested then, is this: greater emphasis on police professionalism has led to more restricted conceptions of the policeman's role. In the case of juvenile work, these restricted conceptions have seen the police separating themselves from those community components feeding youngsters into the police and capable of absorbing them in the diversion process. The result is an increase in the insertion of youngsters further into the juvenile justice system. This progression is particularly interesting because ordinarily the term professionalism is associated with a *maximum* amount of individual discretion. Professionals are credited with the knowledge and skills to make discretionary decisions where nonprofessionals are not. In the case of police, the notion of professionalism seems to have been misconstrued, leading to less use of discretion and more ritualistic, legalistic behavior. Wilson draws the conclusion very succinctly:

> If this analysis is substantially correct, it will suggest several things to the policy maker. First, decisions with respect to *professionalizing* big-city police forces should not be taken without consideration of their effect on the justice meted out in discretionary cases. It is not possible—as we should have known all along—simply to make a police force *better;* these questions must first be answered: "better for what?" and "better for whom?" Students of public administration have argued long and correctly that *efficiency* or *management* can rarely be *improved* without some effect on the substantive goals of the organization. It should not be sur-

> prising that, in police departments, as elsewhere, means are almost never purely instrumental but have their consequences upon ends.
>
> The second implication directly concerns the problem of juvenile delinquency. The training of a police force apparently alters the manner in which juveniles are handled. A principal effect on the inculcation of professional norms is to make the police less discriminatory but more severe. As a political scientist, I cannot pretend to know whether, from the standpoint of *solving* or *treating* the *delinquency problem,* this is good or bad. I find it difficult, however, to believe that the issue is settled.[34]

III. *Diversion and Court Decisions*

One point omitted in the previous section is the effect of recent court decisions on police diversion. These decisions, particularly in the cases of Gault and Miranda, have been taken as supporting insertion as opposed to diversion practices. They have also been interpreted as forcing diversion-oriented police to abandon their approach in favor of insertion as a means of getting youngsters into treatment facilities. A similar trend among judges has been noted by Wheeler et. al.: the more liberal juvenile court judges more often sent convicted youngsters to institutional facilities, presumably because of the greater treatment potentials in those settings.[35]

Gault, Miranda, and similar appelate decisions have, in effect, brought juvenile handling more in line with that of adults. The stress has been at the same time to reinforce concern with the civil rights of juvenile suspects and to deny the past efficacy of the treatment oriented procedures of juvenile courts. Discussions with scores of police juvenile officers and commanders have suggested that some essentially ignore any import of these decisions. A larger number have been influenced by them to use their field and dispostitional discretion with greater care concerning civil rights issues.

However, the most striking (though I do not claim the most common) reaction has been to *use* the court decisions as a *post hoc* justification for preferred actions—insertion actions. The logic goes something like this: "The courts have told us kids should be treated like adults, so if that's what they want, that's what we'll do; no more treatment or getting off easy. They can go to court with their lawyers like anyone else. Our job is to make a good case for the prosecution."

This logic is *not* inherent in the court decisions; these decisions do not pertain to police dispositions, but to adjudication procedures. But they have been used by police separatists to help rid themselves of difficult and sometimes displeasing diversion practices. Accepting the logic has been a very human reaction, but not a particularly professional one in the usual sense of the term. Among other things, it has overlooked the fact that a large proportion of juvenile arrests are for *juvenile status* offenses, those which have no adult counterparts.[36] Finally it does suggest a danger inherent in the continued professionalization of the police (as described above) and the continuing tendency of the courts to provide for juveniles more and more of the trappings of adult criminal justice procedures; namely that we may be turning away from some of the most potent preventive resources in our repertoire—those of the community itself. The detached policeman responding to the legalistic dicta of the court will be hard-pressed to serve as liaison between the juvenile offender and his community. Failure in this direction may well increase our recidivism rates to the point where *diversion* will remain only a footnote in the history of juvenile justice.

IV. *Normalization*

(In this connection it may be noted that the proportion of children's cases compared with those of adults in the Old Bailey sessions is extremely small. In many sessions of the court no children appeared. In one collection of proceedings covering seventeen Old Bailey court sessions during the period February 1683/4-January 1702, only four boys, and no girls, were reported among the six hundred and fifty-four criminals on whom sentences were passed.)—

From accounts available in the British Museum (21)

Normalization, the attitude of responding to possible deviance as non-deviant, seems to raise at least three types of questions. First, is it appropriate for police to adopt a normalization attitude? Second, how do we determine a *proper* amount of normalization; i.e. what is normal and who decides this? Third, what are the major arguments for and against having the police increase their current normalization stance?

For purposes of our discussion, these three questions all pertain to what Lemert most recently has referred to as the *Overreach of Law*.[37]

Available data[38] make it obvious that the police *are* normalizers. They know that the law *overreaches* and dismisses from serious action the vast majority of juvenile behavior which *could* fall within the bonds of actionable behavior as defined by current statutes. The fact that there is great variation between officers and between departments in the amount of normalization undertaken is witness to the conception that delinquency is a function not only of the actor but of the reactor. *Normal* is a definition, not an act. Lerman puts this into its proper context.

> While many judgments about the seriousness of these offenses may appear to be based on the merits of the individual case, delinquency definitions, in practice, employ shifting cultural standards to distinguish between childhood troubles, play fads and neighborhood differences. Today, officials in many communities appear more tolerant of profanity and smoking than those of the 1920s, but there is continuing concern regarding female sexuality, male braggadocio and disrespect of adult authority. In brief, whether or not a youth is defined as delinquent may depend on the era, community and ethnic status of the official as well as the moral guidelines of individual law enforcers.[39]

Different communities and different subcultures define as *normal* a surprisingly wide range of behaviors, with the definitions often in conflict. Each group, of course, considers its definitions to be most proper, whether the group be ghetto residents, suburban housewives, police officers or used car salesmen. In his novel "The New Centurions," Los Angeles Police Sergeant Joseph Wambaugh illustrates the changes in the definition of *normal* that can take place from year to year in a policeman's career.[40] Police must be very careful, therefore, to avoid assuming that *their* sense of normal and acceptable behavior is the only sense upon which to act or not act. They must be alert to other definitions, including even those of their suspects. This means, once again, *greater* use of discretionary powers.

The dangers of failing to normalize many minor infractions have been discussed earlier, and revolve principally around the issues of stigmatizing youngsters and overcrowding the juvenile justice system. Here, we might look more directly at the dangers of too *much* normalizing. For example, noting the large number of youngsters on whom no significant action is taken, Terry suggests that normalization may have the effect of denying access to treatment for many youngsters until it is too late for treatment to curb delinquent careers.[41] David Matza adds an interesting variation with the suggestion that going from the ignoring (normalization) of a first offense to an increasingly more serious response to succeeding offenses may, as a pattern, habituate the offender to minor increments of *pain* that lose their deterrent value.[42] This escalation of sanctions may be analogous to the slow increasing of heat under water holding small animals. The frog, if subjected to slow increases in the heat of a pot of water, never reacts or hops out but dies as the boiling point is reached. Unlike the case of the frogs, the juvenile offender lives in a peer culture in which his experience is viewed by his comrades. If the slow escalation of sanctions serves as a poor deterrent for him, his comrades will learn the same lesson without the need themselves of jumping in the same pot.

Other arguments include those suggested by Wheeler et. al.[43] concerning breaking the cycle of antisocial behavior which tends to develop if its rewards go unchallenged; setting limits for behavior by reacting to that which goes too far; seeking early identification of delinquency-prone youngsters in order to provide early treatment; and the ever present belief in sanctions and deterrents. None of these arguments is new, but they do make it clear that the issues around normalization are clearly two-sided and not to be discounted easily.[44]

V. *Diversion Criteria*[45]

(Generally the Chamberlain sought to smooth out difficulties rather than pronounce judgements. He preferred to arbitrate or admonish and only when these measures proved unavailing did he commit to prison, and even then was ever ready to release the penitent. In the middle of last century the Clerk of the Chamber stated that he, personally, was able to *arrange* five cases out of six without troubling the Chamberlain. [6])

Enough solid empirical work has now been carried out that hunches or prejudices about the use of police discretion can be replaced by factual descriptions. While there is obviously much research yet to be done, it seems fair to dispute the earlier statement from the Crime Commission report: "At this point we know little more than that a multitude of factors governs discretionary judgment. One source of the difficulty in evaluating prejudical disposition is the vast range of pertinent consideration."[46] The discretionary pattern emerges from a listing of major findings reported over the past decade.

1. Goldman[47] cites the primary factors determining diversion/insertion as the subject's age, sex, race, and the seriousness of the alleged offense. Offense seriousness emerged as the single most important factor.

2. McEachern and Bauzer[48] found significant factors to be age, sex, family status, number of prior offenses, probation status, and offense seriousness, but not race. Additionally, they found significant differences from year to year, department to department, and officer to officer. Again, the primary factor was offense seriousness, with departmental and inter-officer differences having secondary importance. Other differences were minor.

3. Sellin and Wolfgang cited a whole series of factors, summarized by Gibbons[49] into eight categories: (1) prior record, (2) type of offense and subject's role in the offense, (3) attitude of victim or complainant, (4) family status, (5) community resources, (6) demeanor and attitude of the subject, (7) availability of detention facilities, and (8) estimates of likely court action.

4. Piliavin and Briar[50] reported initial differences in diversion according to the subject's race but indicated that this could be accounted for by differences in demeanor. Minority youths exhibited more antagonistic attitudes toward the police officers and those with such attitudes—whites or blacks—were more likely to be processed officially.

5. Black and Reiss[51] found particular significance in dispositions of juveniles in the factors of offense seriousness, levels of situational evidence, attitudes (and presence or absence) of a complainant, and attitudes of the subject. This latter finding, in contrast to that of Piliavin and Briar, indicated that an antagonistic attitude *or* an obsequious or over-complaint attitude would tend to bring about an arrest.

6. Speaking specificially to the question of attitudes, Adams[52] lists these as critical questions: "What does he (the subject) say about his involvement? What are his standards of value? Is he remorseful and do his actions indicate that he is not likely to repeat the offense? Is he defiant and likely to form a delinquent behavior pattern? What is his attitude toward authority—the police and the court? Are there any feelings of resentment, animosity, or remorse with regards to his victim?" As a police lieutenant and an instructor in police science courses, Adams' questions exhibit the same fine discrimination in his subject as in the skier's discrimination between a half-dozen types of snow or the gourmet's discrimination among wine bouquets. In the absence of hard data, it increases our confidence that such differences make a difference.

7. Lemert,[53] in noting the great differences in diversion rates among departments, suggests (but fails to document) that "Such differences are largely a function of differences in police organization and in the degree to which they are integrated in a cultural sense with the community areas whose population's they police. They are also associated with cultural differentiation of the police themselves and with variable policies of departments as to what kinds of deviance will or will not be adjusted internally."

Similarly, Wilson[54] has attempted to illustrate diversion differences as a function of departmental policies and styles of operation. Unfortunately, my own research[55] and that of Sundeen[56] largely fail to substantiate these claims despite a determined effort in the attempt. There does seem to be some cause-and-effect residue in the arena of departmental policy, but it is diffuse and weak, suggesting a multitude of causative agents rather than a few. This leaves room for concerted policy efforts to have substantial impact.

Summarizing the data from studies similar to the above, Gibbons draws the conclusion quite properly:

> These four studies add up to a picture of the police operating in a *legalistic* fashion, rather than in terms of prejudices and biases of one kind or another. Apparently the police are more impressed by the nature and seriousness of offenses than by any other factors. The major route to the

> juvenile court appears to be heavily traveled by those juveniles who are most persistently involved in lawbreaking. The four investigations certainly do not provide much factual underpinning for claims than the principal determinants of police action center about such things as economic status or racial characteristics.[57]

It also seems clear that social-psychological factors constitute a second major but secondary category of determinants of police dispositions. Here one could include the attitudes of the victim, offender, complainant and officer, the demeanor of the offender, and the behavioral interactions among the participants in any incident.

The third, but perhaps least clear, category would relate to the police departments themselves—their policies, their styles, their relations to the community, their knowledge and use of resources, etc. In England, Walker[58] suggests that next to age, "The extent to which cautioning is used as a method of dealing with young offenders depends on the policy and instructions of each Chief Constable, and varies remarkably from one police area to another."

Of course, to suggest that dispositional factors can be reduced to these gross categories (the behavioral-legalistic, the social-psychological, and the departmental-community) does not tell us which *ought* to be given priority. Nor does past practice answer the question of what *ought* to be given priority. This is where *professionalism* should come into play, exercising the available discretion among the available alternative actions by consideration of the appropriateness of the three categories of determining factors. Only further research which relates these to recidivism can adequately deal with the *ought* in this issue. Meanwhile, the role of the *trained* juvenile officer must clearly include the exercise of his discretion in such a way as to counter-balance the inexperienced or untrained exercise of discretion employed by field officers in the initial contacts with juveniles.

One cautionary note will conclude this section. Interviews and observations undertaken by my colleagues and me have revealed a rather consistent tendency among police officers to adopt a narrow perspective on suitable diversion and referral cases. The preferred case is a girl, a younger subject, a first offender, a transgressor of a non-serious statute, or some combination of these. The preference should of course be in these directions for both empirical and value reasons. But the perspective is too often *too* narrow. If forced, I would conjecture that a broader definition of divertable youngsters could double the numbers released without undue damage to youth or society. At least, the case for or against a broader perspective could be tested.

VI. *Community Tolerance*

The methods now employed to dispose of delinquent children failing either to reform them or relieve society from their presence, it is certainly expedient a new experiment should be tried—

London, 1829 (137)

Diverting youngsters back to the community is obviously highly dependent upon the community's willingness to report them to the police in the first place and to absorb them following diversions. The greater the community's tolerance, the less diversion needs to take place. In the city of Flint, Michigan, Gold reports that parental knowledge of offenses admitted to researchers was about eight times the knowledge of the police; parents were aware of one quarter of their children's offenses, while the police were aware of only three per cent.[59] This is a measure of one form of tolerance.

Other forms have been described in Carter's report on the communities of Lafayette and Pleasant Hill.[60] Even though absorption levels were already high in those two communities, the project reported by Carter seemed to demonstrate the feasibility of increasing tolerance levels as an approach to delinquency control:

One of the most significant issues in diversion is the question of how actively the police themselves should seek to increase community tolerance. Most would agree that the police (although not necessarily juvenile officers) should attempt to increase the community's receptiveness to referrals. Fewer would agree to more direct intervention. For example, during the Ladino Hills project[69] in Los Angeles, a sixteen year old gang member who had for several years involved himself in minor transgressions was picked up once again for trespassing on school grounds. The investigating juvenile officer learned that the boy had recently been fired (not for the first time) by the manager of a car-wash. The officer called the manager, convinced him to rehire the youngster, and then released the boy with the expected admonishments. A similar instance is recorded by Spergel:

> Officer J. recalled one case in which a youngster had two charges of robbery against him. The employer refused to hire the youngster. The officer checked the record and found that the youngster had been booked twice in a southern town on suspicion of robbery. But on neither occasion had anything been proved against him. The police officer was able to get the employer to change his mind and hire the youngster.[62]

When I have described such instances to juvenile officers, the reactions have been quite mixed. The reaction most pertinent to the issue discussed here is that such interventions by the police seem in danger of *forcing* community tolerance. Whether such forcing is actually possible is problematic, but at least the illustrations highlight the issue of just how aggressive the police ought to be in getting the community to adopt a more tolerant stance toward juvenile misconduct.

Additional tests of the police role are emerging in the wake of newer efforts at coordinating community absorption potentials. Youth Service Bureaus, as centralized referral junctions in the juvenile justice network, can only succeed with the active participation of the police. Their very formation forces the issue of the police role in community and agency tolerance.

A similar forcing of the issue would result from Judge Rubin's suggestion[63] of establishing Neighborhood Juvenile Conference Committees to deal with juvenile status (*pre-delinquent*) offenses. These Committees would tie juvenile dispositions directly to local cultures and situations. This approach, along with Rubin's plea for minority-based absorption agencies, would truly test the universalistic, separatist trend adopted by so many police agencies.

VII. *Absorption Mechanisms*

The Marine Society apprentices vagrant and delinquent boys to sea service on warships.

—1758 (52)

Edwin Lemert has provided a rather thorough review of the absorption potentials represented by the schools, the welfare system, and community organization programs. In each case, he concludes that much is lacking both in operation and in potential.[64] We will be concerned here with four sub-problems, each of which seems to call for discussion of how police activity might yield some improvement. We can label these problems (1) acceptability, (2) suitability, (3) availability, and (4) accountability of absorption agencies.

ACCEPTABILITY: If a police officer is to divert youngsters, he can best do so on the assumption that there is someone or something *out there* that will help prevent that youngster's reappearance. If he is to go beyond this and make an agency referral, he must know of agencies which *he,* the officer, finds acceptable. Ohmart's analysis of California State survey data[65] reveals the content of reported community programs to be in order, drug treatment and prevention, service center or teen center, and *hot line*. Significantly, many police are highly skeptical of just these types of operations. Thus there is a gap between what is available and what is acceptable to the reffering officers.

Our interviews with Los Angeles officers[66] revealed a very consistent negative view of free clinics and similar informal drug facilities. Similarly, these officers shied away from involvement (other than intelligence!) with self-help agencies, ghetto agencies run by residents, agencies with a taste of militancy or radicalism, and so on. Agencies emphasizing lay or volunteer rather than professional staffs were viewed with considerable skepticism. Finally, whether by design or by inadvertent omission, these officers, representing 77 police jurisdictions, failed to mention employment resources even once!

In other words, just as the juvenile police have a constricted view of the types of youngsters who might be diverted and referred, so they have a very constricted view of the kinds of absorption agencies that could be acceptable as resources for them. Add to this that the sorts of agencies officers prefer, such as family service agencies and counseling clinics, are few and far between. Then finally add the strong suspicion that the usual *character-building* program—YMCA, Girl and Boy Scouts, Boys' Club, church groups, recreation clubs—have consistently failed to manifest any significant impact on delinquents. The conclusion which emerges is inescapable; the police must broaden their view of acceptable referral resources.

SUITABILITY: About this problem there is little dispute; a large number of potential community resources have limited suitability because of their policies and practices. Many will not accept certain kinds of cases. Others have hours, such as 9:00 a.m. to 6:00 p.m., which are unrelated to patterns of juvenile misconduct or police referral needs. Still others have restrictive fee schedules, long waiting lists, insufficient personnel and budgets, and so on. The only issue here is whether the police should tolerate and gripe about this situation, or take on a more aggressive role to facilitate the necessary changes.

AVAILABILITY: The Crime Commission has noted the problem of resource availability. Among recommendations to deal with the problem, the Commission included the development of auxiliary staff for the police to increase both available resources and knowledge of them, better training for juvenile officers, and the development of Youth Service Bureaus.[67] These recommendations do indeed seem responsive to juvenile officers' needs. Officers to whom community resources seem unavailable often report that they will insert youngsters into the system—send them on to court—specifically to insure that some form of treatment will be available to them.[68]

But there are two additional problems here. The first is that the availability of a resource is no guarantee of the amount or quality of help a youngster will receive. For many referred youngsters, this *help* turns out to be superficial and unresponsive to *delinquency* prevention. A study of Teele and Levine in Boston[69] illustrates an unfortunately common situation in which referrals (in this case, from the court) simply do not lead often enough to useful consistent intervention. Teele and Levine conclude sadly that delinquency referrals ". . . do not seem to be a central concern of child-guidance clinics." (pg. 125)

The second problem is that of the low level of police knowledge of available resources. Our Los Angeles interviews revealed a surprising lack of information concerning local resources (despite the presence of up-to-date catalogues of such resources often to be found on the shelves in the Juvenile Bureau). Many of our interviewers were taken from a county coordinating agency, and their knowledge of resources for juvenile police work vastly exceeded that of the juvenile officers. Juvenile officers do not seek out, nor are they urged to seek out, suitable referral agencies. By the same token, few private agencies offer themselves as willing absorbers of delinquency. Thus the modal number of private agencies known to our smaller-city juvenile officer respondents in 1970 and 1971 was two! In six cities, the officers in 1970 could not name a single private agency to which youngsters might be referred.

Nor is this *accidental* or temporary ignorance of resources. Exactly half of the 1971 respondents reported *belonging to no* community organizations in the communities they served. Half did not live in the community served. Yet the median number of police associations for these same officers was two and a half.

ACCOUNTABILITY: The final problem in this section is so obvious that it can be stated by noting the contrast between two statements. The first, by MacIver, states the need while the second, from the Crime Commission, states the reality. In referrals, accountability gets translated as follow-through. Without it, when no one is accountable for the process and outcome of the referral, one can legitimately question the value of any referral.

> The selection of an agency should be discriminating and the communication with it fully informative, and there should always be a follow-up to find out what, if anything, has been done. The trained juvenile unit officer is best qualified to undertake this task.[70]

> The absence of followthrough also has ramifications with respect to juveniles referred for nonjudicial handling. Typically the official agency gets in touch with a clinic, social agency, youth board, or similar organization. But the time to explain a referral to the juvenile or a member of his family is short, and in the impersonal, populous districts of an urban area the referral case is often lost. The juvenile may not arrive at the selected place of service, or he may be refused service without the referring official's finding out in time to take other steps. Even where there is a well-articulated referral system with smoothly operating procedures, sheer number of cases may substantially lessen its effectiveness. If the time lapse between apprehension and referral is a matter of days, the subsequent follow-up by a selected community resource may occur at a point when the juvenile and his family have surmounted their initial fear, anger, or regret and concern, and the contact is regarded as an unwelcome reminder of past unpleasantness instead of an avenue of help in time of crisis.[71]

VIII. *Old Stigmata for New*

This next issue is quickly stated and easily illustrated, but not currently resolvable because the perquisite data have not been collected. It is the question of whether diversion away from the justice system and referral into another system—welfare, mental hygiene, scholastic—may not simply avoid one stigmatizing context by adopting another. In terms of the youngster's perspective of himself and others' views of him, do labels like *delinquent, in trouble,* or *bad* do more harm or good than labels like *sick, unstable, weak,* or *stupid.*

Because of this problem, Wheeler et. al.[72] suggest ". . . it is not clear that doing something is better than doing nothing, or that doing one thing is better than doing another." Lemert[73] has summarized the case of the *special schools* which have been developed by school systems in major cities such as New York, Chicago, and Los Angeles, schools designed to deal specifically with recalcitrant and delinquent youths. He concludes very tentatively that they may indeed decrease anti-social behavior related specifically to schools (truancy, vandalism, resistance to teachers), but that the physical, financial and social costs involved may not be justified by the approach or the results. Even more to the point, Lemert points to the problem in these and in regular schools of the labelling process of selecting out youngsters as (negatively) *special*:

> If the teacher feels strongly enough she refers the child to the vice principal, sometimes with the objective of ridding herself and the class of the child's presence. This, of course, is an old practice. What is comparatively new is the bureaucratization of these procedures, with the possibility of additional referrals to school counselors, psychologists, social workers, and sometimes psychiatrists. Cicourel and Kitsuse have concluded from research on this question that the addition of such professionalized service workers to the schools enhances the probability that problems will be perceived in students and that the farther they go along the referral chain, the more serious the problem is likely to be seen. This accrues from the specialized perspectives held by professional clinical people and their reliance on accumulated records about the child from within and outside of the school. Professionals, like teachers, are less likely than lay persons to normalize unusual behavior or deviance, but for different reasons and with differing conceptions of the kinds of problems they *find* in the students.[74]

Thus, to divert an offender from the juvenile court and its institutions may lead to his insertion into another equally enveloping system of labels and stigmata. If there is any validity to the notion of the self-fulfilling prophesy in delinquency labelling—that being handled as a delinquent will increase one's penchant for delinquent behaviors —why should not the same be true in the case of labelling as in need of guidance, therapy, or other intervention forms? This is an issue which cries out for critical research studies, but pending these there is certainly great room for careful consideration of the various alternatives within the police officer's discretionary repertoire.

IX. *Stigmatization: The Burden of Proof*

At this moment, if a child is brought before myself, for example, as a magistrate, I have no power not to award punishment; I am bound to do it; I should be glad to have the power of sending the child to school, instead of sending it to prison. The sending a child to prison is a very serious matter. When you come to reflect upon it; you destroy his or her character probably for life; if you once give them the taint of a prison mark, it is very difficult for them to shake it off; and it is a very great hardship upon a poor infant that he should have this stigma upon him.

—1853 (236)

We have referred throughout this work to the concept of stigmatization or labelling. Lemert[75] defines it as ". . . a process which assigns marks or moral inferiority to deviants; more simply it is a form of degradation which transforms identities and status for the worse." Labelling Theory, as it has come to be known recently, may rank as the most widely accepted unsupported proposition in the criminology of the 1960's and '70's. The problem lies not in the fact of labelling but in its consequences. It is widely accepted that these consequences are largely negative, that in the delinquency field in particular they comprise a further commitment to delinquency and a step down the path to an adult criminal career.

The data available to support or refute these consequences are largely non-existent, although speculation abounds. Labelling theory seems to constitute one of those instances in criminology—much like Lombrozo's work in an earlier era—in which the proposition fits the needs and biases of the field so well that careful empirical investigation has been largely bypassed. The following constitute the bulk of the directly pertinent research.

1. Schwartz and Skolnick[76] have reported on two studies. In the first, job applicants were falsely identified as having court records in a demonstration that such labelling does evoke negative reactions from potential employers. In the second, physicians sued for malpractice were not particularly harmed by the experience. In some instances, in fact, their fellow physicians directed more patients to them as a means of counteracting the effects of the suit. These studies, though often cited and reprinted in the literature, throw little if any light on our problem.

2. Gold, in his Flint, Michigan study, matched twenty youngsters who had been apprehended with twenty who had not but who were equated on their prior offenses (self-reported), age, and sex. Those who had been apprehended were found to commit further offenses in a ratio of eleven to four for their non-apprehended peers. On the basis of these data and others, Gold suggests four processes which might be involved in moving the original apprehension/stigmatization to further apprehensions:

> I suggest that a youngster in this situation is exposed to at least four kinds of pressures to commit more delinquent acts. First, to stop engaging in delinquent behavior constitutes his agreement that he has indeed behaved badly and, by implication, that he is bad; he withholds his agreement and rejects this judgment by offending again. Second, if he stops in the face of threat, he's *chicken;* and if he dares again, he's a cool player of the odds (which usually pays off—rarely are youngsters caught twice). Third, his motives for committing the delinquent act in the first place, whatever they may have been, are seldom changed by the processes invoked by his apprehension; they remain to provoke him. Finally, his apprehension may have just made him mad; so he strikes out.[77]

3. Contrary data are reported by McEachern and his associates.[78] They reported on offenders inserted upward by the police who were or were not made court wards and, in each case, were or were not given probation treatment. They found that labelling (i.e., being made a court ward) was associated with *lower* subsequent recidivism while receiving treatment (i.e., being seen by a probation officer) was associated with higher subsequent recidivism. The condition most directly related to lower recidivism was wardship without treatment,

suggesting that labelling may in fact deter further delinquency if it is not reinforced by further actions.

The same study deals with the possible effects of juvenile detentions. The authors conclude, ". . . while these figures cannot be read to suggest that detention is a cause of improvement (on probation), they can be read as evidence that detention, in these counties, does not constitute a serious obstacle to improvement." Further on, the authors suggest ". . . those who contend that detention is an effective deterrent for delinquents have no support from our findings. Nor can we conclude that detention itself is harmful . . . the effects of detention, so far as simple recidivism is concerned, are still obscure," (pg. 27).

4. Finally, the issue of detention in a juvenile hall has been investigated by O'Connor.[79] He found that alienation among boys with higher delinquency orientations was increased by detention, but otherwise the findings were quite mixed. O'Connor's conclusions emphasize *differential* responses to detention, suggesting a complex interaction between institutional factors and personality variables of the detainees.

Since these studies constitute the bulk of our specific empirical knowledge of the effects on offenders of stigmatization, and since these studies yield such equivocal conclusions, our own conclusion is obvious. We don't know about the good or the harm of stigmatization, even though we use our *suppositions* about such good or harm to justify policies and practices in the disposition of juvenile cases. Surely it is time to admit our collective ignorance, to hold in abeyance the lessons we *believe* we have learned from personal experience, and to support or undertake some definitive research.

X. *Diversion: The Burden of Proof*

By an arrangement which has been in operation at the Birmingham sessions from the beginning of the year 1841 young convicts who are not hardened in crime are, after trial, delivered to the care of their employers or parents, as the case may be.

These persons enter into an engagement to superintend the conduct of their young wards, and to furnish them with the opportunity of earning or assisting to earn their livelihood.

Both guardians and wards are visited from time to time by one of the superior officers of police, for the purpose of ascertaining the conduct of the parties.

The results of this treatment up to October last were as follows: 113 convicts had been so delivered up. Of these 44 were reformed, 40 relapsed, and of 29 the conduct was doubtful.

The majority of these 29 there was reason to fear had relapsed. But all having left their masters, and many having left the town, nothing certain was known of them.

This experiment, which at all events is inexpensive, may be called satisfactory, when it is considered that from the moment the young offender leaves the bar, the Court has no legal control either over him or his guardian, who of course acts gratuitously.

—London, 1847 (179-180)

When I first started my studies of juvenile gangs, the door through which I entered the study of the criminal justice system, I made a point of visiting the juvenile court to learn how it functioned. I was immediately struck by the sermons, admonishments, lectures, and advisements given youths in court by their judges and referees. But when I asked these gentlemen what they hoped to accomplish with their statements, each *without exception* said that they probably accomplished nothing, yet it seemed like the appropriate thing to do. Here, then, we have a case of acting according to the expectations for a role with full knowledge that it is a matter of form, not of substance. Is it only judges who find themselves in this position? Consider the following statement:

Compared with the possible need of a youth for psycho-therapy, how effective can be the solemn little sermon with which a judge or referee in court embellishes his announcement of the disposition of a case? As contrasted with the need to reverse subcultural attitudes fostering delinquency, of what value can be the two or three hours of interviewing and possible advice-giving by a police officer?

Despite the apparent superficiality of such devices, court workers and police officers will continue to do what they see as within their power. Even if found to be ineffectual, they still would be strongly inclined to continue to do these things.

> Yet, in the overall design of delinquency prevention programs by communities it may be significant to know what real contribution to delinquency reduction can be achieved by the relatively *superficial* means. If it is a major contribution then these should be viewed more seriously as components in a community's efforts. If they are useless, there is no point in encouraging well-meaning individuals to fritter away badly needed time and energy going through meaningless motions.[80]

The authors of this quote undertook a study of *effective and ineffective* juvenile officers. They found that, contrary to the question they themselves raised, officer behavior does indeed make a difference. Some officers consistently act as deterrents more than others. Additionally, evidence suggested that both uniformly high diverters and uniformly low diverters failed to deter recidivism as effectively as officers who, through careful use of their discretion, ended up with medium diversion rates.

Strangely, however, a search of the literature turns up no further empirical rather than speculative work on the effectiveness of diversion procedures. My own research group is now in the middle of such research even as this is written, but even this may be more suggestive than definitive. Still, we have hopes; our research involves the active collaboration of almost fifty different police departments many of whom, historically, have been wary of social research. We can at last agree with Wheeler et. al. that the opportunity for turning issue into policy is upon us:

> There was a time when many police organizations were assumed to be distrustful of social scientists and others concerned with delinquency, and they, in turn, assumed that police attitudes toward juveniles were harsh and punitive. The climate of relations is apparently changing in at least some communities. Knowledgeable authorities report that many police organizations are eager to cooperate in efforts to solve the complicated problems of delinquency control. The time seems ripe, therefore, for a renewed examination of the relation between the delinquent, police, and community agencies.[81]

XI. *Youth Service(s) Bureaus*

Of all the proposals to implement police diversion policies, the Crime Commission's suggestion for Youth Services Bureaus has captured the greatest attention (and funding). The spirit of the Commission's recommendation has been captured by Seymour: ". . . the proclamation of a policy to deal with as many juveniles as possible informally obviously requires the development of a flexible, prejudical system able to cope with a wide range of problem children. Hence the importance of youth services bureaus in the re-shaping of juvenile justice."[82]

The general nature of the Commission's recommendation can be gleaned from Lemert's brief summary and from the Commission's chart placing the Youth Services Bureau in the organizational structure of the juvenile justice system.[83]

Describing the bureaus, Lemert noted:

> These were proposed to be local agencies, or part of neighborhood centers, supplying a broad range of services for *trouble-making* youth, referred to them by police, probation departments, schools, and community agencies, or brought in by parents. Suggested services were to be obtained gratis from community agencies, or by contract if necessary. The recommendations for the Bureaus stressed the need to *work out plans* for the rehabilitation of troubled minors through their voluntary participation and that of parents. No detailed means were given for solving the problems of agency coordination but the Bureau staff would be required to observe the principle of accountability in its interagency contracts.[84]

A recent paper by Polk[85] cites a report by the National Council on Crime and Delinquency authored by Sherwood Norman which listed three major functions which Youth Services Bureaus might serve; linking youths to services available to them, developing new resources in the community, and modifying current aspects of the juvenile justice, welfare, educational and other pertinent systems. The NCCD study also identified five rather distinct models which Y.S.B.'s had adopted, identified as (1) a cooperating agencies model, (2) a community organization model, (3) a citizen action model, (4) a street outreach model, and (5) a systems modification model.[86] The fact that Polk was then able to suggest five somewhat different functions for the bureaus[87] is clear evidence of the ambiguity attendant upon the whole concept.

Even in the few years of active consideration of these bureaus, a

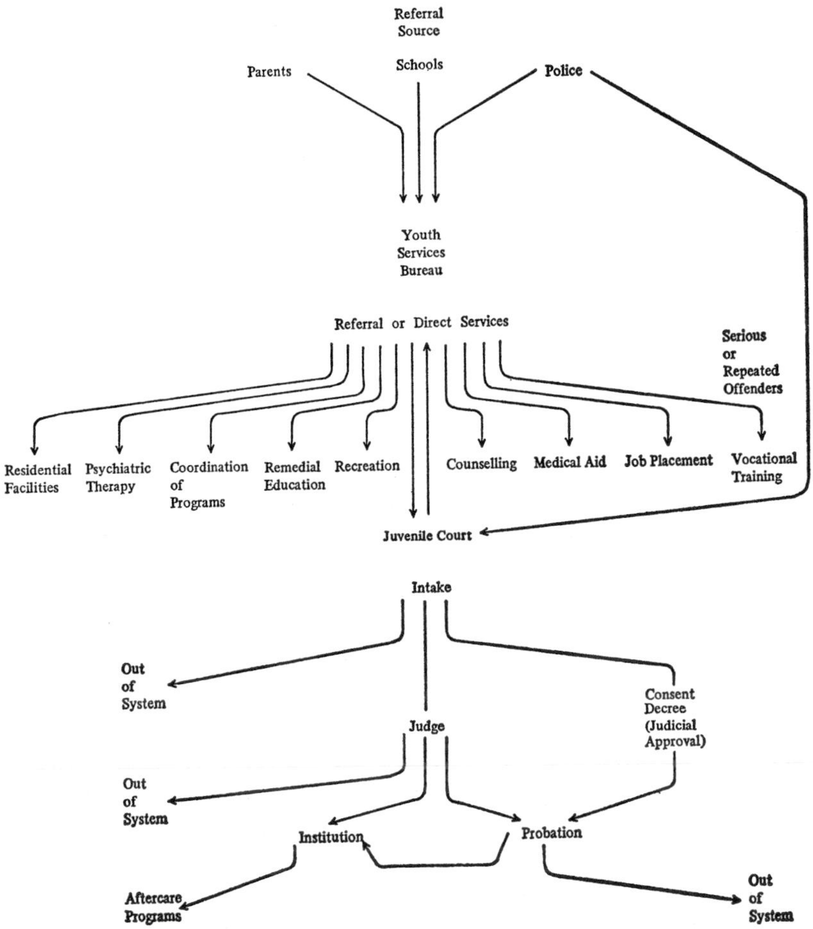

Figure 19-1 Proposed juvenile justice system

number of dangers and failures have been noted by various observers. Among these are the following:

1. A report from the National Institute of Mental Health notes, ". . . the major problem seems to be that coordination of resources—where there are no resources—does not help things very much."[88]

2. Another NIMH report notes two dangers which could apply to any formal referral mechanism. The first is that there might evolve some undue pressure on the diverted youth and family to accept

unwanted treatment. The second is the inadvertent reduction of normalization through what we might here refer to as the *overreach of treatment.* As noted in the NIMH report, ". . . for much of what is now labelled as deviance, the problem is *not* how to treat it but to absorb or tolerate it. . ."[89]

3. Rubin[90] has described the development of one type of Youth Services Bureau in Denver, but indicates that police referrals to the Bureau had not as yet been built into its program or structure. Obviously, such a situation defeats the very design of a diversion program.

4. Lemert [91] has suggested several problems, best stated in his own terms:

> a. The ubiquitous risk is that such Bureaus will become just one more community agency following popular or fashionable trends in youth work, muddying the waters a little more and falling into obscurity.
> b. California's labors so far suggest that something less than stark innovation characterizes planning for its Bureaus.
> c. It is hard to escape the impression of old ideas being recycled when looking at the organizational pattern of some of the Bureaus. (pg. 93)

5. Polk[92] cites the NCCD study of five bureaus and adds his own review of an additional four to point out the diversity of approaches which makes reasonable evaluations problematic at best. A brief resume of the NCCD findings is not encouraging:

> Public and private agencies generally resist working with acting-out children and youth. Existing Youth Service Bureaus tended to limit functions to short-term counseling and referral without follow-up, or failed to develop missing community resources. Only one bureau focused on modifying systems that contributed to delinquent behavior.[93]

6. A two year progress report on the California Bureaus[94] makes no mention of impact, only of information gathering and things the evaluator *will do.* Seymour's paper, however, specifically mentions low police referrals as a major problem in the first year of the California Bureaus.[95]

7. Finally, a report by Seymour of a national conference of

scholars and practitioners makes is painfully clear that the development of Youth Services Bureaus has been haphazard, inadequately coordinated, unresponsive to critical issues, and so on.[96]

Given all of the above, it is no wonder that solid data on the process and outcome of Bureau operations are not as yet available. While this final section of the report might hopefully have reported the results of a major diversion mechanism, we find instead that it can only caution against high expectations. If the value of these bureaus is to be fairly assessed, it may be that the police themselves must see to it that their programs are adequately implemented *with* ample police referrals. Failing this, we have made no gains in the face of increasing pressures to provide some kind of answer to the increasing tide of delinquency.

FOOTNOTES

[1]Useful discussions and reviews of related issues in the areas of court diversion and juvenile detention can be found in two recent publications: Elyce Zenoff Ferster, Thomas F. Courtless, and Edith Nash Snethen, "Separating Official and Unofficial Delinquents: Juvenile Court Intake," and Ferster, Snethen, and Courtless, "Juvenile Detention: Protection, Prevention, or Punishment." Both papers are reprinted in *Diverting Youth from the Correctional System,* Youth Development and Delinquency Prevention Administration, Department of Health, Education and Welfare, Washington, D. C., 1971.

[2]A dramatic illustration of this sequential process has been provided by Philip H. Ennis, "Crime, Victims, and the Police," *Trans-action, 4,* #7 (June 1967) pp. 36-44. Using a survey of potential crime victims, Ennis and his colleagues identified 2,077 victimizations. Of these, 1,024 were reported to the police, 787 received a police visit in response, 593 were called a crime by the police, 120 led to arrest, 50 proceeded to court trials, and 26 resulted in convictions. Note the critical role here of the several police diversion procedures (the decisions not to respond or not to define the incidents as a crime).

[3]A very useful distinction is made by Empey between reformation (rehabilitation) and reintegration, the latter term placing greater emphasis on the role of the community and the offender/community relationship in fomenting and preventing further criminal involvement. See LaMar T. Empey, *Alternatives to Incarceration,* Office of Juvenile Delinquency and Youth Development, Department of Health, Education and Welfare, Washington, D. C., 1967.

[4]This definition, evolving from work in two highly absorbing communities in California, is found on page 22 of Robert M. Carter, *Middle Class Delinquency: An Experiment in Community Control,* School of Criminology, University of California at Berkeley, April, 1968.

[5]This approach, as a technique, is attributed by the authors to *labelling theorists* such as Lemert to whom we shall refer often in this paper. The quote is taken from

a very useful little paper by Stanton Wheeler, Leonard Cottrell, Jr., and Anne Romasco, "The Labelling Process," in Donald R. Cressey and David A. Ward (ed,), *Delinquency, Crime, and Social Process,* New York, Harper and Row, 1969, pp. 608-613.

[6]For the reader seriously interested in working toward a comprehensive evaluation of the effectiveness of the criminal justice system, see Malcolm W. Klein, Solomon Kobrin, A. W. McEachern, Herbert Sigurdson, "Systems Rates: An Approach to Comprehensive Criminal Justice Planning," *Crime and Delinquency,* (October, 1971) and also see Alfred Blumenstein and Richard Larson, "Models of a Total Criminal Justice System," *Operations Research, 17,* #2 (March-April, 1969) pp. 199-232.

[7]Preliminary analysis of this situation involves a description of the characteristics of cases to which this discretionary action has been applied; see Theodore G. Chricos, Phillip D. Jackson, and Gordon P. Waldo, "Inequality in the Imposition of a Criminal Label," Department of Criminology, Florida State University, 1971 (mimeo).

[8]Malcolm W. Klein, "Police Processing of Juvenile Offenders: Toward the Development of Juvenile System Rates," 1970 report prepared for and available from the Los Angeles County Criminal Justice Planning Board.

[9]Nathan Goldman, "The Differential Selection of Juvenile Offenders for Court Appearance," in William J. Chambliss (ed.) *Crime and the Legal Process,* New York, McGraw-Hill Book Co., 1969, pp. 264-290.

[10]David J. Bordua, "Recent Trends: Deviant Behavior and Social Control," *Annals of the American Academy of Political and Social Science, 359* (January, 1967) pp. 149-163.

[11]A. W. McEachern and Riva Bauzer, "Factors Related to Disposition in Juvenile Police Contacts" in Malcolm W. Klein, (ed.), *Juvenile Gangs in Context: Theory Research, and Action,* Englewood Cliffs, Prentice-Hall, 1967, pp. 148-160.

[12]Edward Eldefonso, *Law Enforcement and the Youthful Offender: Juvenile Procedures,* New York, John Wiley and Sons, 1967, p. 102.

[13]John P. Kenney and Dan G. Pursuit, *Police Work With Juveniles and the Administration of Juvenile Justice,* 4th edition, Springfield, Ill., Charles C Thomas, 1970, pp. 223-225.

[14]LaMar T. Empey, *op.cit.,* p. 24.

[15]*Juvenile Delinquency: The Core Problem,* Sacramento, California Council on Criminal Justice (Task Force on Juvenile Delinquency), July, 1970, draft prepared by Howard Ohmart and staff.

[16]Carter, *op.cit.,* p. 61.

[17]Paul Lerman, "Child Convicts", *Trans-action, 8,* #9-10, (July-August, 1971) p. 37.

[18]*Ibid.*

[19]Goldman's work probably merits reading in full, since it seems to have been one of the most influential studies in this area. See Nathan Goldman, "The Differential Selection of Juvenile Offenders for Court Appearance," reprinted in William J. Chambliss, (ed.), *op.cit.,* pp 264-290.

[20]*Task Force Report: Juvenile Delinquency and Youth Crime,* Washington, D.C., The President's Commission on Law Enforcement and Administration of Justice, 1967, p. 18.

[21]This latter point, along with the frequent paucity of community resources, were

presumably instrumental in developing such police *treatment and prevention* activities as police athletic leagues and the Juvenile Aid Bureaus in cities like New York and Philadelphia. These developments are discussed on pp. 54-70 of Edwin M. Lemert, *Instead of Court: Diversion in Juvenile Justice,* Washington, D.C., National Institute of Mental Health, 1971 (available as PHS publication No. 2127).

[22]The surprisingly low level of follow-up in one study can be found in Malcolm W. Klein, "Police Processing of Juvenile Offenders," *supra.*

[23]James Q. Wilson, "The Police and the Delinquent in Two Cities" in Stanton Wheeler (ed.), *Controlling Delinquents,* New York, John Wiley and Sons, 1968, p. 11. The entire selection by Wilson should be read and pondered; if somewhat overstated, it nevertheless provides a highly valuable perspective on the consequences of increased police professionalization.

[24]*Ibid,* pp. 15-17.

[25]This viewpoint is expanded in Klein, et.al., *op.cit.* (footnote #6).

[26]These data and their implications are summarized in Malcolm W. Klein, "On the Front End of the Juvenile Justice System," paper delivered at the meetings of the Pacific Sociological Association, 1971, available upon request.

[27]*Juvenile Delinquency: The Core Problem, op.cit.,* p. 44.

[28]Robert M. MacIver, *The Prevention and Control of Delinquency,* New York, Atherton Press, 1966, p. 143.

[29]Aaron V. Cicourel, *The Social Organization of Juvenile Justice,* New York, John Wiley and Sons, 1968.

[30]Task Force Report, *op. cit.,* p. 10.

[31]*Juvenile Delinquency: The Core Problem, supra,* p. 8.

[32]Task Force Report, *op.cit.,* p. 11.

[33]Joseph D. Lohman, statement before the Subcommittee to Investigate Juvenile Delinquency, of the Committee on the Judiciary, U.S. Senate, 86th Cong., 1st Sess., S.res., pt. 2, "Juvenile Delinquency," pp. 116-117, quoted in Irving A. Spergel, *Community Problem Solving: The Delinquency Example,* Chicago, University of Chicago Press, 1969, p. 208.

[34]Wilson, *op.cit.,* p. 28.

[35]Stanton Wheeler, Edna Bonacich, M. Richard Cramer, and Irving K. Zola, "Agents of Delinquency Control: A Comparative Analysis" in Wheeler, op.cit., pp. 31-60. Some readers may be surprised by the suggestion of a substantial police interest in treatment for juvenile offenders. However, our Los Angeles interviews revealed that, of those officers desiring more resources than were available in their community, the overwhelming majority sought individual or family counseling services, emphasizing the psychogenic bias of proper treatment for the divertable young and minor offender.

[36]For one prominent judge's recommendations in this area, see Ted Rubin, *Law as an Agent of Delinquency Prevention,* Washington, D.C., Youth Development and Delinquency Prevention Administration, Department of Health, Education, and Welfare, 1971.

[37]Lemert, *op.cit.:* note that in this context Lemert cites the words of Roscoe Pound written in 1916!

[38]In addition to studies cited earlier see those (e.g., Terry, Bodine) cited in Don C. Gibbons, *Delinquent Behavior,* Englewood Cliffs, Prentice-Hall, 1970, especially pp. 36-39.

[39]Lerman, *op.cit.,* p. 37.

[40]Joseph Wambaugh, *The New Centurions,* Boston, Atlantic-Little-Brown, 1970.

[41]Robert M. Terry, "The Screening of Juvenile Offenders," *The Journal of Criminal Law, Criminology, and Police Science, 58* (1967), pp. 173-181.

[42]David Matza, *Delinquency and Drift,* New York, John Wiley and Sons, 1964, pp. 186-188.

[43]Wheeler, Cottrell and Romasco, *op.cit.*

[44]Lemert's general handling of the issue, while comprehensive and logically sound, seems to suffer from a somewhat one-sided presentation of the merits of normalization; Lemert, *op.cit.*

[45]A brief but concise review of processes relevant to this issue can be found in Frank W. Miller, Robert O. Dawson, George E. Dix, and Raymond L. Parnas, *The Juvenile Justice Process,* Mineola, N.Y., The Foundation Press, Inc., 1971.

[46]Task Force Report, *o.cit.,* p. 17.

[47]Goldman, *op.cit.*

[48]McEachern and Bauzer, *op.cit.*

[49]Gibbons, *op.cit.,* p. 40.

[50]Irving Piliavin and Scott Briar, "Police Encounters with Juveniles," *American Journal of Sociology, 70* #2 (September, 1964), pp. 206-214.

[51]Donald J. Black and Albert J. Reiss, Jr., "Police Control of Juveniles," *American Sociological Review, 35* #1 (February, 1970), pp. 63-77.

[52]Thomas F. Adams, *Law Enforcement: An Introduction to the Police Role in the Community,* Englewood Cliffs, Prentice Hall, Inc., 1968, p. 180.

[53]Lemert, *op.cit.,* p. 62.

[54]Wilson, *op.cit.*

[55]Klein, *op.cit.*

[56]Richard A. Sundeen, Jr., *A Study of Factors Related to Police Diversion of Juveniles: Departmental Policies and Structures, Community Attachment and Professionalization of Police,* Unpublished Ph.D. Dissertation, University of Southern California, 1971.

[57]Gibbons, *op.cit.,* p. 39.

[58]Nigel Walker, *Crime and Punishment in Britain,* Edinburgh, Edinburgh University Press, 1968 (rev.), p. 179.

[59]Martin Gold, *Delinquent Behavior in an American City,* Belmont, California, Brooks/Cole Publishing Co., 1970.

[60]Carter, *op.cit.*

[61]Malcolm W. Klein, *Street Gangs and Street Workers,* Englewood Cliffs, Prentice-Hall, Inc., 1971. This work includes very extensive discussions and examples of attempts at referrals and absorption.

[62]Irving A. Spergel, *Community Problem Solving: The Delinquency Example,* Chicago, University of Chicago Press, 1969, p. 210.

[63]Ted Rubin, *op.cit.,* pp. 9-12.

[64]Lemert, *op.cit.*

[65]*Juvenile Delinquency: The Core Problem, supra.,* pp. 44 and 45.

[66]Klein, 1971, *op.cit.*

[67]*Task Force Report,* p. 19.

[68]In a search of the relevant literature, I find very few writers who acknowledge this rationale from juvenile officers, although it is one I hear quite often. An exception is Wayne R. LaFave in "Noninvocation of the Criminal Law by Police," in Cressey and Ward, *op.cit.,* pp. 185-208.

[69]James E. Teele and Sol Levine, "The Acceptance of Emotionally Disturbed Children by Psychiatric Agencies" in Wheeler, *Controlling Delinquents, supra.*, pp. 103-126.

[70]MacIver, *op.cit.*, p. 145.

[71]*Task Force Report,* p. 18.

[72]Wheeler, Cottrell, and Romasco, *op.cit.*, p. 611.

[73]Lemert, *op.cit.*, pp. 27-20.

[74]*Ibid.*, p. 24.

[75]*Ibid.*, p. 11.

[76]Richard D. Schwartz and Jerome H. Skolnick, "Two Studies of Legal Stigma," *Social Problems, 10,* #2 (Fall, 1962), pp. 133-140.

[77]Gold, *op.cit.*, especially, p. 108.

[78]A. W. McEachern, Edward M. Taylor, J. Robert Newman, and Ann E. Ashford, "The Juvenile Probation System: Simulation for Research and Decision-Making," *American Behavioral Scientist, 11,* #3 (January-February, 1968), pp. 1-45. See pp. 17-18 and in particular Tables 24, 25, and 26 and the associated text.

[79]Gerald G. O'Connor, "The Impact of Initial Detention upon Male Delinquents," *Social Problems, 18,* #2 (Fall, 1970), pp. 194-199.

[80]William W. Wattenberg and Noel Bufe, "The Effectiveness of Police Youth Bureau Officers," *Journal of Criminal Law, Criminology and Police Science, 54,* #4 (December, 1963), pp. 470-475.

[81]Stanton Wheeler, Leonard S. Cottrell, Jr., and Anne Romasco, "Juvenile Delinquency: Its Prevention and Control," Appendix T of the *Task Force Report, op.cit.*, see p. 420.

[82]John A. Seymour, *Youth Services Bureau,* prepared for a seminar sponsored by the Center for the Study of Welfare Policy and the Center for Studies in Criminal Justice, University of Chicago, January 24 and 25, 1971 (mimeo), p. 4. Seymour's background paper is a marvelously comprehensive review of the issues in the development of the Bureau concept. For those wishing a full and excellently reasoned review, the Seymour paper is by far the best available.

[83]The chart in Figure I is taken from page 89 of *The Challenge of Crime in a Free Society,* the summary report of the President's Commission on Law Enforcement and Administration of Justice, Washington, D.C., 1967. Relevant descriptions can be found in the *Task Force Report, op.cit.*, pp. 20-21.

[84]Lemert, *op.cit.*, p. 93. Useful statements on purposes and organizations of Y.S.B.'s can also be found in John M. Martin, *Toward a Political Definition of Juvenile Delinquency,* Washington, D.C., Youth Development and Delinquency Prevention Administration, Department of Health, Education, and Welfare, 1970, pp. 11-15 and G. David Schiering, "A Proposal for the More Effective Treatment of the 'Unruly' Child in Ohio: The Youth Services Bureau" in Diverting Youth from the Correctional System, Youth Development and Delinquency Prevention Administration, Department of Health, Education, and Welfare, 1971.

[85]Kenneth Polk, "Delinquency Prevention and the Youth Service Bureau," paper delivered at the University of Massachusetts, Juvenile Delinquency Prevention Seminar, October, 1970 (mimeo).

[86]*Ibid.*, pp. 18-21.

[87]*Ibid.*, pp. 23-33.

[88]*The Juvenile Court: A Status Report,* Washington, D.C., National Institute of Mental Health (Public Health Service Publication #2132), 1971.

[89]*Diversion from the Criminal Justice System,* Washington, D.C., National Institute of Mental Health (Public Health Service Publication #2129), 1971.

[90]Rubin, *op.cit.,* pp. 14-15.

[91]Lemert, *op.cit.,* p. 93.

[92]Polk, *op.cit.*

[93]*Research Relating to Children,* Bulletin 27, ERIC Clearinghouse on Early Childhood Education, item 27-KK-1, Washington, D.C., June 1970-February 1971.

[94]*The Status of Current Research in the California Youth Authority: Annual Report, 1971,* Sacramento, Department of the Youth Authority, 1971, pp. 24-26. An earlier report goes into far greater detail on implementation of the California Bureaus. Unfortunately, no impact data were yet available and the data on diversion varied so widely and were of such unequal value that no clear conclusions could fairly be said to have emerged. See Elaine B. Duxbury, *Youth Service Bureaus in California: A Progress Report,* Sacramento, Department of the Youth Authority, January, 1971.

[95]Seymour, *op.cit.*

[96]John A. Seymour, "Report on Youth Services Bureau Seminar," Chicago, Center for the Study of Welfare Policy and Center for Studies in Criminal Justice, University of Chicago, 1971 (mimeo).

REFERENCES

Adams, Thomas F.: *Law Enforcment: An Introduction to the Police Role in the Community,* Englewood Cliffs, Prentice-Hall, 1968.

Black, Donald J. and Albert J. Reiss, Jr., "Police Control of Juveniles," *American Sociological Review, 35,* #1 (February, 1970), pp. 63-77.

Blumstein, Alfred and Richard Larson, "Models of a Total Criminal Justice System," *Operations Research, 17,* #2 (March-April, 1969), pp. 199-232.

Bordua, David J., "Recent Trends: Deviant Behavior and Social Control," *Annals of the American Academy of Political and Social Science, 359,* (January, 1967), pp. 149-163.

Carter, Robert M., *Middle-Class Delinquency: An Experiment in Community Control,* School of Criminology, University of California at Berkeley, April, 1968.

Chiricos, Theodore G., Phillip D. Jackson, and Gordon P. Waldo, "Inequality in the Imposition of a Criminal Label," Department of Criminology, Florida State University, 1971 (mimeo).

Cicourel, Aaron V., *The Social Organization of Juvenile Justice,* New York, John Wiley and Sons, 1968.

Diversion from the Criminal Justice System, Washington, D.C., National Institute of Mental Health, 1971.

Duxbury, Elaine B., *Youth Service Bureaus in California: A Progress Report,* Sacramento, Department of the Youth Authority, January, 1971.

Eldefonso, Edward, *Law Enforcement and the Youthful Offender: Juvenile Procedures,* New York, John Wiley and Sons, 1967.

Empey, LaMar T., *Alternatives to Incarceration,* Washington, D.C., Office of Juvenile Delinquency and Youth Development, Department of Health, Education and Welfare, 1967.

Ennis, Philip H., "Crime, Victims, and the Police," *Trans-action, 4* #7 (June, 1967), pp. 36-44.

Ferster, Elyce Zenoff, Thomas F. Courtless, and Edith Nash Snethen, "Separating Official and Unofficial Delinquents: Juvenile Court Intake," *Diverting Youth from the Correctional System,* Washington, D.C., Youth Development and Delinquency Prevention Administration, Department of Health, Education, and Welfare, 1971, pp. 1-30.

Ferster, Elyce Zenoff, Edith Nash Snethen, and Thomas F. Courtless, "Juvenile Detention: Protection, Prevention, or Punishment," *Diverting Youth from the Correctional System,* Washington, D.C., Youth Development and Delinquency Prevention Administration, Department of Health, Education, and Welfare, 1971, pp. 31-66.

Gibbons, Don C., *Delinquent Behavior,* Englewood Cliffs, Prentice-Hall, 1970.

Gold, Martin, *Delinquent Behavior in an American City,* Belmont, Ca., Brooks/Cole, 1970.

Goldman, Nathan, "The Differential Selection of Juvenile Offenders for Court Appearance" in William J. Chambliss (ed.), *Crime and the Legal Process,* New York, McGraw-Hill, 1969, pp. 264-290.

Gorlich, Elizabeth H., *Guides for Demonstration Projects for Youth Service Bureaus,* Childrens' Bureau, US Department of Health, Education, and Welfare, 1969.

Juvenile Delinquency: The Core Problem, Juvenile Delinquency Task Force, California Council on Criminal Justice, Sacramento, July, 1971 (mimeo).

Kenney, John P. and Dan G. Pursuit, *Police Work with Juveniles and the Administration of Juvenile Justice,* 4th edition, Springfield, Ill., Thomas, 1970.

Klein, Malcolm W., "Police Processing of Juvenile Offenders: Toward the Development of Juvenile System Rates," Los Angeles, L.A. County Criminal Justice Planning Board, 1970 (mimeo).

Klein, Malcolm W., "On the Front End of the Juvenile Justice System," Los Angeles, Public Systems Research Institute, University of Southern California, 1971 (mimeo).

Klein, Malcolm W., *Street Gangs and Street Workers,* Englewood, Cliffs, Prentice-Hall, 1971.

Klein, Malcolm W., Solomon Kobrin, A. W. McEachern, and Herbert R. Sigurdson, "System Rates: An Approach to Comprehensive Criminal Justice Planning," *Crime and Delinquency,* (October, 1971) forthcoming.

Kobetz, Richard W., *The Police Role and Juvenile Delinquency,* Gaithersburg, Md., International Association of Chiefs of Police, 1971.

LaFave, Wayne R., "Noninvocation of the Criminal Law by Police," in Donald R. Cressey and David A. Ward, (ed.), *Delinquency, Crime, and Social Process.* New York, Harper and Row, 1969, pp. 185-208.

Lemert, Edwin M., *Instead of Court: Diversion in Juvenile Justice,* Washington, D.C., National Institute of Mental Health, 1971.

Lerman, Paul, "Child Convicts," *Trans-action, 8,* #9-10 (July-August, 1971), pp. 35-44.

Lohman, Joseph D., "Juvenile Delinquency," cited in Irving A. Spergel, *Community Problem Solving: The Delinquency Example,* Chicago, University of Chicago Press, 1969.

MacIver, Robert M., *The Prevention and Control of Delinqency,* New York, Atherton Press, 1966.

Martin, John M., *Toward A Political Definition of Juvenile Delinquency,* Washington, D.C., Youth Development and Delinquency Prevention Administration, Department of Health, Education, and Welfare, 1970.

Matza, David, *Delinquency and Drift,* New York, John Wiley and Sons, 1964.

McEachern, A. W., and Riva Bauzer, "Factors Related to Disposition in Juvenile Police Contacts," in Malcolm W. Klein (ed.) *Juvenile Gangs in Context: Theory, Research, and Practice,* Englewood Cliffs, Prentice-Hall, 1967, pp. 148-160.

McEachern, A. W., Edward M. Taylor, J. Robert Newman, and Ann E. Ashford, "The Juvenile Probation System: Simulation for Research and Decision-Making." *American Behavioral Scientist, 11,* #3 (January-February, 1968), pp. 1-45.

Miller, Frank W., Robert O. Dawson, George E. Dix, and Raymond L. Parnas, *The Juvenile Justice Process,* New York, The Foundation Press, 1971.

Norman, Sherwood, *The Youth Service Bureau,* New York, National Council on Crime and Delinquency, 1971.

O'Connor, Gerald G., "The Impact of Initial Detention upon Male Delinquents," *Social Problems, 18,* #2 (Fall, 1970), pp. 194-199.

Piliavin, Irving and Scott Briar, "Police Encounters with Juveniles," *American Journal of Sociology, 70,* #2 (September, 1964).

Polk, Kenneth, "Delinquency Prevention and the Youth Service Bureau," paper delivered at the Juvenile Delinquency Prevention Seminar, University of Massachusetts, October, 1970 (mimeo).

Research Relating to Children, Bulletin 27, ERIC Clearinghouse on Early Childhood Education, Item 27-KK-1, Washington, D.C., June, 1970-February, 1971.

Rubin, Ted, *Law as an Agent of Delinquency Prevention,* Washington, D.C., Youth Development and Delinquency Prevention Administration, Department of Health, Education, and Welfare, 1971.

Sanders, Wiley B., (ed.), *Juvenile Offenders for a Thousand Years,* Chapel Hill, University of North Carolina Press, 1970.

Schiering, G. David, "A Proposal for the More Effective Treatment of the 'Unruly' Child in Ohio: The Youth Services Bureau", in *Diverting Youth from the Correctional System,* Washington, D.C., Youth Development and Delinquency Prevention Administration, Department of Health, Education, and Welfare, 1971, pp. 67-82.

Schwartz, Richard D. and Jerome H. Skolnick, "Two studies of Legal Stigma," *Social Problems, 10,* #2 (Fall, 1962) pp. 133-140.

Seymour, John A., "Report on Youth Services Bureau Seminar," Chicago, Center for the Study of Welfare Policy and Center for Studies in Criminal Justice, University of Chicago, 1971 (mimeo).

Seymour, John A., *Youth Services Bureau,* Chicago, Center for the Study of Welfare Policy and Center for Studies in Criminal Justice, University of Chicago, 1971 (mimeo).

Spergel, Irving A., *Community Problem Solving: The Delinquency Example,* Chicago, University of Chicago Press, 1969.

Sundeen, Richard A., Jr., *A Study of Factors Related to Police Diversion of Juveniles: Departmental Policies and Structures, Community Attachment, and Professionalization of Police,* unpublished Ph.D. dissertation, University of Southern California, 1971.

Task Force Report: Juvenile Delinquency and Youth Crime, Washington, D.C., President's Commission on Law Enforcement and the Administration of Justice, 1967.

Teele, James E. and Sol Levine, "The Acceptance of Emotionally Disturbed Children by Psychiatric Agencies," in Stanton Wheeler (ed.), *Controlling Delinquents,* New York, John Wiley and Sons, 1968, pp. 103-126.

Terry, Robert M., "The Screening of Juvenile Offenders," *Journal of Criminal Law, Criminology, and Police Science, 58* (1967), pp. 173-181.

The Challenge of Crime in a Free Society, Washington, D.C., President's Commission on Law Enforcement and the Administration of Justice, 1967.

The Juvenile Court: A Status Report, Washington, D.C., National Institute of Mental Health, 1971.

The Status of Current Research in the California Youth Authority: Annual Report, 1971, Sacramento, Department of the Youth Authority, 1971.

Walker, Nizel, *Crime and Punishment in Britain,* Edinburgh, Edinburgh University Press, 1968 (rev.).

Wattenberg, William W. and Noel Bufe, "The Effectiveness of Police Youth Bureau Officers," *Journal of Criminal Law, Criminology, and Police Science,* 54, #4, (December, 1963) pp. 470-475.

Wheeler, Stanton, Leonard S. Cottrell, and Anne Romasco, "Juvenile Delinquency: Its Prevention and Control," Appendix T. of the *Task Force Report: Juvenile Delinquency,* Washington, D.C., President's Commission on Law Enforcement and the Administration of Justice, 1967, pp. 409-428.

Wheeler, Stanton, "The Labelling Process" in Donald R. Cressey and David A. Ward, Jr., (ed.), *Delinquency, Crime, and Social Process,* New York, Harper and Row, 1969, pp. 608-612.

Wheeler, Stanton, Edna Bonacich, M. Richard Cramer, and Irving K. Zola, "Agents of Delinquency Control: A Comparative Analysis," in Stanton Wheeler (ed.), *Controlling Delinquents,* New York, John Wiley and Sons, 1968, pp. 31-60.

Wilson, James Q., "The Police and the Delinquent in Two Cities," in Stanton Wheeler (ed.), *Controlling Delinquents,* New York, John Wiley and Sons, 1968, pp. 9-30.

Juvenile Offenders

The following bibliography is reprinted from *Diversion from the Criminal Justice System,* National Institute of Mental Health, 1971, pp. 31-33, available from U.S. Government Printing Office as Publication #PHS 2129.

Barrett, Roy Lee. 'Delinquent child': a legal term without meaning. *Baylor Law Review,* 21(3):352–371, 1969.

Chaplan, Abraham A., and Waldman, Ruth. An adolescent health maintenance clinic: a community mental health approach for teenagers. *Adolescence,* 2(5): 53–62, 1967.

Dick, Carroll. A report on the response to a recommendation concerning the placement of dependent children in Washington State. Prepared for the Washington Council of the National Council on Crime and Delinquency. 1969. 35 pp. Unpublished.

Eisner, Victor. *The Delinquency Label: The Epidemiology of Juvenile Delinquency.* New York: Random House, 1969. 177 pp.

Feller, I. W. Children in emergencies. *Federal Probation,* 25(2):12–14, 1961.

Ferster, Elyce Zenoff, and Courtless, Thomas F. The beginning of juvenile justice: police practices and the juvenile offender. *Vanderbilt Law Review,* 22(3):567–608, 1969.

Goldman, Nathan. *The Differential Selection of Juvenile Offenders for Court Appearance.* New York, NCCD, 1963. 133 pp.

Informal disposition of delinquency cases: survey and comparison of court delegation of decision-making. *Washington University Law Quarterly,* No. 2:258–295, 1965.

Juvenile Court Judges' Commission. Additional recommendations for standards in juvenile court-police procedures and for disposition procedures in juvenile court. *Pennsylvania Association on Probation, Parole and Correction Quarterly,* 21(3): 37–46, 1964.

Kelly, Francis. The delinquent child: whose responsibility? *Federal Probation,* 25(4):24–28, 1961.

McKay, Malcolm V. Juvenile court jurisdiction over non-criminal children. Unpublished paper. Cambridge, Mass.: Harvard Law School, 1969.

Mental health consultation to courts and community agencies. In: Szurek, S. A., and Berlin, I. N., eds. *The Antisocial Child, His Family and His Community.* Palo Alto, California: Science and Behavior Books, 1969.

Milne, David S. Public youth agencies: a status report. *Crime and Delinquency,* 9(3):297–305, 1963.

Monahan, Thomas P. National data on police dispositions of juvenile offenders. *Police,* 14(1):36–45, 1969.

National Institute of Mental Health. *Mental Health of Children: The Child Program of the National Institute of Mental Health,* Washington, D.C.: U.S. Government Printing Office, 1965. 65 pp.

New York University. School of Law. Criminal Law Education and Research Center. *The Legal Norms of Delinquency: A Comparative Study.* New York, The University, 1969. 76 pp.

Oklahoma Council of the National Council on Crime and Delinquency. Preventing delinquency: the use of volunteers in providing services to non-adjudicated children in a court setting, by William C. Stephens. Oklahoma City, 1969. 26 pp.

Palmier, Joseph P. Juvenile court intake: form and function. *Willamette Law Journal,* 5(1):121–130, 1968.

Philadelphia. Division of Youth Conservation Services. A review of the Youth Referral Program, 1944–1969. Philadelphia, 1969. 13 pp.

Rector, Milton G. Statement before the U.S. Senate Subcommittee to Investigate Juvenile Delinquency. *Crime and Delinquency.* 16(1):93–99, 1970.

Rubin, Sol. Legal definition of offenses by children and youths. *University of Illinois Law Forum,* 512–521, 1960.

Seattle-King County (Washington). Youth Commission. Juvenile law enforcement bureaus: a survey of their philosophy and practices. Seattle, 1965. 15 pp.

Sheridan, H. Juveniles who commit noncriminal acts: why treat in a correctional system? *Federal Probation,* 31(1):26–30, 1967.

Somerville, James G. A study of the preventive aspect of police work with juveniles. *Criminal Law Review,* August 407–414, 1969.

Szurek, S. A., and Berlin, I. N. *The Antisocial Child: His Family and His Community.* Palo Alto, California: Science and Behavior Books, 1969.

Teele, James E., and Levine, Sol. The acceptance of emotionally disturbed children by psychiatric agencies. In: Wheeler, Stanton, ed. *Controlling Delinquents.* New York: John Wiley, 1968. pp. 103–126.

Teele, James E., and Levine, Sol. Experiences of unsuccessful applicants to child psychiatric agencies. In: Wheeler, Stanton, ed. *Controlling Delinquents.* New York: John Wiley, 1968. pp. 127–151.

Tenney, Charles W., Jr. The new dilemma in the juvenile court. *Nebraska Law Review,* 47(1):67–81, 1967.

Tenney, Charles W., Jr. The utopian world of juvenile courts. Annals of the *American Academy of Political and Social Science,* 383:101–118, 1969.

Thomas, Mason P., Jr. Delinquency and juvenile courts: confusion and diversity. *Federal Probation,* 25(4):47–51, 1961.

Tomaino, Louis. Social work and the prevention of youth offenses. *Child Welfare,* 47(2):85–88, 1968.

U.S. President's Commission on Law Enforcement and Administration of Justice. *Task Force Report: Juvenile Delinquency and Youth Crime.* Washington, D.C.: U.S. Government Printing Office, 1967. 428 pp.

University of California School of Criminology. *The Handling of Juveniles From Offense to Disposition.* Berkeley: The University, 1965. 7 vols.

University of Glasgow. School of Social Study. Police juvenile liaison: practice and evaluation, by J. A. Mack. Glasgow, 1968. 30 pp.

Valukas, Anton R. The juvenile court in operation: substantial improvements needed. *Chicago Bar Record,* 50(7):352–365, 1969.

Wald, Patricia M. The changing world of juvenile law: new vistas for the non-delinquent child—alternatives to formal juvenile adjudication. *Pennsylvania Bar Association Quarterly,* 40(1):37–46, 1968.

Current Project: *After Hours Emergency Child Welfare Services.* Correspondent: Elizabeth C. Biene, Director, Bureau of Child Welfare, 80 Lafayette Street, New York, N.Y. (Project No. 1627 in Information Center files).

Current Project: *Middle-Class Delinquency: An Experiment in Community Control.* Correspondent: Joseph D. Lohman, Dean, School of Criminology, University of California, Berkeley, California, 94720. (Project No. 1283 in Information Center files).

Youth Servies Bureaus

California. Delinquency Prevention Commission. Youth Service Bureaus: standards and guidelines. Sacramento: Youth Authority Department, 1968.

California. Youth Authority Department. Youth Service Bureaus: progress report, by Allen F. Breed. Sacramento, The Department, 1969, 7 pp.

California. Youth Authority Department. Community Services Division. California's Youth Service Bureaus: a study in community action and cooperation, by William A. Underwood. Sacramento, The Department, 1969. 9 pp.

Canlis, Michael N. Tomorrow is too late! *California Youth Authority Quarterly,* 21(1):9–16, 1968.

Moore, Eugene Arthur. Youth Services Bureaus: local community action program prevents delinquency. *Judicature,* 52(3):117–119, 1968.

Norman, Sherwood. An interim report on youth services and resource bureaus. New York: National Council on Crime and Delinquency, 1969. 44 pp.

Rosenheim, Margaret K. Youth Services Bureaus: a concept in search of definition. *Juvenile Court Judges Journal,* 20(2):69–74, 1969.

Special Service for Groups, Inc. Youth Services Bureau: a proposal. Los Angeles, 1969.

Underwood, William. Youth Service Bureau: a new way for offenders. *California Youth Authority Quarterly,* 21(3):12–13, 1968,

Current Project: *Guidelines for Youth Services Bureaus.* Correspondent: Sherwood Norman, Youth Correction Services, National Council on Crime and Delinquency, 44 East 23 Street, New York, N.Y. (Project No. 1873 in Information Center files).

SECTION EIGHT

CORRECTIONS

CHAPTER 20

CONTEMPORARY PROGRAMS FOR ADJUDICATED JUVENILE OFFENDERS: PROBLEMS OF THEORY, PRACTICE AND RESEARCH*

LaMAR T. EMPEY

Introduction

THE FRAMEWORK FOR ANALYSIS. There are two striking and highly contradictory things about the phenomenon called juvenile delinquency. On one hand, there are repeated allusions to the seriousness of the problem and demands from the public that *something be done.* On the other hand, it is a fact that, despite all its wealth and resources, the United States has devoted very little attention to a disciplined assessment of juvenile crime and ways to go about correcting it. "More than 200,000 scientists and engineers," said the President's Commission on Law Enforcement and Administration of Justice (1967a:1), "have applied themselves to solving military problems and hundreds of thousands more to innovation in other areas of modern life, but only a handful are working to control the crimes that injure or frighten millions of Americans each year."

There is nothing new about this state of affairs. It has been cited repeatedly, not only by the recent Crime Commission, but by many other observers as well (Wheeler and Cottrell, 1966; Gibbons, 1965; Empey, 1967a). But unless it can be changed, the problems may

*Summarized from Lamar T. Empey, Contemporary Programs for Convicted Juvenile Offenders: Problems of Theory, Practice and Research. App. 30, Crimes of Violence, Vol. 13, a staff report to the National Commission on the Causes and Prevention of Violence. Prepared by Donald J. Mulvihill and Melvin M. Tumin with Lynn A. Curtis, 1969.

simply grow worse, not better. The lack of investment in scientific research and correctional experimentation probably results from a general tendency to view research on correctional problems through a different prism from that through which research in the physical and natural sciences is viewed. While most people would never be so presumptuous as to suggest that they know the solution for cancer, they would not hesitate to suggest answers for delinquency. Thus, they are disciplined to support the use of funds for research or even to consider it as a useful tool in the quest for solutions. They fail to recognize that answers, if there are any, may only come like answers in the biological or physical realm through a heavy investment in the painstaking and deliberate methods of science, that the only way to interrupt the wandering and bewildering evolution of corrections may be to adopt a more systematic and careful approach.

This particular state of affairs poses a number of problems for any analysis such as this which is concerned with a review of contemporary efforts to deal with the convicted juvenile offender. Because of the pressing need for solutions, there is always a tendency for those who need solutions to believe that answers may already exist and only need to be disseminated. Having adopted this stance, they are anxious for descriptive analyses which spell out action implications without any attention to the complex theoretical and scientific issues involved. This paper, however, will resist the temptation to respond to that point of view and will be concerned as well with the complex issues that make any panaceas seem highly unlikely.

The analysis will be divided into three parts. The first part will be concerned with delinquency in general and will address four major questions:

1. Who is the delinquent? What is delinquency?
2. What should be the basic goals of juvenile corrections?
3. How relevant to basic problems and correctional goals are the theories which underline contemporary programs?
4. What evidence is there relative to the success of existing correctional programs?

The second part will be devoted to an examination of contemporary correctional programs but, rather than simply providing an inventory of those programs, it will be concerned instead with the theoretical bases, operational characteristics and research evidence that relate to the general programmatic approaches that have been applied to juveniles. The analysis will be analytic rather than descriptive.

Finally, the third section will be a summary and conclusion section designed to indicate wherein there seems to be major discrepancies (1) between that which is known and that which in unknown, and (2) between that which is now being accomplished in correctional programs and that which seems to be necessary if rehabilitation and control are to be effective. Hopefully, the analysis might indicate major gaps in existing knowledge and suggest directions for the future.

Part I: General Correctional Problems

QUESTION 1: WHO IS THE DELINQUENT? The evidence is clear that the convicted delinquent with whom correctional programs have traditionally been concerned is most likely a member of the lower-class. Arrest records, probation reports, reformatory data, and demographic studies, over the years, all seem to confirm this conclusion (Shaw and McKay, 1942; Dirksen, 1948; Wattenberg and Balistrieri, 1950; Burgess, 1952; Cohen, 1955; Eaton and Polk, 1961). The major report of the President's Crime Commission (1967b: 56–57) concluded that, "delinquents tend to come from backgrounds of social and economic deprivation. Their families tend to have lower than average incomes and social status . . . It is inescapable that juvenile delinquency is directly related to conditions bred by poverty."

Does this mean, then, that if correctional efforts are successful in changing the lower-class offender that delinquency will be controlled? As a mater of fact, the evidence does not support this conclusion. There is considerable room for disquietude.

Analyses of undetected lawbreaking and of court statutes and practices, as well as official records, suggest that there is a vast difference (1) between the body of offenders who are officially defined as delinquent and the larger number of juveniles who actually break the law, and (2) between the number of delinquent acts that are officially listed and the number that are actually committed. Such analyses suggest that, even if our legal and correctional agencies were totally successful in rehabilitating all juveniles whom they process, delinquency would, by no means, be controlled. By way of illustrating this conclusion, consider the factors that distort the accuracy of official records. Some are well known; others are more subtle and difficult to deal with.

The Questionable Accuracy of Official Records

The questionable accuracy of official records is a well-known fact (cf. Sellin and Wolfgang, 1964). As the Children's Bureau (1965:1) puts it:

> [Delinquency] statistics are affected by several factors. For example, the ages of children and the types of cases over which courts have jurisdiction are established by state law and often vary in different states and sometimes vary within the same state. This discrepancy affects the number of cases reported and, consequently, the comparability of the reports from various courts. Also, the number of children's cases reported by these different courts is influenced by the organization and scope of other agencies. For example, many community agencies suggest cases and refer them to other agencies rather than to juvenile courts; in other communities the juvenile court is one of the few agencies providing social services to children; and in places where social services for children are well established, the juvenile court is sometimes only one of many agencies dealing with children and is used only when its judicial authority is needed. Furthermore, whether or not a child ever comes to the attention of the court is often decided by varying community and parental attitudes toward the child's behavior.
>
> Because of these and other limitations (many of which are not statistically assessable), juvenile courts statistics, when taken by themselves, cannot measure the full extent of delinquency, dependency, or neglect; and they can be particularly misleading when used to compare one community and another. They do, however, indicate how frequently the juvenile court is utilized in dealing with such cases.

Ambiguity of Court Statutes, Policies and Cues

But beyond the mere mechanics of official record keeping, the accuracy of official records is affected by other factors as well, factors that are highly idiosyncratic in character. Members of the juvenile justice system—police, courts and correctional people—are not automatons who respond uniformly and impartially to all juveniles, as the ideals of a rational legal system would suggest, but are people whose changing policies and private philosophies affect their administration of justice. For example, Piliavin and Briar (1964: 209–210) note that, except for the most serious offenses—robbery, assault, grand theft, etc.—the actual violation committed by a juvenile generally played an insignificant role in the disposition of it by the police. The police usually reacted, instead, to *cues which emerged from the interaction between the officer and the youth, cues from which the officer inferred the youth's character.*

Similar observations have been made about the decision-making of the judiciary, and the ambiguous statutes under which they work (President's Commission on Law Enforcement and Administration of Justice, 1967c:25).

> The provisions on which intervention . . . is based are typically vague and all-encompassing: growing up in idleness and crime, engaging in immoral conduct, in danger of leading an immoral life. Especially when administered with the formality characteristic of the [juvenile] court's procedures, they establish the judge as arbiter not only of the behavior but also of the morals of every chld (and to a certain extent the parents of every child) appearing before him. The situation is ripe for over-reaching, for imposition of the judge's own code of youthful conduct. One frequent consequence has been the use of general protective statutes about leading an immoral life and engaging in endangering conduct as a means of enforcing conformity—eliminating long hair, levis, and other transitory adolescent foibles so unsettling to adults. One need not expound the traditional American virtues of individuality and free expression to point out the wrong-headedness of so using the juvenile court; it is enough to reflect that the speed with which such fads come and go is equaled only by the strength of their resistance to outside attack.

Recent Supreme Court decisions, such as the *Gault* decision (George, 1968) may, in the long run, eliminate some of the idiosyncratic decision-making about which the Crime Commission Report complained, but institutional change of the type implied by that kind of decision is relatively slow in coming. The definition of who is delinquent, therefore, is, and may always remain obscured by idiosyncratic decisionmaking. But even beyond that, other factors will also operate to question the accuracy of official records. Consider another body of evidence relative to undetected delinquency.

Undetected Lawbreaking

Delinquent behavior, in official terms, is defined by two essential elements: (1) it is behavior that violates the legal norms of society; but (2) in order for it to become official, it must also evoke official responses from one or more of the various elements of the juvenile justice system (Cloward and Ohlin, 1963:3). Delinquency, then, in official terms, does *not* occur until officials respond. This actually means that official delinquency and actual lawbreaking are two vastly different things. A recent summary of the literature (Empey, 1967b:27–32) indicates the following:

(1) The amount of undetected delinquency is great and the degree of apprehension is low, likely less than 10 per cent.

(2) When self-reported information on illegal acts is obtained from middle as well as lower-class juveniles, the relationships between lower-class membership and delinquency is reduced considerably, especially in smaller cities and towns. Middle—as well as lower-class adolescents are involved in a considerable amount of illegal behavior. Even if lower-class delinquency were controlled, adolescent lawbreaking would still be widespread.

(3) The fact that officials are charged by juvenile court law to respond to poor home and family conditions, neglect and truancy, as well as criminal behavior, may distort the epidemiological character of delinquency and overstress the relationship of lower-class membership to delinquency.

(4) Lower-and middle-class juveniles may tend to commit different kinds of delinquent acts and many of those committed by the middle-class are serious.

Implications for Corrections

There are two major implications that emerge from this question as to "who is the delinquent?" The first has to do with the obvious ambiguity of the phenomenon we call *delinquency*. Short (1960:366–367) has pointed out that delinquent behavior is not an attitude—i.e., "something which one either is or is not, such as male of female, or something which one has or has not, such as measles or mumps." This is an obvious, but often ignored fact. Given the catchall character of the legal statutes which define delinquency, there are virtually no nondelinquents. The ambiguity of these statutes, plus the evidence regarding undetected delinquency, indicates that almost every adolescent has committed acts which, if detected, could have resulted in official arrest and adjudication as delinquent.

Furthermore, the notion that the most delinquent boys spend all of their time in deviant activities is erroneous. Only the smallest of time segments is spent by them in such activities, with the remainder involved in conformist behavior. For example, in observing *typical, tough* city gangs over a 2-year period, Miller (1965: 109, 111) found that assault—the kind of activity about which communities are most concerned—was extremely *un*common. In fact, two-thirds of the male gang members who were observed were not known to have engaged in *any* assaultive crimes over the two-year period and 88 per cent were never charged with such activity. Even among the most violent gangs, then, violence is not a common activity. Instead, verbal aggression seems to be the much more common mode of behavior, accompanied by the distinct tendency on the parts of gang boys to avoid actual violence if they can do so without a loss of status and *honor.*

The implications of these findings, both for the control of lawbreaking and for the rehabilitation of offenders, are profound. On one hand, the fact that law violations among adolescents are widespread means that even if all correctional programs were entirely successful, all lawbreaking would not be controlled. On the other, even if all adolescent lawbreaking could be detected, there is reason to doubt the wisdom of responding to all of it through legal means. Tannenbaum (1938: 12–21), many years ago, expressed concern over what he called the *dramatization of evil.* It was his opinion that many boys who engage initially in mischievous and annoying behavior do not see themselves and that behavior as especially bad, certainly not delinquent. They are made worse, however, by any community which, in hurrying to bring sanctions against them, first defines them as *delinquent* and then causes them to turn to delinquent group associations as a last refuge. Under such circumstances, they find themselves increasingly cut off from association in conventional settings. Murphy, Shirley and Witmer (1946) once put it: "Even a moderate increase in the amount of attention paid to [all undetected lawbreaking] by law enforcement authorities could create a semblance of a *delinquency wave* without there being the slightest change in adolescent behavior."

One must always wonder to what extent the current *delinquency wave* is a function of this very phenomenon and, whether, if attention was focused upon it by other than legal agencies, such attention might be a more important means of control. This is not to suggest that harmful, certainly not criminal, activity should be ignored but it does raise the question as to whether other than legal means might not be a more effective device for the reduction and control of illegal activities, means directed to causes rather than to symptoms.

In support of this conclusion, a brief review of the international scene reveals that an increase in delinquency is not confined merely to the United States, but is an international problem which other countries have been unable to prevent or control. A recent U.N. report (Kvaraceus, 1964: 6) concluded that—

> Even when statistics on delinquency are judged with the greatest reserve —for no neat rows of figures can fully express the extent of the problem— their meaning is clear: delinquency is increasing everywhere. The offenses range from stealing, vandalism and property offenses, petty extortion and gambling to violent behavior, rowdiness, truancy, immoral or indecent conduct, drinking and drug addiction.

The implication is clear: If delinquency is to be controlled, it will probably have to involve communities and agencies other than those who were formerly charged with correcting the adjudicated offender.

In addition, the fact that delinquency is not an attribute, an all-or-none phenomenon, means that some of our traditional ways of viewing the delinquent will have to be changed. That is, the traditional tendency to locate the sole source of difficulty *within* the offender, to see him as either wicked or emotionally disturbed, tends to locate the source of difficulty too much within the individual and to ignore the societal contexts from wihch delinquency springs. It seems likely, instead, that many lawbreakers, even if not officially defined, tend to be more *normal* than *abnormal* measured in terms of mental pathology. It is somewhat meaningless, therefore, to say that *delinquents* are like this, while *nondelinquents* are like that. Instead, actual law-violating behavior is a more or less thing. Juveniles are not either delinquent or nondelinquent; they are more or less delinquent.

All of this muddies up the traditional, punitive and treatment approaches which have been used in corrections. It suggests the need to pay attention to a wide variety of social as well as personal phenomena:

(1) Delinquency may not just be a lower-class phenomenon. It may be widespread among all adolescents, or at least is beginning to spread to all segments of the adolescent population.

(2) The seeming universality of delinquency suggests that it may not be a highly personalized and perhaps pathological deviation. It may be indicative, instead, of a group kind of behavior in which deviant traditions develop among large segments of the youth population in response to prevailing and ill-defined problems within society itself.

(3) The widespread character of delinquency may be indicative of increasing youthful rebellion throughout the world. It seems, in fact, to be taking on political meaning. "Young people," as Polk (1968: 2) suggests, "are not only talking revolution, they are beginning to act." If this is the case, and if more and more young people are drawn into the legal net, the impact on corrections will undoubtedly be profound. In fact, it seems clear that it is impossible for one, narrowly defined and highly formalized legal agency in society to deal with all of these problems, to attempt to control a societal-wide phenomenon, especially if they are expected to act only after illegal acts are committed. The whole field of prevention would be ignored.

These three conclusions, relative to who is the delinquent, have important relevance for the definition of correctional goals. Whose responsibility is it to deal with juvenile lawbreaking as a whole? What does it mean to try to *correct* and to *control* delinquency if indeed it is as widespread as indicated here? Even further, what kinds of systematic knowledge do we have? How adequate is the theoretical base upon which effective correctional programs might be built? First, consider correctional goals as they have been traditionally defined.

Question 2: What Are the Goals of Juvenile Corrections? Existing correctional practices are like a stalagmite on the floor of a cave. Despite the fact that new layers have been added to the basic pillar, despite the fact they add new dimensions to it, they are not independent of the structure. The old and the new are congealed into a solid, often undifferentiated whole. Thus, if one seeks to discover clear and unambiguous correctional goals, one will be disappointed.

The historical and undifferentiated layers of the correctional stalagmite can be conveniently summarized as a succession of three R's: revenge, restraint, and reformation (Glasser, 1964a). *Revenge* was the primary response to lawbreaking prior to the eighteenth century, but was gradually replaced during that, and the following century, by an emphasis upon *restraint,* by the use of imprisonment as the major method for correcting offenders.

When it became apparent that imprisonment would neither work successfully nor would be appropriate for many offenders, adult as well as juvenile, a third major change occurred in correctional philosophy. In the late-19th and early-20th centuries, *reformation* became an important objective. Attention was focused upon the mental and emotional makeup of the offender and efforts were made to alter these as the primary sources of difficulty. Finally, we may be on the verge of yet another revolution in which a fourth concept will be added to the list of R's: *reintegration.* But more will be said on the reintegration issue later. First, let us consider the traditional stalagmite in terms of its triple emphases upon revenge, restraint and reformation.

The reform revolution, of which the juvenile court and the concept of *parens patriae* was a consequence, emphasized the idea that greater justice could be done if both the entire character of the offender and the larger set of circumstances that led to his act could be taken into account when deciding his fate. It suggested that crime is not always a deliberate defiance of social norms, but may be an unconscious response to personal problems; the offender may be sick rather than wicked. His violation of rules may be more an illness than a conscious choice to do wrong. In practical terms, however, the reform revolution placed correctional workers on the horns of a dilemma. It produced a deep-seated and pervasive conflict; namely, the conflict between the older and punitive tradition of revenge and the newer tradition of reform through individualized treatment. These two traditions are inherently contradictory and reflect the conflicting images of man which are found embedded in the correctional stalagmite, indeed in society as a whole.

Since we are concerned primarily in this analysis with juveniles, the history of the juvenile courts since their beginning at the turn of this century provides an excellent case study in the conflict that was generated. On one hand, the reform ideology suggested that the purposes of the juvenile court were "to understand the child, to diagnose his difficulty, to treat his condition, and to fit him back into the community" (Dunham, 1964: 338–339). The child should recognize that he is not being tried for a crime, but rather that the court is acting in lieu of his parents, that it is interested in inquiring into the circumstances which led to the difficulties and insuring his continued welfare. Above all, the child should be treated for his problem rather than punished for his crime.

Presumably, this point of view opened the door for *scientific justice* and the individualization of treatment. Furthermore, because the medical analogy seemed so well suited to the problem, it was quick to appear in the literature, aided and abetted, as Dunham (1964: 344) suggests, by the growing importance of the Freudian point of view. "From the study of neuroses and their emotional manifestations, it was, then, but a short jump to the viewing of delinquent behavior as a symptom of some underlying emotional conflict." The delinquent act was symptomatic of some conflict within the child's personality. Consequently, just as the doctor seeks to restore the physically sick child to health, so the reform ideology urged that a clinical team be utilized to restore the delinquent child to behavioral health, to reduce the delinquent symptoms which have produced his difficulties.

The sharp contrast of this philosophy to that of the revenge and constraint philosophies of earlier periods is obvious. The classical, legal perspective suggests that the legal order is fundamentally an authoritative order deriving its meaning from traditional moral code of society. As Even (1965: 285–286) puts it,

> An implicit assumption of this view is that the exclusive function of law is to reinforce the mores and to provide a uniform and predictable pro-

> cedure for the evaluation and punishment of deviance. That is to say, the function of law is social control and the major problem is one of designing legal sanctions to minimize deviance and maintain social stabiilty.

Thus, one can well appreciate the furious character of the conflict that has been occasioned by efforts to convert the juvenile court into a type of social agency, with traditional, legal procedures deemphasized or eliminated and various treatments introduced in order to *cure* the child. Even if *treatment* were the most likely method of correcting the offender, it is unlikely that the broad-based desire to punish him would be satisfied. The basic philosphical conflict between punishment and reform ideologies remains unresolved and is even heightened under present conditions of youth and racial unrest.

In recent years, the problem has been dramatized by several Supreme Court decisions which substantiate the pervasive conflict between treatment and punishment goals. The court suggests that the juvenile may have gotten the worst of two possible worlds: he has been provided neither with the constitutionl protections of the adult, nor has he received the tender, loving care supposedly inherent in the special provisions of the juvenile court (George, 1968). It is a matter of fact that it is much easier to convict a juvenile than an adult and once he is convicted, he is not likely to receive much better care.

Court decisions imply that legal procedures should be increased in the juvenile court in order to protect the rights of the juvenile, but how this will ultimately be reconciled with the agency functions of the court is difficult to say. How steps can be taken to insure constitutional procedures and yet retain an informal, clinical aura, even if desirable, have not been determined.

Public reactions to this conflict in general, and not just to the juvenile court, reflect ambivalence and bewilderment. In a recent national survey of public opinion, the Joint Commission on Correctional Manpower and Training (1968: 1) discovered that people were highly conflicted regarding the administration of justice and unable to recognize the contradictions inherent in their own opinions. "One must conclude," says the report, ". . . that the public feels that the corrections system is currently inadequate. At the same time, the public is not eager to bring about change. . ."

This public reaction clearly reveals the horns of the dilemma upon which correction is pinioned. So long as the stalagmite upon which corrections is based has contradictory branches emphasizing both punishment and correction, we cannot logically expect correctional workers to be consistent in their methods of dealing with lawbreakers. As Cressey (1968: 31–34) put it, "Correctional workers are called upon to play a game that they cannot win." Their dilemma probably illustrates one of the major reasons that the reform philosophy has not produced a notable improvement in the effectiveness of correctional organizations. Since societal norms are disorganized, correctional goals and practices reflect this disorganization.

As if these problems were not enough, as if correctional goals were not already terribly confused and contradictory, our analysis of "Who is the delinquent?" suggests that, even if correctional goals could be clarified and explicitly pursued, many problems in effectively controlling delinquency would still remain. So long as correctional efforts are directed primarily to dealing with the *convicted* offender, the widespread problems of undetected delinquency will remain. Major correctional efforts will not even be devoted to dealing with them. What, then, are the implications inherent, not only in this conclusion, but in the whole analysis of the goals of juvenile corrections?

Implications of Goals Analysis

There are three major implications inherent in the foregoing analysis:

(1) Correctional goals are badly in need of clarification. An indispensable element in implementing any successful correctional program would be a clear specification of objectives. The process for determining the relevance of any means for addressing correctional problems can be determined only after a set of objectives have been defined and a choice of priorities made among them. One of the major reasons for the failure of many correctional endeavors in the past has been the lack of such a statement and a ratification of it

by key persons, the public and its representatives as well as members of the juvenile justice system.

When objectives are not made explicit, there is no logical means for choosing one approach over another, one kind of staff over another, one program component over another. It would not make much sense, for example, to initiate innovative, correctional programs unless basic and conflicting objectives can be reconciled. Such programs, by themselves, have little meaning unless they are placed in a conceptual framework and are explained by some system of logic.

(2) If efforts at controlling delinquency are to be successful, and this means a heavy emphasis upon preventative as well as rehabilitative efforts, efforts must be made, as Wheeler and Cottrell (1966: 50) suggest, to provide coordination of services between all the possible agencies and especially that there be some unit where firm direction and leadership can be lodged. This is necessary if we are to arrive at rational program priorities. Delinquency is too serious a problem to be lodged in a labyrinth of separate bureaucratic settings with little in the name of logic, program, or coordinating mechanism to tie them all together. This does not mean that a new division or department is necessarily essential. It does mean that a mechanism must be found for guiding the development of the field in a responsible and orderly way. Only then can we anticipate that the federal leadership needed in so many areas of concern for delinquency can really emerge.

(3) The community and its basic institutions should themselves be made the target of change. Much of our discussion to this point has implied that all correctional problems are not inherent in the character of the offender, but in the character of legal and correctional agencies as well. The labeling and stigmatizing processes of society which are derived from an historical emphasis upon punishment and revenge must somehow be addressed and perhaps revised. A growing chorus of writers have been concerned not only with traditional emphases upon revenge, but upon the stigmatizing effects even of current treatment practices. They have been concerned because of the failure of these approaches to address the problem of redefining the delinquent's social position and with it his own conception of himself.

Tannenbaum (1938: 31) suggested that "the process of making the criminal is a process of tagging, describing, emphasizing, making conscious and self-conscious; it becomes a way of stimulating, suggesting, emphasizing, and evoking the very traits that are complained of." Merton (1957: 421–436) described the process as a *self-fulfilling prophecy.* Lemert (1951: 75–76) coined the term *secondary deviation* to describe the outcome of the process-that is, to note that it may add to whatever delinquent tendencies the offender may have brought with him to the correctional scene. Thus, even though we might define the offender as *sick,* rather than *wicked,* we may do little to discourage the notion that he is permanently disabled, either in his mind, in the minds of correctional personnel, or in the minds of society. Although the community investment in keeping him in a deviant status is sustained, the problem of affecting a rite-of-passage back into a nondelinquent status may be seriously hampered. Thus, it is not escape from, but better integration within the community that the offender needs. One major problem for any correctional program, therefore, is in finding ways by which to integrate the offender into ongoing, community life.

It seems without question that more attention will have to be devoted to the devising of strategies by which community involvement and change might be accomplished. At the very least, more effective means must be devised for linking correctional programs and their people, staff and offenders, with external systems-families, schools, employers, and recreational resources.

Question 3: How Relevant Are Contemporary Theories to Existing Correctional Problems and Goals?

Correctional Problems and Goals? "One rather common view regarding the treatment of offenders," says Gibbons (1965: 15)

> is that once an appropriate structure is provided for rehabilitative efforts, including larger budgets, smaller caseloads, wider use of probation, better classification programs, more trained workers in corrections, higher salaries, and the like, dramatic reductions in recividism will quickly follow. This is a position of unbridled and undue optimism, for there is little empirical basis for such a faith. Improvements in correctional structure could have little effect upon recidivism until improvements are also

> made in the practice theory of treatment, and even then, dramatic reductions in delinquency and criminality may be unlikely.

The complex problems which have already been cited in this analysis, some of which have scarcely been identified let alone addressed, attest to the accuracy of Gibbon's observations. If the list of alternatives for responding to delinquency were narrow, well defined and supported by empirical evidence, the task of selecting among them for program innovation would not be difficult. But this is not the case. The choice of alternatives is broad, ill-defined, and lack adequate supporting evidence. There is an obvious need for disciplined, logically valid and testable theories upon which to build broader and more comprehensive programs which seem to have greater promise for addressing the problems of delinquency. How well, then, does correctional theory measure up to this need? How adequate is it for the complex tasks that must be addressed?

"The main task of any theory," suggests Schrag (1967: 229), "is to construct a calculus of relationships among classes of events such that the derived statements are (1) logically valid, (2) accurate in their claims regarding observable data, and (3) useful in describing, explaining, and controlling the course of the events with which they are concerned." Existing theories of delinquency, as judged by these criteria, are weak, especially when one is confronted, as we are here, with the problems of control as well as explanation. There are two reasons for this state of affairs: first, theories of delinquency, like those in social science in general,

> . . . lack the abstract and powerful vocabularies, the precise rules of grammar, and the technical dictionaries that are necessary for translating the philosophy of science into viable procedures for handling their distinctive problems. This means that there are no authenticated methods resolving controversies over the defintions of concepts, the acceptability of assumptions and theories, or even the identification of problems that are unique to (delinquency) as a specialized field of inquiry (Schrag, 1967: 244).

The result is that few, if any, delinquency control theories meet the criteria suggested by Schrag.

Second, most existing theories of delinquency are employed largely for heuristic or descriptive purposes, not for the purposes of explanation and control. They have been of greater interest to scientists as a stimulus to the investigation of the causes for delinquency than to practitioners as the basis for constructing correctional models. Thus, despite a number of critics who lament what seems to them to be an excessive emphasis upon the use of theory in corrections, the facts are that correctional theory does not even meet minimal scientific standards. There are several reasons for this state of affairs.

Attempts to construct and use correctional theory, in any formal sense, have been negligible because of a general distrust of theory. Theory is generally seen by most people, including those responsible for running correctional programs, as being totally abstract and divorced from reality; it does not seem to be applicable to everyday problems. As a matter of fact, they are partially correct in their assessment of the issue.

They are correct in the sense that most existing delinquency theory does not seem to have immediate relevance for them. The reason, as explained above, is that most theorists are concerned more with the logical functions of theory, on an abstract level, than with developing lower-level formulations for guidance in some action or research process. The problem that is created, thereby, is especially acute for the practitioner (cf. Empey, 1964). Theoretically derived strategies which he could use for attacking delinquency problems would require not only a careful specification of the factors with which he should be concerned, but with a further specification as to how those factors might be manipulated in order to achieve his stated objectives. Since it is often difficult for even the scientist to translate the symbolic representations utilized by theory-concepts, terms, propositions-into phenomena that are readily observable in the everyday operation of society, it is even more difficult for the action person to conceive how they could be used in any correctional program.

Yet, it is a mistake to assume that practitioners do not use theory. Although they do not do their theorizing in a very sophisticated manner, most of them have explanations for delinquency-explanations which are not only theoretical, in the sense that they have not been verified, but which tend to become highly rationalized belief systems. These belief systems are intellectual prisms which dictate perception and determine what those who use them will see and on what they will concentrate their efforts. Perhaps even more important, these prisms not only determine what they look for, but what they *overlook* (Glaser, 1956: 433). In other words, most practitioner explanations do precisely what a formally derived theory does: it defines certain factors as important, focuses attention upon them, and explains what the product of interactions among these factors will be. What, then, do correctional people focus upon?

There is no single answer. It all depends upon the general prevailing ethos that tends to characterize any particular correctional organization. In their correctional study, for example, Street, Vinter, and Perrow (1966) found a wide variation of correctional practices and interpreted these varied practices to be a function of differences in the general character of the organizations studied. Furthermore, in any particular organization, the way in which a particular person views the delinquent will depend heavily upon the correctional role he plays. If he is a custodial officer, he will be inclined to see the offender as devious and in need of control. If he is a teacher, he will see the offender as educationally deficient and in need of training. And if he is a therapist, he will view the offender as emotionally maladjusted and in need of therapy. The point is that correctional organizations, themselves, often have confusing and disparate goals, confusing and contradictory emphases which often make the problem worse, not better. The result, too often, is increased cynicism and deviance on the part of the inmate who must somehow survive in an amazingly difficult organization.

Before leaving the subject, a word should be said about the training which professionals in corrections have received. If there is any one practice theory which has characterized the training received by clinical personnel in their professional training, it has been based upon crudely articulated behavioral propositions which suggest that offenders are emotionally maladjusted and in need of individual therapy (cf. Gibbons, 1956: 7). These propositions imply that lawbreakers are *acting out* their emotional problems. The difficulty is, however, that as our knowledge has expanded, it has become obvious that such propositions are inadequate as a total explanation and that if they are to be used, they must be articulated more effectively with a broader body of theory designed to explain the many social and cultural factors associated with delinquency which were mentioned above. Although social factors, and the problems of reintegrating the offender into the community, have begun to creep into the intervention strategies of some correctional programs, this material has not been prominent in comparison to the mass of traditional, psychogenic *theory.*

Many other problems of a complex nature could be cited relevant to existing correctional theory. Enough has been said, however, to indicate that there is a vast difference between the traditional and often vague explanations which have been used to guide correctional practices in the past and scientifically adequate theories. By way of summary, then, let us consider what the implications are that emerge from this analysis.

Implications of Theory Discussion

There are three major implications which emerge from the discussion of correctional theory:

(1) There are vast differences between the ill-defined and conflicting conceptual framework which are presently guiding correctional practices and scientifically adequate theories.

(2) An examination of correctional practices throughout history reveals our preoccupation with understanding why a particular person becomes delinquent and what must be done to change *him.* This is an important perspective, but it is one-sided. Official statistics which reveal that members of ethnic minorities, the working classes, and the poorly educated statistics which reveal widespread delinquency throughout the whole adolescent population, implies that delinquency is a two-sided coin. It represents not only some form of psychological alienation on the part of the offender, but inadequacies in fundamental, societal institutions as well. If correctional programs are to become more relevant therefore, we must develop theories which fit all the parts of the delinquency picture and not just one facet of it. Indeed, if our theories fail to keep in mind the whole, we are not likely to find a satisfactory explanation of the part.

(3) The need for comprehensive theory extends to legal and correctional organizations themselves. Police, court and correctional

agencies are all parts of a single, complex system of justice. Yet, we do not have single explanatory themes by which to understand this total system or the parts of which it is comprised. Quite aside from the personal characteristics of the offender, a knowledge of the way these interrelated parts function is imperative if efforts at the control and rehabilitation of delinquents is to become a more systematic and rational process.

Question 4: What Evidence Is There Relative to the Success of Existing Correctional Programs?

It was pointed out earlier that correctional efforts in this country have been characterized by a wandering kind of evolution. Most of our reforms have been the result of an uneasy series of compromises between punitive aggression and rehabilitative empathy (Morris, 1966: 628–630). Correctional units such as probation, training schools and parole have not been considered on any comprehensive basis as constituting a single system. Instead, new practices such as casework, psychotherapy, remedial education, or group counseling have all been added piecemeal to existing operations and, rather than replacing older philosophies and techniques, have simply supplemented them. Corrections has grown like Topsy. As a result, it is difficult to tell whether new practices contribute to, or only confuse, older objectives and practices.

Consider again the programmatic layers-punishment, reform, and now reintegration-which have accumulated upon the contemporary correctional stalagmite. Begin with punishment. We are ignorant of the extent to which punishment actually deters. In gross terms, the persistence of delinquency seems to belie punishment's' effectiveness. Yet, to be quite accurate, we do not know just what its effects are. It seems likely that punishment does sometimes deter, that it does sometimes educate, but when and how? Perhaps the problem is not one of determining whether punishment deters, but of determining the conditions and degree to which its benefits either exceed or are less than its liabilities.

Similarly, we lack precise information regrading the effects of the reform revolution. "The viability of the reform idea," as Lemert

(1967: 31) suggests, "can be traced to a repressive, puritan psychology reinforced by the propaganda of the mental hygiene movement of the early twentieth century, which helped to produce child guidance clinics, school social work, and juvenile courts." But, concludes Eysenck (1966: 29):

> With the single exception of the psychotherapeutic methods based on learning theory, results of published research with military and civilian neurotics, and with both adults and children, suggests that the therapeutic efforts of psychotherapy are small or non-existent, and do not in any demonstrable way add to the non-specific effects of routine medical treatment, or to such events as occur in the patient's everyday experience.

While such a comment is made about a large and somewhat different population than delinquents, it has extreme relevance for the latter because it reflects the serious gaps in knowledge which confront us.

Our problems stem from the fact that we have failed to approach correctional problems in any way resembling a scientific approach. We have failed to provide means either for avoiding repetitive errors or for pinpointing reasons for successes where successes have occurred.

Yet, as Wheeler and Cottrell (1966: 44) point out:

> No responsible business concern would operate with as little information regarding its success or failure as do nearly all of our delinquency prevention and control programs. It is almost possible to count on one hand the number of true experiments in which alternative techniques are compared; the number of systematic, though non-experimental evaluations is not a great deal larger. We spend millions of dollars a year in preventive and corrective efforts, with little other than guesswork to tell us whether we are getting the desired effects.

It would certainly be hoped therefore, that a greater use of funds for scientific investigation would provide some more conclusive answers.

Implications for Corrections

In terms of its implications for corrections the lack of scientific investigation suggests the need for three kinds of research (Wheeler and Cottrell 1966: 43–45).

(1) The first would be the establishment of information systems by which statistical data, both national and local, could be gathered and used to implement long-term planning and to keep the public informed. Rational and comprehensive planning depends upon adequate, statistical information regarding trends in the amount and types of delinquency and, since it does not now exist, planning must operate in a vacuum. For example, the work of such commissions as the one on the causes and prevention of violence cannot even begin to establish the parameters of the problem accurately because sound data are not available.

(2) Research on the nature and operation of legal and correctional systems, themselves, is badly needed. "For years," says Cicourel (1968: 331), "sociologists have complained about *bad* statistics and distorted bureaucratic record-keeping, but have not made the procedures producing the *bad* materials we label *data* an object of study." Even though recent advances have suggested that the responses of society to juvenile delinquency may be themselves problematic, little has been done to make these responses the object of study. It seems likely that many problems are created by those responses as well as solutions. The process by which this occurs should be examined. Research of this type would itself require attention to two matters.

There is a need for detailed information on the reasons for referral to juvenile courts, on the length of time spent in detention facilities, on the reasons for the dispositions made by the court, on the personnel who work with juvenile delinquents, and on the character of the training schools and other facilities. All these things call for a collection of local, state, and regional data in a national center which can provide statistical analysis and report the results (Wheeler and Cottrell, 1966: 43).

Such research might be labeled *outcome* research and would be of inestimable value in assessing the effects of existing programs on delinquency rates, on cost per inmate, on recidivism and on other outcome criteria.

The second subtype of system research that is needed might be labeled *process* research. It would be concerned with the study of the process by which outcomes were achieved. That is, with the way in which legal and correctional systems operate, in addition to what juveniles do, to produce the success or failures of existing programs. Almost nothing is known about the way in which the policy decisions of authorities, their staffing patterns and beliefs, and their interactions with offenders result in the outcomes that are observed.

(3) Finally, much more basic and experimental research is needed, both on the factors which produce delinquency and on the kinds of theoretically based and innovative programs that might be developed to deal with it. Modern society is in a rapid state of change and if it is to adapt to that change, a continuing flow of information is needed, not only on the nature of the delinquency problem itself, but on the kinds of institutional modifications that will be required to keep pace with it. Such research cannot always occur within the strictures of existing legal and correctional arrangements, but will require new kinds of financial and other supports by which it can be carried out. Hopefully, it might contribute to policy decisions designed to relate changes in the rates and kinds of delinquency to a more flexible societal response.

Part II: Major Approaches To Corrections

This section of the paper is not devoted to an inventory of existing, correctional programs. Instead, it is concerned with an analysis of the different frames of reference that have been applied to juvenile corrections and to the programs in which they have resulted. Although there may be many variations on the major themes that are presented, the major themes will be adequate to pinpoint key issues, especially in light of the problems that were raised above. By submitting major themes to this kind of an analysis, problems left unaddressed, as well as addressed, will be highlighted.

Probation and the Casework-Approach

The historical trend since the mid-19th century has been away from imprisonment and toward the use of community alternatives for offenders. Probation, especially for juveniles, has been the most common alternative. It is a disposition which is available to courts in virtually every jurisdiction.

Probation was introduced initially as a humanitarian measure, not as a scientific endeavor to discover more effective rehabilitative techniques. Early proponents wished simply to keep first offenders and minor recidivists from undergoing the corrupting effects of jail (cf. Glueck, 1933: 228). They were volunteers-ministers and others-whose untrained efforts to help guide and moralize with their probationers were considered adequate. Their philosophy was that the offender was a deprived, perhaps uneducated youngster, who needed help in adjusting to his environment. Their orientation was social in nature.

During and after World War I, as Empey (1967a: 31–31) points out, a marked change occurred in this orientation.

> As probation work continued to expand, there was an ever-increasing demand for professionally educated people, especially trained social workers, to serve as probation officers. And the training of social workers, in turn, was profoundly influenced by the introduction of psychiatric and especially psychoanalytic theory. This theory was preoccupied with the individual and his emotional makeup, and the training of the professional caseworker reflected this concern.
>
> More and more the offender was seen as a disturbed person in whom emotional healing was necessary, and the ability of the probation worker was judged in terms of his capacity to offer psychiatrically oriented therapy. Thus, both the philosophy and administration of probation became a highly complex admixture of psychotherapeutic theory and the older concern with helping the offender to adjust economically and socially to his environment. It remains that way today. The ideology of probation is broad and amorphous, one of generalized beneficence. Ideally, it is supposed to help the offender with all phases of his life, as well as monitoring his capacity for discipline and self-control. Yet, in practice, the individual officer may be expected to maintain a caseload of from 75 to 200 probationers, to conduct pre-sentence investigations, to maintain extensive paper work, and perhaps to carry out other functions as well. It is obvious that the ideology of beneficence has not been reconciled with probation in practice.

It would be fair to say in summary that probation as a correctional device for helping and supervising the individual exists more in form than in substance. Evidence indicates that as a rule very little actual time can be spent by a probation officer with any single offender.

Despite these limitations, probation is widely used. It is used for the preponderant majority of all juveniles and not insignificantly for young adults who are first-time felons. Between one-third and two-thirds of the latter received probation. In many jurisdictions, probation is a county function, in others a city or particular court function, and in others a state function. At the same time, however, there are few central record repositories by which to follow up court dispositions for evaluating probation effectiveness.

Given this brief outline, how might probation be evaluated in terms of the four major questions that were raised earlier: how relevant is probation as a device for controlling the ambiguous phenomenon we call delinquency? How relevant are the correctional goals of probation? What is the nature of the theory upon which probationary practices are based? What is the evidence as to the success of probation?

Probation and Delinquency Control

By definition, probation is concerned with rehabilitation, not prevention. Its main function is to deal with offenders who have been officially defined as delinquent, not potential lawbreakers. To be sure, it is useful as a preventive device insofar as it prevents recidivism. But any controls it may be able to exert will result more from its work with convicted than with undetected lawbreakers. This means, therefore, that if society wishes to control delinquency, probation as it is now organized cannot be expected to exercise that function.

The Nature of Probation Goals

Although the ostensible goal of probation, since its very inception, has been with helping rather than punishing the juvenile, his responses and those of his parents to court action reveal a marked ambivalence. Most offenders do not see the court and its probation agencies as sources of help, but as administrators of punishment (cf. Baum and Wheeler, 1968: 166; O'Keefe, 1948: 31–35). They do not perceive probation and other clinical services as something designed to help, but to punish them. Thus, the conflict alluded to earlier between the traditional concept of punitive versus treatment justice is remarkably well-documented, not just among correctional people and the public in general, but among juvenile offenders themselves.

The fact that this preception exists speaks to the well-known complaint of treatment people that offenders are *unmotivated* to want to change. It indicates why, unless such perceptions by society as well as the offender can be changed, efforts to correct the offender will be difficult. Traditional and simultaneous values favoring both punishment and rehabilitation are in such marked contrast to each other that even the offender is affected by them. The situation is not conducive to much optimism.

A second major difficulty has to do with the administrative and paper work functions of the probation officer (cf. Diana, 1960). His common complaint is that he has to spend so much time preparing court petitions, conducting investigations, writing personal histories of dubious value, and presenting cases in court, that he has no time left to supervise or assist the offender. To make matters worse, the physical location of probation offices is often so far removed from the probationer that actual distance makes supervision difficult, if not impossible (President's Commission on Law Enforcement and Administration of Justice, 1967d: 30). This situation prevails not only in the large city but in rural areas as well. One officer may be responsible for offenders spread over large geographical areas, sometimes over several different counties. Clearly, the juvenile court, as indicated by its administration of probation services, falls far short of its own ideals.

Adequacy of Probation Theory

There are two problems associated with the generic casework theory upon which probation is based. The first has to do with the problem noted earlier in which the administration of probation becomes a highly complex admixture of psychotherapeutic theory and concern with helping the offender to adjust economically and socially to his environment. Historically, the emphasis upon individual treatment, and the correction of emotional maladjustment, has tended to ignore the compelling pressures that are exerted upon the offender by persons living in his community, by the social groups to which he belongs, by the overall culture and, within it, a host of dissonant subcultures. It is this subcultural and cultural matrix from which the offender comes that prescribes his goals and his standards of conduct. And it is this matrix which heavily influences whether he will become a success or a failure, a criminal or a law-abiding citizen (cf. Empey, 1967a: 4).

Consequently, because casework theory has not been concerned historically with institutional and subcultural, as well as individual and familial, change, the probation officer does not have an adequate theoretical base upon which to organize new attempts at intervention.

A second major theoretical problem with which probation must contend is the somewhat incompatible functions which it is expected to perform. Traditional casework theory does not prepare the probation officer both to assist and treat the offender and at the same time to act as an authority figure. Such a stance is difficult to maintain and traditional theory has not provided adequate guidelines by which the officer can be assisted in dealing with hostile persons who are involuntarily assigned to him. The professionally trained probation officer "is not prepared to function within the special structure of corrections in which he is both a representative of the punitive social control system as well as a helper" (Gibbons, 1965: 224–225). This problem extends not only to the possibility that the probation officer might not only have to re-arrest the offender for some new offense, but to censor him for the use of alcohol, staying out late, or being insubordinate in some way to parents or school officials. Not only does the offender have trouble with this situation, but the probation officer himself experiences considerable identity conflict. It seems obvious that new theoretical formulations are needed by which to define the role of a probation officer in somewhat different terms than the traditional casework definition.

Research Evidence on Probation

The research evidence relative to probation effectiveness is both surprising and revealing. On one hand, a number of studies have indicated that despite all the foregoing problems, probation seems to be effective. In a summary analysis of fifteen probation studies conducted in a variety of jurisdictions, England (1957: 667–677) reported success rates which varied between 60 and 90 percent. A survey of probation effectiveness in such states as Massachusetts, California, New York, and a variety of foreign countries provides similar reported results with the modal success rated about 75 percent (cf. Grunhut, 1948: 60–82).

"These findings," says Empey (1967a: 32):

> are not totally valid because they were not obtained under controlled conditions nor were they supported by data which distinguished among the types of offenders who succeeded or the types of services that were rendered. Nevertheless, the success rates were rather uniform and relatively high and cannot, therefore, be discounted totally. They are the product of a variety of kinds of probation administered in different times and places. Even when interpreted skeptically, therefore, they raise some real issues relative to current policy and practice which can only be answered through extensive use of research.

The issues that are raised are these (Empey, 1967a: 32):

> (1) *What proportion of those now being placed on probation could do just as well on a suspended sentence without any supervision?*—Given the fact that probation is able to supply minimal service, if any, suggests that many offenders may be *self-correcting.* Once having been detected and adjudicated guilty, they may not be likely to get in trouble again. Still others might be dissuaded from further delinquency merely through exposure to the limited surveillance which probation supplies.
>
> There is some provocative evidence in support of this conclusion. In their study of over 2,200 delinquents assigned by several juvenile courts to probation, McEachern and Taylor (1967) noted that dispositions of cases fell into four general categories: (a) apprehended offenders who were dismissed by probation departments at intake and received no treatment, (b) offenders who were placed on informal probation without hearing, but who received some treatment, (c) offenders who were made wards of the court but received no treatment, and (d) those who were made wards of the court and received treatment. In following up the recidivism rates of those assigned to these different dispositions, they discovered two significant things. First, they found that those delinquents who were made formal wards of the court (categories (c) and (d) improved significantly more than those who were not (categories (a) and (b)). But, second, and more important they found that those delinquents who were *not* given treatment, that is, were never contacted by a probation officer,

improved more than those who were. The group who committed the fewest offenses during the period of followup were those who were made wards of the court but given no treatment. The authors did not present further data or conjecture to explain these findings but the possibility cannot be ignored that many offenders, after being sanctioned by the court, may be best able to improve without intense supervision.

As Wheeler and Cottrell (1966: 37–38) suggest:

> The court procedures, may be enough to deter the offender from further unlawful activity. He may be less likely to repeat an offense if there is no correctional program put into effect in his behalf. It is precisely this possibility that led the framers of the New York Family Court Act to allow for *no disposition,* following the determination of fact. Relatively little use has been made of this alternative so far, but there is feeling that its use could be systematically increased. This, one very real and possibly very meaningful alternative is simply to invoke no disposition whatsoever.

Certainly such findings should be provocative of further study. Evidence is badly needed as to whether or not arrest, court adjudication and supervision contribute to the development of a delinquent career or whether only parts of this process may be helpful. The important thing would be to determine some balance between the danger of excessive legal and supervisory control versus the dangers of no control whatsoever.

The need for investigation is further reinforced by the conclusion which Berelman and Steinburn (1968) reached regarding the effectiveness of several caseworker-oriented delinquency *prevention* experiments which have been tried. Even though these projects were oriented to preventing delinquency, their results based largely on traditional caswork practices, merit attention. They concluded that—for approximately the past thirty years, delinquency prevention experiments, broadly defined, have yielded but one dismal result: it is yet to be demonstrated that the provision of a preventative service is any more effective in reducing delinquent behavior than no service at all is. This conclusion appears inescapable in light of the control procedures which have distinguished these experiments. But, before pessimism is accepted as the only possible response to these findings, both research procedures and the services rendered subjects in these experiments should be examined with considerable care.

This conclusion, as the authors suggest, does not merit acceptance of the notion that all efforts at community intervention should cease. It suggests, instead, that *outcome* research is not the only kind of research that is needed. Much more information is needed about types of offenders and the kinds of processual happenings that occur within delinquency programs. This need is illustrated by two additional questions which follow.

(2) *How can one identify those who do not require intensive supervision in order to prevent their future violation of the law, and, more important, how can one identify those who do require intensive supervision?*—Obviously, current correctional systems cannot provide the answer. Knowledge-building resources are lacking. Yet, if probation and other casework services are to be improved, some kind of quality control is needed, Hopefully, through research, it might become possible to identify those offenders who are most likely to fail, and, conversely, those who do not require extended surveillance. Probation departments could then concentrate upon that segment of the population for whom probation is most appropriate (cf. Empey, 1967a: 33).

(3) *Is it not possible, given the disarray of existing research evidence, that many offenders who are now commonly committed to institutions rather than receiving probation might be dealt with safely and effectively in the community?*—If the majority of probationers can succeed without much intensive supervision, then perhaps many of those who are incarcerated could do well in the community if supervision were intensified. As Kinch (1962) has suggested, it would be safe to assume that different delinquent types do exist and that, furthermore, these types will vary in their responses to different kinds of treatments, some successfully responding to one kind of treatment, some responding successfully to other assignments. The problem is that typological research is primitive. Very little theory and investigation has been conducted.

In summary, this review of probation reveals a host of startling and contradictory issues which can be answered only by systematic investigation. On one hand, the evidence indicates that probation, as a helping and supervisory device, is highly limited. Its main function, instead, has been that of carrying out the formal rituals of legal and professional processing. On the other hand, the majority of offenders assigned to probation are successful. They do not recidivate. Why? In what way and for whom should probation operate?

Incarceration and Its Impact

The second major approach to juvenile corrections has been incarceration. In commenting upon the use of incarceration as a correctional device, Wheeler and Cottrell (1966: 37) express a common opinion. "The first principle," they say,

> is that traditional forms of incarceration in correctional institutions should be avoided insofar as possible. Such institutions, it is believed, are of dubious value as rehabilitative mechanisms, especially with the inadequate staffing and facilities found in most of them. Extended periods of incarceration in such institutions may prove to be positively damaging to a youth and may reduce the likelihood that he can be rehabilitated. In addition to the stigma attached to assignment to a correctional institution, which may become a serious barrier to the offender's return to a normal social life, there are such added hazards as the loss of contact with conventional society and intensified contact with other offenders. Not only is this form of treatment potentially damaging to the subjects, but the cost of such standard correctional programs is much greater than that associated with most of the alternatives to incarceration. From these considerations, it is clear that this alternative should be used only as a last resort.

That this opinion carries considerable weight and is widely shared is supported by recent figures which reveal that the majority of offenders are not confined, but are in the community either on probation or parole after incarceration (cf. President's Commission on Law Enforcement and Administration of Justice, 1967d: 1–2). Among adults, the rato is two to one-857,000 are under supervision in the community, while only 426,000 are confined—while among juveniles, the difference is even greater, a ratio of four to one-285,000 in the community, with 63,000 confined. Yet, given the prevailing climate of public ambivalence regarding violence and juvenile crime, and given the public's residual faith in punishment and confinement as control and rehabilitative devices, the above conclusions and statistics merit careful consideration. Why should eminent authorities on one hand decry incarceration as an effective device, while the public is inclined to be somewhat supportive of it? A review of our four major questions will help to answer some of these questions but will also highlight the need for more comprehensive theory and research investigation.

Relevance of Incarceration for Comprehensive Delinquency Control

On one hand, it is obvious that incarceration as a device by which to control widespread juvenile delinquency is no more, and is perhaps less effective than probation. The reason is that incarceration is concerned only with adjudicated offenders, not with potential or undetected lawbreakers. As a consequence, its utility as a direct control device can be measured only in terms of its ability to prevent recidivism. Nevertheless, there is a strong and prevailing belief that incarceration is an effective albeit indirect control device because it acts as a deterrent to would-be violators (cf. Empey, 1967a: 1–2).

The rationalist philosophers of the late-18th and early-19th centuries provided the intellectual foundation for our modern reliance upon a theory of social control through punishment. In rejecting the supernaturalism of prior history, they based their corrective policies on the belief that men are rational beings who operate on a pleasure-pain principle, doing that which gives the greatest pleasure and avoiding that which gives them pain. They suggested, therefore, that the purpose of punishment is *not* revenge; its purpose is deterrence. As a consequence, the classical school of criminology, indeed many of our contemporary laws and sentencing procedures are based upon the following set of beliefs: (1) that reactions to crime should be based on a rational, pleasure-pain principle: light punishment for light crimes, heavy punishment for serious crimes, making sure in each case that the pain of punishment slightly exceeds the pleasure of crime; (2) that it is the certainty and the swiftness of punishment, not its severity, which will determine the success or failure of any effort to control crime; and (3) that by utilizing imprisonment and establishing, by statute, a prescribed punishment for each kind of offense, lawbreaking can be controlled most effectively.

The wide acceptance of this theory of social control is easy to detect in modern society. The classical theory of deterrence, with its rationalistic underpinnings became one of the most important bases upon which legal and correctional practices were based. In fact, the writing of many theorists reflected the belief that punishment provides a deterrent effect which serves to maintain social solidarity. Thus, it is not easy to discard the notion that punishment and incarceration are effective control devices.

Whether or not this theory is correct, especially the belief that punishment actually deters potential lawbreakers, is still a matter of continuing debate that remains to be resolved. But whatever may be discovered, there is no denying the popularity of the social control theory of deterrence and the relative simplicity of the objectives that it imposes upon correctional organizations. These objectives are widely accepted and are relatively clear and straightforward: the offender is to be punished and society is to be protected. Imprisonment will not only be humane, but will also deter other rational people from crime. It will be a lesson that crime does not pay.

Yet, the theoretical and ideological bases which gave rise initially to the use of imprisonment as a control device included numerous weaknesses which began, almost from the beginning, to question the theoretical adequacy of the classical school. Both the punitive theory of deterrence and imprisonment have been the subject of attack by correctional and legal scholars almost since their inception. A review of our remaining questions helps to indicate some of the problems that have been noted.

Relevance of the Goals of Incarceration to Delinquency Control

There are inherent difficulties in using places of incarceration as a corrective device. They are what Goffman (1961) calls "total institutions." The total institution, he says, "is a social hybrid, part residential community, part formal organization . . ." which attempts both to punish and, at the same time, to reform the offender. It is a striking example of the problems posed by conflicting punitive and reform ideologies. It is so full of logical contradictions that, while it effectively suppresses the offender, it does little to change him. Why?

The reasons are not difficult to discover (cf. Cloward et al., 1960; Cressey, 1961). Conditions of imprisonment, even among such nondelinquents as prisoners-of-war or mental patients, almost inevitably seem to produce group responses similar to those of delinquents. Captivity, quite aside from one's delinquent or nondelinquent history, quickly precipitates a kind of group climate in which resistance to change by inmates is heightened. The deprivation of liberty, especially for delinquents, only seems to confirm prior, negative perceptions of authority and to heighten resistances to change.

The reason is that places of confinement are typically caste systems

(Empey, 1968: 5-6). Inmates and authorities are divided into discrete groups, and even though the ostensible role of corrections is to have offenders adopt the same values, expectations, and patterns of behavior as staff members, structural conditions in a caste system make it difficult, if not impossible for them to do so.

The reform revolution in corrections, with its emphasis upon individualized treatment, has generally been considered to be an antidote to the caste-like character of correctional organizations and the punishment philosophy out of which they grew. But, paradoxically, there are many who feel that the reform ideology may only have reinforced, not weakened, traditional philosophies and practices. A careful review of the organizational character of *treatment-oriented* correctional programs reveals that they are often castelike in nature. Even though their announced objectives and some of their practices are different from traditional, custodial institutions, many of the same problems remain. On the other hand, there are theoretical arguments in favor of places of incarceration. In order to examine these conflicting, theoretical positions, let us move to the next section which is devoted to that issue.

Theoretical Adequacy of Theories of Incarceration

There are two general theories favoring the efficacy of incarceration.

The first has already been mentioned; namely the belief that punishment is an effective device for changing people and at the same time of utility in deterring others.

The second theory favoring incarceration, or at least removal from the community, is based upon more complex, theoretical foundations. In general, this theory suggests that the offender can benefit from a moratorium, from separation from the complex forces which have led to his delinquency in the first place. By providing in a single setting for all his needs, he can be helped to change, emotionally, educationally, and otherwise, in a protected and safe environment. His problems are of such a nature that correctional organizations must provide substitute resources for training and help in lieu of those which exist already in the community. More will be said upon this later.

The theoretical point of view which opposes incarceration generally emphasizes three major problems: problems arising from the caste-like character of places of incarceration; problems arising from the nature of role relationships, even in treatment-oriented centers; and, finally, the separation of the offender from the community. Consider these problems one at a time.

Contemporary, social-psychological theory emphasizes the idea that an individual's self-concept and behavior are not separable from the social relationships in which he lives. Consequently, the caste-like character of places of incarceration may only reinforce a negative self-image for the offender. The reason is that the most notable consequence of a caste system is to keep the two castes separate (Empey, 1968: 5). While both castes may have complementary relationships of some kind, there is no expectation that membership between the two will be common. *once an inmate, always an inmate, once an authority, always an authority.* Membership in a place of incarceration places the offender in a kind of no-man's land where he is accepted neither by staff members as one of them, nor by the public as one of them. Consequently, the only place he has to turn for a sense of identity and a definition of purpose is to his fellow inmates. Theoretically, at least, this is precisely what we do not want to happen. We want the reverse to happen; we would like the offender to identify with prosocial points of view and take on the conformist characteristics of the nondelinquent, authority caste.

The difficulties for the inmate in doing this illustrate the inherent contradictions of punishment versus reform goals. So long as the primary goal of any system is to punish the offender by maintaining exclusive, superordinate-subordinate relationships between authority and inmate castes, a caste arrangement makes sense. But if the goal of that system is to reduce social distance between the two groups so that they might ultimately share the same goals, aspirations and means, then a caste system does *not* make sense. Applied to corrections, this means that successful change among inmates will require organizational arrangements by which members of the inmate group can adopt new roles and take on the perspectives of a nondelinquent, noninmate person. Only in this way could it be expected that the offender could stop conceiving of himself as delinquent and be stimulated, instead, to conceive of himself as nondelinquent.

In commenting upon places of incarceration, many observers have been pessimistic regarding the effectiveness of such places unless radical changes occur (cf. Schrag, 1961: 329; Polsky, 1962). Conditions have been such as to make it a matter of honor among prisoners not to collaborate with their captors in the interest of change, just as society, in general, considered it a matter of honor for prisoners-of-war not to collaborate with their captors during the Korean conflict. Organizational traditions have made collaboration between staff and inmates, in the interest of reform, difficult.

Some of the same problems are inherent in treatment-oriented places of incarceration. The reason lies in the tendency for the treatment, like the punishment, philosophy to locate the primary source of difficulty within the offender. The problems of change have not really been considered in social-psychological and organizational terms. As a consequence, the treatment philosophy has never seriously challenged the social functions of punishment and indicated the extent to which caste-like, correctional organizations may seriously hamper efforts at rehabilitation.

The tendency for offenders to view whatever is done to them as punishment rather than treatment was alluded to earlier. Part of the reason for this perception lies in the fact that treatment personnel, even if highly trained (and they are in short supply in most juvenile training schools), have a symbiotic relationship with clients which is subtle and paradoxical (cf. Empey, 1967c: 237–328). The status of the professional, his *helping* role, his very place in the whole scheme of things depends heavily upon the client remaining in a subordinate relationship to him. The paradox is, therefore, that although the professional role ostensibly exists to help the client, it is in fact, one which relies upon a superordinate-subordinate relationship. As a result, it is difficult for the client to change unless his relationship to those above him changes also. Organizational arrangements are not available by which to encourage him to stop conceiving of himself as *delinquent, inmate,* or *patient,* and to conceive of himself, instead, as *non-delinquent, employee,* or *student.*

Efforts are beginning in some correctional institutions to move inmates step-by-step into new roles—roles which connote change in some desired direction, which carry with them new expectations and rewards, and which decrease the stigma associated with an offender or inmate status—but these efforts have been limited. There are few correctional organizations which provide means by which the offender can be anything other than inmate or patient. It is difficult, therefore, for him to conceive of himself in any other terms.

In commenting upon the responses of adults to these conditions, Irwin and Cressey (1964: 225–245) have noted three kinds of group adjustments. The first group they label as *thieves.* These are career or sophisticated offenders whose commitment is to criminal subcultures outside of the prison and for whom the prison experience is simply an occupational hazard. They attempt to do their time in the most comfortable way possible. Incarceration for this group may be the most feasible method of protecting society.

The second group they label *convicts.* Convicts are offenders who have long records of confinement in institutions which are likely to have begun at an early age. They have become so conditioned to institutions that it has become a way of life for them. They are uncomfortable in a free world. Paradoxically, therefore, the only way this group may be rehabilitated is to place them in a correctional program in which they have to struggle with the problems of freedom.

Finally, the third group is designated as *legitimate.* This group is made up of offenders who identify with legitimate points of view both outside and inside the prison. Consequently, they are isolated both from *convicts* and *thieves.* The major implication for this group is that they may not have needed prison in the first place. Other alternatives involving a minimum of surveillance, but also maximizing help with occupational, educational or personal problems, may have been far more constructive. One obvious point, therefore, is that research is badly needed by which to identify these three groups and to do a more effective job of providing meaningful alternatives for them.

Finally, perhaps the most devastating criticism of imprisonment in a theoretical and practical sense has to do with the removal of the offender from the community. The crux of any treatment program has ultimately to do with its ability to help the offender adjust to the community, not to a reformatory. Yet, the decisions which lead to success in *doing time* are not of the same type needed for successful community adjustment. Existing conditions of the kind just described may actually be more effective in cementing the offender's ties to a delinquent system than in destroying them. One cannot really talk about increasing an offender's community adjustment unless actual opportunities are made available for him, not just in an isolated correctional setting, but in the community at large. The problem of rehabilitation is a two-sided coin. On one hand, it is obvious that the delinquent, himself, must be motivated to change. He must discard delinquent beliefs and rationalizations and replace them with new beliefs and rationalizations. He must make the kinds of personal changes that will make a conventional community adjustment possible. On the other hand, he cannot accomplish the job by himself, nor can an isolated correctional unit accomplish it either. Not only must any program provide ways by which to motivate offenders to want to achieve in a conventional sense, but do a better job of providing legitimate alternatives as well. A major problem for any program, therefore, is in transferring the changes which might occur within that program to the other major area of a delinquent's life. It seems unlikely that the isolated, correctional institution can accomplish this by itself.

Evidence Regarding Effects of Incarceration

Despite all of the criticisms which have been levied against incarceration, there is little hard evidence to support the view that the sheer avoidance of institutionalization will result in more successful adjustment. It is a lamentable fact that national statistics on recidivism after incarceration are not available. Instead, Costner's review (1968: 14–15) of the subject reveals the following kinds of evidence.

A review of recidivism among juveniles in Federal institutions revealed that slightly over 40 percent were reimprisoned. This was the highest rate of reimprisonment among federal institutions. The rate of imprisonment for juveniles in nine institutions of the California Youth Authority ranged from 31 to 64 percent. However, as Costner (1968: 15) pointed out, "these violation rates were also found to be closely correlated (r=0.87) with violation rates expected on the basis of the *base expectancy* scores of inmates assigned there, i.e., expectations for parole success based on the background factors at the time of commitment (cf. Beverly, 1965). This suggests that if the various institutional programs had any effect at all on parole violation rates, all the varied programs had essentially the same effect.

Glaser (1964b: chap. II) is sharply critical of this kind of information. First of all, he points out that the only conclusive way to find out how many offenders eventually return to incarceration is to follow, for a number of years, all those released in a given period. Too much information is lost simply by observing parole revocation rates or counting the number of offenders who have been incarcerated at some prior time. What happens in the latter case is that two- and three-time losers tend to accumulate in a reformatory or prison because they get longer sentences and are much less readily paroled than first-timers. Consequently, when the focus is only upon those who are incarcerated, we get a biased sample, one which overestimates failures and underestimates success.

A second way which has long been used in science would be to make a direct test of the effects of incarceration by using a random assignment of comparable cases to institutional and noninstitutional programs. We might then be able to judge the effects of incarceration much more systematically. As will be seen later, some new programs are doing this.

In addition, Street (1965) has cautioned against overgeneralizing about the negative effects of incarceration. He found, for example, that inmates in juvenile institutions which have the traditional punitive orientation do exhibit the classic problems that were mentioned above. He also found that institutions that were characterized by a minimum of social distance between inmates and staff members exhibited no such patterns. One might infer, therefore, that the outcome rates of these various institutions might vary considerably. If staff and inmates are close and working together, it might be expected that they would do better upon release than those in which both groups were sharply divided by inmate and official castes. As a matter of fact, the evidence is not yet available to support such an inference.

As Costner (1968: 17) points out, several juvenile institutions in California have attempted to reduce social distance and increase rehabilitation rates by utilizing various forms of group discussion, group therapy and *therapeutic community* concepts. Yet, he says,

> of the three California studies evaluating this general type of program that have been undertaken, none has demonstrated more favorable parole outcomes for boys in these special programs than for boys in the conventional institutional programs. . . . No significant differences were found in parole performance between controls and those in the experimentally varied counseling programs. Thirty months after release, the proportion returned to custody, the proportion removed from parole by revocation or bad discharge, and the per cent of total possible months spent out of custody were very similar for the control and treatment groups at each institution (cf. Seckel, 1965).

In yet another California youth institution, one group of offenders were assigned randomly to a special program emphasizing group therapy, individual therapy, living-unit meetings and special academic and supervised work programs while another group was assigned to regular institutional programs. Yet, twelve months after release, the recidivism rates for these two groups were almost identical (cf. Costner, 1968; Fremont Project, 1965).

Such findings as these are as perplexing as they are distressing. They are analogous to other kinds of research in the behavioral sciences which indicate that under some circumstances, experimental groups may evidence a change in basic attitudes and satisfactions in their relationships with others, yet in terms of some hard criterion variables, they do not differ from control groups. Besides outcome measures of the type just discussed, therefore, we also need much more research on the processual and organizational character of correctional organizations themselves. We need to discover what goes on within programs as well as reviewing their ultimate effects. In the past, *process* research has been almost totally non-existent, even though its purpose would be that of examining the program stimuli that are supposed to produce whatever changes occur. Because of its absence, program operation has been like a mysterious black box, a black box whose internal machinery remains eternally a mystery. Rather than relating the black box to outcome, we have devoted most of our attention to explaining success or failure in terms of age, social class, personality or ethnic status of the offenders involved. This is amazing. It is analogous to trying to understand how steel is produced from several raw materials without knowing what goes into the manufacturing process. We simply do not know in any systematic way whether programs are operating consistent with theoretical design or not and consequently, we do now know where to turn to correct basic problems. If steel companies operated this way, they would still be producing the kinds of lead that corrections is producing.

It is admitted, however, that when one observes inconclusive findings like those just described, he is inclined to harbor the suspicion that no matter what goes on in total institutions, similar lamentable results may be observed. Even so, the inclination to suspicion must be resisted. A better alternative would be to turn to a policy which emphasizes comprehensive planning accompanied by systematic research and evaluation. The goal would be to develop a correctional system in which types of offenders were matched successfully with types of programs.

On one hand, society must be protected against the incorrigible offender. But, on the other, it should not make the problem worse by locking up those who would do better in the community. The need to isolate types of offenders works both ways. As well as identifying those who must be kept out of community programs, it is equally important to identify those who should be kept in them.

A coherent system of alternatives would range from nonsupervisory measures such as fines and the suspended sentence, through increasingly structured community programs, to total incarceration. Hopefully, such a system would result in a more effective and economically efficient allocation of correctional resources. It is possible that a heavier concentration of community alternatives might be run at no extra cost simply by reducing the number of people who are incarcerated.

Efforts to apply new techniques and to increase the number of community alternatives are now taking place. Let us move in our analysis, therefore, to the consideration of some of the innovations that are occurring, both in and out of institutions. They will help further to elicit what must be done if a coherent system of correctional alternatives is to be related to different types of offenders.

Differential Treatment

The suggestion is not new that efforts should be made to match types of offenders to types of programs. It expresses an ideal long-since derived from clinical medicine. As Warren (1967: 1) expresses it:

> One of the few agreed-upon *facts* in the field of corrections is that offenders are not all alike. That is, they differ from each other, not only in the form of their offense, but also in the reasons for and the meaning of their crime. . . .
>
> If one accepts the notion that offenders are different from each other in their reasons for their law violations, the implication follows that attempts to change the offender into a nonoffender will vary in ways which are relevant to the cause. Ideally, the goals of treatment will relate in some direct manner to the causes of delinquency, and the treatment methods will relate specifically to the goals for the various offender subgroups.

Before proceeding to an analysis of recent developments in differential treatment, a moment should be taken to consider the attention that has been paid to the relationship between personality and criminality in correctional theory. As was mentioned earlier, the reform revolution in corrections relied heavily upon the notion that delinquency is a psychological problem, largely independent of any given culture and in need of treatment directed primarily on an individual level (cf. Alt and Grossboard, 1949). The language of medicine crept into the lexicon of words used in thinking about correctional methods. Such terms as *diagnosis, pathology, symptom, prognosis, treatment,* and *cure* occurred in abundance in the literature having to do with delinquents (cf. Hakeem, 1958).

As was mentioned earlier, a number of criticisms have been made of this point of view because of its failure to account for the widespread character of delinquency, the influence of social and cultural factors on delinquency, the likelihood that it is not an attribute which one either has or does not have. But, in addition, an increasing body of evidence has documented the limitations of a strict personality frame of reference.

After examining 113 different research endeavors which attempted to differentiate offenders from non-offenders on the basis of personality traits, Schuessler and Cressey (1950) came to the conclusion that such differentiation could not be documented. Similarly, Hathaway, Monachesi and Young (1960) after many years of endeavoring to relate personality and criminality in some direct way, concluded that personality factors by themselves are relatively weak predictors of law-breaking behavior. These factors, they said, ". . . are much less powerful and apply to few cases among the total samples than would be expected if one reads the literature on the subject."

In their study of the relationship of personality factors to runaway behavior from juvenile institutions, Lubeck and Empey (1968) concluded that the problem may lie, not so much in the total lack of utility of personality measures, but in the static classifications which personality measures have supplied; that is, they have failed to account for the impact on personality of experience in different situational contexts. Their study indicated that personal response will not be unidimensional, but will vary as organizational structure varies. When dramatic shifts occur in the social situation in which individuals find themselves, the various measures of personality characteristics assume lesser or greater predictive power. They reflect the interaction between personal and social systems. It is an awareness of this fact that is represented in emerging correctional programs, especially in efforts to implement differential treatment.

*Current Differential Treatment**

The correctional approach based upon differential treatment which has probably drawn more attention in recent years than any other is the Community Treatment Program sponsored by the California Youth Authority and directed by Marguerite Q. Warren (cf. Warren, 1964; Community Treatment Project; Warren, 1968). This program began initially as an alternative to incarceration and has been followed since by several experiments within institutions as well. This approach is founded on a classic, clinical design prescribing specific types of treatment for specific types of offenders, but it departs from traditional personality classifications and defines offenders according to personal maturity levels.

The maturity typology includes nine subtypes of delinquents classi-

---

*The analysis in this section as well as in the following section on "Group-Oriented Programs" draws heavily on the following source: LaMar T. Empey, *Alternatives to Incarceration,* Washington, D.C. U.S. Government Printing Office, 1967, pp. 40–43.

fied according to the modes of behavior which typify their intersections with the world. The nine delinquent subtypes fall into three larger groupings, and to some extent the subtypes within it, calls for distinctly different approaches to treatment and control. Goals for treatment are individualized in terms of the maturity levels of the delinquent subjects. For example, the maturity classification system "focuses upon the ways in which the individual is able to see himself and the world, especially in terms of emotions and motivations; i.e., his ability to understand what is happening between himself and others as well as among others" (Warren, 1968). Presumably, therefore, if a delinquent were fixed at some low level of maturity, efforts would be made to increase his capacity to relate to others in an effective rather than a delinquent way.

Each experimental delinquent is diagnosed prior to admission to the project and, on the basis of the diagnosis, is assigned to a parole agent who is thought to be skilled in working with that type of delinquent. Thus, types of delinquents are matched with types of agents. Each agent carries an average caseload of eight to ten wards. His contacts with those wards may vary from two to five times weekly and may involve full-day as well as part-time combination—surveillance and firm discipline, individual counseling, psychotherapy, family group therapy, guided group interaction, occasional confinement, or foster home placement.

The effort to make treatment consistent with design has extended to the development of specially designed group homes for particular subtypes who need them. For the type of client who makes his way by manipulating others, a specific home has been set up and is run by a married couple who are trained to frustrate such behavior by exerting firm controls. For the delinquent who needs a considerable amount of assurance and freedom, placement would be in another home designed to operate warmly and permissively. Such homes will operate only for special cases, since most wards will probably continue to live at home.

The community differential treatment project has the advantage of working in the community rather than in an institution. The problems with which it works are those which any young person faces in his daily life rather than the more artificial ones of a total institution. In this way, therefore, this particular program must struggle with community as well as offender resistances to change. Its goals cannot be realized without interaction with the community.

In summary, the classification design of this program is extremely complex. It calls for the differential diagnosis of offenders into subtypes, the selection and training of agents to work with these subtypes, the definition of a treatment plan for each of the subtypes, the development of a host of program resources to be used singly or in combination for the different subtypes, and perhaps even the development of specialized homes in which certain wards would be housed.

The Community Treatment Project is utilizing experimental and control groups by which to compare outcome rates. All subjects come from a common pool of eligibles who have been assigned by the courts to the Youth Authority for what traditionally has been an institutional experience. However, the design permits the random assignment of experimental subjects directly back to the community, while only control subjects are assigned to an institution. Comparative effectiveness of the two programs is being assessed both by parole performance and by attitudinal and behavioral changes.

Differential Treatment Theory

Before proceeding to a review of research findings, a word should be said about the theory underlying the maturity level classification According to Warren's (1968: 10–11) description:

> Seven successive stages of interpersonal maturity characterize psychological development. They range from the least mature, which resemble the interpersonal reactions of a new born infant, to an ideal of social maturity which is seldom or never reached in our present culture. Each of the seven stages, or levels, is defined by a crucial interpersonal problem which must be solved before further progress toward maturity can occur. All persons do not necessarily work their way through each state, but may become fixed at a particular level. The range of maturity levels found in a delinquent population is from maturity level 2. . . to maturity level 5. It should be stressed that interpersonal development is viewed as a continuation. The successive steps or levels, which are described in the theory are seen as definable points along the continuum.

Of the many issues which can and will be discussed about this provocative and complex theory, two may be mentioned briefly here. The first has to do with the fact that *maturity* is often a difficult phenomenon to define. It is relative to time, place and culture. What may represent *maturity* to some, may not represent *maturity* to others. The problem becomes even more complex when one attempts to operationalize it for treatment or research purposes. The maturity classifications which are used in the differental treatment project are extremely complex and will have to be made the subject of considerable research and refinement before complete confidence can be placed in their capacity to distinguish among juveniles in terms of concrete and objective criteria.

Second, even though the maturity concept emphasizes the individual's interpersonal relations with others, it can suffer, if care is not taken, like the personality concept from too singular an emphasis upon the individual. The whole field of mental health, as well as corrections, has been confronted with the problem. Szasz (1956: 279), for example, has been sharply critical about the confusion of social, ethical, medical and legal concepts. He has accused the helping professions of adopting too narrow a view of reality and of assuming that some departure from that view by an offender constitutes a distortion of reality (or perhaps in this case, maturity). The offender's perspective, the lens through which he perceives the world, may be the product of his social and cultural position within that world. His tendency to order the same set of facts into different logical categories may be the product of his socialization in a particular environment, rather than immaturity, as measured by some universal scale. The practitioner must guard, therefore, against interpretations which fail to account for frames of reference which are different from his own. To be sure, successful readjustment on the part of the offender may require some change in maturity level, but it may also require a better awareness both of the unique perspectives which he brings to the correctional scene and of the ways that community institutions, themselves, require change if preventative or rehabilitative efforts are to succeed with him.

Reckless (1955) has also called attention to the fact that the race and social class membership of offenders are by their very nature categories to which people belong quite apart from whatever their maturity or personality levels may be. He calls these *categoric risks* because they reflect differential crime rates among different segments of the population and reveal to some degree the differential responses of officials to different classes of offenders. These categoric risks, by themselves, are predictive of success or failure, quite apart from the personal makeup of the individual, because they also determine how successful he will be in his relationships with others in a competitive achievement-oriented society. How all of these factors relate, then, to personal maturity levels requires further, theoretical explication.

Research Evidence Regarding Differential Treatment

Efforts to evaluate the effectiveness of the differential treatment program reveal many of the complex problems which are encountered in any correctional research. The latest reported figures show that only 28 percent of the experimentals as contrasted to 52 percent of the controls have been parole failures within fifteen months on parole (failures include all revocations of parole, recommitments from the courts and unfavorable discharges). The figures for twenty-four months of community exposure time on parole similarly favor the experimental group, 38 percent vs. 61 percent failure. This difference in favor of the community program is highly significant in statistical terms.

A basic problem with placing complete confidence in recidivism figures of this type lies in a complex number of subtle issues to which attention must be paid. First, these measurements of failure rates occurred while significant numbers of the experimentals and controls were still on parole. Definitive figures cannot be determined until parole has been completed. This is especially important for the experimental groups since parole supervision has been extended to cover a period of years in many cases and results in efforts at control which themselves strongly determine success and failure rates.

As progress reports have noted (Community Treatment Project After Five Years: 6), "part of the differences in failure rates can be explained by differences in decision making with regard to parole restoral following an offense." Several factors have entered into these differences (Palmer and Warren, 1967: Part I, 11–12):

> . . . experimentals have their parole suspended more frequently than do

> controls. Suspensions refer to temporary, rather than permanent, revocations of parole and usually result in a short period of detention.
>
> . . . Parole for experimental cases is rarely revoked on a permanent basis for minor offenses while the same is not true for control cases. Controls are revoked fairly often for such minor offenses as placement failure, poor home or school adjustment, truancy or runaway. An examination of the severity of offenses revealed further that "the controls had been revoked or unfavorably discharged in connection with offenses which had been of significantly *less serious nature* when compared with experimental offenses."
>
> . . . The followup also indicates that the average number of offenses which had taken place during parole was significantly greater for the experimental than for the control group.

The fact that control subjects have been revoked for lesser reasons than experimentals, and yet that the average number of listed offenses was greater for experimentals, while on parole, probably says more about the differential response of treatment personnel to delinquent behavior than about the behavior itself. For example, even though experimentals may have been more delinquent on occasion than controls, their lower revocation rate may be a function of the experimental program, itself. The caseload size and treatment planning is considerably different from regular parole. Experimental agents are able to increase contact and surveillance or to develop new treatment plans for the offender as the need arises, while the same may be less true for regular parole. Furthermore, the decision to suspend rather than revoke parole obviously seems to involve subjectivity on someone's part, and since it seems almost certain that intensive community programs will be used increasingly in the future, more attention will have to be paid both to the treatment and legal issues that are involved. It is not clear in this case, for example, whether experimentals were really any less delinquent than control groups while on parole. The difference in revocation rates may simply reveal differences in correctional approaches by experimental and control staff members. Whether or not one or the other approach is most effective will have to wait further data which provide information on all subjects after they have been released from parole.

Some of the problems just mentioned might be clarified if complete arrest statistics were available. It seems likely that the failure rates mentioned above are possibly clouded too much by parole agent decision making. Information on the frequency of arrests, and their severity, from all agencies of control, might help to clarify the picture.

Arrest data are closer to the point of offense and the frequency and severity of offenses which lead to those arrests are often cloaked in data on court hearings and revocation.

These problems also speak to the exhausting complexities of program evaluation under present conditions. In most cases, adequate funding and staffing resources are not great enough to make the necessary followups. Much of this could be solved if sound information systems were available.

On the other hand, what may turn out to be the most significant aspect of this differential treatment approach is some indication that the most dramatic differences in effect appear when the various delinquent subtypes are considered separately. Some subtypes seem to do better in an institution, while others do better in the community (cf. Warren, 1968). The further explication of these differences and what led to them could be of inestimable value to corrections.

The differential treatment concept, based upon maturity levels, has had tremendous impact in California and elsewhere. It has suggested the possibility of treating a large proportion of the delinquent population in the community in lieu of incarceration. It has led to an experiment in San Francisco in which the differential treatment model is being compared to a group-oriented model (of the type which will be mentioned below) and to traditional institutions. It has stimulated two projects within institutions which have been concerned with developing differential treatment environments more conducive to the needs of specific subgroups within the delinquent population. It has stimulated efforts to more effectively match types of clients with types of workers. Finally, it has made a valuable contribution to the emerging emphasis upon community experimentation and the need for reintegrating the offender more effectively into the community.

Group-Oriented Programs

Based upon a much different set of causation and correctional premises, group-oriented programs have become very common in corrections. The prototype for group-oriented, but small residential centers, is the Highfields Program which was begun in 1950 (cf. McCorkle, Elias and Bixby, 1958; Weeks, 1958). Highfields limits its population to twenty boys, ages sixteen and seventeen, who are assigned directly from the juvenile court. Boys live informally in an old home without usual institutional guards and detailed routine.

Highfields was established on the premise that with intensive group methods, known as *guided group interaction,* rehabilitation could be accomplished in three or four months. Programming is simple and designed to emphasize the problem solving, the decision-making, and the control effects of the group.

During the day, the boys work at a nearby mental hospital, in the evening, the total population is broken into two groups of ten, each of which then meets for a daily group meeting. Formal rules are few. Control, instead, is exercised informally through the development of a group culture which presumably decreases distance between staff and offenders an sponsors the offender in a more active, reformation role. Rather than just *receiving* treatment, he is expected to administer it, along with others, as well. The idea is that individuals are best helped who themselves become capable of helping others. These are the principles which underlie Alcoholics Anonymous and Synanon, the private center for drug addicts run by drug addicts (cf. Yablonsky, 1965).

The general Highfields model has been widely adopted by public correctional agencies in other places; in New Jersey, New York, and Kentucky. Perhaps the most significant variation on the basic theme has been its application in the community where boys who would otherwise be incarcerated continue to live at home rather than in an institution. Two of the earliest of such programs were the Provo Experiment (Empey and Rabow, 1961) and Essexfields (Elias and Pilnick, 1964). A third, The Silverlake Experiment (Empey, Lubeck and Newland, 1966), although residental in nature, kept boys in the community where they attended school, went home on weekends, and so on. All three programs were similar in the sense that they were built around group techniques, were used for older offenders, ages fifteen to eighteen years, and were used as community alternatives to incarceration.

Although there is some danger in treating the conceptual and organizational characteristics of these group programs as one, that will be done in the interest of time and space. Four general assumptions, as stated for the Provo and Silverlake Experiments, have tended to underlie these group programs: (1) that most older delinquents who are eventually processed through the courts are from lower income homes; (2) that the lives of these offenders have been characterized by failure in such conventional institutions as the school or world of work; (3) that this failure is productive of a high degree of strain for them; and (4) that membership in a delinquent group develops as an alternative means for acquiring many of the social, emotional and economic goals which are acquired by other young people through conventional means. The beliefs, rationalizations and points of view of the delinquent groups, it is hypothesized, become important determinants of juvenile, deviant behavior. Delinquency is best understood as a group phenomenon which is collective rather than private, peer supported rather than lonely.

In responding to these theoretical assumptions regarding causation, the following assumptions for intervention were adopted. A program should try: (1) to make the delinquent group the target of change—that is, attempt to change shared standards, points of view, rewards and punishments; (2) to give the delinquent group a stake in what happens to its members by permitting participation with staff in solving problems, exerting controls, and making basic decisions, and (3) to open up conventional opportunities to delinquents in the school, the world of work and other conventional institutions. Reformation on the part of offenders is seen as only one side of the rehabilitative coin. Certain aspects of the community will have to be changed if offenders are to be successfully reintegrated.

In implementing these assumptions, the Provo, Essexfields, and Silverlake Programs were generally the same. Program activities included gainful employment in the community, school, and daily group meetings built around the technique of guided group interaction. This technique as mentioned above varies considerably from traditional group psychotherapy in the sense that all group members, not just staff, are responsible for defining problems, dealing with difficult questions, and finding solutions. Considerable power is shared with offenders. An effort is made to provide means by which offenders can assume more responsibility for their lives and to reward them for help that they are able to give others. The offender is sponsored in an active, reformation role rather than in a passive one in which he is acted upon by others.

The fact that these programs were located in the community meant that the problems with which the groups were struggling were those that confront them in their daily lives: families, friends, school, work, leisure time. It was reasoned that this is one very important strength of a community over an institutional program. The artificiality of institutional life is avoided and concentration can be placed upon the problems of successful community reintegration rather than upon adjustment to institutional norms.

In terms of theoretical adequacy, this approach has not yet attempted to define types of offenders and to differentiate treatment based upon subtypes. Instead, the daily group discussion is used as a diagnostic device by which to identify the *behavioral* problems of offenders and to define new ways of behaving for them which will be less problematic. The main emphasis is upon the need for dynamic analysis based upon the assumption that individual characteristics will change from time to time, altering the kinds of behavioral responses that are needed. Furthermore, it is assumed that the problems to be addressed are less characteristic of personality than of the peer relationships, the attitudes and rationalizations which support a delinquent rather than a nondelinquent adjustment.

Even so, it remains a matter of evidence rather than a theory as to whether these assumptions are valid. It seems highly possible that the group approach is inappropriate for some offenders. Therefore, until efforts are made first, to identify and differentiate delinquent types, and, second, to determine whether program impact varies according to type, it will be difficult to assess the precise effectiveness of the group approach.

Research Evidence Regarding Group Programs

The outcome research on these group programs has been inconclusive. In order to test the effectiveness of the Highfields Program, its graduates were compared to a group of boys who had been committed to the New Jersey State Reformatory for males at Annandale. A lower percentage of Highfields than of Annandale boys recidivated (37 vs. 53 percent). However, the results of the comparison have been debated because both boys were not randonly selected under experimental conditions such as they were in the Community Treatment Program, the Provo and Silverlake Experiments (cf. Tappan, 1960: 502–505). Without such selection, there is some doubt as to whether the groups are comparable. For example, the Annandale boys tended to be a little older, perhaps more experienced in delinquency, and from poorer social backgrounds than the Highfields boys. As a consequence, the most appropriate conclusion is that Highfields has been proven neither less nor more successful than regular incarceration. What is significant, however, is that at least similar results were achieved at much less expense both in monetary terms as well as time saved in the lives of the delinquents. The stay at Highfields was only three to four months and many of the negative aspects of institutionalization were avoided.

An experimental design was used in the Provo Experiment. Boys who were assigned to the experimental program were compared to two control groups, one of which was left in the community on probation, and a second which was incarcerated in a training school. The initial design was such that all three groups could be drawn randomly from a common population of persistent offenders residing in the same county.

As a background for comparing the three groups, a study of court records was made prior to the introduction of the experiment. This study revealed that only about 50 percent of the kinds of persistent offenders who were assigned to the program were succeeding on probation. It will be recalled from the success and failure rates presented earlier for probation that this was a lower success rate than the case for probation in general. It explains why the more intensive experiment was started.

The experiment improved the success rate. Six months after release, only 37 percent of those who were initially assigned to the Provo Experiment, 16 percent of those who eventually completed the program had a record of arrest. Of those who had been arrested, none had been incarcerated. But these were probably not the most interesting findings.

During the same period, the failure rate for the control group under regular probation had gone down almost as precipitously. From its original failure rate of around 50 to 55 percent, the probation department had lowered this rate to almost the same figures as those for the experimental group: 27 percent for all those who were initially assigned to probation, and 23 percent for those who completed it.

Apparently the introduction of the experiment, and the research which accompanied it, had some influence on the operation of court and probation personnel. This reduction in the overall failure rate from 45 to 27 percent was significant. Apparently there was a halo effect, not uncommon in social experiments, which affected everyone concerned and not just the offenders who were subjected to the experimental stimulus. Such findings, of course, indicate the importance of conducting process research by which to identify the factors at work in such circumstances.

In striking contrast to the success for the community groups, the failure rate for those boys who were incarcerated was much higher.

Fifty-eight percent had been arrested after six months, as contrasted to 27 percent for the boys in the community. This finding, however, is subject to the same kinds of criticism as the Highfields and Annandale findings. The reason is that the experiment was never able to fill the control group that was to have been randomly selected and assigned to the training school. The reason is that the judge of the juvenile court was disinclined to commit even persistent offenders to the reformatory. It seems likely that this inclination was affected by the presence of the experiment and resulted in his use of community alternatives in lieu of incarceration. As a consequence, a sample of boys from the training school, who were similar on twenty characteristics to those in the community, were selected as the training school control group. Although when compared on these twenty characteristics, the three groups did not differ considerably, it is still difficult to say whether the two groups were totally comparable. The vast differences in failure rate may have been decreased had they been more comparable.

Other things about this experiment are significant. First, a 4-year followup on all experimental and control groups is almost completed and results will be made available. Second, the costs for community treatment are strikingly lower than the costs of incarceration. At the time of the experiment, the annual cost at the training school was approximately $2,595 per year per boy. The corresponding cost for the experimental group was $1,108. Since the average length of stay at the training school was 9½ months, as compared to only 7 months for the experiment, the actual cost per boy was $2,015 as compared to $609.

The estimated cost for supervising persistent offenders on probation was somewhere around $200 per boy. These differences highlight one real possibility for financing innovation. By removing more offenders from incarceration, and the excessive cost incurred thereby, it might be possible to staff and finance more community experiments at no added cost. The objective would be to develop community vs. institutional controls (Empey, 1966).

The Essexfields Experiment did not benefit from randomly selected experimental and control groups. Instead, it made a comparison of 1,210 youths who were assigned by the Essex County Juvenile Court to one or another of four different treatment programs: probation, group centers (three residental, short term, group therapy institutions), Essexfields, and Annandale, the State Reformatory. Selection for comparison was based upon the following subject criteria: male, 16-17 years of age, no psychosis, severe neurosis, or serious mental retardation, and no prior commitment to a correctional institution. Overall recidivism rates were as follows: 32 percent for probation, 45 percent for group centers, 48 percent for Essexfields, and 35 percent for Annandale, the State Reformatory (Stephenson and Scarpitti, 1967: 94–95). Since assignment to these programs was not random, it is possible only to conjecture about these findings. Two possibilities are suggested: (1) they may reflect the fact that more serious offenders were assigned to Annandale, Essexfields and the group center than to probation; or (2) they may reflect some deleterious effects from institutional supervision, even if in the community.

The Essexfields research made a valuable contribution by noting the number of offenders who failed in each program and who were referred back to court: probation, 28 percent; Essexfields, 23 percent; group centers, 27 percent; Annandale, 2 percent (Stephenson and Scarpitti, 1967: 48). In-program failures refer to those offenders who return to court as unsuitable for their various placements, or because they have gotten into additional trouble. Obviously, Annandale, the Reformatory, unlike community programs, did not have the option so common to community programs, of removing those who are not succeeding. Interestingly enough, the eventual recidivism rates for those who did not complete probation (76 percent) were the highest for three community programs. The next highest was for the group centers (55 percent) and least for Essexfields (48 percent). These figures suggest, of course, that probation was successful in riding itself of high recidivism risks by returning high risk boys to the court for further disposition. The group centers and Essexfields seemed somewhat less inclined to do this (Stephenson and Scarpitti, 1967: 94–95).

Finally, the findings for the Silverlake Experiment are somewhat inconclusive leaving as many unanswered questions as answered ones. In this case, however, experimental and control groups were randomly selected. The experimental group, it will be recalled, was assigned to live-in residence in Los Angeles, while the control group was assigned to a private, open, but total institution in the country. In terms of overall success and failure rates, boys who completed both programs did relatively well. After a 15-month followup, approximately three-fourths of both groups are succeeding. The program is, however, that only about one-half of each group completed their respective programs. The remainder were either defined as in-program failures or run away. This means, therefore, that both programs could be said to be discarding their most difficult cases, or that the most delinquent boys were running away of their own accord. Actually, process research indicates that this may not be the case. In a study of critical incidents in the experimental residence, Empey and Newland (1968) found that there was a considerable sharing of information regarding sensitive and difficult critical incidents, that the majority of these critical incidents were precipitated by a minority of the population, and that their number had declined over time. A program culture seemed to develop which was increasingly efficient as a mechanism for social control. Yet, there was some indication that, because of complex pressures, the approach to critical incidents both by staff and delinquents may have been overly formal, overly punitive. The data suggested that some boys may have been defined as failures by staff and peers or were driven out of the program for reasons other than serious delinquency.

Similarly, a study of runaways by Lubeck and Empey (1968) revealed that structural changes within both experimental and control settings often produced personal strain among offenders. In the experimental residence, personal strain seemed to be the product of an increasingly cohesive system which may have been overly rejecting of the marginal delinquent, while in the total institution, it was disorganization due to a change in treatment philosophy. They concluded, therefore, that the basic issue "may not be that of change vs. no change, or strain vs. no strain, but that of developing a better fund of knowledge by which to construct correctional strategies which can better anticipate and deal with strain."

Finally, although a complete analysis of recidivism data has not been completed as Silverlake, some striking findings have been discovered regarding the ability of experimental and control programs to reduce delinquency. In their preoccupation with whether or not individuals recidivate, correctional and research people have often overlooked the possibility that, even though significant proportions of the offender population may once again get into trouble, their overall involvement in delinquency may have reduced significantly. That is exactly what unpublished data from the Silverlake study indicate. After comparing the *total number of offenses* committed both by experimental and control groups fifteen months prior to their assignment to either program, with the total volume of offenses they committed in the fifteen months after release, the following reduction in offenses was found: for experimentals, a reduction of 76 percent; for controls, a reduction of 72 percent. Similarly, in the fifteen months prior to commitment, the mean number of official offenses per boy for the experimentals was 2.89, and for the controls, 2.83. Yet, in the fifteen months following release, these figures declined to 0.70 for experimentals, and 0.79 for controls. In other words there was a net change of –2.19 offenses per boy in the experimental group, and –2.0 offenses for controls. These are striking findings, indicating that these two programs may have had highly significant results in reducing delinquency, even though traditional measures did not indicate this. Such information suggests that we may only be beginning the task of finding sound measures by which to assess the effectiveness of correctional programs. Such figures as these would provide grounds for optimism rather than pessimism. They seem to indicate the need to avoid treating recidivism as an either-or thing and to determine, instead, the degree of progress offenders make away from delinquency and toward conformity.

Learning Theory and Education Therapy

A recent development has emphasized the idea of administering correctional programs based upon educational, rather than medical models. Learning theory and the application of recent innovations in education have been applied to work with juveniles in two recent pilot programs (Cohen, 1968).

The educational model provides an interesting contrast to the older medical model. Whereas the medical model emphasized pathology and the need to help the offender return to a previous state of health, the educational model emphasizes learning deficiencies, both intellectual and interpersonal. While the medical model was concerned with treating the patient as if he were sick or disabled, the educational model attempts to remedy learning deficiencies.

According to Cohen et al. (1968), delinquents have two basic problems: (1) they are deficient in basic skills and behaviors necessary to be successful academically and vocationally and (2) they lack the kinds of acquisitional and attitudinal patterns by which the needed skills can be acquired. Traditional, educational procedures, both in the community and in correctional institutions have not been adequate as a means of helping offenders to remedy these deficiencies. Yearly promotions, classroom grading, and diplomas are not appropriate goals for learning problems of this type. What must be done, instead, is to *reinforce* the desired behavior by more immediate and meaningful rewards: social recognition, peer approval, money, and creature comforts which money will buy, and which all people seek.

In translating these assumptions into practice at the National Training School for Boys in Washington, several steps were involved. First, each offender's program was based upon the results of a large series of tests given not only upon his arrival, but throughout his stay in the program. It was his major performance, orally and academically, which determined the program he would receive. Second, he was given a set of programmed instructional material based on his present repertoire and its deficiencies. He worked on his own level and progressed at his own speed. Third, learning was elaborately reinforced. One method was a system of points—each point being worth one cent—by which the individual was rewarded for the completion of academic subjects and the passing of examinations. These points could be translated into money by which students could gain immediate gratifications, cokes, snacks, or cigarettes, intermediate goals such as buying their own meals rather than institutional fare and recreational privileges, or long-range objectives in which they could buy such things as their own clothing. By working hard in the program, a student proceeding at his own pace could greatly enhance his standard of living. He could wear civilian clothing, eat non-institutional fare, enjoy the privacy of his own room, and do other things of this type. If he did not wish to work he was put on *dole.* He had to live on institutional fare, wear institutional clothing, suffer the other indignities and deprivations of institutional life. The student was paid off not only in material things, but with recognition as well. Staff and others worked hard to bring any accomplishment to the attention of everyone.

It is quite apparent that this approach is ideologically polar to punishment. While punishment stresses the administration of discomfort for those who do wrong, learning theory emphasizes the importance of reward for those who do right. By reinforcing acceptable behavior, this approach hopes to demonstrate to the offender that a strong investment of effort on his part can be immediately and directly rewarded. New skills and more successful relationships with people will ensue.

In evaluating any program of this type, three questions must be asked: How workable is it by others? Did it achieve its primary goals of increasing educational and social skills? Was it successful in preventing recidivism after release? According to Cohen (1968: 38–41), the answer to the first two questions is affirmative. The technology that was used in the National Training School could be learned and used by others. It is something which other correctional organizations could use. Whether or not this is true, and is monetarily feasible remains to be seen. Second; academic, social, and attitudinal behaviors among the youths in the study were markedly improved. Those who had been past failures, who had been difficult or impossible to teach, had in fact learned a great deal. Third; no post-release data were provided. The eventual impact of the program upon recidivism was not assessed.

Despite the demonstrated achievement of subjects in learning and social skills, the real test of any program such as this must inevitably occur in the community. Its effectiveness will be determined by the degree to which it prepares the subjects to function outside of a special learning environment and in a competitive setting where rewards are less apparent and in which it is necessary to defer gratifications, often for a considerable period of time. What is needed, therefore, is not only a followup study concerned with the recidivism rates of subjects in such an experiment, but the possibility of introducing such techniques for offenders into the community. The idea of redesigning teaching techniques and reward systems so as to encourage acceptable behavior should not be limited to correctional schools, nor should it be limited solely to academic pursuits in the public schools. The two must be joined in some way. More careful designs reinforcing achievement and learning, especially for students who perform poorly under present conditions, should become a part of public school strategies. Such efforts could then be used not only for the purposes of preventing juvenile deviance, but of helping those who are already in trouble.

Part III: Summary and Implications

In the general review of juvenile corrections, four basic questions were examined:

1. Who Is the Juvenile Delinquent?

Definitive answer cannot be given to this question. There is no precise, national information system on delinquency; there is a lack of research evidence on the actual operation of the juvenile justice system; the statutes which define delinquent behavior are ambiguous and imprecise; and juvenile lawbreaking, itself, is widespread, internationally as well as nationally.

Such findings seriously question the adequacy of the approaches that have been used traditionally to control delinquency. Since lawbreaking behavior is widespread, this means that delinquency is not an all-or-none thing, an attribute which juveniles either have or do not have, it is a more-or-less thing in which most adolescents participate. The implications are that, even if all efforts which are now directed to rehabilitating convicted offenders were successful, adolescent lawbreaking would not be controlled. This fact clearly indicates the limitations of taking a strictly legal approach. If delinquency is to be controlled, significant changes will have to be made in many other societal institutions as well.

2. What Are the Goals of Juvenile Corrections?

Correctional workers are asked to play a game they cannot win? Correctional goals are so disorganized, reflecting society's vestigial concern both with revenge and reform, that efforts to be successful are seriously hampered. Coupled with the likelihood that only a minority of adolescent lawbreakers even enter the legal net, this means that two things should probably be done. Greater attention should be paid to preventive and rehabilitative efforts by community institutions and to means by which a more comprehensive and rational approach can be made. "Delinquency," as Wheeler and Cottrell (1966) indicate, "is too serious a problem to be lodged in a labyrinth of bureaucratic settings with little in the name of logic, program, or coordinating mechanism to tie them all together."

3. How Relevant Are Contemporary, Correctional Theories?

Contemporary theories designed to guide efforts at intervention are primitive by any standard of scientific adequacy. They lack the precise rules of grammar, the abstract and powerful vocabularies, the systematic logic of sound theory. They have been directed primarily to the understanding of why a particular individual becomes delinquent, tending to ignore the widespread character of delinquency or the societal and cultural matrices out of which they grow. They do not even take into account the role of the official agencies—the police, courts, and correctional organizations—which respond to delinquency, thus failing to explain the total system of which delinquent behavior, per se, is only a part.

4. What Is the Evidence Relative to the Success of Existing Correctional Programs?

We have failed to approach correctional problems in any way resembling a scientific approach. The lack of investment in correctional research and experimentation, indeed research on social problems in general, probably stems from a value stance which views such research from a different perspective than that from which research in the biological and technological realms is viewed. While society has been willing to expend untold sums on the study of military problems, space exploration, physcial disease and automobile designs, it has expended only a pittance on correctional problems.

Part II of the analysis was concerned with major approaches, old and new, which have been used in corrections.

The historical trend has been away from imprisonment to community alternatives. Probation has been the most common community alternative. Despite undeniable evidence that the supervisory and helpful services provided by probation are severely limited, because of excessive caseloads and bureaucratic responsibilities, it seems to work for the majority of offenders. This finding raises important research questions: (1) What proportion of the offender population needs no supervision? (2) How can those offenders who do need supervision be distinguished from those who do not so that services can be made more efficient? (3) How many offenders now committed to institutions might be safely and effectively dealt with in the community?

Incarceration as a correctional device was evaluated next. Despite the protection which incarceration seems to provide for society, it was pointed out that because of the liabilities imposed by caste-like places of incarceration, because of the conflicting objectives they are expected to realize, and, because of their isolation from the free community, serious questions can be raised about their long-range utility either as protective or correctional devices. Many argue that attempts to rehabilitate in a total institution are futile. Yet, despite these criticisms, the kinds of precise information needed to pinpoint institutional deficiencies, or to indicate when and for whom incarceration may be desirable, are lacking.

Several recent experimental alternatives to incarceration were considered next: differential treatment, group oriented programs, or learning theory approaches. These latter experiments provide the major share of empirical data available on correctional effectiveness. A conservative estimate would be that these studies show that community alternatives are no better nor no worse than incarceration. However, their results are probably achieved at much less expense to society and at far less pain to the offender than incarceration. On the other hand, liberal interpretation would be that not only are community alternatives less expensive, they are more effective.

It is obvious that before this distressing and perplexing set of findings can be replaced with some kind of order, three things will have to be done:

First, society will have to commit the necessary resources to build an adequate knowledge base by which more effective solutions can be suggested. A search, possibly no less expensive and no less time-consuming than that involved in current space exploration or the search for solutions to cancer, will be required. An adequate effort would involve the acquisition of the following kinds of knowledge:

(1) Statistical knowledge on delinquency trends and the effectiveness of overall correctional efforts—an adequate information system is needed;
(2) Knowledge about the nature and operation of legal and correctional systems themselves, on their structures, policy and decisionmaking procedures, their impact on offenders and public alike;
(3) Knowledge derived from basic research concerned with delinquency causation and youth behavior in general; and
(4) Knowledge derived from experimental research devoted to trying new techniques and assessing their impact.

Second, some effort must be made to lodge Federal responsibility for leadership in this knowledge-building task in a single unit. A mechanism must be found for guiding research and program development in an orderly and rational way.

Finally, the social-engineering task of implementing new approaches to youth deviance can proceed simultaneously with, and in fact be a part of, the knowledge-building task. Just as there is a reciprocal benefit gained from the interdependence of theorists, scientists and engineers in space exploration so there can be reciprocal benefit gained from a similar arrangement in this area. Youth deviance and rebellion is not simply a problem of social control to be solved by police or court action, but must involve a wide range of social scientists and practitioners from a variety of fields.

REFERENCES

Alt, Herschel, and Hyman Grossbard

1949. "Professional Issues in the Institutional Treatment of Delinquent Children." American Journal of Orthopsychiatry, XIX (April): 279–280.

Baum, Martha, and Stanton Wheeler

1968. "Becoming an Inmate," p. 166 in Stanton Wheeler (ed.), Controlling Delinquents. New York: Wiley.

Berelman, William C. and Thomas W. Steinburn

1967. "Execution and Evaluation of a Delinquency Prevention Program." Social Problems 14 (Spring): 413–423.

Berelman, William C., and Thomas W. Steinburn

1967. "Execution and Evaluation of a Delinquency Prevention Program." Social Problems 14 (Spring): 413–423.

1968. Delinquency Prevention Experiments: A reappraisal. Seattle: Seattle Atlantic Street Center.

Beverly, Robert F.

1965. "An Analysis of Parole Performance by Institution of Release." Sacramento: Youth and Adult Corrections: Research Report 40.

Burgess, Ernest W.

1952. "The Economic Factor in Juvenile Delinquency." Journal of Criminal Law, Criminology and Police Science, 43 (May-June): 29–42.

Children's Bureau

1965. Children's Bureau Statistical Series, 85. Juvenile Court Statistics—1965. Washington, D.C.: U.S. Department of Health, Education, and Welfare.

Cicourel, Aaron V.

1968. The Social Organization of Juvenile Justice. New York: Wiley.

Cloward, Richard A., et al.

1960. Theoretical Studies in the Analysis in the Organization of the Prison. New York: Social Science Research Council Bulletin.

Cloward, Richard A., and Lloyd E. Ohlin

1963. Delinquency and Opportunity. A Theory of Delinquent Gangs. Glencoe: Free Press.

Cohen, Albert K.

1955. Delinquent Boys: The Culture of the Gang. Glencoe: The Free Press.

Cohen, Harold L.

1968. "Educational Therapy: The Design of Learning Environments." Research in Psychotherapy, 3: 21–53.

Cohen, Harold L., James A. Filipczak, John S. Bis, and Joan E. Cohen
1968. "Case II: Model Project." Research in Psychotherapy, 3: 42–53.

Community Treatment Project
1961-67. Community Treatment Project Reports Nos. 1–8. Sacramento: California Youth Authority.

Costner, Herbert L.
1968. "New Approaches to the Control of Juvenile Delinquency." Paper submitted to the National Commission on the Causes and Prevention of Violence.

Craig, Maude M., and Phillip W. Furst
1965. "What Happens After Treatment? A Study of Potentially Delinquent Boys." Social Service Review, XXXIX (June): 165–171.

Cressey, Donald R.
1961. The Prison: Studies in Institutional Organization and Change. New York: Holt, Rinehart & Winston, Inc.
1968. "Administrative Policy, Staff and Client Opinions Pertaining to the Offender as a Manpower Resource in the Administration of Justice." Washington, D. C.: Joint Commission on Correctional Manpower and Training: 31–49.

Diana, Lewis
1960. "What is Probation?" Journal of Criminal Law, Criminology, and Police Science, 51 (July-August) 189–204.

Dirksen, Cletus
1948. Economic Factors in Delinquency. Milwaukee: Bruce Publishing Co.

Dunham, H. Warren
1964. "The Juvenile Court: Contradictory Orientations in Processing Offenders." In Ruth Cavan (ed.), "Readings in Juvenile Delinquency." New York: Lippincott.

Eaton, Joseph W., and Kenneth Polk
1961. Measuring Delinquency: A Study of Probation Department Referrals. Pittsburgh: University of Pittsburgh Press.

Elias, Albert, and Saul Pilnick
1964. "The Essexfield Group Rehabilitation Project for Youthful Offenders." Correction in the Community. California Board of Corrections. Monograph No. 4(June): 51–57.

Empey, LaMar T.
1964. "The Application of Sociological Theory to Social Action." Social Problems 12(Summer).
1966. The Provo Experiment: A Brief Review. University of Southern California, Youth Studies Center.
1967a. Alternatives to Incarceration. Washington, D.C.: U.S. Government Printing Office.
1967b. "Delinquency Theory and Recent Research." Journal of Research in Crime and Delinquency, 4(January): 28–42.

1967c. "Social Reconstruction in the Reintegration of the Offender." Pp. 235–244 in S. A. Yefsky (ed.), "Law Enforcement: Science and Technology." Thompson Book Co.

1968. "Offender Participation in the Correctional Process: General Theoretical Issues." Joint Commission on Correctional Manpower and Training: 5–21.

Empey, LaMar T., and George E. Newland

1968. "Staff-Inmate Collaboration: Crisis and Consequence." Journal of Research in Crime and Delinquency, 5 (January): 1–17.

Empey, LaMar T., George E. Newland, Steven G. Lubeck, and Anthony J. Manocchio

1966. The Silverlake Experiment, Progress Report No. 3, University of Southern California Youth Studies Center. A final report on the experiment is nearing completion.

Empey, LaMar T., and Jerome Rabow

1961. "The Provo Experiment in Delinquency Rehabilitation." American Sociological Review, 26 (October): 679–696.

England, Ralph

1957. "What is Responsible for Satisfactory Probation and Post-Probation Outcome?" Journal of Criminal Law, Criminology, and Police Science, 47 (March-April): 667–677.

Even, William M.

1965. "Law as an Instrument of Social Change." In W. Gouldner and S. M. Miller (eds.), "Applied Sociology: Opportunities and Problems." New York: Free Press.

Eysenck, Hans J.

1966. The Effects of Psychotherapy. New York: International Science Press.

The Fremont Project

1965. "The Fremont Project: Assessment of a Therapeutic Living Unit." The Status of Current Research in the California Youth Authority. Sacramento: 5. George B. James

1968. Gault and the Juvenile Court Revolution. Ann Arbor: Institute of Continuing Legal Education.

Gibbons, Don C.

1965. Changing the Lawbreaker. Englewood Cliffs: Prentice-Hall, Inc.

Glaser, Daniel

1956. "Criminality Theories and Behavioral Images." American Journal of Sociology, LXV (March).

1964a. "The Prospect for Corrections." Paper prepared for the Arden House Conference on Manpower Needs in Corrections. Mimeographed.

1946b. The effectiveness of a Prison and Parole System. Indianapolis: Bobbs-Merrill, Inc.

Glueck, Sheldon

1933. Probation and Criminal Justice.

Goffman, Erving

1961. Asylums. New York: Doubleday.
Grunhut, Max
1948. Penal Reform. New York: The Clarendon Press.
Hakeem, Michael
1958. "A Critique of the Psychiatric Approach to Juvenile Delinquency." In Joseph S. Roucek (ed.), "Juvenile Delinquency." New York: Philosophical Library, ch. IV.
Hathaway, Starke R., Elio D. Monachesi, and Laurence A. Young
1960. "Delinquency Rates and Personality." Journal of Criminal Law, Criminology, and Police Science, L (February): 439.
Irwin, John, and Donald R. Cressey
1964. "Thieves, Convicts and the Inmate Culture." P. 225 in Howard S. Becker (ed.), "The Other Side." New York: Free Press of Glencoe.
Joint Commission on Correctional Manpower and Training
1968. The Public Looks at Crime and Corrections. Washington, D. C.
Kinch, John W.
1962. "Continuities in the Study of Delinquency Types." Journal of Criminal Law, Criminology, and Police Science, 53(September): 323–328.
Kvaraceus, William C.
1964. "World Wide Story." The Unesco Courier (May).
Lemert, Edwin M.
1951. Social Psychology. New York: McGraw-Hill.
1967. "'Juvenile Justice-Quest and Reality." Trans-Action, 4(July-August): 31.
Lubeck, Steven G., and LaMar T. Empey
1968. "Mediatory vs. Total Institution: The Case of the Runaway." Social Problems Forthcoming.
McCorkle, Lloyd W., Albert Elias and F. Lovel Bixby
1958. The Highfields Story. New York: Henry Holt.
McEachern, Alexander W., and Edward M. Taylor
1967. The Effects of Probation. University of Southern California Youth Studies Center.
Merton, Robert K.
1957. Social Theory and Social Structure. New York: Free Press of Glencoe.
Meyer, Henry J., Edgar S. Borgatta, and Wyatt C. Jones
1957. Girls at Vocational High: An Experiment in Social Work Intervention. New York: Russell Sage Foundation.
Miller, Walter B.
1962. "The Impact of 'Total Community' Delinqunency Control Project." Social Problems, 10 (Fall): 168–191.
1965. "Violent Crimes in City Gangs." Annals of the American Academy of Political and Social Science (March).
Morris, Norval
1966. "Impediments to Penal Reform." The University of Chicago Law Review, 33(Summer): 628.

Murphy, Fred J., M. Shirley, and Helen L. Witmer

1946. "The Incidence of Hidden Delinquency." American Journal of Orthopsychiatry, 16(October): 686–696.

O'Keefe, Daniel

1948. "Mental Hygiene Facilities for the Juvenile Delinquent." Federal Probation, 12(June): 31–35.

Palmer, Theodore B., and Marguerite Q. Warren

1967. Community Treatment Project, CTP Research Report No. 8, Part I. Sacramento: California Youth Authority.

Piliavin, Irving, and Scott Briar

1964. "Police Encounters with Juveniles." American Journal of Sociology (September): 206–215.

Polk, Kenneth

1968. "International Perspectives on Crime and Delinquency, or Nothing Succeeds Like Failure." Salem: Paper presented at the 1968 Annual Conference, Oregon Corrections Association.

Polsky, Howard W.

1962. Cottage Six: The Social System of Delinquent Boys in Residential Treatment, New York: Wiley.

Powers, Edwin, and Helen Witmer

1951. An Experiment in the Prevention of Delinquency: The Cambridge-Somerville Youth Study. New York: Columbia University Press.

President's Commission on Law Enforcement and Administration of Justice

1967a. Task Force Report: Science and Technology. Washington, D.C.: U.S. Government Printing Office.

1967b. The Challenge of Crime in a Free Society. Washington, D.C.: U.S. Government Printing Office.

1967c. Task Force Report: Corrections. Washington, D.C.: U.S. Government Printing Office.

Reckless, Walter C.

1955. The Crime Problems, 2d ed. New York: Appleton-Century-Crofts, Ch. III.

Schrag, Clarence

1961. "Some Foundations for a Theory of Corrections." P. 329 in Donald R. Cressey (ed.), "The Prison: Studies in Institutional Organization and Change." New York: Holt, Rinehart & Winston, Inc.

1967. "Elements of Theoretical Analysis in Sociology." In Llewellyn Gross (ed.), "Sociological Theory! Inquiries and Paradigms." New York: Harper & Row.

Schuessler, Karl F., and Donald R. Cressey

1950. "Personality and Characteristics of Criminals." American Journal of Sociology, LV (March): 476–484.

Seckel, Joachim P.

1965. "Experiments in Group Counseling at Two Youth Authority Institutions." Sacramento: California Youth Authority, Research Report 46.

Sellin, Thorsten, and Marvin E. Wolfgang
1964. The Measurement of Delinquency. New York: Wiley.

Shaw, Clifford R., anr Henry D. McKay
1942. Juvenile Delinquency in Urban Areas Chicago: University of Chicago Press.

Short, James F., Jr.
1960. "The Socio-Cultural Context of Delinquency." Crime and Delinquency (October): 366.

Stephenson, Richard M., and Frank Scarpitti
1967. The Rehabilitation of Delinquent Boys. Final Progress Report. New Jersey: Rutgers University.

Street, David
1965. "The Inmate Group in Custodial and Treatment Settings." American Sociological Review, 30(February): 40–55.

Street, David, Robert D. Vinter and Charles Perrow
1966. Organization for Treatment. New York: Free Press.

Szasz, Thomas S.
1956. "Some Observations on the Relationship Between Psychiatry and Law." American Medical Association Archives of Neurology Psychiatry: 75.

Tait, C. Downing, Jr., anl Emory F. Hodges, Jr.
1962. Delinquents, Their Families and the Community, Springfield: Thomas.

Tannenbaum, Frank
1938. Crime in the Community, Boston: Ginn & Co.

Tappan, Paul W.
1960. Crime, Justice and Correction. New York: McGraw-Hill, Inc.

Warren, Marguerite Q.
1964. "An Experiment in Alternatives to Incarceration for Delinquent Youth: Recent Findings in the Community Treatment Project." Correction in the Community: Alternatives to Incarceration, Sacramento: Board of Corrections Monograph No. 4(June): 39-50.
1968. "The Case for Differential Treatment of Delinquents." Sacramento: Center for Training in Differential Treatment.

Wattenburg, William, and J. J. Balistrieri
1950. "Gang Membership and Juvenile Delinquency." American Sociological Review, 15 (December): 744–752.

Weeks, H. Ashley
1958. Youthful Offenders at Highfields. Ann Arbor: University of Michigan Press.

Wheeler, Stanton, and Leonard S. Cottrell, Jr.
1966. Juvenile Delinquency: Its Prevention and Control. New York: Russell Sage Foundation.

Yablonsky, Lewis
1965. The Tunnel Back: Synanon, New York: Macmillan.

CHAPTER 21

INNOVATIVE CORRECTIONAL PROGRAMS FOR JUVENILE OFFENDERS

JACK COCKS

IN PRESENTING THIS review of current and innovative methods of dealing with juvenile offenders, the tendency is to provide descriptive analyses of action programs in such a way that the reader can assume that many problems have been solved, the answers are available, and the need is only for them to be disseminated. Such, of course, is not the case.

The evolution of corrections programs is not a reflection of a careful and systematic approach, and more often than not the particular program model has been adopted as an empirical or experimental attempt, with little attention given to the development of theory, creation of assumptions, and scientific testing of methods. So, too, is there an unfortunate lack so many times in the examination and evaluation of results—not so much to justify the project or its extension, but to indicate major gaps in existing knowledge and suggest directions for the future.

This report must therefore deal with intuitive and pragmatic explanations of how to meet many of the needs of juvenile offenders rather than scientific or theoretical approaches, although elements of the results of experimental applications are to be found in every action program which contains an evaluative component.

This review will be organized into six parts, utilizing an arbitrary categorization based in part on the frequency with which the respective topics appeared in correspondence or in print in recent months. Part one is a selection of intensive caseload techniques representative, perhaps, of the characteristics taken on by *special supervision programs* as supported by the California probation subsidy program. Part two is oriented around the present deep concern about dealing with those involved with narcotics and drugs. In part three, under the general heading of family education, will be found some of the newer concepts of crisis intervention, conjoint therapy, and behavioral modification.

The subject of part four is related to a new structure for delinquency prevention and avoidance of the juvenile court system as found in Youth Service Bureaus. Parts five and six review some of the newer approaches to use of volunteers and the *new careers* programs which may include the ex-offender or indigenous worker as a relatively new laborer in the vineyard of the juvenile justice system.

The reader is cautioned that these programs are drawn exclusively from those in operation in California, and even here, at the County level almost exclusively. There are two reasons for this; the availability of the material and the assumption that the joint impetus of the Omnibus Crime Bill funds and California probation subsidy funds have achieved as progressive and innovative a set of programs as may be found anywhere else.

The subsidy to counties for improving the supervision of persons placed on probation resulted from legislation enacted in 1965. In essence, the subsidy plan provides that the state encourages counties to keep offenders at home on probation under improved supervision, the costs of which come from the state as a share of savings on institutional expenses. Payment by the state is sufficient to permit the supervision of five times the number of probationers who would be committed to state institutions.

The following terms and definitions are provided to facilitate understanding of several innovative programs.

I Level—Interpersonal maturity classification of psycho-social development.

Transactional Analysis—A system for review of the elements of give and take in human relationships in an effort to identify values.
Operant Conditioning—A term devised by B. F. Skinner to describe a system of rewarding behavior seen as positive, while ignoring that which is seen as negative.
Conjoint Family Therapy—A system of therapy in which problems of family relationships are dealt with by the family and therapist in a family group setting.

Intensive Caseloads

Attempts to develop innovative programs for juveniles have generally been founded on concepts of appropriate but innovative structure, larger budgets, smaller caseloads, better classification programs, more trained workers, and higher salaries. There is, as Gibbons[1] has pointed out, little empirical basis for the faith that dramatic reductions in recidivism will follow the establishment of such improvements. Even so, correctional administrators do have a rational set of beliefs, drawn from their experience, upon which to construct models of treatment and rehabilitation which are departures from the traditional.

A representative focus of juvenile correctional practices in California counties includes the following:

CONTRA COSTA COUNTY[2]—Beginning in 1964, a girls' unit for intensive daytime education (called GUIDE) was established as the first program of its kind in the country. It was seen as an alternative to commitment of a girl to the California Youth Authority, by keeping her with her own family to work with her in the environment in which she must live.

The program is one of daytime activities of school, home-making and recreation activities. There is an opportunity for remedial education and counseling, not only with the girl individually but with her family in family sessions and in monthly parent group meetings. The program is described as one of very intensive treatment. No girl in it can escape learning what effect her individual behavior has, both upon herself and the others in the center. No parents can avoid at least exposure to knowledge of how their behavior, attitudes and ways of communicating have affected their children. The girls have the opportunity to do some part-time work as they progress in the program, with their pay usually taken from donated funds.

The day treatment center approach to delinquency is an effort to rehabilitate a child in the community setting, to redirect energies toward constructive goals and to develop some insight and empathy. It costs the taxpayer considerably less per year than an institutional placement and is believed to cost the youngster and her family considerably less emotional trauma. It is stated that its success rate in Contra Costa County has been high to date and the program is recommended for other jurisdictions as well.

The program has been located in a family residence in a middle-class neighborhood where the livingroom has been turned into a classroom, the pantry into a crafts room, a bedroom into a sewing room, another into an office, and a third into a meeting room with a television set. The dining room and kitchen retain their original purposes. There is nothing on the exterior of the house to differentiate it from any other house on the block. The program has been sufficiently successful that a second, for an additional twelve girls, was established in Contra Costa County in 1968.

This program, of course, is not the only intensive treatment program in Contra Costa County but is taken as representative of a unique and innovative approach to the management of delinquent teen-age girls in a community setting.

FRESNO COUNTY[3]—In 1970, a deputy probation officer in one of the subsidy sections saw the need for group activity for wards on his caseload who were predominantly from a high delinquency area, were of Mexican-American descent, and whose offenses were generally paint and glue-sniffing. A group was formed, known as the Calwa Boys Club. The deputy and several others work at providing alternatives to the boys' usual activities. Originally only probationers were involved; however, non-probationers began attending meetings and activities and have been encouraged to continue. Meetings are held at least weekly, and usually more frequently. Activities have included football, baseball, films, leatherwork, trips to mountains, lakes, swimming and fishing. Refreshments generally are served.

In cooperation with Fresno State College various students who are criminology majors are receiving credit to work with these boys. They have been a big asset to the group. The First Baptist Church of Calwa provides a room for the group to meet and a place to keep equipment.

The Calwa Elementary School serves as a recreational facility. The group picked their own name. The age range has been from eight to eighteen. Service groups have been approached to consider support of the club either in providing equipment or finances, or both. Some limited response has been made so far. State subsidy funds have kept the group going as far as refreshments and equipment are concerned.

The goals of the group have been stated as follows:

1. To provide after school supervised activities.
2. To offer satisfying group activity in lieu of delinquent activities.
3. To deter those who lean toward delinquent activity by providing alternatives and thereby seek to exclude them from the court system.
4. To establish adolescent-adult understanding and communication.
5. Eventually to make the club community sponsored and separate from any county agency.

Fresno County has also established another special project in their boys' intensive supervision unit. This is a first offender caseload and has been in process of experimentation for approximately six months. Essentially it is a minor and parent dialogue program including evening group meetings for participation beyond the single family unit.

San Diego County[4]—A total of nine special supervision units have been established in San Diego County, two of which are restricted to serving adult cases. One of the units works with a disfunctioning family wherein one or more of the members is subsidy eligible, and one mixed unit accepts cases with high commitment potential, whether adult or juvenile. Primary services to juveniles come from two juvenile units located in high delinquency areas together with three community day centers, one for boys, one for girls, and one coeducational. In addition, two group homes are available for supportive services, and contractural arrangements provide for vocational rehabilitation and for teaching services in the community day centers.

The comprehensive training program indicated for San Diego County is of significance. Formal training includes intensive and specialized instruction by appropriate consultants in the I-Level techniques of diagnosis and treatment to develop greater expertise in staff members. There is training in behavior modification and operant conditioning, cultural differences and sub-culture isolation, family therapy, including conjoint family therapy, individual and group dynamics. In addition, Gestalt techniques, transactional analysis, and group counseling are provided for all subsidy personnel. The training is presented at the unit level whenever feasible, and includes use of audio visual equipment to implement all areas of instruction with special emphasis on group interaction, interviewing and non-verbal communication.

SAN BERNARDINO COUNTY[5]—One of the interesting projects established in San Bernardino is entitled *Independence Apartments.* It is essentially a kind of half-way house for youngsters who are unable to remain at home but do not require formal institutionalization. The unique feature of this project is that it is underwritten by a local Kiwanis Club which handles the funds and makes the disbursements. The Probation Department subsidizes the young men placed in the home until they are able to become self-supporting.

A project financed by Federal funds through the California Council on Criminal Justice has been given the name *Neat.* It is a program of diverting youngsters from formal court processing where-ever possible by providing immediate casework and group counseling assistance to youngsters and their parents within 72 hours after the filing of the petition. The project has three groups of 50 cases each. The first group includes youngsters who receive casework and group counseling assistance. The second group receives casework and group counseling plus special medical and psychiatric assistance for which outside services are contracted. The third group is a control group in which the cases are merely identified, to be studied later in the research analysis of the total project. Since this is one of the few programs in which a research analysis component has been so clearly identified, the results should be of significant interest in terms of establishing effectiveness and applicability for other jurisdictions.

SAN MATEO COUNTY[6]—A day care program for delinquents was established in San Mateo County in 1965. The program was reviewed extensively in an article in the October 1968 issue of Crime and Delinquency. The program is based on the concepts of maintaining a juvenile in the community by providing counseling and family therapy as well as educational activities. The program in San Mateo County is for girls and the facility is a part of the San Mateo County Juvenile Hall.

This program received a research evaluation after three years of operation. At that time, out of ninety-eight girls who had participated a total of seventy-one had completed the program. A total of nine who had completed the program and were dismissed from wardship, had subsequent police contact, usually for such activities as runaway. San Mateo County also found that the total out-of-home placements for girls were cut back by about 25 percent after the day care program was initiated. This level has been maintained despite the fact that new referrals for girls have continued to increase at an average of nearly 20 percent per year.

Not only has the program been successful in maintaining girls in their home with a low recidivist rate, but it has been able to do so at a relatively low cost per girl. The average cost for all services and expenses, including staff salaries, for the twenty-four girls in the day care program was listed at $450 per month in July 1969. The average cost is further reduced by the State subsidy program, to an average net cost of $190 per girl per month. A substantial part of this amount is paid for by the parents of the girl involved.

As is true of a number of other counties, San Mateo has a number of innovative programs in other areas which will be covered later.

VENTURA COUNTY[7]—A program with a record of longevity has operated in Ventura County since 1958. It is entitled "School Visitation Program."

There are two deputy probation officers assigned full time to this function. They provide counseling services to those youngsters who are not officially referred to law enforcement or to probation. Students who demonstrate behavior problems at school, habitual truancy, or who are generally seen as potential delinquents are referred to the program.

The school visitation officer interviews the youth and his parents and school personnel. He investigates each case to determine what factors, in the home or otherwise, have contributed to the overt problems in school. He works out a plan involving the youth, his parents, school personnel and other appropriate agencies to offset the delinquency potential. This process occurs without an official referral to the probation department although it is possible that the school visitation officer may place the individual on informal probation or refer him to probation intake for stronger action. School personnel are reported as viewing this program as a positive intervention approach which is successful in deterring a youth from further delinquent involvement and a consequent official referral to the juvenile justice system.

For several years the Probation Department of Ventura County has utilized another alternative to incarceration for court wards. This is the Ward Work Training Program. In lieu of fines and further incarceration, the youth is ordered by the court to put in a specific number of hours at work at a county park or other facility. He is supervised by the regular personnel and his work is evaluated to determine if it meets the criteria deemed acceptable. Benefits to the county are obvious; benefits to the boy are in the development of a greater responsibility for his actions, learning the value of work and learning to work with other people. A recent development of this program is the addition of girls who are required to work in the county hospital laundry.

As with other counties, Ventura County has been able to decentralize services to be more responsive to community needs. Sections of work are now located in Santa Paula, Oxnard and Thousand Oaks as well as in the central office. Noteworthy in the description of these programs is an explanation of a casework technique used by deputy probation officers with both juveniles and adults. This is called *the probation contract* and consists of an agreement between client and officer designed under the limitations set forth by the court order. The probation contract is reported to enhance adjustment for the following two reasons: (1) The probationer, or ward, arrives at a better understanding of the probation orders through the process of reading and understanding the contract agreement; (2) The probationer, or ward, is intrinsically involved in setting the limits of the contract and therefore internalizes the values of the agreement to some degree. In essence, to whatever extent the client accepts the limits he has himself set he will be acting upon self-imposed controls rather than external forces.

Two additional special approaches which might be mentioned briefly include a *warning and grace* period for AWOL probationers and wards. Success has been experienced on numerous occasions in bringing absconded cases back under supervision without formal court action. In practice, the method has consisted of sending word out through the grapevine that a person can voluntarily report to his deputy probation officer by a certain deadline to resolve problems informally. When such report is made the matter is not then officially reported to the court.

The second effective specialized casework tool has been *speaking engagements* by probationers. On many occasions officers have taken clients along to participate in public relations and community resource development efforts. The most common examples of this endeavor have been instances of probationers speaking before community organizations, with all due precautions given to case confidentiality. Such efforts have been by far the most successful endeavor in community relations and are deemed invaluable to the remotivation of the client.

In summarizing this part, it must again be emphasized that this listing is in no way exhaustive or even fully descriptive of all of the ramifications of a particular program. No attempt has been made to recognize the interplay of various approaches which often exists in the implementation of any special program. Accordingly, the same counties will be mentioned in subsequent parts of this presentation as other unique aspects of their programs warrant recognition.

Narcotics and Drugs

No single reason for referral of juveniles to probation or court has increased at so startling a rate as has the offense involving narcotics and drugs. For example, statistical data for San Mateo County show that referrals for *Narcotics, dangerous drugs, liquor, and glue/gasoline sniffing* increased from only 5 in 1960 to a total of 828 in 1970. No county, no community, no neighborhood has escaped the impact of this problem. In developing new programs to meet the needs, the emphasis has been on education and prevention. Actual treatment has generally been seen as a problem for medical care, including components of health and mental health services. Perhaps significantly, none of the models reported using nalline or urinalysis testing for juveniles, and none made reference to a methadone maintenance program for juveniles. To the degree education and prevention programs are successful, these more severe measures may not be required.

Four descriptions of operating programs are as follows:

ALAMEDA COUNTY[8]—A coordinated county-wide drug abuse program has been established in Alameda County. The probation department participates with the Health Care Services Agency, the County School Department, the District Attorney's Office, and indigenous groups and agencies through a grant provided under the Omnibus Crime Control and Safe Streets Act. The Probation Department has established a drug school for juveniles and a specialized drug abuse unit in the department for both juveniles and adults. In addition, a residential treatment center is being contemplated.

SAN BERNARDINO COUNTY[9]—The project in this county is known as the County Juvenile Drug Abuse Project. It is described as a method of diverting youngsters from the formal juvenile court process and has as its unique feature a cooperative arrangement with another State agency, namely, the California Rehabilitation Center, Women's Branch, at Patton. Under this program deputy probation officers are group leaders for a six week parent-child counseling session system. The meetings are held once per week. The leaders receive special training from a staff member at the California Rehabilitation Center and a co-leader is provided by the Center for the women residents there. It is reported that there is a distinct advantage in the two agencies working together and no difficulties have been experienced in the fact that one represents a county and the other the State.

SANTA CLARA COUNTY[10]—The use of volunteers in probation treatment programs has been developed in Santa Clara County in connection with a narcotics and drugs program. It is described as funded by L.E.A.A. and is designed for volunteers to become directly involved in treatment. School teachers and school counselors, clergymen, housewives and other interested persons sign up every two months for group leader training. A part of the obligation is to co-lead a group following completion of the training period. Such techniques as psycho-drama and transactional analysis are used and the training is described as extremely good, thereby accounting for very positive community response.

SAN DIEGO COUNTY[11]—The San Diego program was first presented in March 1969. It was geared specifically to meet the needs of juvenile drug abusers and narcotics offenders. It has proven successful to the degree that it is now included as a regular part of probation services. The program format is simple in nature. It consists of six separate meeting sessions in which attendance by the minor and his parents is mandatory. The meetings occur on Tuesday night each week and continue for six consecutive weeks. The participating minors and parents are subjected to a total 12 hours exposure to the program from their initial enrollment until completion of the course.

The authority for the program is found under provisions of Section 654 of the Welfare and Institutions Code. This section provides for informal supervision by the probation officer under a voluntary agreement with the family involved. The authority for continued supervision may extend to a period not to exceed six months. Excluded from participation are all minors involved in the sale of narcotics to others. In addition, a minimum age of 14 and a maximum age of 17 at the time of offense is also required. The final requirement is that there be a provable narcotics case against the youngster involved. This is necessary because the family is given an option of enrolling in the six session program or the filing of a petition and the submission of the case to juvenile court for formal disposition. Should they select the educational program in lieu of court they are advised that regular attendance is mandatory. Failure on the part of either parent or minor to attend any session will immediately result in the minor's ejection from the program and the immediate filing of a petition alleging the original offense. This approach has the support and backing of the juvenile court.

To further support attendance requirements the minor and parents are required to sign a contract in which they agree to the provisions requiring attendance. The success or failure of the program seems to rest heavily upon the degree of enforcement of attendance requirements. The county reports 100 percent attendance at all sessions to date, indicating excellent structuring on the initial contact with the families involved. The experience indicates that such rigid attendance requirements are necessary for the first meeting only. Once exposed, minors and parents are eager to return for the follow up sessions. The composition of the group provides for separate group discussion sessions. In addition to guest lecturers, the final hour of each meeting provides for separate groups of approximately fifteen persons. One of the characteristics is that the placing of a minor in the same group with his or her parent is avoided. A typical group would include approximately four or five minors and an equal number of parents, plus probation staff.

This program is being evaluated by a two-phase research component. In one, the youngsters are selected through a screening procedure and from the total number a control group of an equal number of those qualifying for the program is being identified. The control group is not enrolled in the program but is withheld from participation and other approaches are being applied. At a later date a comparison will be made by way of record checks and follow-ups to compare the experimental with the control group.

The second research phase requires giving each youngster selected an attitudinal questionnaire developed by the department. After the program is completed and after a three months interval, the minor is again contacted and required to take the same attitudinal test. Differences in responses to the questions on the second test as compared to the first will be attributed to changes in the attitude on the part of the minor, thus providing a second means of determining program validity. San Diego reports that the costs for this program have been minimal. All guest lecturers provide their services on a voluntary basis with no costs involved. Participating staff members are given compensatory time off for each meeting session they attend.

In summary, narcotic and drug education programs lean toward a cooperative approach designed to use the services of other departments or the expertise of particular individuals. Concern about the problems is not limited to probation departments nor is service provided solely at the county level. The city of Pleasant Hill, for example, has a funded project in Discovery House for counseling, guidance and treatment of juvenile drug users. Similarly, the city of Antioch is in its second year of the Reach Project which provides drug prevention and rehabilitation programs for both youths and adults.

Family Education

As a general term, *Family Education* is broadly descriptive of the rather recent upsurge of interest in behavior modification and behavior therapy. As an approach, it finds its roots in the behaviorist school of psychological thought, and certainly is not new. It is simple to understand, being a systematic process of reinforcing positive behavior while at the same time ignoring or exercising negative reinforcements to eliminate unwanted behavior. The approach is sometimes called operant conditioning, as developed by B. F. Skinner, and it concentrates on overt behavior rather than the underlying casual forces. In the attempt to create acceptable new responses to an environmental stimulus, various techniques, such as *contracts* or *transactional analysis* are used. Direct reward of acceptable or positive responses is conceived to be the best method to stabilize intended behavior patterns.

The utility and effectiveness of this type of juvenile treatment program has yet to be established because of the recency of its adoption. Representative of some of these innovations in probation work are the following:

FRESNO COUNTY[12]—A special project of the boys' intensive supervision unit was the establishing of a first offender caseload as an experimental project to develop increased contact between juvenile, parent, and probation officer. At the present time the program has been in existence approximately six months. It includes evening group meetings of both minor and parent, and the experience has indicated a high degree of interest and activity. At the present time this special caseload approach is being evaluated to determine whether it should be continued or not.

ORANGE COUNTY[13]—In cooperation with the community coordinating unit, a grant was secured from the Rosenberg Foundation during 1970 to initiate a program entitled "Project Turn Around." It was established in the Garden Grove area and is an outgrowth of the Westminster Guidance Program as coordinated with the Garden Grove Unified School District and California State College at Fullerton. The program is designed to offset those factors contributing to the development of delinquent behavior. These would include truancy, academic deficiency, incorrigibility, and unstable family environment among students aged nine to twelve enrolled in elementary schools. Non-professional volunteer workers are utilized to provide counseling and guidance to young people experiencing these adjustment difficulties. These services are likewise provided to their families. Program emphasis is given to attendance, citizenship, academic achievement, and increased parental ability to meet a child's needs. Every effort is made to develop a strong working relationship between student, family, volunteer and teacher. The research component of the project is being conducted by the Sociology Department, California State College at Fullerton.

SANTA CLARA COUNTY[14]—As an outgrowth and expansion of subsidy developed programs, Santa Clara County has extended their innovative services to an agency-wide program. These include both I-Level and Transactional Analysis techniques. The county is in the final phase of training all casework staff in a newly developed style of family behavior modification to include at least one of the supplemental techniques such as transactional analysis. The specific and selective use of the particular treatment method is based on an I-Level classification verified by a team of six supervising probation officers.

SAN DIEGO COUNTY[15]—A project entitled "Simplified Analytical Methods of Behavioral Systemization" has been proposed as a new method of approaching the problem of the incorrigible juvenile. The intent is to establish a structured educational program for the parent in more effective ways of controlling behavior. The project anticipates modification of the child's behavior as the parent becomes more expert in good behavior modification techniques. It is predicated upon the idea that most parents have a primary interest and ability in being the control agent for their child and that faulty systems are correctable.

The program proposes involving each family in a series of ten sessions, consisting of one hour of actual teaching experience conducted by a psychiatrist and one hour of reinforcing group discussion. Additional time is provided for discussion between group leaders and the psychiatrist. It is estimated that the program would involve between 250 and 500 families in a one-year period. These families would be drawn from new referrals to the juvenile court system as well as existing wards of the court. Involvement with the program would initially be by contract for informal supervision although provision is made for the program to run concurrently with the juvenile court process for a juvenile who is a ward of the court.

Research will be provided in order to establish whether the new approach contrasts favorably to more traditional methods. It is hoped that the approach will provide a model including video tapes and curriculum guides for both psychiatrist and group leaders which would be adaptable in other communities. Evaluation of the project is to be developed involving personnel at California State College, San Diego, and utilizing the standard techniques of developing an experimental and a control group for analysis and evaluation of program results.

As an intervention strategy, family education represents both expansion and refinement of traditional casework approaches toward dealing with family problems of socialization and resocialization. The long range potential appears good although the appropriateness of the service as essential to the juvenile justice system may be open to question.

Youth Service Bureaus

In 1967 the President's Commission on Law Enforcement and Administration of Justice recommended the expanded use of community agencies for dealing with juveniles non-judicially.[16] It was suggested that such agencies might be located in community centers and should serve both delinquent and non-delinquent youth by providing coordination of all community services for young people.

California has established nine of these recommended agencies as Youth Services Bureaus, with enabling legislation passed in 1968 (Sections 1900–1906, Welfare and Institutions Code). Two of these Bureaus will be described here, plus a recap of similar approaches developed in Orange County as a part of a comprehensive delinquency prevention program.

San Mateo County[17]—The San Mateo County Delinquency Prevention Commission was alarmed by the youth problems in Pacific during the summers of 1968 and 1969 when there were serious youth disturbances. They were of such community magnitude that numerous youth and adults were arrested and serious damage resulted to stores and to police equipment. The Commission applied for a grant to establish a Youth Service Bureau, which was funded through the Department of the Youth Authority on October 1, 1969. Beginning July 1, 1971 the funding will be from the California Council on Criminal Justice. The primary purpose of the Bureau is the diversion of youth from the juvenile court system by the provision of meaningful services at the community level. Staffing is accomplished primarily through the means of detachment of personnel from the county and private agencies on either a full or part time basis to counsel and to help develop the delinquency prevention program. Agencies contributing direct service staff include the San Mateo County Probation, Health and Welfare Departments, the Catholic Social Service, and the Family Service Agency. Other sources provide consultation.

Diversion has been accomplished primarily by receiving and servicing referrals from police, schools, families and citizens. The services normally take the form of family counseling, crisis intervention, screening and referral to appropriate ameliorative agencies and the provision of aggressive casework services. Every attempt has been made to involve as many of the referred youth's family members in the crisis intervention program as possible. Predictably, there has been a residue of clients for whom no appropriate service was available elsewhere in the social service structure. Such clients, though few in number, have become part of an active caseload involved with lay community volunteers and college students who have been given an intensive training program and who work under the direct supervision of a staff member.

Additional projects initiated throughout the year utilized trained volunteer youth and adults as *street-workers* to dissuade and divert troublesome youth to positive experiences. Family education seminars were initiated to provide a base for families to re-think their role and function. A tutoring program was developed to provide personal and academic growth for youthful clients who were experiencing school as well as behavioral problems. Community service projects were initiated so that clients and youthful volunteers could have a means of expressing their energies toward correcting the ills of their society and their community.

The main evaluation component of the project is conducted by the California Youth Authority. There are two major objectives to be evaluated. These are to determine whether the Youth Service Bureau can (1) divert a significant number of youth from the juvenile court system, and (2) utilize community resources in a more coordinated manner. It is intended that data will be developed to give information as to the Youth Service Bureau's impact on delinquent behavior. The issues to be looked at include: (1) Is there a greater use of probation services; (2) Are more petitions sustained from this group than from the rest of the country; (3) Of those sustained petitions, are there more out-of-home placements made?

San Diego County[18]—The Youth Service Bureau of San Diego County is a pilot project in delinquency prevention originated by the Probation Department. It was originally funded through the California Youth Authority and now has been funded by the California Council on Criminal Justice. It has been in operation for a two-year period. Approximately 1,000 referrals have been handled during that time. Approximately one-third of the referrals are from law enforcement, another third from probation, schools and other agencies, and approximately one-third directly by parents or youngsters. At any given time the average caseload for each staff member would be approximately sixty-five. Other agencies contribute staff or services to the cooperative effort. These include the San Diego Police Department, County Welfare Department, Community Mental Health, San Diego City Schools, California State College at San Diego, Claremont Women's Club, Claremont Adult School, and the Junior League of San Diego, Inc.

Policy for the Bureau is determined by an executvie board made up of representatives of the contributing agencies, the community served, and the youth served. The Bureau functions under the general auspices of the Delinquency Prevention Commission of San Diego County. Individual counseling has been the basic tool of the Bureau in working with youth and their parents, supplemented by group counseling, psychiatric consultation and evaluation.

The Bureau has engaged in numerous other activities including the following:

1. Rap Sessions—These are weekly unstructured meetings with youth of the neighborhood to discuss matters of concern ot them.
2. Adult Education Programs—A four week course is run each semester dealing with problems of the pre-delinquent.
3. Drug Abuse Program—A six week program of information giving and small group counseling, operated in conjunction with a similar program established by the Probation Department.
4. Narcotic Identification—The Youth Service Bureau is equipped and

authorized to identify drug substances for parents and youth with questions without jeopardy of arrest.

5. Delinquency Prevention Presentations—Staff has conducted a prevention conference attended by 15 community agencies. Members of the Youth Service Bureau regularly talk with community groups, schools, and clubs on subjects relating to the prevention of delinquency.

The Youth Service Bureau has been free to experiment with specially geared programs to meet the needs of the individual youngster or community. To meet the needs of a negatively oriented school drop out the Bureau set up a teachers aid program. Faced with a school expulsion, the Bureau set up a junior high school program complete with mandatory physical education courses, curriculum guides, accepted texts, staff and a student body.

Evaluation of the Bureau has been favorable. In a study of juvenile arrests in the target area versus the entire city, the target area had a decrease of 4 percent while the overall city rate went up 5.6 percent and another similar area went up 5 percent. In a 1970 study done by graduate students at California State College, San Diego, both the number of arrests and the severity of arrests were significantly decreased following referral to the Bureau. Currently the California Youth Authority is conducting a study to determine longer range changes. Continuing evaluation of the Bureau will be the responsibility of a special research group from the Youth Authority who will be able to contrast not only the San Diego Bureau but all other bureaus in the State.

ORANGE COUNTY[19]—In June 1970 the Board of Supervisors approved establishment of a community services project in Orange County. This was the result of extensive planning on the part of a committee including the County Administrative Office, Director of Community Mental Health Services, the Health Officer, Superintendent of the Department of Education, and the County Probation Officer. A total of fourteen cities in Orange County were interested in being the site for the initial program. Selection was made of the city of Placentia, based on attitudes as well as socio-economic distribution within the city which seemed to provide the greatest number of potential applications for other cities.

In March 1971 the project was given the opportunity to expand to include a city of the second type. As a result of the opportunity offered by the Youth Development and Delinquency Prevention Administration, the city of Fountain Valley was also included in the project. The program is designed to work with these two cities for a three to five year period to develop a model for other cities in the county. In this model the advice and participation of as many residents as possible will be sought to develop community action programs to more effectively deal with current problems as well as retard or prevent the development of new ones. The goal of the program is to create a cooperative climate in which the existing institutions will be more responsive to the needs of the community and citizen participation will stimulate the development of new and innovative approaches.

The project places a multi-discipline staff at the disposal of the community. At the present time the team consist of a supervising probation officer, a public health nurse and a social worker. The major role is to be that of catalyst. The team will develop the communication link between the various segment of the community. Additionally, since the staff members come from various county departments they will increase awareness and communication between departments. In this way needs will be identified, cooperative programs developed, and duplication of effort minimized. The staff team will reach out and attempt to involve the total community and its institutions in both the decision making and implementation of action programs.

Another project in Orange County has been given the name "Alternative Routes." It is an effort by the police, schools, and probation department to find new and more effective ways of dealing with the problems of youth. In so doing it is hoped that a greater number of young people will be diverted from the juvenile justice system and that more effective and enduring solutions can be found for the problems experienced by these youth and their families.

For an eighteen month period three youth service officers from the probation department will be located in each city, which will give them an opportunity to become more familar with the local agencies and the resources they offer. It will afford the community an opportunity to become acquainted with youth services officers, who are a special class of deputy involved in community development and community relations service. They will work closely with the police department, schools, and parents. The youth services officers will be available to provide services to parents and youth upon request and will have a small caseload for informal supervision. They will counsel with minors and their families, evaluate problem areas and assist in developing programs to aid individual families to more effectively use existing community resources. The Alternate Routes project will provide the opportunity for the police, the schools, the community and the probation department to work together in a program which not only provides benefits to the entire community but may be the forerunner of a team effort in many areas of the judicial process.

Volunteers

The use of volunteers in probation work has a history of more than twenty years. It was in 1959 that a pioneering program began in Royal Oaks, Michigan, to provide services to persons seventeen and over charged with misdemeanors. A history of that program, described by its sponsor and president, Judge Keith J. Leenhouts, may be found in the December, 1970, issue of Federal Probation.[20] In a similar article, Dr. Ivan H. Scheier of the Boulder (Colorado) Juvenile Court and director of the National Information Center on Volunteers in Courts has listed over 100 ways courts can use volunteers.[21] It is possible to obtain excellent literature, a Volunteer Court Newsletter, and other services by contacting him at the Hall of Justice in Boulder, Colorado. Data furnished from these sources indicate more than 600 courts are known to be making substantial use of volunteers today; there were only about twenty-five in 1967.

It would be safe to say that almost all of California's counties have been using or have been influenced by the use of volunteers in juvenile correctional services. Representative programs include the following:

Los Angeles County[22]—A program known as Visto (Volunteers in Service to Offenders) is operated by the Los Angeles County Probation Department. It began as a pilot project in two area offices of the department, in March 1968. It was originally funded by the Office of Economic Opportunity. Within a year results exceeded expectations and the program was expanded to 16 different work locations. Visto is a project in which community volunteers are continuously recruited and trained to work with probationers. Volunteers are required to make monthly reports on a special form indicating the number of contacts made, the number of hours contributed, and a brief summary of the volunteer's impressions of achievement during the contacts. Problems which arise are discussed with a member of the Visto staff or the deputy probation officer responsible for case supervision.

Volunteers perform any type of service for which their individual abilities provide and which would meet the specific diagnosed needs of a probationer. Typical services include transportation to take a child to a doctor or a mother to camp to visit her son. Volunteers take groups of juveniles to ballgames or museums or other activities of a similar nature. Families are helped with budget or housekeeping problems and even emergency babysitting. One of the most important services is to provide tutoring to juveniles to help them find employment, to assist with job training and to provide opportunities to graduate from high school.

The Visto project has served as a catalytic agent in bringing together indigenous community groups and organizations to work cooperatively on community betterment programs. Examples of these services include a narcotics treatment and educational program for teenagers, a new career program for young adults involving aptitude testing, career counseling, prevocational training, remedial tutoring, and special courses in trade school or college. Within the first nine months of the Visto service a total of 309 probationers had received some kind of service from 150 volunteers. A total of 5,513 volunteer hours was provided. The test of a volunteer program is the effect it may have on a rate of recidivism. By December of 1968, of the 309 probationers who were involved for varying periods of time, only ten had to be terminated before the requested service was completed. The Visto program is seen to be important because of the involvement of volunteers and various indigenous groups by which the community is gaining first-hand knowledge of its own problems and is becoming involved in doing something about them in a postitive manner.

ORANGE COUNTY[23]—Two volunteer programs have been established in Orange County. One is called "Volunteers in Probation," or

VIP. It was initially established to provide services to adults and was subsequently extended to include juveniles. A number of orientation and training sessions were conducted for the benefit of department staff members and volunteer applicants. It was thought important to include discussions of the role and obligations of the volunteer, the goals of the department, and an overview of probation, the courts, and the institutional and treatment programs. The training meetings are conducted for groups of approximately ten volunteers at a time and are led by departmental volunteer group leaders. Each volunteer is required to attend one orientation session and two training meetings.

In order to provide accurate information to the public, a volunteer speakers corps was established using the services of six staff members who volunteered to meet with groups and community agencies to present the information. One of the programs established was for services to juveniles described as truants. Through the efforts of a deputy probation officer a number of rap sessions were organized and volunteers utilized to assist in the group discussions. From an initial beginning of two groups, a total of four have now been established. Similarly, a program involving the solicitation of campership opportunities for youngsters was developed. This program is now in its second year and has a a goal of 250 camperships for this current summer. Another program utilizing volunteers is entitled "Operation Santa Claus." This involves the sponsorship and support of a civic league and junior women's club and involves the solicitation and distribution of gifts to children under the supervision of the probation department and residing in their own homes, in foster homes, or in institutions.

The second program established by Orange County is called VISA (Volunteers Influencing Student Achievement). In the program, volunteer citizens provide 4th, 5th, and 6th grade students with assistance in the area of social relationships and scholastic achievement. With the approval of their parents, selected older students will be matched with carefully chosen volunteers. Efforts are now under way to recruit, screen and train sufficient volunteers to meet the needs of approximately 150 students. The volunteers will be recruited from church groups, civic organizations and other interested citizens. It is expected that a screening process will be used involving a record check at the Orange County Sheriff's Office, a check with the California Criminal Identification Index, the Department of Motor Vehicles and the local Police Department. As a general rule no one will be considered to become a volunteer if he has a record of criminal offenses. Subsequent to record checks, applicants are interviewed by members of the project staff.

Factors considered include concern about the individual's philosophy regarding authority, his willingness to assume responsibility for the entire length of the project, healthy mental attitudes, adaptability, warmth of personality, flexibility, emotional stability and the attitude of the volunteer's family toward the project. Selected volunteers will meet in at least three training sessions. The first will be an orientation to their responsibilities as volunteers. The second and third sessions will deal with the role of the volunteer and with techniques of listening, counseling, dynamics of individual and group interaction. It is expected that additional meetings will be scheduled on a regular basis to provide an opportunity for sharing of experiences and for further training. It is expected that other volunteers will be selected and trained in the administrative processes of Visa.

Under the direction of probation staff the administrative volunteers will assist with the responsibility for recruiting, screening, and selection of volunteers to be assigned to the students. Further, they will participate in matching volunteers with students selected by the school staff. They will coordinate the activities of these volunteers through the school year and it is expected that the demonstration will provide a model so that the program could be adapted to any school or school district in the county with minimal guidance from the probation department.

It is expected that the Visa program will be available initially to all elementary schools in the Placentia Unified School District. The administrator at each school will appoint a staff member to coordinate with probation staff and with the administrative volunteers. It is expected that the school staff member will become a resource person upon whom the volunteer can call for information relative to the child's progress in school. It is expected in the future, as a part of Visa, to develop a program for parents. The conception is that parents would appreciate an opportunity in an informal setting to discuss with other parents the problems that they may be experiencing in communicating with their children.

San Diego County[24]—In January 1970 a program entitled "Volunteers in Probation" was initiated as an innovative program in San Diego County to provide differential treatment to juveniles. The initial recruitment attracted 48 persons who had formerly been employed as professional staff of the probation department. Second steps involved contacting other groups, and, for example, 90 students from California State College at San Diego volunteered at the initial invitation. The response to VIP was so great that for a few months the supply of volunteers exceeded requests for services. For the last three months of the first year virtually no formal recruitment was used yet people still responed as they learned of the program from those who were already active.

In the first year over 20,000 hours were devoted to VIP from a total of 320 persons. Approximately 40 percent of the volunteers were men and approximately 80 percent were college graduates. Every effort is made to select mature, stable, reliable persons to serve in VIP. Each applicant must attend orientation classes, submit an application, and appear for an in-depth interview. Police, sheriff, and probation records are checked but an arrest record does not necessarily obviate membership. VIP includes former offenders who contribute much to the program. The applicant's attitude, not his record, is the final determining factor. Reference letters are sent to three people named by the applicant. Usually the application is approved when two favorable references are recorded.

The VIP orientation involves two evening sessions totaling seven hours. The first meeting includes an overview of VIP, the philosophy and organization of the probation department, a group exercise in values, theories on *how to help* from a former offender, and the film "The Dangerous Years." The second session includes a talk by a clinical psychologist. This is followed by small group discussions, with each group being led by a professional probation officer and a volunteer co-leader. Volunteers accepted into VIP are classified as unpaid county employees. Though unpaid, volunteers are covered by Workmen's Compensation and by liability insurance.

Most volunteers work on a one-to-one basis with dependent children, wards, or with adult probationers. The majority are involved in performing a supportive, companion role with the minor. Others provide tutoring service, employment counseling, visit children in institutions, teach home-making skills and provide other services that are needed. Some volunteers work with groups and do group counseling or serve as co-leaders. They have been involved in a number of special projects, such as developing a program for giving swimming lessons, a sports program, recrutiment of foster homes, communications, and drama, employment counseling, drivers training lessons and job procurement instructions.

There are three paid staff members provided to coordinate and administer the volunteer program. Much of the administrative work is done by volunteers. After a volunteer is accepted into the program he is assigned to a volunteer advisor who lives near him. The volunteer advisor serves as a liaison between the district advisor and five to twenty volunteers. The district advisors are also volunteers and are supervised by the volunteer services coordinator who is the paid staff member responsible for the program.

A volunteer newsletter entitled "The Docket" is published quarterly by volunteer staff. It is distributed to volunteers, staff supervisors, judges, juvenile justice commission members, the press, and other key persons in the community. It serves to increase community awareness, give recognition to volunteers, inform staff of the scope of volunteer activities, present instructive articles to volunteers, list unfilled jobs and unmet needs and also serves as a recruitment device. Most public relations activities are performed by the volunteer services coordinator. However, additional work is being done by volunteers and some are now giving talks to community groups and preparing radio announcements and press releases.

Volunteers In Probation is incorporated as a tax exempt charitable organization. It administers a *crisis and rehabilitation fund* and funds are solicited from various sources to meet special or emergent needs of clients. Staff education is an ongoing process and the volunteer services coordinator meets with training classes for new probation officers and with other staff units as well.

Evaluation of the program is currently being initiated with the development of an evaluation report form. It is reported that very few serious problems developed with volunteer personnel during the first year of operation. Volunteers were responsive to staff supervision and used mature judgment. However, approximately 10 percent of the volunteers failed to fully complete their volunteer assignments. Overall, it is felt that the strengths of the volunteer program far outweigh weaknesses. Volunteers are providing much needed highly individualized services to clients at no cost to the county program. Use of volunteers increases citizens' awareness of the function of the probation department, and involved citizens become more cognizant of the complex factors involved in crime and delinquency. Enlightened volunteer members communicate client and agency needs to the community with a result that increased support improves the climate for progressive sound probation services.

San Mateo County[25]—In September of 1969, the San Mateo County Probation Department initiated a citizen volunteer program with the hope that qualified volunteers would enrich and complement probation services to probationers by providing such services as job counseling, big brother and big sister relationships, tutoring, emergency transportation and by planning and conducting special activities in juvenile hall. Shortly after the start of this limited program the juvenile court initiated a court work program whereby certain court wards were ordered to complete a given work assignment with some charitable or public agency as a condition of probation. The newly created volunteer office was asked to coordinate this program. The probation department developed approximately eighty active volunteers to work with probationers and was managing the program through the half-time service of a volunteer coordinator.

In August of 1971 however, the California Council on Criminal Justice approved a two year program to fully finance a Director of Volunteers position and an expanded program to recruit and select additional volunteers and to coordinate and expand the court work program. In addition, public information and fund raising will be included and special volunteer activities will be accomplished as proposed by division directors.

Of significant interest in the San Mateo Project is a six point evaluation program. Since the use of volunteers is expected to reach approximately 500 individuals, it is expected that a research program can be established to provide both experimental and control groups of approximately fifty cases for each group drawn from populations to be of approximately equal size, similarly chosen, and with members who have committed offenses similar to those of the control group. The control group will receive traditional probation services and the experimental group will be assisted by citizen volunteers. Pertinent information to be recorded will include the group size, reasons for individual referrals, type of treatment received during probation, recidivistic acts and final dispositions. This review will be continued and evaluated after six months, nine months and one year periods of time.

In addition, overall program evaluation will be measured by a questionnaire designed subjectively to assess the value of the volunteer program in the opinion of the offender, the volunteer, and the probation officer.

A third evaluative component includes a measurement of community response. This will include accurate accounting of all property, goods and monies donated to the program. An evaluation form requesting suggestions, criticisms and reactions to the program will be submitted to each community organization interested and providing support to the volunteer services. This will allow for a critique to emanate from community participants.

Further, overall effectiveness will be interpreted by the director and analyst from data maintained on the number of volunteers, their activities, number of man hours, number of court wards assigned to the court work program, number and types of work resources utilized and the number of court assigned work hours completed by the probationer. Finally, an in-depth report will be submitted after six months of program experience. This will guide the project orientation and serve as the basis for substantive alteration if needed. After one full year of operation an annual report will be submitted to the California Council on Criminal Justice.

SANTA BARBARA COUNTY[26]—A specific example of the use of volunteers to focus on a specific community problem is exemplified by the Santa Barbara Special Supervision Units' Trust Company. Trust is a made-up word meaning Training For Responsibility Utilizing Subsidy Techniques. The project is made up of probationers, probation officers and volunteer members of the community interested in the rehabilitation of juvenile offenders. The Trust Company was begun in the summer of 1969 because of the sharp increase in crime in one of the delinquency prone areas of the eastern part of Santa Barbara. There was growing resentment among juveniles, most of whom were gang members, toward law enforcement and the establishment. Much of this hostility was contributed to by the readiness with which many crimes were indiscrimately attributed to the gang. Most of the juveniles involved were Negro and Santa Barbara at that time had only one black police officer.

Utilizing leadership already designated to certain youths in the area by other young people, a nine member Board of Directors was elected to head up the Trust Company. In August of 1969 the Board of Directors obtained use from the Santa Barbara Recreation Department of an old club house in one of the eastside parks. The club house has been made available on a regular basis, rent-free, since that time. The club house was in a general state of disrepair and the first project was painting and refurbishing. This called for the recruiting of volunteers from the University of California at Santa Barbara, from Santa Barbara City College, and from Westmont College. In addition, volunteers were solicited in the community.

The program of activities which was finally developed involved approximately one-hundred-fifty young people per week. The program includes general rap sessions, films, speakers, employment counseling, job finding, and recreational activities. The highlight of the week's activities is a Friday night *Gig*. At all times the Trust Company is managed and directed by the juveniles themselves, who take full responsibility for the enforcement of their rules. If any fund raising activities are conducted all monies are handled by the juveniles, and to date no money has disappeared.

In the current year the probation department has made available a small amount of financial support to provide for purchase of arts and crafts supplies, atheletic equipment and tools for task oriented groups. In addition, parents of youngsters have been involved and are making valuable contributions to the group. Activities of the Trust Company have included basketball games, preparing and servicing booths at the Santa Barbara Drug Alert Project and the

Santa Barbara Schools Festival to distribute anti-drug information, and juveniles have served as aides and advisors to professional staff of the department, making suggestions in the areas of counseling, guidance, and tutoring of younger children. At the present time a summer project is under way utilizing resources of the neighborhood youth corps so that approximately fifteen gang members will receive pay for work done in cleaning and maintaining picnic areas and restoration of the presidio which was begun by the local historical society.

The Trust Company is described as a community based correctional program with emphasis on the incorporation of local persons and agencies to allow offenders to relate to the community in a positive fashion. The intention is to help prepare young people to cope with basic life requirements in a satisfactory manner that leads to self respect and dignity.

New Careers

The use of indigenous aides or new careerists, some of whom may be ex-offenders, as a manpower source in corrections is a growing but contradictory concern. On the one hand, the desirable features of using persons familiar with problems to help solve the problems of others, of developing new kinds of permanent jobs, and of adding personnel to meet the growing need for services for which there will not be enough professionals available are on the positive side of the ledger.

In opposition, and representing serious difficulties to overcome, are the statutory or administrative prohibitions against the employment of probationers or parolees by state agencies in 40 states. In 422 local probation and parole agencies surveyed, nearly three fourths (72 percent) are prevented from hiring a person with a felony record or who is on active probation or parole. Not only regulations but public opinion about offenders and ex-offenders will stand in the way of employment of new careerists. Even more contradictory are likely to be the attitudes of correctional personnel. A survey of these attitudes, conducted by the Joint Commission on Correctional Manpower and Training, showed that half of the national sample of correctional personnel interviewed felt that it would not be a good idea to hire ex-offenders in their agency.[27] While these views and prohibitions apply specifically to ex-offenders, there is a similar set of attitudinal restrctions related to new careerists per se.

Again, the probation subsidy program has provided opportunity to bring new careerists into county employment as Community Workers. The counties of Ventura and San Diego, for example, use ". . . ex-offenders and/or indigenous community members to assist the community-based special supervision units by providing liaison with the probationer's neighborhood, peer group, and sub-culture; motivating the *hard core* unemployed probationer toward obtaining and maintaining empolyment; assist in locating employment and training opportunities; act as co-leaders in group counseling; serve as behavior models; assist probationers with transportation; and provide liaison between the probationer and community resources for education, recreation, cultural enrichment, and constructive social experiences."

At least two counties, Los Angeles and San Mateo, have major problems worthy of a more detailed presentation:

LOS ANGELES COUNTY[28]—The program developed in Los Angeles County beginning in March 1967 has been called RODEO (Reduction of Delinquency through Expansion of Opportunity). It is a concept of reducing or preventing juvenile delinquency by intensive in-community probation supervision actively supported and assisted by all of the forces which can be brought to bear positively to influence a young person's life and behavior. The program began as an alternative to placing seriously delinquent minors outside of the community in probation camps or institutions, or commitment to the California Youth Authority. Initially the funds were provided through the Office of Econoimc Opportunity. Currently RODEO is supported under State Aid to Probation Services. The principal goals of the RODEO program are described as, (1) To open up the community's opportunity structure to young men and women who are often cut off from such opportunities; (2) To explore ways in which indigenous personnel can be used to work with delinquent youth; (3) To help families become aware of, and use their own strengths and potentialities for change; and (4) To study the records of the younger siblings in the family to learn the extent to which they may be prevented from becoming delinquent in the course of their exposure to the RODEO program.

Implicit in the RODEO concept is the belief that four approaches, in their broadest sense, are the most effective ways to bring about changes. These four ways include the team approach, in which a deputy probation officer is team leader with two community workers as his assistants, and the expanded team to include the juvenile, his family, his church, school and neighborhood members who are interested in him. The concept includes an orientation toward strengthening the family. Experience in RODEO indicates that the most significant predictor of success is the degree of family strength, interest, stability, and support.

The group process is also a concept of the RODEO program. All of the minors participate in groups led by the deputy officer. This has two purposes: using the group process to modify behavior and providing and additional vehicle for intensive supervision. Finally, the concept includes broad community involvement. RODEO staff are involved in the decision-making process as well as the implementation level with significant community organizations. The RODEO facility reaches out to the surrounding community and encourages residents of the neighborhood to view the office as a service location. Community groups are encouraged to use the facility for some of their meetings and to invite others to participate in the program.

One of RODEO's contributions to the field of corrections has been its demonstration of the tremendous reservoir of untapped skills which become available through adding indigenous personnel to the supervision team. These benefits accrue not only to the client and to the community workers themselves but also the professional staff. Several cautions should be observed in developing a community worker program. The candidate for the position of community worker may be expected to have a variety of personal problems. Other factors being equal, an applicant should not be ruled out unless the problem is so gross that modification seems too difficult for him to work out even with help. In other words, if the applicant seems to have basic qualities needed for social service and to want the job, he should be screened in if at all promising, rather than screened out.

The following factors are recommended to be considered when selecting community workers:

1. Applicants should be older than clients, with 21 years as a flexible minimum age.
2. Applicants must have a valid driver's license and an automobile that can be operated.
3. No formal educational requirements should be specified although applicants need to be able to read and write well enough to make informal reports on daily activities and to do simple arithmetic such as that required to make out a mileage claim.
4. General health must meet civil service requirements. Physical appearance and apparel should conform to minimum standards for office attire and grooming.
5. Additional selection factors to consider include the applicant's feelings about authority, his leadership qualities, his potential for job responsibilities including punctuality, regular attendance and conscientious application to duties, and his value system relating to his ability to work within the framework of the department and its philosophies and goals.

Experience in the RODEO program has indicated that it is almost inevitable after community workers have been on the job for awhile and feel they know their way around that they will begin to question, overtly or covertly, the difference in their salaries and duties as compared to those of the deputy probation officer. It is recommended that this situation should not be treated lightly or handled on an individual basis. It is best managed as an agenda item for an all-staff meeting. It should be pointed out that under present value systems, and until other avenues are developed, the way up a career ladder in our bureaucracy is through education. It is important to recognize the responsibilty of having indigenous assistants to work with top management and with civil service personnel to upgrade positions and make additional opportunities available. The director of a new careers program should understand that problems which arise with community workers must be handled quickly and explained fully and with the awareness that although the community worker does not know all the technical rules his assessment of feeling is likely to be accurate.

In the RODEO program, training for community workers has been approached in the following ways:

1. A six-week training course of four hours per week is conducted for initial orientation. The main focus is toward agency policy and procedures. Lectures and discussion are supplemented by outside speakers on various subjects. Audio-visual presentations are made and field trips are conducted.
2. On-going in-service training is geared to the agency's program and toward remedial, functional education. This would include training in how to make a speech, how to present a case, or understanding the civil service process.
3. A suggested reading program has been developed. The aim is to encourage the habit of perusing current literature and keeping abreast of articles and books in the field of corrections.
4. Counseling aimed at helping the new careerist identify his potential and planning with him to implement a realistic program of self education has been found to be important.
5. Required enrollment in a new careers course at a college has been found to be useful. A number of colleges and universities are developing these academic programs leading to an A.A. certificate in Social Services. If possible, such a program should include provision for time off from work or overtime credit up to a specified number of hours for the training which is received.

The principles and program elements which were developed in the RODEO program are now being applied to larger areas through the Model Neighborhood Program.

San Mateo County[29]—In 1968 the Probation Department in San Mateo County created its first area office to service the predominantly black community of East Palo Alto and East Menlo Park. 80 percent of the staff in this office are Negro and new concepts of utilizing community manpower and personnel were adopted by creating new classifications of community workers and new career trainees. The distinction lies in the fact that new careerists are college students of minority background who are enrolled in a career academic program in addition to a part-time aide assignment in the probation department. Those assigned to the East Palo Alto Office are learning the role of the probation officer and how to assume responsibilities equivalent to those of the probation officer and the community worker. The long range goal is to assist the new careerist through graduation from college in the hope that he will become a full-time member of the probation staff. The title of community worker is used for the indigenous or neighborhood person who has been recruited to assist in the ongoing daily programs.

The San Mateo project is called Watoto. This is a Swahili word meaning children. The staff and program are dedicated to a total community involvement as the best means of meeting the needs of children under supervision. As a community based service not only is the office located in the community but so are the roots of many of its programs. An integral part of the staffing of the service is the community worker group. All of these persons are residents of the service area. Each possesses an intimate knowledge of the community and demonstrates an ability to relate to the disadvantaged family as well as the probation staff in the correctional process. Community workers assist when incidents of community disturbance occur. They participate with groups planning community-wide programs, aid in the development of foster homes, and participate with groups of children in special activities. In addition, community workers are assigned a joint responsibility with probation staff to work directly with probationer and his family. In many cases a close counseling relationship is established, while in other instances the community worker relates to those agencies and groups which have an impact on the satisfactory adjustment of the minor.

Interesting components of the Watoto project include the fact that a citizens' advisory committee composed of 26 members who reside in East Palo Alto and Menlo Park assisted in the development of the program. Credit must be given to the Urban League of the Bay area for entering into the agreement with the San Mateo County Board of Supervisors to provide community workers for the Watoto project.

The five basic goals of the project are as follows:

1. Utilizing community residents in the treatment, rehabilitation, and goal direction of youth from the communities.
2. Developing a new careers program for college students from the communities.
3. Maintaining community identity in the composition of staff.
4. Improving probation services through intensive involvement with wards

of the court and in developing realistic programs of a preventive nature.

5. Bridging the communication gap between residents of the community and the probation department.

The project staff and the community workers have engaged in a number of activities in pursuit of their goals. They have recruited foster homes and developed group homes. They have developed emergency and temporary housing facilities and developed a youth counselor's program utilizing young people from the community being served in an employed capacity in the probation department. They have expanded the new careers program and have assisted in seeking employment for youngsters and were helpful in college placement. They have pursued a working relationship with business and industry to assist deprived families and have adopted flexible program hours to accommodate to resident's needs.

The Watoto project was developed to assure the possibility that black staff would be available to counsel residents of the black community. It is reported the program has already brought about a major change in the area and is having positive effects on youngsters and the community. The California Youth Authority's Outstanding Service Award for 1971 was presented to the San Mateo County Probation Department for their imaginative programming in developing the Watoto project. Recognition for the success of this program is credited to the communities it serves, to the dedicated staff, and to the Probation Department.

Summary

This review of current innovative programs in a number of California Counties reveals on the one hand how many different programs have been developed and on the other how there is a relatively consistent theme running through these programs as described in the four preceding sections. It would be difficult to assume that the same considerations are not to be found in other jurisdictions where the same kinds of problems must be dealt with (particularly narcotics and dangerous drugs offenses) and the same urgency is present to develop new and different approaches and to expand resources through use of volunteers and para-professionals. In this sense, then, the recent experience and development in California is probably transferrable to other locations where local adaptations can be made to meet local conditions.

There are a number of significant factors revealed by this analysis. There is, first, a significant amount of attention being paid to preventive programs which include great emphasis upon family (parent-child) education and new techniques, such as operant conditioning, which a few short years ago would have seemed strange indeed in a probation setting. Secondly, there is evidence of a rather wide discrepancy between precise anf factual data which would describe the actual operation of the juvenile justice system and the relationship of the innovative programs described herein to the solution of problems in the system. There is no question that juvenile lawbreaking is widespread but the statutes describing delinquent behavior are ambiguous and imprecise. Accordingly, programs have been developed and are operating with little reference to a strictly legal approach which must include consideration and protection of the legal rights of minors. This is perhaps most clearly perceived in the lack of investment in the necessary correctional research designed to establish the relationship of innovative measures to those more traditional.

Thirdly, in evaluating the evidence relating to success of these innovative programs, the evidence is considered to be either *premature* or *speculative*. The rapidity with which change is occurring in the field is of course related to this phenomenon, yet credit must be given to the requirements of new funding programs to include a research and evaluation component in order to qualify a project's eligibility for funds. To the extent that these findings can be integrated into an information system, the availability of research evidence will be increased and the duplication or replication of similar approaches may be avoided.

Finally, in acknowledging respect and appreciation for the progressive actions which have been described, recognition must be given to those public administrators who have found, within their bureaucratic and traditionally oriented organizations, the opportunity to become social engineers. The task may be described as developing a change agent approach toward progress and improvement in solving the problems of social control of juveniles. Not the least of the attributes of these administrators is their knowledge about the nature and operation of the legal and correctional systems themselves, about their structures, policies and decision-making procedures, and about their impact upon offenders and public alike. Given all these, the willingness and courage to take risks in the pursuit of new goals and strategies is most gratifying.

FOOTNOTES

[1]Gibbons, Don C., *Changing The Lawbreaker,* Englewood Cliffs: Prentice Hall, Inc., 1965.

[2]For additional information contact John A. Davis, County Probation Officer, P.O. Box 791, Martinez, California 94553.

[3]For additional information contact Frank L. Bailey, Probation Officer, Room 700, Courthouse, Fresno, California 93721.

[4]For additional information contact Kenneth F. Fare, Chief Probation Officer, 2901 Meadow Lark Drive, San Diego, California 92123.

[5]For additional information contact Stewart C. Smith, Chief Probation Officer, 175 West 5th Street, San Bernardino, California 92401.

[6]For additional information contact Loren A. Beckley, Chief Probation Officer, 21 Tower Road, Belmont, California 94002.

[7]For additional information contact Frank Colston, County Probation Officer, Courthouse, Ventura, California 93001.

[8]For additional information contact James D. Callahan, Chief Probation Officer, 400 Broadway, Oakland, California 94607.

[9]See No. 5 above.

[10]For additional information contact Robert E. Nino, Chief Probation Officer, 840 Guadalupe Parkway, San Jose, California 95110.

[11]See No. 4, above.

[12]See No. 3, above.

[13]For additional information contact Margaret C. Grier, County Probation Officer, 301 South Manchester, Orange, California 92711.

[14]See No. 10, above.

[15]See No. 4, above.

[16]The President's Commission on Law Enforcement and Administration of Justice. Task Force Report: Juvenile Delinquency and Youth Crime. Washington, D. C., 1967, 19–21.

[17]For additional information contact Ralph Rutley, Director, Pacific Youth Service Bureau, 160 Milagra Drive, Pacifica, California 94044.

[18]See No. 4, above.

[19]See No. 13, above.

[20]Leenhouts, Keith J., "Royal Oak's Experience With Professionals and Volunteers in Probation," Federal Probation Quarterly, December 1970, p. 45.

[21]Scheier, Ivan H., "The Professional and the Volunteer in Probation: Perspectives on an Emerging Relationship," Federal Probation Quarterly, June, 1970.

[22]For additional information contact Kenneth E. Kirkpatrick Chief Probation Officer, 320 West Temple Street, Los Angeles, California 90012.

[23]See No. 13, above.

[24]See No. 4, above.

[25]See No. 6, above.

[26]For additional information contact Clifford C. Romer, Probation Officer, Box 1379, Santa Barbara, California 93102.

[27]"Offenders as a Correctional Manpower Resource," Joint Commission on Correctional Manpower and Training, June 1968, p. 3.

[28]See No. 22, above.

[29]See No. 6, above.

SECTION NINE

RESEARCH AND EVALUATION METHODS

CHAPTER 22

THE EVALUATION OF POLICE PROGRAMS

ROBERT M. CARTER

ALTHOUGH RESPONSIBLE POLICE administrators are concerned with and anxious to use evaluation as a tool in the management of their agencies, there has been some considerable confusion about the nature of evaluation. The President's Crime Commission noted that university-trained research personnel frequently approached organizational problems from an academic frame of reference or were almost completely unacquainted with operational problems of the agencies. They used a mysterious language of *contingency coefficients* and *multiple linear regressions* and their techniques and methodologies for evaluation were equally alien to administrators. Conversely, administrators were generally neither well versed in a social science approach to evaluation nor able to envision the creation of an ongoing research and evaluation program within their agencies. It is not suprising that this background has produced some considerable confusion and suspicion about the nature and process of evaluation. And yet, the process of evaluation is not a stranger to the police administrator. Evaluation—based upon sound data—is the key to decision-making, and it is the decision-making capability which is of primary importance among all administrative activities. Careful assessment and evaluation mark the appropriate decision; inadequate or partial evaluation most assuredly limit the administrator's capacity for sound judgments.

At bottom, however, the process of evaluation is not especially complex—particularly when it is dissected and analyzed through its major component parts or elements. There are four identifiable parts in the spectrum of evaluation: objectives, programs, standards, and methodologies. These will be examined separately and then joined together into a simple model for evaluation.[1]

Evaluation of a program (or process) must begin—not with the program—but with a clear and explicit *identification of the objectives toward which it is geared.* The police administrator must be able to outline his goals or purposes, not only in general terms, but also as precise clear objectives . . . *objective number one is* . . ., *objective number two is* . . ., and so on. Further, it must be recognized that the objectives may be of two levels: a *need to achieve* or primary objective and a *nice to achieve* or secondary objective. There may be one or more of each type of objective and accordingly a priority or special emphasis may be placed upon accomplishment of one objective rather than another. For the purposes of model construction, the objectives may be represented as a target as in Figure 22-1.

In the target figure, there are two equally important primary objectives represented by the two segments of the bull's-eye. There are also two secondary objectives, not of equal importance, assigned to the 5 and 1 rings.

Emphasis is placed upon the fact that the administrator should be aware of the objectives and, where appropriate, their priorities without recourse to *outside* consultants or experts.

The second component of the evaluation process is the explicit *identification of the program (or process) to include its component parts.* As was the case with objectives, the police administrator who tells us that *he has a delinquency prevention program* has in fact told us very, very little. To understand his program would require some considerable detail about such basics as who is involved and why, and how did they get involved and when, the degree or extent

[1]The approach outlined below has been successfully utilized for program evaluation at the Delinquency Control Institute of the University of Southern California and at the California Youth Authority Juvenile Law Enforcement Officers' Training Course. Police participants, examining police programs and following the model step-by-step, have found the procedure to be useful.

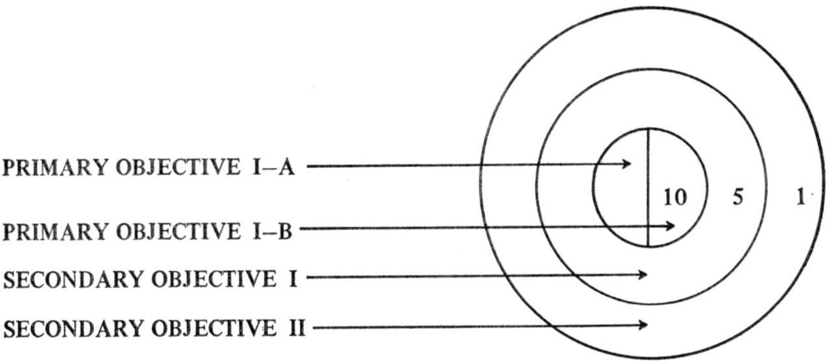

Figure 22-1 Objectives

of involvement, the specific nature of the program and so on. For model construction purposes, a neat symetrical representation of *program* is inappropriate, for if all the components of a program cannot be identified: there are pieces which are elusive or hidden and there are some, the existence of which are unsuspected. Accordingly, our model presentation for program, Figure 22-2, is somewhat *amoeba-like* with most, but not all, components identified. The unknown elements are identified by *x*.

When objective and program are fused together into the model, the thrust of evaluation becomes evident, as shown in Figure 22-3. Programs are evaluated against—or in terms of—objectives.

Evaluation cannot exist in a vacuum and be solely an examination of program components and objectives. There is a requirement for development of a type or types of measures to determine how well programs and objectives mesh. Thus, the third element in the process of evaluation is the *development of one or more measures or standards or criteria* for evaluation. These measures may be few or many, simple or complex; but, as was the case for objectives and programs, they should be precise, explicit, and identifiable by the police administrator. Since these standards serve as the measuring device to determine the fit of program to objective, the model utilizes a simulated ruler as in Figure 22-4. The ruler for this model is six units long, with units here representing cost, time, personnel, ease of operations, politics, and effort required. The ruler may be longer or shorter with finer or coarser units, or with different and varying units of measure.

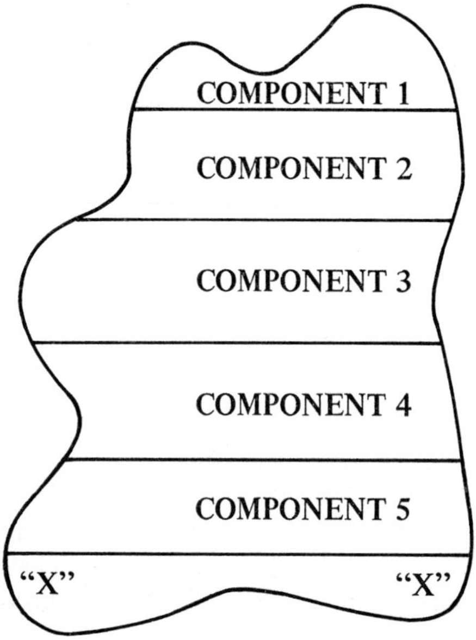

Figure 22-2 Programs

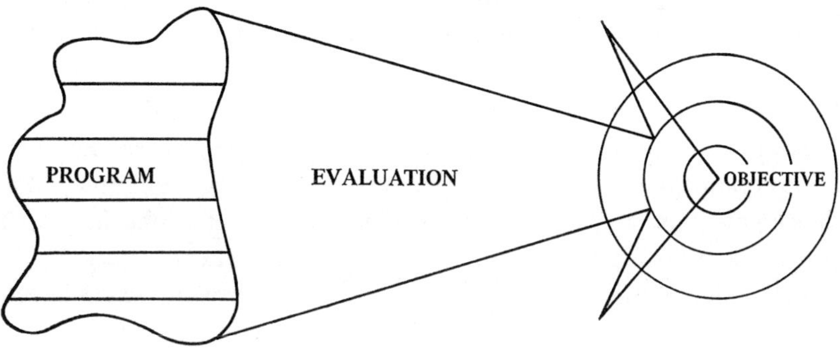

Figure 22-3 Direction of evaluation

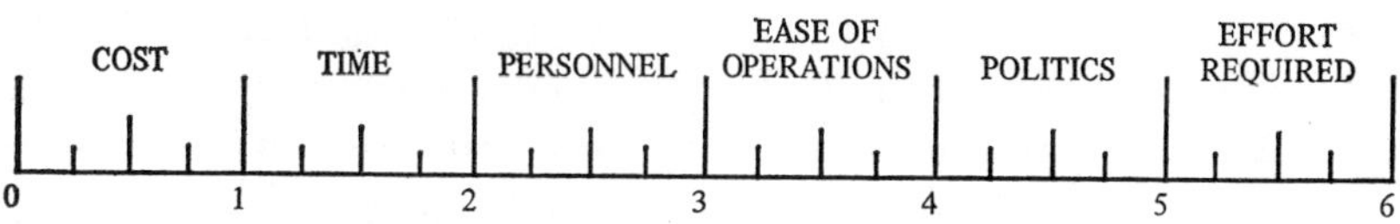

Figure 22-4 Measures, standards or criteria

At this point, three of the four elements of evaluation have been identified: objectives, programs and standards, and it has been pointed out that the police administrator should have fairly complete knowledge of the specific components of each of these three elements without recourse to *expertise* from outside his agency. The fourth element of concern is methodology. *Methodology provides the techniques for evaluation* and focuses on four questions—who, when, where, and how? These questions may take the following form: "*who* will do the evaluation—the agency itself or consultants from the outside?"; "*when* will it be done—at the beginning of the program, during the life of the program, or at program termination?"; "*where* will the evaluation be done—within the agency, in a research division, on a campus?"; and, "*how* will the evaluation be done—by computer, by subjective techniques, or by tic marks drawn on a yellow tablet?" Although it is possible that the administrator will not know the answers to these and related methodology questions, he should be aware of the questions. They are recurring regardless of the nature of the evaluation task. Figure 22-5 presents the completed model for the evaluation process.

The model presented has focused on the evaluation of a single *program* against one or more *objectives* by a set of *standards* utilizing a specific *methodology*. The model did not assume the existence of alternative programs—that is, a Program *A and* a Program *B, or*

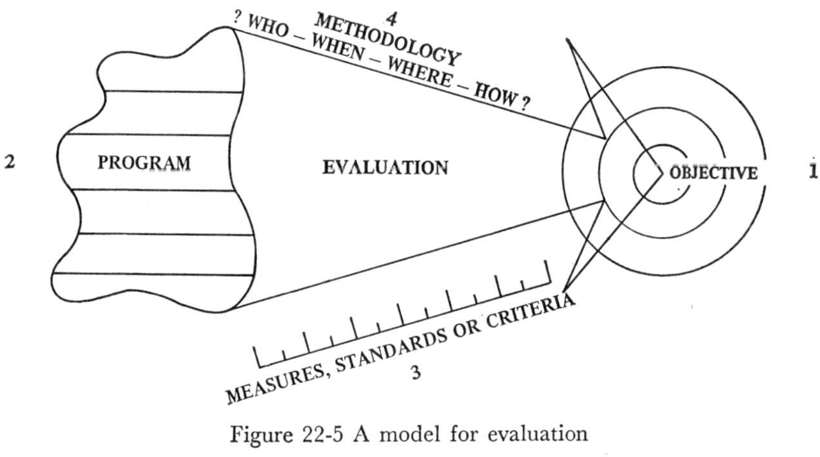

Figure 22-5 A model for evaluation

C. But if alternatives exist, and this is the common experience, there must be a determination as to which of the program alternatives available is most appropriate in terms of the agency and its operations.

In comparing two or more programs, it is absolutely essential to recognize that an accurate evaluation is impossible if there are different standards or methodologies or changed objectives. Simply put, Program *A* and *B* cannot be evaluated, one against the other, if objectives are changed or if different sets of standards or methodologies are used. One simple evaluation guideline exists for comparison of programs. Of the four variables, objectives, programs, standards, and methodologies, *only* programs may be varied; all else must remain constant. In short, programs cannot be compared if we use different targets, different rules for measurement, or different questions or methodologies. The model for this kind of evaluation appears in Figure 22-6. Note that only program varies.

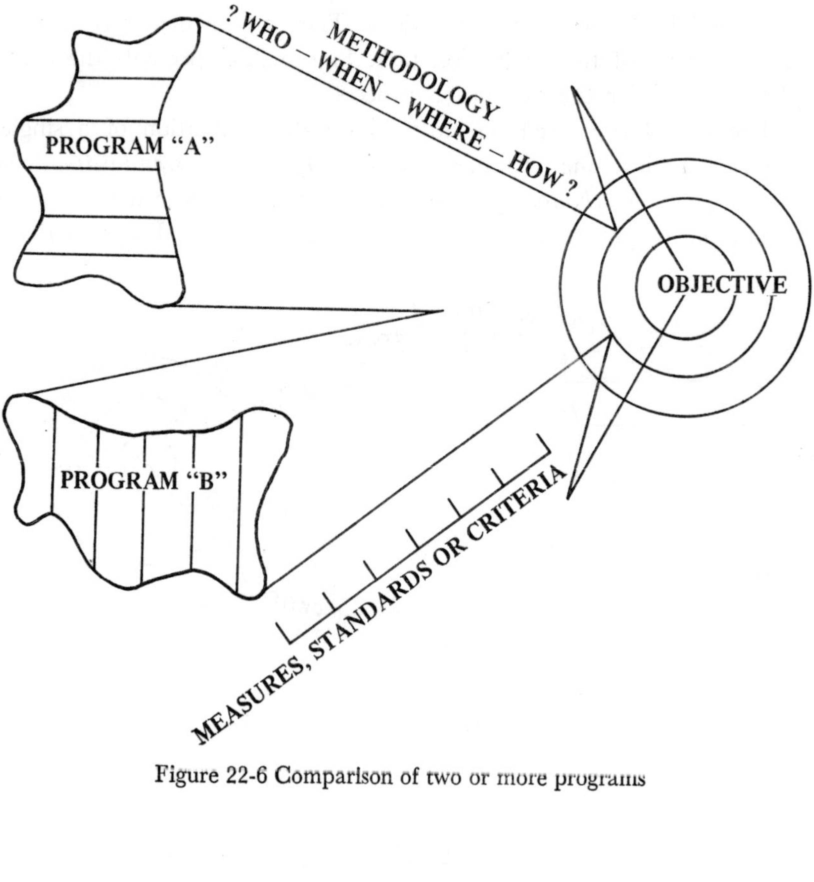

Figure 22-6 Comparison of two or more programs

When alternative programs are evaluated against identical objectives, using common standards and the same methodology, a determination as to which program is the most appropriate of the alternatives is made by the use of two criteria. The first is *best fit;* the second is an analysis of the alternatives by each of the standards. *Best fit* is simply the determination of how well each program achieves the stated objectives. Program *A* covers or achieves less than one-half of the target objective; Program *B* encompasses all of the primary objectives and part of the secondary objectives. Clearly *B* is the *best fit* of program and objectives.

In the event two different programs have a similar *best fit,* a comparison of the program is made by *analysis of each of the standards in order of their priority.* Under this condition, and using a ruler similar to that presented earlier, the two different programs would be examined by establishing first a priority of standards, i.e., first priority is cost, second is operational ease, third is effort, and so on, and then determining how the programs compare one with the other. Thus, we ask . . . how do these programs compare as to cost?, how do they compare in the ease of implementation into current operations?, and how do they compare as to effort required? If minimum cost is the essential standard and *A* is three times that of *B,* then *B* is the obvious choice. If the costs are identical, but *A* may become operational with less difficulty than *B,* and all other standards are more or less equal, *A* is the appropriate choice. If cost and operational ease are similar for both programs, we proceed to the next standard —and the one after that—until one alternative is a clear choice over

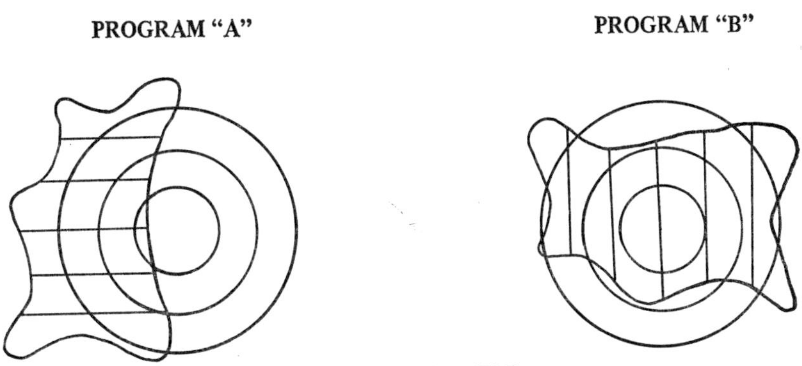

Figure 22-7 "Best Fit"

the other. A simple format for such a review of standards appears in Figure 22-8. In that illustration, Program *A* has a clear advantage over *B*.

In summary, evaluation has been examined as a process and in terms of a simple model which indicates that there are four major

PROGRAM "A" PROGRAM "B"

PRIORITIES (High → Low)

MEASURES, STANDARDS OR CRITERIA	PROGRAM "A"	PROGRAM "B"
"BEST FIT"	=	=
COST	+	-
TIME	+	-
PERSONNEL	+	-
EASE OF OPERATIONS	-	+
POLITICS	=	=
EFFORT REQUIRED	+	-

Figure 22-8 Different programs with identical "Best Fit" and review of standards

and essential components. It has been suggested that a plan for evaluation starts with objectives and flows through programs, standards, and methodologies. As a practical matter, these components may be combined in the development of a plan of evaluation, but it must be emphasized that they are independent of one another and, at some point, must be isolated and examined separately. Further, it has been noted and emphasized that the police administrator must have first-hand knowledge about the objectives, programs, and standards and should at least be aware of several basic questions as related to methodology.

Substantial funds under various federal and state legislation are currently available to law enforcement agencies for innovative crime prevention programs and other activities. Almost without exception, application for research-based, action or demonstration grants require a plan for evaluation. The police administrator must become familar with the process of evaluation, whether seeking grant funds or simply making decisions about ongoing or contemplated operation. Evaluation is a function of administration and a requirement for the administrator.

SECTION TEN

LEGAL ASPECTS

CHAPTER 23

THE CURRENT STATUS OF JUVENILE LAW

MARTIN LEVINE

I. INTRODUCTION

THIS REVIEW OF the current state of juvenile court case law and statutes is intended for those working within the juvenile justice system who seek a systematic summary.

It should be taken with several grains of salt.

First, the doctrine outlined here is not that of any given jurisdiction, but a nation-wide synthesis.

Second, doctrine varies from practice—as the practitioners have always known, and as the legal realists have drummed into the heads of the scholars.

Also to be considered is the intractability of the world to the most well-intentioned of man's plans for both these reasons.

Third, announced purposes differ from actual effects. (The sociologists have a phrase about the *unanticipated consequences of purposeful social action.)*

Juvenile courts were set up to provide minors with all the benfits of an enlightened and informal paternalism, and to save them from the rigidity of the criminal law. In recent years, scholars, courts and legislatures have drawn back from this classic stance—not sure that the paternalism has been of much help to the juveniles, and suspecting that the protection of criminal law procedure may do the young offender more good than harm.

This counter-current has two immediate results for those studying juvenile law: The high-minded rationale propounded by some is subjected to cold-eyed scrutiny by others; and one must therefore tread with caution in predicting whether the future development of any given rule with favor traditional, informal paternalism or the more recent analogizing with criminal law.

II. THE PHILOSOPHY OF THE JUVENILE JUSTICE SYSTEM

A. *The System in General*

The juvenile justice complex includes the juvenile court, law enforcement agents,[1] probation officers,[2] other corrections officials,[3] and social workers.[4] The court itself may be a special and independent entity whose sole task is to handle juvenile matters or it may be a special branch or session of a trial level court with general criminal or civil jurisdiction.

The *philosophy* of the juvenile justice system differs from that of the criminal or civil courts in several ways. Most obvious is its goal—*rehabilitation* of the child rather than punishment, or settling of disputes. As to procedure, juvenile courts are traditionally nonadversary in form,[5] the stress has been on informality, and great discretion is granted to police and *intake* officers to dispose of the case at early stages, diverting the juvenile from the court.

B. *The Rehabilitative Model*

The juvenile justice system, in theory, is totally committed to serving the *best interests of the child,* and thus to rehabilitation. For example, the juvenile court holds its records confidential so that a citizen formerly involved in juvenile proceedings may answer *no* if asked if he has ever been *arrested, detained,* or *involved.*[6] Early reformers believed that the system's role in dealing with juveniles was to ascertain "What he is, how has he become what he is, and what had best be done in his interest and in the interest of the state to save him from a downward career."[7] To do this, the most effective procedure would be to abandon the procedures with which courts dealt with adults and instead to have the judge "seated at a desk, with the child at his side where he can on occasion put his arm around his shoulder and draw the lad to him."[8]

C. *The Legal Model*

Whether or not the juvenile courts were successful in helping to meet the social and psychological needs of the children who came before them, many critics felt that they were not observing procedural fairness. One response has been statutes such as the New York law which recognizes also the purpose "to provide a due process of law" in juvenile courts.[8a]

Another reaction has been in the courts, most notably the constitutional protections recently enunciated by the United States Supreme Court. Not until 1967 did the Supreme Court first speak directly to the juvenile court institution, and since that time several major decisions by the court have been handed down. These decisions by the court dealt with the so-called *waiver* and *adjudication* stages in which it is decided whether to deal with a youth as a juvenile or *waive* him into the criminal system, and whether the youth is to be adjudicated as subject to the court's authority as a *juvenile delinquent*. In *Kent v. United States,*[9] a waiver case, the Supreme Court held that there must be "procedural regularity sufficient in the particular circumstances to satisfy the basic requirement of due process and fairness,"[10] specifically that a juvenile is entitled to representation by counsel, a hearing, access by council to the *social records* and other reports presumably considered by the court in rendering its decision, and a statement of reasons by the juvenile court for its decision.

The following year, the court went beyond *Kent* in requiring extensive procedural safeguards in adjudication proceedings which could lead to commitment. *In re Gault*[10a] required that advance notice be given of the adjudication hearing; that the juvenile have the right to counsel; that he have the right of confrontation and cross-examination; and that he be afforded the protection of the privilege against self-incrimination.

The court broadly criticized the informality which persumably had been justified by the rehabilitative purposes of juvenile courts:

> The absence of substantive standards has not necessarily meant that children receive careful, compassionate, individualized treatment. The absence of procedural rules based upon constitutional principles has not always produced fair, efficient, and effective procedures. Departures from estab-

lished principles of due process have frequently resulted not in enlightened procedure, but in arbitrariness.[11]

The Supreme Court again spoke to the juvenile court adjudication stage three years later. *In re Winship*[12] held that the case against the child must be proven beyond a reasonable doubt.

After these three cases, one might have concluded that all of the procedural protections previously help applicable to adult criminal trials were hereafter to govern juvenile proceeding as well. However, in a 1971 Supreme Court case, *McKiever v. Pennsylvania,*[13] the court rejected the contention that juveniles are entitled to a jury trial in the adjudication stage (as essential to fundamental fairness, and therefore constitutionally required.) The court declared that establishment of such a right would remake the proceedings into a fully adversary process and that there would be no longer a reason for the juvenile court system's separate existence. Instead, the court retained the idea of an intimate, informal, protective system.

D. *Future Statutory Development*

The development of juvenile court statues in the foreseeable future is likely to be influenced by two recent model proposals both of which reflect a counter-reaction against traditional informality.

The Uniform Juvenile Court Act was prepared by the National Conference of Commissioners on Uniform State Laws in 1968, and has already been adopted by at least one state.[14] One writer thinks it will eventually be adopted by most states.[15] The most salient characteristics include the following: The statute would provide extensive procedual rights to children and their parents appearing in the juvenile court, including the right to counsel, at public expense if necessary;[16] it would provide a classification of *unruly* children[17] covering offenses applicable only to children, such as smoking and truancy; simplified procedures for interstate juvenile problems; and a review of commitments at least every two years.[18]

Another statutory proposal[19] was developed in 1969, and takes an even stronger stand on procedural rights than the Uniform Act. It provides for a non-waivable right to counsel in delinquency and need of supervision cases;[20] and includes provisions barring double jeopardy.[21] It also stresses the use of community agencies other than the courts to deal with juveniles, when possible,[22] and provides for time limits to speed up the court processes and prevent long delays before hearings, especially where the child is held in detention or shelter care.[23]

Recommendations as to the next steps in juvenile justice will be forthcoming in 1972 from another source. The Institute of Judicial Administration is formulating national standards of juvenile justice under a grant from the National Institute of Law Enforcement and Criminal Justice, a United States Justice Department agency. The advisory committee of judges, scholars and lawyers is headed by United States Circuit Judge Irving R. Kaufman.[23a]

III. SUBSTANTIVE LAW

The *substantive law* of the juvenile courts defines which children fall within the authority of the court:[23b] in general, the categories of *delinquents, persons in need of supervision,* and those who are *neglected.*[23c]

A. *Criminal Conduct by Children—"Delinquency"*

A common statutory definition of *delinquency* is conduct that violates penal law, including a state criminal code, municipal ordinance, and federal law (as well as, at times, the laws of sister states).[24] In addition, *delinquency* may include acts that would not be criminal if done by adults.[25]

Sometimes the fact that a child is involved is taken account of by the court in differentiating between the categories of children's *delinquency* and adult's *crimes*. For example, while Section 602 of the California Welfare and Institutions Code provides that any minor who violates "any laws of this state" that define a crime, comes under the jurisdiction of the juvenile court, the Supreme Court of California has held that in order for a child under the age of fourteen to become a ward of the court under Section 602, clear proof must be shown that at the time of committing the act the child appreciated its wrongfulness.[26]

The Minor Ordinance as a Special Case—the Problem of Overinclusion:

The argument has been made that our society has over-relied on the criminal sanctions,[27] and this point has special force in the area of juvenile court jurisdiction. A jurisdiction encompassing *all* penal law violations includes such activities as littering the streets, and behavior so broadly defined cannot be taken as always identifying a child who is in need of rehabilitative help.

Existing laws sometimes attempt to narrow slightly the scope of jurisdiction in this area. For example, the Texas Juvenile Act,[28] defines a delinquent child as one who "*habitually* so deports himself as to injure or endanger the morals or health of himself or others," (emphasis added) and the statute was recently upheld against an attack on the grounds of unconstitutional vagueness,[27] (although a petition alleging only that a child "habitually violated the penal ordinances" is too vague to give the court jurisdiction where it did not also specify *which* ordinances were violated.[30])

The Serious Offense as a Special Case:

Some states provide that the most serious offenses—such as murder or rape—must always be tried in a criminal court, regardless of the age of the offender. However, the tendency of legislative reform has been toward eliminating these exceptions. In Massachusetts now, for example, a child within the appropriate age limits is within the exclusive jurisdiction of the juvenile court regardless of the offense charged.[31]

The Defense of Insanity:

The courts have split as to whether the defense of insanity should be allowed to bar an adjudication of delinquency. The Wisconsin Supreme Court has upheld insanity as a defense to a charge of juvenile delinquency, barring any adjudication in such a case.[32] On the other hand, a New Jersey Juvenile and Domestic Relations Court has recently held that an insanity defense does not bar the adjudication itself, though a juvenile who has been adjudicated delinquent based upon an anti-social act committed while insane cannot be subjected to penal sanctions.[33]

It is possible to reconcile these seemingly contrary results by recognizing that each court was following its state's available procedure for committing the child to an inpatient treatment institution.

Confinement:

A common problem is that children are being confined for a much longer period than would adults convicted of the same offense. In a Texas case[33] the child, aged sixteen, argued that he faced confinement for a period of almost five years for carrying a switchblade knife, while an adult who engaged in the same conduct could not be confined for over one year. This difference in treatment, he claimed, violated the equal protection and due process clauses of the Fourteenth Amendment.

The Court upheld the difference in treatment: finding the varying terms of confinement rational in view of the announced purposes of the juvenile system in educating, treating, and rehabilitating the child, rather than in punishing him for a crime. Thus an announced non-punitive purpose was held to justify infliction of a greater sanction.

Other courts have used much the same rationale to justify different periods of confinement for juveniles and adults who have engaged prohibited conduct.[34]

Non-Criminal Conduct—"Semi-Delinquency"

Unruly children and PINS (Persons In Need Of Supervision). The Uniform Juvenile Court Act includes within the juvenile court's jurisdiction *unruly* children,[35] while the New York statute includes *persons in need of supervision.*[36] Children brought under the court's powers under these semi-delinquency headings are also defined as those who are in danger of leading *an idle dissolute, lewd, or immoral life.*[37] These terms have generally been upheld against attacks for unconstitutional vagueness.[38]

The Necessity of Specifying *Need for Treatment:*

Some states have legislation requiring that more than deviant behavior be found in order for a child to be brought under the jurisdiction of the juvenile court. Thus the New York Family Court Act provides that in a petition in a delinquency case, the allegation must be made that the child "requires supervision, treatment, or confinement,"[39] while a petition to adjudicate a child as in need of supervision must state that he "requires supervision or treatment,"[40] It has been suggested that such a requirement is necessary in order to justify, under the constitution, the departure from criminal procedures.[41] Whether the evidence in specific cases—or in any case, given the state of knowledge of behavioral science—can support such a finding, remains an open question.

Traffic Offenses:

Most juvenile court acts which create jurisdiction on the basis of violations of the penal law include traffic offenses within that jurisdiction,[42] leaving it open to the juvenile court to waive jurisdiction and remand to the traffic court.

The trend in legislation, however, seems to be to exclude from juvenile court jurisdiction those children who violate traffic laws.[43] At least one court has noted that sometimes the interests of a juvenile traffic offender require the help of a juvenile court, and in a case of vehicular homicide has decided that for jurisdictional purposes it would be treated as a felony, within the jurisdiction of the juvenile court.[44]

Regulation of Juvenile Behavior Through Police and Courts

Many things which adults may do lawfully become matters of concern to the police and the courts if a minor does them.

The excuse is sometimes given that only the law enforcement apparatus has the access to information and the personnel needed to deal with juvenile behavior problems. The police department is the only agency with men on the street, in all areas of the city, twenty-four hours a day ready to receive complaints, intervene promptly, and follow through till an authoritative disposition is made.

Objections have been raised that using law enforcement to handle juvenile problems results in stigmatizing the young persons involved, depriving them of the measure of autonomy other young persons possess, and exposing them to brutalizing experiences. These objections are sometimes answered by invoking the paternalistic philosophy of the juvenile courts. And whether the objections are valid depends on the extent police and courts can approximate the ideal of a benevolent juvenile system.

Occasionally the courts have acted to strike down a substantive rule which would render juveniles—but not adults—subject to the intervention of police and courts for *non-criminal* behavior. Thus, juvenile curfews have been held unconstitutional as unlawful discrimination[45] and as "unlawful invasion of personal rights and liberties."[46]

C. *Neglect and Dependency*

Most statutes allow juvenile courts broad discretion over the custody and control of *neglected* or *dependent* children through the doctrine of sovereign power of guardianship over minors, *parens patriae.* Neglect may be held to arise on the basis of parental omission or commission, such as abandonment of a child, or failure to provide *necessities* for a child's health and well-being.[47] At times the statute will refer to some fault on the part of the parents, or to *improper guardianship.*[48] Cruel and excessive corporal punishment may also be deemed to constitute parental neglect,[49] as well as giving rise to a criminal charge of assault and battery.

Dependency statutes make no reference to the child's *fault.* A child may be deemed *dependent* if he has no parent (or guardian), or if he lacks proper care due to the physical or mental incapacity of his parent; or if his parent *with good cause* wishes to give up his responsibilities for the child.[50] The trend in legislative thinking, however, is to limit the scope of the dependency jurisdiction of the juvenile court and instead utilize administrative handling by social welfare agencies.[51]

There may well be overlap between the juvenile court's neglect and dependency jurisdiction, on the one hand, and its delinquency jurisdiction, on the other. For example, a child may be adjudicated *delinquent* for the violation of a penal law, but the reason for his criminal behavior may be because of his home environment, so that he is also *neglected.* To handle a situation such as this, the New York law allows the court, on its own motion, to substitute a neglect petition instead of an original petition alleging either delinquency or the semi-delinquency status of a "person in need of supervision."[52]

IV. THE ROLE OF LAW ENFORCEMENT AGENTS

A. *In General*

The functions of law enforcement agents with respect to juvenile offenders encompass several roles:[52a]

—questioning,[53] searches,[54] and other investigation;[55]

—screening out cases which come to the attention of the authorities, before they arrive at the juvenile court;[56]

—initiating juvenile proceedings by taking the juvenile into custody;[57,58]

—taking measures to prevent juvenile delinquency.[59]

B. *The Role of Police in Taking the Child Into Custody*

Sources of the Governing Law:

The law pertaining to taking juveniles into custody is based on general arrest statutes, juvenile court statutes, the common law, and constitutional limitations on official interferences with personal freedom.

Stop and Frisk:

The Constitution permits police to detain an adult suspect on the street in order to question him, for an adequate cause less conclusive than that which would sustain an arrest;[59a] and a limited search for weapons dangerous to the officer is permitted incident to this investigative stop.[60] A similar power as to juveniles was approved in *In re Lang,*[61] where in response to a report of an impending gang fight, police went to the street where the fight was to occur. The Family Court of New York County held that in such a situation, even though there was no cause at that time for an arrest, the police were authorized to detain boys on the street for questioning and search.

Arrest for *Crime*[61a]

As to adults, arrest is possible with or without a warrent, but in either case the federal Bill of Rights determines the limits of the law enforcement process, and the police must meet the requirement of probable cause to believe that a felony took place and that the suspect did it—warrantless misdemeanor arrests are further restricted to these *viewed* by the officer. As to children, "all of the juvenile court acts grant a wholly unqualified right to arrest a child who has violated the penal law."[62] This statutory power may be interpreted as subject to the same Constitutional requirements, however, since the case *of In re Gault* held that juveniles are entitled to the *fundamental fairness* guaranteed by the Fourteenth Amendment Due Process Clause;[63] (it should be noted, however, that McKeiver v. Pennsylvania has held that the requirements of fundamental fairness do not necessitate the application to juvenile court proceedings of *all* the safeguards given to adults in criminal proceedings.)[64]

Protective Custody and *Arrest* of Semi-Delinquents:

While the Fourth Amendment sets limits to arresting activity, it is nevertheless true that a child may constitutionally be taken into custody in situations which would not justify arrest of an adult. Statutes and court decisions grant this enlarged power out of a *paternal* concern for protecting children from harmful surroundings. The Uniform Juvenile Court Act of 1968, for example, authorizes taking a child into custody if there are reasonable grounds to believe that the child is suffering from illness or injury or is in immediate danger from his surroundings, and his removal is necessary.[65]

The authority to take a child into temporary custody without a warrant is not always coextensive with the scope of the juvenile court's jurisdiction over children, as granted by juvenile court statutes. In some states, not all, police may act if the court could make a finding of delinquency or waywardness with respect to him; or who has violated an order of the juvenile court; or who has escaped from a reform school; or who should be taken into custody *for his own protection.*[65a]

Non-Arrest Proceedings:

Criticism has been leveled at permissive authority for taking children into custody without warrants. Especially with respect to the neglected, the truant, and the disobedient, it is contended that these children should not be taken from familiar surroundings and exposed to the uncomfortable and perhaps traumatizing experience of being arrested. Instead, the suggestion has been made that the legal process begin with a summons to the parents, with a summons also to the child if he is old enough to understand the obligation to appear in court.[66]

C. *Detention and Notice*

Alternatives for the Arresting Officer:

Once a case has come to the attention of the authorities, an officer may have a wide range of alternatives with which to deal with the juvenile, often including all of the following: (1) field release of the child, perhaps with an informal warning, but without making an official record or taking further action; (2) field release of the child, but writing up a *field report* for the juvenile bureau; (3) taking the juvenile to the station house and later releasing him to the custody of his parents; (4) referring him to a community social service agency; (5) immediately turning the youth over to the juvenile bureau; (6) taking the juvenile directly to the station house for juvenile court processing; (7) referring the case directly to the juvenile court.[67]

Arrest and the Requirement of Notice to Parents:

An arresting officer is commonly required to give notice to a child's parents after he has been taken into custody,[67a] usually after the child has been taken to the station house.

This practice of immediately taking a child to a police facility has been criticized on the grounds that the child should be spared such an intimidating experience, especially since the system of juvenile justice purports to place his welfare in a paramount position. The suggestion has been made that the child should always be taken immediately to a special juvenile facility, with no stopover whatsoever at the station.[68]

Police Screening: Standards for Decision:

The importance of the police screening power may be seen from the statistics showing that the majority of juveniles who appear in court are police referrals, and that half to two-thirds of all police contacts are handled without referral.[69]

In some cities, police hold hearings to determine whether or not a case requires the attention of the court.[70] If a child confesses at the hearing, officers still have open to them several of the alternatives listed above.

Standards for deciding how to deal with the child, whether or not a police hearing is held, may include any of the following critieria: the seriousness of the offense allegedly committed; whether the child has previously appeared before the juvenile court; whether the child and his parents have been unable or unwilling to cooperate with the non-authoritative agencies or benefit from them; and whether the juvenile has a record of repeated delinquency extending over a period of time.[71] Sometimes referral to the juvenile bureau, probation department or court is made mandatory by a juvenile court statute, especially if the offense involved is a felony or a crime of violence.[72]

D. *Questioning the Child*

The Application of the Miranda Rule:

The requirements of *Miranda v. Arizona*[73] should be followed in the juvenile court process.[74] In accordance with this procedure, a child in custody must be advised that he need not answer questions or make a statement; that anything he says may be used against him; that he has the right to have an attorney with him during any discussion with police, and that if he cannot afford an attorney, one will be provided for him; and that he may discontinue answering questions at any time.

The child should also be told "the crime he . . . may be charged with, the seriousness of the crime, the penalty and the punishment that could be inflicted."[76]

And the juvenile's claim that he is an adult is not sufficient to excuse the officer from the duty of properly warning him.[77] The child's parent should be notified of the proposed interrogation and—some authorities say—it should take place in their presence, and in the home.[78]

Waiver:

The Supreme Court has noted in excluding confessions obtained from juveniles, that they may not fully appreciate a warning of rights or have full freedom of choice in waiving them.[79] The child's maturity, his intelligence, his knowledge of the rights he is waving, the situation in which he is being questioned, are all relevant to the determination of validity of the supposed waiver.

In determining whether a juvenile has the legal capacity to waive his *Miranda* rights, the same problems arise as are discussed as to waiver in the paragraph The Problem of Searching the Child's Home below. Some guidance may be had from a recent decision of the California Supreme Court, *In re M.*,[80] where a fifteen-year old boy was informed two separate times of his *Miranda* rights before making statements, and where the juvenile appeared to be of normal intelligence; the court held that *the totality of circumstances* did not lend itself to the conclusion that the boy should be held incompetent to have waived his rights.

The Exclusionary Rule:

Admissions made by a child without a lawyer during in-custody questioning may be introduced into evidence only by the normal *Miranda* showing that the applicable warnings were given and that the rights to silence and to counsel were intelligently and knowingly waived without coercion.[81] A recent Supreme Court case has modified the *Miranda* doctrine itself, however, to allow even statements prohibited by *Miranda* to be used for impeachment purposes if the defendant decides to testify at trial.[82] Statements obtained by physical or mental coercion would remain totally inadmissible at trial.[28a]

E. *Searches*

Sources for the Law:

Unlike the matter of arrests, searches in delinquency cases are usually not controlled by juvenile court statutes. The juvenile system has established few guidelines for those investigating juvenile delinquency. This has primarily been the result of reliance on the doctrine of *parens patriae,* which assumes that because the state is acting in place of the parent and is doing what is best for the child, there is no reason to protect the juvenile from unreasonable governmental interference. Thus the applicable law in this area deals mainly with constitutional limits on searches and seizures.

Searches of Body and Place Arrested:

Juvenile court statutes considering the right of an officer to search a child frequently follow the law developed in adult cases. Thus in

People v. Marsh,[83] the court used the general rule in search and seizure cases that a search without warrant is reasonable if made incident to an arrest, and if probable cause exists for that arrest.

The *Marsh* holding must be limited by more recent adult cases. When an arrest is made, the United States Supreme Court has held *reasonable* the arresting officer's search of the *person* arrested. Further, an arresting officer may also search the *area* within the arrestee's *immediate control* in order to remove any weapons which might be used to resist an arrest or effect an escape, but such a search without a warrant may not extend to rooms other than that in which the arrest occurs.[84] This rule has been further elucidated in a recent Supreme Court decision, holding that if the search of a house without a warrant is to be constitutionally valid as incident to an arrest, the arrest must have taken place *inside* the house.[85]

The Problem of Searching the Child's Home:

Search of a home, without either a search warrant or an arrest, may be legitimate if consent is given, which essentially is a wavier of Fourth Amendment rights. When consent to such a search is made by a juvenile, the problem arises as to whether he has the legal capacity to waive that Constitutional protection. Considerations to be taken into account in determining a child's legal capacity are his maturity, his intelligence, and his knowledge of the rights he is waivng.

A further problem concerns the child's standing to waive his parent's right of privacy. It has been said that a minor living in the home probably cannot give a valid consent to a search of the parental home in the absence of his parents.[86]

The converse problem is raised when consent to search the home is given by the parent, not the child. Although ordinarily one may not waive another's constitutional rights, in cases where a child has objected to evidence obtained from searches with the parent's consent, the objection has generally been rejected and the evidence admitted.[87]

Searches in the School:

In a recent case, a juvenile was instructed by his high school principal to empty his pockets and complied by taking out some marijuana and placing it on the principal's desk. The juvenile argued that the marijuana was recovered by unreasonable search and seizure in violation of his Fourth Amendment rights. The Court of Civil Appeals of Texas rejected that argument, concluding that the principal, in insisting that the boy empty his pockets, acted in a *private capacity* in *loco parentis,* and not as an arm of the government.[88]

In a case reaching a similar result by another line of reasoning, it was held that a high school principal fulfilled an appropriate function in inspecting a suspected delinquent's locker, in that the school official had a right to prevent lockers being used to harbor stolen property or harmful substances.[89]

F. *Other Aspects*

Lineups and Other Forms of Identification:

The United States Supreme Court has held that an accused has the right to counsel at a police lineup. In order for in-court identification by a witness, based on such a lineup, to be admitted, counsel must have been present at the lineup (unless the right to counsel was waived).[90] The rule has already been held to apply to juvenile cases by at least one court.[91]

As far as fingerprinting is concerned, most states imply authority for the use of such a procedure, though there may be restrictions on the fingerprinting of juveniles in certain circumstances.[92] Although arguments have been made against the fingerprinting of juveniles, other authorities see a need for positive identification.[93]

Discovery:

According to some authorities, police may have a duty of informing the child or his attorney of evidence gathered.[94] An important consideration here is that discovery is a rapidly changing field, and recent statutory and case law in the local jurisdiction must be consulted to insure that the appropriate procedures are being followed.

The Preventive Aspect of Police Work:

The prevention of crime through recreation and *character-building* programs, as well as counseling services, has been undertaken by police departments in many communities.[95]

V. THE ROLE OF THE JUVENILE COURT (PROBATION) OFFICER—INTAKE AND ADJUSTMENT

A. *In General*[95a]

If a juvenile is released to his parents after being taken into custody, he is brought to the attention of the juvenile court by a "paper referral."[96] An officer of the juvenile court, usually a member of the probation staff, evaluates the facts of each case to determine how it should be handled. Through his inquiry the intake officer determines whether the juvenile court has jurisdiction,[97] makes judgments as to the sufficiency of the evidence, and decides whether or not court action is desirable.[98] In 1967, 53 per cent, (423,000) of all cases referred to juvenile courts were handled without a judicial decision.[99]

Although statutes in many states seem to require that there be an intake investigation,[100] it has been held that proceedings may begin even though no investigation has been made.[101] The statutes seldom make provisions for the juvenile to be represented by counsel at the intake hearing,[102] but the constitutional privilege against self-incrimination has been recognized as applicable in many of the juvenile court acts.[103] For example, the New York Family Court Act prohibits the use of statements made at the intake conference in a later fact-finding hearing.[104]

Another function of the intake procedure is to screen out of the judicial process children who are mentally ill. If a psychiatric problem is found, the officer may have the alternative of procuring therapy rather than proceeding with a petition. Some states allow the filing of a petition other than one alleging delinquency in order to permit the court to order treatment. For example, in California a person under the age of twenty-one may be adjudged a dependent child of the court "who is physically dangerous to the public because of a mental or physical deficiency, disorder or abnormality."[105]

B. *Procedure*

The first question facing the intake worker is whether the complaint appears to be within the jurisdiction of the juvenile court, whether the juvenile is within the statutory age limit.[106] The intake officer must next decide whether the evidence is sufficient to support the allegations of delinquency made in the complaint.[106a] The extent of the investigation made by the worker varies from jurisdiction to jurisdiction: in some areas the officer simply reviews the evidence presented, while in others he has to gather it.[107]

C. *The Decision to File a Petition*

Finally, the intake officer must decide whether the filing of a petition will be in the best interest of the child and the public.[108] At this time especially the officer may wish to hold a hearing, inviting the juvenile, his parents, and any complainants.[109] At such a conference, the officer may attempt to make an *adjustment* that will make further, i.e. involuntary, proceedings unnecessary.

The typical juvenile court statute provides that petitions should be filed when formal adjudication is in the interests of the public or the child, but it fails to specify the criteria which are to be used in making this decision,[110] leaving it solely to the discretion of the intake officer.

Other departments, however, supply strict standards which must be followed. For example, in New York City the juvenile court has given an express set of standards to the intake department: all contested cases, all crimes of violence or other serious offenses, and all cases involving juveniles with significant records must be referred to the juvenile court for adjudication.[111] In addition, a further check on the intake process is provided by the New York Family Act, which specifies that the intake officer has no power to prevent the filing of a petition in the court if the juvenile or his parents so desire.[112] A study of intake workers and their criteria for referring cases to the juvenile courts has shown that the usual practice is to adjust only admitted offenses; contested cases are regularly referred to the judge;[113] also important are the following factors: age of the child; previous record; family background; seriousness of the offense; and the attitudes of both the juvenile and his parents.[114] The significance of two additional factors has been suggested[115] the time of day when the act took place, and whether the child's home neighborhood is a high delinquency rate area. Also, the intake department may *adjust* certain cases though a complainant requests formal court action, in a case involving, a trivial or first offense which ordinarily would be dismissed without further action.[116]

D. *Alternatives to Trial*

Informal Adjustment (Probation):

Adjustment, or informal probation, represents an attempt to satisfy the complainant with a less severe remedy than juvenile court adjudication.[117]

Statutes dealing with adjustment procedures generally provide for three major elements: there should be voluntary adjustment conferences between the parties and the intake officers, statements made at such conferences should not be used against the child later in a fact-finding hearing, and adjustment conferences should continue only for a limited period.[118]

The use of informal probation with periodic conferences has been the subject of much controversy. For those who advocate its use, the argument is made that this procedure avoids the evils of formal adjudication and saves judicial time.[119] On the other hand, the criticism has been made that these procedures are too informal and do not offer sufficient protection of the juvenile's rights. For example, it has been noted that although informal procedures should be based on consent, it is doubtful whether there can be any real consent under the present processes[120] which are inherently coercive. The practice has been rejected by the Children's Bureau which would limit nonjudicial adjustment of delinquency cases to referral to a social agency and very brief conference with the child and his family.[121]

Referral to Another Social Agency:

Another alternative available to the intake official is referral of the case to another social welfare agency. The effectiveness of this referral in terms of help to the child depends to a great extent on whether there are enough child welfare agencies in the community, and their own policies regarding the juvenile court and children who have had court contact—(some refuse to take *troublemakers*).

Closing the Case:

The intake officer may, if the complaint is unwarranted, or the case is the child's first and involves a trivial offense, close the case without taking further action. The worker, of course, may take this opportunity to lecture the child and warn him against engaging in any nonconforming behavior in the future.

E. *Alternatives for Complainant if Petition not Filed*

The juvenile court acts provide conflicting answers as to whether the persons initiating the original complaint against the child need rest satisfied with the adjustment. For example, the New York statute provides that "the probation service may not prevent any person who wishes to file a petition under this article from having access to the court for the purpose."[122] California law gives the decision of the intake officer slightly more weight by giving the complainant the opportunity, not to file a petition with the court, but rather to have the officer's decision reviewed by the juvenile court.[123] On the other hand, the Uniform Juvenile Court Act takes a stronger stand, forbidding the filing of a petition unless an authorized official has determined that it "is in the best interest of the public and the child"[124] for the action to be commenced.

F. *Controversy in the Area*

The major controversy in this area surrounds the validity of discretionary, unofficial handling of juveniles by intake officers. In addition to the criticism of potential violations of the child's constitutional rights, there has been concern, particularly among law enforcement agents, that a case serious enough to be referred to the juvenile court should not be handled by an informal release of the child, with the intake officer rather than a judge assessing the danger to the community of such release.[125]

The President's Commission on Law Enforcement and Administration of Justice has furnished suggestions for intake procedures in the hopes of providing a more effective system:[126] Written guides and standards should be formulated and taught in an inservice training course; staff resources should be expanded; there should be full awareness of service opportunities and programs in the community; the staff should be able to gather sufficient background information on the child to make an intelligent selection of alternatives; the intake officer's discretion in deciding whether to dismiss the case or file a petition should be retained, but overly informal methods of control which are easily subject to abuse (such as informal probation with the filing of a petition as a penalty for violation) should be discarded in favor of institutionalized nonadjudicatory methods.

Another suggestion frequently made is that a role be provided for the lawyer at the intake stage.[127] Although officials usually feel that the advantage of the intake procedure is its informality and non-adversariness, it has been argued that this stage is the ideal point for legal representation to begin. The lawyer can, among other things, speak to legal jurisdictional requirements and make sure they are met, determine from the evidence if a prima facie case has been made out, and interpret the situation to the child and his parents.[128]

VI. THE ROLES OF JUDGE AND COURT OFFICER—THE HEARING PROCESS

A. *Pretrial Detention*

In General:

Juvenile Court Acts commonly require law enforcement agents to bring a child taken into custody to the court or to a detention facility if he is not released to his parents.[127] At either place the decision must be made whether to detain the child until the court hearing or to release him to his parents, and whether a petition should then be filed.

A decision to detain at this stage can be effective only for a limited time, usually for forty-eight hours,[128] within which time either a petition must be field against the child, or a detention hearing is held by the judge, or both, if the detention is to continue.[128c]

The Pretrial Detention Hearing:

The juvenile court statutes vary widely regarding the nature of the judicial detention hearing. In most jurisdictions, the law provides that the judge may continue the detention of a child pending trial, with no requirement that a hearing need be held on this issue.[129] On the other hand, other states provide not only for a hearing, but also for the child's right to counsel, privilege against self-incrimination, and notice of the charges.[130]

Criteria for the Decision to Detain:

Although some juvenile court acts do not provide any standards for the pretrial detention decision,[131] others give such general criteria as the need to insure public safety as well as to protect the child. The Uniform Juvenile Court Act, for example, sets forth the following guidelines:[132] "A child taken into custody shall not be detained or placed in shelter care prior to the hearing on the petition unless his detention or care is required to protect the person or property of others or of the child or because the child may abscond or be removed from the jurisdiction of the court or because he has no parent, guardian, or custodian or other person able to provide supervision and care for him and return him to the court when required."

In addition to statutory provisions, several courts have spoken to certain aspects of the pretrial detention hearing. The Supreme Court of California recently struck down a juvenile court's determination of detention, holding that the nature of the alleged offense cannot in itself constitute the basis for dentention.[133] The juvenile court had failed to consider the youth's case on its individual merits, and instead held him in custody under the court's policy that all those who had allegedly sold marijuana should be detained prior to the jurisdictional hearing. The U. S. Court of Appeals for the District of Columbia Circuit has held that the juvenile court judge may order detention for a child only if the court can "secure for him custody, care and discipline as nearly as possible equivalent to that which should have been given him by his parents."[134]

The Right to Bail:

Juvenile court statutes are divided on the question of whether a child in custody has a right to release on bail.[134a] Some states have expressly provided that the rules as to bail in criminal actions shall apply to juvenile court proceedings;[135] others have expressly provided that those rules shall not apply.[136] Statutory provisions for release to parents are regarded as an adequate substitute for bail,[137] and courts which have held that the constitution requires a hearing on probable cause, meeting due process standards, before children may be held in pretrial detention, have refrained from holding that there is a constitutional right to bail.[137a]

Considering this issue, one court has recently held that even though a juvenile has no right to a grand jury indictment, he does have a conditional right to release pending the adjudication hearing.[138]

B. *The Steps of the Hearing*

The Filing of the Petition:

Formal proceedings in the juvenile court begin with the filing of a document called the petition. Thereafter there is an attempt to obtain personal jurisdiction over the parents, and over the child if he is not in custody.[139]

As discussed above, the juvenile court acts vary in their requirements as to who may file the petition: from a state like California, which authorizes only the probation officer,[140] to a state like Illinois, which permits anyone to file a petition,[141] with states like New York specifying persons who may file the petition.[142]

The contents of the petition, usually governed by statute, commonly include the name and age of the child, the names and addresses of the parents, and a statement as to whether or not the child is in detention.[143] Other acts insist on an allegation of the child's need for treatment or confinement.[144]

Where the statute requires a statement of facts in the petition that brings the juvenile into the court's jurisdiction, there may be a question of whether sufficient facts have been alleged. In response to this problem, courts have held that specificity will be measured by the same standards as are required in criminal indictments or informations.[145] Unspecific allegations cast in the conclusory words of a statute, such as that the child *habitually violated penal ordinances*[146] or was a *delinquent neglected child,*[147] have been held insufficient to bring a child within the jurisdiction of the juvenile court. It has been held that where the petition alleges delinquency based on specific criminal conduct, and the evidence proves another crime, in such a situation a finding of delinquency cannot be sustained because of the variance.[148]

Jurisdictional Requirements:

Statutory provisions for children coming within the jurisdiction of the juvenile court usually contain two elements: age and conduct.[148a]

Although most legislation defining delinquency contains no lower age limit,[149] there is a common law tradition that no child under the age of seven years can be guilty of any crime.[150] For the few states which do specify a lower age limit, the policy of immunity for the very young is continued with respect to the delinquency jurisdiction of the juvenile courts.[151] It has been noted that even in states whose legislation does not specify a minimum age there have been no reported cases involving an allegation of delinquency against a child under the age of seven.[152]

As to persons in need of supervision,[153] also, some statutes do not provide a lower age limit, and most juvenile court legislation provides no lower age limit for cases within the court's neglect jurisdiction.[154]

Children between the ages of seven and fourteen years have also traditionally constituted a *special* class. At common law, juveniles within this group were presumed to lack the capacity to commit a crime, and the prosecution was required to prove beyond a reasonable doubt that the child knew right from wrong before he could be convicted.[155] Although efforts to assert this common law defense have been almost uniformly rejected,[156] the Supreme Court of California has recently upheld its application to delinquency proceedings.[157]

The juvenile court acts are uniform in providing some upper age limit for the court's jurisdiction. Most often that age is eighteen, a fact which the state must prove in a delinquency proceeding in order to establish the jurisdiction of the court.[158] Some states, like Illinois, provide a higher age for girls than for boys (seventeen and sixteen respectively).[159]

If a child commits a delinquent act while he is within the juvenile court age and is not brought to court until he has passed the age, most appellate courts have held that a juvenile court may not try the child for delinquency.[160] Others, however, have held that the court's jurisdiction is determined by the child's age at the time of the alleged offense.[161]

The Requirement of Notice:

It has long been held a requirement of due process that a court,[162] including a juvenile court,[163] may make an order affecting the rights of an individual only if it has acquired personal jurisdiction over him. In order for a court to have such jurisdiction over a party to an action, adequate steps must be taken to give notice to that party.

The U. S. Supreme Court has emphasized the notice requirements necessary in a juvenile court proceeding in the landmark decision of *In re Gault*[164]: "[t]he requirements [are] that the child and his parents or guardian be notified, in writing, of the specific charge or factual allegations to be considered at the hearing, and that such written notice be given at the earliest practicable time, and in any event sufficiently in advance of the hearing to permit preparation. Due process of law requires notice of the sort we have described—that is, notice which would be deemed constitutionally adequate in a civil or criminal proceeding."[165]

Juvenile court legislation generally provides for written notice, in the form of a summons, to be given to the child and his parents.[165] Service of the summons may be in the manner provided for in the rules of civil litigation,[167] generally requiring personal service of notice on the parent; on failing to locate him or his address service by publication; or else a certified mailing to his address.[168]

The Supreme Court in *Gault,* while requiring notice, also recognized the traditional rule that a court may obtain personal jurisdiction when the parents appear voluntarily in the court, thus waiving the right to timely written notice.[169]

Since the New York Family Court Act expressly states one of its purposes as providing due process in juvenile delinquency hearings, the juvenile has the right to a bill of particulars adding specificity to the petition's general notice.[170]

Venue and Transfer:

Since there are many juvenile courts sitting in different places in each state, it is important to know which court is the proper location to hear a child's case—in other words, where is venue proper.

Proper venue is generally covered by the state juvenile court act.

The laws are generally permissive, typically allowing the case to be brought, for example, in "either the juvenile court in the county in which a minor resides or in the county where the minor is found or in the county in which the acts take place or the circumstances exist which are alleged to bring [the] minor within the [jurisdiction] of the juvenile court."[171]

It is common for the court in which the case originates to have the discretion to transfer the matter to another county. For example, the Uniform Juvenile Court Act makes transfer to the county of residence discretionary prior to final disposition, but compulsory if the child has been found delinquent and other proceedings involving the same child are pending in the county where the juvenile resides[172]

The courts have split as to whether a child has a right to demand a change of venue. While the Maryland courts have found that the juvenile has no such constitutional or statutory right, the Indiana Supreme Court has reasoned that since a juvenile proceeding is a civil case, the question should be governed by the right to change of venue under the civil rules of court.[174]

The Right to Counsel:

The United States Supreme Court case of *In re Gault,*[175] considering the due process requirements governing delinquency proceedings which may result in commitment, expressly determined that the child and his parents must be notified of the child's right to be represented by counsel retained by them, of if they are unable to afford counsel, that counsel will be appointed to represent the child.

In determining whether a waiver of right to counsel is voluntary, one court spoke of considering the *totality of circumstances,*[176] while another held that the record must affirmatively show that the child and his parents, if indigent, were advised that an attorney could be provided for them, and refused, or if able to retain counsel elected not to do so.[177]

Juvenile Court acts often parallel the judge-made law py providing that the child and his parents must be "advised by the court of their constitutional rights," including "the right to be represented by counsel at every stage of the proceedings."[178]

The Plea:

Juvenile court legislation does not normally specify the type of formal response the child may make to a petition alleging circumstances which would bring him within the jurisdiction of the court.[179] However, whether the child denies the facts alleged or enters no plea,[180] a fact finding hearing is set up and the case proceeds to that stage of the process. In most cases, the child does not deny the charge. An admission from the child's attorney that the charges are valid is unacceptable;[181] the juvenile court judge must determine that the child himself has made the admission.

C. *Waiver Into The Adult Criminal Process*

In General:

The juvenile court has the discretion to exclude certain children by relinquishing its jurisdiction over them, leaving it to the prosecuting official to decide whether to proceed against them in a criminal court. This action may be known as waiver, transfer, or certification.[181a]

The consequences of waiver for a juvenile may be drastic. For example, in a recent case a fourteen year old tried in a criminal court as the result of a waiver received a sentence of life imprisonment.[182]

Juvenile court legislation has been interpreted as conferring upon the child a right to waiver proceedings in that court, and a failure to provide them has been held to deny a criminal court jurisdiction to hear the case.[181] Similarly, the record of the waiver hearing must reveal evidence upon which the juvenile court judge could have based his waiver decision.[182]

The Waiver Hearing:

The first United States Supreme Court case reviewing the actions of a juvenile court was *Kent v. United States*[183] involving a waiver hearing. A sixteen year old boy charged with housebreaking, robbery, and rape was waived into the adult criminal process by the Juvenile Court of the District of Columbia. No hearing was held; no findings were made by the court; the court stated no reasons for the waiver; the boy's counsel was denied access to a social service file which presumably was considered by the juvenile court in determining its waiver decision. At a jury trial, Kent was found guilty of housebreaking and robbery, and was sentenced to thirty to ninety years in prison. The Supreme Court reversed and remanded, holding that it is precondition to a valid waiver order that the juvenile be allowed representation by counsel, a hearing, access by counsel to the social records and reports considered by the court, and a statement of reasons for the juvenile court's decision.

The state courts have split as to whether the result in *Kent* was based on congressional legislation, so that the states would not be bound by the holding,[183] or was required by the Federal Constitution, so that the ruling would govern the states.[184] Where *Kent* is not considered as stating constitutional requirements, it has been held, for example, that the absence of a written statement of the reasons for the waiver decision is immaterial.[185]

The Waiver Investigation:

Juvenile court statutes commonly require that there be a background investigation and report made by the court staff to be considered by the judge in determining whether to waive a case. For example, the California law states: "the court shall cause the probation officer to investigate and submit a report on the behavioral patterns of the person being considered for unfitness."[186] If such a study is not made, it has been held that the waiver is not valid and any subsequent criminal proceedings are void.[187]

In *Kent,* the Supreme Court emphasized the right of the juvenile's attorney to access to any reports which would be considered in the waiver decision. State legislation often extends a similar right. Colorado, for example, provides that "Written reports and other materials relating to the child's mental, physical, and social history may be considered by the court, and the person or persons who prepared the report and other material shall appear and be subject to both direct and cross-examination."[188]

Criteria for the Waiver Decision:

Three criteria are commonly listed by juvenile court legislation for determining which children within the court's otherwise exclusive jurisdiction may be *waived:* the age of the child, the offense allegedly committed, and a prediction as to whether the child will continue to commit criminal offenses if juvenile court jurisdiction is retained. A fourth has been suggested by the Uniform Juvenile Court Act's prohibition of waiver with respect to a child who is committable to a mental institution.[189]

As to age, most statutes specify that only children in the upper reaches of the juvenile court's age jurisdiction may be waived.[190] The legislation refers to the child's age at the time the offense was allegedly committed.[191]

As to the offense, most legislation mentioning this criterion restricts waiver to children over the specified ago who are alleged to have committed an act which would constitute a felony if committed by an adult.[192]

As to prediction of future conduct, one form requires consideration of whether it is possible through the juvenile court system to help the particular child. For example, Alabama law allows waiver for a child who "cannot be made to lead a correct life and cannot be properly disciplined under the provisions of this chapter."[193]

Some courts have held that the juvenile court must adjudge a child delinquent before it can proceed to the question of whether or not he is amenable to juvenile court treatment;[194] others do not require proof of the offenses alleged in the petition.[195] The Uniform Act takes a middle course by allowing waiver only when "the court finds that there are reasonable grounds to believe that the child committed the delinquent act alleged."[196]

The court will also consider whether the minor is functioning as an adult—i.e., is he working? living away from his parents? married?

The Right to Counsel:

Courts interpreting *Kent* as constitutionally-based have therefore held that a juvenile has the right to counsel at a waiver hearing.[197] Statutory provisions often grant attorney representation.[198]

Review of Waiver:

Several methods exist to review the juvenile court's waiver decision: a motion in the criminal court to dismiss the indictment;[199] direct appeal;[200] writ of habeas corpus;[201] writs of mandamus and prohibition to compel the juvenile court to keep a case and forbid a criminal court to proceed with it;[202] or on a finding that the waiver procedure was faulty, reversal of the criminal conviction for lack of jurisdiction in the criminal court.[203]

Reverse Waiver:

It should also be noted that, under California practice, an individual between eighteen and twenty-one may be arrested under adult procedure, and then certified to juvenile court if consideration of the facts as outlined above seem to so warrant.

D. *Adjudication of Delinquency*

The Jury Trial:

The United States Supreme Court has recently declared that the juvenile has no constitutional right to a jury trial. In *McKiever v. Pennsylvania,*[204] Mr. Justice Blackmun, writing for a plurality of the Court, reasoned that the juvenile court proceeding is not a criminal prosecution, and that ". . . one cannot say that in our legal system the jury is a necessary component of accurate fact-finding."[205]

Reaching a conclusion different from *McKeiver v. Pennsylvania,* Massachusetts' highest court recognized the juvenile's right to jury trial. In Massachusetts, juveniles appealing to the Superior Court for a trial de novo on the delinquency judgment have a statutory right to have their case heard in *like manner as appeals in criminal cases.* This includes the right to trial by jury—not withstanding that the juvenile is to be treated as a child in need of aid, rather than as a criminal.[206]

The Burden of Proof:

In another case recently reviewed by the U. S. Supreme Court,[207] a judge in the New York Family Court had found that a twelve year old boy had entered a locker and stolen $112.00 from a woman's pocketbook. The judge conceded that the evidence might not establish guilt beyond a reasonable doubt, but held the boy delinquent by using a standard of *preponderance of the evidence* as provided by

New York Law.[208] He ordered the child confined for a period which might extend as long as six years. The U. S. Supreme Court reversed, holding in that the adjudicatory stage of a delinquency proceeding the case against the child must be proved beyond a reasonable doubt. Whether this rule applies to the juvenile court's semi-delinquency jurisdiction is unsettled:

The Right to a Public and Speedy Trial:

Most juvenile court acts expressly state that the proceedings are not public. This policy against shielding children from detrimenal publicity has recently been upheld by the Supreme Court.[209]

As far as the child's right to a speedy trial is concerned, state courts considering the question have determined that the child does have such a right.[210]

The Rules of Evidence:

The receipt of evidence at a trial is controlled by rules designed to contribute to the accuracy of the fact-finding procedure and to promote other goals of the law. Evidence must be relevant to a fact at issue,[210a] for example, and hearsay evidence is generally not admissable.[210b]

Some evidentiary rules have been held to be derived from the U. S. Constitution. For example, verbal or physical evidence obtained in violation of a juvenile's constitutional rights is not admissable.[211] In addition, *In re Gault*[212] required certain evidentiary procedures on due process grounds: "Absent a valid confession adequate to support the determination of the juvenile court, confrontation and sworn testimony by witnesses available for cross-examination were essential for a finding of *delinquency*."[213]

Other evidentiary rules are specified in the juvenile court acts. For example, New York allows only *evidence that is competent, material and relevant* to be admitted at an adjudicatory hearing.[214] In California, when it is alleged that a child has violated the law, only that evidence may be admitted which is *legally admissable in the trial of criminal cases;* but in the court's semi-delinquency jurisdiction anything *relevant and material to the circumstances or acts* may be admitted.[215]

Judgment and Findings:

Even if it is established that a child has committed a delinquent act, it is not necessary that he be adjudicated delinquent. For example, California law provides for an order of probation without adjuding the juvenile a ward.[216]

Since the juvenile court has limited jurisdiction, its judgment must affirmatively show the facts which have been found to bring the child within its powers. It has been held insufficient merely to recite that the child has been found delinquent.[217]

Transcribing the Proceeding:

Juvenile court acts rarely contain clear requirements that a record be kept, and speak instead of minutes kept by the judge.[218] The Supreme Court in *Gault,* while not ruling on the point, suggested that keeping a record in the juvenile court would help to create "a healthy atmosphere of accountability,"[219] and the trend in recent legislation is to require a complete record of adjudicatory hearings.[220]

Finality of a Determination:

The constitutional prohibiton against double jeopardy has been held to apply to juvenile delinquency proceedings, so that once a delinquency petition has been dismissed the state cannot bring a second petition on the same offense.[221]

E. *The Decision on Disposition*

Disposition as a Separate Determination:

A fundamental change in recent juvenile court legislation is a requirement that the question of the child's disposition be kept separate from the question of the sufficiency of the facts to bring him within the jurisdiction of the court.[222]

Most statutes allow the disposition hearing to be held immediately following a finding that a child is delinquent or within the jurisdiction of the court, although they may provide for the hearing to be continued to allow gathering of the evidence relevant to the disposition decision.[223]

The Social Study:

Since it is the announced goal of the juvenile court system to obtain individualized justice, the judge in his disposition decision has the benefit of information, usually gathered by a probation officer, about the child, his school experiences, his family, and his other relationships.[223a]

The New York law provides that "Such reports may not be furnished to the court prior to the completion of an adjudicatory hearing, but may be used in a dispositional hearing."[224] The California Supreme Court has similarly held that a judge's review of the contents of the social report prior to making the jurisdictional decision was reversible error because some of the report was legally incompetent.[225]

As to whether the child and his attorney may have access to the social study before the disposition hearing, the proposed Texas Juvenile Code[226] requires, for example, that "prior to the disposition hearing, the court shall provide the attorney for the child with access to all written matter to be considered by the court in disposition."

The Right to Counsel:

Whether a juvenile has the right to representation at the disposition stage of the juvenile court process is not covered by the court holding of *Gault*. Nevertheless, most courts which have considered the issue have decided that it is constitutionally required.[227] Further, most statutory provisions granting right to counsel are broad enough to include the disposition stage.[228]

F. *Review*

In General:

The Supreme Court has not determined whether a child has the constitutional right to appeal a juvenile court decision. Juvenile court statutes commonly provide for appeals.

A usual description of one who has standing to appeal is "any party aggrieved,"[229] including the child, a parent deprived of the custody of his child or even one whose child was placed on probation.

"[T]he state or a subdivision of the state" may also be granted standing to appeal.[230]

Some states, such as Arizona, provide no appeal.[231] Such a rule has been held not to violate the federal constitution.[232]

Methods of Review:

Legislation sometimes provides for *de novo* review, the appellate court giving the juvenile court decision no weight and the whole case being reexamined starting from scratch.[233] More commonly, however, an appeal constitutes a review, rather than redetermination.[239] Some statutes provide for a rehearing in the juvenile court before the case goes up on appeal, so that the first proceeding can be informal and without a reporter, while the rehearing may be recorded as the basis for an appeal.[235]

If the child is in custody, the legality of his confinement may be challenged collaterally by a petition for writ of habeas corpus,[236] testing both the legality of the child's custody and whether the conditions of his confinement are valid.[237]

The Record on Appeal:

The record must show that the issue raised on appeal was also raised in the juvenile court,[238] except for errors that go to the jurisdiction of the court.[239]

As to whether an indigent child has a right to a free transcript for use on appeal—the Supreme Court has held that for adults an adequate form of the trial record must be provided for the convicted indigent person[240]—some courts have held so on the reasoning of *Gault*,[241] and others have similarly decided on analogy to felony cases.[242]

The Right to Counsel on Appeal:

Although *Gault*[243] held that an indigent juvenile has the right to counsel at a hearing which might result in his commitment, it is not clear whether there is a constitutional right to assigned counsel at the appellate level. The Iowa Supreme Court has held that *Gault* requires Iowa's statutes to be interpreted so as to grant the right of counsel on appeal.[244] Juvenile court legislation providing for counsel "at every stage of the proceedings"[245] may be sufficiently broad to include the right to representation on appeal. The language of other statutes, however, suggests that those states feel no duty to appoint counsel on appeal.[246]

VII. THE ROLE OF THE CORRECTIONS OFFICER— DISPOSITION ALTERNATIVES

A. *In General*

Statutes generally permit the juvenile court great discretion in deciding what is to be done with a child adjudicated to be within the jurisdiction of his court. For example, the Iowa code allows the juvenile court judge, after making a finding that the child is delinquent, to order one or more of the following dispositions:

(1) Continue the proceeding from time to time under such supervision as the court may direct;

(2) Place the child in the child's home under the supervision of a probation officer or other suitable person;

(3) Transfer legal custody of the child to a child placement agency, or a probation officer, or a *reputable individual of good moral character;*

(4) Commit the child to the state board of control for placement at a training school;

(5) Commit or place the child in any private institution or hospital, or in a public institution not under the jurisdiction of the state board of control, for care and training;

(6) Order any necessary special treatment or care provided for the child's physical or mental health; or

(7) Order the child released from its control, terminating the proceedings, at any time during which the child is under the court's jurisdiction.[247]

The court's discretion, however, is bound by certain restraints. The judge must choose from among the alternatives that are authorized by the applicable juvenile court act.[248] In addition, some statutes allow commitment to a reform school only in cases where the child is found a delinquent, excluding cases where the child is adjudicated a person in need of supervision or otherwise within the court's semi-delinquency jurisdiction.[249]

B. *Suspended Judgment*

Some statutes give the juvenile court judge discretion, in effect, to suspend pronouncement of adjudication, by refusing to make a delinquency finding even when the evidence establishes sufficient grounds.[250] In other states, however, a suspended judgment (the least severe disposition), may be entered only if there has been a formal adjudication of delinquency. Such a judgment may be entered on conditions similar to those which would be imposed if the child were placed on probation; or the conditions may be directions to the child's parent, rather than to the child.[251] If the juvenile is adjudged to be a person in need of supervision, the juvenile court judge has the authority to terminate the proceedings without any conditions being imposed.[252]

Where a statute provides authority for avoiding a finding or suspending judgment, there is often some time limit to the conditions that may be imposed on the child—usually six months or one year.[253]

C. *Probation*

In General:

As probation is conceived within the juvenile process, it is intended to contribute to changing the juvenile's behavior. Probation tries to achieve this change through retention in the community, avoiding institutionalization. Some juvenile court legislation authorizes probation in all cases, regardless of the conduct on which the delinquency finding is based.[254]

There are rival emphases for probation, and it is sometimes suggested that *effective* supervision and treatment combine them: surveillance, service and counseling.[255] With respect to surveillance, the probation officer should keep in touch with the child, his parents, his school, and other concerned persons, to see how well the probation plan is being carried out. This may also show the child that society, as represented by the court officer, is interested in helping him avoid further nonconforming behavior. The officer may help serve by helping the child and his family use available community social services to deal with problems they face. The probation worker is often expected also to counsel all concerned, to help them understand and confront the existence of the personal or environmental problems which have helped produce the child's delinquency.

The child's period of probation may not exceed the time limit set in the applicable statute, often two years. It may be possible, however, to renew the probation for an additional statutory period.[256] In Los Angeles County, the maximum period of probation is one year. At that time a report is submitted to the court recommending (depending on the minor's progress) dismissal or continuance.

Conditions of Probation:

Juvenile court statutes generally do not specify conditions of probation to be imposed by the court, typically requiring that the child be placed on probation "under conditions and limitations the court prescribes."[257] California adds that the conditions imposed must be "fitting and proper to the end that justice may be done and the reformation and rehabilitation of the ward enhanced."[258]

Juvenile court orders are sometimes as vague as the statutory provisions. For example, appellate courts have upheld a condition that the juvenile "stay out of all trouble."[259]

A special case which has been treated explicitly by the courts involves the imposition of conditions regarding religion. In *Jones v. Commonwealth,*[260] a case which has often been followed, the juvenile court's probation order required, among several conditions, that the juvenile attend Sunday school and church each Sunday for a period of one year. The Supreme Court of Appeals of Virginia struck down the order as a violation of religious freedom, stating that "No civil authority has the right to require any one to accept or reject any religious belief or to contribute any support thereto."[261]

Restitution as a Special Condition:

There is one special condition that juvenile court statutes often mention as to probation: that the child may be required to make restitution or reparation.[262] In some states the obligation to pay may extend only to property damage caused by the child and not to personal injuries.[263]

A disposition ordering restitution should be imposed only if consistent with the juvenile court system's goal of teaching the child to be responsible. In one case, a seventeen year old boy, adjudged delinquent for striking a pedestrian, was placed on probation on condition he pay $1,040.00 at the rate of $10.00 per week for a period of two years, payable through the court.[264] The Superior Court of Pennsylvania struck down the restitution order. It conceded that the juvenile court "undoubtedly may impose such terms as will bring home to the minor a realization of the seriousness of his delinquency;"[265] however, it concluded that by its severity this particular order invited further delinquency and revolt against the authority of the court, instead of working towards the boy's reformation.

Quality of Supervision:

The compliance with probation depends in part on the quality of supervision available, (as well, of course, on whether the child wants to change his behavior pattern.) In many areas, probation may mean little more than the child reporting to the court at specified intervals to give assurance that all is going well. Probation should involve active contacts by the officer, including visits to the home; even then the worker's heavy case load may preclude all but the most superficial relationships with individual children.

Revocation of Probation:

Proceedings to revoke probation are generally provided for in the juvenile court acts. Often revocation commences with the probation officer taking the child into custody, utilizing statutory authority to act as peace officers.[266] Such law enforcement authority may create problems for the probation worker, however, because he tries to achieve a trusting and confidential relationship with the child in order to fulfill his counseling and guidance duties. The Uniform Juvenile Court Act, reacting to this problem, expressly provides that "a probation officer does not have the powers of a law enforcement officer," and that he may take his probationer into custody only under circumstances where "the child's health or safety is in imminent danger," or there is the possibility that the child will run away, or he is so ordered by the juvenile court.[267]

Proceedings following the taking into custody are dealt with in varying detail by the statutes. The New York Act simply provides for a *hearing,* requiring that violation of probation be evidenced by "competent proof"[268] Other states apply all the rules for notice and hearings that would be used in a new petition charging delinquency.[269]

In addition, the courts have established rights for the juvenile faced with probation revocation. For example, New York courts have extended to the child adjudged a person in need of supervision the right to a hearing on probation revocation.[270] Further, a case which is often cited holds that the juvenile has a right to counsel in a probation revocation proceeding.[271]

Probation revocation for semi-delinquents may differ from that for delinquents. If a semi-delinquent child is placed in some child caring institution or agency and proves to be disruptive there, some states allow the juvenile court to then commit him to an institution for juvenile delinquents,[272] while others limit the court to the dispositions originally available.[273] A juvenile's probation may be revoked, not only for violating express conditions but also for non-complicance with the implied condition of good behavior.[274]

In California it is rare for a juvenile probation to be revoked. Instead the minor is usually taken back to court by the police on the new charges.

D. *Commitment*

In General:

Commitment, the most severe disposition available to the juvenile court judge, is generally available at his discretion unhedged by statutory limits.[275] Some codes, however, do provide that a child may be removed from his home only when "the court shall secure for him custody, care, and discipline as nearly as possible equivalent to that which should have been given him by his parents."[276]

Imposing some limitations on the juvenile court judge's discretion, one court has held that before committing a child to the custody of the Department of Public Welfare, the juvenile court judge is obligated to conduct an *appropriate inquiry* to explore alternatives to commitment.[277] In another recent case, commitments to industrial school were reviewed on the merits on appeal and reversed. It was found that the children had no previous record, were remorseful, had made restitution, and had turned themselves in on the day after the offense.[278] Further, a disposition for a person in need of supervision ordering him placed in a state training school was recently reviewed on the merits of appeal and struck down when a psychiatric report stated positively that such placement would be harmful to the child.[279]

Length of Commitment:

Traditional legislation allowed the child to be placed in the custody of a reform school until he reached the age of twenty-one. Even though this might mean that a child could be kept in an institution up to fourteen years—much longer than an adult who had committed the same acts, appellate courts had not found such differences in treatment unconstitutional.[280] In a recent decision, however, the Supreme Court of Pennsylvania held that there can be no constitutionally valid distinction between a juvenile and an adult offender which justifies making one of them subject to a longer maximum commitment in the same institution for the same conduct.[281]

The more modern legislation sets a maximum time for a child to be held in custody.[282] Yet many of these statutes may also provide that the original period of commitment may be renewed for an additional period.[283] Even in states where the original period of commitment may last until the child is twenty-one,[284] renewal is allowed if it has been determined by the committing court that the child "would be physically dangerous to the public because of [his] mental or physical deficiency disorder, or abnormality."[285] The court may order an additional two year commitment an unlimited number of times, so that a life sentence is in theory a possible result.[286] The usual California practice is commitment for a 90 day observation period, followed by a parole decision to release the minor back into society.

Recent decisions have held that after his statutory release time, a juvenile offender's confinement cannot be extended without a jury trial on whether he is dangerous enough to require further *treatment;*[287] and the extension period must be based on the same factors relevant to adults, and cannot exceed two years.[288]

The Training School:

Training schools, camps, halfway houses, and other training facilities function to provide a specialized program for children who must be committed to be treated. Normally these are juveniles considered somewhat *hardened* or *unstable*. The program has been characterized as being a preparation for the ultimate test of returning to community life.[289] Many of such facilities are moving away from the old *reform school* theory, trying to teach the juveniles the difference between right and wrong, and towards a concern with what the behavior means to the delinquent himself.[290] The stress is on new programs such as community-based treatment and group treatment.[291]

Juvenile detention houses are subject to court supervision in disciplining juveniles, and may be required to report such punishments as solitary confinement and involuntary drug injections to parents and guardians ad litem.[292]

Transfer to an Adult Penal Institution:

In several states it is possible to transfer a committed child from a juvenile reform school to an adult penal institution.[292] It has been suggested that two types of criteria are used to determine the need for transfer: incorrigible behavior, and the inadequacy of the juvenile institutional program to meet the needs of the child.[294]

Some courts have upheld the constitutionality of a transfer even without a hearing, reasoning that persistent incorrigibility might seriously impair the well-being of the juvenile training school.[295] Others have ruled that it is a denial of due process to impose imprisonment as a result of a hearing lacking the constitutional protections of a criminal trial.[296] *McKeiver vs. Pennsylvania,* while not speaking to this precise issue, has recently held that not all of the rights possessed by an adult in a criminal trial must constitutionally apply to juveniles.[297] It may thus follow that a transfer to an adult penal institution, even without a full criminal trial-type hearing, is constitutional if it is based on procedures which do not violate the requirement of *fundamental fairness.*

E. *Care and Protection Orders*

Often children having problems sufficient to bring them within the jurisdiction of the court also have problems in their relationships with their parents. Some juvenile court acts provide for this situation by allowing the court to make an order regulating the activities of the parent. For example, in New York the juvenile court may "set forth reasonable conditions of behavior to be observed by a person who is before the court and is a parent or other person legally responsible for the child's care . . . Such an order may require any such person . . . to refrain from acts of commission or omission that tend to make the home not a proper place for the child."[298] A protective order may be made at any stage in the proceedings.[299]

F. *Aftercare*

In General:

Juvenile aftercare has been characterized as the release of a child from a training school at the time when he can best benefit from life in the community under the supervision of a counselor.[300] Its purpose is to provide for the child an individualized plan for making a successful return to life outside the institution. The plan for reentry must consider both the effects of institutional life on the juvenile and the attitudes of the community to which he is returning.[301]

The organization of aftercare services vary widely among the states; such administration may be the responsibility of a lay board, an adult correction program, a public welfare agency, a youth authority, or the training facility itself.[302]

The extent of aftercare supervision provided for the juvenile varies from area to area, but in most cases "supportive, sustained, and positive implementation of an aftercare plan is, more often than not, rare."[303] Because of the small number of workers and the large number of cases, contacts by the staff are usually crisis-oriented—the worker will see the child only when an emergency arises. In many states, supervision generally consists of a monthly report written by the juvenile and mailed to the state office.[304]

The Decision to Release:

The authority to release children from state training schools may rest with any of a variety of agencies, including the youth authority, the state training school board, the state institutions board, the department of correction, the department of public welfare, the parole board, and the state board of control.[305] In most cases, these authorities are composed of members appointed by the Governor of the particular state. It has been suggested that the decision to release a juvenile is not solely a question of the child's emotional and social readiness to return to society. Instead, the decision may be determined by limitations of the training school program, inadequate budgets, and the need to make room for new arrivals.[306]

Revocation of Parole:

The cases are in disagreement as to whether a child must be given a hearing on revocation of his parole or aftercare order. One recent case has found that there is no constitutional requirement of a hearing to determine the return of a child to a state training center if the superintendent has decided that such action is in the child's best interest.[307] On the other hand, another court has held that the child should be allowed a hearing as to whether his aftercare should be revoked.[308]

If a hearing is held on revocation of aftercare, the child is usually not afforded the same protections afforded one newly brought before the court; including the rights to have court-appointed counsel, a fact-finding hearing on the allegations, confrontation and cross-examination of witnesses, and presentation of witnesses on his own behalf.[309]

VIII. CONCLUSION

A. *The Supreme Court's View*

Justice White's concurring opinion in *McKeiver v. Pennsylvania* sets out the traditional model of the juvenile court in words eloquent enough to be quoted at length:

> The criminal law proceeds on the theory that defendants have a will and are responsible for their actions. A finding of guilt establishes that they have chosen to engage in conduct so reprehensible and injurious to others that they must be punished to deter them and others from crime. Guilty defendants are considered blameworthy; they are branded and treated as such, however much the State also pursues rehabilitative ends in the criminal justice system.
>
> For the most part, the juvenile justice system rests on more deterministic assumptions. Reprehensible acts by juveniles are not deemed the consequence of mature and malevolent choice but of environmental pressures

(or lack of them) or of other forces beyond their conrtol, hence the state legislative judgment not to stigmatize the juvenile delinquent by branding him a criminal. His conduct is not deemed so blameworthy that punishment is required to deter him or others. Coercive measures, where employed, are considered neither retribution nor punishment. Supervision or confinement is aimed at rehabilitation, not at convincing the juvenile of his error simply by imposing pains and penalties. Nor is the purpose to make the juvenile delinquent an object lesson for others, whatever his own merits or demerits may be. A typical disposition in the juvenile court where delinquency is established may authorize confinement until age 21, but it will last no longer and within that period will last only so long as his behavior demonstrates that he remains an unacceptable risk if returned to his family. Nor is the authorization for custody until 21 any measure of the seriousness of the particular act which the juvenile has performed.

Not only are those risks that mandate juries in criminal cases of lesser magnitude in juvenile court and adjudications, but the consequences of adjudication are less severe than those flowing from verdicts of criminal guilt. This is plainly so in theory, and in practice there remains a substantial gulf between criminal guilt and delinquency, whatever the failings of the juvenile court in practice may be.[309a]

The Supreme Court's opinion in *Winship* notes the beneficial aspects of the juvenile court: In the pre-adjudicatory stage, distinctive procedures; in adjudication, an informal, flexible, speedy process; in the post-adjudicatory stage, a wide-ranging review of the child's social history and individualized treatment; also, in terms of sanction imposed, avoidance of stigma through confidentiality of the process, the denomination of the adjudication as other than a criminal conviction, and the absence of laws depriving one adjudicated of the civil rights a felon would loose.[310]

However, both justice Whilte's opinion,[311] and Justice Blackman's opinion for four members of the Court, recognize how the juvenile courts have, in practice, fallen short of their announced goals. As Justice Blackman puts it:

The devastating commentary upon the system's failures as a whole. . .[312] reveals the depth of disappointment in what has been accomplished . . . The community's unwillingness to provide people and facilities and to be concerned, the insufficiency of time devoted, the scarcity of professional help, the inadequacy of dispositional alternatives, and our general lack of knowledge all contribute to dissatisfaction with the experiment.[313]

Justice Blackman's opinion goes on to quote from the Crime Commission's task force report on juvenile delinquency:

> What emerges, then, is this: In theory the juvenile court was to be helpful and rehabilitative rather than punitive. In fact the distinction often disappears, not only because of the absence of facilities and personnel but also because of the limits of knowledge and technique. In theory the court's action was to affix no stigmatizing label. In fact a delinquent is generally viewed by employers, schools, the armed services—by society generally—as a criminal. In theory the court was to treat children guilty of criminal acts in noncriminal ways. In fact it labels truants and runaways as junior criminals. In theory the court's operations could justifiably be informal, its findings and decisions made without observing ordinary procedural safeguards, because it would act only in the best interest of the child. In fact it frequently does nothing more nor less than deprive a child of liberty without due process of law—knowing not what else to do and needing, whether admittedly or not, to act in the community's interest even more imperatively than the child's. In theory it was to exercise its protective powers to bring an errant child back into the fold. In fact there is increasing reason to believe that its intervention reinforces the juvenle's unlawful impulses. In theory it was to concentrate on each case the best current social science learning. In fact it has often become a vested interest in its turn, loathe to cooperate with innovative programs or avail itself of forward-looking methods.[314]

It is the gap between aspirations and achievements that has evoked the counter-currents against the traditional juvenile court model; perhaps most important is the very fact that the juvenile courts make use of *(as treatment)* sanctions so similar to those the criminal courts impose as *punishment*. In *Winship* the Supreme Court explains that what it did in *Gault* was to make

> clear that civil labels and good intentions do not themselves obviate the need for criminal due process safeguards in juvenile courts for [a] proceedings where the issue is whether the child will be found to be delinquent and subjected to the loss of his liberty for years is comparable in seriousness to a felony prosecution.[315]

B. *Future Trends*

As the juvenile court process—and the adult criminal justice process develop, they grow more like one another.

The recent Supreme Court opinions on juvenile law have imposed many of the procedural protections of the adult criminal court on the adjudication phase of the juvenile justice process. These opinions do authorize the juvenile court to depart in certain ways from procedures historically required in criminal courts. But perhaps the departures permissible for juveniles are also permissible for adults.[316]

Many, if not all of the special characteristics of the juvenile court thought to justify *non-criminal* procedures may perhaps be exported to the adult criminal court.

1. For example, in the intake stage:

The juvenile court may obtain a background report on the individual at the beginning of the court process without waiting for a finding of guilt and ordering of *presentence report.*

There is frequent use of a *consent decree* arrangement wherein the parties agree on what the best interests of the individual and the community seem to require.

The decision on going forward into formal adjudication is typically made by one who—by training—is more likely to be a social worker than a lawyer and who—by official role—is a court officer rather than a prosecutor.

2. As to adjudication:

Closing of the case without an adjudication of *guilt* is seen as a successful resolution for law enforcement—if the case warrants that disposition—not as a defeat for the People. Perhaps in recognition of the limited efficacy of our present knowledge or *rehabilitation,* absence of formal adjudication is seen as being—in many cases—the most helpful thing the court can do. (As the physician's maxim has it, the first rule of treatment is not to make matters worse.)

3. As to disposition:

The range of disposition alternatives is, at least ideally, defined to include the full range of resources available in the community, private as well as public and informal as well as formal. Authorization of institutionalization is seen as a last resort.

4. As to the *substantive law:*

The list of behavioral situations indicating need for community intervention—and authorizing authoritative reordering of the individual's life—is recognized as different from the list of behavioral situations recognized by society as the evils expected to be eliminated. Thus in juvenile law, one does not view stopping children from running aways as a goal of the law; running away is recognized as a symptom indicating the need for action to *prevent* more serious problems. In criminal law, on the other hand, the code of substantive offenses functions as an index both of ends of the law and as the occasions of its invocation.

The "juvenile court often appears," as the British Committee on Children and Young Persons has noted:[317]

> to be trying a case on one particular ground and then to be dealing with the child on some quite different ground. This is inherent in combining the requirement for proof of a specified event or condition with a general direction to have regard to the child's welfare.[17]

All of these aspects of juvenile law should be examined for their applicability to the adult criminal process.

On the other hand, juvenile law has yet to fully assimilate the great lesson of criminal procedure: that the rules of law serve as a protection of the liberty of the citizen by circumscribing the power of officials.

For example, in *McKeiver v. Pennsylvania,*[318] the court noted that jury trials help protect subgroups in the community from the oppression of those whose representatives control law enforcement. As the dissent in *McKeiver* pointed out,[319] Black youths in the South involved in civil rights demonstrations, the juveniles in one of the companion cases, are just such a group in need of protection.

Perhaps youths in general are deserving of recognition as a *minority group*—with less power, wealth, status, and individual autonomy than the majority. The whole arrangement is justified by the general understanding that they are less wise, in need of care by the stronger and generally happier and better-off because of their less-than-equal status. The justification is of course true, at least from the point of view of adults, unlike the use of similar ideologies in past history for helots, serfs, Africans, or women.

If youths are a minority group (at least for some purposes) then perhaps society should go out of its way to provide them the fullest protection, of due process from the effects of possible bias by members of the governing (adult) group.

Thus it may well be desirable to extend the protection of criminal law on an equal basis to the young—and also to extend most of the features of juvenile justice on an equal basis to adults.

Such a development, if it occurs, may happen not because of inherent tendencies within the legal system, but as a reflection of trends in our society. There may be a beginning of an integration of the young within the general society. Similarly, there may be changes within our culture as to how adults perceive *misbehavior* by youths. Youths, after all, must remind adults of the youths they know well—their own children—and the youths they knew most intimately—their own young selves. And changes in our legal system for the young may thus reflect psychological changes within the family and within the minds of the ex-children who are the adults.

FOOTNOTES

[1]See section IV, *infra.*

[2]See section V, *infra.*

[3]See section VII, *infra.*

[4]The social workers are frequently "court officers," though "court officers" may be probation officers without social work training.

On the several roles involved in the process, see generally Newman, *Functions of the Police, Prosecutor, Court Worker, Defense Counsel, Judge in Aiding Juvenile Justice,* 13 *Juv. Ct. Judges J.* 6(1962)

[5]The effect of the recent developments discussed below have been to cast the procedure in a more adversary mold. Thus under current California practice, for all petitions under *Calif. Welf & Inst. Code* §602 (West), [hereinafter *Cal. Code*] the District Attorney prosecutes and the Public Defender defends. See Lois R v. Superior Court, Cal. Rptr. (Sept. 3, 1971)

[6]I.N.G., a Minor v. Superior Court, Cal. (Cal.Sup.Ct., May 6, 1971).

[7]Mack, *"The Juvenile Court,"* 23 *Harv.L.Rev.* 104, 119–120 (1909).

[8]*Id.* at 120. But this very informality, it has been suggested, may leave the child in a Kafkaesque insecurity devoid of fixed reference points. See Studt, *The Client's Image of the Juvenile Court, Justice For The Child* 203–04 (M. Rosenheim, ed., 1962) [cited hereafter as *Justice For the Child*].

[8a]*N.Y. Family Ct. Act.* §711 (McKinney) [hereinafter *N.Y. Act*], see generally Elson, *Juvenile Courts and Due Process,* in *Justice For The Child 96*

[9]383 U.S. 541 (1966)

[10]383 U.S. at 553

[10a]387 U.S. 1 (1967), see generally Dorsen & Reznick, *In re Gault and the Future of Juvenile Law, 1 Family L.Q.* 1 (1967)

[11]387 U.S. at 18–19.

[12]397 U.S. 358 (1970).

[13]397 U.S. 358 (1970).

[14]See *N.D. Century Code* 27-20-01 *et seq.*

[15]Arthur, *The Uniform Juvenile Court Act,* 19 *Jur. Ct. Judges J.* 153 (1969).

[16]*Unif. Juv. Ct. Act* [hereinafter cited as *Uniform Act*] §2(d).

[17]*Uniform Act* § 26.

[18]*Uniform Act* § 366.

[19]*Children's Bureau, Dept. of H.E. & W. Legislative Guide For Drafting Family and Juvenile Court Acts (Pub. No. 472).* (1969) [hereinafter cited as *Legislative Guide*].

See also the earlier *Children's Bureau, Dept. of H.E. & W. Standards For Juvenile And Family Courts* (Pub. No. 437 (1966) (hereinafter cited as 1966 *Standards)* and *Children's Bureau, Dept. of H.E.& W., Standards For Specialized Courts Dealing With Children* (1954) (hereinafter cited as 1954 *Standards).*

Among the proposals of the *National Council on Crime and Delinquency* are *N.C.C.D., Council of Judges, Model Rules For Juvenile Courts* (1969) (hereinafter cited as *Model Rules)* and the *Standard Juvenile Court Act* (1959), in the *1966 Standards.*

The Uniform Juvenile Court Act [cited herein as *Uniform Act*] has been previously mentioned.

[20]*Legislative Guide* at § 25.

[21]*Id.* at § 27.

[22]*Id.* at § 14. This, of course, is one of the most vital reforms in the area.

[23]*Id.* at §17.

[23a]In announcing the 27 member advisory committee for the study, the Institute of Judicial Administration said in a statement:—

> Recidivism among juveniles is discouragingly high. According to one source, 74 per cent of juveniles found guilty of an offense will later be re-arrested. Critics of the present juvenile system argue that rather than rehabilitating youthful offenders, the system is creating future criminals.
>
> The statement noted that "public concern about crime and the availability of Federal funds make this an excellent time to start significant reforms in court proceedings as well as such important related areas as police and correctional practices." It went on:
>
> "The standards which result from this project would provide the basis for model codes and administrative guidelines for such diverse topics as the selection and training of judges and other criminal justice personnel, the role of prosecutors and defense attorneys, probation and parole procedures, diversion of cases for nonjudicial treatment, and correctional programs."

[23b]Substantive law is sometimes defined as the law addressed to citizens in general, and procedural law as the law addressed to courts, lawyers and officials. Thus substantive criminal law defines the behavior denominated criminal, and so identifies which individuals are properly subject to the authority of the law enforcement

authorities. Procedural criminal law, in great part, sets out rules to limit the behavior of law enforcement authorities.

[23c]In the California statutory scheme, *Cal. Code* § 602 provides jurisdiction over youths who have violated a law, ordinance or juvenile court order; *Cal. Code* § 601 for those disobedient, truant, or in danger of leading an idle or immoral life; *Cal. Code* § 600 for those neglected, uncontrolled or dangerously mentally disturbed.

[24]E.g., *Or. Rev. Stat.* § 419–476(a); *Uniform Act* § 2(2).

[25]In Massachusetts, for example, it is a criminal offense, punishable by six months in jail, to be a "'stubborn child." *Mass. Gen. L. Anno.*, c. 272, § 53.

[26]In re R., 1 Cal.3d 855, 83 Cal. Rptr. 671, 464 P. 2d 127 (1970).

[27]*See H. L. Packer, The Limits of the Criminal Sanction* (1968).

[28]*Texas Juvenile Act,* Art. 2338–1.

[29]E.S.G. v. State, 447 S.W.2d 225 (Tex. Civ. App. 1969).

[30]Johnson v. Texas, 401 S.W.2d 298 (Tex. Civ. App. 1966).

[31]*Mass. Gen. L. Anno.* c. 119, § 52.

[32]In re Winburn, 32 Wis.2d 152, 145 N.W.2d 178 (1966).

[33]Smith v. State, 444 S.W.2d 941 (Tex. Civ. App. 1969).

[34]*E.g.*, State in Interest of K.V.N., 112 N.J. Super 544, 271 A.2d 921 (J. & D.R. Ct. 1968).

[35]*Uniform Act* § 2(d).

[36]*N.Y. Act* § *712 (b).*

[37]*Cal Code* § 601. The repeal of this jurisdictional bases is being considered in California. See *L.A. Daily Journal,* October 20, 1971. pp. 1, 10: In 1970, the State Assembly's Interim Committee on Criminal Procedure, recommended repeal of Section 601, claiming that "Courts. . . have never been and are not now capable of acting effectively as agencies of social welfare. The best the court can really hope to do in a 601 case is control the minor's future behavior. . .

"Unfortunately, the court is not able to cope with the real underlying problems of the minors brought before it on Section 601 petition. In fact, it is hardly able to cope with the symptom."

The Los Angeles County Superior Court judges wrote section 601 should be repealed because it "in effect permits irresponsible parents, overworked and ineffective school personnel. . . to 'put a record' on a youngster who, in most cases, is not the one primarily responsible for the activity involved."

The judges say that by bringing family matters into the court, the relationship between parent and child is even further deteriorated.

It does "unjustifiable harm to children" to involve them in a court process "because they can't get on at home," Juvenile Court Presiding Judge Marvin A. Freeman has said.

[38]E.g., People v. Deibert, 117 Cal. App.2d 410, 256 P.2d 355 (1953); State v. L.N., 109 N.J. Super. 278, 263 A.2d 150 (1970); *contra* Gonzales v. Maillard, F.2d, *prob. juris.* noted, U.S. (19).

[39]*N.Y. Act* § 731(c).

[40]*N.Y. Act* § 732(c).

[41]*Uniform Act* § 29, Comment.

[42]*S. Fox, The Law of Juvenile Courts in a Nutshell,* 50–52 (1971) [hereinafter cited as *Fox*].

[43]See, *e.g., Colo. Children's Code* § 22–1–3 (17) [hereinafter cited as ***Colo. Code***].

[44]I.R. v. People, 464 P.2d 296 (Colo. 1970).

[45]Hayes v. Municipal Court, 9 Cr. L. 2423, 2424 (Okla. Ct. Crim. App., Aug. 28, 1971).

[46]Aves v. Justice Court, 306 P.2d 601, 605 (Cal. 1957).

[47]See, *e.g., Colo. Code,* § 22-1-3 (19) (a), (d), (e).

[48]*N.Y. Act* § 312(b).

[49]In re Carl, 174 Misc. 985, 22 N.Y.S.2d 782 (1940).

[50]*Ill. Juv. Ct. Act* § 702–5.

[51]*Uniform Act* § 2(5).

[52]*N.Y. Act* § 716(b).

[52a]See generally *R. Myren & L. Swanson, Police Work With Children* (Children's Bureau, Dept. of H.E.&W., Pub. 62–399); Piliarin & Briar, *Police Encounters With Juveniles,* 70 Am.J.Soc. 206 (1964).

[53]See section (d), *infra.*

[54]See section (e), *infra.*

[55]See section (f), *infra.*

[56]See section (c), *infra.*

[57]See section (b), *infra.*

[58]See section (c), *infra.*

[59]See section (h), *infra.*

[59a][footnote omitted].

[60]Terry v. Ohio, 392 U.S. 1 (1968), Sibron v. New York U.S., 88 S.Ct. 1889 (1968).

[61]44 Misc.2d 900 (1965); the *Terry* authorization would also, by its own reasoning, extend to juveniles.

[61a]Of course the juvenile has generally not committed a *crime* because the behavior is willful violation of law that is defined as *crime* for an adult, is usually defined as *juvenile delinquency* for a juvenile. Similarly the police seizure of the juvenile's person is denominated a *taking into custody* which *shall not be deemed an arrest. Standard Act* §16. This terminology is intended to suggest, that the child is being afforded a *protective service for his benefit* by the police. *Remington,* et al., *Criminal Justice Administration* 971 (1969).

[62]255. N.Y.S. 2d 987; see, *e.g. Standard Act* § 16(a) and (b); *N.Y.Act* § 721.

[63]In re Gault, 387 U.S. 1 (1966).

[64]McKiever v. Pennsylvania, 403 U.S. 528 (1971). Since the Fourth Amendment guarantees promote privacy rather than accurate fact-finding, under McKiever's approach they may be held not to govern juvenile proceedings.

[65]*Uniform Act* § 13(a) (3); accord *Standard Act* § 16(c). Run-aways may also be taken into custody. *Standard Act* § 16(d).

[65a]For example, the *Standard Act* § 16(d) permits a peace officer to take a child into custody without warrant if there are reasonable grounds to think him a runaway, § 16 (d), and also, to protect the child *if* he is *seriously* endangered and *immediate* removal seems necessary. The *New York Act* does *not* extend to "persons in need of supervision"—apparently even those seriously and immediately in need of supervision—and instead mandates use of summons in such cases, § 721, Committee Comment. On the other hand, Ohio case law states that the law of arrest does not apply to juvenile proceedings because they are not criminal *in nature,*

and, without benefit of statute, allows a police officer to take a child into protective custody on reasonable grounds to think him either delinquent or wayward or dependent. *In re James L. Jr.*, 250 Ohio 2d 369, 194 N.E.2d 797 (Juvenile Ct. 1963).

[66]See *N.Y. Act* § 721, Committee Comments.

[67]See the discussion in Note, *Juvenile Delinquency: The Police, State Courts and Individualized Justice,* 79 *Harv. L. Rev.* 775, 776 (196) [hereinafter cited as *Harvard*] The *New York Act* § 724 expresses a preference for release to parents, subsec. (b) (i) & (c) although allowing taking the child to family court or approved facilities, Subsec. (b) (ii) (iii); and forbids taking the child to the station house (unless it has been designated by the courts as a suitable facility) *Ibid;* see In re Rytane, 234 N.Y.S.2d , 778 (19).

And New Jersey forbids taking those under 16 to a police station, N.J.S. 2A: 4–33, except for temporary questioning. State v. Smith, 32 N.J. , 532, 164 A2d , 520 (19).

[67a]E.g., *N.Y. Act* § 724(a); see In re State in Interest of Carlo, 47 N.J. 224, 225 A.2d 110 (1966); *1954 Standards* at 39. Failure to notify parent or probation officer as statute requires may render a confession thus obtained inadmissable. State v. Shaw, 93 Ariz. 40, 378 P.2d 487 (1963); In re Williams, 49 Misc.2d 154, 267 N.Y.S.2d 91 (Family Ct. 1966).

[68]*Fox* at 110. Unlike the criminal process, in juvenile law a judicial *guilty verdict* is not the usual goal, but only a last resort. Diversion from court referral is the norm, and entails great discretion on the part of intake officers and police.—As to police, such dis-discretion is widely recognized as appropriate, even though the police role is rarely provided for by legislation, often not supported by training or articulated standards, and sometimes extending the restraints on juveniles outside the substantive jurisdiction of the courts. *Remington* 997.

[96]Compare *Fox* at 776 with *Remington* at 998.

[70]*Harvard* 778–84; *President's Commission* 81–83.

[71]*Ibid,* Chicago Police Dept., Manual of Procedures, *(Section III—Basic Factors and Considerations in The Processing of Juveniles)* (1965) in *Remington* 1011–1014. See *Eldefonso, Law Enforcement and the Juvenile Offender: Juvenile Procedures* 100 (1967). Wertham & Piliarin, *Gang Members and the Police,* in *D.B. Ordua The Police* 72–75 (1967) mention magnitude of the offense, previous contacts with police, and parental control—criteria similar to those listed in the text—but emphasize *attitude* as the *major* determinant of police dispositions in half of the cases. Cicourel is cited for his emphasis on speedy confession as leading to leniency, and Nathan Goldman for emphasizing defiance as leading to a court referral. The defiant youth "has also symbolically rejected the normative basis for conforming to the law and the police are likely to process him formally, utilizing detention and the courts."

[72]*Harvard* 775.

[73]384 U.S. 436 (1966).

[74]In re Creek, 243 A.2d 49 (D.C. Ct. App.); see Dorsen & Rezneck, *In Re Gault and the Future of Juvenile Law,* 1 *Family L O* 1 (1967); Ketcham, *Guidelines from Gault: Revolutionary Requirements and Reappraisal,* 53 *Va.L.Rev.* 1700 (1967). *Contra* In re Rust, 278 N.Y.S. 2d 333, 342–43 (1967).

[75]387 U.S. 1 (1966).

[76]In re Juvenile, 9 Cr. L. 2452, 2453 (R.J.Fam.Ct., August 4, 1971).

[77]*Ibid.*

[78]See note 67a, *supra.* Questioning of the juvenile in his parents' presence and at home are said to be "not at all unusual" in a publication of the International Association of Chiefs of Police, which nevertheless suggests that the choice should be left in the hands of the police officer. *G. O'Conner & N. Watson, Juvenile Delinquency and Youth Crime: The Police Role* 58 (1964) (Note the *Policy Guides* on disfavored tactics), Statements by youths in custody at the police station, in the absence of parents and counsel, have been held inherently unreliable. In the Matter of Four Youths, 89 Wash. L. Rptr. (Juv. Ct., D.C., April 7, 1961, reported May 9, 1961).

[79]Haley v. Ohio, 332 U.S. 596, 601 (1948); Gallegos v. Colorado, 370 U.S. 49, 54 (1962); See also in re State in Interest of Carlo, 48 N.J. 224, 225 A.2d 110 (1966); Note, *Waiver in the Juvenile Court,* 68 *Colum. Law Rev.* 1149 (1968).

[80]70 Cal.2d 444 75 Cal Rptr. 1, 450 P.2d 296 (1969).

[81]In re Creek, 243 A.2d 49 (D.C. Ct. App. 1968); *contra* In re Rust, 278 N.Y.S.2d 333, 342, 343 (1967).

[82]Harris v. New York, U.S. (1971).

[82a]The rules on involuntary confessions apply to juveniles. In re State in Interest of Carlo, 48 N.J. 224, 225 A.2d 110 (1966) (lengthy incommunicado questioning); Haley v. Ohio 332 U.S. 596 (1948); Gallegos v. Colorado, 370 U.S. 49 (1962). More generally, confessions obtained unconstitutionally are inadmissible in juvenile court, as are in-court admissions which are their fruits. In re Teters, 264 C.A.2d 816, 821 Cal. Rptr. (1968).

However, the "harmless error" rule has been held in at least one case to be relaxed for juveniles, so that admission of an unconstitutionally obtained confession did not constitute reversible error where there was other substantial evidence sufficient to support the finding. *Id.* at 827. *Contra* for adults, People v. Spencer, 66 Cal.2d 158, 163. Compare In re Donnie H. 5 C.A.3d 781, 790, 791 (1967) (reversal) as to child when there is little other substantial evidence; cites Spencer (1907)).

[83]40 Ill.2d 53, 237 N.E.2d 529 (1968). As to unreasonable search and seizure see also In re Donaldson, 269 C.A.2d 509 (1969).

[84]Chimel v. California, 395 U.S. 752 (1969).

[85]Vale v. Louisiana, 399 U.S. 30 (1970).

[86]May v. State, 199 So.2d 635 (Miss. 1967).

[87]*E.g.,* U.S. v. Stone, 401 F.2d 32 (7th Cir. 1968); People v. Clark, 252 Cal. App.2d 479, 60 Cal. Rptr. 569, 402 P.2d 856 (1967); State v. Vidor, 75 Wash.2d 662, 452 P.2d 961 (1969).

[88]Mercer v. State, 450 S.W.2d 715 (1970).

[89]State v. Stein, 203 Kan. 638, 456 P.2d 1 (1969).

[90]U.S. v. Wade, 388 U.S. 218 (1967).

[91]In re Carl T., 1 Cal. App.3d 344, 81 Cal. Rtpr. 655 (1969).

[92]Apparently, no state has a total prohibition. Friker, *The Fingerprinting of Juveniles,* 43 *Chicago-Kent L. Rev.* 144 (1966). Some states prohibit both fingerprinting and mugging unless a court order is obtained, or unless necesssary for the "detection and apprehension of an unknown offender." *Idaho Code Ann.* §16–1811 (6) (1965 Supp.). (Identification of a supposed offender must be meant, as the fingerprinting of one *already in custody* cannot be needed in order to apprehend him). Strict rules are set for the circulation and destruction of the fingerprint card. *Ibid.*

[93]*Eldefonso, op. cit. supra,* note 71, at 115; *G. O'Conner & N. Watson Juvenile Delinquency and Youth Crime: The Police Role* 64–65 (1964).

[94]*Fox* at 137. Evidence favorable to the defendant must be disclosed by the prosecution. Brady v. Maryland, 373 U.S. 83 (1963).

[95]*Eldefonso, op. cit. supra,* note 71, at 86.

[95a]See generally Sheriday, *Juvenile Court Intake,* 2 *J. Family L.* 139 (1962).

[96]*Harvard* at 775, 778 (1966).

[97]See, *e.g., Mo. Rev. Stat.* § 211.031 (1959).

[98]See, *e.g., Mo. Rev. State.* § 211.081 (1959).

[99]*Children's Bureau, U.S. Dept. of H.E. & W. Juvenile Court Statistics,* 1967 at 11 (1969).

[100]*E.g., Cal. Code* § 652.

[101]In re Bacon, 240 Cal. App.2d 34, 49 Cal. Rptr. 322 (1966).

[102]Handler recommends a "defense probation officer" who together with an "investigative officer" will present the case to a "hearing probation officer." Handler, *The Juvenile Court and the Adversary System: Problems of Function and Form,* 1965 *Wisc. L. Rev.* 7, 41–44. Compare Rosenheim & Skoler, *The Lawyer's Role at Intake and Detention Stages of Juvenile Court Proceedings,* 11 *Crime & Delin.* 167, (1965).

[103]In the practice in Los Angeles, for example, before an intake investigation begins, the minor is told his constitutional rights. He must acknowledge he understands and effect a waiver before the investigation can continue. On the minor's competency to waive his rights, see below.

[104]*N.Y. Act* § 734; see also *Uniform Act* § 10(c).

[105]*Cal. Code* § 600(c).

[106]See generally Ferster, *et al., Separating Official and Unofficial Delinquents: Juvenile Court Intake,* 55 *Iowa L. Rev.* 864, 869 (1970).

[106a]A California study done as a basis for juvenile law revision showed that only one-fourth of the counties responding did probation officers mention this as a criterion used in dismissing a referral. *I Shaw & W. Burkhart, A Study of the Administration of Juvenile Justice in California,* pt. III, 36–39 (1960).

[107]Ferster, *op. cit., supra,* note 106, 870.

[108]See 1966 *Standards* at 148.

[109]See *Harvard* at 779.

[110]See, *e.g., Iowa Code Anno.* § 232.3 (1966); *Okla. Stat. Anno.,* Tit. 10, § 1103 Supp. 1968–69).

[111]*Harvard* at 789.

[112]*N.Y. Act* §§ 333(b), 424(b), 734(b), 823(b).

[113]*Harvard* at 788.

[114]*Ibid;* see also Shain & Burkhart, *op cit supra,* note 10(a).

[115]Sheridan, *Juvenile Court Intake,* 2 *J. Family L.* 139, 150 (1962).

[116]Ferster, *supra,* note 106, at 878–79.

[117]See, e.g., *Cal Code* § 654.

[118]See, *e.g., Ill. Anno. Stat.* ch. 37, §§ 703–8 (Smith-Hurd Supp. 1967); *Md. Anno. Code,* art. 26, §§ 70–2, 70–6, 70–8 (Supp. 1969). See discussion of the "consent decree" in *President's Commission* 83–84, *op.cit.infra* note 126.

[119]*President's Commission on Law Enforcement and Administration of Justice, Task Force Report: Juvenile Delinquency and Youth Crime* 16 (1967) [hereinafter cited as *Task Force Report*].

[120]Sheridan, *Intake Through Disposition, Proceedings of the Alabama Work Conference for Juvenile Court Judges* 36 (1965).

[121]*1966 Standards* at 57–60.

[122]*N.Y. Act* § 734(b).

[123]*Cal. Code* § 655.

[124]*Uniform Act* § 19.

[125]*See F. Remington, et al., Criminal Justice Administration* 1015 (1969).

[126]*The President's Commission on Law Enforcement and Administration of Justice, The Challenge of Crime in a Free Society* 83–84 (1967). [here cited *President's Commission*].

[127]See note 67 *supra.*

[128]See Rosenheim & Skoler, *The Lawyer's Role at Intake and Detention Stages of Juvenile Court Proceedings,* 11 *Crime and Delinquency* 167, 169–70 (1965).

[128a]See, *e.g., Uniform Act* § 16(a).

[128b]See, e.g., *Uniform Act* § 17.

[128c]In California, for example, the judge can extend the detention for up to fifteen judicial days. *Cal Code* § 635, 636 (1966).

[129]*E.g., Mass. Gen. L. Anno.,* c. 119, § 68. Thus there is only a "paper review."

[130]*E.g., Cal Code* §§ 630, 631, 632, 633. In California, the hearing must be held within three judicial days of the taking into custody; see also In re Macidon, 240 Cal. App. 2d 600, 49 Cal Rptr. 861 (1966).

[131]*E.g., Colo. Code* § 22–2–2.

[132]*Uniform Act* § 14; see also *Chic. Police Dept., Youth Div., Manual of Procedure* (1965), reprinted in *Remington,* et al., *Criminal Justice Administration* 995 (1969).

[133]In re M., Cal.3d 89 Cal.Rptr. 33 473 P.2d 737 (1970). For an example of the overlays between the detention decision and consideration of adjudicaiton, see the description of the detention hearing in *First Ann. Inst. for Juv. Ct. J. & Ref., Proc.* 10–12 (1962).

[134]Fulwood v. Stone, 394 F.2d 939, 943 (1967).

[134a]See Annot., 160 A.L.R. 287 (1946). Many juveniles are detained unneccessarily. In one study, almost two-thirds of those detained pending hearing were thereafter released on probation or without adjudication. N.Y. *N.Y. St. Legis. Comm. on Ct. Reorg., Pt. II, The Family Court Act.* 11 (1962).

[135]*E.g., Ark. Stat. Ann.* § 45–227; *Mich Stat. Ann.* § 27, 3178; *W. Va. Code Ann.* § 4904. See Trimble v. Stone, 187 F. Supp. 483 (D.C. 1960).

[136]*Ky. Rev. Stat. Ann.* § 208.110; *Ore. Rev. Stat.* § 419.583.

[137]*E.g..* Baldwin v. Lewis, 300 F. Supp. 1220 (E.D.Wisc. 1969); In re Castro, 243 Ca. App.2d 402, 52 Cal. Rptr. 469 (1966); *Cal. Code* § 628.

[137a]See discussion in section VI(a), *supra.*

[138]In re John Doe, 9 Cr. L. 2390, (Alaska Sup. Ct., Aug. 9, 1971).

[139][Omit].

[140]*Cal. Code* § 650.

[141]*Ill. Juv. Ct. Act* § 704–1.

[142]*N.Y. Act* § 331 (neglect); § 733 (delinquency, and persons in need of supervision).

[143]*Fox* at 144.

[144]*N.Y. Act* §§ 731, 732; *Uniform Act* § 21(1).

[145]In the Matter of Walsh, 59 Misc.2d 917, 300 N.Y.S.2d 859 (1969); In the Matter of Richard, 449 P.2d 809 (Wash. 1969).

[146]Johnson, v. State, 401 S.W.2d 298 (Tex. Civ. App. 1966).

[147]In re Long, 184 So.2d 861 (Miss. 1966).

[148]In re Glassberg, 230 La. 396, 88 So.2d 707 (1956). However, where the offense which is proved is a lesser included offense of the one charged, the child may be adjudged delinquent. In re Taylor, 62 Misc.2d 529, 309 N.Y.S.2d 368 (1970).

[148a]Since a finding as to conduct is a prerequisite, not only to the determination of the juvenile's status (as delinquent, semi-delinquent, or in need of supervision) but also to the very jurisdiction of the court, the adjudication hearing is sometimes termed the jurisdiction hearing.

[149]*E.g., Uniform Act* § 2(1).

[150]See, e.g., Walker's Case, 5 N.Y. City Hall Recorder 137 (1820).

[151]*E.g., N.Y. Act* § 712(a); *Cal Code* § 602.

[152]*Fox* 18.

[153]E.g., *N.Y. Act* § 712(b).

[154]*Fox* 20.

[155]Godfrey v. State, 31 Ala. 323, 70 Am. Dec. 494 (1858).

[156]Juvenile Court of Shelby County v. State ex rel Humphrey, 139 Tenn 549, 201 S.W. 771 (1918); Borders v. United States, 256 F.2d 458 (5th Cir. 1958).

[157]In re Gladys R., 1 Cal.3d 855, 83 Cal. Rptr. 671, 464 P.2d 127 (1970).

[158]State v. Mendenhall, 21 Ohio App.2d 135, 255 N.E.2d 307 (1969).

[159]*Ill. Juv. Ct. Act* § 707–2.

[160]*E.g.,* State ex rel Koopman, v. County Court Branch No. 1, 38 Wis.2d 492, 157 N.W.2d 623 (1968); Lowry v. Commonwealth, 424 S.W.2d 841 (Ct. App. Ky. 1968).

[161]*E.g.,* State v. Jones, 220 Tenn. 477, 418 S.W.2d 769 (1966); United States v. Fotto, 103 F. Supp. 430 (S.D. N.Y. 1952); see *N.Y. Act* § 714.

[162]Pennoyer v. Neff, 95 U.S. 714 (1878).

[163]Harris v. Soulder, 233 Ind. 287, 119 N.E.2d 8 (1954).

[164]387 U.S. 1 (1967).

[165]In re Gault, 387 U.S. 1, 33 (1967).

[166]*N.Y. Act* § 736; *Colo. Code* § 22–3–3(B); *Uniform Act* § 22(a).

[167]In re Dell, 56 Misc.2d 1017, 290 N.Y.S.2d 287 (1968).

[168]*See, e.g., Uniform Act* § 23.

[169]In re Gault, 387 U.S. 1, 34 (1967); see also *N.Y. Act* § 736.

[170]In re Edgar, 9 Cr. L. 2127 (Kings Co. Family Ct., April 20, 1971).

[171]*Cal. Code* § 651; see also *Uniform Act* § 11.

[172]*Uniform Act* § 12(a).

[173]In re Fletcher, 251 Md. 520, 248 A.2d 364 (1968).

[174]State ex rel McClintock v. Hamilton Circuit Court, 232 N.E.2d 356. (Ind. 1968).

[175]387 U.S. 1 (1967).

[176]In re R.M., 105 N.J. Super. 372, 252 A.2d 237 (1969).

[177]In the Matter of Haas, 5 N.C. App. 461, 168 S.E.2d 457 (1969).

[178]*E.g., Colo Code* § 22–1–6 (1) (a).

[179]*Fox* 157.

[180]McClintock v. State, 253 N.E.2d 233 (ind. 1969).

[181]In re M.G.S., 267 Cal. App.2d 329, 72 Cal. Rptr. 808 (1968). The rule is the same in criminal law. See, *e.g.,* United States ex rel Thurmond v. Mancusi, 275 F. Supp. 508 (E.D. N.Y. 1967).

[181a]The waiver is not to be made after adjudication, but either during the adjudication hearing (People v. Brown, 13 C.A.2d 876, 881, (1970)) during the detention hearing (Brace M v. Superior Court, 270 C.A.2d 566 (1969); or in a separate hearing (seemingly required by People v. Arauz, 5 C.A.3d 523, 529, (1970)).

[182]Hall v. State, 284 Ala. 569, 226 So.2d 630 (1969).

[182a]Haziel v. United States, 131 App. D.C. 298, 404 F.2d 1275 (1968); Peyton v. French, 207 Va. 73, 147 S.E.2d 739 (1966).

[182b]Hall v. State, note 182 *supra.*

[183]383 U.S. 541 (1966).

[183a]*E.g.,* Powell v. Sheriff, 85 Nev. 684, 462 P.2d 756; Knott v. Langlois, 102 R.I. 517, 231 A.2d 767 (1967).

[184]Steinhauer v. State, 206 So.2d 25 (Fla. 1968); Templeton v. State, 202 Kan. 89, 447 P.2d 158 (1968).

[185]Eilman v. Superior Court, 9 Ariz. App. 6, 448 P.2d 878 (1969).

[186]Cal. Code § 707 (Supp. 1969).

[187]*E.g.,* M v. Superior Court, 270 Cal. App.2d 566, 75 Cal. Rptr. 881 (1969); Tilton v. Commonwealth, 196 Va. 774, 85 S.E.2d 368 (1955).

[188]*Colo. Code* § 22–3–8(3).

[189]*Uniform Act* § 34(4) (ii).

[190]*E.g., Colo. Code* § 22–3–8(1). (children sixteen years of age or older).

[191]*E.g., Cal. Code* § 707; *Uniform Act* § 34(a) (1).

[192]*Colo. Code* § 22–3–8(1).

[193]*Code of Ala.,* Tit. 13, § 364.

[194]*E.g.,* Seagraves v. State, 279 Ala. 621, 189 So.2d 137 (1966).

[195]*E.g.,* Stephenson v. State, 204 Kan. 80, 460 P.2d 442 (1969).

[196]*Uniform Act* § 34(a) (4) (i).

[197]*E.g.,* Hopkins v. State, 290 So.2d 841 (Miss. 1968); Summers v. State, 248 Ind. 551, 230 N.E.2d 320 (1967).

[198]*E.g., Colo. Code* § 22–3–8(2); *see also Cal. Code* § 634.

[199]State v. Naylor, 207 A.2d 1 (Super. Ct. Del. 1965).

[200]In re Doe I, 444 P.2d 459 (Hawaii 1968).

[201]Powell v. Sheriff, 85 Nev. 684, 462 P.2d 756 (1969).

[202]M v. Superior Court, 270 Cal. App.2d 566, 75 Cal. Rptr. 881 (1969).

[203]*E.g.,* Summers v. State, 248 Ind. 551, 230 N.E.2d 320 (1967); Hopkins v. State, 209 So.2d 841 (Miss. 1968).

[204]403 U.S. 528 (1971).

[205]403 U.S. at

[206]Commonwealth v. Thomas, 9 Cr. L. 2145 (Mass. Sup. Jud. Ct., April 29, 1971).

[207]In re Winship 397 U.S. 358 (1970).

[208]*N.Y. Act* § 744(b).

[209]In re Barries, 39 *U.S.L. Week* 4777 (1971) ( ).

[210]*E.g.,* Piland v. Clark County Juvenile Court, 85 Nev. 489, 457 P.2d 523 (1969); State v. Henry, 78 N.M. 573, 434 P.2d 692 (1967).

[210a]Thus the court at the adjudication hearing may not consider the probation officer's *social study* of the child, which contains material relevant to disposition but inadmissible and prejudicial as to adjudication. In re Corey, 226 C.A.2d 295, Cal. Rptr. (1968); In re Gladys R., 1 Cal.3d 855, 861; 83 Cal. Rptr. 671, 464 P.2d. 127 (1970).

[210b]See *Model Rules, Rule* 25, 16 *Crime and Delinquency* 255, 257; *1966 Standards* quoted with approval. In re Gault, 387 U.S. 1, 56–57 (1967).

It has been held that the report of the juvenile probation officer may be considered at the adjudication hearing even though it contains hearsay, In re Garcia, 201 C.A.2d 662 (1962), since the probation officer acts in behalf of the court to investigate and report 27 Op. A.G. (Cal.) 292, 295 (1956). To the extent that the rule against hearsay incorporates the constitutional values of confrontation and cross-examination, the Garcia holding is inconsistent with Gault.

[211]*E.g.,* In re Marsh, 40 Ill.2d 53, 237 N.E.2d 529 (1968). See also text at notes 73–82.

[212]387 U.S. 1 (1967).

[213]387 U.S. at 56.

[214]*N.Y. Act* § 744(a); this is the same principle as the *1966 Standards.*

[215]*Cal. Code* § 701.

[216]*Id.* at § 725(a).

[217]Powell v. Gregg, 118 Ga. App. 225, 163 S.E.2d 251 (1969); *see also N.Y. Act* § 752.

[218]*E.g., Ill. Juv. Ct. Act* § 704–8(1); *Cal. Code* § 702.

[219]In re Gault, 387 U.S. 1 (1967).

[220]*E.g., Colo. Code* § 22–1–7; *Uniform Act* § 24(c).

[221]Richard M. v. Superior Court, 9 Cr. L. 2028 (Cal. Sup. Ct., March 24, 1971).

[222]*E.g., Cal. Code* § 702 (Supp. 1969).

[223]N.Y. Act § 746(a) (Supp. 1969).

[223a]Thus the rules of evidence (e.g., the hearsay rule) are relaxed. The National Council on Crime and Delinquency so recommends, 16 *Crime & Del.* 255, 258 (July 1970). As New York's highest court has stated, however, "hearsay, opinion, gossip, bias, prejudice, trends of hostile neighborhood feelings, the hopes and fears of social workers, are all sources of error and have not more place in Children's Courts than in any other court." People v. Lewis, 260 N.Y. 171, 178, 183 N.E. 353, 355 (1932). *Accord, Minnesota Juvenile Courts Rules Symposium,* 54 *Minn. L.R.* 201, 386 (1969).

[224]*N.Y. Act* § 746(b).

[225]See note 210a, *infra.*

[226]§ 24.04(b) (1970); *see also Ill. Rev. Stat;* ch. 37, § 705–1 (2) (1967).

[227]*E.g.,* In the Matter of F, 30 A.D.2d 933, 293 N.Y.S.2d 873 (1968); Steinhauer v. State, 206 So.2d 25 (Fla. 1968).

[228]*E.g., Uniform Act* § 26(a). For material on the role of counsel in the juvenile process, see excerpts in *Remington* 1072–1084 and bibliographical note at 1084.

[229]*Tex. Civ. Stat.,* Art. 2338–1, § 21 (Vernon).

[230]*Uniform Act* § 29(a).

[231]*See* In re Gault, 387 U.S. 1, 8 (1967).

[232]In re Brown, 7 Cr. L. 2378 (3d Cir., July 10, 1970).

[233]*See, e.g., Mass. Gen. Laws Anno.,* c. 119, § 56.

[234]*N.Y. Act* § 1011.

[235]See, In re Jenkins, 210 Pa. Super. 501, 234 A.2d 49 (1967); *Or. Rev. Stat.*, 419.498, 419.561.

[236]*Fox* at 247.

[237]Creek v. Stone, 126 App. D.C. 329, 379 F.2d 106 (1967).

[238]Smith v. State, 280 Ala. 241, 192 So.2d 443 (1966).

[239]State v. Sluder, 463 P.2d 594 (Ore. 1970).

[240]Griffin v. Illinois, 351 U.S. 12 (1956).

[241]*E.g.*, Chambers v. District of Dubuque County, 152 N.W.2d 818 (Iowa, 1967).

[242]E.g., In re Boykin, 39 Ill.2d 617, 237 N.E.2d 460 (1968).

[243]In re Gault, 387 U.S. 1 (1967).

[244]Chambers v. District Court of Dubuque County, 152 N.W.2d 818 (Iowa, 1967).

[245]*E.g., Colo. Code* § 22–1–6 (1) (a).

[246]*E.g., N.Y. Act* § 249.

[247]*Iowa Code* § 232.34 (1966).

[248]In the Matter of Drywalski, 26 A.D.2d 894, 274 N.Y.S.2d 670 (1966).

[249]*E.g., N.Y. Act* §§ 753, 754 *Uniform Act* §§ 31, 32.

[250]See *Cal. Code* § 725(a).

[251]*N.Y. Act* § 753(a); *Family Court Rules, Rule* 7.5

[252]*N.Y. Act* § 754(a).

[253]See *Fox* at 210.

[254]See, *e.g., N.Y. Act* § 753(c).

[255]See *President's Commission on Law Enforcement and Administration of Justice, Task Force Report: Corrections,* Appendix A at 32 (1967).

[256]See, *e.g., N.Y. Act* § 757(b); *Uniform Act* § 36(e).

[257]*Uniform Act* § 31(2).

[258]*Cal. Code* § 730.

[259]In re Green 203 So.2d 470 (Miss. 1967), *Cert. denied* 392 U.S. 945 (196).

[260]185 Va. 335, 38 S.E.2d 444 (1946).

[261]38 S.E.2d at 448.

[262]*Cal. Code* § 730.

[263]In the Matter of Bordane, 33 A.D.2d 890, 307 N.Y.S.2d 527 (1969).

[264]In re Trignani, 148 Pa. Super. 142, 144, 24 A.2d 743, 744 (1942).

[265]148 Pa. Super. at 145, 24 A.2d at 744.

[266]See, *e.g., Cal. Code* § 584.

[267]*Uniform Act* § 7(5).

[268]*N.Y. Act* § 779.

[269]*E.g., Colo. Code* § 22–3–18(3).

[270]State ex rel Cox v. Appelton, 62 Misc.2d 403, 390 N.Y.S.2d 290 (1970).

[271]McDaniel v. Shea, 108 App. D.C. 15, 278 F.2d 460 (1960).

[272]*E.g., Cal. Code* § 730; *Uniform Act* § 32.

[273]*E.g., N.Y. Act* § 775.

[274]In re Litdell, 232 So.2d 733 (Miss. 1970).

[275]*Fox* at 218.

[276]*E.g.*, 16 *D.C. Code* § 2316(3) (Supp.V, 1966).

[277]In re Elmore, 127 App. D.C. 176, 382 F.2d 125 (1967).

[278]In the Matter of Walker, 172 N.W.2d 903 (N.D. 1969).

[279]In re P., 34 A.D.2d 661, 310 N.Y.S.2d 125 (1970).

[280]*E.g.,* Commonwealth v. Fisher, 213 Pa. 48, 62 Atl. 198 (1905); Abernathy v. United States, 418 F.2d 288 (5th Cir. 1969).

[281]In re Wilson, 264 A.2d 614 (Pa. 1970).

[282]*E.g., Colo. Code* § 22–3–14(3) (a) (two years; *N.Y. Act* § 758)(c) (three years).

[283]*E.g., Colo. Code* § 22–3-14(3) (a).

[284]*Cal. Code* § 1769.

[285]*Cal. Code* § 1800.

[286]*Cal. Code* § 1802.

[287]In re Gary W., 9 Cr. L. 2357 (Cal. Sup. Ct., August 7, 1971).

[288]People v. Smith, 9 Cr. L. 2359 (Cal. Sup. Ct., August 7, 1971).

[289]*Op. cit. supra,* note 255, at 141.

[290]*Id.* at 142.

[291]*Id.* at 149.

[292]In re Owens, 9 Cr. L 2415 (Cook Co., Ill., Cir. Ct., August 9, 1971).

[293]*E.g., Wis. Stat.Ann.* §§ 48,52 (Supp. 1969).

[294]*Children's Bureau, Dep't of H.E. & W., Delinquent Children in Penal Institutions* 7 (1964).

[295]Wilson v. Coughlin, 259 Iowa 1163, 147 N.W.2d 175 (1966); Shone v. State, 237 A.2d 412 (Me. 1968).

[296]In re Rich, 125 Vt. 373, 216 A.2d 266 (1966).

[297]McKiever v. Pennsylvania, 403 U.S. 528 (1970).

[298]*N.Y. Act* § 759(e).

[299]*N.Y. Act* § 740.

[300]*Op. Cit. supra,* note 255, at 149.

[301]See *id.* at 150.

[302]*Ibid.*

[303]*Id.* at 154.

[304]*Ibid.*

[305]*Id.* at 152.

[306]Elliot, *Parole Readiness: An Institutional Dilemma, Federal Probation* **27** (March, 1964).

[307]Bernier v. State, 265 A.2d 604 (Me. 1970).

[308]Velasquez v. Pratt, 443 P.2d 1020 (Utah 1968).

[309]Loyd v. Youth Conservation Comm., 387 Minn. 12, 177 N.W.2d 555 (1970).

[309a]McKeiver v. Pennsylvania, 403 U.S. 528, 551–3 (1971) (White, J., conc.).

[310]In re Winship, 397 U.S. 358, 366–67 (1970).

[311]Note 309a, *supra,* at 553.

[312]The reference here is to the *Task Force Report* at 7–9.

[313]McKeiver v. Pennsylvania, 403 U.S. 528, 544 (1971).

[314]*Id.* at 528, quoting from *Task Force Report* at 9.

[315]In re Winship, 397 U.S. 358, 366 (1970).

CHAPTER 24

GUIDELINES FOR JUVENILE COURT IMPROVEMENT

MANY STATES ARE CURRENTLY in the process of revising their juvenile court laws because of the interest of juvenile leaders and concerned citizens.

Following is a brief selected bibliography of suggested standards and guidelines which can be of assistance to legislators, juvenile justice personnel and others in their deliberations on appropriate revisions. These materials have been prepared by federal departments and by professional organizations which have been working toward juvenile justice progress for many years.

U.S. Governmental Publications

Law As An Agent of Delinquency Prevention.
Ted Rubin. Youth Development and Delinquency Prevention Administration, Department of Health, Education, and Welfare. (SRS-JD-173) 1971.

Legal Bibliography for Juvenile and Family Courts. (1969).
Department of Health, Education, and Welfare.

Legislative Guide for Drafting Family and Juvenile Court Acts.
Prepared by William H. Sheridan. Department of Health, Education, and Welfare. Publication #472—1969.

Non Governmental Publications

Publications of the National Council on Crime and Delinquency.
NCCD Center, Paramus, New Jersey 07652:

Guides for Juvenile Court Judges
Guides for Juvenile Court Judges on News Media Relations
Guides to the Judge in Medical Orders Affecting Children
Juvenile Traffic Offenders—A Policy Statement
Model Rules for Juvenile Courts
Procedure and Evidence in the Juvenile Court
Provision of Counsel in Juvenile Courts
Standard Juvenile Court Act, 6th ed.
Standards and Guides for the Detention of Children and Youth, 2nd ed.

Uniform Juvenile Court Act.
National Conference of Commissioners on Uniform State Laws, 1968. 1155 E. 60 Street, Chicago, Illinois 60637.

APPENDIX A
FEDERAL SOURCES OF FUNDS FOR SYSTEM IMPROVEMENTS

THE TWO MAJOR ADMINISTRATIVE SOURCES of federal funds for system improvement are: (1) The Law Enforcement Assistance Administration of the U.S. Department of Justice, and (2) The Youth Development and Delinquency Prevention Administration of the U.S. Department of Health, Education, and Welfare.

The Law Enforcement Assistance Administration

The Law Enforcement Assistance Administration (LEAA) was created by the Omnibus Crime Control and Safe Streets Act of 1968.

Congress held that law enforcement efforts must be better coordinated, intensified and made effective at all levels of government. It thus became the responsibilty of LEAA to improve the entire criminal justice system. The criminal justice system in the United States has grown up as separate jurisdictions and as separate components within those jurisdictions. Only rarely has it been considered in its entirety. Instead separate planning has gone ahead for law enforcement, for courts, for corrections and for the other components of the system.

LEAA Operation. Congress also held that crime was primarily a state and local problem and therefore the principal responsibility for meeting it should not rest with the federal government. The principal focus of LEAA activity thus became the administration of block action grants to the states. These are called block grants because they are allocated to the states on the basis of population. They are action grants because they are designed to implement the plans which states have already made. These plans are drawn up by state planning agencies (SPAs) which were established with LEAA planning funds and which are maintained by LEAA planning grants. The state plans call for comprehensive improvement in the criminal justice system within the state. When LEAA has approved a comprehensive state plan, the state is eligible to receive its full block action grant.

TYPES OF GRANTS. The first grant LEAA gives to a state is a planning grant, to either establish or to maintain a state planning agency (SPA) to draw up a comprehensive plan.

After that plan has been approved the state may receive the full amount of its state block action grant that will implement the program.

In order to meet necessary needs which might not come either under planning or block action grants Congress also authorized LEAA to give discretionary grants, which are action grants given at LEAA's discretion to states or cities or other agencies. LEAA also provides technical assistance to help improve police, courts, and corections agencies.

Congress also provided funds for academic assistance—to help improve the overall criminal justice system by improving the quality of criminal justice personnel. These funds are used to provide in-service education for people actively involved in the criminal justice system and also to assist those who are preparing for professional careers in the field of criminal justice.

Finally, to provide the new knowledge and discover the new techniques necessary for continued improvement, Congress provided LEAA with research funds, to finance grants and contracts for research and development in the field of criminal justice.

Requests for most grants are made through regional criminal justice councils which process them through the state criminal justice council for final approval.

Additional assistance and information is available through LEAA Regional Offices as follows:

Region #1-Boston

Joseph R. Rosetti, Regional Director
Law Enforcement Assistance Administration
U.S. Department of Justice
Post Office and Courthouse Building, Room 1702
Boston, Massachusetts 02109
617/223-7256

Region #2-Philadelphia

Arnold J. Hopkins, Regional Director
Law Enforcement Assistance Administration
U.S. Department of Justice
928 Market Street (2nd Floor)
Philadelphia, Pennsylvania 19107
215/597-7846

Region #3-Atlanta

George M. Murphy, Regional Director
Law Enforcement Assistance Administration
U.S. Department of Justice
730 Peachtree Street, N.W. (Room 985)
Atlanta, Georgia 30308
404/526-3556

Region #4-Chicago

John J. Jemilo, Regional Director
Law Enforcement Assistance Administration
U.S. Department of Justice
O'Hara Office Center (Room 121)
3166 Des Plaines Avenue
Des Plaines, Illinois 60018
312/299-3339

Region #5-Dallas

Norval Jesperson, Regional Director
Law Enforcement Assistance Administration

U.S. Department of Justice
500 S. Ervay Street, Room 407-C
Dallas, Texas 75201
214/749-2958

Region #6-Denver

Edwin R. LaPedis, Regional Director
Law Enforcement Assistance Administration
U.S. Department of Justice
Room 5619, Federal Building
Denver, Colorado 80202
303/297-4784

Region #7-San Francisco

Cornelius Cooper, Regional Director
Law Enforcement Assistance Administration
U.S. Department of Justice
1838 El Camino Real (Suite 111)
Burlingame, California 94010
415/341-3401

Youth Development and Delinquency Prevention Administration

The Youth Development and Delinquency Prevention Administration, of the Department of Health, Education, and Welfare, dispenses funds made available through the Juvenile Delinquency Prevention and Control Act of 1968. Financial assistance to States and communities are provided to:

—develop programs with respect to the increasingly visible youth culture existing across the Nation at this very time;

—direct national efforts at basic changes in important institutions;

—upgrade services in the areas where delinquency and crime rates are highest, and identify and provide special services to youth who are too often neglected merely because they live in areas where delinquency and social disorganization are low;

—make further improvements in the services available within the juvenile justice system so that the youth passing through it will not stand in danger of continuing their delinquent careers.

The recent decentralization of the program through the placement of full-time Associate Regional Commissioners for Youth Development and Delinquency Prevention Services in each of the 10 Departments of Health, Education, and Welfare Regional Offices is designed to provide for a strengthened effort through the development of closer working relationships among the Federal, State and local levels of government. By providing a vehicle for close liaison between the administering agency and the State agencies, immediate access is afforded to the technical assistance and expertise of these specialists in the development of plans and programs.

APPENDIX B

SELECTED BIBLIOGRAPHY

General Publications

American Law Institute, *Standards, Guides, and Model Acts,* Model Penal Code. Proposed Official Draft., Philadelphia, 1962.

Blake, Mary E. *Selected Annotated Readings on Group Services in the Treatment and Control of Juvenile Delinquency;* Children's Bureau Juvenile Delinquency Facts and Facets 3. Washington, U.S. Government Printing Office.

California Youth Authority, *Standards and Guidelines for Youth Service Bureaus.* Department of the Youth Authority and California Delinquency Prevention Commission, 1968.

California Youth Authority. *Standards for Juvenile Homes, Ranches, and Camps,* Sacramento, 1965.

Carter, Robert M., Glaser, Daniel, and Wilkins, Leslie. *Correctional Institutions.* New York, Lippincott, 1972.

Children's Bureau, U.S. Department of Health, Education, and Welfare. *Selected Films on Child Life,* Children's Bureau Publication 376. Washington, U.S. Government Printing Office, 1962.

Children's Bureau Publication 365. *Youth Groups in Conflict;* Washington, U. S. Government Printing Office, 1958.

Children's Bureau Publication 353. *Health Services and Juvenile Delinquency;* Washington, U. S. Government Printing Office, 1955.

Children's Bureau Publication 347. *The Adolescent in Your Family;* Washington, U. S. Government Printing Office, 1954.

Children's Bureau Publication 349. *Parents and Delinquency:* Washington, U. S. Government Printing Office, 1954.

Correctional Research Association. *Community Work on Alternatives to Imprisonment (Principles and Guidelines);* Washintgon, U. S. Government Printing Office, 1967.

Empey, LaMar T., *Alternatives to Incarceration,* Washington, U. S. Government Printing Office, 1967.

Empey, LaMar T., and Libeck, Steven G. *The Silverlake Experiment.* Chicago, Aldine-Atherton, 1971.

Glaser, Daniel, and O'Leary, Vincent. *The Control and Treatment of Narcotic Use,* Washintgon, U. S. Department of HEW, U. S. Government Printing Office, 1966.

International Association of Chiefs of Police, Research, Development and Planning Division. *Guides for Police Practice: Fundamental Phases of Curriculum Development and Instruction in Police Training with Emphasis on Juvenile Subjects,* Washington, 1965.

Joint Commission on Correctional Manpower and Training, *Offenders as a Correctional Manpower Resource,* Washington, U. S. Government Printing Office, 1968.

Milliken, Rhoda J. *The Role of the Police in Mental Health;* Public Health Service Publication 360, Washington, U. S. Government Printing Office, 1955.

Myren, Richard A., and Swanson, Lynn D. *Police Work With Children,* United States Children's Bureau Publication No. 399, 1962.

National Advisory Commission on *Civil Disorders,* Waskhington, Government Printing Office, 1968,. New York, Bantam, 1968.

National Commission on *The Causes and Prevention of Violence Report;* Washington, Government Printing Office, 1969.

National Council on Crime and Delinquency. *Strategy for Action in Establishing Alternatives to Training Schools.*

National Council on Crime and Delinquency. *Standard Probation and Parole Act,* 2nd ed.

National Council on Crime and Delinquency. *Standards for the Selection of Probation and Parole Personnel;* (by NCCD Professional Council), Rev. 1968. .

Piliavin, Irving, and Briar, Scott. *Police Encounters with Juveniles,* Washington, Department of HEW, Social and Rehabilitation Service, Office of Juvenile Delinquency and Youth Development, 1966.

President's Commission on Law Enforcement and Administration of Justice:
The Challenge of Crime in a Free Society (Commission's General Report)
Task Force Report: The Police
Task Force Report: The Courts
Task Force Report: Corrections
Task Force Report: Juvenile Delinquency and Youth Crime
Task Force Report: Narcotics and Drug Abuse
Task Force Report: Crime and Its Impact—An Assessment
Washington, U. S. Government Printing Office, 1967.

Pursuit, Dan G., Gerletti, John D., Brown, Robert, and Ward, Steven. *Police Programs for Preventing Crime and Delinquency.* Springfield, Thomas, 1972.

Rubin, Ted, and Smith, Jack F. *The Future of the Juvenile Court,* Implications for Correctional Manpower and Training, Joint Commission on Correctional Manpower and Training, Washington, 1968.

U. S. Children's Bureau. *Institutions Serving Delinquent Children—Guides and Goals,* Prepared in cooperation with the National Association of Training Schools and Juvenile Agencies, 1962.

Werthman, Carl, and Piliavin, Irving. *Gang Members and the Police,* Washington, Department of HEW, Social and Rehabilitation Service, Office of Juvenile Delinquency and Youth Development, 1966.

Witmer, Helen L. *Delinquency and the Adolescent Crisis,* Washington, U. S. Department of HEW, Welfare Administration, Children Bureau, 1960.

Criminal Justice Management

Alexander, Myrle. *Jail Administration,* Springfield, Thomas, 1957.

Amos, William E. and Manella, Raymond L. *Readings in the Administration of Institutions for Delinquent Youth,* Springfield, Thomas, 1965.

Becker, Harold K. *Issues in Police Administration;* Metuchen, The Scarecrow Press, 1970.

Becker, Harold K., Felkenes, George T., and Whisenand, Paul M. *New Dimensions in Criminal Justice,* Metuchen, The Scarecrow Press, 1968.

Bittner, Egon. *The Functions of the Police in a Modern Society;* National Institute of Mental Health, Center for Studies of Crime and Delinquency, Washington, Government Printing Office, 1970.

Bordua, David J. *The Police;* New York, John Wiley, 1967.

Bradley, Harold B., Smith, Glynn G., Salstrom, William V., et al. *The Non-Prison;* Saint Paul, Brice, 1970.

Bristow, Allen P. *Effective Police Manpower Utilization;* Springfield, Thomas, 1969.

Bristow, Allen P. (ed.) *Police Supervision Readings;* Springfield, Thomas, 1971.

Burpo, John H. *The Police Labor Movement: Problems and Perspectives;* Springfield, Thomas, 1971.

Carter, Robert M. and Wilkins, Leslie T., *Probation and Parole. Selected Readings,* New York, John Wiley, 1970.

Conrad, John P. *Crime and Its Correction,* Berkeley, University of California Press, 1965.

Eastman, George D. and Eastman, Esther M. (eds.). *Municipal Police Administration,* Washington, International City Management Association, 1969.

Galvin, John J. and Karacki, Leon. *Manpower and Training in Correctional Institutions,* Staff Report of Joint Commission on Correctional Manpower and Training, Washington, 1969.

Germann, A. C. *Police Executive Development,* Springfield, Thomas, 1962.

Glaser, Daniel. *The Effectiveness of a Prison and Parole System,* New York, Bobbs-Merrill, 1964.

Gourley, G. Douglas. Effective Municipal Police Organization, Beverly Hills, Glencoe, 1970.

Hanna, Donald G. and Gentel, William D. *A Guide to Primary Police Management Concepts,* Springfield, Thomas, 1971.

Horwitz, John J. *Team Practice and the Specialist: An Introduction to Interdisciplinary Team Work,* Springfield, Thomas, 1970.

Iannone, Nathan Floyd. *Supervision of Police Personnel,* Englewood Cliffs, Prentice-Hall, 1970.

Joint Commission on Correctional Manpower and Training, Staff Report. *Perspectives on Correctional Manpower and Training,* Washington, January, 1970.

Kenney, John P. *Police Management Planning,* Springfield, Thomas, 1959.

Kenney, John P. and Pursuit, Dan G. *Police Work With Juveniles and the Administration of Juvenile Justice,* Springfield, Thomas, 1970.

Kenney, John P., and Williams, John B. *Police Operations: Policies and Procedures,* 2nd ed., Springfield, Thomas, 1968.

Kobetz, Richard W. *The Police Role and Juvenile Delinquency,* Gaithersburg, International Association of Chiefs of Police, 1971.

Leonard, V. A. *Police Patrol Organization,* Springfield, Thomas, 1970.
Leonard, V. A. *Police Personnel Administration,* Springfield, Thomas, 1969.
Leonard, V. A. *The Police Communications System,* Springfield, Thomas, 1970.
McCorkle, Lloyd, Elias, Albert, and Bixby, F. Lovel. *The Highfields Story,* New York, Holt, Rhinehart and Winston, 1958.
McIntyre, Donald M., Jr. *Law Enforcement and the Metropolis,* Chicago, The American Bar Association, 1967.
Melnicoe, William and Mennig, John C. *Elements of Police Supervision,* Beverly Hills, Glencoe, 1969.
Miller, Frank W., Dawson, Robert O., Dix, George E., Parmas, Raymond I. *The Juvenile Justice Process,* Mineola, The Foundation Press, 1971.
National Advisory Commission on Criminal Justice Standards and Goals, U.S. Department of Justice, 1973.
Niederhoff, Arthur. *Behind the Shield: The Police in Urban Society,* Garden City, Doubleday, 1967.
Nelson, Elmer K., Jr., and Lovell, Catherine H. *Developing Correctional Administrators,* Research Report of Joint Commission on Correctional Manpower and Training, Washington, November, 1969.
Newman, Charles L. *Personnel Practices in Adult Parole Systems,* Springfield, Thomas, 1971.
Norman, Sherwood. *The Youth Service Bureau,* Paramus, National Council on Crime and Delinquency, 1971.
Newman, Charles L. *Sourcebook on Probation, Parole and Pardons,* Springfield, Thomas, 1968.
Pell, Arthur R. *Police Leadership,* Springfield, Thomas, 1967.
Saunders, Charles B. *Upgrading the American Police,* Washington, The Brooking Institution, 1970.
Schul, Bill D., ed. *Community Planning for Youth,* Topeka, Office of the Kansas Attorney General, 1964.
Siegel, Arthur I., Federman, Philip J. and Schultz, Douglas G. *Professional Police-Human Relations Training,* Springfield, Thomas, 1970.
Smith, Bruce. *Police Systems in the United States,* New York, Harper and Row, 1960.
Spergel, Irving. *Politics, Policies and the Delinquent Problem,* Washington, Office of Juvenile Delinquency and Youth Development, 1966.
Street, David, Vinter, Robert D. and Perrow, Charles. *Organization For Treatment,* New York, Free Press, 1966.
The President's Commission on Law Enforcement and Administration of Justice. *Commission Report: The Challenge of Crime in a Free Society,* Washington, Government Printing Office, 1967.
The President's Commission on Law Enforcement and Administration of Justice. *Task Force Report: The Police,* Washington, U. S. Government Printing Office, 1967.
The President's Commission on Law Enforcement and Administration of Justice. *Task Force Report: Corrections,* Washington, U. S. Government Printing Office, 1967.
Weston, Paul B. *Supervision in the Administration of Justice: Police, Corrections, Courts,* Springfield, Thomas, 1965.
Whisenand, Paul M. *Human Relations: Law Enforcement in a Changing Community,* Englewood Cliffs, Prentice-Hall, 1971.

Whisenand, Paul M. *Police Supervision: Theory and Practice.* Englewood Cliffs, Prentice-Hall, 1971.

Whisenand, Paul and Tamaru, Tug T. *Automated Police Information Systems,* New York, John Wiley, 1970.

Wilson, James Q. *Varieties of Police Behavior.* Cambridge, Harvard University Press, 1968.

Wilson, O. W. *Police Administration,* New York, McGraw Hill, 1963.

Wiilson, O. W. *Police Planning,* Springfield, Thomas, 1958.

Wilson, O. W., and McLaren, R. C. *Police Administration.* New York, McGraw-Hill, 1971.

JUVENILE JUSTICE PUBLICATIONS

The following items have been published by the Youth Development and Delinquency Prevention Administration, U.S. Department of Health, Education, and Welfare, and are available from the U.S. Government Printing Office, Washington, D.C. 20402.

A Bibliography on the Inhalation of Glue Fumes and other Toxic Vapors—A Substance Abuse Practice Among Adolescents

Includes brief introduction to the problem. Also lists recent projects, and political jurisdictions that have enacted legislation to control glue sniffing. 21 pages.

A Community Mental Health Approach to Drug Addiction

Includes a provocative discussion of the history of drug abuse. Advocates the use of innovative methods to learn more about the problem and deal with it more effectively. 135 pages.

A Situational Approach to Delinquency Prevention

Suggests a systematic approach to long-term prevention strategies through understanding the interrelated elements of the delinquent act.

Alternatives to Incarceration

Provides a general view of correctional systems and philosophies, and a detailed examination of several recent approaches toward furnishing youth with alternatives to incarceration. 88 pages.

Analyzing Delinquent Behavior

A short essay relating a new case and neighborhood assessment, methodololgy for the study of delinquent behavior. 30 pages.

Conference Proceedings/Inhalation of Glue Fumes and Other Substance Abuse Practices Among Adolescents

Reprints of papers presented at a conference dealing with youthful substance abuse practices. 140 pages.

Delinquency Prevention Strategies

Describes models based on different sets of program priorities, differing conditions in a community and differences in the nature of youth deviances.

Delinquency Today: A Guide for Community Action

An overview of the problem and concepts of delinquency, past and present, and a suggested blueprint of community programs to deal with the problem today. 24 pages.

Education and Training for Criminal Justice: A Directory of Programs in Universities and Agencies, 1965-67.

Lists various education and training programs in the field of criminal justice. 136 pages.

Helping Youth

A profile of six community programs designed to develop comprehensive action programs to deal with basic causes of delinquency. 80 pages.

Juvenile Courts Statistics

Various statistical information on delinquency cases handled by juvenile courts. Updated annually. 20 pages.

Law As An Agent of Delinquency Prevention

Suggests ways of improving California Juvenile Court laws increasing the process of diversion.

Neighborhood Legal Services

Discusses the general problem of providing legal services for the poor, and describes several projects designed to provide effective legal aid. 79 pages.

Neighborhood Service Centers

Describes the multitude of services offered and focuses on some basic issues that need to be resolved in order for these centers to make a more vital contribution toward meeting a community's needs. 111 pages.

Nonmetropolitan Delinquency: An Action Program

Briefly describes the problem of delinquency in nonmetropolitan areas and how it differs from urban delinquency. Includes an action program for curbing nonmetropolitan delinquency. 27 pages.

Personal Characteristics and Parole Outcome

Describes the role selected personal characteristics play in determining the success or failure of parole. 24 pages.

Pros and Cons: New Roles for Nonprofessionals in Corrections

Examines current experimentation employing nonprofessional personnel in correctional institutions and the community. Explores ways of providing new career opportunities for youth, and furnishes guidelines for agencies interested in job development. 127 pages.

State Responsibility for Juvenile Detention Care

Describes the role States should play in providing adequate detention care for juveniles. 16 pages.

Statistics on Public Institutions for Delinquent Children

Various statistical information on children in institutions including: numbers of institutions, average length of stay, number of children by sex and State, and expenditures. Updated annually. 13 pages.

Take Your Trouble to the Hotline

A magazine reprint describing Hotline as an important new resource for crisis intervention.

The Alcoholic Offender

Discusses the general problem of alcoholism and crime. Describes the role of intoxicants in determining parole failure or success. 31 pages.

The Control and Treatment of Narcotic Use

Contains an overall view of narcotic use and describes methods of aiding addicts. 41 pages.

The Crisis of Qualified Manpower for Criminal Justice: An Analytic Assessment with Guidelines for New Policy

Assesses the problems facing the field of criminal justice with respect to qualified manpower. Suggests guidelines for new policy. In three volumes: volume 1—Probation/Parole; volume 2—Correctional Institutions; volume 3—Law Enforcement (in preparations). 240 pages.

The Culture of Youth

Examines the phenomenon of the emergence of a distinct subculture comprised of youth. 29 pages.

The Juvenile Delinquency Prevention and Control Act of 1968

Official print of the law. 12 pages.

The Reentry of the Offender into the Community

Examines the most salient features of the parole process and how it often fails in its obligation to assist the offender to reintegrate into society. Offers suggestions for improving the parole process. 22 pages.

The Sentencing and Parole Process

Discusses the relationships between the sentencing and parole processes. Describes a "Model" penal code and a "model" sentencing act. 26 pages.

The Violent Offender

Describes the problems parole boards must face in deciding whether or not to release violent offenders. 39 pages.

Toward a Political Definition of Juvenile Delinquency

A look at the juvenile justice system and its relationship to those with whom it comes into contact. 16 pages.

Treatment in the Community

Brief discussion of the need of employing community-based alternatives to incarceration. Reprinted "Trial" magazine. 2 pages.

Using Volunteers in Court Settings

Provides a "how-to-do-it" manual for using volunteers in court probation programs. Contains detailed information on developing and managing volunteer programs. 227 pages.

Volunteer Programs in Courts

Collected papers detailing major program areas for using volunteers in courts probation programs; a companion volume to "Using Volunteers in Court Settings." 268 pages.

Why Children Are in Jail and How to Keep Them Out

Describes the jailing of children, and offers specific suggestions for stopping this practice. 8 pages.

Youth and Violence

An in-depth examination of the relationship of youth and violence, including a discussion of contemporary youth. 48 pages.

Youth as Advisers to Adults

Describes a simple technique whereby youth and adults can exchange meaningful views. 6 pages.

Youth Involvement

Brief history of youth involvement, including several models untilizing the youth involvement concept. 30 pages.

Youthful Drug Use

Includes an overview of the drug problem and, based on past drugabuse projects, offers recommendations that may be used as guidelines for control programs. 39 pages.

SELECTED ANNOTATED BIBLIOGRAPHY ON MANAGEMENT FILMS

Appley, Lawrence A. *What Management Is,* American Management Association.

We frequently hear phrases such as *management and labor, management and government, mnagement and education*—phrases which imply that management is some kind of class or group of people, or even a particular economic level.

"But management is not a class," Mr. Appley points out. It is an activity within itself, an activity unlike any other activity." There is, he notes, management within labor, management within government, management within education. There is even management within the home.

What exactly is management? To this question Mr. Appley gives a clear, concise answer-one which explains why he believes that no activity has as much influence, as much impact upon human beings as does the leadership under which they work. It is an answer which explains why he believes management is the most important activity in the world, save religion.
Black and White, (16mm) 30 Minutes

Appley, Lawrence A. *The Management Process,* American Management Association.

If management can be defined briefly as the art of getting things done through people, how does the actual process work? In this talk, Mr. Appley describes the three steps which make up the management process. The steps sound simple but the process is not.

First, the manager must have a clear idea in his own mind of the action he wants taken—he must know what he wants done. Second, he must transfer this idea into the mind of the person he wants to do the job. This step is where most managers stumble. Mr. Appley estimates from his experience that more than 90 percent of the instructions and requests given to people are inadequate for these people to do as well as their supervisors would like to have them do. Third, the manager must motivate the person he wants to do the job. This is where most workers balk. People just don't like to be told what to do. To motivate a man successfully, the manager must make that person feel that the action to be taken is his own idea or a good part his own, thus committing him to its accomplishment.

Ideally, as Mr. Appley shows, the three steps should be taken concurrently to ensure the highest motivation and the most positive action.
Black and White, (16mm) 30 Minutes

Appley. Lawrence A. *Management the Simple Way,* American Management Association.

"Do unto others as you would have them do unto you" is the main principle of good management put in its simplest form. In this program Mr. Appley shows how adhering to the Golden Rule makes management "the simple way" possible.

He examines the natural process of leadership, and the responsibilities of planning and control as expressions of the management function. Citing employee relations as the single most important factor contributing to company success, he explains why "management is personnel administration." He probes twelve universal truths about human beings, their motives and desires —truths that must be recognized if we are to achieve sound employee relations.

Six simple steps to good managmeent are also set forth by Mr. Appley, six steps that can be taken easily by any intelligent manager—with astounding results.
Black and White, (16mm) 30 minutes.

Appley, Lawrence A. *What's Different?,* American Management Association.

We all rush around proclaiming our differences, our own personal uniqueness. We protest too much at times. One of those times is in the area of managing, when being able to find—and use—our likenesses can pay off.

In this first session Lawrence Appley shares with you his techniques for getting things done through other people. He reveals how you can develop a sensitivity to people and situations which, in turn, can increase your own effectiveness.

Mr. Appley emphasizes that basically people are the same; they will respond to certain fundamental approaches, react to certain basic values. Whether they speak Swahili, French, Russian or English, whether they have much or little education, whether they are low or high—placed in life—you can find the values that will direct, motivate and inspire. He tells you what, in his opinion, some of these values are, and how you can interpret or enlarge upon them to suit your own situation—values like being of service to others, doing more for others than they do for you, contributing to the welfare of the group, having a mission in life, working for freedom of equality and oppor-

tunity. Values that are as applicable to your private life as to your public life.
Black and White, (16mm) 30 Minutes.

Appley, Lawrence A. *Setting Your Target,* American Management Association.

If you've no target to aim at, chances are you won't make a very big hit. That's as true in business and private life as it is in sports, according to Mr. Appley. And it's the reason why he is a staunch believer in long-range planning.

In this session Lawrence Appley examines the principles of long-range planning and tells you, first, how to gain the perspective necessary for successful planning of any kind. He follows through with hints on target-finding—how to see yourself or your business or your position within a business as it is now, and how to estimate how far you can go. Then he shows you how to zero in on your future.

In all, six basic steps to the successful long-range planning are covered in detail: How to determine the nature, the size of the enterprise; the rate, the nature of growth; the pricing and the financial policies of your endeavor. These are steps which Lawrence Appley says not only will help you to run a more successful business but also to have a more effective, successful personal life.
Black and Whihte (16mm) 30 Minutes.

Drucker, Peter. *Managing Time,* B.N.A. Films.

Discussed here was the concept of managing an executive's time. A revealing episode which exposes the overly efficient executive as ineffective—utilization at the executive training level.
Color, (16mm) 28 Minutes.

Drucker, Peter. *Focus on Tomorrow,* B.N.A. Films.

A summary of what appears in Drucker's book *Managing for Results.* Discussing the subjects such as, *this is our business, knowledge is the business, making the future today, key decisions and business strategies.* Utilization should be at the middle management and executive levels.
Color, (16mm) 28 Minutes.

Drucker, Peter. *The Effective Decision,* B.N.A. Films.

Discusses the collection of facts and the making of a decision. A key point discussed in this film was making the right decision on the wrong problem which is a situation which leaves no savable alternatives. However, if the individual makes the wrong decision on the right problem, he always has an alternative of adjusting his decision to make it the right one. Film utilization

here or training utilization could be at the supervisory, middle management, or executive level of training.
Color, (16mm) 28 Minutes.

Drucker, Peter. *What Can I Contribute,* B.N.A. Films.

A middle management or executive level insight into what happens in an organization when the organization man does not get promoted. What sets one man apart from another within the organiztion. This could be used at the supervisory, middle management, and executive training level.
Color, (16mm) 28 Minutes.

Drucker, Peter. *Staffing for Strength,* B.N.A. Films.

A discussion of the problem of staffing within an organization. That is, what is it that an individual can do or cannot do. It seeks to point out alternatives in dealing with the change in organization structure. The training utilization level would be executive heighth.
Color, (16mm) 28 Minutes.

Green, Edward J. *The Impact of Change—The Problem,* American Management Association.

Much has been said about the impact of change on management—and much of what has been said has been contradictory and confusing. Any attempt to solve problems imposed on management by this age of change must be based on a clear understanding of the nature of change itself. Here, Mr. Green points out, is where a lot of the confusion arises—for change today is not what it was twenty or even ten years ago. The revolutions going on in so many areas of our life—in knowledge, research and development, education, technology, marketing—have changed the very nature of change. The difference is not just quantitative—not just an acceleration in the rate of change—it is qualitative. Change itself is changing. Mr. Green takes a close look at this situation and defines the problem as it relates to the fundamental goals—and means—of management.
Black and White, (16mm) 30 Minutes.

Green, Edward J. *The Need for Better Planning in Management,* American Management Association.

We can only cope with the problems of the age of change through more effective management, Mr. Green asserts in this program. And more effective management can only result from more effective planning. But it will have to be a new kind of management—and a new kind of planning. Instead of trying to make philosophers out of middle management, he suggests, perhaps we should devise methods to enable the average manager to perform in a

superior fashion. However, in doing so, he cautions, we must be sure to strike the right balance between the planning and doing part of a manager's job. What should the planning part consist of? First, Mr. Green says, the manager should plan for his own area of responsibility. Second, his plans must be coordinated with those of his colleagues. Third, his plans must support the over-all company objectives.
Black and White, (16mm) 30 Minutes.

Joynt, John B. *Basic Principles of Organization,* American Management Association.

How can your managers perform effectively if the organization of your company holds them back at every turn? It is Mr. Joynt's profound belief that the first step in management improvement is organization improvement. And, in this presentation, he describes the most advanced concepts and basic principles of effective organization. He not only discusses the broad role of organization in determining objectives, designing structure, developing people, and achieving results—he defines in the greatest detail the responsibility for organization planning at different levels of management. . . the company plan and ideal plan of organization. . . and the need for simplicity, stability and flexibility to accommodate the growth and building of managerial competence.
Black and White, (16mm) 30 Minutes.

Oncken, William. *Motivation by Communication,* American Management Association.

Explore communications not as a technique or device, but rather as an integral part of the motivating process. It depicts communications as a means, not an end. It relates the basic needs of employees for opportunity, recognition, belonging and security directly to the managers communications responsibilities and shows how to develop a more effective organization by motivating through communications.
Black and White, (16mm) 26 Minutes.

Oncken, William, Jr. *Communication Downward,* American Management Association.

This program develops an understanding of the importance of downward communications, particularly in increasing employee confidence, job satisfaction, loyalty and awareness of his contribution to the objectives of the enterprise. It examines the *why, what,* and *how* of communications and helps to better establish communications objectives and to develop and implement both long and short-term communications plans.
Black and White, (16mm) 20 Minutes.

Oncken, William, Jr. *Communications Upward,* American Management Association.

This program identifies and analyzes common blocks to upward communications and helps to apply a new approach to the task of conveying information and selling ideas to top management. It will help make oral, and written messages more meaningful and improve person-to-person, person-to-group, and group-to-group communications.

Black and White, (16mm) 26 Minutes.

Oncken, William, Jr. *Communications and Organization Lines,* American Management Association.

This presentation concerns itself with the how-to-do-it method of effecting better and more efficient horizontal coordination and cooperation. Through the case history and workshop approach, it will demonstrate how others have achieved greater effectiveness, while at the same time, simplifying and streamlining their lateral communications systems.

Black and White, (16mm) 21 Minutes.

Oncken, William, Jr. *Leadership—Leadership Characteristcs,* American Management Association.

In this presentation, Mr. Oncken defines leadership by examining the types of authority a person can exercise. He describes four types of authority—position, personality, competence, and character and shows how they function in getting work done through people.

Black and White, (16mm) 23 Minutes.

Oncken, William, Jr. *Delegation,* American Management Association.

"Have you been doing more things lately, but can't seem to get anything done?" It's this problem that Mr. Oncken cites as he discusses the process of delegation. Delegation, he emphasizes, is concerned exclusively with results, not with the assignment of tasks. And, he examines in detail the three main aspects of delegation: (1) Responsibility—your subordinates must know the kinds of situations to which they are expected to respond; (2) Authority—they must know the sort of action they should take in response to these situations and (3) Accountability—they must provide the kind of full disclosure of results from these actions so that they can judge at any time how well your work is progressing. Mr. Oncken shows how to promote this understanding throughout your staff.

Black and White, (16mm) 21 Minutes.

Oncken, William, Jr. *General Management—Managing a Manager's Time,* American Management Association.

One of the most prevalent characteristics of effective management is the manager's ability to plan his time. . . to make the hours spent on the job more productive. Mr. Oncken offers a very different view of where and how a manager spends his time. He points out why time is absorbed by different duties and functions and what a manager can do to increase the results he is getting in proportion to the amount of time he devotes to a job. The very realistic discussion of a manager's problem in apportioning his time focuses on three demanding areas—time the manager must devote to his own work, time spent in organizing work, and time given to delegating work to others.

Black and White, (16mm) 24 Minutes.

Urwick, L.F. *The Principle of Organization,* American Management Association.

Starting with the definition of organizations as "the function of arranging and correlating the tasks the group must carry out," Colonel Urwick establishes and explores the ten basic principles of organization. He catalogs objectives, specialization, coordination, authority, responsibility, correspondence, definition, span of control, balance, and continuity as organization principles. He then relates the contribution that each of these make to organization effectiveness, and demonstrates how they influence operational functions.

He distinguishes effectively between organization considered as a structure of positions, and its true purpose as a device to secure effective communications to make it possible to realize established goals.

Black and White, (16mm) 36 Minutes.

SELECTED ANNOTATED FILM BIBLIOGRAPHY ON JUVENILE JUSTICE

"Boy in Court"—12 min/Produced by National Probation Association (now NCCD)

What might happen to a boy in police court and prison is contrasted with his treatment in a model juvenile court and under a probation system.

Supplier: Audio-Visual Center,
University of Indiana
Bloomington, Indiana

"Headed for Trouble"—33 min/plus 7-1/2 min trailer/Produced by Potomac Films for Public Affairs Committee

Urges cooperation of community to redirect the child headed for trouble.

Stresses unique role of police. Concluding panel discussion led by psychiatrist and various police officers. Illustrates how a good police department juvenile bureau should function.

Supplier: Public Affairs Committee
381 Park Avenue South
New York, New York 10016

"Seduction of the Innocent"—10 min/Loaned Free

This film is designed to hit the problem before it becomes a reality. It is a dramatic story of two young people, a boy and a girl, who during the trying teen times become victims of narcotics. Through a need to belong and a desire to go along with the group and its youthful zest to try something new, they begin a one way journey to self destruction. The film points out danger signals along the way and shows the tragic aftermath when those signals are not obeyed.

Supplier: Texas Department of Public Safety

"The Current Scene"—26 min/B&W/Produced by KCET-Los Angeles

An intimate glimpse of a young people's *pot party* and the making of marijuana cigarettes from raw blocks of the weed, with an added discussion of law enforcement problems of smuggling and detection. Narcotics agents, users of marijuana, and non-users are interviewed for their opinions on the moral issues involved in the drug's uses. Considerable attention is paid to the detection of smuggled marijuana from Mexico and the use of this drug by High School students, *ghetto-area* residents, and servicemen.

Supplier: NET Film Service
Indiana University

"The Dangerous Years"—30 min/Produced by Wolper Associates for Kemper Insurance Company

Through real life situations and frank interviews with juvenile officers, probation officers, policemen, juvenile court judges, and hardened young criminals, the documentary explores juvenile crime in our country today. Considers some possible solutions; raises questions for the responsible citizen to consider.

Supplier: Kemper Insurance
National Advertising Supervisor
Mutual Insurance Building
4750 Sheridan Road
Chicago, Illinois 60640

"This Question of Violence"—59 min/B&W/Produced by NET

An in-depth report on the historical, social, and psychological factors that seem to underline violence in modern life. Psychiatrists discuss the problem of aggression, which often comes from neglect and deprivation. It tells how this leads to violence.

Supplier: National Educational Television Film Service
Indiana University
Audio-Visual Center
Bloomington, Indiana 47401

"Youth and the Law"—37 min/B&W/Produced by McGraw-Hill

Film from Pennsylvania Department of Public Welfare outlining the role of the Juvenile Police Officer.

Supplier: International Film Bureau
322 So. Michigan Avenue
Chicago, Illinois 60604

or McGraw-Hill Book Co.
330 W. 42nd Street
New York, N.Y. 10036

The following films are available on loan, for free showing, by writing: National Audiovisual Center (GSA), Washington, D.C. 20409. (Please try to allow three weeks in advance of proposed viewing date and, if possible, provide alternate viewing date. These films may also be purchased; write the above for prices.)

The Image Changers

A timely discussion of the relationship between the police, the community, and youth. Black and white—28:10 minutes.

Look Further Than Tomorrow

Discusses Washington, D.C. summer youth programs emphasizing youth involvement. Touches upon both negative and positive aspects. Black & white—33:30 minutes.

The Quiet Summer

Describes a youth-run project operated during the summer of 1965 in Hampton Beach, New Hampshire, that successfully ended a pattern of annual youth rioting that begain in 1961. Black & white—28:15 minutes.

APPENDIX C
DELINQUENCY CONTROL INSTITUTE

OBJECTIVES

TO PROVIDE A SPECIALIZED academic and practical training program of ten weeks, designed to aid law enforcement officers and others to work more effectively with youth and community problems.

Since police officers annually contact from 5 to 10 percent of the juveniles in their communities, the DCI offers professional training to do their jobs more effectively.

The DCI was conceived in 1942, and began operating in 1946. It has since conducted more than 57 classes, graduating 1500 law enforcement officers engaged in juvenile work.

The participants in the training program learn to:

1. Understand the existing laws relating to juveniles and keep pace with new legislation.

2. Organize and manage a police juvenile program using modern principles of administration.

3. Understand delinquent behavior and the multiple factors contributing to it.

4. Make effective dispositions of cases and secure cooperation of treatment agencies.

5. Plan citizen participation in the development of community-wide delinquency prevention programs.

6. Interpret law enforcement to the public and create a realistic new image of the police.

7. Develop more effective coordination throughout the juvenile justice system.

CURRICULUM

The Institute offers classroom instruction and seminar discussion in four major categories:

I. Crime and Delinquency Causation. Emphasizes growth and change in childhood and adolescence; utilizes the contributions made by the behavioral sciences.

II. Delinquency Prevention and Control. Stresses the role of the police and total community resources in coordinated planning and development of effective programs.

III. Police Administration and Techniques, Special emphasis upon administration of police juvenile programs and the role of the law enforcement officer in today's changing society.

IV. Leadership, Human Relations and Community Relations. Stresses the skills of decision making, problem solving, and communication. Administration is viewed as an active creative process.

METHOD

The fourfold attack on the basic problems as presented in the classroom by regular faculty members of the University of Southern California is reinforced by a wide-range of interdisciplinary specialists representing major resources of the Los Angeles metropolitan community and the State of California. Classroom instruction is supplemented by research field work and field visits to important agencies and institutions engaged in juvenile work.

PARTICIPANTS

Fifty persons are admitted to each class and are selected from police departments, probation and parole departments, district attorneys' staffs, school districts, or citizens interested and qualified in youth counseling. Each class is divided into two sections to facilitate participation.

FEE

Tuition of $1000 is paid by the agency sending the student, by his community, by the student himself, through a scholarship granted by the Institute or through L.E.E.P. funds. The tuition fee covers selected classrooom materials. California enforcement agencies qualify for reimbursement by P.O.S.T.

SCHOLARSHIPS

A number of scholarships are offered by the Automobile Club of Southern California, The American Legion Child Welfare Foundation Inc., the Farmers Insurance Group, Hollywood Turf Associated Charities, Los Alamitos Charity Foundation, Sears-Roebuck Foundation. All inquiries regarding these scholarships should be directed to the Delinquency Control Institute.

CREDIT

Twelve units of university credit within the School of Public Administration is available to qualified candidates upon graduation.

ENROLLMENT

To be accepted for the Institute, applications should be accompanied by a written recommendation from the applicant's department head.

For Additional Information:

Delinquency Control Institute
John and Alice Tyler Building
University of Southern California
Los Angeles, California 90007
Phone: (213) 746-2497 or 746-2498
Director, Robert M. Carter

NAME INDEX

SUBJECT INDEX